BRINGING IN THE SHEAVES
ECONOMY AND METAPHOR IN THE ROMAN WORLD

The annual harvesting of cereal crops was one of the most important economic tasks in the Roman Empire. Not only was it urgent and critical for the survival of state and society, it mobilized huge numbers of men and women every year from across the whole face of the Mediterranean. In *Bringing in the Sheaves*, Brent D. Shaw investigates the ways in which human labour interacted with the instruments of harvesting, what part the workers and their tools had in the whole economy, and how the work itself was organized.

Both collective and individual aspects of the story are investigated, centred on the life-story of a single reaper whose work in the wheat fields of North Africa is documented in his funerary epitaph. The narrative then proceeds to an analysis of the ways in which this cyclical human behaviour formed and influenced modes of thinking about matters beyond the harvest. The work features an edition of the reaper inscription, and a commentary on it. It is also lavishly illustrated to demonstrate the important iconic and pictorial dimensions of the story.

BRENT D. SHAW is Andrew Fleming West Professor of Classics at Princeton University.

THE ROBSON CLASSICAL LECTURES

BRENT D. SHAW

Bringing In the Sheaves

Economy and Metaphor in the
Roman World

UNIVERSITY OF TORONTO PRESS
Toronto Buffalo London

© University of Toronto Press 2013
Toronto Buffalo London
www.utppublishing.com

Reprinted in paperback 2015

ISBN 978-1-4426-4479-3 (cloth)
ISBN 978-1-4426-2922-6 (paper)

Library and Archives Canada Cataloguing in Publication

Shaw, Brent D.
Bringing in the sheaves : economy and metaphor in the Roman world / Brent D. Shaw.

(Robson classical lectures)
Includes bibliographical references and index.
ISBN 978-1-4426-4479-3 (bound). – ISBN 978-1-4426-2922-6 (pbk.)

1. Wheat – Harvesting – Rome – History.   2. Wheat – Harvesting – Social aspects –
Rome – History.   3. Wheat – Harvesting – Economic aspects – Rome – History.
4. Labor – Rome – History.   5. Romans – Agriculture – Africa, North – Biography.
6. Africa, North – History – To 647.   7. Rome – Social life and customs.   8. Rome –
Economic conditions.   I. Title.   II. Series: Robson classical lectures

SB191.W5S53 2013   633.1′150937   C2012-905713-4

This book has been published with the help of a grant from the
Canadian Federation for the Humanities and Social Sciences, through the Awards
to Scholarly Publications Program, using funds provided by the Social Sciences and
Humanities Research Council of Canada.

University of Toronto Press acknowledges the financial assistance to its publishing
program of the Canada Council for the Arts and the Ontario Arts Council, an agency of
the Government of Ontario.

 Canada Council   Conseil des Arts
for the Arts   du Canada

University of Toronto Press acknowledges the financial support of the Government of
Canada through the Canada Book Fund for its publishing activities.

this one is for shauna

ὅς τ᾽ ἔπειτ᾽ ἔφυ,
τραικτῆρος οἴχεται τυχών,
Ζῆνα δέ τις προφρόνως ἐπινίκια κλάζων
τεύξεται φρενῶν τὸ πᾶν
τὸν φρονεῖν βροτοὺς ὁδώσαντα,
τὸν πάθει μάθος
θέντα κυρίως ἔχειν.

Aeschylus, *Agamemnon*, 171–8

Contents

List of Illustrations

List of Tables and Maps

Introduction/Preface

This is not a book. Not at least in the ordinary sense of a compact and unitary piece of writing. It is rather the reflection of a series of oral presentations on questions about a peculiar human activity, that of harvesting. This trek of mine through the problems posed by the work of reaping cereal crops in Roman antiquity began with a gesture from Alison Keith. Her invitation to deliver the Robson Classical Lectures at the University of Toronto provoked me to think, again, about a conundrum whose various dimensions of work, action, technology, and thought had occasionally piqued my curiosity in the past. Frustrating as the investigations themselves became, the lectures were the happy occasion of many acts of generosity and hospitality. If I cannot recollect them all, it is because the profusion and number of what the Greeks called *xenia* put me so deeply in the debt of my hosts. Of the graduate students who made the occasion so enjoyable, I must thank Ms Jaclyn Neel and Jessica Westerhold, and all of their peers, for their daily assistance in matters technical and inquisitorial. And there are these other thanks, too: To the generous Wallace McLeod, whose introduction to the architectural history of Victoria University was an education in itself, and whose high-level tour of the heights of Victoria College, and the breathtaking perspectives of the University from its roof-top eyrie, were a challenge to an acrophobe. He was my Pausanias. To the hosts on different evenings: Christer Bruun and Andreas Bendlin; my old Cambridge friend Jonathan Edmondson and his (then) new colleague, Ben Kelly; Michael Dewar, Erik Gunderson, and the intriguing Katherine Blouin; and Ben Akrigg and Ephraim Lytle, the latter one of my students from my days at Penn. A not so fortuitous encounter (it was purposefully suggested by my vigilant host) with an old acquaintance from Lethbridge days, the New Testament scholar John Kloppenborg, brought me a rich and unexpected harvest of information and scholarship. In the end, I must return to Alison Keith, who provided the first incitements that caused this critical inquiry to be contemplated. Otherwise, it probably would never have happened and certainly not in this fashion.

The non-Toronto acts of gratitude that helped in the production of the lectures, and then the writing of book, are numerous. Taken in anodyne alphabetical order they are: first, to my wonderful colleague and fellow Canadian at Princeton, Jeremy Adelman, for the inspiration of his work on agricultural labour in the great wheatfields of Canada and Argentina, for the loan of papers and books from his personal research collection, and for his introduction to the fascinating Georgina Binnie-Clark; to Jairus Banaji for drawing my attention to what I should already have known; to Benedetta Bessi for tears, death, and De Martino – and for a lot of inspiration; to Life Blumberg for her prompt to take another look at Thomas Hardy, Terrence Malick, and the heavenly days – she was right about the last, since I had casually disregarded something so obviously underfoot; to Catherine Coneybeare for pointing me back to Agnès Varda and the combine harvester; to my good colleague Marc Domingo Gygax for answering transatlantic e-mail queries on his beloved Catalonia; to Michael Flower for jogging a feeble memory on a Greek tyrant; to Andrew Ford for Pindar, Wordsworth, and reminding me – how *could* I have forgotten? – of Traffic and John Barleycorn; to John Kloppenborg for one of the great happenstance gifts ever given to a chance inquirer, and on wine no less; to Ariel Lopez for drawing my attention to an unusual portrait of Caracalla, and for his generous grant of permission to use his diagram of the historical ecology of the Nile River valley; to Jocelyne Nelis-Clément for reminding me of Alain Corbin; to Eric Rebillard for helping make available the necessary photographs from the deep archives of the Louvre; to Sitta von Reden for allowing herself to be pestered about contracts; and to Dorothy Thompson for more of the same. All have helped in different ways, and I am grateful for their many acts of scholarly generosity. Finally, another Canadian note. Almost by accident, I must confess, I happened upon the insightful work by George Grantham that proved so helpful to the arguments that I was attempting to make. He responded generously to my queries, and I thank him here. Finally, in an acme of gratitude, I must put on record my debts to the referees for the University of Toronto Press. They produced some of the finest critiques that I have ever received. Their reports revealed a careful and focused reading and analysis, and what is more, a real understanding of the argument, its problems, and the ways in which it might be improved. I am truly grateful to them. May other writers be so fortunate. If I have not been able to redeem all of their insights, the shortfall is mine.

Notes of gratitude must also be put on record for those who, in addition to suggesting ideas, offered more pragmatic assistance in finding or acquiring materials necessary to this study. To my fine colleague, Nino Luraghi, for his interventions over the Ostia mosaics from the Tomba della Mietitura. My former graduate student Gil Gambash, now at Haifa, for his interventions with the Hecht Museum at Haifa University to arrange for the reproduction of a reaper amulet. My best friend of many years, Professor Gabriel Herman at the Hebrew University Jerusalem, for setting up connections with Professor Ze'ev Weiss to obtain permission to reproduce the synagogue mosaic at Zippori (ancient Sepphoris), which he was generous in permitting. Professor Helmut Reimitz, from the Department of History at Princeton, for his communications with Professor Günther Hölbl at Vienna concerning the Edfu temple reliefs, and to Professor Höbl himself for granting permission. And Dr Alan Stahl, also of Princeton, for his kind help with the coin images, both in his explication of them, and for his acting as intermediary with the American Numismatic Society and its resources.

Of my other colleagues at Princeton, Bob Kaster came to my rescue with his careful reading of several chapters and the most important of the appendices, saving me, with his usual acumen, from more than one embarrassing misstep. He's just the best. And to Margaret 'Stevi' Stephens, a lifetime friend, is owed a special note of gratitude for her close reading of the whole. Her acumen in spotting comma abuse and awkward expression is without peer. The production of the book by the staff of the University of Toronto Press has been a pleasure. I must thank them for their guidance, technical assistance and, above all, their moral encouragement and enduring patience. Suzanne Rancourt, the Humanities Editor at the Press, and Barbara Porter, my production manager, were foremost among these Toronto helpers. Finally, a paramount act of gratitude, to Shauna, who, once again, read the whole damned thing over and over again, making a host of useful suggestions, mark-ups, and critical observations, all of which prompted thinking and rethinking, and which aided considerably in improving the readability of the text. What is more, she ferreted out, unearthed, and extorted e-data from sources so arcane that only the most skilled of electronic detectives could find them. Her abilities in digging up things deeply hidden on the net are such that she ought to be hired by CSIS or the SVR. It is for this, and for much else beside, of which only she can know, that the dedication is made.

What follows is an experimental sortie into a subject of some importance. Although the final production demanded the more formal treatment of a book, the arrangement of the chapters, some of the style, some of the repetition, and the odd rhetorical indulgence have preserved the sense, as well as the limitations, of the oral form of the lectures on which they are based. Like most such lectures, they cannot and do not pretend to be a comprehensive whole. There is so much more that would have to be done, but these initial test probes might indicate some of the parameters and some possible directions that another interested mind might take. I had simply determined *a priori* on a subject and an angle of attack that I imagined concerning an action that must have involved a very great number of all the inhabitants of the empire in recursive behaviour of some considerable economic significance. My focus settled on the practice of harvesting, and then narrowed to the harvesting of cereal grains – not, for example, the equally significant vintage or the olive harvest – and then it narrowed further to the specific task of reaping. I believe that this was a hugely important economic task with a large number of potential spin-offs and entailments about how humans have thought. It was these tracks that I wished to follow. Not everyone sees these matters as having the same economic size or significance. The recently published, truly monumental *Cambridge Economic History of the Greco-Roman World*, for example, has not a single word to say on the whole subject of harvesting, with all this has to suggest about our priorities in studying the ancient economy. Sometimes, I think, simple hard work, useful labour, tends to get lost in the shuffle of high conceptual thinking.

The investigation is like five test trenches cut into the evidence, five different angles of perspective on the process of reaping as it is attested in selected regions and times of Roman imperial history. The focus on north Africa, and, in particular, the life of one anonymous reaper from that land, was determined in part by the survival of some of the best corpora of evidence on the subject from this region of the empire, and partly by the author's own proclivities and areas of expertise. If, in my historical comparisons, there seems to be a perhaps unusual emphasis on Canadian conditions, and the role of Anglo-Scottish and Ukrainian grain farmers, especially those who settled the high plains of the Canadian West, the reader is asked to remember the context of the lectures and the audience. What is on offer here is determined in many ways by the original form of the presentation: three lectures, a graduate seminar, and then a supernumerary piece that resulted from pushing the limits of death. But they are only a number of experimental sallies. Needless to say, there is a wider scope for more detailed and deeper research. So I wandered, sometimes very far afield, from the confines of the ancient Mediterranean. The manifest justification is that I am touching on human activities and modes of thinking that have a very long-range story that intersects and runs through the more restricted confines of the history with which I am most familiar. One purpose of these diversions is to gesture to these other times, places, and peoples. If either intrigue or dissatisfaction with what I have done incites and encourages more work on these problems by others, then so much the better.

My story lies on the other side of a great revolution in labour that is a recent convulsion. When this revolution first took place in the nineteenth century in the land that was the avatar of the modern industrial economy, its rapid and pervasive effects were experienced within the existence of one generation. One man, in his own lifetime, could mark the tremendous effect of the change. In the year 1912, in prefacing the reprint of his novel *The Mayor of Casterbridge*, first written and published in the mid-1880s, Thomas Hardy drew attention to this fact. At the beginning of the second decade of the twentieth century, readers of the reprinted version of his novel, he warned, could no longer be expected to have any natural empathy with the conditions described in it. 'Readers of the following story who have not yet arrived at middle age are asked to bear in mind that, in the days recalled by the tale, the home Corn Trade, on which so much of the action turns, had an importance that can hardly be realized by those accustomed to the sixpenny loaf of the present date, and to the present indifference of the public to the harvest weather.' That simple indifference to what Hardy calls 'the harvest weather' is at the centre of my story. Although the great revolution in agriculture, to which Hardy avers, took place all of a sudden, in a generation or so, it separates us from our ancestors as irrevocably as any revolution can. In a bit of table talk on one of those pleasant evenings in Toronto, Christer Bruun and I agreed that it was a hopeless thing for us to expect our students to have any personal empathy with this now-distant world – even if we ourselves had once been close to it. We had both felt the frustration of trying to describe these other places and times of rural economy and life to those who had no connecting experiences with them.

The problems are not just those of distance and time, but also of individual lives and of evidence. Our story circles around the narrative of the life of one man from late antique Africa. It is perhaps fitting that by the fragmentation of the very stone that records his story he is nameless, an unknown. This whole aspect of the problem raises the aspect of 'the life of an unknown' as does the exciting exploration of more modern archives by Alain Corbin. Our man, from the Roman town of Mactaris in Africa, made his life as a reaper of cereal grains rather than as a *forestier* and a maker of clogs, but he has had his life, like Louis-François Pinagot, made well known, even famous, by modern-day historians. But I made the selection of my man and his occupation in the service of a rather different purpose. If large numbers of persons in a given social order repeatedly engaged in a social (and economic) action year after year, then what were some of the less tangible effects of just doing this important thing?

Good and bad are thoroughly mixed in real life as it is lived. If everyone today, as we are vouchsafed, will have their own fifteen minutes, they might also have their own more modest quinquennium. In beginning to hunt down the remnant tracks of evidence in the life story of the African harvester who is at the centre of my inquiry, I never quite knew where I was going or where I might be headed next. In the end, I found myself in a place where I certainly did not wish to be. I followed the tombstone that was the departure point of my investigation as far as logic and technical skill would permit. But the whole process, I must confess, never resembled the deliberate and purposive work of reaping. It was more like Agnès Varda's cinematic insights into the grubby world of gleaning: gathering, hopefully, to useful and creative purpose, leftovers, throwaways, and discards – in my case, the fortuitous castoffs of long-vanished times. At one point, it seemed certain that the end was in sight when the path then began diverging again, strangely, in other directions. The first signs of this distress surfaced in a lively discussion of the cold and anodyne economics of my problem in a sunny but cool San Diego in January of '07. In that discussion, I benefited from the comments of many. But when I was asked directly by Cam Grey what on earth my presentation was all about, I replied, 'I don't know, but I think that I'm headed in the direction of death.' 'Well that's where we're all going, mate,' he retorted. In his wonderful Oz-like way, he put the whole matter better than I ever could.

BDS
Princeton
10 May 2010

BRINGING IN THE SHEAVES:
ECONOMY AND METAPHOR IN THE ROMAN WORLD

CHAPTER ONE

Under the Burning Sun

In listening to verses composed at the dawn of Greek poetry, we hear the vivid story of how the divine blacksmith Hephaistos forged a new suit of armour for the warrior Achilles. The rhythmic words in which Homer details the decoration of the hero's new shield feature the first harvesting scene known in Western literature.[1] In describing how Hephaistos hammered out the picture of reapers at work on the warrior's shield, the poet depicts a basic economic activity that underwrote the existence of the community in both war and peace.

> He placed on it the estate of a great man where the hired men
> with sharp sickles in their hands were cutting the crop.
> Of the handfuls of cut stalks, some fell to the ground
> along the lines of reaping, one after another, while
> the sheavers were binding the other handfuls with ties.
> Three of the binders were standing over the sheaves and
> behind them boys were gathering up the bound sheaves,
> carrying them in their arms.
> The lord stood there in silence, sceptre in hand,
> at the head of the reaping rows, rejoicing in his heart.
> And off to the side, beneath a spreading oak,
> the lord's servitors were setting out the harvest feast.
> They were preparing a great ox they had slaughtered
> for the reapers' dinner, while the women helpers
> generously sprinkled white barley over it.

The *basileus* or great lord stands, sceptred, gazing over the bounty of his lands.[2] The hired hands, the *erithoi*, sweat and labour at the heavy work of reaping, assisted by household dependants who undertake the secondary tasks of sheaving, binding, and carrying the cut grain to storage.[3] A perhaps surprising observation is that the subsequent thousand years and more of Greek and Latin literature offer no comparably vivid scenes of harvest labour. There are, it is true, fragmented allusions to individual elements of the harvesting process found here and there in the canonical literary texts of the time. Following this classical interlude, allusions to harvesting in agrarian metaphors were liberally employed by Christian bishops in their writings and by Christian preachers in their sermons. When the scene in Homer is compared with the allusions and metaphors from these later times, it is apparent how little had changed in the intervening millennium and more of Mediterranean civilization. The basic harvesting operations remained labour intensive. They required the same participation of groups of seasonal workers, and the same struggle and sweat under the burning sun to cut the cereal crops.[4]

If ancient literary pictures of harvest labour, like the scene described by Homer, are idealized distillations of a common work activity, they also betray small consistencies and differences that signal that they are scenes from a particular phase of Mediterranean antiquity. An equally well known fictional representation of cutting crops, from Leo Tolstoy's *Anya Karenin*, where the landlord Konstantin Levin joins his peasants in the hard work, replicates many of the same features of the ancient descriptions, including the presence of the landlord. But there are small differences. The protagonist of the piece and the peasant labourers on his estate wield scythes, not hand-held sickles or reaping hooks.[5] Not as much an ekphrasis as a vivid replaying of life, the scene in Tolstoy indicates a special ecology of harvesting and a labour process, that of mowing, that is different from the harvesting of cereal grains. It also indicates peculiar sensibilities of self-representation. There is no hint in Homer's *basileus* or in the great Roman landlords later described by Christian writers, like Augustine and Ambrose, of the likelihood that they would personally have joined in the grit and the pain of reaping the cereal crops.

Of course, there were always a few back-to-the-soil idealists, ascetic heroes like the elder Cato who, like Tolstoy, were happy to advertise how they were willing to share in the toil and sweat of their farm workers.[6] But there is still a difference. In the Roman instances there is not the same quality of evident joy prompted by the aesthetic beauties of the visual geometrics of the mowing or, more important, such fulsome praise of the sheer enjoyment of the hard work itself. More disturbing than these aesthetic distinctions is the fact that ancient depictions of an activity that was so widespread, that engaged such great numbers of people, and was filled with manifest meaning are very rare and different when compared with the representations of Tolstoy's time. The contemporary paintings of Alexei Venetsianov, for example, offer good pictorial parallels to Tolstoy's interest in fine verbal descriptions of peasant harvest work. It should also be noted that in their own time these paintings were a near-revolutionary departure from the ages-old

1.1: Alexei Venetsianov, *Harvesting: Summer*, 1827.
The State Tretyakov Gallery, Moscow; ArtResource

norms of portraying rural life and peasant farmers and, even more, the hard field work itself.[7] We should never expect too much from the field of representation, but the differences are there in the record to be seen.

The paucity of reflections of rural work in the artistic canons of the past is difficult to explain, in part because of the manifest ubiquity and the natural importance of the labour. The plain fact is that the grain harvest was of enormous economic significance to premodern societies. As a historian of Victorian England has noted, marking the obvious dimensions of scale: 'Perhaps the first thing we should say about nineteenth-century harvesting is that it was an immense activity.'[8] The same immensity must also have been true of the Roman world. Other than war, few activities mobilized manpower resources as consistently and over such wide expanses of the Mediterranean as did this annual agricultural task. Given the analogy, it is useful to note that standing armies had ready-made organized manpower that was often turned to this other productive work. In modern times, but before the full blast of modernity, the same connection is found. During the First World War, when the labour on the Canadian prairies needed for the harvest was in too short a supply, the army furloughed soldiers to make up the deficit.[9] Given the immensity of the demand on manpower, a balance between military work and harvest labour is generally found in the past.[10] In Egypt of the Ptolemies, the recruiting and movement of soldiers could be done in tandem with the mobilization of reapers. The two were connected, the one with the other.[11] In Roman Africa, reaping and mowing were collective activities that could similarly involve whole units of the army. A vexillation or detachment of the Third Augustan Legion was temporarily moved to the small town of Casae, about a dozen miles north of the legionary base at Lambaesis, to mow a crop of hay.[12] These were working soldiers, just like the ones who were employed by Caesar in his campaign in Britain in 55 BCE: men who laid down their arms to reap cereal grains.[13]

It is hardly surprising, then, to find armies in antiquity 'taking crops' wherever they moved. While some of these instances are ones in which soldiers compelled locals to deliver crops as requisitioned, not a few of them reveal the soldiers themselves, like Caesar's legionaries, engaged in the work of reaping.[14] The numbers could be considerable, amounting to many thousands of men committed to a single reaping operation.[15] The manpower relationship between harvesting and military service was therefore inversely connected and proportionally related. Intensive military recruiting in the harvest season could have a severe impact on the reaping of the crops. The author of the account of Caesar's African War of 46 BCE claimed, perhaps with some degree of exaggeration, that no harvest had been taken off in the previous year because the enemy, the faction of Pompey, had recruited so heavily from local manpower.[16] In Rome's war against Macedon, in 171 BCE, Perseus the Macedonian king provides another case.

Perseus had remained for a few days in his camp at Sykurion ... he heard that the Roman soldiers were bringing in grain that they had reaped from the fields round about, and that each man, in front of his own tent, was cutting off the heads of the grain with his sickle so that the grain might be threshed more cleanly, and (he also heard) that they had made great piles of straw throughout the camp ...[17]

Knowing about the heaps of straw in the Roman camp, Perseus decided to attack it with firebrands. Having reaped all the crops in the lands around their base, however, the Roman forces had shifted their camp to Krannon and, having reaped the crops there, they had then moved again to reap the fields around Phalanna. When Perseus learned from a Roman deserter that the Roman troops were wandering around the fields of the latter town engaged in reaping, he took advantage of their dispersal to attack them. He slaughtered a great number of the Romans and captured 'a thousand' wagons, presumably including the ones used to transport the grain that the legionaries had reaped.[18]

In all these cases, we find the same pressures on limited mobile manpower that had to be distributed between harvest work on the one hand and military work on the other – the same pressures that were encountered in Canada during the First World War. If the fixed numbers of able young men who formed the same pool of draftees in each time period are considered, we are faced with a variant of a zero-sum game. The heavier demands of the one kind of work vitally affected the availability of labour for the other. To fulfil both tasks, if conditions required, soldiers as soldiers were engaged in reaping cereal grains. In visual terms, the standard illustrations of the imperial army on the move pictured on Trajan's column show that legionaries routinely foraged and that they were commonly involved in the labour of reaping.[19] It was a pattern that continued to the very end of Roman antiquity. In a harvest in the region of Noricum in the early sixth century, it was necessary for the grain to be defended against the pestilences of mildew and locusts, and for it to be reaped quickly. In response, soldiers from the local army detachment were sent into the fields to help take off the crops.[20]

Not unnaturally, the analogy of these two kinds of work affected processes of mental representation. The work for the one task, that of reaping cereal crops, was preparation for the other: reaping the lives of men on the battlefield.[21] The agricultural field, the *ager* or the *campus*, with its cutting to be done came to merge with images of cutting on the *field* of battle, as with the *campus Martius* at Rome. The field was a common denominator. To be 'on campaign' – that is, literally, to be 'in the field' – signalled not just the violent competition of cutting plant life in the harvest field, but also the reaping of lives on the field of battle. In this way, to be 'in the field' or 'on campaign' came to indicate any comparable martial-like contest, such as the electoral campaign waged by McCain and Obama, and their

1.2: Roman legionaries reaping: Trajan's Column, Rome, Italy. Cichorius, *Traianssäule*, Tafel lxxxi, scene cix–cx, 291–2; *Dritter Textband: Commentar zu den Reliefs des zweiten dakischen Krieges* (Berlin: Georg Reimer, 1900), pp. 199–202, on Bild cx, Tafel lxxxi, scene 292–3

cohorts, in the late summer and fall of 2008.[22] The 'fielding' of men offers another extension of this way of thinking. The metaphor was already in mind in antiquity. In a petition made by a Ptolemaic landlord against his tenants, one Antimachos complained that his farmers had agreed in their contract to go out to his fields at the time of harvest and to hire reapers, and not to stay at home, as they had done. Whether going out into the field or doing the reaping, Antimachos uses the same verb meaning 'to be on (military) campaign': *strateuein*.[23] In Roman antiquity, the connection was direct and manifest. It was felt and often experienced by the men who were both peasant farmers and recruits for the army and, in the Republic, voters in the citizen assemblies. Along with his sword, every Roman legionary carried a harvester's sickle as part of his standard equipment. This cutting instrument was present as often as his sword and it was probably used more often.[24] Given the rural background of many of the recruits to army service, the engagement of soldiers as reapers was a logical one. Which is ironic, since harvesting was one of the arduous agricultural tasks that they had hoped to escape by serving in the army.[25] Resentment naturally surfaced when soldiers were compelled back into the hard rural grind that they thought they had left behind – when, as foot soldiers, they found themselves pressed into service as common day labourers in the fields.

Given the analogy and the reality, it is not without grounds that the civilian harvester's cutting and mowing was, by turns, likened to the violent actions of the soldier, and that the harvester was later compared to the holy warrior and the Christian martyr.[26] These metaphors are found, and pervasively, in writings, including modern ones, on the migrations of harvest labourers. One such account from 1904 describes '*the army* that moves northward from Oklahoma to Canada harvesting the wheat.'[27] The metaphor was not without a basis in real working conditions. A reporter interviewing men going to the wheat fields of the American West in 1902 was met with the remark: 'and a lot of us have been in the army.' The harvester of the time was similarly described in military terms, in a simile, as a 'medium-sized wiry healthy-looking fellow, such as from the United States cavalry.'[28] Sometimes both metaphors were combined, as in the reference to 'the *crusade* of this civilian army' used to describe the movement of seasonal harvesters in Canada in this same period.[29] Similar metaphors were also found in all Mediterranean lands in antiquity because of the equally pervasive and eternally recurrent annual cycle of labour that mobilized millions of peasants, soldiers, contractors, seasonal workers, holy men and monks, as well as the women and children of each rural household, all set in motion with the advent of each harvest season.

Into this sweeping Mediterranean panorama, I wish to place a single ordinary life. It is the story of a man from the African provinces of the Roman empire. Since we do not know his name, he is conventionally known in our modern histories as the Maktar Harvester. He has received this name from the small town of Mactaris, adjacent to modern-day Maktar in Tunisia, where his tombstone was discovered (see fig. A.2.1). The Maktar Harvester's story is important not just because of the personal interest of the man's life, but also because he is mentioned in nearly every handbook and history of the empire's economic and social relations. In the long epitaph on his tombstone he boasted, in verse no less, of his own wondrous rise from base poverty to the ranks of municipal decurion and town censor. His dramatic elevation in wealth and status was founded on the manual labour of reaping cereal crops in the grain fields of Numidia. This one man's rise from being a landless peasant upwards to the highest ranks of the decurial order of his home town raises more questions than it ostensibly answers: elementary questions about the nature of work and wages in the Roman empire. To come to terms with this one man's life, we must not only understand the bigger picture of the social relations in which he was embedded, but we must also essay a few queries about economic processes.

From the details of his story, there is no doubt that the harvester from Mactaris fashioned his social elevation out of the hard manual work that he performed in harvesting cereal crops in the expansive grain fields that stretched over the high plains of Africa. In pragmatic terms, one still has to wonder: How did he do it? How was his rise to high social status possible? What is the background against which this manual work for profit was formed? It is a truism of the modern writing of ancient history that much of the history of labour is less about the work and work regimes themselves than it is a second-best history that does what it can with the existing legal and literary sources. It tends to reduce the actual dynamics of hard work to a history of ranks, statuses, rights, and obligations.[30] We have to do better. Even so, there is a distressing absence that must be confronted. There can be no doubt that the harvesting of crops was an intense labour activity that involved a great part of the rural population in the lands of the Mediterranean every single year in a huge mass of backbreaking work. Yet what is known about the work regimen of harvesting and about the harvesters themselves, especially those who were free labourers, amounts to almost nothing.[31]

The Maktar Harvester's story is therefore something of a paradox. The important events of his work life and his public career are known in some detail. As far as the surviving historical records go, however, his tale is a solitary one. His is yet another illustration of those economic occupations where we know that the number of persons involved was immense and that the work was of paramount importance, but where the appearance of the workers themselves in our literary and epigraphical sources is so slight as to be almost non-existent.[32] It must first be admitted that our historical knowledge of free hired labour in agriculture in general is not impressive.[33] When it comes to cyclical, repeated, and necessary tasks like harvesting, we seem to be almost as ignorant about them as the work itself was ubiquitous.[34] If it is as true for Mediterranean antiquity as it was for eighteenth-century England that the harvest was 'the heartbeat of the economy,' it is equally true that its labour regimes are obscured by a singular lack of interest on the part of the writers of our historical sources.[35] Perhaps more poetically, Olivier de Serres, the great Protestant innovator of French agriculture in the late sixteenth and early seventeenth centuries, summed up the importance of the harvest to the premodern world: 'The harvest is the crown of agriculture, the reward for the expenditures and the sweat of the labourer, the hope of his family, the security of the master, the life and wealth of the whole state.'[36] More than this, we know that the cereal harvest, where it was a dominant factor in the rural economy, set a repeated and consistent annual rhythm of labour demands that produced cyclical highs and lows of employment in the economy as a whole.[37] For Roman society and the empire, it would have been no different. But in the extreme deficit of the required evidence, to estimate anything useful about the labour involved, the historian of Roman antiquity is compelled to seek wider comparative fields, such as the early modern European agrarian economies witnessed by de Serres, from which to sketch some tentative generalizations.[38] Closer to the ecology of the Roman empire, studies of small scale rural Mediterranean societies by anthropologists, historians, and sociologists might reveal similarities of practice and form, and indicate some of the parameters of our problem.[39] It is with these limits that a beginning must be made. We might usefully begin with problems of scale.

How Much Work?

To make a reasonable estimate about the mass of the work required, we must confine ourselves to a particular part of the entire harvesting process. It is also necessary to establish some estimates of quantity, no matter how speculative. Our inquiry will therefore be restricted to the specific case of the harvesting of the major cereal crops of wheat and barley. It will not encompass other kinds of harvests, such as the cash crops of olives and grapes.[40] For the purpose of analytical precision, our focus will be even narrower. Except as they are necessary to our story, there will be no consideration of many important aspects of the harvesting of cereal grains, including the operations of transport, threshing, and storage. Because my interests are focused on work, mobility and migration, contracts and disputes, expectations and fears, and on the ideas generated out of these behaviours and sentiments, my attention will be concentrated directly on reaping, one of the two main parts into which harvest operations have been analytically divided.[41] In economic terms, a broad bisectorial division of labour is found in agricultural work between front end tasks such as ploughing and reaping, where the labour inputs are approximately proportional to the area being worked, and back end operations like binding, transporting sheaves, and threshing, in which the labour inputs are roughly proportional to the level of outputs.[42] This division reflects a real-life separation of harvest labour into two distinct, if connected spheres that had implications for the systemic organization of the whole process of the harvest. It involved the management of the labourers and their tools, and the gendered division of the work. The customary bifurcation of labour in the harvesting of cereal crops justifies a corresponding analytic division into two parts. In focusing on the single 'front end' operation of the cutting of the crops and on the persons who did the reaping, I am deliberately selecting the part of the harvest that is most clearly defined in terms of work and concept.[43] Even presuming that there was seasonal hiring of the labour needed for the various operations of reaping, we might ask: What was the work

HARVESTING LABOUR PROCESS

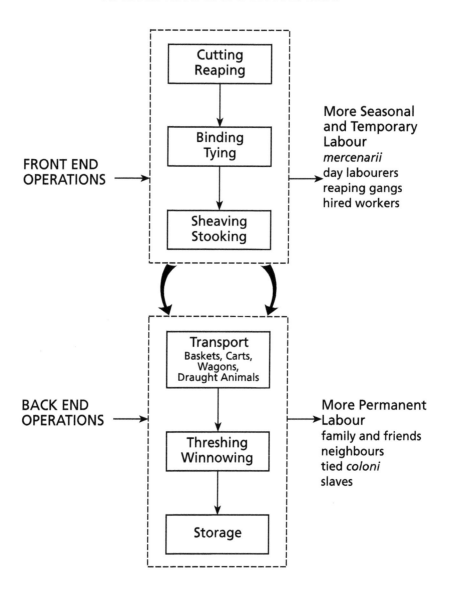

1.3: Elements of the harvesting labour process (author)

of reaping like? How demanding of labour? How cumulative were its effects? And how rewarding was it?

Modern analysis of conditions that approximate the premodern set of factors involved in cereal production in the Roman Mediterranean indicates that between 5.7 to 7.5 man-days of labour were needed to grow a hectolitre of wheat (in Roman terms, about 28 to 30 modii) to the point where it was reaped and stored. For the 300,000,000 modii of cereal grains produced annually in Roman Africa, the general labour requirements were therefore enormous. Something in the range of 60 million man-days of work per annum would have been required. But the critical factor that determined the allocation of labour in performing this task was the seasonality of the collective labour requirements. Only a portion of this work was directly involved in the reaping operations themselves. For the sake of comparison, we can note that for the three week harvest period in eighteenth-century France, it was a rule of thumb that about 15 to 20 harvesters were needed to reap an area that had been ploughed and seeded by four workers. That is to say, the seasonal work demands of reaping were about four to five times normal labour requirements.[44] The general scale of these work demands also ought to be noted.

The sheer magnitude of the [labour] flows in and out of the corn [sc. wheat]-growing sector meant that the markets coordinating them were a critical nexus of early modern and early industrial economies. In particular, the organization of non-agricultural production had to be compatible with temporary interruptions caused by migration to harvest work in response to temporary wages that were often twice as high as the normal industrial wage.[45]

If the scale of movement of the seasonal labourers needed for the reaping of cereal grains attained anything like that in late eighteenth-century France (about 1 per cent of the adult population) then we can postulate the need for something on the order of half a million persons on the move each year in the Roman empire to cope with the reaping of cereals at harvest time.[46]

Given the magnitudes and the disruptions entailed, one would think that the agricultural handbooks of Roman antiquity, from Cato the Elder to Palladius, would provide answers to questions concerning the labour. Although they do furnish us with some practical details, it is frustrating that they confront us with yet more questions and problems. Pliny the Elder, writing in the 70s CE, sets the beginning of the mowing season – perhaps for his homelands in northern Italy – at 1 June, but he says nothing about the labour needed to carry it out.[47] Also, Pliny is referring to the mowing of hay crops and not to the reaping of cereal grains. Writing in the mid-first century CE, Columella comments on agricultural operations in the first two weeks of May in central Italy. He notes that a competent worker could mow about a iugerum, or approximately two-thirds of an acre, of meadowland in a day, and that a second worker who collected the sheaves could bind 1,200 *manipuli* in a day, each of them weighing about four pounds.[48] In another passage, when speaking about the last two weeks of July, he repeats that one worker could mow one iugerum of hay in a day. Columella notes that by this time the harvest had already been completed in temperate places near the sea, and within thirty days of the cutting of the grain, the straw which had been cut was gathered in heaps. Obviously these are general estimates and so important cautions must be noted. These include the fact that Columella, like Pliny, is writing about the cutting of hay and not about the reaping of cereal grains, a slower and more arduous process that required more time and manpower. And he was writing about the specific conditions in central Italy reported by his sources, a region in which he himself owned farms, and where many of his literate and learned readers did as well.

The problem is that when Columella finally approaches the specific subject of the reaping of cereal grains (which he does only in brief asides) he suggests that the labour required was about the same as that needed for mowing hay: one and a half days for one man to reap a iugerum of wheat and one day for a man to reap a iugerum of barley.[49] In giving these estimates, he was repeating the figures provided a century or more earlier by Varro in which that writer claimed that the reaping of one iugerum of cereal grain on easy or level ground required approximately one day's work from one man. He notes that additional work will be needed to carry the cut grain in baskets to the threshing floor.[50] Even if the cutting operations described by Columella are for mowing hay and not reaping grains, his estimate of the labour requirements for reaping is barely possible. Other problems and doubts subsist. Although Varro adds the qualification that it takes *about* one day's work 'on favourable terrain,' his low estimates conflict both with other ancient evidence and with modern observations. These numbers suggest that Varro was probably using an odd one-off source and that Columella was copying Varro in following traditional wisdom, not a very happy situation for the modern historian who is left grasping at straws.

What little we can glean from other agronomists confirms that the reaping of cereal grains was markedly more labour intensive than was the mowing of hay. The fifth-century Latin agronomist Palladius more credibly states that the reaping of five modii of barley (the *modius* is about one-quarter bushel) was something that could be done in one day by an expert reaper. But he adds that an average reaper could probably cut only three modii, and a poor one in the lower ranks of the less skilled even less than this.[51] Translated into amounts of land, these figures suggest that a competent and experienced reaper could harvest about two-thirds of a iugerum a day (that is, about half an acre) but that an average harvest worker could only cut about half a iugerum in the same time.[52] The best direct evidence for work and pay rates under real conditions in classical antiquity is found in the harvest contracts from Roman Egypt.[53] What we read in these contracts is that despite the different sizes of the individual harvesting gangs, the amount of land to be harvested by each man is roughly the same, about three-quarters of an aroura, that is, approximately three-quarters of a iugerum, for each reaper. In Egypt, however, it is important to note that reaping was usually done in optimum weather conditions and on planar terrain. These reaping rates would surely not have been the average ones in the less favourable conditions found elsewhere in the empire.

Modern estimates for the non-mechanized harvesting of cereal crops in comparable areas of the Mediterranean suggest higher levels of *per diem* labour requirements for reaping. Figures for the grain harvest from the early nineteenth century, before the introduction of mechanized reapers, indicate that about one and a half worker-days per acre were needed for reaping done with a scythe and three to four worker-days per acre for reaping cereal grains with a hand-held sickle.[54] Since the iugerum was about two-thirds of an acre, at these rates it would have taken about three worker-days to cut the equivalent of a iugerum. Other high rates have been found. In one case, an estimate has been derived from the harvesting of barley crops in rural and remote areas of the Greek islands of Amorgos and Karpathos in the early 1980s. For workers primarily using hand-held sickles, it is reported that the reaping and binding operations consumed a range of between four and five worker-days of labour per hectare.[55] Given the fact that elderly women constituted the bulk of the labour force in these unusual cases, it has reasonably been suggested that under normal circumstances where hired labour was used (where even the locals said that much faster rates were expected) the lower of the two rates would surely be closer to normal expectations.[56] Some modern data also point to greater efficiencies in nineteenth-century England, where it was sometimes thought that one man with a sickle could reap about an acre a day. But these rates are considerably above what is known for most Mediterranean conditions and for continental Europe. Such estimates must represent best case or ideal situations.[57] Where modern historians have access to reasonably good statistics on the reaping of cereal crops, on the whole they point to significantly lower average rates on the order of half an acre a day, or less, as closer to the norm (see tables 1.1 and 1.2a–b).

Comparative statistics from early modern and nineteenth-century Britain (tables 1.1–2) show that in high cutting with the hand-held sickle one worker could reap about 0.4 to 0.5 acres a day. This rate suggests that about two worker-days would be required to reap an acre of wheat. Since barley was almost invariably low cut, the requirements were slightly higher at about three worker-days per acre.[58] These figures are equivalent to about one and a half worker-days per iugerum for the reaping operations alone.[59] But these rates are for the more amenable conditions of nineteenth-century England, which had better cutting instruments and technologies than were available in antiquity. The worker-day rates per iugerum for the wheat fields of Roman Africa must have been higher. Comparable statistics for indigenous reapers from the modern Maghrib are difficult to come

1.4: Traditional modes of reaping on the Argive Plain, Greece, c. 1900. 'Primitive Method of Harvesting Grain on the Plains of Argos, Greece' c. 1901: LC-USZ62-65927: Library of Congress, Public Access

by. One set of figures presented in a standard handbook on 'indigenous agriculture' in the colonial period claims that for local non-European reapers, who always used sickles, it took 8 to 12 days of labour to reap a hectare (approximately 3.75 iugera) of wheat or barley.[60] Making the appropriate calculations, this would indicate that higher rates of between 2 and 2.5 worker-days of labour would have been required to reap a iugerum of cereal grains. These data point to approximately the same order of labour requirements to reap a unit of standing grain in the Maghrib when premodern harvesting tools and techniques were used.

Table 1.1: Comparative efficiency of reaping methods: early modern England

	Cutting rates per diem		Worker-days per iugerum
	acres	[iugera]	
Wheat harvesting			
High reaping (sickle)	0.5	[0.8]	1.3
Low reaping (sickle)	0.4	[0.7]	1.4
Scythe	1.7	[2.8]	0.4
Manual reaper	15.0	[25.0]	0.04

Source: Overton, *Agricultural Revolution in England*, table 3.21, p. 124. Overton's figures are expressed in acres; for the sake of direct comparison, they have been translated into Roman iugera.

Table 1.2: Cereal grain reaping and mowing rates: nineteenth-century England

A = Cutting rate per worker-day per acre [iugera]
B = Ratio of linkage workers to reapers
C = Total worker-days per acre [iugera]

Reaping method	A	B	C
Wheat crops			
High reaping: sickle	0.35 [0.56]	1:7	3.6 [2.3]
Low reaping: sickle	0.25 [0.40]	1:5	4.8 [3.0]
Low reaping: reaping hook	0.33 [0.53]	1:5	4.0 [2.5]
Mowing: binding-sheaving	1.10 [1.80]	2:1	2.7 [1.7]
Barley and oats			
Low reaping: sickle	0.33 [0.53]	1:5	4.0 [2.5]
Low reaping: reaping hook	0.40 [0.64]	1:5	3.3 [2.1]
Mowing: binding-sheaving	2.00 [3.2]	2:1	1.5 [0.9]
Mowing: loose sheaves left in swathes	2.00 [3.2]	0.5:1	0.8 [0.5]

Source: Collins, 'Harvest Technology and Labour Supply in Britain, 1790–1870,' p. 460 and 'Labour Supply and Demand in European Agriculture 1800–1880,' p. 82: all of the figures given by Collins are in acres; I have given the equivalents in iugera in square brackets.

Such per unit labour requirements do not in themselves provide any measurement of the general scale of the work required, much less an estimate of how much of this labour was mobile or specific to the season. Even for more modern and recent times, just before the advent of machine-driven agriculture, it is still difficult to acquire good estimates of the overall dimensions of the movement of seasonal harvest labour. The author of a standard treatment of migrant agricultural workers in one of our best documented historical cases, nineteenth-century Britain, confesses that there are in fact no hard reliable statistics.[61] Even in this case, however, in the nascent era of the mechanization of harvesting, it is reasonably certain that there were more than several hundred thousand men and women on the move as part of itinerant harvesting gangs. At the height of these migrations, they included between sixty and a hundred thousand Irish harvesters who annually crossed the Irish Sea to work in the grain fields of England.[62] We must remember that the harvesters who were counted were the Irish and foreign labourers alone, and that these numbers do not take into account the more numerous internal migrations of English itinerant labourers within the country. The movements of seasonal workers were on an enormous scale for the time. As late as the early twentieth century, when important parts of the harvest had already been mechanized in the United States, the numbers were tens of thousands for individual American states. By the late nineteenth century, the total numbers required for the wheat harvest were already over a hundred thousand men a year.[63] In the same early decades of the twentieth century, the bringing of thirty to sixty thousand seasonal harvest workers to the wheat fields of western Canada 'involved the largest mass movement of men organized to meet a single peacetime need.'[64]

Statistical studies of the annual distribution of workloads on English farms in this same period estimate that, even under conditions of incipient mechanization, about a third of all of the labour required in a given year was needed for harvesting operations. When crops were cut by hand, well over half of all the annual labour requirements for a farm were concentrated in the time of the harvest. The same relative proportion is found for the grain fields of the United States and Canada in the late nineteenth and early twentieth century.[65] Even more significant is the scale of the general labour demand produced by the widespread farming of cereal grain crops under premodern conditions. At least as late as the eighteenth century in France, the labour demands for this one sector of the economy directly affected the labour available for all other sectors of the economy.[66] The need for additional seasonal labour generally depended on the scale of the farming operations. For smaller peasant farms, the task would probably be within the range of the individual family with some assistance from friends and neighbours.[67] Modern cases indicate that for large farms about half of all the labour required in the grain harvest season had to be acquired from outside.[68] This suggests comparable levels of demands for external mobile labourers in the harvest season for Africa in Roman antiquity. Given the vagaries of weather and local conditions, a family of six, with some additional help allocated for the reaping process, might be able to cope with about forty iugera or so. Such a regimen assumes ideal conditions, which were not always the case. Of the less-than-ideal conditions, adverse weather was the big and constant threat that curtailed reaping operations.

Given these constraints on the process of reaping, it is possible to acquire a general estimate of the labour needed for cutting the harvest each year for the Roman provinces of Africa where the Maktar Harvester worked. From the indications given by the ancient sources, the total average cereal production for Roman Africa – albeit with considerable annual and decadal fluctuations above and below the average – can be estimated on the low side at about 300,000,000 modii of cereal grains per annum.[69] Modern post-war figures for the Maghrib indicate that the total grain production for the eastern Maghrib (not including Morocco or Tripolitania) averaged about 255,000,000 modii of wheat and about 105,000,000 modii of barley for a total of about 360,000,000 modii per annum.[70] With returns of 20 modii per iugerum representing lower average annual yields, the area that would have had to be reaped to yield cereal grain production on this scale would have been on the order of 15,000,000 iugera of land.[71] The most reliable modern statistics that we have for 'indigenous' agriculture in Tunisia and Algeria for the late nineteenth and early twentieth centuries, when the work was not mechanized and almost all the reaping was done by hand, indicate averages of about 5 to 6 quintals per hectare for wheat and barley crops, that is, about 18 to 20 modii per iugerum in Roman terms. An important caution that must be repeated about these figures is that the yields are *averages*. Annual per unit yields in antiquity varied, as they have in modern times, between lows of about 3 quintals per hectare (i.e. 10 modii per iugerum) to highs of about 7 quintals per hectare (about 25 modii per iugerum).[72]

If on average it took about two men one day to reap a iugerum of cereal grains, then in Africa this annual task would have required 30,000,000 worker-days of labour. If the harvest season for any given region lasted about thirty days, and one man could account for the reaping of 15 iugera in that time, then something on the order of a million men would be required for the reaping process alone. In most large land areas that are characterized by some difference in ecological conditions, harvest seasons are more normally calculated at two months or an eight-week cycle.[73] In this case, each man could account for up to 30 iugera, and therefore half a million men, or so, would be involved in the cutting process. But not all workers would be on the move across the whole face of Africa. The majority of harvest labour, one must suspect, worked on local fields and would not be applied much further afield. For Egypt, the other great cereal grain producer and exporter in the empire, about 9,000,000 arourai (an aroura being, like the iugerum, about two-thirds of an acre) were sown to wheat. At two-thirds to three-quarters an aroura reaped per day by one worker (the requirements set in the reaping contracts from Egypt) around 12,000,000 to 13,000,000 worker-days would be required to cut the wheat crop alone.[74] When the other major cereal crop, barley, is added to the crop mix, about a quarter to a third additional worker-days for reaping would be required, for a total of about 15,000,000 worker-days for the reaping of cereal crops in general.[75] Over a thirty-day reaping cycle, these figures suggest that something like half a million men would be directly involved in reaping.

The labour requirements for reaping would easily have to be doubled or trebled to account for the carting, threshing, winnowing, and storage of the grain. The scale and the intensity of the work were enormous. On the other hand, the real surplus demand on labour supply – that is, work in addition to that provided by the domestic unit and its surrogates – should not be exaggerated. Much of the required work force would already be fixed and in place. Many peasant families could use their own resources, with occasional help from friends and neighbours, based on a mutual exchange, to take off their own crops. But in general the labour demands for the harvest were simply huge, requirements that had to be met by both local permanent labour forces and by mobile harvest workers. Deciding on what portion of the total of millions of worker-days would be filled by seasonal workers on the move is an important part of our problem. The best empirical evidence, again, comes from Roman Egypt. Data from the mid-third-century Heroninos archive indicate that larger estates acquired something like a third or more of their labour from casual or temporary sources at low points in the annual agricultural cycle. However, as much as three-quarters or more of all the labour required for the harvest season was drawn from temporarily hired outside workers.[76] What we need to know, therefore, is how much cereal land in Roman Africa was worked in operational units that were larger than those that could be worked with familial labour and which therefore required additional seasonal workers for the harvesting process.

Confirmation that our estimate of the general order of scale of the labour required to take off the amount of cereal grain produced in Africa in antiquity is at least probable is found not only in comparative figures for premodern harvest labour in the Maghrib. It is also found in an imperial constitution of the year 422 issued by the emperor Honorius to Venantius, the *Comes rerum privatarum*, the chief court official who was in charge of the administration of imperial properties. It is a constitution that concerned the emperor's lands in the provinces of Proconsularis and Byzacena.[77] The imperial decision was given in reply to petitions submitted by the proprietors (more properly, the principal lessors on behalf of the tenant farmers who were working for them) for tax relief for their lands that were not under cultivation. The decree informs us that in the proconsular province some 9,002 centuries (one century contained 200 iugera) and 141 iugera were lands that were being worked, while 5,700 centuries and 144.5 iugera were exempt from tax because they were not being cultivated. Similarly, the decree states that in the province of Byzacena, some 7,460 centuries and 180 iugera were being cultivated, while 7,615 centuries and 3.5 iugera were permitted to be

Map 1.1: Africa of the Maktar Harvester

exempt from taxation because they were not under production. The data seem credible. They were most likely based on official land-tax registers, and they match the ratio of uncultivated to cultivated lands that was true of these same regions during the 1950s and 1960s.[78]

The land based fiscal data preserved in the imperial constitution of 422 indicate that a total of 1,800,541 iugera in the province of Proconsularis and 1,492,180 iugera in the province of Byzacena were under cultivation, for a total of 3,292,721 iugera in the two provinces. It is important to note that the figures apply only to these two provinces. No comparable ones exist for Mauretania Sitifensis or

Numidia, the two other great grain-producing regions in Africa. Another problem with assessing the general significance of the law is that its numbers apply only to lands in the ownership of the emperor. If imperial lands amounted to about one-sixth to one-fifth of all arable lands, then there must have been something on the order of about 15 million iugera under cultivation in Proconsularis and Byzacena. Since Numidia and Sitifensis would have had something on the order of two-thirds to three-quarters of this amount under cultivation, the sum total of arable land would have been in the range of 30 million iugera. About half of the total amount of arable land in the Maghrib has been under cereal cultivation in any given year (as opposed to lands devoted to arboreal crops or vines), and so these figures suggest that *approximately* 15 million iugera were sown to cereal crops each year.[79]

In Africa of the Roman period, a rural economy based on the agricultural surpluses of cereal crops and olives flourished. Unlike the production of olive crops and the processing of olive oil, which have left a vast archaeological residue for modern study, we know rather little from material evidence about the labour invested in the cereal crops that produced much of Africa's wealth.[80] Epigraphical texts can help make up some of the deficit, but here, too, there are difficulties. The well-known regulations of the great imperial domains in the Bagrada Valley, from the northern regions of the proconsular province, record specific tasks that could be demanded from the tenants. They were allowed to cultivate lands around the periphery of the core areas of the large estates in return for the performance of labour obligations on the main domain. The regulations divide the additional work contributions into various kinds.[81] This information is of little use for our purposes, since the quantities of work-days or *operae* owed by the sharecropper for all kinds of extra tasks were arbitrarily set at two days per year for each specific task. No more than two days could be demanded of the tenant for ploughing and seeding, two for weeding, and two for harvesting. The regulations indicate the kinds of farm tasks for which extra labour was most required, but they give no idea of the totality of such needs from the perspective of the men who managed the farm lands for the emperors. There appears to be no adjustment in levels of demands for labour of the kind that appears, for example, in arrangements for villein tenancies in twelfth-century France where the labour requirements in man-days of work varied, increasing substantially during the harvest season.[82] In the case of the Roman imperial domains in Africa, all tasks, whether ploughing, weeding, or harvesting, were set at the same rate of two days per task for the whole year. At harvest time, under this regime, the manager of the estate would have to recruit more of the available two-day units (or, perhaps, commute them from ploughing and weeding). The problem is that the labour demands were calculated from the point of view of the individual sharecropper and not from the perspective of the seasonal needs of the domain manager. In fact, the arrangements assume that the manager would acquire the additional labour needed for the harvest by means that did not primarily depend on the local tenants.

For the purpose of understanding the life of our harvester from Mactaris, we must consider the specific problem of how much of the total harvest labour had to be met by mobile seasonal workers. The proportions in past times and places varied, sometimes considerably. For the grain fields of the United States and Canada in the late nineteenth and early twentieth centuries, estimates of migrant labour as a proportion of all harvest labour requirements varied from one-third to two-thirds of the annual total.[83] Any estimate for north Africa would depend on how much of the total area devoted to the cultivation of cereal grains was in the management of larger farms or estates that could not have reasonably been harvested by dependent peasant families using their own resources. Without Roman land registers or census declarations, we are left in the realm of speculation. As has already been stated, the late imperial land-tax constitution issued by Honorius in 422 permits the deduction that imperial estates accounted for about one-sixth to one-fifth of all of the arable land in the provinces of Byzacena and Proconsularis.[84] There is nothing to make us suspect that the proportion would be much different for Numidia or Mauretania Sitifensis, the other two important wheat-producing provinces in Africa. The huge landed property holdings that were held by senators and other wealthy landowners separately from the imperial lands give every impression of being equally considerable. Indeed, they might even have been much greater in extent than those held by the emperor and the imperial fisc. If the emperors, senators, and other large landholders managed between half and two-thirds of all lands in larger operational units, this would give us some idea of the level of demand for additional seasonal labour.[85] The cold truth, however, is that we cannot know. Many imperial domains, or substantial portions of them, were probably run in small units that were let out to long-term lessees. But there are indications that wealthy landowners ran some of their estates in larger operational units. Even if only half of the lands owned by the great landowners were run in this fashion, the scale of the seasonal labour demands produced by them would require very large numbers of men to be on the move each summer to reap the cereal crops. The whole purpose of running all of these numbers is simply to indicate general parameters of scale: whatever the specific figures that applied in Roman antiquity, there can be no doubt that something on the order of tens of thousands of men must have been on the move each summer to do the reaping and that, in consequence, there must have been many hundreds of contractors of seasonal harvest labourers.

An Urgent Thing

The need for seasonal labour was prompted not just by the quantity of the additional work demands, but also by their intensity. How soon would the reapers have to march out to the fields to do the reaping? The time was determined by the weather conditions of each particular year, by the latitude of the fields being reaped, by the elevation of the land, and by other factors like local hydrological conditions and soil types. Apart from the year's weather, mainly too much or too little rain or sun, most of the other conditions were reasonably constant and led to normal expectations. In the plains regions of central Italy, the mowing of meadowlands, then as now, started around mid-May and lasted until the middle of June.[86] The reaping of the main cereal crops, barley and wheat, usually began about the middle of June and lasted to the middle or the end of July.[87] The summer solstice was taken as a normal benchmark for the beginning of these last operations. For the most part, the start dates and reaping times are confirmed by many literary sources, the singular and striking exception being the *menologia rustica* that place the reaping of barley in July and the reaping of cereal grains in August.[88] These are a full month off the known modern norms, as well as those attested in Italy for antiquity, so an explanation must be sought for the anomaly.[89] In the topsy-turvy ecology of Egypt, these start points were different and peculiar to its own environment. For cereal grain crops, reaping typically began in the third week of April in the more arid lands of the south, but in late May for the lands in the Delta.[90] In the prime wheat-growing lands of Africa, on the high plains of the interior, the greater aridity, different soil types, and lower levels of humidity conspired to make the start dates a month or more earlier than those in central Italy. The reaping of oats and some of the early barley crops usually took place in May, and the reaping of late barley and all of the wheat crop took place over the last weeks of May and the first weeks of June, with threshing occurring at the end of June.[91] It was only in exceptionally humid regions with very good soils in enclaves along the northern coastline that the harvesting of the wheat crops might take place as late as the first weeks of July.[92]

Roman agricultural writers warned that it was an urgent matter that ripe wheat and barley crops be harvested quickly. Any delay, as Columella emphasized, could be very costly, since birds and other wild animals would begin to consume the standing crops. Another problem was that the ripe heads of the grain would begin to fall from the stalks and could only be recovered by intensive and costly gleaning operations.[93] He repeats the same advice, with greater urgency, for the harvesting of barley. It must be reaped more quickly than other cereal grains since the heads shattered easily and, if there were delays, much of the grain would be lost.[94] In the rush to take off the crops, however, the reaping could also take place too soon. The

1.5: *Les Très Riches Heures* of the Duc de Berry: mowing in the month of June.
Musée Condé at Chantilly, France; ms. 65, f. 6 v.; ArtResource

hired harvester or the dependent tenant who reaped prematurely, since the crop was not his own, could face a legal action for damages under the terms of the Lex Aquilia.[95] Whatever the risks, there was a clear sense of urgency that overrode all other considerations. In the midst of one of the greatest political crises that faced the late Republican state, when Tiberius Gracchus was running for re-election as tribune in 133 BCE and it was a matter of utmost importance that citizens come in from the countryside to vote for him, they failed to do so and it became clear that he was going to lose the election. Many of Tiberius's supporters, so went the story, simply did not come into the city to vote, responding instead to the more urgent demands of the harvest that year.[96]

The times set for harvest were so fundamental that they were governed by the imperial legislation of the state. By the later empire, among the recognized state holidays on which formal court actions could not be heard were the First of January, Sundays, Easter, and the days in the months when the harvesting of the major cash crops occurred, usually from 24 June to 1 August.[97] Even the strict measures of the imperial law recognized the urgency of the harvest season. In an order issued by the emperor Constantine to his Praetorian Prefect Aemilianus in the year 328 concerning the considerable latitude and powers available to governors in the process of tribute collection (and this in years when the western government was hard pressed for income) he specifically exempted farmers who needed to perform harvest labour.

If a farmer should be urgently occupied with the business of farming or in taking off the harvest, he shall never be hauled off to the performance of extraordinary tributary impositions, since it is a matter of wisdom to satisfy such [i.e., economic] necessities at the required season.[98]

This seems to have been a general exemption, and one that was specifically maintained by the emperor Justinian as late as the sixth century.[99] When the emperor of Rome, even when he was under fiscal pressure, referred to the 'necessities' and the 'required season' and made allowances for them that superseded the demands of the tribute system, he knew what he was doing. These had been long-standing practices, ones that had been enforced following standard regulations that governed the running of municipalities in the provinces of the empire. The *duumviri*, the two mayors of a town, were permitted to postpone the official business of the local government either for the harvesting of cereal grains or for the vinting of grapes. They were permitted to do this twice (for two thirty-day periods) during their annual term of office. These local regulations mimicked the ones that applied at Rome, ones that regulated the affairs of the metropolis in the context of the agricultural cycles of central Italy.[100] At a less exalted level, the individual farmer who was a usufructuary of agricultural land was not permitted to do many things basically to alter its conditions. He could not, for example, construct buildings on the land. An exception was made, however, for a building that was necessary for the harvesting of crops.[101] If it was for the purpose of taking off a harvest, the owner was permitted to move on to lands that were in the hands of a usufructuary.[102] So, too, a person could not be hauled before a court if he was a farmer engaged in the harvest. It was a right that was long and well established, and one whose force was confirmed by a legal declaration, an *oratio* uttered by the emperor Marcus Aurelius (although, obviously, exceptions were permitted).[103] To make the legal standing of this special time explicit, each governor had to declare publicly what was to be 'the time of harvest,' according to the custom of each region in his province.[104]

Other threats that made the harvest an urgent thing were the dangers of severe winds and storms of mid-summer that could be ruinous for the unprepared farmer. The Elder Pliny mentions the case of one Democritus who warned his brother Damasus, who was taking off his crops in the extreme heat of mid-summer, to leave what remained of the crop in the field and to hurry to get what he had already taken off under cover. The prophetic warning, says Pliny, was confirmed. A few hours later a savage rain and windstorm attacked the part of the crop that was left standing.[105] High winds and pouring rains could ruin the ripened crop, even if it was already lying in cut sheaves on the ground. It was recognized in the law that 'this superior force, which the Greeks call Divine Power,' and which the jurists were supposed to take into consideration, was a principal cause of crop losses suffered by landowners and tenants.[106] Just as important are the ways in which the malignant power of inclement weather was construed by literary talents. Gale-force winds and lashing rains were threats of such a primal order that the Roman poet could compose fearful evocations of them in his words on the risks of farming.

> Why should I speak of the storms of autumn and the stars,
> when the days are already shorter and the season milder,
> and of things against which men must guard? When rain-
> bearing Spring pours down showers, when the spiked heads
> of grain in the harvest fields bristle, when the milky-coloured
> grain is ripened on its strong stem? Just when the farmer has
> marched his harvest gang into the golden fields and is busy
> stripping the barley heads from their fragile stalks,
> many times I myself have witnessed the combined assault
> of the winds rushing together to tear up the heavy crop from its
> very roots, and tossing it skywards into the heavens.

> In the same way, Winter with its blackened blast sends the
> light straw and stems flying. Often the immense battle line of rains
> attacks from the sky, piling up a savage storm with its darkened
> downpours, marshalling clouds from on high. The peak of the
> heavens falls and deluges the happy crops and the labours of oxen.
> The drainage ditches are quickly filled, and once-empty river beds
> burst with roars, the waters raging and boiling in their twisting
> courses. The Father himself, in the midnight of the clouds, wields a
> glowing thunderbolt in his right hand. With a great crash the earth
> trembles. Wild animals run amok. Fear levels the hearts of ordinary
> mortals, striking them to the ground ... Fear these things and
> carefully watch the months and stars ... and, above all, worship the
> gods and celebrate the annual rites for Great Ceres ...[107]

Frightful apparitions of almost cinematic terror engulf the readers and listeners. A few of them would sympathize from real experience. Excited by the poet's images and by the stories told by relatives and friends, they would relive the wholesale destruction of a year's labour and their future hopes. The passage is violent and filled with militant allusions to the clash of battle.[108] It is for these compelling reasons, warns Vergil, that the farmer must carefully observe the signs of the seasons. The purpose was to determine the time for the reaper to arrive.

Because of these very threats, as Palladius emphasized in his *Opus agriculturae*, there should be absolutely no delay in taking off the crop. The farmer should even risk taking the crop off early and allow some post-reaping ripening on the threshing floor, he advised, rather than suffer loss because of slowness or inaction.[109] The same basic risks were reported some two millennia later as the causes that made getting additional seasonal labour to the wheat lands of the Canadian and American West an urgent matter for the mobilization of manpower.[110] Inclement weather was always a malign force that both overshadowed the beginning of reaping and threatened to disrupt harvest operations. A litany of testimony, ancient and modern, specifies that perilous weather, especially high winds and heavy rains, was the main culprit. Barring a beneficial act of God, there was nothing that the landowner could do to get the men back to work once the threat had materialized.

Bad years like these are reported in literary sources for late antiquity and the early medieval west. In the year 820, torrential rains did widespread damage to animals and caused grain crops to rot in the fields.[111] The same threat is attested for County Kildare in early sixth-century Ireland, as is reported in the life of the holy woman Brigida or, as she is better known in her Christian guise, St Brigit.[112] Harvesters and day labourers had been summoned to the region from far and wide. The reapers had gathered in great numbers to take off the crops, but exceptionally heavy downpours of rain kept them from getting to their work. It was only the divine presence of the saintly woman that kept the bad weather from harming her lands. Her crops remained dry and the harvesters who had gathered from the whole of the neighbouring region went to work, reaping from early morning to late at night to take off the ripened grain.[113] The aura of the saintly holy woman had its beneficial effect.

The story of St Brigit is not unique. Inclement weather was just as pressing a problem in the Gauls in late antiquity, where, as in Ireland, it was a much-feared force that was thought to be under the control of evil persons and that therefore required the intervention of equally powerful sacral figures to fend off.[114] A sacred narrative from Gaul centres on the holy man, the Abbot Aridius from the region of Limoges (the ancient *civitas Lemovicinorum* with its city centre of Augustoritum in Aquitania) and his involvement with weather and reaping. In his story, one that dates to the late sixth century, the same terror recurred.[115] A heavy rainstorm stopped the harvesting of the crops.[116] The rains poured and lashed downwards for so long that the dampness threatened to regerminate the grain. The local people begged Aridius to intervene. The holy man emerged from the local church and begged God to calm the skies, with the immediate and happy result that the clouds dispersed and the heavens became serene. The harvesters went out to the fields to complete their work.

There is the equally dramatic tale of an Irish missionary saint resident in Gaul, the holy Columbanus, who similarly intervened with his saintly powers to rescue a reaping season. Once again, the cause of fear and danger was destructive weather.

The time had come to store the supplies of grain in the granaries, but the violent winds had not stopped piling up storm clouds. Without doubt, hard necessity was pressing everyone onward so that the heads of the ripe crop of grain on the stalks, already beginning to germinate, would not be lost. There was a man of God at the monastery at Fontanae where a new field had yielded a rich crop. Violent blasts of wind drove on the rains and the clouds in the heavens did not cease to pour waters onto the earth. The man of God, in some anxiety, considered what he should do in these circumstances. Faith armed his mind and taught him to seek the right course of action. He summoned all the men and ordered them to start reaping the crop. They were surprised by the Father's order. No one could understand what he meant. They all came and began to reap the grain with their sickles in the downpours of rain, and then looked to see what the Father would do. He placed four men filled with the faith, one at each of the four corners of the field: Comininus, Eunocus, and Equonacus, who were Scots by origin, and a fourth, named Gurganus, who was a Briton. Having arranged them in this way, he himself with the others reaped the grain that was in the middle. What a wondrous miracle! The rain storms retreated from the grain fields and the rainwaters were dispersed in every direction. The heat of the sun burned down on the men who were reaping in the middle area and a strong warm wind blew as long as they collected the grain. Faith and prayer were so powerful that the rain was driven off and there was sunshine in the midst of the storms.[117]

Columbanus was, no doubt, well acquainted with such threats, since he himself had often worked as a reaper in taking off harvests. The stories of Brigit, Aridius, and Columbanus are ones that happen to survive because of the production of Christian narratives that focused on these ordinary matters of daily life as if they were of epic importance.[118] What the tales document is the special sacrality of harvest time and the heightened significance of a season riven with an unusual intensity of possible rewards and losses, hopes and fears. All three stories play on the urgent conditions that demanded the widespread collation of surplus agricultural labour.

The threats and pressures of reaping time generated dominant emotions of apprehension and fear. In the age of the Maktar Harvester, Augustine was well aware of this pervasive fear, and he speaks of it with eloquence from personal experience.

How great and how often do the farmers, and indeed all men, fear disasters for their crops from the sky, from the land, and from all kinds of destructive animals. Usually they finally feel secure when the crops have been reaped, gathered, and stored. And yet I know certain cases when a sudden and unexpected flood, causing men to flee, has swept the finest grain harvest from the granaries and destroyed it.[119]

Given the threatening conditions, it is hardly surprising that sermons delivered by Christian preachers in Africa in the age of the Maktar Harvester could draw together all of these elements – the immensity of the labour required, the sense of impending threats, and the final success – into a single large metaphor.

The crop is reaped only with great effort, it is transported to the threshing floor, it is beaten and threshed, and it is winnowed. After so many threatening dangers of weather and storms, and after so much hard work of the peasant labourers and the anxieties of the landowners, the clean grain is finally stored in the granary. Winter comes and the grain that had been cleaned is brought out and scattered on to the ground. This [i.e., the rescattering of the grain so carefully collected back on the ground] seems to be nonsensical, but it's not silly because hope makes it not foolish.[120]

In bringing these elements of life in the fields before his parishioners, Augustine was using each of the stages of the harvest as a symbol of a process involved in the Christian vision of life, death, and redemption.

Where could landlords or farm managers go to find the extra manpower that they so urgently required to fend off potential disaster? In almost all known cases, seasonal work in harvesting has been transferred from areas with surplus labour to regions with a deficit of workers.[121] The reserve labour pool out of which the labour was drawn existed partly because normal familial and agricultural practices sustained its reproductive costs.[122] In Roman antiquity, the different sources of such seasonal labour parallel what is known from comparable circumstances in modern-day Europe and the Americas. For the early twentieth-century United States, we have Donald Lescohier's surveys of tens of thousands of itinerant harvest workers in the United States in the early 1920s. Even with the mechanization of agriculture in the American West at the time, the need for additional manual labour for the harvest was still immense.[123] Lescohier's surveys specified three main sources of seasonal workers.[124] About a third of them came from existing rural farm environments. These were usually men who were hoping to supplement their existing farm incomes. This was a consistent source of seasonal labour in most premodern societies. The great majority of Irish harvest labourers making their way to England in the nineteenth century were small landholding peasants who needed extra wages to add to their marginal annual incomes. But need alone is not sufficient. The districts of Ireland that contributed most of the itinerant labours were not necessarily the most indigent or hard pressed. Rather, they were those that were better connected in the communications that linked supply areas with regions of demand in England.[125] Another third of the harvesters in the American cases studied by Lescohier were unskilled migrant manual labourers. These men picked up harvesting jobs as part of a cycle of itinerant work in construction, logging, and mining. The remaining third of the seasonal workers were men from urban areas who went into the fields for the purpose of supplementing their incomes.[126] Most of these flows of labour were extensions of existing movements internal to a given region. In this sense, the seasonal circulation of harvest workers was parasitic on normal population movements.[127]

In Africa of the Roman period, there were also three common sources of surplus labour for the harvest. One was rooted in the populations in the more heavily urbanized region in the north of the proconsular province: in Carthage and in regions in its deep hinterland, including the town of Mactaris. The denser settlements of the Carthaginian hinterland harboured rural and urban proletariats who needed the additional seasonal employment. That town and village dwellers took advantage of the extra employment and pay by decamping into the countryside each year is confirmed by evidence from antiquity. As for existing population movements, it might be noted that the reserve pool of seasonal labourers matched the recruiting pool of young men for the army.[128] The same pattern of recruitment was found in other parts of the Roman Mediterranean, as in the annual trek of townsmen from Edessa, Carrhae, and other towns to the farming districts in upper Mesopotamia.[129] On 26 November of 502, the Saracen chief Na'aman, who was an ally of the Persians, was able to take 18,500 prisoners in a raid against these cities because so many of their inhabitants had gone out into the surrounding rural regions to help with the harvest.[130] In Egypt, men left large urban centres to seek employment in cycles of rural work, including the harvest. Like one Kastor, they had their travel plans determined by the advent of the harvest. In his case, he promised his brother Apollonios that he would return to Heptakomia for a hearing, but only 'after the harvest.'[131] It was assumed that seasonal workers moved from nearby towns and villages out into the countryside, and governed their lives accordingly.[132]

A second regional labour source that is difficult to estimate for Africa in Roman antiquity was the population of the mountain zones, especially the highlands of the central Maghrib that surround the high plains of Numidia. To the south, these were the inhabitants of the Aurès mountains; to the north and west, the peoples of the Biban and Babors, the Hodna and the Greater and Lesser Kabylie. These montane zones have traditionally been densely populated. There is every reason to believe that the movement of peoples from the highlands down to the plains, taking their animals in search of pastures and themselves in search of work, was not just an early modern or a medieval phenomenon.[133] This same source of labour recruitment based on the employment differential between mountain and plain was also found in early modern Europe.[134] The broad flat plains regions that were planted mainly to cereal grains were often less densely inhabited than were the mountain and hill regions that surrounded them. The former were in need of the extra seasonal labour which the latter could provide.[135] Finally, in Africa of the Roman period it is almost certain that a third major source of seasonal workers was the extra manpower provided by the transhumant pastoral nomads who were migrating northwards in annual treks from the fringes of the Sahara desert to their summer pastures in the high plains of Numidia.[136] In good years, they would propitiously reach their summer pastures in the north just as the crops had to be taken off, and they had surplus manpower and plenty of draft animals to hand.

In all known instances where there has been any substantial commercial growing of cereal grains, particularly wheat and barley, it is perhaps worth re-emphasis that the need for additional labour is immense. Even in the first age of mechanized agriculture in the American West in the late nineteenth and early twentieth centuries, the demand for seasonal harvest labour required the movement of hundreds of thousands of men, most of whom were outsiders to the regions to which they had come to work. In 1912, 85 per cent of the seasonal harvest labour required by Kansas farmers came from out of state. That percentage might have been one of the highest, but it was not wholly unusual in scale.[137] Although some regions could recruit much of the extra labour that they required locally, in other places, such as Kansas and Oklahoma, more than half of the entire mobile workforce was continually on the move, going from one county to the next at harvest time.[138] The fact that so much of the labour was on the move and originated from areas external to the regions where the reaping was done was always potentially problematic. Given the sometimes divergent sources that fed the streams of seasonal migrations, there have been historical debates over the nature of these movements. Are they to be considered part of the multitudinous motions of small groups, like Marc Bloch's 'Brownian movements,' that pullulate on the fringes of a solidly anchored agrarian world to serve its needs? Or are they the result of the marginalization of outcast elements who occasionally burst into the solidity of local agrarian society only to be cast out again after use has been made of them?[139] The better view, surely, is that the movements were endemic parts of all social and economic systems. They enabled a mass of minor connections to be made, more in some historical circumstances and environments and less in others.[140] Nevertheless, there was almost always a cost. The considerable dislocation of manpower on the move, even if in response to a genuine need, created upheavals and disturbances, sometimes violent ones.

Natural Threats

It was not just the large numbers of itinerant reapers on the move that contributed to distress and violence. More commonly, it was the uncertainty from one year to the next about how much additional labour would be required. In the American West, 'the flow of labor within the Wheat Belt during [the] harvest was erratic, resulting in an abundance or oversupply of labor in some areas and shortages in others.' This was the prime cause of disruption and violence: the local harvest economy could not absorb the additional labour.[141] As has been remarked, the problem of acquiring sufficient harvest labour was never a simple problem of supply and demand.[142] The discrepancy between the demand for and supply of workers occasioned both labour concerns on the side of the hirers and fear of serious local disruptions among the locals.[143] Sudden downturns in production were caused mainly by unfavourable environmental conditions. Inclement weather and pestilential infestations were the main adversities. Even in the conditions of more modern communication in the later nineteenth and early twentieth centuries, dramatic changes in the demand for additional labour caused by bad weather conditions or by invasions of pests could not easily be communicated to the men who followed a given regional seasonal work circuit year after year. In premodern conditions, all one could do was to hope and, literally, to pray to avoid these dangers. A magical curse tablet was found buried in the ground south of the town of Aradi, just to the northeast of Mactaris. The words inscribed on it call on the fearsome spirits and demons of the underworld to protect the lands and the crops growing on them from hail, rust, the furious blasts of the drying desert winds, and the swarms of evil-doing locusts.[144]

For standing cereal crops in Tunisia in the early modern age, the two greatest threats were local versions of these same dangers: the superheated blasts of the *ghibli* or *scirocco* that suddenly swept in from the Sahara and the curse of the locust. Dark clouds of the airborne insect predators could suddenly shadow the entire skyline. An observer in Tunis in 1764 described their arrival in near-epic terms: 'On the 24th of February at ten o'clock in the morning the sky was darkened by a dense cloud of locusts that covered the whole horizon. In the space of the two and a half hours that the flight of these insects lasted not one ray of the sun could be seen.'[145] The large swarms of locusts that periodically infested Italy, just to the north, were borne there on winds from Africa.[146] The effect of these attacks in Africa itself must have been no less terrifying than they were in Italy, where the people, riveted by fear, sought refuge in the extreme remedies dictated by the Sibylline Books. Locust attacks could be so severe that they dislocated more than just crops. One such hopper attack forced the whole populace of an African town to abandon their city.[147] In the region of Cyrene, the pests were regarded as so dangerous that the city passed a law requiring that war be declared on locusts three times a year. In the first phase the eggs of the locust were to be crushed, in the second stage the grubs were to be killed, and in the third the fully grown insects were to be eliminated. The penalty imposed on men who shirked this duty was the same as that for army deserters.[148]

The dangers presented by locust invasions persisted throughout the Roman period when the threat was taken seriously by the provincial government of Africa. The career of a municipal aristocrat from Thugga in the mid-first century CE lists one of his offices – one whose powers extended over the whole territory of Carthage – as 'official in charge of locust control.' He was the *curator lucustae* whose authority probably extended as far as Mactaris to the south.[149] In standard economic transactions and agricultural production, in addition to other faults, legal authorities had to take into account the damage done to crops by locusts.[150] The combined movements of human helpers and biological pests sometimes collided to produce tragic results, but even when they did not the threat was always present. The almost predictable result of a severe downturn in cereal grain production caused by detrimental environmental forces were large numbers of underemployed young men wandering around seeking rural work that was not available. What followed was distressing, or worse.[151] In these bad years, the pastoral nomads would arrive at their northern pastures too soon, with little in the way of compensatory work for them. The large annual movement of people and

1.6: Pieter Bruegel, *Aestas/Summer*. 1568: Kunsthalle, Hamburg; ArtResource

animals that took place under these uncertain conditions naturally produced fearful apprehensions and social tensions.

Quality of Work

The erratic nature of the labour demands created uncertainties about employment, wages, and work conditions that led to serious contentions between employers and those seeking employment.[152] Even under normal conditions, however, the work was hard and exacting in the extreme. As with most harvest work, reaping was done, almost by definition, in the torrid temperatures of midsummer days.[153] In Bruegel's evocation of *Aestas* or Summer, a representation of peasant labour in the Low Countries, drawn around 1570, we see the male reapers wearing broad-brimmed hats, one of them quenching his gargantuan thirst.[154] In picture and word, the burning heat of the sun defined the nature of the work.[155] In Roman mosaics and paintings, we see the headgear worn by the harvesters to protect

1.7: Roman reaper with hat: Summer in a fresco from the catacomb of San Ponziano, Rome. J. Wilpert, *Le pitture delle catacombe romane*, 2 vols. (Rome, 1903), p. 34, no. 6

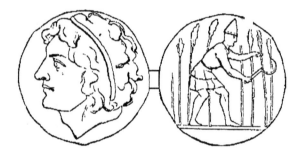

1.8: Reaper with a conical hat: drawing from a Ptolemaic coin. J. Pellerin, *Recueil de médailles de rois*, vol. 1 (Paris–Francfort et La Haye, 1762), p. 208

themselves from the incessant pulverizing heat of the sun's rays.[156] Conical, wide-brimmed hats appear to have been so much the norm around the Mediterranean that they were used to identify reapers on miniature images produced on small intaglio amulets and also on the bronze coins of Alexandria from the reign of Antoninus Pius. The headgear was traditional; it was featured much earlier on coins of Ptolemaic age.[157] Later, the hats are found in representations of the season of harvesting in the figure of the harvester with sheaf and sickle on a synagogue mosaic from Sepphoris in the Galilee (see fig. 4.19).[158] The protective headgear is also visible on representations of medieval mowers as much as it is on Bruegel's early modern harvesters (see fig. 4.3).[159] And the head coverings are described in ethnographic reports on the apparel required of reapers in modern north Africa.[160]

The pulverizing heat could not be escaped. Logically, the common symbols for the months of mowing and reaping found on African mosaics of the time were fans to cool the body and jars of water to slake thirst.[161] On one of the Roman amulets that features the reaper's hat, we also see the reaper stripped down because of the heat, his tunic thrown over the branch of a nearby tree. Because of the heat, reapers worked mostly in the nude or they wore only a very light garment known in the East as the *theristron* or *theristrion*, a summer dress.[162] Harvesters in late antiquity are described in the same way: 'In the whole day, nothing is brighter than at midday, when the sun burns red from the middle of the sky and pours down its light like a boiling hot spring over the whole of the earth – when the nude harvester is roasted alive and, gasping for breath, he strives at the magnitude of his work. Then the cooling dew is most welcome, if only because the morning damp makes the dried stalks of grain easier to cut.'[163] Along with the sun and the burning heat came the insects. Harvesting in the grain fields meant being bitten by flies and mosquitoes, and stung by wasps, or worse. The vexatious insects were sometimes so savage that only the powers of a holy man could alleviate their attacks. The saintly Friardus in late antique Gaul worked as a harvester in the fields, bent over collecting the cut sheaves.[164] The reapers and sheavers with him were being mercilessly attacked by wasps. The holy man fell on his knees and prayed to God. He then approached the wasps' nest and made the sign of the cross over their home. All the wasps hid themselves and the saint and his fellow reapers were able to cut the grain close to the nest, unharmed.

Comparison with later ages and times reveals the same verities. In the American and Canadian wheat belt, a similar work regimen meant that men usually laboured ten to sixteen-hour days, under punishing conditions in the summer heat, in harsh temperatures that sometimes reached upwards of 110–120 degrees Fahrenheit.[165] The words of Richard Jefferies, who worked in the wheat fields of nineteenth-century England, empathetically picture the arduous nature of the work.

The next day the village sent forth its army with their crooked weapons to cut and slay. It used to be an era, let me tell you, when a great farmer gave the signal to his reapers; not a man, woman, or child that did not talk of that ... These [the harvest workers] were so terribly in earnest that they could scarcely acknowledge the presence even of the squire. They felt themselves so important, and were so full, and so intense and one-minded in their labour ... More men and more men were put on day by day, and women to bind the sheaves ... for as the wheat fell, the shocks rose behind them, low tents of corn. Your skin or mine could not have stood the scratching of the straw, which is stiff and sharp, and the burning of the sun, which blisters like red-hot iron. No one could stand the harvest field as a reaper except he had been born and cradled in a cottage, and passed his childhood bareheaded in July heats and January snows ... The edge of the reap-hook had to be driven by force through the stout stalks like a sword, blow after blow, minute after minute, hour after hour; the back stooping, and the broad sun throwing his fiery rays from a full disc on head and neck ... they [the harvesters] were liable to be struck down with such internal complaints as come from the great heat. Their necks grew black, much like black oak in old houses. Their open chests were always bare, and flat, and stark ... The breast bone was burned black, and their arms, tough as ash, seemed cased in leather. They grew visibly thinner in the harvest field, and shrunk together – all flesh disappearing, and nothing but sinew and muscle remaining ... So they worked and slaved and tore at the wheat as if they were seized with a frenzy; the heat, the aches, the illness, the sunstroke, always impending in the air ... No song, no laugh, no stay – on from morn to night, possessed with a maddened desire to labour, for the more they could cut the larger the sum they would receive ... So hard, you see, is the pressure of human life that these miserables would have prayed on their knees for permission to tear their arms from the socket, and to scorch and shrivel themselves to charred human brands in the furnace of the sun.[166]

Conditions were surely no different in Roman antiquity. The reaper not only worked in the ferocious heat of the sun and in the dust and dirt of the fields, amid the flies, mosquitoes, and other annoying insects, but he hacked at the stalks and gathered them, remorselessly. In addition, the reaping action of the hand-held sickle required that he bend over at the hips with his back permanently arched for hours on end. A little relief would be had when the reaper stood upright to grasp the whetstone that was usually stored in a piece of hollow horn tied to his waist, with which he repeatedly sharpened the blade of his sickle.[167] The arduous bending over again and again produced typical back injuries and chronic problems of sciatica – so much so that the figure of the reaper was used metonymically to represent the aches and pains of the affliction. Magical amulets are found throughout the Mediterranean that feature the profile of a reaper on the one side and the word for sciatica – σχίον, a form of ἰσχίων, 'of the hips or legs,' or the words σχίον θεραπία, 'for the healing of the hips'—on the other. They were meant to ward off or to alleviate the pain and the suffering of this affliction so characteristic of the reaper.[168]

To sense some of the harshness of the work in late antique Africa one has only to listen to a story from the Vandal court of the late fifth century. In order to inflict severe punishment on some miscreant courtiers in the aftermath of his edict of 18 June 477, Huniric, the Vandal king of Africa, sent them out to harvest in the lands around Utica. It was the burning heat of the sun that they felt beating down on them. The reaping was so arduous that they later remembered the savage work as a kind of martyrdom.[169] It was not, remarks Victor of Vita, in an unnecessary explanation, the work of delicate men. *Delicati*. The word drips from his lips with acrid condescension. He might just as well have said 'women's work.' Envisaged as the backbreaking part of harvest labour, reaping was always construed as quintessential men's work. Women not only worked, but worked hard in the harvest.[170]

1.9: Reaper amulet for sciatica. Hematite stone, Egypt of Hellenistic
or early Roman date; ArtResource

But they were habitually thought of, and therefore portrayed, as mainly involved
in the back end of the process, in its second stage: the gathering of the sheaves
and the collecting of the grain (not gleaning, we should note) in the strict sense of
cleaning up the remnant grains for the landlord.[171] This was probably not objec-
tively true. There is plenty of comparative evidence from the Mediterranean and
elsewhere to show that women have been directly involved in reaping, even if not
in great numbers.[172] But the evidence is sparse, and it is regionally specific. For
example, no women are attested in any of the Egyptian harvesting contracts or
household accounts as being involved in reaping. Here it was manifestly seen as
'men's work.'[173] The evidence for manual reaping in modern north Africa is mixed.
In some regions women have been involved in reaping, in others not.[174] But the

1.10: Reaper amulet. Courtesy of the Hecht Museum,
University of Haifa, Israel

attitude in Victor reflects what seems to have been a division of labour that is
apparent in the depiction of it through the twelfth and thirteenth centuries.[175]
In the northern lands of Europe, although men predominate in the reaping of
the harvest, women are pictured as reapers and participated in the cutting of the
crops. In Italy, on the other hand, it is men who are pictured as doing the reaping, almost to the total exclusion of women. It has been postulated that this is not
just a Mediterranean attitude, but a pattern found in global divisions of labour
in the harvesting process.[176] Although it might not always have been so in reality,
there are arguments to indicate a gendered division of harvest labour that broadly
distinguished Mediterranean from western European norms.

The cut stone miniatures of reapers, to which reference has already been made
above, no matter how small and schematic they might be, are evidence of the bodily pain and physical impairments that were induced by reaping. The same incised
stones document the typical elements of the reaper's tools and attire, including
his sickle and broad-brimmed hat. These, too, hint at the difficulties of the work.
Sometimes the reapers wore special leggings, probably to protect against minor lac-
erations, the scratching of the stalks, and the bites of insects.[177] As the weariness of
long hours of cutting and sheaving dragged on and exhaustion set in, there was the
propensity to lose concentration. Because the reaper wielded the sickle blade with
considerable force, it was possible to miss the mark and hit one's hand or fingers.

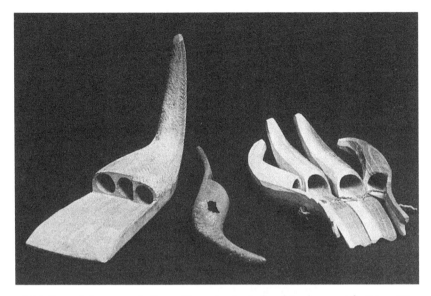

1.11: Reaper's finger guards. Bryer, 'Byzantine Agricultural Implements,' fig. 20, p. 77; permission courtesy of the author

It happened to a reaper in late sixth-century Gaul. He cut right through one of his own fingers, but he was lucky enough to have a holy man nearby who was able to heal the digit dangling from his hand by a thin strip of skin.[178] In more modern times in the eastern Mediterranean, protective 'gloves' or finger guards made of wood or bone are known. It has been guessed, rightly I think, that there must have been ancient equivalents that have simply been lost from the material record.[179] We know from medieval European writings that such finger or hand guards existed and these were habitually used even though they never appear in manuscript illustrations or in paintings of rural labour.[180] Modern examples made of wood, bamboo, and even stitched segments of tin are known.[181] They are also attested as part of the normal equipment of reapers in modern north Africa.[182] The ways in which they were constructed, used, and discarded means that ethnologists have widespread evidence for them, but for archaeologists to find surviving examples from antiquity is very difficult.[183]

Seeing the Work

The processes involved in reaping, and their connection with the successive steps of the whole of the harvest, are difficult to visualize from the few illustrations that we have from Africa of the Roman period. The illustrations of relief sculptures found on some funerary stelae, however, provide an almost eerie step-by-step pictorial commentary on a contemporary sermon ascribed to Augustine. They offer an opening to redescription and interpretation. When expatiating on the meaning of martyrdom, a problematic subject that frequently provoked recourse to harvest metaphors, the African preacher describes the process of reaping and carrying in the sheaves:

For when the cut sheaves have been carefully bound by the hands of the reapers, the sheaves are not cut loose there, but are thrown as whole bundles onto a wheeled cart. In the same way, the bodies of the holy *like* whole sheaves are lifted onto the carriage of the body of Christ.[184]

The process by which the sheaves were collected is also alluded to in a contemporary African commentary mistakenly ascribed to Augustine:

We bless you in the name of the Lord. Likewise so that you, leaving aside fruitless and arid works, will sow those things which will fill up both the hands of the harvesters and the laps of the arms of those who gather up the sheaves.[185]

The reaper walked forward, cutting a handful of grain with his sickle, and he then laid it on the ground. When several of these had been cut, he would bind them together with a string or he would use lengths of prepared straw as ties. He would then gather the tied or bound sheaves in his arms and carry them to be loaded onto a transport wagon. In another sermon to his people, in which he is trying to evoke a common experience that they themselves had witnessed, a preacher refers specifically to this tying operation:

Joseph ... as if standing in the open fields with his own brothers, [was] busy tying up the sheaves of grain, and admiring the sheaves of his brothers and his own sheaf.[186]

Paulinus of Nola refers to the initial sequence of actions in cutting. The reaper first cuts and collects the handful of grain with his hand. He then collates the sheaves in the cradle of his arm.[187] In another sermon to his parishioners, while elaborating on the metaphor of the days of the Final Judgment as a harvest in which the angels appear as harvesters to collect the souls of Christians, Augustine recounts the process by which an individual harvester collected the stalks of grain and then collated them into a bundle or sheaf in the cradle or lap of his arm.

The harvesters will come and they will gather the wheat into the storage barn, but they will tie up the weeds and will throw them into the fire ... the harvester does not fill his hand with that [other grain]. The verse follows and it says: *The harvester did not fill his hand, nor did he gather the handfuls.* And the Lord says: *The harvesters are the angels* [Mt. 13:39] ... Some are those who collect the sheaves, others are those who are passing by them on the road ... Who are those who collect the sheaves? Harvesters. Who are the harvesters? The Lord says: *The harvesters are the angels.*[188]

In Africa, the Latin word *gremium* became the colloquial term for a sheaf of grain. It was the word for the stalks of grain that are described as cradled or gathered *in sinum* – that is, 'in the lap' – of each sheaver or bundler as he placed the individual 'handfuls' of grain that he picked up into the crook formed by his arm.[189] Although the sheaves were usually called *manipuli* outside Africa because they were gathered 'by the handful,' in Africa the local Latin word *gremium* became the standard term. We see it repeatedly in citations from the old African Latin translations of the Bible, as in the Psalms whose well-known verse, 'they shall come rejoicing, bringing in the sheaves,' is cited by African Christian writers from Cyprian to Augustine, using *gremia* not the Italian Latin *manipuli* for the sheaves of grain.

Walking out they walked and they were weeping as they broadcast their seed; coming back, they shall come rejoicing, carrying their sheaves.

Ambulantes ambulabant et plorabant mittentes semina sua, venientes autem venient in exultatione tollentes gremia sua.[190]

The words express the manual operations and the ways in which the mind was focused on different gestures and actions. Grasping the stalks to be cut with the right hand as opposed to the cradling of the cut stalks for placement on the ground perhaps conditioned a different definition and word for the sheaf. We can see these sheaves depicted on mosaics, bound into units with straw ties, as on a season mosaic portraying the month of July from a house of a Christian landlord at Thebes in Greece.[191] But low cutting and sheaving were themselves peculiar labour operations which, as we shall see, were not followed everywhere, even within Africa. Were these recursive manual actions ones that configured both the mental images and the ways in which the reaping process was seen and pictured?

The instruments and the actions of harvesting were standard themes of the funerary stelae erected in connection with the cult of the great African deity Saturn. Some of the more striking of these stelae have been found not far from Mactaris, in the region of Siliana to the north of the town.[192] The so-called Boglio stele is perhaps the most impressive of these peculiar Saturn stelae.[193] In reviewing the pictorial program on the stone, which is composed of four super-

1.12: Reaper bringing in his sheaf: mosaic from Thebes, Greece; fifth/sixth century CE.
Thebes Archaeological Museum; permission courtesy 23 Ephoreia, Byzantine Antiquities

imposed registers, it is important to remember that we are dealing with a funerary stele. The context is death. The top register represents a temple, with the picture of an eagle, symbol of the god Saturn, set in the tympanum. Under the roof of the temple, Saturn is seated on a recumbent bull. Beneath this panel, an inscription was cut in a band across the stone, noting that the landowner Cuttinus had fulfilled his promises to the god.

Saturno Aug(usto) Sacrum / P(ater) n(oster) Cuttinus votu(m) sol(vit) cum suis. B(onis) B(ene)

Sacred to the August God Saturn / Cuttinus, our father, with his family, has made good his promise [i.e., to the god]. May there be good things for good people![194]

Under these words, in the second register, is an illustration of the sacrifice directed by Cuttinus. To his right, his wife is holding up a basket of fruits. The bull and the ram to be sacrificed are pictured here, as are two *canistrarii* or assistant sacrificers who flank the borders of the scene. But it is the tableaux in the third and fourth registers that most directly interest us. In the third register, to the left, a man driv-

1.13: The Boglio Stele, Siliana Region, Tunisia. The Bardo Museum, Tunis; ArtResource

ing a pair of oxen with a plough represents the sowing of the crop. To the right is a scene of two men engaged in harvesting a field of wheat. The harvesters have just cut the stalks of grain, and they are in the process of binding them into *manipuli*, or *gremia* as the Africans would have said in their Latin. The final and lowest register displays the transport of the sheaves to the granaries on the home domain. This

1.14: The lower registers of the Boglio Stele. The Bardo Museum, Tunis; ArtResource

is done by means of three two-wheeled carts, each of which is drawn by a pair of horses. The sheaves of grain are stacked high on each of the carts, in the manner described by Augustine. Based on nothing other than stylistic grounds, the stele has been dated to the Tetrarchic period, but a later date is just as possible.[195]

Who were the labourers whose sweat and exhausting work took off the harvest for the landlord Cuttinus? Were they free men who hired out their labour? And if they were, a brief investigation of the status of occasional or seasonal workers quickly reveals that persons of free status who hired out their work for pay were often regarded as being *like* chattel slaves, castigated because of their slavish dependence on their employers. 'The lot of the hired man is almost invariably presented throughout Greek and Roman history in an unpleasant light.'[196] The overlap between the two statuses was so pervasive that an argument has been proffered that most hired workers or *mercenarii* were in fact slaves whose labour was hired out by contractors who owned them.[197] There is some evidence for the presence of slaves who were used in this fashion. In fourth-century BCE Attika, for example, there are instances of farm managers who contracted with persons for the reaping of crops in which it is reasonably certain that the contractor was the owner of the slaves who were being leased out for that purpose.[198] This may well have been an arrangement used in the more intense and concentrated economic networkings of rural Athens. Generally speaking, however, the fourth-century rhetors assume that reapers were hired men of free status. When Aeschines protested against being charged with having a 'friendship' or *xenia* with Alexander, Demosthenes in making his riposte to this protest states that he would not be so rash as to make a claim like this 'unless a person is to speak of *reapers or other wage earners* as the *philoi* of those who hire them.'[199] The objection might still be made, as it often has been, that even if the reapers, like other wage earners, *misthotai*, collected or earned a wage, they could still be doing so as slaves working and earning wages for their owners and contractors. If the general truth of this claim has been successfully challenged, the attitude that was fixed in the perspectives of the wealthier landowning classes remains an important force in forming their general attitudes to labour.[200] Whatever the prevalent attitudes of the social elites towards seasonal labourers, it is manifest that most of the men reaping the crops in Africa – even if many of them were caught up in various types of dependent relationships with their social superiors – were not slaves but rather persons of free status.

These observations draw our attention back to the structuring of the harvest scene on the Boglio Stele. In its spatial hierarchy, the illustrative program of the stele highlights the superior place of the landlord, Cuttinus, and his wife, the *domina*, who are pictured in its upper register. They are engaged in rituals appropriate to their class. The other identity problem that is suggested in the hieratic formalism of the relief centres on the anonymous men who are doing the hard work, the ones who are figured at the base of its order. What were *their* stories? In a singular instance from Africa it is possible to retell the tale of one such harvester, even if his name and identity remain as anonymous as the figures of the harvesters in the register at the bottom of the stele. It is to him and to his story that we now turn.

CHAPTER TWO

Primus in arvis

First in the Fields

The town of Mactaris was a typical municipality in the African provinces of Rome's western empire. A small but prosperous rural centre, it was set in the rugged hills of the Dorsal, the mountainous backbone and watershed that divides the northern and southern ecologies of present-day Tunisia. As a peripheral community, Mactaris was fixed at the extreme southwestern edge of a zone of dense urban settlements that fanned outwards from the provincial capital of Carthage. At a little over ninety miles southwest of the great metropolis, the town was also set at the junction of important east-west and north-south ecological frontiers. Perched above valleys that wound through the highlands of the Dorsal, it was a natural communications node. Control of the valley passes through the Dorsal mattered in both ancient and modern times. Vicious little combats over these defiles were fought between Allied and Axis forces in the first months of 1943. And with them came death and tombstones. A temporary American cemetery for the war dead, with wooden slats from ration crates serving as grave markers, was laid out at Maktar.[1] In Roman antiquity, as early as the reign of Augustus, Mactaris was on the major highway that connected Carthage on the coast with the large army base at Ammaedara (modern Haïdra) deep in the interior.[2] One road ran southeastward from the town through the flatlands of Byzacena towards Thysdrus in the Sahel. Another, to the northeast, followed the valley of Wadi Siliana to join the main highway to Carthage. Other roads ran northwest from Mactaris to Sicca Veneria, and southwest, through the lands of the tribal Musulamii, to Theveste, the gateway to the plains of Numidia. In all periods of antiquity, from pre-Roman Africa to the last days of Byzantine domination, Mactaris served as an administrative point of political control. It was a centre for tribute collection and for the enforcement of justice. Its situation was also liminal. The town could be thought of as either eastern or western, northern or southern. In the Diocletianic downsizing of the provinces of the empire, Mactaris was moved out of the proconsular

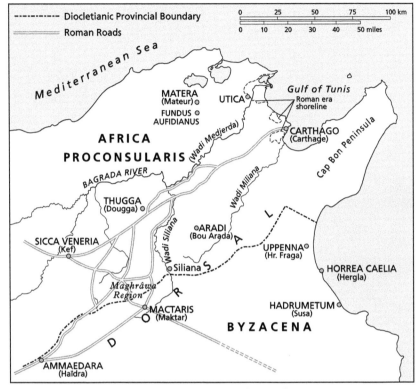

Map 2.1: Roman Mactaris (Maktar) and region

province to just inside the northern border of the province of Byzacena to the south.[3] It could fit just as well either way.

During the first phases of its efflorescence as a Roman town, Mactaris was fitted out with a triumphal arch celebrating the emperor Trajan, a monumental aqueduct, an amphitheatre, public baths, a forum and a plaza with a Capitolium, a governmental basilica, and other public buildings, as well as temples to some of the major deities of the imperial pantheon, including Apollo and Dionysus in his guise as Liber Pater. And a temple to the great and omnipotent African god Saturn newly constructed in the early third century.[4] Most of the impressive public structures can be dated to the ebullient age of the Antonine and Severan emperors. With its built-up urban core, Mactaris was in every respect a typical agro-centre of the Carthaginian hinterland. No matter how intensely developed the Roman towns of Africa might have been, like Mactaris and the densely packed monuments of its centre, they were strictly defined and compressed islands of urbanity

2.1: Roman Mactaris: the Forum (author)

set in extensive and profoundly rural territories. Although they manifestly counted as cities by the standards of the time, they were more directly connected with their rustic surroundings than are most modern towns of our own experience. They were similar to the typical agro-villages of late nineteenth-century England, as one of them was described by Thomas Hardy.

Its squareness was, indeed, the characteristic which most struck the eye in this antiquated borough, the borough of Casterbridge – at that time, recent as it was, untouched by the faintest sprinkle of modernism. It was compact as a box of dominoes. It had no suburbs – in the ordinary sense. Country and town met at a mathematical line.[5]

The connections that extended out of Mactaris into both neighbouring and more distant regions, and well as its close links with the surrounding countryside and its economy, made it an ideal place from which a man on the move might strike out and know where to go, from that same mathematical line.

In 1883 a singularly striking Latin inscription was discovered in the urban environs of Mactaris. It was an epigraphical text that has since come to assume a paradigmatic importance in the social and economic history not just of Africa, but of the entire Roman empire.[6] The stone on which the text of the inscription was engraved is a tall rectangular stele, slightly more than a metre in height and about half a metre in width. The inscription itself is a lengthy funerary epitaph written in verse. It is inscribed in an elegant script that consciously imitates the pleasing aesthetic elements of a fine formal handwriting. This florid script had been invented in Africa and was widely used by its writers in the Roman period.[7] What is most important about this peculiar script, variously categorized as uncial or semi-uncial, was that it was part of an innovative African tradition of handwriting. The use of the script in the production of documents and manuscripts coming out of Africa, one of the great centres of production of Latin literature, was so characteristic that it came to define one of the four main categories of handwriting formally recognized in early medieval Europe: African Letters or *Litterae Africanae* as they were called.[8]

Written as a first-person narrative, the poem recounts the rags-to-riches story of a poor peasant who rose from tilling a small plot of land and working as an itinerant farm labourer to become a respected citizen of means and social rank in his home town. The deceased's name is missing from the lost topmost part of the inscription. Since harvesting was the labour by which he acquired his new-found wealth, the anonymous subject of this success story has come to be known simply as the 'Maktar Harvester.' The harvester's story is told in a verse epitaph of about thirty lines, twenty-eight of which can still be read. It is composed in distichs of variable metric and artistic quality.[9] The aesthetics of epigraphical poems like this reflected the ideals of what might be called the middling ranks of municipal society in the western provinces of the Roman empire. As in other notable cases, such as the great celebratory verse paean to the members of the redoubtable municipal family of the Flavii from Cillium (modern Kasserine in south-central Tunisia), the personal details embedded in the poem presume a degree of consultation between the client and the professional poet who had been commissioned to create the

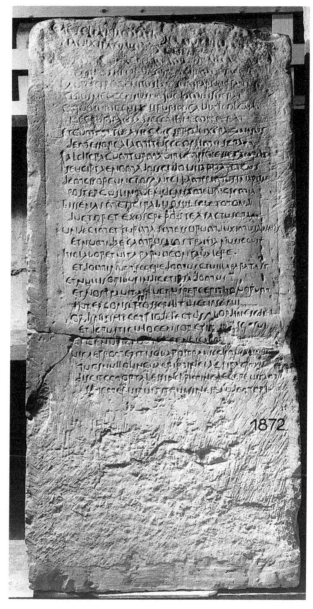

2.2: The Maktar Harvester inscription. The Louvre, Paris;
permission courtesy of the Louvre

final artistic product. It reflects the misunderstandings and the other social and cognitive gaps that such commissions entailed.[10] In brief compass, the patron, our man, had the poet celebrate the heroic achievements, as he saw them, of his own humble but honourable life. The words on the stone tell the following story.[11]

His Story

I was born from a poor family and to a father of meagre means
 who had neither municipal wealth nor his own house.
From these beginnings by birth, I lived by cultivating the soil. 5
 Never was there any rest for me or my land.
When each year produced the ripening crops, then
 I was the first harvester out to cut the stalks
When our sickle-bearing band of men marched out to the fields,
 whether to seek the nomad plains of Cirta or those of Jupiter. 10
Before everyone else, I was the first harvester into the fields,
 leaving the land behind my back thick with sheaves.
I reaped twelve harvests beneath the raging fire of the sun.
 Then I rose from field-hand and became a foreman.
For eleven years I led the bands of harvesters, 15
 and my gang cut the fields of Numidia.
This work and life was good to a man of small means.
 [line missing]
It made me the owner of a house and provided a farm
 – the house itself does not lack for any luxuries.
And my life has reaped a harvest of honours: 20
 I was registered in the ranks of the town's senators.
Chosen by them, I too sat in the council's holy chamber.
 From being a poor peasant, I even rose to be town censor.
I fathered, and lived to see my sons and my dear grandsons,
 [line missing]
I have passed the bright years of my life as I have deserved, 25
 years that no savage tongue can harm with blame.
Learn, mortals, to live a life free of wrongdoing.
 He deserved to die thus, he who lived a life free of deceit.

In the decades following its publication and subsequent inclusion in the standard corpora of Latin inscriptions and collections of Latin verse epigraphy, the story of the Maktar Harvester came to play an increasingly important role in modern histories of Roman social relations. It served as an example of the real possibilities of raising one's social status in the hierarchical society of the time. There is scarcely a survey of the empire, especially those devoted to life in its provincial regions, that does not include a reference to this inscription. It has been used to sustain arguments on everything from the place of slave and free labour and the values placed on manual labour, to the potential for social mobility in the ranks of the Roman imperial order.[12] Differences of opinion, sometimes rather sharply argued, have been registered over the typicality of the harvester's ability as a poor labourer of free status to raise his standing by dint of sheer hard work. Views of the man's typicality or otherwise correlate fairly closely with what might be called the political sentiments of a given historian on the nature of the ancient economy. The more conservative and optimistic the historian is about the modernity of the empire's economy, the more the harvester's story is seen to exemplify a pattern of beneficial mobility in wealth and status that was typical of imperial society. The more radical the historian of Rome is on the economic disjuncture with the past and the more pessimistic he or she is about its modernity, the more the harvester's life is presented as a strange oddity to be regarded as an exceptional instance of one man's social advancement by personal labour. His success is a quirk to be set against a pervasive background of slavery and other forms of dependency and servitude. To such interpreters, our man is not a paradigm, but a paradigm breaker – an odd exception to the prevailing repressive values placed on manual labour and low social status.

For the great historian of the empire's economic and social order, the Russian liberal Mikhail Ivanovich Rostovtzeff, Maktar's native son was a model small landowner grown great by his own efforts. He was a typical *agricola bonus* who by unstinting hard work won his way into the local bourgeoisie of a Roman town in the Antonine age.[13] To the more conservative Gilbert Charles-Picard, creator of the canonical portrait of Romano-African civilization, the harvester was not just any example. He was typical of the ebullience and social mobility of municipal life in Africa in the epoch of the Antonine and Severan emperors.[14] By contrast, the more leftish (to put it politely) Geoffrey de Ste Croix dismissed the harvester's significance with a curt 'the man was probably a very rare exception.' Ste Croix held our man to be as typical as the exceedingly rare case of the Christian bishop who actually deigned to work with his own hands.[15] That is, almost as rare as the proverbial hen's teeth. An economic oddity. Moses Finley, working from a similar perspective in his influential work *The Ancient Economy*, was a little more expansive, but of much the same opinion. In reply to persons who had staked claims about the importance of free wage labour in the Roman economy, Finley retorted: 'I shall be reminded of the third-century funerary monument from Maktar … memorializing a farm labourer who ended his life as a local senator. I pay my respects to the defunct, but until a few more such epitaphs are discovered, I shall remain unpersuaded by the attention this "Harvester Inscription" receives in modern accounts, including such not uncommon nonsense that it "bears proud testimony to the material and spiritual rewards of that life of toil and frugality idealized in Vergil's *Georgics*."[16] So much for typicality.

Even within the confines of the regional history of the African provinces, the same patterns of interpretation can be observed. No serious survey of the provincial society of Africa of the Roman period, popular or scholarly, fails to mention our harvester and to argue much these same divergent points of view.[17] For all of its significance as a proof text for the social and economic history of the empire and its provinces, surprisingly few detailed analyses of this evocative epigraphical poem have been made.[18] This is a shame, because, in the rush to judgments, technical difficulties with its dating and context, matters that are fundamental to its meaning, have been left unaddressed. The answers to both these questions are more usually assumed than they are critically investigated. Then again, there are broader, also unexamined claims that have been made about the work regime central to our agrarian hero's life, namely the labour of harvesting. Harvesters were as ubiquitous a phenomenon in the past worlds of the Mediterranean as our exemplary harvester is in modern scholarship, and about as anonymous. But modern day historians of labour in the Roman empire have no cause to complain on this score. The evidentiary situation is not much different for historians of early modern and modern rural labourers: 'these farm workers [i.e., harvesters] have been left in an historiographical "no man's land," in no small part because of their social anonymity.'[19] Although this is noted of rural seasonal labourers in late nineteenth and early twentieth-century western Canada, and of their contemporary history, it is no less true of most other historical times.

The career of labour highlighted in the poem demands a consideration of the harvester's social context, and it provokes a host of questions. We might begin with a simple one: What historical periods marked the long history of Mactaris, and from which of them did our man come? Formally established at the end of the second century BCE by Numidian and Punic overlords, the highland agrotown became the main administrative and fiscal centre for the surrounding region.[20] After the Roman conquest of 146 BCE, the town gradually mutated, becoming a cultural melting pot that contained an amalgam of African, Punic, and Roman elements and institutions. As with many towns in the proconsular province of Africa, Mactaris finally shed most of its Punic culture in the public sphere only by the age of the emperor Trajan, some two and a half centuries later.[21] In the early decades of the Roman state's takeover, it attracted a resident community, a *conventus*, of Roman citizens who were not only settlers on the land but also men involved in business and investment. Not the least among these latter persons were men connected with the collection of tribute for the Roman state.[22] Their presence at Mactaris is explained in part by the fact that the town had already served as the centre of a large tribute collection district both for the Carthaginian state and under the aegis of the African kings. And it continued to fill this role after the Roman takeover. In this capacity, Mactaris had administrative connections with a large number of surrounding towns.[23] These governmental functions provoked movements that connected the town with the outside world, like the ones that led a servitor of the Roman tribute system from Mactaris to take up residence at Ostia.[24]

Like all larger towns in the *pertica* or formal territory of the great colony of Carthage, because of the unusual domination that the provincial metropolis had over its *territorium,* the titular municipal advancement of Mactaris was artificially retarded.[25] The town was formally recognized with the status of a Roman colony, the *Colonia Aelia Aurelia Mactaris,* only late in the Antonine age.[26] In the later age of the fourth and fifth centuries, Mactaris remained just as large and just as busy as it had been at the height of the Antonine summer. For administrative purposes, however, the town was now located in the new Diocletianic province of Byzacena to the south.[27] The shift reveals the town's liminality and its continued importance as a connector between different economic regions: the highly urbanized zone of the Bagrada Valley to the north and the more open agricultural lands to the south and to the west. In the last half of the fifth century, the whole region witnessed the construction of elaborate fortified farmsteads built by wealthy peasants and large landowners.[28] The texts of the Latin inscriptions of persons who lived in this second age of late antiquity reflect a rich and vibrant town life at Mactaris. Among others, they include three *honestae feminae* or women of high social rank, a renowned medical doctor or *archiatros*, and a teacher of rhetoric.[29] It was also an age when Christian basilicas came to have a dominant place in the town and in which each of the two major factions of the Church in Africa maintained its own bishop in the community.[30] The town boasted its own martyrs, including the noble Felix.[31] Its Christian writers were still lively in the later Byzantine age when Cassiodorus informs us that one of them, the bishop Victor, was busy revising and correcting the works of John Cassian.[32] But where in this wide range of local history is our harvester to be placed?

A Conundrum of Time

We might begin with some technical matters concerning the inscription itself. One seeming certainty about the poem has been its date. A once dominant paradigm of the history of Roman Africa assumed that the high points of the land's economic prosperity matched the long waves of economic development of the empire as a whole. The harvester's life strikingly exemplifies buoyancy, optimism, and an ascent through the social order based on the acquisition of wealth chiefly by means of hard work. He was an African Samuel Smiles. There are no apparent hints in his story of the depressing effects of servitude, deserted farmlands, or the deleterious colonate that were once supposed to mark the empire in decline. It was therefore assumed that the inscription must have been produced in a bright and halcyon epoch of the empire, in Gibbon's golden and happy days of the Antonines; or, as more work was done on the economic history of Africa, perhaps slightly later in the flourishing African baroque of the Severan emperors.[33]

At the time of the poem's original publication, Charles Tissot expressed an opinion on its date. His conscious links between African prosperity and the date were to be echoed again and again: 'We are inclined to think that this inscription was contemporary with the age of the Severi and with the age of the great industrial and agricultural prosperity that Africa enjoyed under these emperors.'[34] Such assertions affected the placement of the harvester in time and, in turn, the interpretations of what his life meant. Gilbert Charles-Picard, with his peerless knowledge of the Latin culture of Rome's African provinces, was certain that even greater precision was possible. 'If the harvester died towards 270,' Charles-Picard postulated, 'he could have been born around 190, and the acquisition of his wealth would have been gained around 210–235, when Africa was in the full flower of its prosperity.'[35] It is this halo of 'great industrial and agricultural prosperity' that has cast its beneficent glow on the harvester from Mactaris and on the narrative of his personal success. Judgments made by writers of general histories of the imperial social and economic order have been equally bold. In his history of the social classes of the Roman empire, Jean Gagé was certain that this 'African Georgics,' as he put it, could not be imagined until the results of the Antonine epoch's effects on the economy of local imperial society had manifested themselves. Our harvester was therefore a scion of the greatness of Africa's Severan age.[36]

The scholarly consensus that emerged regarding the time to which the poem belonged consistently linked the ebullient optimism and triumphant success of the harvester's personal story to the parallel fate of the empire at large. This fixed unanimity is strange because when the inscription was discovered, the immediate predilection of its first commentator, who did not have much time to think beyond matters of form and content, was to suggest a much later date.[37] Even in the face of significant comparative evidence from late antiquity on the existence of men like the harvester from Maktar, the consistent predilection was to place him in an earlier age of African history on the grounds that he could not have existed in a time of political chaos and retrenchment, cultural decline, and rural immiseration – that is, in the later empire.[38] More recently, within the now better known local perspective of the Latin culture of the town of Mactaris, the problem of dating the inscription has been reduced to specifying the age of Africa's 'prosperity' in which the harvester is to be located.

The issue of temporal location is not a trivial one, since it has been argued that, even within the confines of the small town of Mactaris, our man was not alone. In the exuberant days of the High Empire, he already had peers. Excavations in the town, it has been claimed, have uncovered other written records that offer more exemplars of poor men's rise to wealth and power.[39] One of these is the case of a 'mere farmer' who built a grand mausoleum just outside the town.[40] On closer inspection, however, none of these instances parallels that of the harvester. Whereas it is true that the man who built the mausoleum bore the *cognomen* Colonicus, the name alone does not signify much. Even if it reflected his status as a *colonus*, that is, a cultivator or a farmer (a piece of guesswork that is far from certain, even improbable) it would not necessarily link him with the world of an itinerant harvester. Based on his name, one could even postulate that he was a substantial landowner.[41] But 'Colonicus' is nothing more than a personal name, so it is probably best to abandon uncontrolled speculation about any other significance that it might have had. Pinarius Mustulus, another possible parallel from Mactaris, is a more interesting case. In his funerary epitaph, Mustulus boasts of having increased his property holdings and of having made profits by non-fraudulent means.[42] Unfortunately, the funerary inscription is so fragmentary that not much more can be said about it. The words reflect sentiments common to men who desired to present themselves as *boni patresfamilias*. They were good dependable men who did not allow their family wealth to be impaired or diminished. Rather, they left their patrimony in an improved condition for their heirs and descendants. A man whose family and resources were already significant, and one who ranked in the town's decurial class, could easily boast on his tombstone that he had preserved or increased his inherited wealth. Such a social background and the attendant sentiments are far removed from those of our harvester.

A different type of analysis, that of literary genres and types, specifically of poetry as a form of cultural expression, has led to efforts to place the harvester inscription in the context of the fifteen or so Latin epigraphical poems known from Mactaris. These verse inscriptions, it must be cautioned, are distributed over the whole chronological range of the town's existence as a Roman municipality, from the second to the sixth centuries CE. Based on content and form, it has been argued that the metrical inscriptions from Mactaris can be divided into two broad groups. The first contains themes and language that are more typical of celebrations of the deceased in the high Roman empire. By contrast, epitaphs in the second group highlight phrases and ideas that are normally found in the Christian epigraphy of the later empire. The harvester's poem has been placed in the first group because, like the other poems in it, his epitaph is considered to be a traditional Roman *elogium* that recounts the life of the deceased and which celebrates the protagonist's virtues and past achievements. The ideals shared by the verse epitaphs in the first group evince no concern with any post-mortem future, largely because their subjects did not envisage one. These verse epitaphs, it is asserted, are therefore to be dated to an earlier pre-Christian phase in the history of the town.

In the metrical inscriptions of the second group, whose epitaphs are oriented towards the coming life-after-death, the future is a time of the greatest consequence for the deceased. Personal values and achievements are adjusted accordingly.[43] One can certainly agree that this distinction in basic values is apparent in the poetic inscriptions from Mactaris and that the difference could have some basis in the changing social conditions of the time. It might further be agreed that the values do indeed reflect a predominantly non-Christian world in the one category and a Christian set of values in the other. But it is dubious that content alone is sufficient to determine the date for any specific inscription, or that all of the inscriptions in the first group necessarily predate Christian times. There were many so-called pagans to be found in the cities of Africa in the fourth and fifth centuries. The traditional values of the old social elites still dominated the high secular culture of the towns and cities of Africa of the time. An upwardly mobile man like our harvester would have had every reason to mimic the values of the town's upper ranks. Such mimicry might even have made him a more acceptable candidate for adlection to its formal offices.[44] We also know that Christians at Mactaris, as in other African towns in late antiquity, sometimes preferred to retain these traditional classical elements in the self representation of their lives.[45] As has been noted of the Christian epitaphs from the town: 'One is struck by the importance of their pagan heritage, not only in their expression ... but above all in the themes developed in them, the great majority of which have nothing Christian about them.'[46]

In this respect there was nothing unusual about Mactaris. It must be remembered that many urban centres that were similar to it in size, type, and function, towns like Calama and Sufes, were ones in which non-Christians were still an important element in the urban population as late as the age of Augustine in the fourth and early fifth centuries. In these years, indeed, both of the above towns witnessed spectacular anti-Christian riots. They were places where the local senates and their magistrates were dominated by secular interests that were, if anything, latently hostile to Christians and their strange off putting ideas.[47] This was certainly true of Mactaris in late antiquity where the author of a study of its Christian inscriptions, as we have just noted, remarks on the surprising power and strength of pagan themes and language in them.[48] Neither on the basis of easy assumptions about the nature of the long waves of economic development in Africa nor in any typology of generic content are there good grounds for rejecting dates later than the Severan age for the harvester's tale.

The uniform assumption shared by historians who were attempting to date the harvester inscription is that it must belong to a period of prosperity and for

bijjenaj mejjej pabido jub jole totondi
ductor et exopere postea factus eram
undecim et turmas messorum duximus annii
et numidae campos nostra manus jecuit

a b c d e f g h i l m (∞) n o p q r s t u x

n ba ro ere sp.

2.3: Lettering of the Harvester inscription. *Ephemeris epigraphica* 5 (1984), 279, p. 277 = CIL 8.11824, p. 1223

Mactaris and Africa this age must have been in the efflorescence of wealth under the Antonine or Severan emperors – not, at any rate, in the gloom and depression, and the more rigid social hierarchies, of the later empire. This is rather strange, because there are plenty of signs that it is to this later age that our harvester should be assigned. In an attempt to find the chronological place of his epitaph, we might begin with the technical matter of the script in which it was incised. In order to interpret the cursive writing found on wooden waxed tablets of the Vandal age that were discovered in the late 1920s on the Saharan frontier of the Algerian and Tunisian borderlands, the editors of the *Tablettes Albertini* engaged in a thorough survey of writing styles in Africa. After noting that the Maktar Harvester inscription had been dated to the third, fourth, or even the sixth century, they remarked that the question of its dating required a total reassessment.[49] Based on the criteria that were accepted by the editors for the analysis of the writing on the tablets of the Vandal period, in their view the harvester inscription seemed to belong to the years of late antiquity and not to those of the high empire.

The verse text of the harvester's story furnished such a striking example of the extensive use of the so-called cursive script in a stone inscription that, in the very year it was published, Emile Hübner made reference to it in his set of stereotypes of epigraphical letter forms. He published these in an adjunct volume to the *Corpus Inscriptionum Latinarum* that he intended as a technical publication to assist in understanding the development of different types of epigraphical writing.[50] The chronological and geographic limits of any given type of script were of considerable interest to its editor.[51] At the time, Hübner referred to the inscription as a good example of an uncial script and noted that it was not surprising that

2.4: African script: the Vocontius Publius Flavius Pudens Pomponianus inscription.
Thamugadi: Cagnat, *Cours d'épigraphie latine*, 4th ed. (Paris, 1914), pl. xv.4

soon after the development of uncials for manuscripts, the script made its way to writing on stone. The early dated examples that Hübner cited were from Italy, the earliest of which dated to the year 314 CE. On closer inspection, however, it can readily be seen that these early inscriptions are not in the African script. The majority of Hübner's examples that *are* close in type to the script of the harvester's epitaph are of much later date. Some are from the late fourth century and the fifth century, but most come from the sixth.[52] The same pattern seems to be true of the specific African examples that he cites.[53] The chronological limits of the African inscriptions incised in the unusual script, some of which are from Mactaris, are difficult to ascertain since most of them do not bear any obvious dating markers.[54] Some of the inscriptions in the 'uncial' script from Africa that Hübner lists, however, do have indications of their temporal provenience. Among them is a career inscription for the senator Vocontius Publius Flavius Pudens Pomponianus incised on a statue base from Thamugadi, modern Timgad.[55] The public celebration of Pudens's career produced a second inscription at Thamugadi in the same unusual script.[56] Another example, also from Thamugadi, is a career inscription in honour of Marcus Virrius Flavius Iugurtha, an *eques Romanus*. He was *flamen*

2.5: African script: Vocontius Publius Flavius Pudens Pomponianus, Thamugadi. CIL 8.2391, lines 1–4 and 6: Hübner, *Exempla*, no. 1147, p. 411

2.6: African script: the Virrius Iugurtha inscription, Thamugadi. CIL 8.2409, lines 1–3: Hübner, *Exempla*, no. 1148, p. 411

perpetuus and *decurio* at the imperial colony of Carthage, named the *splendidissima colonia* in the inscription, and he served as *curator rei publicae* at Thamugadi.[57] Iugurtha's posts and the nature of the language used in them would place him, probably, in the last quarter of the third century CE.

Against the later date for this script indicated by these parallels, Jean Mallon argued, based on epigraphical grounds, that the script of the Maktar Harvester inscription had first appeared much earlier than had usually been postulated. He found confirmation for his hypothesis in a funerary stone discovered at Mactaris that preserves a lengthy verse epitaph of a young woman named Beccut.[58] She had died a premature death. Her elegant epitaph was inscribed on her tombstone

2.7: African script: the Beccut inscription, Mactaris. Charles-Picard, Bonniec, and Mallon, 'Le cippe de Beccut,' fig. 21, p. 161; permission courtesy of *Antiquités africaines*

in a cursive script similar to that used for the harvester. Mallon found the editor's dating of the text to 260/270 CE congenial, since it confirmed a hypothesis that he had formed about the African origins of this unusual 'uncial' script.[59] But the date of about 260/270 for the verse epitaph of the woman Beccut was itself based on the editor's own antecedent hypothetical dating of the Maktar Harvester inscription. In Charles-Picard's view, the dates of the two are interconnected. The method is manifestly arbitrary and circular. The plain fact is that the Beccut inscription offers few clues to its own date. It cannot be dated by reference to the Maktar Harvester inscription, which itself has been dated by the 'feeling' that it must belong to a high period of Africa's economic development. In the welter of these hypotheses, Mallon did present some persuasive arguments in favour of the first appearance of this type of script in a mid-third-century context in Africa.

But the earliest possible appearance of the script, especially in permanent stone monuments, is hardly a necessary or sure indication of the temporal location of the Maktar Harvester's verse autobiography. Furthermore, while the whole pre-history of the script on the perishable media of papyrus and vellum is not to be denied, it should not be used as a necessary benchmark for estimating the time of its transfer to the more durable medium of stone and for its use in public display, assumptions that probably affected Mallon's judgments. Nor is there any reason to think that the harvester inscription should necessarily be located at one temporal extreme of the whole range of the data on the use of the unusual script on stone. In lieu of other evidence, one could just as powerfully argue for a later date close to the end of the wide spectrum of possible dates for the script, that is, in the sixth century. In the face of the lack of decisive evidence for the date of the use of the script, it is surely best to opt for the middle of the range of dated examples. This is not to deny that an early date for the harvester's story is *possible* but that, based on the closest parallels to the inscription, other alternative dates – much later ones in fact – are just as likely.

At the time of the discovery of the stone, and based on the economic expecta-tions argument, Charles Tissot dated the inscription to the age of the Severi. On the basis of its script and its style, however, Emile Chatelain immediately argued against Tissot's hypothesis and stated that a date as late as the sixth century was equally possible.[60] Despite Mallon's preference for what might be considered a rather early date in the third century, the use of the unusual so-called uncial script indicates a date in the mid- to late fourth century or even later. It is clear that the unusual form of writing, widely found in inscriptions and in manuscripts of Afri-can origin from the third to the eleventh centuries CE, is a type of lettering that is indebted to a long tradition of African manuscript production that has largely been lost to us.[61] Our harvester was a person of low status. He was someone who was at pains to advertise his humble origins. Yet he was also someone who was eager to mimic a high style set by his betters. It seems more probable that by his time there was already a track record of the unusual script being used by wealthy and powerful persons, often as public officials, for public display on stone. Theirs was an influential style that set a pattern for the harvester and his hired stone-cut-ter to imitate. This hypothesis suggests a date later than the earliest run of exam-ples where the innovative script was used to celebrate the careers of senators and other high-ranking imperial officials. Then there are the contents of the text itself.

Poetic Words

An evaluation of the words of the harvester's self-portrait furnishes additional clues to the inscription's probable location in time. The subject presents him-self, honestly it must be thought, as something of a social upstart. The disarming naïveté with which he describes his rise from low to high is a not inconsiderable part of the charm of his tale. The same is true of the way in which he presents his career as culminating in the high rank that he achieved in his home town. In this presentation, he was imitating the standards set by his social betters. He surely did not initiate either the epigraphical mode of verse in celebration of the self or the use of a literary script on stone in its public presentation. Rather, the poet and the workshop that he hired mimicked models with which they were familiar and which had already been established as stylistic norms. Such workshops existed in Mactaris. One of them produced the interesting verse epitaph, noted above, that celebrated the young woman with the unusual name of Beccut. But hers was just one of a series produced by the same workshop that had access to cutters who could produce a script in beautifully shaped capital letters, the traditional writing used for elevated public subjects. Or they could produce something in the fancy new script, if the customer required.[62] The corpus of Latin verse inscriptions from the western provinces of the Roman empire reveals that this particular mode of presentation of the self was normally used by persons who entered the ranks of local municipal society. They were men and women who were important locally, but who were still only in the middling ranks of a grander imperial society.[63] The harvester was following a type. He used his death and the erection of a funerary stele, one of the most frequent occasions for this purpose, to offer a typical advertisement of the self, to vaunt a transformation in the life course of a low-born person. It is not without reason that he has been seen as a latter-day Trimalchio.[64]

These few observations indicate that the Maktar Harvester inscription should probably be placed in a time no earlier than one in which there already existed a significant number of upper-class models and styles to be imitated. Comparisons from the northern regions of the proconsular province made on this basis suggest a date no earlier than the fourth century. The question must then be asked: Is the later fourth century a probable social and economic context in which to locate the mobile and profitable career of the harvester from Maktar? Some decades ago, the answer would have been a resolute 'no.' Such an upwardly mobile career would have been thought to be very unlikely in Africa of late antiquity, which was then viewed within a general paradigm of empire-wide decline. Recent decades of archaeological research, however, have permanently overturned all of these assumptions. It is now manifest that Roman Africa of the fourth and fifth centuries, even if by default, was a prime beneficiary of political and military disintegration elsewhere in the empire. As an isolated foyer of relative peace in the Mediterranean, Africa experienced an economic boom during these later times, especially in the sectors of agricultural production. Far from appearing odd or unusual in this later context, the Maktar Harvester's career now seems more rather than less probable. Even marginal lands in the arid southern frontiers were becoming more intensely developed and, as their communities assumed new forms of municipal organization, they too engaged in the epigraphical habit.

Then there is the matter of the technical vocabulary used in the inscription – to be precise, its poetic diction. For example, while some earlier examples can be found for the use of the word *gremium* for a sheaf of wheat or barley, almost all of the known examples are found in Latin texts of the late fourth century or later. Most of the instances from Africa, drawn mainly from the writings of Augustine, are from the 380s, the 390s, and even later. Similarly, the reference to the building in which the local *ordo* or town council met as a *templum* finds an almost exact parallel in an inscription from the colony of Lambaesis in Numidia that is dated to the 380s. Then there is the use of words and expressions that are not found in Latin in earlier ages in Africa. One of these is the use of *demessor* for harvester. Repeated twice in the inscription to identify our man, it is never once found in the whole corpus of classical Latin before the end of the Severan age. It *is* found, as are many such compound nouns beginning with the emphatic prefix *de*, in the later age of the fourth and fifth centuries. Nor is *progenitus* found earlier but it is used, both here and elsewhere, in texts of the late fourth century and later, including epigraphical ones. And it is frequently found in the writings of Augustine, but not in earlier patristic writers from Africa. Similarly, there is the unusual usage and form of the word *postea*, which, as has been acutely noted, is not used in this fashion until the fourth century and later.[65] In a poetic discourse that consciously mimics Vergilian forms, chronological clues like these are not numerous. They might be refuted individually, but collectively they suggest that Chatelain's suspicions were correct. The flourishing career of our harvester probably took place in the later part of the fourth century, or in the fifth, but not earlier.

Self-Representation

Like other Africans who had their family stories set in verse for public display, the harvester adopts a tone that emphasizes personal success. There are some parallels in the famous verse epitaph of the Flavii of Cillium, inscribed about the middle of the second century CE. Cut onto the outer walls of the tall Afro-Punic Roman funerary mausoleum, the 110-line poem is the longest epigraphical verse epitaph known in Latin. In it are expressed some of the same sentiments that are found in the harvester's epitaph.[66] The deceased, Titus Flavius Secundus the elder, is lauded for his acquisition of money and other forms of wealth. He is praised for having achieved his fortune by investment of labour in agricultural production: for example, by instituting the use of irrigation to cultivate vines.[67] In the same way, our harvester was also proclaiming 'I am a success.' Nevertheless, from the time of the discovery of the harvester inscription, almost every student of its verses has remarked on the difference of tone between our man's story and the more formally pompous presentation of the success of Titus Flavius Secundus and his family.[68] For a man whose origins were rooted in poverty, the harvester's achievements were equally impressive. He was part of the African economic boom of the fourth century that witnessed an immense extension of land under cultivation. This movement was especially manifest in the development of marginal lands along the Saharan periphery. But it was just as evident in the extension of existing cereal and fruit production in regions further to the north. He was the peer of a man named Bion, a pious Christian octogenarian farmer who celebrated the planting of 4,000 olive trees near Uppenna in the northern Tunisian Sahel.[69] Such hard working men were not alone. They are a few of the known named beneficiaries of a rural expansion in the late fourth century Maghrib.

The success of the harvester from Maktar was made possible, in part, by this late agrarian development coupled with the heightened demand for the services that he offered. And boasting about the improvement of one's wealth and substance by means of hard labour was not unusual in Africa of late antiquity. There is, for example, the case of the farmer and citizen of the town of Bihensi Bilta, located to the south of Matera, modern-day Mateur, in the region to the north of Carthage. He is vaunted as having restored a farm called the *fundus Aufidianus*. Through hard work and ingenuity, he improved the olive crops by implementing a new process of grafting. He dug a new well, set out a new orchard, and planted new vines under the trees.[70] Rural improvers like the man from Bihensi Bilta were continuators of the successful agricultural entrepreneurs from the days of the high Principate, like the industrious Aelius Timminus from the town of Madauros: 'hard and patient in his labours, frugal, alert, and sober, he managed the affairs of a not well off family and raised a poor household to equestrian rank.'[71] That is to say, Timminus presents himself as having achieved high social status by dint of hard personal effort.

In the presentation of one's life successes in verse, a factor as simple (or perhaps not as simple) as that of style and fashion must be considered. For whatever reason, there are an unusual number of poetic self-portraits in the Latin epigraphy from Mactaris and its surrounding region. Successful hard-working farmers are known from elsewhere in Africa, but they represented themselves in the medium of prose.[72] Influences of exemplary behaviour, however, might have been even broader in the ranks of persons of high social status. Such achievements were not wholly unparalleled. There were Africans of the time who followed these other paths of social mobility. Perhaps best known from the later empire, in the 380s, was Aurelius Augustinus. Coming from the agrotown of Thagaste, he used the advantages of education rather than manual labour to fuel his social elevation. He was not alone; nor was the form of boasting. The personal story lines of some of these men had similarities to ones of our harvester. Sextus Aurelius Victor was a young man with limited resources (so he says) who rose from a small town in Africa to become Prefect of the City around 389. His story was as follows: 'I was born on a small rural farm and had a father who was poor and uneducated, but now, because of my brilliant studies, I live the life of the better sort of people.'[73] Again we witness a similar path of ascent, although in this case it was gained by the means of mental rather than manual labour.

Marvellous exemplars of upward mobility from the nameless ranks of rural idiocy, poverty, and depression to higher rank and municipal excellence are also known and celebrated in several different modern literatures. There were men like Thomas Hardy's Michael Henchard, an itinerant rural labourer in late nineteenth-century England. Henchard's occupation as a hay-trusser makes him someone whose work was similar to that done by the harvester from Maktar. He was a rough, hard character who made his living on the road engaged in seasonal employment as a worker who followed behind the reapers and tied the mowed hay into bundles. Before his eventual fall back into his lowly origins where he belonged, Henchard rose to become mayor of the rural South Wessex town of Casterbridge, a latter-day Mactaris. He was like a modern duumvir. He is a good example of a type. Admittedly, there are rather few of these literary types. But that is the point. At least Henchard had a writer who could invent and imagine him, a writer who had a form in which he could express his subject's life, and a large enough readership interested in a story like his. Our man from Mactaris, by contrast, had to invent himself and advertise his own life, admittedly with some literary assistance. Otherwise, no one would have been sufficiently interested to create him and to place him in the upper-class literature of the age. The death notice was a type of self-produced 'literature' that was within his grasp.

On the Road

So how did the harvester from Maktar make his fortune? Although he specifies that it was at harvesting, he certainly does not mean that he was a simple individual reaper who happened to make a lot of money. The improbability of a story like that would be extreme. Various words and terms used in the poem, although poetic and not strictly legal, reveal that he was a leader or an organizer of gangs or *turmae* of harvest workers. That is to say, he was a contractor who gathered together large numbers of men on a seasonal basis and took them on the rounds of the high plains of Africa to reap cereal crops. Although the 'Fields of Jupiter' that he mentions defy sure identification, the location of the 'nomad plains of Cirta' is almost certain. The high plains of Numidia lying north of the Theveste-Lambaesis highway, the main route that ran along the northern slopes of the Aurès

Mountains, are surely the 'fields of Numidia' to which our harvester refers. The 'nomad plains' might also have included the lands to the southeast of Cirta around the town of Tigisis. It is in this region that the winter pasturelands of the tribes of the Nicibes and Suburbures were located. The pastoral nomadic groups belonging to the Nicibes moved northwards out of the Saharan periphery each summer to reach their pasturelands.[74] And these lands might also have included plains areas even further to the west, like the extensive grain-growing flatlands around the colonial city and provincial capital of Sitifis.

The 'Fields of Jupiter,' given the identification of the king of the gods, Jupiter, with the African deity Saturn, could refer to another well-known feature in the landscape. Perhaps, as has been suggested, the location refers to one of the flatlands close to Carthage that was particularly identified with one of the most important Saturn shrines.[75] Although the latter identification is speculative, the geographic connections that it suggests would make sense from what is known of the usual practices followed by harvesting gangs elsewhere in the western Mediterranean and Europe. It is also strongly suggested by the known pattern of the sequential seasonal ripening of the wheat and barley crops attested for the modern-day Maghrib. Harvesting gangs would begin their rounds in the high plains of Numidia around Cirta/Constantina and Sitifis in the west. They would start reaping in the driest and hottest regions where the grain crops ripened first. Then they would work their way gradually northwards and eastwards towards the heartlands of the proconsular province north of the Dorsal: the Siliana Plain and the valleys around el-Fahs. It is a logical guess. Such circuits are typical of most recurrent harvest labour regimes once the types of crops, the operational units, and the patterns of ownership stabilize.[76] Under these conditions, both the managers of the itinerant labourers and the workers themselves become well acquainted with the normal rounds. The same was true in nineteenth-century England.

The most independent class of day workers were those who travelled in companies, leap-frogging from job to job. They planned a route so that they were fully employed throughout the harvest season, and could take on the most profitable jobs. These travelling bands were usually made up of young men, who were prepared to work long hours and to travel far. They created their own 'harvest circuits,' and trod the same elliptic path year after year, leaving home to mow the early hay and returning for the corn harvest in their own locality.[77]

Similar harvest circuits would have been encouraged in Roman Africa by the variable temporal cycles in which the different crops matured. Seeded earliest in the year, barley was also the first crop to ripen, beginning in March in the lands closest to the fringes of the Sahara in the south and then progressively later, in April and May, in more northerly and westerly lands. The reaping of the wheat crops would usually begin a month later, in May and early June, in most of these same regions.[78] This was also true of the American West at the end of the nineteenth and the beginning of the twentieth century, where the 'armies' of seasonal labourers worked northwards from Oklahoma, following the ripening harvests. They then worked their way backwards, from north to south, following the complementary seasonal demands of the lumbering industry.[79]

It was on a circuit of the grain-growing regions of Africa that our man, a contractor of harvest workers, led his gangs each year. As a contractor, he would probably not march an entire gang from the Mactaris region out to the far west. More likely, he would take a few workers with him, acquiring more men en route to the high plains, and then collecting others from local sources (e.g., pastoral nomads and montane highlanders) when he arrived at his destination. In their recruitment, the gangs who reaped the high plains of north Africa were, in all likelihood, composite conglomerates. The contractors, usually known as *conductores*, were a normal part of the labour process. They assembled the gangs out of various manpower sources. They were also the men who stood between the farmer or his agent who needed the work done and the men who were looking for employment in the fields.[80] Both the men who were hired and the contractors would know the usual regional cycle of the ripening of the crops and the need for labour. The process is perhaps best documented for Roman Egypt, where the grain harvest began earlier in the more arid and hotter lands of the south, in the nomes of central upper Egypt in late April – at Hermoupolis on 30 Pharmouthi (about 25 April). The harvest time varied according to the weather conditions of each year, but in Upper Egypt, it was centred in the months of Pharmouthi and Pachon (roughly, April and May).[81] The harvest moved to the months of May and June for the Delta Region of Lower Egypt, and to slightly later times yet for regions along the Mediterranean coast.[82] The ecological conditions that marked the onset of the first days of harvest in each region drew harvesting gangs along natural annual circuits of work.

In Africa seasonal labour was drawn from two basic sources. One was the light but more mobile populations of pastoral nomads. The other was provided by the dense centres of population: both the regions of intense urban development in the east, especially the network of towns inland of Carthage and the heavily populated mountain highlands in the west. In the case of the towns, the additional manpower was there in abundance, ready to be organized and set into motion, from east to west, for the taking off of the harvest of cereal grains. To recall and affirm a point already made, these same sources of surplus labour also provided the main body of recruits for the Roman army in Africa.[83] Similar patterns of labour recruitment were found in modern times in Canada and Argentina. The main sources of manpower for the army and for harvesting gangs were found in regions of denser urban development. Both countries also had the same cyclical patterns

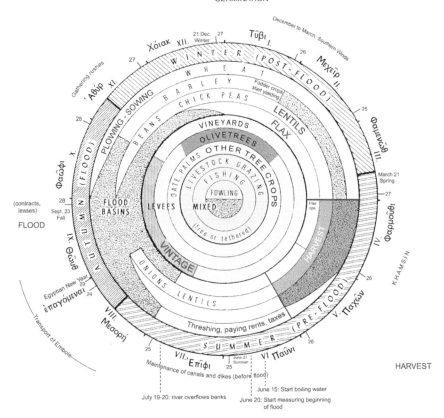

2.8: Reaping in the ecological cycle of the Nile River Valley;
permission courtesy of Dr Ariel López

of the movement of men out to the fields and back to regions of heavier urban settlement.[84] The town of Mactaris was ideally positioned on the *limen* or threshold interface between the two worlds of surplus population and higher seasonal labour demands. Our harvester came from the right place.

Even so, how was the Maktar Harvester's wealth possible? A logical answer the question about the source of his wealth is that it was gained by piling up a large number of tiny increments of profit. That is to say, an accumulation of small units of anything could bridge the gap between the low and the high. This process has parallels in other sectors of the economy of the Roman Mediterranean, of which one example will have to suffice to illustrate the possibilities. The land transport of a wide range of commodities was as basic to the ancient economy as was the annual cycle of harvesting operations. The hauling of a wide range of goods required the employment and provisioning of various kinds of vehicles for carting and a range of draught animals. Given the limited availability of hard-topped roads and the ubiquity of rough terrain, goods often had to be transported on the backs of pack animals, in most cases the hardy and dependable mule. The profession of the *mulio* or mule driver filled this important economic need. If performed by a lone individual in a modest way, the profession afforded only a modest income. If it was done on a larger scale, using the combined instruments of ownership, agency, hire, and the management of greater numbers, the factor of scale enabled the accumulation of considerable returns.[85]

An illustration of successful mule driving on a large scale is provided by Publius Ventidius Bassus, the suffect consul of 43 BCE. Ventidius Bassus had risen from base origins to a position of considerable wealth and power through his involvement in the business of mule transport. His low origins and the means by which he escaped them earned him the pejorative nickname of *mulio* from the likes of Cicero and others.[86] We therefore know that there existed a general class of energetic entrepreneurs who met low-level mass demands and who made fortunes from such business. The career of Ventidius, and of others like him, is a useful model for what involvement with otherwise small and despicable things might achieve for an energetic man.[87] The rewards of meeting mass demands like transporting goods or reaping cereal crops produced an odd conflicting mix of low-class sources of wealth and high-rank incomes. Note the connection: the existence of men of low social status who by their involvement in necessary tasks acquired wealth and position. By doing so, they astonished persons of higher rank and in the process drew upon themselves the merciless criticism of these others. Our harvester certainly did not reach anything like the consulship in the Roman state, but he did attain an analogous position of rank and authority in his home town of Mactaris. He did not have to make millions or tens of millions, but probably something amounting to a tenth of the latter figure: a hundred thousand or so.

The emperor Augustus might be able to lay claim, vicariously it is true, to a noble ancestry going back to the foundations of Rome, and beyond. But the reality was nowhere near as perfect or as illustrious. Marc Antony was able to taunt Octavian with the fact that his great-grandfather was a freedman and a rope-maker from the countryside around Thurii, and his grandfather nothing more than a money changer.[88] The slurs – both were surely intended as such – might have been useful abuse, but they cannot be dismissed. They were probably true.[89] And this truth hints at a hugely underinvestigated world of connections between high and low. By these means, among others, not only labour but ideas, including, as in this case, vituperation, ritual abuse, and polemic, passed up and down the social order. Such mobility, from servitude to the heights of wealth and power, was possible. In this case, it took four generations to ascend from the bottom to the very top. Our man from Mactaris did not have to manage and collate resources on the scale of a Ventidius Bassus, but rather on the scale, say, of the father of Flavius Petro, the ancestor of Vespasian, who was able to settle down and become a notable in the municipality of Reate in central Italy. The Maktar Harvester was able to achieve a similar elevation in much the same fashion: because he was *not* an individual worker, but a man who collated and organized the labour of others. In more modern times, the process was frequently repeated, with young entrepreneurs who provided harvest labour making real wealth in the process.[90] In antiquity, such men might not have been as common as they were in more modern economies, but they were certainly known and present in appreciable numbers.

The World of the Contractor

In technical and legal terms, our anonymous man was a *manceps* or a contractor of labourers. In the business of contracting labour, the *manceps* was the middle man. He organized and hired the labourers, sometimes trained them, and then put them to work for a landowner with whom he made a contract to take off the harvest. As has already been noted, the father of Titus Flavius Petro, the great-grandfather of the emperor Vespasian, was reputed to have been just such a contractor of farm labourers. He was said to have led his gangs of seasonal workers from Umbria on annual rounds of agricultural work in the Sabine lands of central Italy.[91] In Italy of the first century BCE, there must have been many such men. In Petro's case, it is his distant relationship to a Roman emperor that caused him to be noted in a literary source. In like manner, there must have been very many harvest contractors and great numbers of *turmae* or gangs of harvesters in Africa during the fourth and fifth centuries. Much of the labour would have been strongly cyclical in nature, setting up patterns of predictable routes that the gangs would follow and regular clients with whom the contractor would deal year after year.[92] Because of the structural nature of the labour demands and the management of supply, the figure of the labour contractor is frequently found between the landowner and the workers to be hired. He was not peculiar to the Roman world alone. The many dozens of labour contracts that survive from Babylonia of the eighteenth and seventeenth centuries BCE richly attest the existence of these useful intermediaries.[93]

Cato's handbook on agriculture includes model contracts that give us an idea of the terms that were usually found in contracts for seasonal agricultural work. Despite the fact that it is of middle Republican date and applies to the taking of a crop in central Italy, his model contract for the acquisition of a seasonal workforce for the harvesting of olives contains general terms that are analogues to those that applied to the harvesting of cereal crops in later times outside of Italy.[94] In the agreement, the harvest work contractor made a contract with the owner of the land on which the crops to be harvested were grown, with the manager of the farm, or with the person to whom the crop had been sold. High on the list of caveats are concerns with the suspected propensity of workers to thieve part of the crop. The owners' fears led to the demand that oral oaths be sworn by the workers that they would not steal the crops that they were about to harvest. In some cases, it seems that the contractors had to put up surety monies to guarantee the performance of the contract: that the numbers of men promised would actually turn up on the dates agreed and that they would do the job as it was prescribed. Every failure to perform according to the terms of the contract subjected the contractor and his men to fines or deductions from their final pay or from the advanced surety monies. On the other hand, bonuses and incentives that encouraged the harvesters to execute their tasks as efficiently as possible were also specified.

The most detailed evidence that we have on these seasonal labour agreements and on the contractual conditions of employment comes from the surviving records of written harvesting contracts from Roman Egypt.[95] Although these written agreements are an excellent guide to the real conditions of the work, we must assume that most reaping contracts were made orally.[96] Even where written contracts existed in abundance, as for example in Old Babylonian–period Mesopotamia, there were still oral dimensions to them that complicate their interpretation.[97] We might also reasonably presume that the few written contracts that have survived encapsulate a range of normal terms of work and pay that were found in the more common verbal contracts. A dozen or so of these written contracts have survived from Roman Egypt in reasonably complete condition.[98] A typical example comes from the last decade of the first century CE.

[about 20 missing letters...] in the year of our Lord Caesar: 54 arourai, 6 arourai to each. As the wages for reaping, you will give to [each of] us 5/6ths of an artaba [i.e., about 3.75 modii] of wheat for each aroura [i.e., about a iugerum]; and after the harvest you will measure out the above-mentioned wage for the above-mentioned aroura, on the condition that you, Eudaimon [i.e., the landowner], are responsible for gathering the sheaves of wheat. You will also supply us with drinking water until we finish the reaping of the said arourai of land. If any one of us is idle at any time, we will be required to substitute another man in his place for the same day. The above-mentioned wheat you will pay to us according to the Athenian sixth-part measure, and in addition you will give us a *keramion* of beer on the last day. We shall be required to begin reaping on the 30th of the present month, Pharmouthi, in the present 10th year [i.e., of the emperor Domitian]. For each aroura in wheat that is reaped you will pay us the stated 5/6ths of an artaba of wheat. The 10th year of the Emperor Caesar [Domitian Augustus. Month Neroneus Augustus] 25. Theon [about 25 missing letters][99]

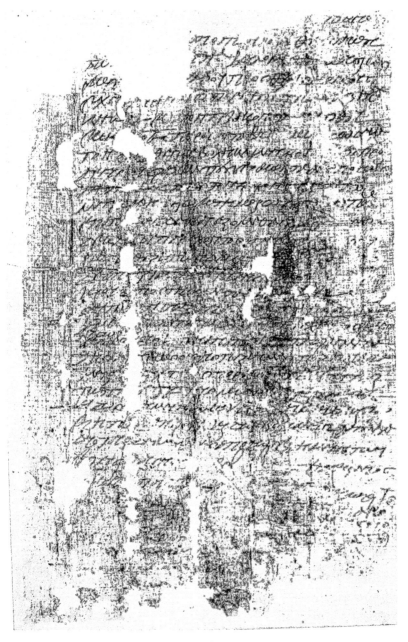

2.9: Harvesting contract from Roman Egypt, the Sarapion Archive, 125 CE. P. Sarap. 51: Schwartz, *Archives de Sarapion*, pl. iv

From the terms found in almost all of these contracts, a general outline of the standard contracting process can be ascertained. The reapers usually travelled to the fields in groups of up to a dozen men and with their leader they bargained with the landowner. The offer of the price to do the job came from the men themselves. They were allowed to inspect the field and to estimate the amount of reaping to be done; then they haggled with the owner over recompense. The men reserved the right to inspect the land so as to be able to confirm the amount of land to be reaped for which they were contracting. It was expected that each man would reap about three-quarters of an aroura per diem (roughly the same portion of a iugerum). In some cases, the daily pay was made in kind and was calculated as a proportion of the crops reaped. Rates ran from six-sixteenths to twelve-sixteenths of an artaba a day, depending on the circumstances.[100] In terms of the value of an artaba of wheat immediately after harvest (i.e., at the low end of the annual value cycle), this indicates that the reapers were receiving between 3 and 4.5 drachmai per diem.[101] Other sources, however, like the account books of estate managers, contain standard line items in which the per diem wages for reapers are calculated in coin, suggesting that a money payment was made.[102] In these records, it is money pay that is described, in one case 2 drachmai and 3 obols for each aroura that was reaped.[103] The discrepancy between the wheat payments in kind and the payments of hard coinage might reflect the greater immediate use value of the latter to reapers on the move, as opposed to the greater ease of payment in kind for the landowner. The labour services of the hired harvesters are specified as 'for reaping,' *pros therismon*: for the cutting and the binding of the sheaves. In some cases, the individual sheaves, the *dragmata*, were collected and bound into larger units.[104] The owner was expected to provide his own labour for the collecting of the sheaves and for transporting them either to the threshing floor or to a storage facility. The reaping was for specified wheat crops and fields whose dimensions would have been well known to the negotiators, since they were located in familiar localities.

The reapers sometimes found their labour in heightened demand. They were then able to ask for and receive advances, normally of up to 4 drachmai per man, probably to tie their obligations to a specific landlord who needed their services. The date on which the reaping was to begin was sometimes set by the landowner, but more often, it seems, it was a mutually agreed date. The salary was to be paid immediately 'after the reaping,' *meta ton therismon*, or, sometimes, in the month following the completion of the work. When made in kind, the payment was to be dispensed on a pro-rated basis in 'x' amount of wheat or barley that was to be calculated according to the standard measures that were locally in force. On his side, the contractor guaranteed to provide a force of 'n' number of men. If that number fell into deficit for any reason (for example, sickness or failure to show) then it was the responsibility of the contractor to make good the promised number. Finally, the contractor agreed to have his men work from the day of the inception of the work until its completion without interruption. The emphasis in the contracts is on the need for continuity in the reaping.

As for his part of the obligations, the landowner or hirer assumed several responsibilities beyond paying the men their wages or their recompense in kind. He had to supply the ties for binding the sheaves. He had to promise to provide for the transport of water to the men during the reaping and, on the last day, to give them a jug of beer, or double that amount in wine. In addition to the monetary part of their salary, the landowner or his manager also promised to provide various amounts of food to each worker: an artaba of beans, two free sheaves of wheat, and a fig cake. Some of these latter additions were presented as goodwill gifts or gratuities offered to the men by the landowner. The reapers, in turn, reciprocated (or, at least, claimed that they would do so) by promising to work an extra day for the landowner for free. These same gratuitous items are found in other labour service contracts in Egypt, where they were given as a form of tip called a *thalios* or a *thallion*, or as an honorarium that was given *eis timên* or *hyper timêma*.[105] Gratuities, perks, benefits, and extra payments remained something that owners and their agents continued to take into consideration through the age of the Maktar Harvester, all of them as additional incentives to encourage good work in their fields.[106]

Sometimes the men who contracted with the *manceps* of the reapers were the landowners or *domini* themselves. More often in practice, however, it was the agents who managed the farms – the *vilici*, *procuratores*, and *actores* – who struck the deal.[107] As in the detailed harvesting contracts known from ancient Babylonian centres, there is every reason to believe that at least some of these contracts (as attested on the contracts from Roman Egypt) were made months in advance of the harvest, with down payments of some type given to the contractor to guarantee later performance.[108] Because of the intensity of the demand for the urgently needed labour, the harvest workers had be imported from regions where the labour was in surplus. These were zones of relative underemployment. Labourers had to be moved in groups in an organized fashion to the rural zones where their employment was suddenly required. Economic pressures produced the movement.[109] The migration of harvesters in groups to the place of harvest each year was one of the most important ways in which the harvest workforce was obtained. In Egypt in late antiquity, the monks of the great monastic establishments represented just such a reserve pool of seasonal labour. Rufinus notes that they would move down the Nile river valley 'in flocks,' as he puts it, at harvest time. They would earn enough pay in one harvest season to survive for the rest of the year and even have some left over to be able to make charitable donations.[110]

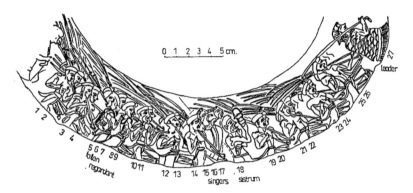

2.10: The harvesters on a Minoan vase. Younger, *Music in the Aegean Bronze Age*, pl. 2; permission courtesy of the author

Many of the elements in the process remained the same over time because they were structurally set by the nature of the labour demand and supply. In nineteenth-century rural England, we find much the same process.

It was quite a business when the harvest men met with the farmer each year to fix the price per acre for tying, shocking and carting. First of all they would inspect each field in turn, then the farmer would leave the men to talk the matter over for a while before coming back to hear their decision. Often they would argue for as much as half a day, but in the end they would always come to some agreement. Then the farmer would send for some beer to seal the bargain and a start could be made on the work.[111]

The status of the contractor who was at the centre of the entire process was therefore commensurately high even if his personal magnitude was limited and temporary in nature. In England the contractor who discussed the terms of the labour contract with the landlord or his agent was known as the 'King of the Harvest.'[112] The Roman *manceps* of the harvesting gangs was no less powerful a person. A combination of contractor, manager, and tyrannical boss, he appeared like a regal figure commanding huge numbers of men throughout the countryside. In an African sermon dating to the sixth century, pseudo-Fulgentius compares him to another royal personage, King David of the Bible:

It is pleasing to witness the fields of wheat crops filled with ripening golden stemmed stalks … these crops are like the passions of the martyrs … For in this same way, our blessed David, like a *manceps* before his harvesters, sings out loud accompanied by his lyre a harvester's song about the reddened blossoms of the martyrs and the harvest crops about to be cut.[113]

The Roman *manceps* not only hired out the labour of the harvesters but also supervised the sometimes difficult men under his command. He was an imposing figure. He was like the superintendent in charge of the seasonal harvesters reaping the immense Dalrymple farm in South Dakota in 1880, who, as he commanded his men from his elevated position on a superb horse, is reported to be '*like* a brigadier directing his forces,' albeit of men who were 'fully armed and equipped, not with swords, but with the implements of peace.'[114] This impressive man, who leads out the parade of his harvesting troupe, might be identified with the figure on the famous Minoan 'Harvester Vase' who is leading a gang of twenty-two men, fourteen of them pictured as engaged in singing and chanting. He is notably attired in a grander style than the others and is armed with a long baton.[115] On occasion, such might have been the assertive air of authority exuded by our harvester from Maktar. He rose through the ranks from being a simple reaper or cutter of crops, a *demessor* as he calls it, to become a *ductor* or a leader of harvesting gangs. *Ductor ex opere postea factus eram*: 'Then I rose from a field-hand and became a foreman.' We can imagine that he, too, might have led his men in a formal procession on what the poet Vergil called the grand Day of the Harvest, the *messis dies*, when the harvester marched his gang of reapers, military fashion, into the fields.[116]

The Work: Hire and Pay

The most urgent operations and the most intensely demanding of labour were those that involved the cutting of the cereal crops: the cutting, binding or tying of the sheaves of grain, and, where required, their shocking or stooking. The labour required for these operations usually had to be met by recruiting occasional workers, often from outside the community: day labourers, migrants, hired men, and other aliens who arrived either as individuals or in groups. The second part of the harvest encompassed the processing of the cut grains: the carrying or the carting to the threshing floor, the threshing, and then the storage of the threshed grains. This second component of the harvest was less urgent, with the result that landowners ordinarily depended on whatever permanent labour was available locally. Family, friends, neighbours, slaves, permanently tied workers, sharecroppers, and year-round hired hands – the owner or the farm manager mustered them in a kaleidoscope of variations.[117] In Sicily of the first century BCE, it was during this second part of the harvest, after the grain had been reaped and brought to the threshing floor, that the slaves who were the permanent labour force on the farms were assembled in large numbers to begin work. It was the time when the human wealth of the latifundist's household was on display for all to admire.[118]

As this example shows, the normal place of slaves in harvest labour was usually limited to the sphere in which the permanent workers of the household were engaged. For Italy of the first century BCE, Varro assumed that tasks such as reaping and mowing involved not the permanent slave labour of the domain, but rather *mercenarii* or hired hands who, as free persons, contracted their work.[119] The contractors, however, sometimes worked with mixed workforces made up of slaves and free hired workers, both of whom could be designated as either hired hands, *mercenarii*, or more specifically as day labourers, *operarii*. Christian commentators in late antiquity, usually remarking on a brief passage in the Gospel of Luke on hired labourers in the service of a master, refer to both kinds of workers.[120] An African preacher of the time could discourse at length on how every great house had all these kinds of labour at its disposal: hired workers, slaves, and sons, in that order.[121] Legal provisions for the use of slaves in harvest work suggest that surplus slave labour in the possession of any given owner could be lent, leased, or sold to other landowners. In one such case, a testator left eight of his country slaves to his concubine with the proviso that she would become responsible for maintaining them with provisions. Problems arose because their former master, the testator in this case, had been accustomed to sending them out at harvest time, at which time he himself had *not* provided them with victuals. The question therefore arose: Was his concubine to benefit from the same exemption?[122] The presumption is that owners of slaves sometimes transferred or lent them to others, presumably neighbours and acquaintances, to use at harvest time.[123] In which case it was now these others who were responsible for providing the slaves, as harvesters, with the daily food rations that they would normally have received from their master.[124]

It is important to note that in a society where whole sectors of economic production were dependent on slave labour, the use of slaves for reaping was *not* a general practice in Africa during the Roman period. It is true, however, that slaves were available and could be used. Sometimes they were a more flexible form of permanent labour who were lent or rented precisely in these conditions of urgent demands. The practice is found in Roman Egypt in the early fourth century at the town of Hermonthis (modern Armant), located about a dozen miles south of Thebes. A landowner in the town used his slaves as a mobile labour force, reassigning them to work in the fields when the harvest season arrived. We might consider a slave named Philokyrios, who bore the servile name 'Master Lover.' In the 'down' months of the work year, he was paid an irregular disbursement when he was resident on the home farm, but when harvest time came, he was dispatched to the fields with the other workers.[125] Slaves could also be hired out as reapers. The usual recourse of landowners, however, was to hire workers in the ordinary sense of *misthôtai*: free men who were paid a wage for their work. A man named Sion, who was managing the harvest for his master Isidoros, wrote to him, noting with some alarm that the young men who had been working the fields had simply taken off, probably for higher-paying offers of employment.[126]

2.11: A reaping gang in Algeria, c. 1900. 'Harvesting with the Reaping Hook – Algeria,'
in Buck, Kratzner, and Owings, *Harvest Scenes*, p. 10

I have spoken to Didymos about sending along other hired hands so that they will do the
work here. But he tells me that he doesn't have the money. If you wish, you can send me
there to hire workers and I'll work with them and clean up the fields. Write back to me.
See that you don't forget to write back to me about this matter. You know that it's the time!

Kairos estin. There is a sense of urgency in the letter, with its plea not to forget
to write back immediately. Now is *the* time. The work had to be done now. The
men involved were persons of free status who hired out their labour. They were
probably locals whom Sion could acquire for pay. In other cases involving greater
distances and larger numbers, it is manifest that the men on the move were free
to do so.

Given the known manpower requirements for harvesting, a small landowner
who owned more land than a family and neighbourly helpers could reap – say,
forty or fifty iugera at the outermost – needed smaller crews of half a dozen to a
dozen men to complete the reaping. Numbers on this order are suggested by the
harvesting contracts from Roman Egypt, where the size of the reaping gangs was
commonly between six and a dozen men.[127] The reaping gangs mentioned in the
rich documentary evidence from Old Babylonian period Mesopotamia similarly
appear to have been hired in units of six, with twenty-four as the normal upper
number of men in them.[128] And we see gangs of this size harvesting in premodern
conditions of manual labour in the nineteenth-century Maghrib. A landholder
who had much larger amounts of land to be harvested (say, between two and
four hundred iugera) required several hundred worker-days of labour to do the

reaping. If the task was to be completed in a week, he would have to contemplate hiring forty to fifty men. Total numbers like this are also attested. They are found not as much in the smaller grain fields of the Nile Valley, as in the broader, more expansive fields of Gaul. A late Gallo-Roman landlord hired about seventy men for one of his harvesting operations.[129] The real need is to estimate how many farm units in Africa were above the size where the harvest could be managed by the deployment of the labour of the proprietor or sharecropper's family, friends, relatives, and neighbours.[130] The problem is that we do not have, and are unlikely ever to have, the statistics needed to make this calculation.[131] The distribution, moreover, would have varied considerably from one region to the next, depending on the size of larger farms and on the range of crops that were being harvested.[132] But the scale was surely significant. Even based on the most modest of estimates, the numbers of hired men on the move every year must have run into hundreds of thousands. For these large numbers of mobile labourers, the seasonal work afforded critical extra money and other resources.

In societies where the connection between harvest labour and the landlord needing the work was one of organized or formalized dependency, recompense often took the form of a proportion of the grain harvest and not much else. In fourteenth-century England, where peasant tenants were required to provide labour for demesne lands, for example, 'reaping ... was commonly rewarded with one sheaf for each half-acre, a half-acre representing a day's labour.'[133] In almost all societies that had a strong monetized sector in their economy, however, harvesters were ordinarily paid wages according to day rates. In the Canadian and American wheat belts of the early twentieth century, even with the advancing mechanization of agriculture, a *per diem* pay system prevailed. Men would bargain with the landowner on the spot about their wages, which in the year 1921 varied according to the time, demand, supply, and the region, and ranged from three to five dollars per day. Only a year earlier, however, when different circumstances had produced a greater demand for labour, the wages in some regions had run as high as eight dollars a day.[134] Since harvest was a time of intense labour demand, pay often rose above the normal day-wages in the same season of the year by as much as half again or even double the normal rates.[135] Reapers in particular received significantly higher recompense than did those who performed ordinary agricultural work during the remainder of the year, sometimes by as much as three times the normal pay rates.[136] The same order of wage differences was also found for harvesters in premodern north Africa. In the late nineteenth and early twentieth centuries, an ordinary field labourer was paid about one franc a day, a reaper received from 2.25 to 2.75 francs a day, while the manager of a gang of reapers was paid 3.5 to 3.75 francs a day.[137] But even these rates of pay could rise, and sometimes substantially, given any one of a number of exogenous factors that affected the availability of labour. The significant decadal rises and falls, along with marked increases and decreases in labour productivity, however, are hidden from us for Roman Africa.[138]

Our best evidence from Roman antiquity, harvesters' contracts from Roman Egypt, confirms that reapers received higher than the normal rates of pay for agricultural work. Their wages varied from six- to twelve-sixteenths of an artaba (the artaba being about four modii) per diem, which amounted to about one and a half times the normal daily pay rate for general agricultural labour in the same season. It was as much as double the pay rate for other seasons in Egypt.[139] Compared to rates of per diem pay for unskilled workers in Egypt over the long term, a similar picture emerges. When commuted to wheat equivalents, harvesters received between 15 and 25 litres of wheat equivalent pay per diem, while long-term normal rates of recompense fell in the range of 3.5 to 6.5 litres of wheat equivalent per day. In these terms, harvesters in Egypt were getting day wages that were approximately three times (and sometimes more) the normal per diem pay rates attested for unskilled labourers over the long term between the third century BCE and the eleventh century CE.[140] For day labourers, the normal daily rates of pay in the nearby lands in Syria-Palestine seem to have run at about a denarius a day, but they were well above this level in times of high demand, sometimes by as much as a factor of four in the case of harvest labour.[141] In addition to their pay, it was always assumed that the harvesters would be fed and provisioned. In Roman Egypt, as with other workers, these provisions included gratuitous rations of beer.[142] The little direct evidence that we have from Roman antiquity, as well as comparative data from the early medieval West, confirms that among the victuals that the reapers received was drink, ordinarily water, but also special provisions of wine or beer.[143] Legal texts on contracting for seasonal harvest labour assume that these were obligations that had to be borne by the owner or the tenant farmer of the lands that were being reaped, and these additional costs included various forms of material recompense and sustenance.[144]

Daily payment was rarely limited to shares of the crops that were harvested or to money wages, but rather was composed of some combination of these. As in other times and places, the harvesters expected food, drink, and temporary shelter as part of their earnings, and it was up to the landlord to provide these additional elements of recompense. In the story of Boaz and Ruth, a biblical harvest narrative much retold and commented on in late antiquity, the landlord Boaz tells his foreman not to harass the young woman Ruth, but to provide her with the same lunch and drink that he was providing for the reapers in the field.[145] The prophet Habbakuk, likewise, is reported to have prepared a pot of hot soup and a jug of mixed wine to take to the harvesters in the fields when he was suddenly told by an angel to take it to feed Daniel in the lions' den.[146] Gregory of Tours reports a typical incident of feeding reapers which threatened to turn violent when a bad event happened in Arvernian lands.[147] A landlord had ordered a large vat of beer to be prepared as drink for the harvesters who were arriving to take the crops off his lands. Beer was a normal part of a reaper's pay in the region.[148] Unfortunately, the landlord's slaves, who had been left behind at the farm when he was detained in town, drank most of the beer, 'according to the way that slaves usually behave,' the narrator explains. They left almost nothing for the landowner to give to the harvesters. The notable was embarrassed when the large gang of harvesters turned up to reap his crops. Before beginning their work, they had inspected the quality and quantity of the beer and, naturally, they had found it wanting. In the midst of his shame, we are told, the baron was suddenly inspired by God. He turned to the tankard and called out the names of the holy angels to make the small remaining amount in the container increase enough so that the day labourers would have sufficient drink. And, *mirum dictu*, says Gregory, for the whole day there was no lack of beer for the harvesters, until night finally put an end to their work. So here it is – an alcoholic riff on the miracle of the loaves and the fishes played out in late antique Gaul. It is therefore difficult to estimate the part of the whole recompense which came as monetary wages. A harvester's entire reimbursement was usually a per diem payment that was an amalgam of money, payments in kind of the produce itself, and living arrangements during the harvest that included shelter, food, and drink.[149]

The propensity to use the labour of free men on a hire system was true of the temporary seasonal labour for the harvest in all parts of the empire. Whether it was in Italy of the Principate or Africa of the late empire, Judaea of New Testament times or the post-Roman Gaul of Gregory of Tours, the seasonal harvesters are spoken about, without exception, as hired men who are paid a wage. In almost every case, the assumption was that these were men of free status who were selling their own labour. It was such a commonly accepted fact that it was the basis of everyday comparisons and similes of the time. The hiring of harvest labourers was so normal that it was paradigmatic. In proverbial sayings and popular generalizations, the expression 'to hire *like* harvesters' seems to have been a usual illustration of work for wages.[150] In the case of the late Roman landlord in Gaul and his miraculous beer, the men whom he hired to take off his crop were separate from the slaves who made up the permanent workforce on his domain.[151] The writer of the Gospel of John, in his evocation of the Last Times as described by Jesus, states:

> Already the reaper receives his wages,
> already he is bringing in the grain for eternal life,
> so that the sower and the reaper can rejoice together.[152]

Jesus is speaking about the reaper collecting his wages, his pay or *misthos*, as the normal means by which his labour was recompensed.[153] We must envisage hundreds of thousands of men from all over the Mediterranean being involved every year in a supplementary wage cycle of real significance.

Any attempt to estimate the economic value of this cycle is something that is not much above the level of educated guesswork. But let us try. Let us take a notional reaping gang of twenty men. This is slightly larger than the larger gangs attested in the Egyptian papyri, but reaping gangs probably were larger in the more expansive plains ecology of Africa. At 2 to 3 denarii pay rates per diem for each man, we can estimate that the total income per diem for the whole gang would have been 40 to 60 denarii. If the reaping gang worked for two harvesting rounds of thirty days each, we are envisaging approximately 2,400 to 3,600 denarii, equivalent to about 10,000 to 15,000 sesterces in total. This is for the reaping alone. If the gang leader's hired men were involved in other operations, or a third cycle of harvesting was attempted, this estimate would have to be modified upwards. It is uncertain whether the contractor of the harvest gang would get a portion of the total recompense for his whole gang or a sum separately contracted with the landowner. If the contractor's earnings were a proportion of his men's pay and that share was set as low as one-tenth, this would suggest a total of 1,000 to 1,500 sesterces for a season (although he probably earned more for additional work). But if, as we have seen in the comparative data, the contractor was paid directly at three times (or so) the pay level of the ordinary reaper, or 6 to 9 denarii a day, he would have acquired not less than 360 to 540 denarii, equivalent to 1,500 to 2,200 sesterces for the working season. (This is about the same range as the proportionate take for him that we have estimated above.) In either case, the manager of the work force would be receiving in cash two to three times the net pay of a legionary footsoldier. This would be for managing reapers on the move for just part (albeit a very intensive part) of the entire work year. And this pay would be in addition to his normal income as a farmer. Furthermore, despite the wonderful talk of the Maktar Harvester's life being 'free of deceit,' we cannot rule out the distinct possibility that contractors like him were not averse to exploiting the men under their control.

As the comparative history of harvesting shows, seasonal workers involved in reaping tended to fall into two broad categories. The first comprised large organized groups that were hired on a regular annual basis by big landowners. The second category was made up of individual labourers and small groups of men who were picked up directly on an 'as needed' basis by landowners or their agents. What little evidence exists concerning seasonal hired labour for the harvest indicates that men in the latter category tended to congregate at marketplaces to sell their work power. In the eastern Mediterranean these venues were found in the *agora* of a town or at *panêgyreis* in the countryside. In the western Mediterranean, the labourers tended to be found in the *fora* of the towns and villages or at the *nundinae* or periodic markets in the countryside.[154] If the parable of the vineyard in the Gospel of Matthew is a typical example of the practices involved, the men assembled or loitered in the local marketplace (in this case, the *agora* of the village), where they waited for an employer or his agent to offer them a contract for a day's work.[155]

By going with the agent, the men seeking employment agreed to the usual rate of pay. In the gospel parable, the pay for ordinary manual labour in the fields was a denarius a day. The parable plays with the fact that the day labourers hired early in the morning on a particular day later grumbled about those men who had worked for only part of the day but had received full pay. They felt that the recompense for the latecomers' work should have been pro-rated. But the employer probably did pay a flat per diem rate for every man whom he hired for a given day. Acquiring harvest labour on a daily basis by seeking individual unemployed workers in the city or town marketplaces was typical of many labour markets around the Mediterranean. It was the injustices often found in this type of hiring that John Chrysostom, as was his wont, railed against. In one sermon, he castigates landlords for paying the peasants whom they hired paltry sums of money and not allowing them even a small part of the harvest itself.[156] In saying this, Chrysostom was alluding to the practice of allotting some of the harvest crop itself to the harvesters in a combination of money wages and payments in kind.

These seasonal agricultural labourers, acquired by daily pay under written or oral contract (more frequently the latter) through the aegis of contractors or more directly from those who congregated at local market centres, dominated the task of reaping in Africa in the age of the Maktar Harvester. They were the seasonal workers to whom the Christian bishop Optatus of Milevis referred in his narration of the violence around the town of Bagaï in southeastern Numidia in Africa during the 340s. From what Optatus says it is clear that labourers habitually gathered at local periodic market centres precisely because the markets functioned as labour exchanges where landowners or their agents could acquire reapers on a daily basis.[157] To find the workers that they needed, the owners or agents would go to nearby marketplaces where they knew that men in search of work would congregate. A standard modern handbook from the 1920s on indigenous agriculture in North Africa reveals similar practices in the early twentieth century.

The indigenous workers are paid by the day. During the period of the hardest and largest scale work, they arrive in numerous groups, often from far afield. Not having lodging provided for them, they sleep rough, often under the open sky. In certain regions, the indigenous women work in the fields on the European farms … [158]

If conditions in the modern day pre-war Maghrib are anything to judge by, a number of common elements in recruiting and pay remained in place.

Except for the odd case, harvest workers are usually recruited at the market places where they gather, congregated in groups according to their own (i.e. regional or ethnic) origins. The employer negotiates with them concerning their salary which is fixed according to generally accepted rates for each region year by year. This is a function of the market for this sort of labour and it therefore tends to vary up and down over the whole season. The salary is fixed in money. Food and shelter are added.[159]

In many of the provinces of the Latin West in the fourth century, where much of the countryside was divided into great estates under the aegis of one landowner, the quantity of seasonal labour needed for a given harvest might have been considerable. On a recurrent annual basis, it was easier and surely more typical for large landowners and their agents to deal with labour contractors who could provide large numbers of workers on a predictable basis. As we have noted, just such a landowner in late Roman Gaul needed a force of seventy men (presumably in addition to the regular workforce on his domain) to bring in the harvest.[160] In sixteenth- and seventeenth-century England, the larger harvesting gangs tended to be on this order of magnitude. Some of them were much larger. In Pembrokeshire, the landowner George Owen recruited a workforce of up to 240 men to bring in his harvest.[161] The recruitment drew from any large pool of underemployed younger males who were conveniently grouped to be drafted for this purpose.

Analogous labour pools were provided by existing institutions, like the army, that collected men together in large numbers, but also by new ones that entered into the repertoire of Roman society. In late antiquity, the monastery was just such an institution. It was a ready recruiting ground both for seasonal workers and, as we shall see later, for providing the occasional men needed for organized violence.[162] Monasteries provided the extra strong male hands and arms required for heavy work. It was a practice that had a long history. As early as the 330s and 340s, monks from Macarius's community at Sketis in the western desert of Egypt, about forty miles west of the apex of the Delta, would supplement their incomes by going up country to hire themselves out to work in the harvest.[163] At the same time, or perhaps a bit earlier, in the age of Pachomius, monks from the monastic settlement of St Simeon's at Aswân in Upper Egypt were similarly involved in harvesting for hire.[164] It was a systemic pattern of the emergence of a seasonal labour market that repeated itself every year. In the late sixth century, the monks from the same community at Sketis were still hiring themselves out as harvesters at day rates of pay.[165] This is a case that we get to learn about precisely because it was institutionalized and reported upon, although for purposes completely different from those that concern us. In his history of the monastics of Egypt, Rufinus of Aquileia reports on a certain monk named Serapio in the Arsinoïte nome. Serapio was the Father of many monasteries in which there were 'something like ten thousand monks.' The total (a *myriad* in the Greek text) was simply conventional for a very large number. It is what Rufinus reports about the activities of these monks and the fact that they were typical of *almost all monks in Egypt*, rather than their numbers, that is interesting for our purposes.

From the profits of their own work, all the monks ... give monies. They acquire these funds especially at the time of harvest from the pay for their manual labour. They give the greatest part of this money to the above mentioned Father, Serapio, and it is ear-marked for the support of the poor. Moreover, this is the custom not only of these men alone, but of almost all the monks of Egypt. They hire out their labour at the time of harvest for the operation of reaping. And from their pay they each acquire eight hundred modii of grain (more or less) and part of this they offer for the support of the poor. Not only the poor of the region itself [i.e., the Arsinoïte nome] are fed, but ships loaded with grain are sent to Alexandria for the support of persons locked in prisons or foreigners stranded (in the city) or simply those who happen to be in need.[166]

The average value of 800 modii of grain in Egypt at this time was about 18 to 20 solidi.[167] The value of 800 modii of cereal grains in the high empire, at a rate of about 3 to 5 sesterces per modius, would have been between 2,500 and 4,000 sesterces.[168] In a period when an ordinary Roman footsoldier's annual pay packet was about 1,200 sesterces per annum, but only 300 to 600 sesterces a year net after deductions had been made, the seasonal harvest workers were acquiring a considerable amount of cash or cash equivalent in one short period of intense work.[169]

Although such sums of money are not huge, they are still substantial. Nor are we compelled to believe the exaggerated numbers of the often mendacious Rufinus as exactly true. They seem to have been inflated to advertise the scale of the benefactions being made by the monks. But the numbers, if even generally indicative, are significant since they suggest that the cash that the monks acquired in this manner was a seasonal windfall of real importance to manual labourers. Again, for what it is worth, comparative evidence demonstrates much the same economic significance of seasonal agricultural labour, especially harvest work. The total wages of itinerant harvesters in western Canada in the first decades of the twentieth century amounted to between 100 and 200 dollars a season at a time when the annual day rates for other manual labour would have netted a worker about 300 to 600 dollars a year.[170] That is to say, in a regular two-month harvesting season, the harvester would accumulate about a third of a year's income for other manual day labourers. Such scales of significance are also indicated for nineteenth-century England, where a host of figures suggest that mowing and reaping operations for a rural worker of the time produced approximately a quarter of his family's entire annual income.[171]

The Man Himself

The events of our harvester's brief verse autobiography are set in his *patria*, the municipality of Mactaris.[172] Can we determine anything more about his background? His story is presented as one of epic achievement in a heroic mode. As a latter-day Odysseus who wandered the Numidian plains of Roman Africa, it is perhaps fitting that he has been left with no name. But in this anonymity, there are some clues. He says that he began with nothing. His parents were poor. The technical language of the inscription indicates that they were landless and had no home of their own. The fact that his family had no *domus* does not mean that they literally had no roof over their heads, but rather that in the status-bound categories of the time there was a manifest distinction between a house that counted and one that did not. They might have lived in a makeshift African-type hut called a *mappalium* or perhaps in something a little better, but which still did not count as a proper house. Such mud and straw huts, *tuguria* as they were called in Africa, were known as the habitations of people who were so poor that they worked as seasonal harvesters. It has been averred by some, among them the great historian of antiquity Mikhail Rostovtzeff, that the first lines of the poem indicate that the harvester was a small independent landholder who had worked hard to add to the exiguous economic base that he already had in order to make himself wealthier. The words *ruri mea vixi colendo* could bear this interpretation, but it seems unlikely in the light of the first lines of the poem as they survive.

Later in the poem, in its twentieth line, the harvester states: *et nostra vita fructus percepit honorum.* The words are not only a delightful poetic trope on which to form the turning point in his career, but they are also a revealing piece of legalese. *Fructus percipere* means 'to take off the produce' from a piece of land, which is precisely what he was doing. By the end of his life, the harvester had reversed this situation. His successes had enabled him 'to reap a rich harvest of offices.' If this later success mirrors his earlier life, the words seem to suggest that he began life as a partiary *colonus* of the type well and widely known from Africa, in effect a sharecropper. This better reflects his sense of epic accomplishment in acquiring land and property by the use of the labour of his own bare hands. Whatever else we can deduce from the words of the poem, two specific statements in it indicate the nature of our man's character. He was hard-working, persistent, and entrepreneurial. He began by reaping the fields of Numidia as an ordinary field worker for twelve years (l. 13). Working year after year in the fields, he gained hard-won experience in doing the basics of the job. Using these skills, he then served a further eleven years as the foreman or manager of a reaping gang (l. 15). The words describe a career of hard manual labour that began, probably, around age twenty or so. Then, in his early thirties, having achieved experience and the authority of an older man that would be respected by the strength of youth, he undertook the more profitable managerial role of harvest contractor that lasted into his early forties. It was then, with his accumulated wealth, that he began his social career at Mactaris where he emerged as a municipal worthy.

It has been claimed that this feat of upward mobility was wholly unusual. But there are so many ordinary pieces that went into making our harvester's life that it is difficult to believe that there were not others, indeed many others like him. Similar first-person narratives are available from other ages and places. Although they are not cast in elegiac verse and do not exactly replicate the precise rise to power of our man, they nevertheless reflect some of the same attitudes and accomplishments. Take the recollections of one Joseph Arch of Warwickshire, a harvester in late nineteenth-century England.

I went into different English counties, and also into Wales, hedge-cutting. I got good jobs, and very good money, and was in great request. Not only was I master of this branch of my craft, with men working under me, but as I had taken to mowing when sixteen years of age, I had now become a master hand at that also, and had almost invariably a gang of from twenty to twenty-five men under me in the field. This was my reward for having caught slippery old Father Time by his fore-lock. I made very good mowing contracts with larger graziers; they would give me five or six shillings an acre. The farmers were not so liberal by half, as they seldom paid more than three shillings an acre. Still, taking one contract after another, I did well and could put more money into my pocket than I had ever done … Wherever I had worked … I was conscious of increased strength, and vigour of mind and body; I had learned where I stood among my fellow-workers, and consequently I was more than ever determined to carve out an upward path for myself, and be a somebody in the world of working men.[173]

The critical elements of the form are here in a first-person narrative, in its 'I' form. There is the pride in hard work, the itinerant nature of the tasks, the command of large gangs of men, and the service as the contractor of seasonal labourers – and the good money to be made.

The pay for harvesting was always better than the pay for other agricultural tasks and in other seasons. In times when the agricultural sector of the economy is doing particularly well, harvest wages rise proportionately higher. That is a benefit to individual workers, but it is an even greater boon to the man who can organize gangs of labourers. In repute at least, and perhaps in fact, the income made from such a livelihood was able to found the fortune of a direct ancestor of a Roman emperor. As we have already noted, only four generations before Vespasian was wealthy and powerful enough to ascend the throne of the empire, his great-grandfather had earned enough to make the transition in status from labourer and harvest foreman to that of a small-town burgher at Reate in Sabine country. The feat was accomplished over the decades of the 70s and 60s BCE, in the last century of the Republic, in a bustling rural region close to the booming metropolis of Rome. Regions like that around Reate were ideally positioned to supply the growing demands of the city, no doubt at much higher prices than obtained elsewhere. Some four and a half centuries later our anonymous African *manceps messorum* from the small municipal town of Mactaris achieved a similar success. He did this by much the same means, in an age when the fields of Africa, like those close to Rome in an earlier age, were ideally positioned to supply produce for a mass market at good prices. By the time the grandsons and great-grandsons of whom *he* so proudly boasts in his epitaph were of age, a Roman empire would no longer exist in which they could have risen to become *principes omnium*.

In his own day, however, whom did our happy man command on those annual rounds? It is by a peculiar but logical connection that some relevant evidence has survived. Because of the involvement of some of their numbers in the sectarian violence in fourth- and fifth-century Africa, the same age as the one in which our man from Maktar worked, we know something about these wandering gangs of harvesters. In the colloquial African Latin of the time, they were called *circumcelliones* or men who hung out around a *cella* or a storage room. The circumcellion harvesting gangs in Africa are rarely represented as functioning as haphazard collections of men looking for work. Rather, they worked under the direction of *mancipes* or contractors who acted as labour organizers and managers who negotiated harvesting contracts with the landowners. If anything went wrong, these *mancipes* had made the contract and they were, in this and other matters, legally liable for the behaviour of their men.[174] They were like the hirers and contractors of labour who are mentioned in other contexts, notably in the parallel case of the gangs of wandering monks of late antiquity.[175] In this sense, the *manceps* was like a *conductor*: someone who took up labour contracts and who stood between the owner and the workforce that was to be employed.[176] Although the agricultural manuals on running estates, from Xenophon to Cato, supported the ideal that the landowner himself should participate in the harvest operations by engaging in the process of reaping, evidence for the participation of landowners in the Roman imperial period in the manual labour is slight to non-existent.[177] Almost all writers who attempted to indicate the real conditions of the harvest speak of the owner himself or his agents acquiring or dispatching harvest labourers to the fields, but nothing more.[178] Since the owner was assumed to effect the hiring of the seasonal workers through his agents, slave or free, who acted as extensions of his own person, the man in the middle remained as anonymous as the workers themselves.

What does the scale of the demand for seasonal harvest labour and the example of this one man demonstrate? The fact that there are not many more such entrepreneurs who boast of their own background in epigraphical texts, or who appear in our formal literary texts, is hardly surprising. There is so little evidence about the organization and the employment of harvest labour in general that to expect a flurry of autobiographical accounts, poetic or not, of reapers is to expect too much. No one doubts that sea-going merchants existed in very large numbers, yet there are few first-person narratives authored by them that survive. Some part of this is surely connected to the banausic status of manual labour and to persons closely connected with the world of trading that was perceived as hucksterism. In a paean to the virtues of life on the land, a radical stoic of the early empire could rhetorically ask his readers: 'Are not planting, ploughing, and vine-dressing honourable work? And sowing, reaping, threshing – are not these all free skills, suitable for good and honest men?'[179] The manner in which the questions are pitched shows that Musonius was advocating an unusual, if not a radical, idea to the prosperous and learned of his own society that they manifestly did not share. That *attitude*, and not the bare economic relationships and realities, is surely what coloured the propensity to self-celebration in certain aesthetic modes.

Whatever the power of the prevailing artistic, aesthetic, moral, and representational filters, Augustine repeatedly refers in a completely offhand manner to the widespread existence of the *mancipes* or contractors of seasonal agricultural workers. They surely existed in considerable numbers for Africa alone. If less than a third of the annual cereal harvest involved gangs of such hired men, and if all of them worked in groups as large as fifty men or so (which seems unlikely), then there were, at the very least, many hundreds of such labour contractors operating in any given year. That should warn us against taking the few known mini-biographies and self presentations of such men that have survived and reading them as direct measures of *economic* significance – in this case as indicators of their *economic* insignificance. The aesthetic and moral canons governing the advertising of one's life and status were so strong that we do not commonly get to see these men in the process of their daily work in all modes of representation. We do not get to see them even as much as we are able to see public celebrations of powerful and wealthy former slaves or freedmen in Italy.[180] The labour contractors are just another case of a status group trapped in a space and time where there were few choices open to them other than for themselves to present their own lives and their work. Should *they* fail to do so, the representation simply would not happen. If the rarity of descriptive pictures of ordinary workers and contractors is a measure of the power of social and moral barriers, and of aesthetic standards, it is surely an abuse of this type of evidence (or its absence) to read it as a straightforward indicator of *economic* realities. This is not the only screen between our eyes and the realities that we wish to see. Equally hidden from us by this same aesthetically determined discourse is the history of the implements that were used. This is the different history of how reaping was done in a complex interaction between humans and the ever changing ways in which they exploited their environment.

CHAPTER THREE

Sickle and Scythe
Man and Machine

For his third memory image Ricci chooses the Chinese character *li*, meaning profit. To compose an image that the Chinese will remember, he divides the ideograph for *li* vertically down the middle, thus yielding two new ideographs, one of which means 'grain' and one 'blade' or 'knife.' From these two components Ricci composes his memory picture, 'a farmer holding a sickle, ready to cut the crops in the field.'[1]

The great transition out of the endless and remorseless regimen of hand labour that had ruled the world of the grain harvest from the dawn of agriculture happened in the long nineteenth century. In a whole host of sectors, this new age marked a watershed between the premodern and the modern worlds, and not only in the realm of technology. In the field of harvesting it was no different. The year 1831 witnessed the invention of a machine that could reap. The development of a mechanical reaper was part of an amazing kaleidoscope of scientific and technological innovations and applications that made the world in which we now live. Although it was only a small part of these innovations, its effects were huge. As has been remarked, if this invention had not been made, a very large portion of the current population of the United States and Canada would still be involved year-in and year-out in the annual task of taking in the grain harvest. Instead, a truly exiguous number of persons, both proportionately and absolutely, currently perform this task (indeed, are involved in the whole agricultural sector, period).[2] This theoretical scenario is itself a secondary fiction, since the much larger population of our own age would not have come into existence in the first place had it not been for a significant number of technological innovations in agricultural production and distribution. Of these, the mechanical reaper was one of the most important.

In the same vein as these imaginary hypotheses, there is another thought experiment and a nagging question. The Roman empire was technologically advanced compared with preceding economic and social orders, not a few of which still subsisted in the lands over which it ruled and in regions immediately adjacent to its frontiers. But if the empire's core economy was so technically developed, so market permeated, and so immense in the scale of its demands and productive capacities (and these suppositions are without doubt true), why did a labour intensive task such as that of harvesting crops, and specifically reaping, not provoke the move to a more technologically efficient mechanical means of doing the work? The question about technological advance has badgered historians of the Roman economy. As one of them phrased the problem: 'We must be able to perceive the value of an important priority: An explanation for why Roman society failed to rise any further once it had reached the peak of its development, why there was no transformative impulse of the kind that Pirenne identified in Europe after the year 1000.'[3] He is precise in specifying that by 'transformative impulse' he includes the emergence of a wide range of new technologies that would mark such an economic revolution.

The general question is not quite as theoretical as it might at first appear. It can be subdivided into smaller subquestions specific to each mechanical and technical process that was implicated in the conjunction of human, animal, and natural forces with a given array of tools and methods. It also has a special relevance to the problem of agricultural labour in antiquity. Although the first effective and widely implemented mechanization of reaping was initiated in the nineteenth century, there is good evidence that tentative steps in this same direction had been taken some nineteen centuries earlier in lands that were part of the Roman empire. There survive literary and pictorial data on reaping machines, however primitive the contraptions were by today's standards, that were employed in harvesting operations in the northwestern regions of the empire. In certain important aspects, these machines resemble the precursor models of the first modern reaping machines: Rube Goldberg–like contrivances imagined, modelled, and sometimes actually built in the early nineteenth century.[4] The modern inventions, however, became part of a linear and unbroken process in a series of steps that led to the mass production of reaping machines. By the last decades of the century in which they were invented, they revolutionized agriculture on a global scale.

We might wonder what forces led to the first attempts at mechanical reaping in the Roman empire. We might also ask why these early machines did not experience an economic and technical takeoff similar to the modern ones. It was not for the absence of the idea or even for the lack of its long-term application in harvesting operations. This process can be considered in terms of the large-scale nature of reaping operations on an ecological stage as extensive as the world ruled by the Roman empire and on a scale as small as one man reaping cereal crops in Africa in late antiquity. But the question requires a much larger perspective than that of a large empire. Our purview must be one that will engross the domestication of

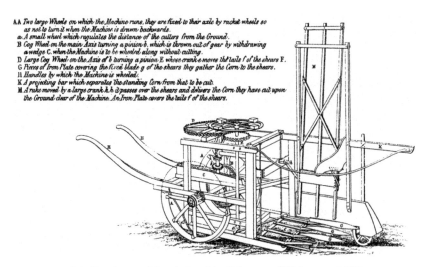

AA Two large Wheels on which the Machine runs, they are fixed to their axle by racket wheels so as not to turn it when the Machine is drawn backwards.
a. A small wheel which regulates the distance of the cutters from the Ground.
B Cog Wheel on the main Axis turning a pinion b, which is thrown out of gear by withdrawing a wedge C. when the Machine is to be wheeled along without cutting.
D Large Cog Wheel on the Axis of b turning a pinion E. whose crank e moves the tails f of the shears F.
G Pieces of Iron Plate covering the fixed blade g of the shears they gather the Corn to the shears.
H Handles by which the Machine is wheeled.
K A projecting bar which separates the standing Corn from that to be cut.
M A rake moved by a large crank h.h. it passes over the shears and delivers the Corn they have cut upon the Ground clear of the Machine. An Iron Plate covers the tails f of the shears.

3.1: Reaping machine designed by Solomon of Woburn, c. 1807.
Specifications of English Patents for Reaping Machines, append. B. Woodcroft
(London: Eyre and Spottiswode, 1853)

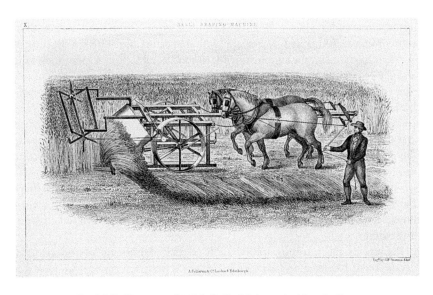

3.2: Patrick Bell's reaper of 1826. Oxford Science Archive; ArtResource

cereal grains and the relationship of human communities to these domesticated crops over a very long term. In short, how did the human technologies of reaping change, why did they do so, and with what effects on human perceptions and ideas?

It is with these questions that some of the real problems emerge. Like the Maktar Harvester, the Gallo-Roman harvesting machine has been repeatedly selected as a prime indicator of significant economic and technological trends.[5] The machine was used, and not for the first time, by Moses Finley in a much-quoted and debated essay on the problem of technical innovation and progress in the ancient world.

Neither increased productivity nor economic rationalism (in Max Weber's sense) was ever achieved in any significant measure, so far as we can tell. Someone in Gaul invented a rude ox-powered mechanical reaper which was used on the *latifundia* in the northern districts of that province, but it neither inspired landlords elsewhere in the Empire to imitation nor inspired anyone to seek labour-saving devices in other branches of agriculture. By contrast, an English translation of the fourth-century Latin writer Palladius, who gave a brief description of the Gallic device, was the direct stimulus for the invention of 'Ridley's Stripper,' which had a useful and profitable career in Australia for forty or fifty years (at least to 1885).[6]

The rhetoric about rudeness aside, these words express rather directly a series of assumptions and questions about the nature of technical innovation. As with its subscription to Weber and its concerns with the 'before' and 'after' in the birth of Western modernism, the argument tends to conflate all technical innovation onto a single ecological plane. It then becomes a fundamental problem if agricultural innovations made in a given region in northwestern Europe were *not* adopted by landowners in the Mediterranean and the Levant. Unfortunately, artificial contrasts of this kind have been a staple of the history of technical innovation and development. From water mills to three-field crop rotation, the Romans and the peoples in the core areas of the Mediterranean have been faulted and found wanting for not adopting and implementing technical developments on the scale in which they were instituted and then spread throughout the lands of western Europe. Sometimes, as in the case of water mills, the substance of the accusations, along with the attendant theoretical claims, have been shown to be false or misleading.[7]

Because of the historiographical problem that the history of technological development has been and because it remains a marginal concern to most students of Graeco-Roman antiquity, the discipline never makes such banausic questions primary items on the research agenda of ancient historians. A not infrequent result has been that a hypothetical 'fundamental insight' made by a nineteenth or early twentieth-century érudite has become an established truth more often than not by default because of the simple lack of systematic investigation and testing of the hypothetical claim. One of the most famous (at one time, it was repeated as gospel) was Lefebvre des Noëttes's famous conclusion that Greek and Roman methods of harnessing draft animals, mainly horses and mules, imposed serious limits on the combined load-carrying capacity of the carts and wagons drawn by draft animals, and therefore on the nature of bulk transport in antiquity.[8] Once historical investigators began looking more thoroughly at the evidence, serious questions and doubts arose. The result was that the truism was found to be in need of substantial revision and refinement.[9] Not only was the conclusion wrong in important respects, it also configured the ecological background and the typical use of draft animals in a misleading fashion.

To return to the specifics of the case of the reaping machine, we must wonder why the ancient reaper was invented where it was and not in the apparently more developed core of the empire. And why was it not widely adopted in the Mediterranean? Let us begin by getting some of the more obvious and simplistic explanations out of the way. The first and most frequently reiterated of these is the malign influence of slavery.[10] Why invent machines when cheaper and more effectively coerced human labour is to hand? This attitude has become more nuanced in recent years, but it was given sufficiently brutish expression by Heitland at the turn of the last century. After outlining what he saw as obvious defects in the harvesting machine, he offered his general observation: 'The lack of interest in the improvement of tools has been noted as a phenomenon accompanying the dependence on slave labour.'[11] There are two good reasons to doubt the explanation, at least at the general level at which it has often been pitched (as it was here by Heitland). As we have seen from our history of reaping, the first reason is that most of the harvest labourers who are attested on record were workers who were free in status. The plain fact is that the more intensive harvest tasks that were ideally suited for mechanical devices were the same ones that were done by contractors of *free* labour. It is possible that there was a significant servile involvement in the work that is hidden from our view, or absent in our surviving evidence. But the data that exist on the problem are manifest in what they suggest about the general labour situation. A second objection to this assumed blocking effect of slavery is the observation that the presence of slaves and the institution of slavery were not always hostile to the emergence of new technologies or to the invention of new devices, mechanical or otherwise, to improve efficiency in the labour process.[12]

The story of the invention of the modern mechanical reaper, which is reasonably well documented, tells against easy assumptions that postulate slave labour as a general impediment to technological innovation.[13] It is worth the retelling.

The modern reaping machine that took the world stage and became widely diffused outside its point of innovation was invented by Cyrus Hall McCormick. Its effective operation was first demonstrated to the public near the village of Steele's Tavern, Virginia, on a hot summer day in July 1831. As with many nineteenth-century innovations, caught up in a roiling cauldron of invention and rethinking, from Darwin and Wallace to Watt and Newcomen, who precisely was the true and first inventor of such a reaping machine is a subject of debate and controversy.[14] Even within the confines of American concerns, there were disputes and legal wranglings involving Cyrus McCormick and Obed Hussey, another prolific autodidact inventor of the time. The case was a close-run one, the various merits of either man debated by their proponents in pseudo-dispassionate and 'disinterested' manners, with collections of documents and testimonia in support.[15] As one partisan in the disputes noted, the problem was never with the idea itself: 'As to the *theoretical* portion of the business [i.e., the *idea* of a machine reaper], the enquiry might be greatly extended; indeed, for past centuries, as we have imperfect accounts of Reaping Machines used by the Romans.'[16] The same problem bedevils the invention of the stripping machine for harvesting wheat that was invented in response to a competition in South Australia in 1843. Probably John Ridley was the 'true' inventor, but others, including one John Wrathall Bull, put in credible claims.[17] Despite all the near misses and good ideas, however, there is no doubt that the first into this field on a worldwide scale was the machine tested in the early nineteenth century in Virginia, a heartland of antebellum slavery in the United States. But that is not the end of the story. The scene of the invention and the first demonstration of the reaper was recollected by Cyrus McCormick's grandson.

His father [i.e., the father of Cyrus McCormick], who had spent so many years trying in vain to build a reaper, may have hoped for success for the boy, but feared that the problem would prove insolvable. His mother stood a little apart, lovingly proud of her tall son whether his reaper worked or not, ready with comfort or praise or renewed encouragement. Jo Anderson was there, the Negro slave who, through the crowded hours of recent weeks, had helped build the reaper. There were also harvesters, men who had been toiling in the adjacent fields and had laid down their scythes and sickles to come and watch the new-fangled cutting machine.[18]

Although the later importance of some of McCormick's partners in this venture, like Colonel James McDowell and Colonel William Massie, is noted, the role of the black slave Jo Anderson is emphasized again by McCormick's grandson.

Most of all, the name of his Negro helper, Jo Anderson, deserves honor as the man who

3.3: First public trial of the McCormick Reaper near Steele's Tavern in 1831. Lithograph, 1883: McCormick, *Century of the Reaper*, 1931, plate between pp. 2 and 3

worked beside him [i.e., Cyrus McCormick Sr] in the building of the reaper. Jo Anderson was a slave, a general farm laborer and a friend ... the Negro toiled with him up to the hour of the test and after. It is pleasant to know that in later times, when old Jo's productive days were over, Cyrus or his son provided for his declining years.[19]

Through the felicitous veils of paternalism and self-congratulatory praise that cover this glowing remembrance or perhaps more accurately this happy fiction, we see not only the central role played by a slave, Jo Anderson, in the process of invention, but also the whole background of the institution of slavery in ante-bellum Virginia. The same sentiments are also mirrored in the imagined and reconstructed visual of the scene painted by N.C. Wyeth to celebrate the one hundredth anniversary of the achievement.[20] Slavery is ever present in the production of the wealth out of which McCormick himself arose and which helped to create the large-scale agriculture that provoked the invention in the first place. Not unimportantly, it was also central to the position of men who could sustain the free time and the fiscal burdens required by the invention. The two big financial backers that McCormick specifically notes, Colonels McDowell and Massie, were slaveholders and plantation owners in the Virginia Piedmont. As members of families of considerable social standing in Virginia society, both men provided monetary support for McCormick's invention, surely because his technical efforts converged with their own agricultural and economic interests.

By the mid-1850s, working out of a production plant in Chicago and using a

3.4: The gift of the New World to the Old. *Implement and Machinery Review*, January 1901

much improved version of his mechanical reaper, Cyrus McCormick had revolutionized agriculture and achieved worldwide fame. His reaper won the highest recognition at that cynosure of Victorian progressivism, the Crystal Palace Exhibition of 1851, where the McCormick reaper was awarded a Great Medal for *the* technical invention that had transformed the age.[21] It came to be represented as the quintessential technological gift that the New World had bestowed on old Europe. For our purposes, it is sufficient to note that in the invention of the mechanical reaper at the dawn of the modern era the institution of slavery was central. Far from preventing or impeding such an invention, especially in the sphere of agriculture, chattel slavery was integral to the process.[22] At least three of the great industrial innovations of the age – the mechanical reaper, the riverboat steamer, and the automatic cotton engine (the cotton 'gin) – emerged from the context of the slave South. All of them were not only sustained and provoked by chattel slavery, but they platformed a huge expansion of the system of slave agriculture.[23] This being so, we still have to understand the story of the mechanical reaper of Roman times. How and why did it come into existence, and why did it not have the resplendent transglobal success and influence of Cyrus McCormick's invention of 1831?

The same story can be looked at differently. A poor inventor named Obed Hussey had a good claim to being the inventor of the mechanical reaper. In his case, we are speaking of small points of difference and of a year here or there in the America of the 1830s. The son of Quaker parents from Maine, he moved to the newly developing agro-centres of the Midwest around Cincinnati where, in 1833, he designed and produced a working mechanical reaper.[24] Hussey patented this machine six months before McCormick did his. Hussey, too, displayed his invention at the great Crystal Palace exhibition. And initially he out-produced and outsold McCormick. On balance, it seems that it was McCormick's superior managerial and marketing acumen that won the day and that finally drove Hussey, who died in a tragic accident in August 1860, out of competition in the market. What background wins in invention? Is it the slave-based plantation agriculture of antebellum Virginia of a Cyrus Hall McCormick, or the hard-driven rational thinking, cheese-paring Protestant ethic of the free yeoman farmers and the inventive machine and tool shops of the American Midwest of the Quaker Obed Hussey? Each side, with its supporters and proponents, compiled large dossiers of testimonia and official documents to demonstrate that they were the first. The manifest caution is that any combination of the right kinds of forces could get the job done. Although the drivers of technical innovation might be as various as those seen in the cases of McCormick and Hussey, they still seem to be limited in kind.[25] For us the question is: What relations among the factors of climate, soil, crops, land ownership, labour forces, and the organization of work and tools produced the different track of technology in reaping in northern Gaul in Roman antiquity?

Techniques in Roman Reaping

Everywhere in the Roman Mediterranean for all of antiquity, and indeed for long after, the sickle was the standard instrument used for the reaping of cereal grains. The sickle had many technical and regional variations but it remained a sickle. And it remained the dominant instrument used in the work of reaping in Mediterranean lands well into the early modern era.[26] In Roman antiquity, the reaping sickle was recognized as one of the fundamental farm implements, the *instrumentum fundi*, that every farm was expected to have.[27] Before the advent of machine technology, the physical dictates of the reaping process meant that individual men and women, using the reaping instrument invented at the very beginnings of agriculture, had to work furiously under the scorching heat of the midsummer sun. The gruelling labour was essential to bringing in the cereal crops required to sustain life over the following year.[28] The peculiar nexus of demands on manual labour in harvesting and the types of crops in their ecological settings in the Near East and Mediterranean meant that there was little impetus to change the basic tools of work. Not until the end of the nineteenth century and in some of the most advanced agrarian economies of western Europe was as fundamental a general change as that from the sickle to the scythe made in the reaping of cereal grains.[29] But there had been earlier shifts from the sickle to the scythe for this same purpose. Although these changes can be documented, they were never permanent. The tendency was always to revert to the use of the sickle. It is therefore important to understand under what circumstances these back-and-forth shifts occurred.

It is surely no accident that it was the high-demand, urgent, and most labour-intensive part of the whole process, the front end of the harvest, the task of reaping, that was replaced by machines. These were the mechanical reapers that, over the last decades of the nineteenth century, in both western Europe and the Americas, began finally and irrevocably to replace the gangs of human hands. Even so, it was an uneven and lengthy process. In these same regions, it was not until the early decades of the twentieth century that hand reaping finally became an anachronism.[30] From these modern cases, we know that it was the labour demands and the organizational requirements concerned with the cutting of cereal grains that first attracted innovation. The labour process of the harvest was strongly dimorphic in the distinction between the front end work of reaping and the back end functions of gathering, transporting, threshing, winnowing, storing, and processing (see fig. 1.3). This dimorphic division was gendered, with men dominating the front end of the reaping and women found in the back end, primarily collecting and gathering the cut sheaves.[31] This model of harvest labour is complicated in Roman antiquity by the presence of slaves. Slaves were usually employed in the back end of the harvest where tasks were performed at a slower pace and in a more deliberate fashion. Only then were human slaves or draft animals ordinarily used, for example in the milling of the grain into flour. In a mid-fourth century rural jacquerie in Africa, rebellious slaves on large agricultural estates freed themselves from the grist mills and ostentatiously strapped their former masters to the millstones that they had been turning, making them turn the stones 'like the most contemptible of animals, under the whip.'[32] The words were part of a rhetoric of maltreatment that focused on the extremes of slave labour. They point to the normal place for this labour that was outside the seasonally intense world of the reaper and his sickle.

These observations on harvest work demand the posing of more precise questions about the nature of the labour process. How, exactly, was the reaping done and how did this affect the work demands of harvesting? In Africa, the reaping process usually involved a worker holding a sickle, bending downwards to cut the grain stalks below knee height.[33] The reaper then gathered the cut grain into bundles which he bound and left behind him in long rows on the ground. Unlike the mowing of hay, the reaping of cereal grains was almost universally done with the hand sickle and not the scythe as the standard cutting instrument. The individual reaper who cut the wheat or other cereal crop had to be supported by a line of ancillary workers who were involved in the gathering, binding, raking, transporting, and cleaning up operations. The links in these processes, necessarily marked by significant regional variations, are described by Varro for regions in Italy close to Rome. He first discusses haying and then the cutting of cereal grains.

First, the grasses grown long in the hay meadows should be low cut with the sickle when they stop growing and begin to dry out from the heat. Having been cut they should then be turned over with forks while they are drying. When the hay has completely dried, it should be made into sheaves and transported to the farmstead. Then the loose hay from the meadows should be raked up and added to the piles of cut hay. When this has been done, the pasture should be close cut. That is to say, the stalks that the mowers have missed – leaving the field lumpy, as it were, because of the uncut grass – must be cut again with sickles.[34]

Having described the basics of the mowing of hay, Varro then turns to the harvest proper: the taking off of the cereal grains.

The word *messis* is the word appropriately used for those things that we measure, *metimur*, above all for cereal grains … and so the word 'harvest,' *messis*, is derived from that word (i.e. *metire*).[35]

Putting aside Varro's etymological interventions, Columella's description of this same process, which was written a century later, does not add much to the account of the earlier writer, most probably because the modes of organization, the basic tools, and the types of labour had remained much the same.[36] Even for the circumscribed region of central Italy around Latium, however, Varro could specify three distinctive modes of reaping. Each of them had different types of links with the other parts of the labour process that were involved in the harvest.

Both high-cutting and low-cutting methods of reaping cereal grains were found throughout the ancient Mediterranean. The method used varied from one microregion to another. Varro's three types of reaping included two variants of high cutting and a third technique that combined both low and high cutting of the stalks of grain. The first method, that of double cutting, is one that Varro suggests was commonly found in Umbria to the north of Rome. It was a method in which the reaper cut the stalk of cereal grain close to the ground, leaving most of its length attached to the head. In this form of cutting, the reaper was left with a bundle of stalks and heads called a 'handful' or *manipulus* which he then let fall to the ground. In the Umbrian practice, rather than carrying the stalks and heads as whole sheaves to a threshing floor near the farm buildings, a secondary cutting operation was conducted in the field in which the reaper cut the heads of grain from the tops of the stalks. The transfer of the cut grain heads to the threshing floor or storage area was then done by others using carrying baskets.[37] In a tertiary labour task, the long stalks of straw left in the fields were gathered into heaps for later use as fodder.

Varro next refers to a second method of reaping which he claims was typically found in Picenum in east-central Italy. Although this was an unusual method, it provides us with information vital to our later discussion of the problem of the development of the mechanical harvester. The type of cutting involved the use of a comblike instrument. The harvesting tool was a curved wooden stick that had a series of serrated teeth made of iron at its end. The harvester used this instrument to move up under the heads of wheat or barley, coming up along the line of the stalk. He then manipulated the iron-toothed ends to break off the heads of the cereal grain, leaving the straw standing in the field.[38] This method must also have employed basket carriers who collected the heads of grain directly from the reapers and then transported them to the threshing and storage facilities on the home farm. The deheaded grain stalks were left standing in the field to be cut in a later reaping operation.

The third type of reaping described by Varro is a method which was found around the city of Rome and in many other places in Italy. In this method, also one of high cutting, the reapers simply grabbed the cereal grain heads near the top of the stalk and cut them off. The stalks minus the cereal heads were left standing in the field. They were cut later in a secondary reaping or mowing operation that dealt with the stalks as straw. Since the cutting of the heads of grain was the crucially important task, the reapers who performed this high-value task were paid at higher rates. The later cutting of the straw left in the field was not urgent. This mowing could be done according to normal modes by the men who cut the straw, and so it merited nothing more than normal pay.[39] The reapers who cut the grain heads and the little bit of the stalk that was attached threw them into baskets by which they were carried to the threshing floor.[40] This type of high cutting appears to be one of the more common means of reaping in the Mediterranean because it efficiently linked the labour process of the reapers with the work of the men and women who used baskets to transport the grain heads to the threshing floor or directly to the storage facilities.[41] Where this method of reaping was followed, the ancillary back-end labour had to be organized to effect a continuous and close connection between the reapers and the basket collectors.

The latter two methods of reaping described by Varro for various regions of central Italy were different types of high cutting. These were intensive and not very flexible methods of work, since the basket carriers had to be fairly numerous.

3.5: Reapers and assistant with carrier basket on the cornice frieze of Tomb NB, Ghirza, Tripolitania. Romanelli, 'La vita agricola tripolitana,' p. 62

They also had to follow the reapers closely to allow them to throw the cut heads of cereal grains into the basket containers. Despite its apparent disadvantages, high cutting, or secondary high cutting as in the case of the Umbrian method, combined with the use of baskets to transport the cut grain heads, appears to have been a method of reaping found in many areas of the Mediterranean and in some isolated regions in north Africa, like Tripolitania. In describing the taxing labour of the 'hardened harvester,' Ovid uses a standard image to describe how Vertumnus 'in disguise as a reaper' placed the heads of reaped grain into the carriers' baskets.[42] The harvester's basket, integrally connected with these methods, was such a common item that it could easily be used in the city of Rome as a form of concealment.[43]

It should be kept in mind that, just as in central Italy, the methods of reaping varied from one region to the next in the Roman world. In Britain, for example, it seems that a method of high cutting was used in which only the cereal heads were transported to the threshing floors and storage chambers.[44] Bronze coins from Alexandria issued in the reign of Antoninus Pius suggest that a type of high cutting, as indicated by some agricultural accounts, was also the norm for Egypt.[45] But all three methods, and other ones of low cutting, as well as simply the crudest method of 'pulling,' can be documented for various periods of the history of Pharaonic Egypt. A complex of regional, social, and temporal factors was always in play.[46] The high cutting of cereal crops, however, does *not* seem to have been the common method found in Africa in the reaping operations in which the harvester from Maktar would have been involved. A problem bedevilling the interpretation of iconographic evidence like the coins from Alexandria is the concern that representational conventions might not reflect regional realities. Another problem is that changes in crop types, work organization, and economic forms meant that there were temporal shifts from one method to another. For example, whereas carrying baskets appear to have been used in the grain harvest in Egypt in the Pharaonic period, by Ptolemaic and Roman times the use of pack animals, including donkeys (both alone and pulling wagons) and camels, to carry sheaves to the threshing floor appears to have become a common practice.[47] This shift points to a gradual transformation in reaping methods in which low cutting replaced high cutting. It is the former method of reaping that was the common one in Africa during the Roman period.

The reaping operations involved in the mowing of fodder crops were analogous to cutting cereal grains but they were different in technique. Pliny says that in Italy the mowing of hay crops began around the first of June. Displaying his usual cheeseparing concerns with *conpendia* or savings, he claims that the mowing operations of earlier times had been more expensive, since mowers had to import Cretan whetstones to sharpen their scythe blades. They also had to pay for olive oil for whetting that was kept in horns tied to their legs. In his own day, by contrast, innovations in Italy had provided a whetstone that could be used with water. Despite its deleterious effects on the blade of the scythe, the new method was less expensive.[48] This matched the work rationale of mowing itself. The mode of cutting with a long swing-blade was a rough and approximate one that sacrificed some returns for speed and gross production. The cutting of the mowers was so rough that Pliny recommended redoing the field with men using sickles in a secondary cutting of the stands not properly cut by the mowers.[49] It is in this context that he states that mowers using the Italian blade, apparently halfway between a sickle and a scythe in design, could cut a iugerum of hay in one day.[50]

For the African fields of the Maktar Harvester, pictorial representations and verbal descriptions indicate that low cutting was the norm. As stated above, there are some exceptions, like those found in the depictions of reaping on the tomb reliefs from Ghirza in the predesert of Tripolitania. These reliefs picture the high-cutting technique of reaping. High cutting makes sense where the crops are more isolated and concentrated in dispersed patches in the field and where the stalks of wheat or barley are sparse – conditions that were found in the great wadi valleys of Tripolitania.[51] Almost everywhere else in Africa, pictures and texts refer to low cutting of cereal grains and the binding of sheaves as the normal method of reaping. Since the reapers are allowed to reap and move independently of the sheavers and carriers, this type of reaping is marginally more efficient than most types of high cutting. In low-cutting operations, the harvesters cut the stalks closer to ground level. The reapers then let the handfuls of stalks and heads of grain, or *manipuli*, fall to the ground in rows. Once they had finished the cutting, the reapers no longer needed to be concerned with the sheaves, nor did they have to worry about maintaining constant contact with the binders and carriers. The men and women who collected the sheaves worked independently, at their own pace, first binding the sheaves and then gathering them from the ground. Next they either carried the sheaves directly to the threshing floor or, if distances were prohibitive, they loaded them onto wagons or the backs of mules or camels that transported them to the threshing floor or to the storage facilities.[52]

Whatever the regional variations, the fundamental process of reaping cereal crops was basically the same for all parts of the empire from Judaea to Britannia, from the Scythian lands in the northeast to the Mauretanias in the extreme southwest, and over the whole of the empire's existence. The sickle in the hand of the individual harvester was the way that the grain harvest was performed every year – with one solitary exception. For reasons that are unclear, and with consequences that are equally obscure, communities in the extreme northwestern parts of the empire, regions along and adjacent to the lower course of the Rhine and in the rich plains of northern Gaul, invented and used a reaping machine. The evidence relating to its creation and its fate demands further investigation.

The Machine: Contemporary Reports

The first caution is that the data, while striking and decisive, are few and problematic. They consist of two literary references and less than half a dozen fragments of stone relief sculptures that depict the reaping machine.[53] Since the data are so exiguous, we might consider the literary evidence first. Only two written sources, separated by four centuries or more in time, refer to the reaping machine. The one was written by a Roman equestrian who flourished in the mid-first century and the other was composed by a late Roman landlord.

(i) Pliny, *NH*, 18.72.296. In the earliest dated reference to the machine, the Elder Pliny, in his survey of different types of harvesting, provides a brief allusion to its existence.[54]

There are different methods of harvesting. On the *latifundia* in the Gauls there are very large containers with teeth placed on their edges. Mounted on two wheels, they are driven through the crop by a draft animal harnessed behind them, in such a way that the heads of grain torn off in this manner fall into the container.

Messis ipsius ratio varia. Galliarum latifundis valli praegrandes, dentibus in margine insertis, duabus rotis per segetem impelluntur, iumento in contrarium iuncto; ita dereptae in vallum cadunt spicae.

(ii) Palladius, *Opus Agric.* 7.2.1–4. In his late Roman handbook on agriculture, which probably dates to the early fifth century, Palladius refers to the harvesting machine, again identifying it with specific ecological regions of the Gauls.[55]

The inhabitants of the plains regions of the Gauls have a method of harvesting which saves on labour since, other than the labour of men, it requires the work of only one ox to reduce the time of an entire harvesting operation.[56] That is how there emerged this moving container mounted on two small wheels. The surface of the carrying box, which is square, is furnished with sides that slope outwards such that the upper part is larger than the lower. Its boards are not as high on the front side of the vehicle as they are at the back. There, along the front, numerous small separate teeth were spaced closely together, set at the height of the stalks of grain, with the teeth curved upwards. Attached to the rear of the bin are two short poles, similar to those of carrying litters, and an ox is harnessed to these poles, with the aid of a yoke and traces, with its head facing towards the carrying box. It goes without saying that this ox must be calm so that it will not outrun the pace of its driver. The ox pushes the carrying box through the crop to be harvested and all the heads of the grain are seized by the teeth with which it is armed, and in this way they are separated from the stalks, which remain outside while the heads of grain pile up in the carrying box. The ox driver, who follows behind, does this by raising or lowering [the carriage] as often as necessary. This way it takes no more than a few goings back and forth to take off the whole crop in a relatively brief space of time. This method is good for flat lands where the terrain is even and also for those where it is not considered necessary to keep the straw.

2. … Pars Galliarum planior hoc conpendio utitur ad metendum et praeter hominum labores unius bovis opera spatium totius messis absumit. Fit itaque vehiculum quod duabus rotis brevibus fertur. 3. Huius quadrata superficies tabulis munitur, quae forinsecus reclines in summo reddant spatia largiora. Ab eius fronte carpenti brevior est altitudo tabularum. Ibi denticuli plurimi ac rari ad spicarum mensuram constituuntur in ordine, ad superiorem partem recurvi. A tergo vero eiusdem vehiculi duo brevissimi temones figurantur velut amites basternarum. Ibi bos capite in vehiculum verso iugo aptatur et vinculis, mansuetus sane, qui non modum conpulsoris excedat. 4. Hic ubi vehiculum per messes coepit impellere, omnis spica in carpentum denticulis comprehensa cumulatur abruptis ac relictis paleis, altitudinem vel humilitatem plerumque bubulco moderante, qui sequitur. Et ita per paucus itus ac reditus brevi horarum spatio tota messis impletur. Hoc campestribus locis vel aequalibus utile est et his quibus necessaria palea non habetur.[57]

The first reference to the machine reaper by Pliny might date to the mid-70s CE when he was imperial procurator of Gallia Belgica, a province whose area covered the regions where most of the pictorial representations of the machine have been found – where he even might have seen the contraption. Or he might have made these observations earlier, in the late 40s CE, when he was serving one of his *tres militiae* in the same region.[58] Pliny certainly took care to observe other aspects of agricultural life in the region, such as the extraordinary fertility of winter wheat, which he noted (as he often did with unusual phenomena) as one of its peculiarities.[59] The second reference to the machine is by the late Roman *illustris* Palladius. He reveals a more detailed knowledge of the reaper, almost certainly derived from a first-hand acquaintance with its workings. For Pliny the tool is something of a local curiosity on which he reports, whereas for Palladius it is a practical instrument whose construction and operation he knows and is able to describe in some detail.[60] The two reports confirm that the device was widely used for a time span that extended over at least four centuries. The machine was not a strange and idle curiosity. It was a functioning tool that was put to practical use over significant areas of Gaul, and it had a real longevity.

The harvesting machine has conventionally been called a *vallus* because Pliny uses this word in his description of it. Palladius, however, uses the term *vehiculum* for the machine. Although *vehiculum* came to have the more general sense of 'vehicle,' it also maintained the basic meaning of 'carriage' because it was thought of as a container that carried things. In a rural context, it meant precisely what it does in Palladius: a boxlike structure for collecting and carrying agricultural produce.[61] In the same way, the word *vallus* designated the bin or container mounted on wheels into which the heads of grain fell, and not necessarily the whole machine.[62] The word *vallus* seems best understood as a feminine form derived from the diminutive of *vannus* meaning 'winnowing basket.'[63] The large hopper in the machine into which the heads of grain fell was seen to be a variant of the harvesters' baskets that were used in the normal cutting process in which the heads of grain were carried from the field to the threshing floor. In an analogic process of invention, the machine collected the heads of grain in the place of the baskets in which they were ordinarily collected in the comparable high cutting hand-reaping operations.[64] In the usage of both Pliny and Palladius, the whole machine took its name from its main part – the collecting box on which the cutting teeth were located. This connection might furnish a clue about the process of its invention.

The Iconographic Evidence

An evidentiary supplement to the exiguous number of literary references for the mechanical reaper is the slightly larger number of stone relief sculptures that picture the reaper. These have been discovered in a geographic triangle to the west

Map 3.1: Northern Gaul: heartland of the reaping machine

of the lower parts of the Rhine in northwestern Europe. The sites are located between Reims, Roman Durocortorum, in the west, a parallel point on the Rhine to the east, and Koblenz, Roman Confluentes, at the juncture of the Rhine and the Moselle to the north.[65] The representations, which date, speculatively, to the late second or early third century CE, demonstrate that Pliny and Palladius were not imagining a fictitious thing.[66] The earliest of them is found on the reliefs in the great central vault of the so-called Gate of Mars at Reims. These reliefs were known and studied in the nineteenth century. The physical appearance of the mechanical harvester was therefore well known to modern scholars a long time before the 1950s. Nevertheless, the extraordinary discovery at the hill promontory of Montauban, about two kilometres south of Buzenol, in the tiny province of Luxembourg in the extreme southeastern corner of Belgium, on 16 May 1958, was a scholarly and media surprise.[67] It featured the fullest and most striking stone relief sculpture from Roman times of the harvesting machine in operation. The discovery provoked widespread popular interest. American reporters rushed to the site. On 30 June 1958, an initial report appeared in *Time* magazine, and *Life* magazine devoted an entire page to the site and the relief in the 11 August issue of the same year.[68] Thousands of tourists flocked to see the site in the first months after the announcement of the discovery.[69]

The relief sculptures at Buzenol were cut onto the surface of blocks that were reused for the defensive retaining wall of a hilltop refuge constructed towards the end of the third or the beginning of the fourth century. The stones had originally been part of funerary monuments, no doubt located at Roman sites in the plain below the hilltop defensive site. Almost certainly, the reliefs were originally parts of typical Gallo-Roman funerary monuments that were located along the main Roman highway that ran from Reims (Roman Durocortorum) to Trier (Roman Augusta Treverorum), by way of Arlon (Roman Orolaunum), just to the north of the site at Buzenol. The way in which the reliefs were found in settlements strung out along the highway from Reims to Koblenz (see map 3.1) suggests that this communications route played no small part in the making of the reliefs. It connected the artisanal shops of the sculptors and suggested common themes to patrons. The urgency of the construction of the refuge at Buzenol is signalled in part by the plundering of local burial places to acquire the stone to build the walls around the crest of the hill that rose about 70 metres above the surrounding valleys.[70] Eighteen of the forty limestone blocks in the defensive wall that were unearthed in 1958 have decorative reliefs on them.[71] All of the reliefs are illustrations that were connected with funerary themes appropriate to the original tomb monuments from which the stones had been plundered.

One of these blocks, no. 19 contains two scenes that are relevant to our interests. On one face, no. 19a, we see the representation of a banquet that was surely intended to be a funerary 'last supper.' Two women are lying recumbent on cushions, while to the left a servant fills one of their cups, in the evocative words of Mertens 'in a gesture worthy of a Vermeer.'[72] To the right, a curtain hanging from rings gives the impression of an indoor scene as would be seen by an external viewer. Although this picture has its own attractions, it is an example of a typical scene of which several good examples have survived from the Gallo-Roman repertoire from the regions in the lower Rhineland.[73] The other side of this same stone block, no. 19b, features the harvesting scene that is of special interest to us. The

3.6: The Gallo-Roman reaping machine: fragment from Montauban-Buzenol. Mertens, 'Sculptures romaines de Buzenol,' fig. xiv, p. 81; permission courtesy of the Musée Gaumais

relief is manifestly of one of the harvesting machines described by Pliny and Palladius. To the left, a man holding a long polelike tool is guiding the stalks of grain into the teeth of the machine. The machine itself is mounted on a two-wheeled axle. To the right can be seen elements of the long poles to which a mule or an ass is harnessed. This illustration was part of a series of other scenes that depicted agricultural life on the domain of the landlord to whose funerary monument these blocks originally belonged. Another block, no. 25, contains scenes on both sides. One side, no. 25b, is a realistic scene of two peasant farmers. I cannot better Mertens's description of one of them.

… at the left [there is] a man in peasant garb, clothed in a short-sleeved tunic over which has been thrown a cloak with a large hood out of which the man's head appears. With his left hand, he is holding a three-pronged fork over his shoulder. Portrayed with a striking realism, the man's head has been sculpted by the hand of a master. His hair short and curled, his forehead, mostly bald, and his moustache and short beard depict a man prematurely grown old. His somewhat touching expression of fatigue, the movement of the lips, and the fixed stare gives us, in sum, the living picture of a rough peasant returning to his home after a day of very hard work, there to be received by his wife.[74]

In this evocative description there is an exercise of imagination, but the reading of the sentiments is credible. Perhaps as many as five funerary monuments had their stones robbed to construct the wall. The decorative reliefs on them were parts of a common repertoire of images that were found in a large cultural area centred on the lower Rhine and Moselle. Within this inventory, certain types of representative art, like the relief panels on the impressive funerary monuments of the landed elite, featured realistic scenes of life, labour, and commercial exchange. One of the best-known and most studied of these tombs is the funerary pillar monument of the Secundini from Igel.[75] This famous monument, however, is only one of a type that was commonly found throughout the geographic zone between sites on the Rhine to the east and the valley of the Moselle to the west. All of the relief sculptures on these monuments, whether they featured scenes of agricultural life, as at Buzenol, or commercial dealings, as at Igel, were meant to be read metaphorically.

The discovery of the Buzenol relief had the effect of refocusing attention on a similar but less well preserved piece of relief sculpture that had been found over a century earlier in 1854. The discovery had been made at Arlon, also in the province of Luxembourg in southeastern Belgium, only some fifteen kilometres to the northeast of Buzenol. Because of its poor state of preservation, the relief had been neglected and misinterpreted.[76] The stone relief was seen as representing everything from a horse rider to a merchant laden with his goods for market, but it was the insightful Rostovtzeff who had the perspicacity (as so often) to see its true significance. It was another relief depicting the reaping machine described by Pliny and Palladius.[77] Originally part of a funerary monument, the relief depicts a man standing between two guide poles in the act of directing something attached to the poles through a field of grain. Probably it was Rostovtzeff's acute sighting of the tail of the draft animal and its haunches, barely visible in the extreme left of the damaged stone, that enabled him to make the connection with the literary descriptions of Pliny and Palladius. Alfred Bertrang, the museum director at Arlon, had the insight to take the Buzenol and Arlon reliefs as furnishing different parts of the same machine and to combine them to provide what was the first reasonable facsimile of the original representations of the reaping machine. Although the joining of the two different reliefs to produce a uniform picture of the entire machine has been disputed, the general impression imparted by the restoration is surely valid.[78]

The creation of the single perspective of the machine from the combined Buzenol and Arlon reliefs permitted the identification of fragments of representations

3.7: The Gallo-Roman reaping machine: fragment from Arlon. Musée Luxembourgois, Arlon, Belgium; ArtResource

of this same machine from other locations in the Rhine and Moselle corridors. In 1964, a fragment of a relief originally discovered in 1890 in a field behind the Landesmuseum at Trier was identified as part of a representation of the mechanical reaper. The fragment shows one side of the lower part of the machine, including one wheel and a part of the catcher bin or *vallus*, part of one of the harnessing bars, and the front leg of the horse or mule that was pushing the machine. It was literally a case of putting the cart before the horse. Heinz Cüppers, the director of the Landesmuseum, was able to put this newly identified fragment together with the ones found at Buzenol and Arlon to reconstruct a complete picture of the original machine. Five years later, in 1969, another block was discovered at Koblenz on the lower Rhine that was a fragment of a similar relief of the reaping machine.[79] Koblenz, as is evident from its Roman name of Confluentes ('the Confluence'), was situated at the point where the Moselle flowed into the Rhine. The city was a major connector on the Moselle line of communications through the region. The fragment of the relief, discovered near the bridge across the Moselle,

3.8: The Gallo-Roman reaping machine: fragment from Trier. Fouss,
'Le *vallus* ou la moissonneuse des Trévires,' fig. 3, p. 128

3.9: A reconstruction of the Gallo-Roman reaping machine. Cüppers,
'Gallo-römische Mähmaschine auf einem Relief in Trier,' fig. 1, p. 152

is broken and heavily worn. It pictures a draft animal, perhaps a horse, harnessed
to one of two draw bars by a trace line that runs up over its lower neck as it pushes
the wheeled catchment vehicle in front of it.

I suspect that there are more reliefs of the machine that remain to be discovered
in this same cultural zone. They were lost to sight when the funerary monuments
of which they were part were dismantled to construct defensive and other works
during the long fourth century. That four of them have already been identified, all
from this same region, is no accident. The concentration must signal something

3.10: The Gallo-Roman reaping machine: fragment from Koblenz.
Raepsaet and Lambeau, *La moissonneuse gallo-romaine*, p. 42

of cultural and economic significance. Despite minor variations in depictions, in all of the reliefs we see a reaping device that is reasonably fixed in its elements and modes of use. The basic parts of the machine are a wooden box or container to collect the heads of grain as they were reaped, and the axle and set of wheels on which it was mounted. The motor power for the reaper was provided by a draft animal, usually a mule or an ass. A horse is represented in one case, perhaps, it has been guessed, less from reality than from the elevated status suggested by the equine. The draft animal pushed rather than pulled the cart-like device.[80] The animal's driving power was harnessed by the means of two long poles, one mounted on either side of the cart collector. The mule or ass that stood between these poles faced the wheeled machine that was placed in front of it. The draft animal then pushed the whole contraption forward through a field of cereal grains, guided by a driver who either followed along beside and slightly behind the animal and machine or who stood at the rear between the two harnessing poles.

How the reaping of the cereal grains was actually effected by this machine is somewhat unclear. The machine was not so modern that it could do the cutting itself; it was not mounted with moveable metal teeth in the manner of a modern combine harvester. The teeth mounted along the upper leading edge of the *vallus* or collecting box were intended, basically, to force the stalks of grain into narrow fixed spaces where they were held by the force of the machine as it was driven forward. In some if not most cases it seems that a second man moved in front of the machine. He used a hard edge at the end of a long pole to help force the heads off the stalks of grain, using the teeth and the upper front edge of the container box as leverage for the stripping operation. The operation might have been even cruder than this, and the pole instrument might only have been used to direct and push the heads of the grain into the spaces between the teeth. The heads of the grain stalks would be snapped or broken off and they would then fall into the collecting box. The mounting of the collecting basket on a two-wheeled axle allowed the driver to move the leading edge of the machine with its teeth up or down, adjusting the height of the teeth to the height of the grain heads that were to be cut.

The tombstone reliefs of the Moselle-Rhine region that enable us to see the machine redirected attention to an earlier representation of the mechanical harvester that was created as early as the second century CE. It was found at a location in northern Gaul well to the south and west of the Rhine-Moselle triangle where all of the other representations have been found. All of the reliefs described above had originally been decorative parts of funerary mausolea. By contrast, the earliest illustration of the machine was part of a public and congratulatory monument, not a funerary one. It was sculpted as part of a series of relief panels that decorated the high central vault of the monumental triumphal arch at Riems named the Porte de Mars after the nearby temple of the god of war.[81] Riems, the Roman city of Durocortorum, the *civitas* centre of the Remi, was located in the middle of a panoramic expanse of fertile agricultural plains. A system of centuriation to the west of the town has been revealed by aerial photography. Durocortorum possessed the beneficial status of a 'free city' or *civitas libera* that left it with greater autonomy to run its own municipal affairs. A Roman-style agriculture that was based on villas came relatively late to the region, but it was quick to develop when it did, incited in part, it is thought, by the large legionary camps along the Rhine that elevated the demand for market-oriented provisions.

The triumphal arch of the Porte de Mars was one of two such arches that marked either end of the *kardo* of Roman Durocortorum. These two arches were complemented by two other less impressive arches that marked either end of the city's *decumanus*. The Mars Gate was a massive three-gated arch. Indeed, at over 32 metres in width, it was one of the largest in the empire. Sometimes claimed to have been constructed in connection with a visit by Hadrian to the city in 132, the arch is more probably a late second or early third-century construction.[82] The decorative panels on the ceiling of the middle vault of the central arch of its three great archways feature the reliefs that concern us. It is unfortunate that these are now in a rather bad state, having suffered serious degradation over time since the casts were taken and the drawings were made by the architect Narcisse Brunette in the middle of the nineteenth century. His drawings, and those made by J.M.S. Bence which were included in the Comte de Laborde's *Monuments de la France*, are the firmest basis that we shall probably ever have for our knowledge of their contents.[83] Care must therefore be taken with their interpretation.

The relief panels in the central archway originally constituted a complete calendrical series picturing typical rural activities associated with each month of the year. From what survives of the reliefs on the vault of the central arch, we possess scenes that represent the seven months of the year from June to December. The remains of these reliefs, and the central panel around which they are arranged, show that they were centred on a seated deity who was accompanied by representations of the four seasons. The pictures on the adjacent panels are a typical development of the agricultural seasons motif. The first panel covers the months of spring, featuring the raising of horses for the month of June, something for which the inhabitants in the region around Durocortorum were renowned. The panels that follow at the end of the arch similarly reflect typical scenes from the months that are found almost everywhere in the calendrical tradition. September is represented by scenes of the hunt, October by the vintage, and November by the butchering of pigs. It is the two panels that follow the initial panels representing scenes of spring, the ones that feature the summer months of July and August, that are most relevant to our argument. They are pictures that illustrate field work in the summer season, including the harvesting of cereal grain crops.

As best as these panels can be reconstructed, based on Brunette's casts and Bence's drawings, the first of them, for the month of July, illustrates three men who are involved in mowing the hay crops. The importance of the illustration is that all three men are wielding scythes.[84] The man furthest to the left is shown resting on the handle of his scythe. The man in the middle is pictured in a standard pose used for sharpening a scythe. He is holding his scythe upended with the cutting blade at head height so that the whetstone used to sharpen it can be applied more easily and efficiently with his right hand.[85] The man to the right is shown in the motion of cutting. The relief might represent three different figures in sequence, or it might be intended to illustrate the same man going through the motions of mowing, sharpening his scythe, and then returning to mowing.[86] In this panel, the convention of scything as signalling the mowing of fodder crops is maintained. It is the panel that follows this one that is particularly important for our purposes. It is meant to offer a typical scene of agricultural labour for the month of August. It is not a scene of mowing, but rather one of the reaping of cereal crops. It is this panel that illustrates the reaping machine at work. The relief

3.11. Relief from the central vault of the Porte de Mars arch at Reims.
After L.J. [Comte] de Laborde, *Les monuments de la France: classés chronologiquement ete considérés sous le rapport des faits historiques et de l'étude des arts,* 2 vols.
(Paris: P. Didot l'Ainé, 1816–36), vol. 1 (1816), pl. cxiii, p. 91

shows a mule pushing the cutting machine with its toothed front edge and a man walking in front holding a long tool that he is using to force the tops of the stalks and the heads of the grain into the machine's teeth. A figure at the bottom of the panel is holding a basket to carry away the heads of grain that have been collected in the hopper of the machine.

The importance of the Reims arch lies in the peculiarities of the reliefs on mowing and reaping: the panels dedicated to the months of July and August. First of all, they reveal a sensitivity to local ecological conditions for cutting hay and cereal crops. The representations for mowing and reaping in Mediterranean calendrical illustrations are usually attached to June and July respectively. The moving forward of the reaping season to later months reflects the realities in the different conditions in northwestern Europe. These different months, for example, are consistently reported in early medieval sources for the region as the times for mowing and reaping.[87] This forward movement of the reaping season is also found in medieval calendrical illustrations.[88] On all other such seasonal or calendrical representations in Roman antiquity the sequence is normally a scene of mowing fodder and hay crops, usually with the use of long-bladed sickles, which is followed by a scene indicating the slightly later process of the reaping of cereal grains, again with the use of sickles. The Reims reliefs were following a well-established sequence of motifs, but they did so with important modifications. Instead of using a long sickle for mowing, the reapers are employing proto-scythes. Instead of using conventional sickles for the harvesting of cereal grains, the reapers are using a machine. The reliefs on the arch therefore represent two parallel moves, and it is surely not implausible to see them as linked in the mind of the designer. The advance from long-bladed sickles to scythes in the mowing of hay was somehow linked to the parallel use of the reaping machine in the harvesting of cereal grains.

Agricultural Innovation: The Plough

Why the machine reaper was so closely identified with a microregion in the northwestern empire is suggested by several factors. It has been noted that important technological advances and inventions tend to come in batches when different inventors happen to discover similar answers to the same problem.[89] Such persons are members of networks in which exchanges of similar kinds of knowledge are taking place. The members of these 'colleges' are usually confronting comparable problems and they are dealing with the same kinds of technical materials. In complex and dense networks of agricultural production, the manufacturing of tools therefore tends to become more concentrated and focused. The rapidly developing rural economy of England in the sixteenth and seventeenth centuries is a good example. The village of Norton, Derbyshire, became an important centre for the manufacture of scythes. It was only here and 'in a couple of parishes on the Worcestershire-Staffordshire border' that scythes were made for the national market of the time. Harvesting sickles for the same national English market were manufactured by 'an even more concentrated group of families' in a nearby parish.[90] The striking concentration of the production of these tools was not a happenstance. In the case of the manufacture of scythes, the makers themselves were among 'the richest of the rural metalworkers, and with the largest farms.'[91] The concentration of technical innovation and production had an ecological and an economic logic.[92] The same type of concentration of manufacture and supply might have happened in Roman Italy as well. Cicero, for example, twice refers to a specialized neighbourhood of sickle manufacturers in the city of Rome, which no doubt served markets in Latium and central Italy.[93]

The need to understand the nexus of interlinked networks of knowledge exchange and of persons faced with similar ecological problems has caused a rethinking of the whole problem. In reconsidering the existing work done on the Gallic reaping machine up to the late 1980s, a leading agricultural historian outlined the major unresolved problems concerning its invention and use. How was the apparatus able to be invented, and based on what existing techniques? Why is it attested only in Gaul? And if we are to judge from the five known representations, only in a single region in Gaul? And finally, why did it apparently disappear from use some time after the fifth or sixth century CE or, at any rate, before the ninth century?[94] This same historian objected to the existing technical explanations for its invention and use: to cut down on losses, to save on labour, and to take advantage of the efficiencies allowed in the harvesting of cereal crops on relatively planar surfaces.[95] All of these conditions, he rightly noted, existed in many places in the Mediterranean, and in abundance in the wheat fields of Africa. So why was the harvesting machine not developed there, but in a specific region of northwestern Europe? And even if it was not invented in Africa, why did its use not spread rapidly to the grain fields of the Mediterranean?

The emergence of a technical innovation and its rapid and widespread deployment are dependent on a host of existing networks: 'sa totale imbrication et dépendence des systèmes techniques environnants,' as it has been nicely phrased.[96] This fact, in turn, is not separable from the total history of invention and technology, from the globalizing tendencies of effects, no matter how tiny and regionally specific the first appearance of any new thing. As we have noted, the effects of innovation usually condense and concentrate in certain regions where colleges of persons faced with similar problems connect with one other. They tend to trade information in ways that link the members to the development of new ideas. For whatever reasons, the lands of northern France, Belgium, Luxembourg, the west central Rhineland, and the southern parts of the Netherlands were just such a region of shared interests and knowledge in the development of rural economies.[97] Importantly for our purposes, this region had a long pre-Roman history as a foyer of agricultural innovation and development. The concatenated series of innovations in agricultural tool kits in this region draw our attention to it. The developments involved not only the mechanical reaper, which cannot be seen in isolation, but also implements like cutting tools used for reaping crops and ploughs used to break the soil for seeding.

These developments were already apparent in the pre-Roman Iron Age in the plains of northern Gaul and in the Moselle and Rhine corridors, but the Roman period brought further expansion and the extension of cultivation into marginal zones that had not previously been exploited.[98] We should emphasize that the unusual intensity of agricultural development in this particular region was well underway before the imposition of Roman military and administrative control. Basic shifts in agricultural technology had already taken place that were responses to the distinctive ecology of the region. By the later Iron Age, light scratch ploughs had been replaced with heavier ploughs that were capable of the one-time straight furrow ploughing of heavier soils instead of the repeated cross-ploughing by lighter scratch ploughs. Although no archaeological evidence has yet confirmed the further combination of a plough with wheels to make it more mobile and manoeuvrable, we know that such ploughs did exist and they were a distinctive peculiarity of the region.[99] They are mentioned, notably, by the Elder Pliny. He says that these wheeled ploughs were used in an area north of the Alps which he rather enigmatically calls Gallic Raetia.[100] The nature and origin of the wheeled plough has occasioned much debate.[101] Like the mechanical reaper, it was a technical innovation that enabled a better use of labour. This is an aspect of its use that Pliny notes: that by harrowing the land as it ploughed, the new instrument obviated the need for the intensive work of manual raking after the initial ploughing.[102] The notice by Pliny, with the evidence of archaeology and linguistics, has spawned a host of studies arguing that the origin and diffusion of the new plough emanated from the European northwest.[103]

The claim has been disputed, but there is no doubt that the deep-furrow plough is another case of the development of new tools in response to environmental prompts. In farming in the Mediterranean, including Italy, the plough of the Roman period, the rather simple ard or scratch plough, remained the standard instrument through the medieval period.[104] In lands around the Mediterranean, this standard ard plough remained singularly resistant to change, because it was so well suited to the light soils that it worked. It was well adapted to the tasks that it performed.[105] Detailed archaeological investigation has unearthed evidence for the development in northern Gaul and the Rhineland of a plough with a share and coulter as early as the second century CE. It was a new plough which in some cases might have been provided with a wheeled forecarriage in the manner described by Pliny. Further modifications to this new plough took place in the third and fourth centuries.[106] The main point for our argument here is *not* that there was a sudden invention of the front-wheeled deep plough, but rather that a series of innovations were pieced together to create a plough more suitable to turning the heavy soils of the north Gallic and German plains.[107] In fact, some ploughs found in German sites near the Rhine from this period exemplify a mid type in this long stream of development. One of them, found in the fifth-century hoard of iron tools at Osterburken, was discovered with a large number of scythes of the new type.[108] The innovations were happening as parts of a package of responses to a common set of environmental problems. As with the harvesting machine that was known by Palladius, the wheel-drawn plough was also known in northern Italy.[109] Whether this type of plough that was better adapted to the exploitation of heavy soils was invented in the northern plains of Gaul, in the Po Valley region of northern Italy, or in the Danubian basin is something that is not yet settled.[110] It is perhaps surprising that the new plough, unlike the mechanical reaper, did not figure on the reliefs of funerary monuments.[111] Since scenes of ploughing were an integral part of depictions of the seasons and an important metaphor of the steps between birth and death in the life cycle, it is a not inconsequential problem.

There is a basic lesson to be learned from this little history of the deep-furrow plough. It is simply that the new plough and the adaptations associated with it, such as the front-wheeled carriage, the wheeled harvesting machine, the new long-handled scythe, the special angle-hafted versions of the long blade, the use of new field systems, and new patterns of seeding and storage, were all parts of a constellation of interrelated changes that were specific to the plains regions of western Europe. It was between the Seine and Marne on the one hand and the Moselle and the Rhine on the other where these innovations seem to have been concentrated, where they were joined with new combinations of work regimes, and where they assumed their most intense form of development. In short, they should be seen more as localized regional ecological adaptations than as specific individual inventions. The larger purview within which these developments must be viewed is one of human work processes and tools as extensions of human capabilities. Agricultural tools were part of a continual interaction between humans and their environment. And just as the instruments changed, so did the specific words, terms, names, and ideas that were connected with them.

The Coming of the Scythe

If the machine reaper was a solitary thing in these strands of development, it might be seen as something of a fortuitous and accidental discovery. But there are indications that other significant innovations in harvesting were being made in the same context. When speaking of the cutting of hay crops or *faenum*, the agronomists report the use of different types of sickles, generally known as *falces faenariae*, for most areas of the Roman Mediterranean.[112] Since the purpose of getting hay was to cut the entire stalk so that it could be used as fodder, low cutting was by far the most efficient means of bringing in the crop. The response to reaping these species of grasses was to develop a significantly longer cutting blade that could be used with a sweeping motion of the whole arm and back – a long blade that was better adapted to the cutting of these crops. With this point of development, it was not a big step to the concept of attaching the larger blade to a long stick-like handle by which it could be wielded with a more powerful sweeping motion.[113] The move to connect the sickle blade and the haft does not require great intelligence, but only a modest ability to innovate, exactly as Roman soldiers on campaign in Judaea did with their sickles.[114] The long handle meant that this kind of reaping was easier on the back. At the same time it enabled a more powerful mechanics of cutting, using the power of the whole body by means of the simultaneous use of both hands and arms in the cutting action. Once again, there is both literary and pictorial evidence relevant to this innovation. Although the data are slighter in this case, they match the patterns that are reflected in the development of the reaping machine.

> (iii) Pliny, *NH*, 18.67.261; from the mid-first century CE.[115]

> Of reaping or cutting blades, there are two kinds. The Italian type is the shorter and is useful even on ground covered with brambles. The types used on the domains of Gaul are larger ones requiring less expenditure [of work] since they cut the grasses at mid-height and do not touch those which are too short. The Italian mower cuts with one hand, his right one, only.

> Falcium ipsarum duo genera: Italicum brevius ac vel inter vepres quoque tractabile, Galliarum latifundiis maiores conpendio quippe medias caedunt herbas brevioresque praetereunt. Italus fenisex dextra una manu secat.

Just as he did with the harvesting machine, Pliny asserts an unusual piece of knowledge and (surely not accidentally) he uses almost precisely the same technical language as he does for the machine harvester. The tool was typically found, he claims, on large domain lands in Gaul, the *latifundia Galliarum*, and it had been brought into use for the same reasons as the mechanical harvester. The identical technical term, *conpendium*, used by Palladius in connection with the machine harvester is used by Pliny for this farm tool. The new type of *falx* was brought into use as a labour-saving device. It was a precursor, in some fashion, of the true scythe. Pliny contrasts the manner of its use with the Italian *falx*. The latter tool was swung using one hand only, whereas the heavier and larger Gallic *falx* required the use of *both hands*. In conceptual terms, however, it came under the general Latin word used for such a cutting device. It was still called a *falx* since, in their mind, it was not a thing so clearly separated and different from, say, a large sickle as to provoke a wholly new term for it. Given the fact that the Elder Pliny provides this reportage, it is hardly accidental that the few undisputable Roman illustrations that we have of the innovation, the two-handed Gallic scythe, come from Reims and from the same region of northern Gaul and the greater Moselle that was also the home of the harvesting machine. As has already been shown, it is on the panelling of the central arch of the Porte de Mars in Reims that there is pictured a scene of mowing with the use of the long-handled scythe.[116] The blade of the implement is unusually long. One of the mowers rests on the tool, which logically suggests that it is long-handled. The other, the central figure, is sharpening the blade on his scythe, which is clearly attached to a long handle. Several other reliefs, all from northern Gaul and the Rhine, demonstrate the existence of this scythe in the high Roman empire.[117] But how close is this tool to the later western European scythe? *If* – and it is a considerable 'if' – the early nineteenth-century drawing by Bence is faithful in its replication of the original relief and not some imagined confection (which is possible), then we are witness to an intermediary stage on the road to the later development of the true scythe.

The new scythe was a reaping tool with a long shaft, at the end of which was mounted a blade in the fashion of a reaping sickle. That the artist of the Reims reliefs knew the sickle is guaranteed by the fact that it, too, appears in another panel: the one for the month of May.[118] What the artist represents is a marriage of the ordinary balanced sickle blade of the period with a long shaft with which to wield it. The idea was to take an existing cutting technology, that of the sickle or mowing blade, and to enhance its cutting power by enabling the use of the whole body weight and the directive power of two hands and arms in the swinging motion of the tool. This is almost certainly Pliny's *falx Gallica*, whose development he specifically identified with the large landed domains of Gaul and the drive to save labour costs. But the pictures of it and Pliny's simple description, which emphasizes the longer blade and the longer haft or sned, conceal other important changes. One was the evolution of a larger, straighter blade and a shift of the placement of this long blade on the sned, moving it at an increasing angle to the handle so that a reaper could use it in one sweeping motion while keeping the blade parallel to the ground. This is the important development that the archaeological finds of scythe blades from the core region along the Rhine, including the huge cache of iron tools found at Osterburken, show had taken place in this same region.[119] As with the harvesting machine, we have testimony from the

3.12: Detail of Reims arch relief. Close-up from the drawing of de Laborde, as in fig. 3.11

same source, the Elder Pliny, that was probably derived from a similar personal experience. We also have a pictorial representation of the implement on a monument that features one of the reaping machines. As with the machine, we witness the long-term use of an innovation in harvesting that extends over a period of four centuries and more. And it is attested in the same developmental region in northern Gaul and the Rhineland.

The archaeological evidence that connects southeastern Britain, the Low Countries, the Rhineland, and northern France in a single material cultural zone reveals similar patterns in the development of reaping tools. In the case of the sickle, the data reveal a movement from flint-based sickles of the so-called Neolithic, through a limited range of bronze sickles, to a much larger range of different iron types.[120] In the subsequent Roman period, the iron scythe made its appearance in considerable numbers. Here too there was a wide range of variation in styles, but with a basic subdivision into two types of scythes: those armed with long and those with short blades. The shorter-bladed scythes appear to be earlier in date. The long-bladed scythe was a later development, but one which had a real impact on reaping, to judge from its appearance in large numbers in iron hoards like that at Great Chesterford in Essex.[121] Much this same pattern of development, with slightly different chronological horizons and distinct regional variations, can be found on the continent facing Britain.[122] A survey of the reported archaeological finds of sickle and scythe blades in Roman Gaul reveals their concentration in the sites of the northern plains of France from Picardie in the west to Lorraine in the east, with significant concentrations in the Moselle (see map 3.2). The distribution also reveals, admittedly for bronze sickle blades, a special foyer of metallurgical production of blades centred in the Haute-Savoie. As for scythe blades, there are concentrations of them in Picardie, in the Champagne-Ardenne region (perhaps significantly, the centre of the Reims arch reliefs), and also in the Moselle. It is hardly merely fortuitous that these regions are the same ones where the literary evidence, the iconographic data, and the archaeological remains all converge to indicate the special significance of sickle and scythe technology.

Nor does it seem to be mere happenstance that this region was not just the one where the first true scythes were developed, and from which they subsequently dispersed to other areas of Europe and the Mediterranean, but that it remained the area that was noted for continued innovations in the design and use of this tool. These included the more extensive use of scythes in the mowing of pastures in the fourteenth century in Flanders, a development that was accompanied by the invention of a special light scythe called the Hainault scythe that was used to mow the marginal areas of fields.[123] The reapers in this same region had the option of moving the scythe to the reaping of cereal crops in addition to the mowing of hay fields. It was here that the *sape* or 'small scythe of the north' first appeared.[124] Its use extended over the same region in northwestern Europe centred on the known centres of the ancient harvesting machine: Hainault, a province just west of Luxembourg in southern Belgium, and Flanders and the Artois, regions that communicated with southeastern England across the Channel.[125] It was also here that the innovation of a forked rack-like attachment that would catch the falling stalks of cereal grain and considerably ameliorate the losses of cereal heads was invented. This idea, too, spread out from this regional centre of development to the rest of Europe.[126]

The history of the increased use of the heavy scythe for reaping cereal crops points to the same developmental zone as the epicentre from which the new idea flowed. Rather than any unilinear chronological shift from the Roman world of

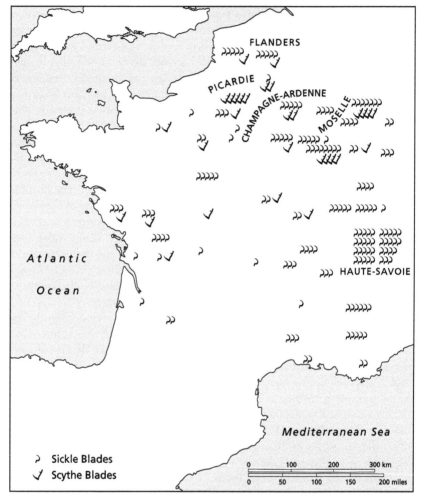

Map 3.2: Distribution of sickle and scythe finds in late prehistoric and Roman Gaul

the Mediterranean to the tool kit found in the feudal economy of western Europe, all these developments point to long-term ecological factors that were focused in this zone in northwestern Europe as opposed to environments in the Mediterranean. The importance of this creative zone for the development of new technologies which then spread outwards is well known. Take the following brief statement of the facts.

Up to the mid-eighteenth century the sickle and the reap hook were the predominant corn [wheat] harvesting tools in Europe. The scythe was confined to south Britain, the Low Countries, the Rhineland and a few areas of Denmark, France and Switzerland. Nowhere, except in Flanders and Hainault, had the practice of mowing been much extended to the bread grains, wheat and rye. Yet by 1900 the scythe or the heavy hook had become the chief and in most places the exclusive harvesting tools through western Europe and was soon to become so in eastern Europe and the Balkans. Only in Portugal, Italy and Spain was reaping with small tools still the common mode.[127]

Greece should also be added to this list. Furthermore, given the indications of the data, one must suspect that this pattern was also true of late La Tène and Roman antiquity, although the core historical problem for the Roman age is the difficulty of finding the evidence.

Few classical literary sources cover this region, and even fewer of them deal with aspects of farming life. To cite literary passages or illustrations from medieval manuscript sources as the first evidence for any of these innovations, moreover, is fundamentally misleading. Data drawn from early medieval manuscripts, generally ones of early Carolingian date, give a false impression of things described or pictured in them as beginning suddenly when they are first reported in this particular medium. It may well be that the 'earliest' representations of the scythe are pictures found in manuscripts like the Martyrology of Wandalbert or the Kalendarium of Salzburg, both of early ninth-century date.[128] It may well be that the earliest dated mention of a scythe called a *side* in English is found in an Anglo-Saxon glossary of 725.[129] But these claims have all the compelling power and interest of witnessing a dog chasing its own tail. Since these are among the earliest manuscripts that are counted as 'medieval,' it is only logical, indeed necessary, that they provide the earliest known examples of 'medieval' inventions in this medium. This is measuring a category of *evidence*, and not much more. A fuller range of data relevant to the problem needs to be considered.

Ecology and Human Concepts

Why did the Gallic reaping machines not experience takeoff? The answer might lie in another innovation that seems to be tied to the same region and time period in which the machine was developed and used, and which was closely linked to it. Pliny and Palladius both claim that the machine was invented to save on labour and therefore on the costs of work. The machine was used because it was a *compendium laboris* or a saving on labour expenses.[130] The general situation was one in which there were constant challenges among different alternative modes that were experimented with in taking off the harvest. In and of itself, a shortage of labour was not the sole driving force needed to create mechanical innovations in antiquity. It certainly was not always the critical factor in the adoption of techni-cal innovations after they came into existence.[131] The only competition among harvesting tools was between the existing tool for reaping cereal grains, the hand-held sickle, and other analogous bladed instruments. Under constant pressures, both specific and sporadic, bearing on its use, the sickle went through a large number of permutations from the fourth and third millennia BCE onwards, but especially in the last millennium BCE and the first CE. The multitudinous types of sickles, connected as a series of interrelated developmental forms, are material reflections of ongoing responses to environmental pressures and to the entice-ments of change.

Innovations, adaptations, and changes that aimed at improving the efficiency of the labour process were parts of continuous experiences and responses. The invention and the spread of the long-handled scythe is surely to be connected with the many variant regional modifications that were made to the sickle as a harvest-ing tool: the shift in the making of the blade from flint to metal, at first copper and then bronze; and then the move to the production of more efficient blades made of iron. The appearance of *iron*-bladed sickles at indigenous sites in inland Sicily in the age of the Greek colonization of the island has rightly been taken as a sign of the intensification of a rural economy based on cereal crops, especially the production of wheat.[132] Perhaps the single most significant innovation in the sickle was the production of the 'balanced' type. This new sickle design was pro-duced by moving the blade of the sickle at an angle along the axis of the handle, thus making it more balanced, easier to hold, and more powerful in its cutting sweep.[133] Although its widened use and distribution took place as part of the communication networks that were part of the Roman empire (and hence com-mon claims about its invention in the Roman period) its invention and early use antedate Roman political and military domination in western Europe. In fact, the region in which the balanced sickle was first developed and used appears to have been the cultural area covered by La Tène sites in Gaul, that is to say, the selfsame area on either side of the middle Rhine where most of the other developments in reaping of which we have been speaking took place.[134] Some time in the last half millennium before the Roman intrusion into the lands of western Europe and in response to the problems posed by harvesting cereal crops in these lands, local iron-working technology made a significant advance in reaping technology which subsequently made its way into the Mediterranean.

The single most thorough study of the permutations through which the reap-ing sickle has gone over time makes clear that there was one simple hand-held innovation for the mowing of grasses and the reaping of cereal crops that stands apart and is separate from them all. This is the reaping scythe.[135] The conventional claim has been that the scythe, like the balanced sickle, was an invention made in

Table 3.1: Relative work efficiency (area reaped per man per day: acres per diem)

Tool	Smooth sickle	Serrated sickle	Sape/Volant	Scythe
Median	0.17	0.5	1.0	1.5
Range	0.12–0.21	0.38–0.63	0.88–1.13	1.5

Source: Comet, *Le paysan et son outil*, p. 190

(See also tables 1.1 and 1.2a–b, at p. 17 above)

the time of the high Roman empire.[136] Perhaps. But as has also been perceptively noted, the nature of harvesting tools stood in a constant relationship to the ecological forces of which they were part. For millennia of human harvesting of cereal and forage crops there were only two reaping tools: the sickle and the scythe. And over thousands of years they continued to coexist, twinned side-by-side in the work of the harvest in a form of codependence.[137] There was never any automatic or permanent transfer from the one to the other. Rather, there were fluctuations in terms of greater or lesser preferences for the one or the other, choices that depended on a matrix of factors that included the quality and quantity of labour and the types of plants being harvested, among others. There is no doubt that the scythe was in a bare mechanical sense more efficient than the sickle in terms of the quantities of grain it could reap in the same time frame (see table 3.1). But this simple efficiency was never the only factor that determined the preference for the scythe over the sickle.

Multiple historical measures and records have demonstrated the greater efficiency of the scythe as an instrument for cutting cereal grains. In local or indigenous agricultural conditions in north Africa in the late nineteenth and early twentieth century, it took about 2 to 3 worker-days to reap the equivalent of a iugerum of land with a sickle. One good worker with a scythe could reap a hectare of cereal grains in 2.5 days, which is to say that he could reap the equivalent of a iugerum in two-thirds of one day.[138] These figures agree with the data collected for reaping rates in medieval and early modern Europe. Although the work was done much faster with the scythe – up to three times as quickly – it was widely recognized that there was a serious loss of grain heads caused by the violent hitting action of the scythe's blade in the process of cutting the grain stalks.[139] The benefits of speed had to be balanced against the losses of significant amounts of the crop that could only be reclaimed by extensive recoupage operations. In addition to the technical matter of crop losses, communities that adopted the scythe for the harvesting of cereal grains had to confront the social disruptions that it would cause.

The widespread use of the scythe for reaping cereal grains, for example, reshaped

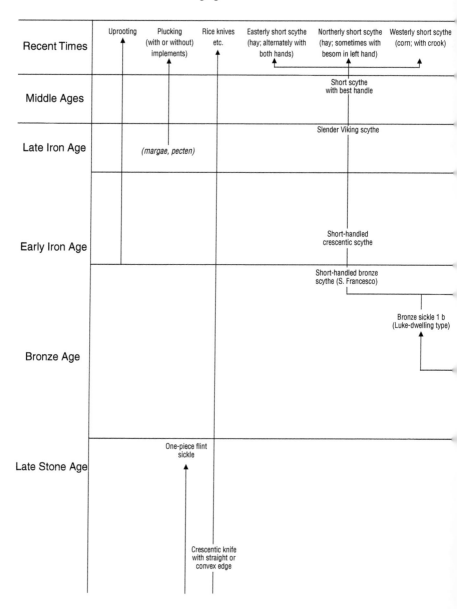

3.13a: The evolutionary development of the sickle. Steensberg, *Ancient Harvesting Implements*, foldout

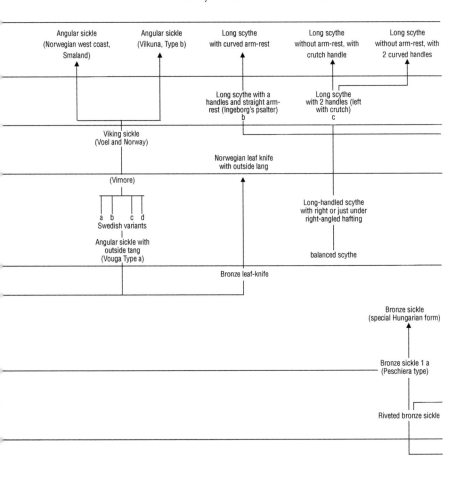

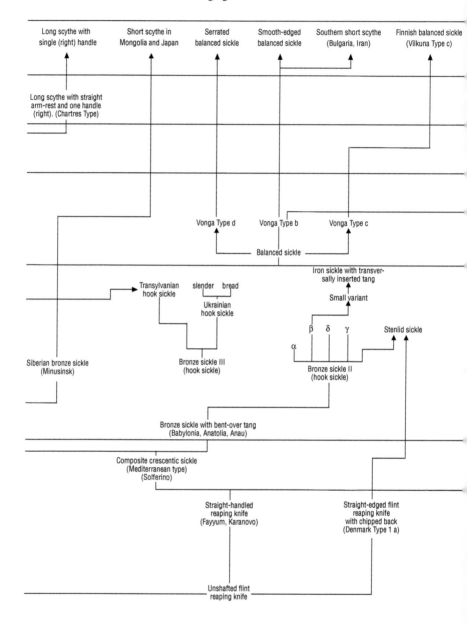

3.13b: The evolutionary development of the sickle. Steensberg,
Ancient Harvesting Implements, foldout

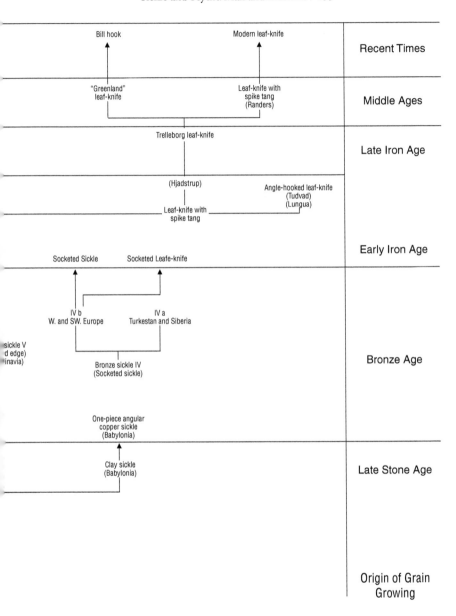

the gendering and the age structure of field labour. A massive change like this was an additional social cost of a new technology of cutting. Deep and pervasive effects on existing social relations were caused by the shift to the use of the scythe in cutting cereal crops.

The complexity of the economic adjustments involved in this situation is illustrated by the problems that emerged when farmers tried to substitute scythes for sickles in [cereal grain] harvesting. The main source of temporary labour had always been the vast local army of women, children, and old people who emerged from the household economy of small-scale farming and rural industry to complete their annual subsistence income with earnings from the use of the sickle. Because the scythe's more rapid rate of cutting was not matched by a parallel improvement in the productivity of labour employed in stooking and binding the cut grain, its introduction created an imbalance in the proportions of young and old and of male and female workers demanded to reap, bind, and stook. The imbalance was exacerbated by the fact that scythers tended to be outsiders, owing to the greater skill and strength required to handle the tool.[140]

As long as the hand-held sickle was in use, medieval and early modern depictions of reaping from western Europe consistently show that women worked in the cereal harvest. But they are almost never shown wielding a scythe in the mowing of forage crops.[141] Possible objections based on ideologies or aesthetics of representation are not convincing. The evidence, both iconic and literary, where it specifically refers to mowing, and the use of the scythe, consistently indicates the absence of women workers.[142] 'The increased size and weight of the scythe emphasized the strength and stature required of the mower, effectively confining its use to the strongest men.'[143] If reaping cereal grains with the sickle was arduous and backbreaking work, the work involved in mowing or reaping with a scythe was regarded by a host of contemporary witnesses of the early modern period as taxing the outer limits of brute strength.

The shift to the reaping of cereal crops with large handle-hafted scythes entailed turning one's back on the huge reserve labour force constituted of women and, to a lesser extent, of children and older persons. The later move to mechanical reapers, beginning with the machines devised by Bell, Ridley, Hussey, and McCormick, might provide some parallel clues, but the factors are so different that discerning underlying similarities is problematic. The big move to mechanization, primarily marked by the use of machine harvesters from the late 1880s through the 1920s, was encouraged by the growing problems of acquiring the needed manual labour. The work of women and children, for example, was being siphoned off by the urban factories. The shift was also favoured by the availability of machines and by profits from sales of produce at prices that were sufficiently high to enable the owners to disregard crop losses. These factors in combination encouraged the acquisition of expensive, if potentially wasteful, machines.[144] The one process drove the other in sequence, but the problem of acquiring the necessary labour and the availability of options to substitute for the sickle were central to the shift in technology. It must be kept in mind that a basic change in tools fundamentally altered divisions of labour, the gendering of work, concepts of loss and gain, rapidity of process, and consequently dominant images of what the harvest was.

Conpendium Laboris?

If the Elder Pliny and Palladius both state unequivocally that innovations like the Gallic scythe and the machine harvester were brought into use to save on the costs of labour, it must have been manifest to them that this was a prime cause of the use of these new technologies. This factor must have been one of the necessary compelling causes, but it was certainly not the only cause nor even a sufficient one. There were many places in the empire where there were shortages of labour, but where no new reaping tools or machines appeared. On a reasonable and credible estimate of the factors involved, the Gallic reaping machine was approximately three times as efficient as the hand reaping of cereal crops with sickles. This was about the same level of improved efficiency as the scythe.[145] What Pliny and Palladius must have meant in speaking of *conpendium laboris* is something like 'all other things being equal in this particular set of ecological circumstances,' a saving on labour was a significant calculation. Furthermore, the concept of labour shortage is a complex one that does not correlate easily with either a sparse or a dense local population. A shortage is in no sense easily deducible from the archaeological facts of poverty or wealth, or of the thinness or density of settlement patterns. And on more than one count, the presence of slave labour was not the core problem. Slaves were no certain impediment to technological innovation, especially in agricultural and resource-extraction sectors, as, for example, in mining. In any event, chattel slave labour was very far from being the dominant mode of rural labour in agrarian production in the Gallic regions of the empire in which these technical innovations, including the mechanical reaper, are attested.

These obvious facts have not impeded all kinds of unwarranted suppositions about labour regimes being made on the evidence of the reaping machine alone. Let us consider one of them.

Among the Remi, the diffusion of this amazing harvester [machine] assumes, at its base, the existence of a class of skilled persons of some high technical ability who were able to conceive, to develop, and to repair these machines – skilled workers who could operate them, and, what is most important, a peasant world composed not of great wealthy landowners who had at their disposal an abundant supply of cheap labour and for whom the urgent need to take off the harvest quickly posed no problem but, on the contrary, a world of small and middling producers who were closely tied to artisans and workers.[146]

Based on the hard evidence known to us, every one of these claims is open to question. First of all, the levels of technical skill required to make, operate and repair the machine were not that elevated. The mechanical reaper was made by cobbling together some fairly simple aspects of existing carriage, wheel, and harnessing technology. These were areas of technology in which the Gauls already excelled.[147] They are elements of carriage and harnessing that are illustrated on the set of stone reliefs at Buzenol that also featured the reaping machine.[148]

The next claim, namely that the invention necessarily presumes a world not of wealthy landowners but of small peasant landholders, seems almost perverse, since both Pliny and Palladius explicitly state that the opposite was the case. Even so, great landowners and latifundist estates were not *necessary* elements. A purely happenstance visit to a museum in eastern Pennsylvania in the autumn of 2007 revealed a nexus of provocations that had led a few inventive farmers in the region in the late nineteenth and early twentieth century to produce a harvesting machine that bears a striking resemblance to the Roman reaper.[149] No matter how useful it was and how in need of being invented, this machine went nowhere. Even though it was used by many farmers in the region, and was something of a success, it remained a thing unique to Bucks County. It was not reproduced, manufactured, or distributed on any significant scale. The two examples on display in the Mercer Museum are the only ones that are known.[150] So here is an example of a machine (so called by persons of the time) which was designed by a local farmer out of the basic components that were also found in the Gallic reaper. Technically the invention was not difficult. Just unusual, perhaps.

We might begin with the basic fact that the Gallic reaper was not as much a reaper as it was a stripper or, as the Pennsylvania machine from Bucks County was called, a header. Like the clover header, the Gallic machine might well have been designed for a special crop that was ecologically well adapted and widely grown in the particular region in which the machine is most attested. Just as the Pennsylvania cutter was specifically designed for the heading of clover to collect seed, it has been hypothesized that there was a close causal connection between the Gallic reaper and the cereal crop of spelt, *Triticum spelta*, which was widely grown in this particular region in antiquity.[151] The reason, it is speculated, is that the hard heads of the spelt, unlike those of wheat and barley, were relatively easy to detach and to strip from the stalk, and that this known fact would provoke the idea of a machine that could perform the needed task. The main components that went into the idea of a device that would strip the heads of spelt were wheels, animal traction or force, a collecting box, and reaping teeth. The first three elements, as has already been noted, were widely available in local carriage technology.

The use of reaping teeth was perhaps suggested by an existing reaping tool that was called a *mergae* or *mergites* or 'divers,' but sometimes simply *pecten* or 'comb.'[152] These were toothed instruments or separate stick-like fingers used in a comb-like fashion to strip the heads of cereal grains.[153] Still known from their use in modern times in the Republic of Georgia and in Asturias on the Atlantic shores of northern Spain, where they are called *mesorias*, their existence in Roman antiquity is attested by both Varro and Columella.[154] The name *mergae* for the reaping instrument was connected with the swooping action of sea birds who dove beneath the sea to catch fish, since their action was likened to the hand manoeuvre of the reaper who used the device. Like the sea bird, the reaper swooped the tool down under the heads of grain and then up again to break them off.[155] This is almost certainly the same comb-like instrument to which reference is made by Ovid.

> At set times of the year he ties the cut grasses
> and he combs the sheared earth with a wide-toothed comb.

> Temporibus certis desectas alligat herbas
> et tonsam raro pectine verrit humum.[156]

In late sixth- and early seventh-century Iberia, Isidore of Seville refers to a comparable agricultural implement that had teeth that were used to comb or to rake the ground.[157] It is significant that it is the Elder Pliny who noted the use of the comb-like reaping tool in Gaul, again probably based on his own observations.[158] And it is surely not accidental that he mentions this comb-toothed tool in the same passage in which he describes the mechanical harvester and with some of the same verbiage: compare *rare pectine* with the *denticuli … rari* of Palladius. Just as significant, he matches the instrument with two specific crops grown in Gaul: panic grass or *panicum*, and millet or *milium*. Although the comb was gradually abandoned as a reaping tool in northwestern Europe, a memory of it is still found in medieval French texts.[159] Such headers or strippers were well known as late as the end of the seventeenth century in the southern United States.[160]

In the case of the Gallic reaping machine, we can be more specific about the nature of the labour saving that it enabled. It was limited to the reaping or cutting process. If the Reims relief is accurate, and since it depicts a man holding a basket that is certainly part of the transportation of the cereal heads collected in the *vallus* of the stripper, the labour saving ended quickly at the point where the cereal grains had to be transported to storage. A similar development in a different historical

3.14: The Ridley Stripper: South Australia, mid-nineteenth century. G.L. Sutton, *Wheat-Growing in New South Wales Australia* (Sydney, 1910)

period and place points in the same direction. It is the history of the closest technical analogue to the Gallic reaper, the Ridley Stripper, invented in South Australia in 1843. This harvesting machine, designed to take off wheat crops, was very successful in Australia. It was also successful in reaping the wheat fields of Argentina and South Africa where Ridley Strippers or rival versions were exported or where they were produced locally in considerable numbers. Also relevant to the problem is the fact that John Ridley, its inventor, was directly influenced by reading Pliny and Palladius and by seeing an imaginative drawing of what the Gallic reaper might have looked like. In the course of his invention, it was specifically noted that the Roman machine was *not* a mechanical reaper. An author who, in 1854, was debating the priority of McCormick's claim to have developed the first true workable reaping machine remarked as much.

If the ancients were successful in making a practical implement for reaping, by horse, or ox power, as some ancient writers assert, we certainly have no correct or reliable account of a machine that would be considered efficient or useful at the present day; a machine to save or tear off the heads only – as described by Pliny and Palladius – would more properly be termed a gathering machine, and not at all suited to the wants and habits of modern farmers.[161]

It is notable that the Ridley stripper had little or no success in western Europe, England, or North America. The main reasons for its successes and failures were ecological. It was not the specific crop – wheat, or *Triticum aestivum*, in most cases – but rather something closely related that determined its success or failure. It was the condition of the wheat heads at the point of their reaping.[162] In the Australian and the other cases of its success, the conditions of heat and aridity produced hard grain heads that detached readily and easily from the stalk of the plant.[163] The same pattern can be observed in North America in modern times, where header machines were also known. Pushed and not pulled by animal power, just as in the case of the Gallic machine, the header's limited use can be precisely mapped. The confines were defined: 'The header in particular adapted to areas where wheat usually develops a short, stiff straw and where the harvesting season is normal[ly] dry.'[164] In more humid and damp climates, like that of Britain, the stripper was not an effective reaping device because the wheat heads would not easily detach.

The modern history of a comparable machine supports the idea that in the conditions of northern Gaul in the late Roman empire the crop that the reaping machine was designed to harvest, probably spelt, was well adapted to the peculiar stripping action of its teeth, and vice versa. This points the way to a possible answer to the question of why use of the reaper declined in post-Roman years. It was a huge exogenous factor that affected this whole ecological zone. It was a more humid and colder phase of climate in western Europe identified, since La Roy Ladurie's dramatic evocation of it, with a late medieval 'little ice age,' the chronological sweep of which was somewhat broader than was first thought.[165] As the environment changed, there was a general shift away from growing spelt to the planting of soft wheats as the main cereal crop in the region.[166] The transition from late Roman conditions and those of the early medieval warm phase to the damper, wetter conditions of the later period produced harvest conditions that militated against a device that was a stripping machine. The prompts to the creation and development of a given tool and the factors in the expansion or recession in its use were environmental and ecological. The same observation applies to the scythe that was born in this same region and gradually expanded out of it. It too was not widely adopted in the ancient Mediterranean. Greek farmers did not select the scythe for reaping or mowing but tended to retain the sickle as their main tool for both tasks.[167] No new word was devised in Byzantine or early modern Greek for the scythe, as happened in the European northwest. All cutting tools of this kind remained, simply, *drepana*.[168]

Another important clue to the invention and development of the Gallic reaper is provided by the transition on the Reims arch relief that depicted the use of the harvesting machine. As work on premodern England has shown, in a system where human muscle power remains the norm, it is the employment of hand tools that is the greatest single constraint on the productivity of agricultural labour in the fields.[169] So it is to changes in tool design and use that our attention should be drawn. On the Reims reliefs, the usual sequence of representations for June/July and July/August: that is, the normal pattern of mowing hay with a large sickle or a small scythe followed by the reaping of cereal crops with a sickle experienced a double displacement. Mowing in July became cutting with true large scythes, followed by the August cutting of cereal crops with a reaping machine. The first question that is prompted by this move is: Why not shift to use the scythe for the harvesting of cereal grains?

The loss of grains caused by reaping with the scythe could only be justified and sustained where the aim was to reap more grain more quickly and where the losses were compensated by the large scale of the operation. The transition to this last stage, the displacement of the sickle by the scythe for the reaping of cereal crops, began in England around 1800. But the transition took a generation or more, with scythes not coming into general use for this task until after 1835.[170] Next in sequence came the reaping machine, which finally began to displace the scythe by the 1880s. This is the same sequence that is suggested by the Mars Gate reliefs at Reims, but with the sickle being replaced by a reaping machine instead of by a scythe. The historical ecology of the shift in post-Roman times is interesting. At some time before the mid-eighteenth century, the shift to using scythes to harvest cereal crops had begun on the large farms of northern France and on those in the southeast of England. It seems that this technological diffusion began in the Low Countries and northwestern Germany.[171] It is surely not accidental that a similar concatenation of forces was witnessed in these same lands by the elder Pliny in the first century CE, whose later developments we can trace in literary and archaeological sources. In both cases, the shift was made because other large wage-earning sectors were drawing manpower away from the pool of seasonal harvest labour.[172]

The use of the scythe in the reaping of cereal grains is an indicator that larger landowners were moving upscale partly because of the *conpendium* or saving of labour costs of which the ancients spoke. That such movements were the results of decisions made by landowners or their managers is plausible. It certainly happened as part of a continuous process at the beginning of the nineteenth century which eventually led to the introduction of reaping machines. But this move was only the most recent change in this region of northwestern Europe. The shift had been made earlier and for the same reason: for the *conpendium laboris*, that is, as an answer to increases in the cost of labour. There was a move to use the scythe in harvesting wheat and other cereal crops in western German lands and Flanders around 1300. A similar shift happened thrice in the next century, again in periods when rural wages were high: in 1348–52, 1389–1402, and 1411–29.[173] The reason was that the move to the use of the scythe produced significant savings on labour costs. But the scything of cereal grains was never a preferred method of reaping, if only because of the significant losses of cereal grains entailed by this method. The trend was always back to the use of sickles.

Only a select sector of the whole agricultural economy devoted to cereal production made the shift to reaping with scythes, and then it happened slowly and against a background of continuity in the existing methods of reaping. At the end of the eighteenth century in England, approximately nine-tenths of the entire cereal grain harvest was still reaped with sickles: 'There was no simple progression from one technique to another. Machine reaping appeared on large farms in the 1850s, but hand cutting continued on small farms for a hundred years.' In fact, the majority of the cutting of cereal crops was still done with sickles.[174] The scythe was only a possible interstitial ecological response. In the pre-Roman and Roman northwest of Europe it stood, temporarily, between the sickle and the harvesting machine. Similarly, its flourishing in the nineteenth century was short lived – about a thirty- to forty-year interval between the age of the sickle and the arrival of the harvesting machine.[175] The move to the scythe for reaping cereal grains presumed a distinction between small farms and large ones: like the difference between small operational units and *latifundia* in late Roman Gaul, or between yeoman farms and plantation-sized estates in early nineteenth-century Virginia. Given the environment in which the larger units of cereal production tended to arise, the shift to the use of the scythe and then to the harvesting machine in Britain was made mainly in the extensive flatlands that were devoted to cereal growing in the southeast of England and in East Anglia.

A perhaps amazing thing is that it was seeing a mockup or a picture of the Gallic reaper that provided the direct model for a modern invention used for much the same purpose.[176] Beginning with the primal modern field manual of Pietro de' Crescenzi's *Ruralia commoda*, first put into print in 1471, there were a series of references to Palladius's reaping machine in agricultural handbooks down to the time of John Loudon's standard reference work published in England in 1825.[177] It was on seeing a picture of it published in Loudon's *Encyclopaedia of Agriculture* that John Ridley acquired the idea of how to produce a similar stripping machine that would answer *the labour problems* that were bedevilling the taking off of the wheat harvest in South Australia in the 1840s.[178] There is no reasonable doubt that the Gallic machine, which was a type of stripper, would have considerably improved productivity. In South Australia in the early 1840s, Ridley's Stripper, a machine with much the same design and mode of operation. The main difference was that it was usually pulled by a team of horses under the guidance of a single observant rider, rather than being pushed as was the Gallic reaper. The new machine was easily able to outperform manual reapers. At the competition of 1843, the stripper was able to reap 70 acres of wheat land in seven days, a rate of about 10 acres a day, considerably above the one acre a day that a good man could cut with a scythe. The machine was responsible, at least in part, for an enormous increase in land sown to wheat crops in a fifteen-year period between 1840 and 1856.[179] As with other agrarian inventions, like the cotton 'gin, the stripper permitted not just a more efficient processing of the cereal crops, but itself contributed to a significant expansion in the agricultural production of which it was part.

A Peculiar Region?

In any attempt to explain the phenomenon of the Gallic reaping machine, the one thing that is immediately manifest in the evidence, both literary and archaeological, is its specific geographical distribution. The literary references mark its presence in the expansive plains regions of Gaul. All the relief sculptures are confined to a zone of northwestern Gaul and the Roman Rhineland, in a sector on a line between Reims, Trier on the Moselle, and Koblenz on the Rhine (see map 3.1 above). The territorial triangle in which the evidence for the mechanical reaper is concentrated has a baseline running west of the Rhine to Reims, with its apex above Colonia Agrippinensis on the lower Rhine. But the wider plains regions of northern Gaul to the west of this triangle were certainly also centres of its use. Some explanations have emphasized local features that might excite an interest in a machine as a more efficient means of harvesting cereal grains. These include flatter plains and a topography that, in contrast to many regions in the Mediterranean, did not suffer from the sort of accidence of terrain that would impede the convenient progress of a wheeled machine. But this is certainly not a sufficient explanation since, despite common intense topographical variation, there were many flat plains areas in the Roman Mediterranean. One of the most famous grain-producing regions in all of the empire, the high plateaux of Africa, the very plains to which our anonymous harvester from Mactaris led his gangs each year, in many places had uninterrupted planar surfaces that sometimes extended to the limits of the visible horizon. Here, if anywhere, one would presume that a reaping machine would have worked to maximum advantage and, in theory at least, the need for it might have been great.

In considering this problem, the important factors of frontiers, peripheries, and communications come to the fore, just as they did in Cyrus McCormick's Virginia of the 1820s and 1830s. The middle Rhineland, the Moselle valley, and the general region between the Seine and the Rhine, with its riverine highways and tributaries leading in a line from the heart of the empire to its outermost northern peripheries, were corridors of broad economic significance.[180] More than once, it is has been pointed out that the geographic triangle, anchored in the lands of the Treveri and the Remi, and those lying immediately to the west, was an unusual zone of intense economic activity.[181] It might be nothing other than an accident that this same zone would later be the foyer of a late medieval and early modern economic revolution centred on intensive agriculture and cloth production. Perhaps. But I think not. It can hardly be accidental that there was a manifest pattern of economic development in the larger triangle that is bounded by the Rhine on the east, the Ile de France to the south, and the Maastricht-Aachen area at its peak.[182] In the heavy distribution of Roman-style agricultural villas in northern Gaul, this region has one of the densest concentrations attested in the archaeological record.[183]

The Rhone-Rhine corridor and the neighbouring micro-regions of northern Gaul were hot spots of agricultural development. The vineyards developed in this region are one example of an intensified agricultural production for sale and trade that was a driver of economic innovation in the region. Appearing first in ecologically privileged areas, innovations gradually spread outwards from the zones of their first development.[184] Linguistic evidence for the other shifts in agricultural technology that we are examining points in the same direction. Words in modern languages derived from the Latin *falx* mean sickle everywhere *except* in northern Italy and in northern France, where the derivative terms like *falce* and *faux* are used to mean scythe.[185] Ordinary language use points to a common ecological frame that was different from the core of the Mediterranean to the south where the sickle remained the harvesting instrument par excellence for cereal grains. Both of these scythe-using zones were inhabited in antiquity by Gallic peoples who were linked to one another by culture, language, and other modes of communication. It has long been recognized that some early Carolingian illuminated manuscripts contain illustrations of scythes. Two of the most important of these come from Trier, which is hardly just another accident.[186] These north Italian/ Gallic connections are doubtless part of the reason why Palladius knew of the reaping machine.

In an assessment of the role of technological innovation in this region, one writer confesses that 'in fact, the conscious desire systematically to connect theoretical research, experimentation, and applied technology is a phenomenon that does not seem to have appeared before the end of the Middle Ages.'[187] It must be admitted that, when measured against early modern inventions, the technological improvements in the reaping part of harvesting operations in this development zone in the pre-Roman and Roman period were often small and incremental. They were ones that could easily be effected and applied by farmers and workers on the ground. Even if individually minor in type and scale, they had a significant cumulative impact. The history of the shift to different types of sickles in England is a warning. In the nineteenth century, in not a few regions the harvest was still taken off by sickle, but at twice the speed and efficiency of the Roman period. The reasons were simple ones: a slightly different type of tool, a different technique in its use, and a metal blade of higher quality that permitted sharper and cleaner cutting.[188]

These sometimes complex facts bring us back to the iconography. The illustrations should not be seen in isolation. Rather, they should be viewed as part of a milieu of artistic production, a local tradition in a specific region where the land-owners produced demands, to which artisans responded, for more realistic artistic representations that highlighted scenes from their everyday professional life.[189] These scenes range from representations of agricultural tasks such as ploughing and seeding to the well-known and widely studied icons of the commercial production, trading and sale, and transport of woollen textiles that were inscribed on the famous monument at Igel. The decorated tower monument of the Secundini was one of the impressive funerary mausolea that were characteristic of this economic and cultural zone. These observations suggest that it was something about the nexus of forces in the region, rather than any single factor, that explains the emergence of the reaping machine.

Surveys of the economic development of northern Gaul and the Rhineland over the entire period from the late Iron Age or La Tène culture (of which this was the homeland) through the Roman period to a new and distinctive phase of economic development that occurred in the ninth and tenth centuries CE emphasize a number of common factors. First of all, agriculture was not just the backbone of the economy; it was by far and away its largest sector. Next, the most characteristic constructed feature of the high phase of the Roman development of the country-side and of this rural economy was the villa, through which the exploitation of the land was managed in its leading sectors. Pertinent to this second observation, it has been shown that there were three major zones of villa development in the Gauls and the Rhineland. First, there was a southern zone of development in regions close to the Mediterranean where there was a tremendous diversity in range and design of the villas that reflected the highly diverse, fragmented, and variegated ecological forms of this area. The second zone, in the middle hinterland of Gaul, was marked by varied and dispersed villa types. By contrast, in the northern zone, in lands close to the Rhine and its tributaries, there developed a different rural culture where the villas were characterized by 'a remarkable uniformity in design, which are relatively simple in type, and were of a very functional character.'[190]

It is the northern region that is of most interest to us. The density of villas in this region was simply staggering. The true scale of villa development was revealed, in the first instance, by aerial surveys that were conducted under the aegis of Roger Agache in the 1970s. The regions of the Beauvaisis, Soissonais, the Artois and Cambrésis, and the neighbouring areas in Belgium, Luxembourg, and those adjacent to the Rhine, were places where 'one is struck by the homogeneity and the regularity of the orthogonal "rational planning" of the sites, perfectly set out and sharing an astonishing similarity of type.'[191] That is to say, the entire region was set apart by a peculiar emergence of large, wealthy villa complexes that dominated the countryside and which formed nodes in the interconnected economic links that controlled the rural spaces around them. The villas in the regions of modern day Belgium and Luxembourg, and nearby regions in northern France, have been justly described as 'veritable palaces,' with design features that highlight regularity and a rationalizing logic.

As has also been remarked upon in one of the surveys of this vast rural wealth and power: 'It is clear that the settlement of the villas, the driving motors of the rural estates, is above all found in a close relationship with the natural, topographical, and climatic conditions of the region.'[192] The same survey further notes: 'If there is one requirement that stands out above all others, it is the fertility of the soil. In Gaul, the villas were systematically set up in the middle of the richest agricultural lands. That is the golden rule. Because the villa is, above all, we repeat, an agricultural concern, linked to a large rural domain whose activities it directed and whose daily life it commanded.'[193] The dense and territorially huge estates in the northern region that existed in such profusion could only have been producing goods for markets. It is also manifest that most of the estates were placed in lands that were best adapted to the production of cereal crops. They would easily have produced surpluses greatly in excess of any peasant demand. Local urban markets appear to have been few and weak. In comparison with the more heavily urbanized areas of the empire, the towns in northern Gaul were small in number, not large in size, and were dispersed over greater distances. Part of the standard argument is that it was the large and constant demands of the Roman army in its bases along the Rhine and in Britain that provided the impetus to production. The army's huge, systematic, and predictable annual purchases of food supplies, it is claimed, set up a recurrent cycle of demand, purchase, and supply that fuelled the development of the large villa and domains that we see on the ground. Without doubt, the supplies required by the army must have been important, but even the most liberal estimates of army requirements do not provide the quantities of demand needed to produce the extensive agricultural development which has been confirmed by archaeology. There must have been other markets and a mass demand, even within the region, that sustained the complex rural development.

Work, Invention, Metaphor

The combination of forces that produced an ecological region within which specific economic developments occurred, including technical innovations, and the links that connected this region to others must be taken into account. In the Roman period, the ecological zones of the Rhine and northern Gaul were especially well connected with an unusual hyperdeveloped villa-centred social order in the countryside that was at the heart of the most complex and large-scale agricultural production. It was in connection with its ecological needs and economic enticements that the reaping machine was developed. For this reason alone, the reaper was an innovation that might not have had a very wide attraction or potential for application in a quite different Mediterranean ecology. To say that the classic Roman agronomists remained 'totally ignorant' of the innovation is to compare developments and innovations on radically unequal terms.[194] In this case, the transfer of technology would depend on decisions made by men like Pliny or Palladius who would understand the reaping machine's utility for the harvesting of cereal grains, for example, in the fields of Africa. Pliny had served as a procurator in Africa and possessed first-hand knowledge both of its ecology (geography in his terms) and agro-fiscal nexuses.[195] In comparative terms, one might note that agriculture in the Roman world did not draw the attention of the state to the degree that it did, for example, in contemporary Han Dynasty China. The major writers of agricultural treatises address their concerns mainly to private landowners and to the ways that they could, as individuals, increase their own incomes.[196] But there is no inherent reason why the dispersal of new ideas through successions of private landowners committed to increasing their incomes would not have worked just as well in dispersing new technologies as would a state-directed development achieved by governmental fiat. Palladius, like Pliny, was constantly attentive to innovation. A lot of it, he claims, was based on personal experience: what he had been told and what he had seen, that is to say, information derived from oral communication and direct experience.[197] There was no inherent mental impedance to the transfer of useful information.

The case of the reaping machine raises difficult questions about technological change in simple agrarian economies. The interdependence of human communities, environmental forces, and exploitative technologies produced continuous recursive chains of effects. The tools and the mechanisms of harvesting cereals, for reaping in particular, critically affected every human action and attitude. As one stands in a field of grain, one has to gaze at the grain and think 'these plants have domesticated us as much as we have domesticated them.' Ideas of how tools are connected with their environments point in sundry directions. Some indicate the supposed paramount importance not of the technologies themselves, but rather of the social structures surrounding them.[198] The innovations provoked by new ideas and their formation recursively moved back through the same processes of thinking to produce yet new ways in which the matrix of instruments, tools, and labour might induce novel modes of thinking. Concepts of path dependence emphasize the combination of all of these in a complicated and continuous feedback process in which every new instance cumulatively influences all subsequent choices.[199] At every point, these recursively affect the way humans think, not only about the labour process itself but also about other unrelated matters. The sudden and massive intrusion of the scythe produced a significant number of different ways in which the producing and taking of basic materials for sustaining life were perceived. The front-end labour process was now viewed as almost entirely masculine and more violent in nature. Speed and energy were applied with a harsher and more violent cutting motion to the taking of the crop. Efficiency and the attendant losses that it induced were sustained in the name of a harder calculation of gain and loss. The manner of the work and the technology conditioned a perspective in which one was willing to risk greater losses in search of greater gains.

Just as individual parts of a given technological process were involved in a continuous feedback loop that linked human minds, the tools, and the tasks, the innovations in reaping fed back into the mental images of the reaper. They further empowered those who represented both his actions and ones that were perceived to be analogous to them. After all, the Gallic harvesting machine, as we have seen it pictured in all of its hard reality, was not just a decorative element boasting of technical progress. It was the signifier of something quite other than the cutting of cereal grains. As Matteo Ricci understood of Han script, machines and tools could be used to represent and to display mental ideation. And this problem takes us back to Augustine's concerns with the reaper and his cutting blade not just as a source of labour and technology, but as a bearer of meaning. Our interests in reapers are peculiar analytical social and economic ones that he did not have. Augustine's interests in them were tied not to function and profit, but rather to violence and belief, both of which point to different and darker aspects of thinking about the harvest, and to the threatening figure of the reaper himself.

CHAPTER FOUR

The Grim Reapers

Count Dracula: To die, to be *really* dead, that must be glorious!
Mina Seward: Why, Count Dracula?
Count Dracula: There are far worse things awaiting man than death.[1]

The reaping scene hammered onto the shield of Achilles calls to mind the harvest accompanied by exultant feelings of triumph and joy. Such celebratory emotional responses are understandably associated with sentiments of happiness and exuberance that were evoked by the jubilance of the season: the rolling gold, the bumper crops, and all the bounty. The spirits of rejoicing were surely like the emotions evoked by the composers of the songs in the biblical book of the Psalms, especially the verses frequently quoted by Christian preachers in the late antique world of the Maktar Harvester.

> Those who sow in tears
> shall reap with songs of joy;
> those who go out weeping
>   bearing the seed for sowing,
> they shall come home rejoicing
> bringing in their sheaves.[2]

One of these preachers, Augustine of Hippo, in commenting on this same Psalm in one of his sermons, made manifest the metaphor at the core of the Psalm. It is death.

Where are they going? And from where are they coming? What are they sowing in tears? What are the seeds? And what are the sheaves? They are going to death, they are coming from death. Going by being born, coming by rising again. They are sowing good works, they are reaping the eternal pay. The seeds are ours: whatever we will have done as good persons. The sheaves are ours: what we shall receive in the end. But if the seeds are good, that is, good works, why then (do they sow) 'with tears,' since God loves the joyous giver?[3]

As Augustine goes on to say, the answer to the last question makes sense if his listeners understand that the words of the Psalm applied to the martyrs of the faith. The images that connected sowing with life and reaping with death were well known, coming, as they did, out of proverbial sayings and everyday observations of the links between reaping and the routines of daily life. An important form in which they were remembered and propagated (as here in the Psalms) was in the songs that were sung as the harvest was being reaped. For the landlord, the sheaves were his by right of ownership. For the reaper who did the good work, they were part of his remuneration: he had earned them. These real-life experiences were tied to mental images set in a sequence: the seeding of cereal grains, the reaping of the crop, and the reaper's pay at the end of the harvest. Produced by the actions of everyday living, the images were powerful and logical extensions of commonplace experiences. Augustine was not saying anything new. The Christian mental picture could be reworked within traditional thematics. In a brilliant floor mosaic from Thebes, Greece, the month of July is portrayed as a reaper bringing in his sheaf. Notably, it is a Christian period piece embedded within the long-worked theme of the seasonal cycle of life and death found in calendrical mosaics.[4]

The way in which the new faith, from its inception, exploited images of reaping and their meaning is demonstrated by the apostle Paul in a letter that he had written more than three centuries earlier to the Christian community at Corinth.

And mark this: The man who sows sparingly will reap sparingly; the one who sows generously, will reap generously ... Each one should give as he has chosen in his own heart ... for *God loves the joyful giver* ... The One who freely gives seed as a gift to the sower and bread for eating will provide you with all the seed you need and will make *the harvest of your good deeds* a full one – becoming wealthier in every way, you will be able to engage in every kind of benefaction ...[5]

From the perspective of Paul's disciplinary eye the use of the trope of reaping was modestly threatening, but it was also encouraging, connecting, as it did, the mundane experiences and images of everyday labour with the ideology of euergetism and civic benefaction: the one who reaped bounteously could also give bountifully. The encouragement was to give and to bestow favours on the Christian community, especially on its mendicant and needy leaders, and to give generously. In the manner of a person sowing a crop, the returns for such generosity would be enhanced by means of a divine quid pro quo. The returns would be multiplied, just as seeds produced enhanced yields at harvest time, especially since the gifts were not to civic officials or to members of a civic community, one's fellow citizens, but rather to the new slaves of God, his professional servants. The words therefore allude to ideas of freely given benefactions and the rewards that the giver will reap. The latter benefits were assured because, as Paul states, it was known that God loved a joyful giver. The preacher could then expatiate on the joyful Christian gift, following the natural temporal sequence of harvesting and reaping.

And his seed will be blessed ... His seeds are what he will leave behind; therefore, what he sows here now, he will reap later. For the apostle says: 'Let us not grow weary of doing good, for in His own time we shall reap with no weariness. So while we have the time,' he says, 'let's do good for everyone.' *This* is your seed that will be blessed. You commit it to the earth and you collect so much more ... You can see this same seed specifically named by the apostle when he is speaking about alms. He says: 'The one who sows little, sows and reaps little, but the one who sows blessings, reaps blessings' ... Here we cast our seed in sufferings, trials, pains, and groanings. But consider another psalm: 'Going they went out, and they were weeping as they sowed their seed.' But *now* pay attention: 'Their seed will be blessed. Coming back, they will come leaping for joy, carrying their sheaves.'[6]

In the midst of this same passage, the preacher emphasizes that alms-giving is needed, and now. Only at that later time, after death, in Paradise, will there be no thirst, no need of water; no hunger and no need of bread.

The Psalmist's use of the image was not so happy. His less joyful perspective suggested not the happiness of benefactions, but rather the spectre of death. If the believer was to reap the harvest of his good work, an accounting that calculated what he owed was to be made when the person himself was reaped. The centrality of death cannot be disregarded, and at least some residue of its power lay behind the happier use of the metaphor by the apostle Paul. This connection with death determines the shape of most of our data. It must be remembered that we only know of the harvester's story from Mactaris because it was inscribed on his tombstone. To understand the darker implications of the Psalmist's verses, we might begin by considering the refrain of a modern evangelical hymn that echoes his words: 'they shall come rejoicing, bringing in the sheaves.' The hymn was reputedly one of the most popular sacred songs in America during the late nineteenth and early twentieth centuries, when a great portion of the entire population was directly involved in agricultural production, including the work of reaping.[7] In its words is found a strong allusion to what lay immediately beyond the completion of the harvest. On the one hand, there was the joy to which the words of both the ancient Psalm and the modern hymn refer: plentiful food finally in store for the forthcoming year. But those who sang about the harvest in this joyful sense also knew that it was the bleakness of winter that would soon follow. For the singers, the connection between harvest and the threat of death was manifest.

The linkage was readily understood because the rhythms, work routines, and cycles of production were shared by large numbers of people. Their common experiences produced mental templates that their minds could manipulate for new and different purposes in communications among themselves. The connections were possible because the participants in the discourse knew the points of reference from their world of experience. The progression from a widespread economic routine to metaphor is perhaps obvious: large numbers of people do the task and then they think in terms suggested to them as mental extensions of what they do. It is this facet of metaphor that will concern us here.[8] This is how new concepts and words emerge and then merge again. Something as apparently impersonal and objective as modern scientific thinking is not exempt. Take, for example, the tropes of change involved in biological evolution. Why did Darwin, Wallace, and a large number of other persons caught up in the heavily industrializing capitalist societies of western Europe all converge simultaneously on the same idea of competitive advantage and selection in adaptation to a given environment? It has plausibly been suggested that the reason was the contemporary economic circumstances in which they were involved: 'The perceived structure of the competitive economy provided the metaphors on which evolutionary theory was built.'[9]

Part of the reason for the compulsion to form extended mental images is the hard-wired drive in the human mind to produce explanations in the form of narratives.[10] The same mental process in antiquity moved from production and the social organization for work to the mind and language, and then back again. The narrative was implicit, since the work process was inextricably bound up in a larger natural cosmic order. The cycle of the seasons that determined rural work also determined the mental place of ploughing, seeding, and reaping in a given and predictable sequence. The fact that the reaping that helped to produce the necessary sustenance for the next year's life cycle was itself divinely ordained contributed to sacralizing the instruments of production. And the fact that the tool was a cutting instrument like a martial blade meant that this extension of the hand, like the Samurai's sword, absorbed a sacral aura of taking life. The sickle was ordinarily represented among the tools of agriculture that were vowed or devoted to gods upon the successful completion of the annual cycle. In the case of the sickle, the dedication was to Demeter or Ceres, the goddess of grain.[11] Africans knew of the practice and the idea, and they could write about it at length, as did Apuleius, in his book about life changes, the *Metamorphoses*. In developing his extensive allegorical narrative of Cupid and Psyche – Love and the Soul – he describes Psyche's desperate search for her Lord.

4.1: Ceres harvesting grain: House of Icarios, Oudna, second century CE.
The Bardo, Tunis; ArtResource

She immediately began to quicken her pace to the place [i.e., to the temple that she had seen from far off]. Although she was exhausted from her continuous efforts, hope and desire urged her onwards. When she had energetically ascended to the highest heights, she went in close to the immortal couches. There she saw some sprigs of grain piled in a heap and others woven into a crown; and she also saw sprigs of barley. And there were sickles and all the tools of harvest labour, but they were lying scattered about, here and there, carelessly discarded from the workers' hands in the summer heat, as is usually the case.[12]

Soul sets about organizing these items as if they should not be left in such a chaotic disorder and, apprehending the approach of the goddess Ceres, begs her protection from the fury of Venus. Note the evocation of the real-life world of reaping: the tools of cutting are strewn around, carelessly tossed aside by workers weary from working under the fires of the midsummer sun, *as is usually the case*. The image of the goddess Ceres, the reaping and the piling up of cereal grains, and the wearing of a crown woven out of stalks of grain is pictured on a contemporary mosaic from Oudna, Tunisia.

The connections between the progression of the seasons, human labour in producing agricultural crops, and the stages of life are perhaps so obvious as not to require much conscious reflection. THE COURSE OF LIFE = THE SEASONS OF THE YEAR is a fundamental metaphor shared by almost all human cultures that experience a distinctive progression of seasons.[13] A life narrative was like the annual cosmic narrative. As part of this process, the passage of time was envisaged as a sickle that cut through all things and destroyed their existence. Embodied as a person, Time was seen as a divine being who reaped by killing or destroying all things with a harvesting sickle.[14] This knowledge could be played upon and elaborated by the creative human writer or artist. Just so, Vincent Van Gogh created a series of paintings of grain fields that highlighted the ripening of the crops and the final harvest of the wheat. Given his interest in the sequences of the seasons in nature and the ways in which these implicated the natural human life cycle, his decision to settle on the themes of growth and gathering was not unusual. It required no knowledge of the long history of reaping and harvesting that we have outlined, much less the specific economic conditions and Christian thematics of late Roman Africa. As a modern western European artist, Van Gogh shared the interests of a coterie of nineteenth-century interpreters of rural life. Jules Breton, Léon L'Hermitte, and Jean-François Millet, and others formed an influential background to some of his main themes. Zola in his *La Terre* also shared the same aesthetics of the age and he produced similar pictures, only in words.

From the second week of August, the work went ahead. The reapers started from the fields lying to the north and were working their way down to the ones along the Algre valley; sheaf by sheaf, the vast expanse of wheat fell beneath the semi-circular sweep of their scythes. These tiny insects, submerged in this gigantic labour, were winning the day. Behind their slowly advancing line, the level earth was reappearing under the hard stubble through which the women gatherers were slowly wading, head downwards. It was the time of the year when the mournful, lonely plain of Beauce was at its gayest, full of people and enlivened by the constant flow of workers, carts and horses. As far as the eye could see, the teams were working away in the same rhythm, moving along sideways with the same sweep of the arm, sometimes so close to each other that you could hear the hiss of the steel, while others stretched out in long black lines, like trails of ants, right up to the skyline ... For the last few days, the heat had been overpowering ... the stubble was crackling in the drought and, above it, the still heads of wheat, as yet uncut, in the burning air seemed to be glowing with their own flame in the shimmering light of the sun. And not one leaf to offer a touch of cool shade, nothing but the foreshortened shadows of the men on the ground, since morning soaked with the sweat of the fiery sky ... [15]

Contemporaries in England who created analogous scenes in paint, like Max Michael, George Clausen, John Linnell, Alfred Glendenning, Henry Parker, Robert Gallon, and precursors of theirs like George Stubbs, felt the same impulse. Among Russians, we have already referred to Alexei Gavrilovitch Venetsianov. But others like Kazimir Severinovich Malevich and Boris Mikhailovich Kustodiev, who were painting in Russia at the time, followed this same path. The desire for artistic success and commercial viability was part of the motive and the interest,

4.2: Vincent Van Gogh, *Wheat Field with a Reaper*, 1889.
Van Gogh Museum, Amsterdam; ArtResource

but not all of it. All of these works were pieces of the same realist stream of creation that allowed the similar 'realistic' evocation of the reaping scene by Tolstoy that we have already described above, at the beginning of our investigation.

Death

These factors do not explain Van Gogh's choice of the particular scenes that he painted, nor the manner in which they were finished. That he executed these paintings in a particular time frame, between mid-June and the end of July in 1890, however, is significant. They were the last six weeks of his life.[16] And in this case, we have the artist's own words about the connections that were being drawn in his mind – words that explain the meanings that he envisaged when he painted the figure of a harvester in his *Wheat Field with a Reaper* at Auvers-sur-Oise in midsummer of 1889. He wrote to his brother Theo.

I am struggling with a canvas begun a few days ago before my indisposition. A reaper. The study is all yellow, terribly thickly impasted, but the subject was beautiful and simple. I then saw in this reaper – a vague figure struggling like a devil in the full heat of the day to get to the end of his work – I then saw in it the image of death, in the sense that humanity would be the wheat being reaped. So, if you like, it's the opposite of The Sower that I tried to do before. But [there's] nothing sad in this death. It takes place in broad daylight with a sun that floods everything with a light of pure gold ... The Reaper is finished ... It's an image of death as the great book of nature speaks to us about it. But what I sought is the 'almost smiling.' It is all yellow, except for a line of violet hills, a pale blondish yellow. I find it odd that I saw it like this through the iron bars of a cell.[17]

There might be debates about how one can connect his final paintings with the self-inflicted gunshot wound when Van Gogh walked out into the same wheat field at Auvers on 27 July 1890 and killed himself. But the undeniable aura is there. The picture of the reaper is, as Van Gogh himself specifies, the image of a kind of death. By a violent act, the artist literally made himself at one with the forces of nature that surrounded him. He reaped himself. The whole of this fascination was prefigured and confirmed a year earlier, in September 1889, when, at Saint-Rémy, he followed the painting of *Wheat Field with a Reaper* with two more figures in imitation of Millet: the *Reaper with Sickle* and *The Reaper* (with a scythe).

The aspects of death and violence that inhered in the reaping of the grain could be turned inwards, but they could also be unfolded outwards, as the artist himself phrased it, into an 'an almost smiling.' Seeing and contemplating reaping as seen and pictured by this artist could, in turn, provoke further extensions by another writer and poet, again based on a common dread and apprehension.

> Acres of rolling gold I now survey through the bars,
> the bumper crops of summer under sunset –
> there in the midst a reaper battling all that bounty;
> he is death, death as the great book of nature paints him
> all but smiling ... yes, I can almost feel him in me,
> warm with labor, laughing with the harvest –
> gold for every stroke of his sickle ...[18]

But if experiences of facing death are as individual as death is common, the fact only serves to remind us of the problems of ubiquity and scarcity. If some ancient literary depictions of the work of reaping do exist, it hardly needs to be pointed out how rare they are. Any attempt to collate all the descriptions with the hope of eking something useful out of them is bound to produce a disappointing harvest. The question then arises why a process that was so widespread, important, large scale, and part of daily work in every region of the Roman Mediterranean left such a sparse record in all forms of ancient literary and artistic production. This peculiar absence is also true of poetic creations that logically ought to have made something more of the mechanics of the harvest, like Hesiod's *Works and Days* or Vergil's *Georgics*, where there is next to nothing. More disconcerting, perhaps, is the fact that this lack is also true of the agricultural handbooks where, we might imagine, the single most critical and labour-devouring operation of the whole agricultural year should have left a more discernible footprint.[19]

The problem with the representation of the work of the harvest seems to be a general one that bedevilled other ages as well. We might consider the apparent distinction between the picturing of the work of reaping in the medieval cal-endrical tradition and its odd absence in the agricultural treatises that began to appear at the end of the same period.[20] Part of the problem with the early modern agricultural treatises, beginning with Pietro de' Crescenzi's *Ruralia Commoda* of 1305, is that they were so heavily indebted to the classical tradition from Cato to Palladius.[21] The void in the treatment of labour in these works is so manifest that even the dullest scribbler could not fail to notice the absence. Without doubt, some of the refusal to discuss rural labour can be attributed to literary type. As can be seen from a study of the earliest agricultural handbooks produced in Eng-land and western Europe in the fifteenth and sixteenth centuries, these works were not only cast in a lordly crypto-utilitarian genre, but also in an ideologi-cal and aesthetic space in which the entire subject of hard work was assiduously avoided. Of the ancients, upon whom they depended so much, even Palladius, who was moved now and then to note the problem of the costs involved in agri-cultural work, almost wholly avoided treating the operational sides of farming that involved the problems of labour: 'Plus etonnant encore que certain bizarreries de composition ... est le silence presque total que fait notre auteur sur les problèmes proprement économiques ... ceux que posent la gestion du domaine rural et son mode d'exploitation.'[22] Given the aesthetic mode, tools for working the fields, for example, are described in loving detail, but the ways in which they were manufac-tured or put to use is very much underplayed, even deliberately avoided.[23] Since harvesting operations were an intensely plebeian time of tough, sweaty, and sordid work, it is perhaps not surprising that they were ignored in the production of idyllic pictures of the countryside and its life.[24] The agronomists' distaste for dis-cussing the practical and technical problems of labour supply is more difficult to explain. Given the overpowering impact of certain kinds of aesthetics on writing, we might perhaps understand *some* of their hesitation, but the resulting absence and its effects on the long term history of the writing of agricultural manuals are still a frustrating puzzle.[25]

This same reluctance does not seem to be as true of different forms of repre-

4.3: Pieter Bruegel, *The Harvest/August*, 1565.
The Metropolitan Museum of Art, New York; ArtStor

sentation found in other ages. One can easily refer to the well-known paintings of Pieter Bruegel. His canonical pictures of the idyllic joys of peasant life in the Low Countries of sixteenth-century Europe are much imitated and reproduced.[26] Painted at a time contemporary with the first modern agricultural manuals in print, Bruegel's panoramas have come to be a kind of acceptable high-culture artifact. We find echoes of them in a thousand and more pedestrian modern representations of the joys and communal solidarities of harvest time. Even so, as one student of the social world of these artistic creations has emphasized, the premodern paintings, etchings, and drawings that celebrate the social ebullience of harvest, so frequently replicated in modern-day art and history textbooks, were a rather minor genre at the time when they were produced.[27] By the nineteenth century, illustrations of reaping were becoming more numerous, but they were still part of a convention apparently limited to certain modes. For the most part, they are absent from decorative ceramics, for example.[28] And they are not found at all in other popular media where one might have reason to expect them.[29] That is to say, they had a particular market.

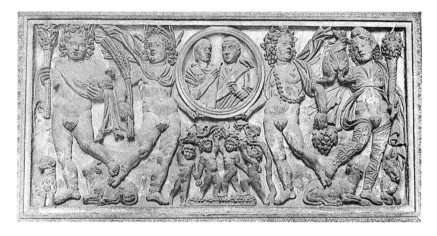

4.4: Reapers on a Late Roman sarcophagus, Rome, Palazzo Mattei. F. Matz
and F. von Duhn, *Antike Bildwerk in Rom*, 3 vols. (Leipzig: Breitkopf und Härtel,
1881–2); vol. 2, p. 306, no. 3022

The same problem of distribution in variant media was also found in Roman
antiquity, but with different valences. There are numerous examples of reaping
scenes as part of the sequence of the seasons on funerary sarcophagi, for example, in Italy and in some of the western provinces of the empire, although they
are hardly found at all in Africa.[30] The imbalance in distribution is explained,
in part, by the relative paucity of finds of sarcophagi in Africa, the home of our
harvester. Taken from a larger strategic purview, however, the total number of
harvest themes found in reliefs on sarcophagi (i.e., where the numbers of surviving
and catalogued sarcophagi are significant) remains a rather constant proportion of
about a fifth of all thematic representations found on these burial monuments in
both pre-Christian and Christian periods.[31] And this is for a mode of burial where
a fair number of the clients consistently came from higher social strata, mainly
the ranks of the clarissimate in the fourth century.[32] When the harvest themes are
taken with the other dominant themes found on the sarcophagi, such as bucolic
or hunting scenes, one can easily see the manifest connection with death. Within
this context, it also makes sense that some themes, like Dionysiac parades, circus pomps, or, especially, the heavy emphasis on philosophical scenes in the pre-
Christian sarcophagi, fade or disappear among their Christian successors. But the
harvest does not. Its seasonal signals remain the same. This test case demonstrates
the fatal context of death, whether 'pagan' or Christian, as the critical frame of
metaphorical representations of the harvest in antiquity, and in particular of reap-

ing. It is within the realm of death that the presence of the reaper is weighty and constant.

Critical historical analysis of the artistic and literary production of the same reaping theme in more recent times has suggested that the early modern paintings were part of the search for acceptable plebeian social images in an age when the tension between peasants and the new burgeoning urban classes was becoming acute. These latter social ranks, it is argued, were becoming 'anxious' about the threat posed by the former. Therefore, artists on canvas responded in kind.[33] But then why not in other similar ages of tension and social change? If the tensions were so profound and novel, why was the new response so specific and targeted? Anxiety always worries everyone nowadays, but it explains rather little. And it might also be noted that these happy communal pictures had a fundamentally different context from almost the entire repertoire of ancient representations of the harvest and of reaping. The early modern images were produced with paint on canvas, paper, or vellum, as portable pictures or on the leaves of even more portable books. That is to say, they were deliberately manufactured as items of commerce. Although the Bruegel paintings, of which the summer harvest is one, were part of a series whose context was rooted in the seasonal cycle of medieval sacred texts, they were commissioned by a wealthy Antwerp merchant to be displayed in his home.[34] This aesthetic does not seem, on the surface at least, to be connected with any fear or apprehension of peasants as much as with a personal anxiety to acquire the appropriate household décor.

This was *not* true of most of the ancient visual representations of reaping. It was not true of Graeco-Roman iconography, nor was it true of the brilliant paintings and frescoes from Pharaonic Egypt. Here there is a huge difference between the ancient figures and the Western early modern and modern illustrations of the harvest. Compared to typical representations of the annual cycle of the seasons in the pictures of plenitude and happiness in the rural scenes of a Bruegel or in other painters of his time, the ancient picturings are fundamentally different. This is because the immediate and primary context for them was not life, but death. The game here was death-ritual in a more direct and unmediated sense, and not primarily the affect of commerce and personal acquisition. The ancient figures are largely depicted on heavy, fixed media. Representations on media other than wall frescoes, relief sculptures, and mosaics are rare. Of these other forms, reapers and scenes of reaping are sometimes found on lamps and other ceramic media in late antique Africa, but only infrequently, and even here they were death objects.[35] They were a functional iconography needed for social inspection and funerary ritual: they were decidedly not crudely commercial in nature. Of all the pictorial representations of harvesting that I have employed, from the wall paintings of the rock-cut tombs of the Theban nobles of Middle Kingdom Egypt, to the relief

4.5: Noble husband and wife reaping in the afterworld: tomb of Sennedjem, 1280 BCE, Deir el-Medeina, Thebes. The Metropolitan Museum of Art, New York; ArtStor

sculptures on the mausolea of the Romano-African lords of rural Tripolitania, and the sarcophagi from late Christian Italy, Gaul, and Spain, none would have existed were it not for the celebration of death.

Among the most striking and complete of these tombstone illustrations of the seasonal cycle of agricultural tasks in the context of death, including the task of reaping, are the mosaics from the *Tomba della Mietitura* in the Isola Sacra at Ostia. As one enters the tomb complex, a large central floor mosaic worked in dramatic white and black features the funereal motif of the Alkestis myth at its centre.[36] The central Alkestis panel is surrounded by six smaller mosaics of typical agricultural scenes that the viewer would see on entering the portico, illustrations that represent the cycle of birth to death. In sequential order, the scenes are ones of ploughing, hoeing and weeding, reaping, carrying the cut grain to the threshing floor, threshing, and, finally, winnowing. There is no doubt that the magnificently wrought picture of two reapers (the tomb is rightly named after them) cutting their way through a field of wheat, in a flowing and sweeping movement, was meant to symbolize the part of the life cycle in which life was taken. This life was then metaphorically collected, stored, and adjudged in the subsequent frames. The connection of this cycle with the death and rebirth experience of Alkestis imparted meaning to the whole. The meaning of the restoration of the reborn wife

4.6: Reapers on the sarcophagus of Junius Bassus, Rome, 359 CE. J. Wilpert, *I sarcofagi cristiani antichi*, 3 vols. (Pontificio Istituto di archeologia cristiana, 1928–36), vol. 3, pl. 271

to her husband through the intervention of Herakles, and what this signified for the person buried in the tomb, would have been manifest to most Roman viewers.

The tombstone reliefs of the great mausolea of the grandees of the predesert communities in Roman Tripolitania furnish the same kind of evidence and context, but in a provincial milieu and in the medium and style of relief sculpture. The scenes carved into the frieze of the 'B' mausoleum in the north cemetery at Ghirza replay the same sequence of seasonal agricultural tasks that are seen in the mosaic of the tomb at Ostia, albeit in distinctive regional cultural modes. In the ploughing scene from the Tripolitanian predesert the ploughs are drawn by camels and not by oxen as they are at Ostia.[37] Here, too, the scenes of threshing and winnowing follow that of reaping in sequence.[38] Again, the scene of the reapers in the field, whose appearance is quite different from their Italian counterparts, since they are almost wholly nude as they toil in the burning heat, is part of a larger narrative of seasonal labours that replays the sequence from birth to death, and beyond, as it pertained to the great lord buried in his splendid desert mausoleum.[39] Even with their regional peculiarities, these reliefs use the same symbolic language.

All of these representations conceive of reaping as part of a unified sequential process that pictures the steps from life to death, and beyond, in a narrative sequence. The fuller sequence of equivalencies or metaphors that is seen, for example, in the *Tomba della Mietitura* mosaics might be represented schematically as follows.

4.7: Tomb mosaic of the seasons: Tomba della Mietitura. Isola Sacra, Ostia. (Baldassare, [1990]). fig. 45, p. 97; permission courtesy of Professor Irene Bragantini, and Dottoressa Anna Maria Morretti, Soprintendente, Soprintendenza Speciale per I Beni Archeologici di Roma e Ostia

4.8: Two reapers in the field: Tomba della Mietitura, Isola Sacra, Ostia (Baldassare, [1990], fig. 49, p. 101; permission courtesy of Professor Irene Bragantini, and Dottoressa Anna Maria Morretti, Soprintendente, Soprintendenza Speciale per I Beni Archeoligici di Roma e Ostia

PLOUGHING/SEEDING	=	BIRTH OF LIFE
HOEING/WEEDING	=	LIFE AS LIVED
REAPING	=	DEATH
TRANSPORT	=	JOURNEY BEYOND DEATH
STORAGE	=	STATE OF REST

With these elements in mind, it is easy to see how the images can be manipulated, shifted, ornamented, replaced, redone, and abbreviated as was appropriate or required. In the case of the reliefs on the tower tombs from northern Gaul the figure or figures of men reaping with sickles could be replaced by the picture of a man with a reaping machine. The meaning was still the same, although it was represented in a regionally different and ecologically conditioned form. Most often, because of the constraints of space, such as the field available on a small funerary stele, abbreviation was required, so the entire sequence of metaphoric pictures was not presented to the viewer. In these cases, usually only the two most important elements in the sequence, those of ploughing and reaping, were retained. The

4.9: Reapers and pile of cut grains on the cornice frieze of Tomb NB, Ghirza, Tripolitania. Romanelli, 'La vita agricola tripolitana,' p. 62

scenes of ploughing and reaping were understood to be signs of a larger sequence of birth, growth, and death in the annual agricultural cycle and of the greater zodiacal cycle of the cosmos. By themselves they bookended the intervening steps and so represented the entire process. This schema makes sense of a pair of bronze coins that was issued at Alexandria in the fifth year of the reign of Antoninus Pius. One illustrates a ploughman wielding a goad with which he drives a yoke of oxen pulling a plough, and the other features a reaper cutting three stalks of wheat.[40] The two coins represented the whole of the life cycle. They were connected with a set of coins that Pius issued at Alexandria in year 8 of his reign, 144–5 CE, that featured the signs of the zodiac.[41] Once again, the ploughman and the reaper were shorthand symbols for the whole series of steps that connected birth, death, and the beyond.

The constant availability of the abbreviated version of the whole sequence leads me to suspect that there are probably more illustrations of the Gallic harvesting machine than have currently been accounted. The simple reason is that archaeologists, museum curators, and scholars who were studying and cataloguing funerary reliefs in the nineteenth century were unaware that the metaphoric substitution of MAN REAPING WITH SICKLE = MAN REAPING WITH HARVESTING MACHINE was possible. Therefore, they only represented and drew what they saw as possible in the mind's eye of the time. For example, when they saw a ploughing scene and something that looked like a farm cart in the other half of the scene, they drew a cart.[42] Almost certainly, however, the cart is not a cart but a harvesting machine, armed

4.10a: Coin of Antoninus Pius, Alexandria: Figure ploughing. ANS 1944.100.60251. rev.1795; permission courtesy of the American Numismatic Society

4.10b: Coin of Antoninus Pius, Alexandria: figure reaping. ANS 1944.60255.rev600; permission courtesy of the American Numismatic Society

with the *vallus* and its harnessing poles. The example to which I have just referred was discovered near Arlon, which surely adds probability to the claim, located, as it is, at the epicentre of several other known representations of the theme.

On the Boglio stele, where the scene of ploughing is twinned with the scene of the reapers cutting the crop, the pair of pictures bears the obvious metaphoric meaning of the whole sequence of life to death (see figs. 1.12–13). It is surely not

4.11: Relief of plough and 'cart' from Arlon, Belgium G.-F. Prat, *Histoire d'Arlon*, vol. 1, pl. 64

purely accidental that the poet who composed the verses for our harvester from Mactaris began by having him cultivating the soil and ended with him reaping the crop. The poet was replicating the same sequential pattern about our man's life and death. Other pictorial representations of reaping, like the one on an oil-burning lamp from Late Roman Africa, could simply be decorative motifs. Given the widespread presence of Christian themes on lamps of the period, however, it seems more likely that they too signify death and the divine reapers. Almost all the representations of reapers appear as illustrations on funerary monuments, a fact that is true even of the apparently pedestrian bas-relief sculptures of the Gallic harvesting machines.[43] To our eyes, the illustrations might seem to be used to boast of technical innovation (that is, after all, our interest in them), but their original cultural and material context was that of death and burial. In seeing these images, people of the time never gazed at them, as we do, isolated in museum displays. They saw them in their monumental and cultural context. Seeing a scene of reaping on a tomb face, the viewer of that time was always powerfully reminded of the darker undertones of the harvest season, signalling, as it did, the end of life. This was so even if the symbolism used harvesting machines, the latest in the high-tech of the time, to convey this same message.

The connection between reaping and death was a primal one, going back as far as the domestication of plants and animals that was part of the new human ecol-

4.12: Reaper on late Roman lamp from Hr. es-Srira, Tunisia. Renault, *Cahiers d'archéologie tunisienne*, 3 (Tunis, 1910), fig. 6, p. 127

ogy of agriculture and the more complex social orders that gradually emerged with it. The ideas and thinking connected with these developments evolved in complex ways. They are found, for example, in Egyptian concepts that were eventually incorporated as a consistent canon in the Coffin Texts of Middle Kingdom Egypt and the later text of *The Coming Forth by Day*, the so-called Book of the Dead. In both cases, they are illustrated with scenes of the deceased involved in reaping. The spells in the Coffin Texts that are numbered 464 to 467 contain descriptions of travels of the dead by boat to the lakes of the afterworld where they arrived at the Field of Hetep ('Peace, Contentment').[44] In the first of the spells, the deceased addresses Hetep.

I furnish this your field, O Hetep, the field which you love … so that I may be content and mighty in it, that I may eat and drink in it, that I may plow and reap in it, that I may make love and awaken in it, and that my magic may be mighty in it.[45]

One of the following spells (CT 466) names all of the various places in the Field

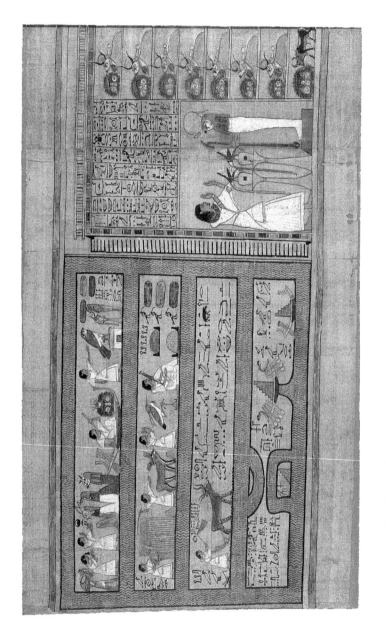

4.13: Scene of reaping in the afterworld, illustrating chapter 110 of the Book of the Dead. Sekhet-Hetepet from the Papyrus of Ani, c. 1420 BCE; ArtResource

of Hetep and makes clear that the activities of ploughing and reaping are virtually the only activities taking place in it.[46] The most complete description of the activities of the deceased in the Field of Hetep (CT 467) shows how reaping enables the dead man, as a mighty figure, to possess, to feed, and to offer other provisions to 'his people.'

I travel, I plow, and I reap for I am Hetep in the god's city … I am mighty and glorious in the Field of Hetep. I eat and travel about in it. I plow and reap in it. I make love and rest in it … BEATING PLACE. I have come into you … knowing the name of the god … When he reaps, I plow and reap … SEEING THE FIELDS, THE CITY, AND THE DISTRICTS, PLOWING AND REAPING, SEEING RE, OSIRIS AND THOTH EVERY DAY, HAVING POWER OVER THE WATERS AND THE WINDS, DOING EVERYTHING THAT ONE WANTS LIKE ONE WHO EXISTS IN THE ISLE OF THE FLAME. LIFE IS IN HIS NOSE SO THAT HE CANNOT PERISH. AS FOR THE ONE WHO IS IN THE FIELD OF HETEP, HIS PLOTS OF LAND AND HIS OFFERINGS ARE IN IT FOREVER AND EVER.[47]

The magical empowerments of these writings functioned in the context of funerary rituals and ceremonials, of which the brilliant painted frescoes of the burial chambers of the power elite were also a part.[48] The purpose of the reapers, it seems, was not to reap the deceased or to represent the taking of life, but rather the opposite: to enable the deceased to be provided with victuals. Beyond the Gate that permitted the deceased entry into the Sixth Division of Tuat, there is an illustration of five men with harvesting sickles who are followed by a second group of seven reapers armed with their sickles. The god Re declares that these men are to reap in the fields of Tuat so that the deceased will have the appropriate food and sacrificial offerings.

These are the men who have their sickles and who reap the grain in their Field. Re says to them: Take your sickles and reap your grain, for this is granted to you … your habitations and to join yourself to the Circle of Hidden Forms. Hail to you O reapers! Their food is of bread cakes and their drink is of tescher ale and their libations are made with cool water. Offerings are made to them on earth as being those who reap the grain in the Fields of the Tuat.[49]

The reaped grains are turned into loaves of bread. These, in turn, are connected with the concept of Ma'at as the governing principle in the judgment of the deceased.[50] The scenes of reaping are connected with death, but with a life-beyond-death that is different in fundamental ways from other Mediterranean and later Christian visions. It did not separate life and death by as severe a polarity, or represent it in the context of ideas of time laden with almost tangible concepts of futurity.[51] In the Sekhet-hetep or the Field of Peace, the deceased ploughs and reaps *as if* in his or her own life.[52] The reaping is not so much connected with a transition effected by a single act of violence, a sudden and dramatic deprivation of life, as it is with a mirror like imaging of two realities that are vitally and continuously linked.

Speaking and Thinking

Harvest experiences connected the repeated annual activity of reaping cereal crops, huge and all-encompassing in its overall scale but intensive in its impact on individuals, with modes of thinking. Purposive actions create conditions for the extension of concepts and ideas, but there are also common experiences imposed on the individual as conditions of living that have much the same effect. Experiences with ordinary types of illness, for example, have provoked the means by which unrelated matters could be conceived and spoken about.[53] Although not as dramatically personal as a fatal disease, the reaping of cereal crops and the use of harvesting sickles was a repeated and recurrent use of tools that had a close experiential relationship to production and value. The use of domestic instruments for the manufacture of food or clothing, for example, likewise produced a host of metaphors applied to a range of unrelated matters.[54] The widespread recursive use of a common instrument like money in the form of coinage has been argued, rightly I think, to have worked fundamental changes in modes of conceiving and speaking about other matters that had nothing to do with economic exchange, but a lot to do with more general concepts of value.[55] As an embodiment of value, money is admittedly a rather special case where the metaphoric impact on thinking is understandably particularly impressive.[56] These instances, and others, suggest that repeated actions and work tasks, and the ways in which they were involved in the larger annual cycles of daily existence, provided fertile grounds for extensions of categories of thinking and speaking.

That common experiences of agricultural workers and of peasant farmers as expressed in metaphors could find their way into the written discourses of social elites was a fact of which the latter were well aware. When Cicero remarks that metaphor or *translatio* was instituted because of the poverty of language, but that pleasure and enjoyment made its use frequent, he adds that it is well known that *even* peasants or *rustici* say that vines have produced 'gems,' that pastures are 'luxurious,' and that harvests are 'joyful.'[57] The word 'even' reflects the social prejudices of a Cicero. There are no good reasons for believing that *rustici* would have been less prone to metaphorical thinking than their superiors who self-consciously deployed the *translatio*. Quintilian notes more of this same type of behaviour:

peasant farmers speak of 'a gem' on the vines, crops that are 'thirsty' and fruits that 'are suffering.'[58] There must have been many other metaphors of this kind, not deliberately discussed as such, that were known and adopted by the literate elites of the time.[59] The high social literati thought of such expressions as popular in origin and they believed that they were derived from everyday experience in the fields. As the Ostia mosaics of the *Tomba della Mietitura* show, when the representation of reaping appeared as a specific picture, it was still embedded in a larger pattern of meaning that linked the annual tasks of production to stages of life. In the calendrical representations of the months and the seasons from Roman antiquity, the reaper and the sickle never stood alone. They were always embedded in a greater cosmic ebb and flow of cyclical movements in nature. Since real-life harvesters appeared in each village and rural region at the same time every year, and their arrival was connected with plants that were harvested at the same time each year, it made sense that the persons and their instruments were connected with the cycle of time.

Among the main iconic contexts in the Roman world in which reapers are found were illustrated calendars that symbolically pictured the months of the year or the seasons, or both in combination.[60] In their various forms, the calendrical icons encapsulated two different but interrelated traditions. On the one hand, they portrayed the annual cycle of the zodiac with its links connecting divinities, symbols, and seasons. On the other, they featured the civic ceremonial holidays of the year that marked the annual cycle of official days and agricultural activities that were celebrated by a given community.[61] A calendrical mosaic from Thysdrus in Africa, probably of fourth-century date, offers a mixture of both traditions, with civic ceremonials dominating the months from October to May, whereas the critical months of June to September are marked by seasonal themes connected with the harvest.[62] The rural *menologia* were also part of a tradition that united both elements in a single form. It is significant that the most influential agricultural handbook of late antiquity, Palladius's *Opus Agriculturae*, was organized in this same zodiacal fashion. In effect, it was a large literary *menologium*.[63] In this tradition, the symbolic figure representing summer or the month of the cereal grain harvest is shown as a lightly clothed young man holding a flaming torch, although sometimes the torch alone is represented. Both symbols highlighted the burning heat of the summer sun that incited the ripening of the cereal crops.

Season of the Sun

The heat of the sun was so identified with the growth of grain in the fields of Africa in late antiquity that the image of the summer sun and the growing crops could be used, metaphorically, to describe the rebirth of cities and their walls.[64]

4.14: Figure of June from the Codex Calendar of 354. Vindobonensis ms. 3416, f. 7 v.: Osterreichische Nationalbibliothek, Vienna in J.H. Herrmann, *Die illustrierten Handschriften und Inkunabulen in Wien* (Leipzig, 1923)

That metaphoric power remained the same in modern north Africa, where the time of reaping was often regulated by the elders of villages who set the Day of the Harvest.[65] The representation of the sun's generative warmth not only recapitulated the principal economic activity of the season and the month, but also indicated the civic celebrations that marked this point in the year. Throughout the later empire, 24 June was known as the Day of the Torches. Its special significance in Roman Africa was also official. The entire system of centuriation or land survey that extended inland from the provincial metropolis of Carthage was oriented along the lines of the rising sun as seen from the Byrsa at the point of the summer solstice.[66] The land, the place of the people on it, and the networks of production and taxation were all fitted into a formal grid pattern based on a zodiacal system governed by the sun.

In some regions, like central or northern Italy, this same day marked the time of harvest when seasonal labourers would congregate in the towns before going out to finish the reaping of the crops.[67] In most of the regions in Africa where our harvester and his gangs were reaping, the harvesting of cereal grains would have been completed by the end of June. In these places, the Day of the Torches must have been thought of as marking the end of the reaping and the successful conclusion of the harvest.[68] The 24th of June was appropriately celebrated at night by the joyous parading of torches. It has remained the same to the present day in the Maghrib, where the summer solstice is marked by the harvest in the same fashion and celebrated in the same manner: by the joyous lighting of fires.[69] The day was also tied into the great cosmic cycle of the year, and it was conventionally regarded as one of the very important turning points in it. For our purposes, for the Christian world of late antique Africa, the day was regarded as the end of the harvesting season when great assemblies of the Church could be called, and it served as a focal point in the year that could mark the beginning or the end of important cycles for sacral business.[70] Fulgentius the mythographer, writing from Carthage at the end of the fifth century, makes clear the significance of the symbols of the day.

Ceres means 'joy' in Greek. They selected her to be the goddess of grain, since where there is plentiful increase in crops, joy must also abound. They wish to see Proserpina as the crop, which is 'crawling' [i.e., pro serpens] through the earth with its roots … Her mother, Ceres, is said to search with the light of torches for her daughter who had been raped so that the Day of the Torches is dedicated to Ceres obviously for the reason that it is at this time that the crops are sought out with torches – which is to say, the heat of the sun – to be reaped with joy.[71]

The heat of the sun and the colour of the crop, its whiteness, are not written into this text from literary artifice alone, but rather from experience, just as in the modern-day Maghrib, where the growing heat of the sun sets the tempo of work as it moves towards the harvest, towards the Days of White.[72] The linking of the celebration with Demeter/Ceres and Korê/Persephone is intriguing. On the one hand, the principal festivals identified with these deities in the big urban centres of the Mediterranean were ordinarily held in either the spring or the fall, and they were usually connected with sacrifices to chthonic deities.[73] But the connection with death and the underworld could also be sought in the identification of the Day of the Torches with the end of the harvest in Africa, with the beginning of the season when the crops no longer grew. This different emphasis links the festival that Diodorus Siculus witnessed in his native land of Sicily, perhaps in his home city of Agyrium, with the one that was celebrated in Africa. Certainly from the time of the Carthaginian hegemony in the fourth century BCE, if not earlier, in both lands Demeter/Korê and Ceres/Persephone were the deities who were

4.15: Figure of Summer: mosaic from La Chebba, Tunisia.
Bardo Museum, Tunis; ArtResource

identified with the cereal grain harvest. In the vast grain-growing hinterlands of Carthage, the wealthy and fertile lands of the Bagrada River valley, the cult of the Cereres, as the two goddesses were called, became a dominant civic agrarian cult.[74] The public cult of the Roman Ceres might have been initiated at Carthage in connection with the establishment of the Caesarean colony in the mid-40s BCE. This makes good sense, given the orientation of the huge system of land survey that extended southwestward out of Carthage. By late antiquity, however, the different agrarian deities had coalesced in a general identification with the harvest and with the underworld.

The same symbolic representations and meanings were embedded in public displays of wealth by the great landowners in Africa, in whose fields the wheat and other cereal grains were grown and harvested. The urban and rural houses of the *dominus* class in Africa have produced a large proportion of all the known mosaics that feature the natural cycle of seasons and work.[75] If there was a single event and figure that the mosaics of Africa identified with the season of summer it was the harvester, armed with his sickle, labouring under the torch of the sun's heat. On a

4.16: Saturn stele from Vaga-Sicca Veneria region:
Saturn as Lord of the Four Seasons. Leglay, *SAM* 1, pl. vii.4

mosaic from Thysdrus (modern el-Jem), Tunisia, summer is represented as a reaper brandishing his sickle and carrying a sheaf of wheat.[76] There are many known variants on this theme, as we can see in the brilliant mosaic from Chebba, near Ruspe on the Tunisian coast. The theme of the seasons is also found on Saturn stelae and reliefs, such as the one from the Sicca Veneria region to the northwest of Mactaris. It features figures representing each of the four seasons – the one wielding a sickle represents summer – all under the watchful aegis of Saturn.[77] Similar associations are seen on the famous seasons and months mosaic from Saint-Romain-en-Gal on the Rhone.[78] In this monumental mosaic, as with the other seasons, summer is illustrated by its zodiacal totem: the lion. Each of the totemic animals that represented the different seasons as animal signs of the zodiac (the wild boar for winter, the bull for spring, and the panther for autumn) is mounted by a rider, as is the lion of summer, who is ridden by a cute miniature *genius* armed with his equally cute reaping sickle. The sign of the Lion reflected not just the savage heat of the summer sun under which the reapers worked, but also the sun deity himself, the prime star who moved the entire procession of the seasons.

The literary descriptions and the brief poetic captions that sometimes accompanied the illustrations of the season of summer, or the months of summer, spell out the relationship between the two temporal modes. The symbol of the sickle, for example, signalled the month of July.

> July leads the sickles through the lush green meadows.

> [Iulius educit falces per prata virecta.][79]

So depictions of the month of July feature the reaper with his sickle as symbolic of the whole season.[80] Naturally, reference to the symbol varied according to the ecology of the writer. The month of August was normally celebrated in verse for the new name that connected it with the first emperor, but sometimes it, too, was recognized for its significance in the rural economy.

> August, leaning into the task, cuts the grain with the reapers in a long battle line.

> [Augustus Cererem pronus secat agmine longo][81]

The idea pictured in these descriptions of the zodiacal cycle of the year and of the seasons is also illustrated in the reliefs of the seasons on funerary sarcophagi.

Another way in which this same symbolism was reflected in popular mass experience was in the circuit taken by the chariot-racing teams in the great hippodromes of the empire. The oval of the racing track represented the circuit of the seasons. As such it fell under the aegis of the sun and was marked by the signs of the zodiac. So it was in the circus at Carthage where the three pillars at its centre held up symbolic statues: Seia, named for the sowing of crops, Messia for reaping, and Tutulina for the guarding of the sheaves.[82] Here, too, the standard colours of the racing teams, red, blue, green, and white, were thought to be connected with the seasons, with red representing the glowing heat of the summer sun.[83] Both types of representation not only had communal importance, as did the calendars; they also had personal significance in which the movement of the zodiac or the cycle of the year was connected with the life of the individual. Through each person's spiritual death and rebirth, the interlinked spheres worked both on physical reality and on belief, as was recognized at the pinnacle of his ritual experience by the African Apuleius.[84] In this way, the community and the individual person, public and private, were knitted together into a great cosmic cycle.

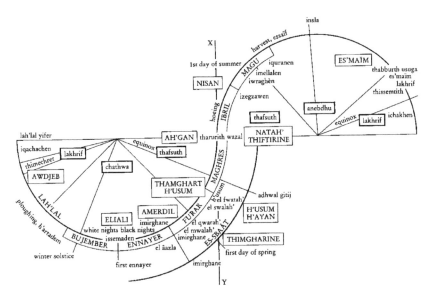

4.17: The Abstract Calendar. P. Bourdieu, *The Logic of Practice*, fig. 1, p. 203

None of this should surprise. But where does it all come from? Beyond the iterations of traditional symbols and representations, the similarities were underwritten by the observations and narrative experiences that connected the living of life from end to end in a given year, and then by having the narrative reinforced year after year. Perhaps the finest description of the process is one that is (fortunately for us) focused on a north African case: the pattern analysed by Pierre Bourdieu in his aptly entitled *Le sens pratique*.[85] By carefully observing the annual activities of the village inhabitants of the Kabylie, he saw that the actually experienced living-in-world, the *habitus*, through the different seasonal movements of the year, and the seasonal agricultural labours, formed a work-thought world in which people lived.[86] Although these concepts were constantly mutated to fit the strategies and tactics needed to live in a particular situation, the combined experiences tended to coalesce into a pattern of experiential knowledge that was represented to the villagers themselves as an annual cycle. The course of experiences, from the rural activities of ploughing and seeding at one end of the year to the cutting of the harvest at the other, produced a general schema. Its form mapped all of the most significant communal events in the year, often according to oppositions, like gender (and gendered activities, like weaving), that were parts of an overarching prospect of activities and meaning.[87] This annual cycle was then writ large, so that one year becomes the truly one Big Year, a cosmic cycle in which the small replicates the patterns existing in the large. The rituals that marked the passage through the seasonal activities of the year were mapped onto an individual life as it passed through a world of life experiences from birth, through various stages of growth, to being taken when it transited into the time of death.

The homologies of these ideas with those found in the Roman calendars that illustrated the cycle of the seasons and months with death are exact. The single best known example of an illustrated calendar that has survived from late antiquity is the so-called Codex Calendar of 354. For our purposes, it is sufficient to note that it was produced under the aegis of Furius Dionysius Filocalus, and that the single achievement for which he is most famous is his development of an impressive monumental script. Pope Damasus used this script, in the 360s, to mark the tombs of the illustrious Christian martyrs in the catacombs of the city of Rome with verse epitaphs. It was here that the martyrs watched over the Christian dead.[88] The one project was vitally connected with the other. The whole purpose of the calendar was to emplot the new Christian map of death on the traditional Roman civic calendar. The death of Christ, and the deaths and depositions of bishops and martyrs, were now set inside a traditional Roman grid of time.[89] In the illustrations for the Codex Calendar of 354, the month of June is represented by a nude figure of a youth carrying a torch, with a sickle floating, symbolically, off to his left side (see fig. 4.14).[90] Like the Day of the Torches, these other traditional symbols of the harvest season were now being filled with Christian significance.

The still-life pictures, the sculptures in the round, the decorative relief panels, and the brilliant mosaics were all part of a larger world of living rituals and beliefs. They provoked and reflected the ideas that were integral to the practices. In some of these symbolic acts the harvest was associated with ritual laments for the dead. In different parts of the Mediterranean, the laments assumed regionally peculiar forms, but at some point all of them intersected with the idea of the cycle of the seasons representing the course of life ending in death. In doing so, they also associated the real-life work of the reaping of cereal grains with the end of life.[91] This connection, however, is only part of a wide range of similitudes that are drawn between the course of life and individual humans as different types of plants that grow, bloom, and are then picked. In the modern Greek tradition, 'Men are identified with tall, strong cypress trees; women with lemon trees and orange trees. People are also equated with apple trees, vines, roses, and other flowers.'[92] In a structural sense, it could be said that the metaphor was intended to mask the differences between the two terms: human and plant life. The trope suggested, perhaps optimistically, that human lives, being reaped or plucked, are like plants that will continue to have a cycle of life after death: 'the metaphor seeks to mediate the opposition between life and death.' The assertion asks the interpreter to accept the masking function of ideology as primary. Perhaps more than mediating, the metaphor was a way of acting and thinking, of lamenting, which was, after all, the functional context in which the poems and songs are found.

In metaphors that are signalled by figural representations, the point is perhaps made in terms of belief and local agricultural practice in a series of zodiacal mosaics that decorated the main halls of synagogues in the Galilee in the age contemporary with the Maktar Harvester.[93] In these large floor mosaics, brilliant illustrations of the zodaical cycle are usually set in the centre of a larger scheme of cosmic significance. The corners of the mosaics are replete with figures of the four seasons. In the lower right corner of the mosaic from Sepphoris, modern Zippori, Israel, the figure of Summer is portrayed with a sheaf of wheat to her left and the symbol of the denticulated reaping sickle to her right. The figure is captioned so that there can be no doubt of her significance: ΘΕΡΙΝΗ ΤΡΟΠΗ (Season of Summer = HEAT) in Greek to the left between the sickle and the hoe, and *Tequfat Tammuz* (Season of Tammuz = SUMMER) to the right below the sheaf.[94] The significance of Summer as the heat that scorched the earth and brought the crops to the point of death where they were reaped was placed inside the larger zodiacal cycle of meaning. This was the time of Tammuz, a time whose special significance in these arid lands was marked in Babylonian ritual as a time of mourning. The summer solstitium was celebrated with a six-day-long funeral for the god that was marked by the singing and chanting of funerary dirges and laments. The death of the god was also marked by torchlight processions. Similarly, everywhere in Jewish and Christian sacred iconography, the pictures represent the harvester and his reaping tools as both the reality of the harvesting operations of the year and the violent end of life. If the religious significance of this repetition was represented zodiacally in the form of a perfect circle, the ecological cyclicality on which it was based is perhaps better pictured by the unending wave patterns suggested by Bourdieu's diagramming of the cycle of Kabyle agricultural life.

The metaphors and images were therefore connected with the ritual funerary dirges sung by the harvesters as they cut the last life from the final sheaves that they reaped.[95] As the reaper made the final swing of his sickle and the last sheaf fell to the ground, he sang a lament. One of these harvest dirges was connected with the story of a man named Lityerses, who was sometimes claimed to have been one of the illegitimate sons of King Midas of Phrygia. Lityerses was renowned as a strong and violent reaper. By repute, he was a big man armed with an equally heroic appetite. He had only one bad habit. As part of his annual task of reaping the fields near the Meander river, Lityerses would force any man who happened to pass close to his fields to join him in taking off the crops. When the reaping was completed, Lityerses would tie the stranger into the last of the sheaves and decapitate the man with his harvester's sickle. He would then throw the headless

4.18: The zodiac from the Synagogue Mosaic at Sepphoris, Israel; permission courtesy of Professor Ze'ev Weiss and the Sepphoris Excavations; drawing Pnina Arad

4.19: Summer and the sickle from the Synagogue Mosaic at Sepphoris, Israel; permission courtesy of Professor Ze'ev Weiss and the Sepphoris Excavations; photograph Gabi Laron

body of the poor victim into the nearby river.[96] Lityerses' bad behaviour was later interpreted as a ritual, a sacrifice performed by him to ensure a good harvest in the following year.[97] The metaphors implicit in this story – SHEAF IS A HUMAN BEING // SHEAF IS A LIFE // REAPING IS TAKING LIFE // REAPING IS BRINGING DEATH // THE REAPER IS A BRINGER OF DEATH – were basic ones found in most Mediterranean lands, although with important cultural variations.

Just as significant as the violence was the fact that the word *lityerses* was used to designate a traditional harvester's song, one that was both violent and threnodic in tone.[98] Lityerses finally met his come-uppance when a stranger who wandered by during one of the harvest seasons happened to be none other than Herakles. When the day of reaping was finished, and Lityerses attempted his old trick, Herakles bound Lityerses into a sheaf and decapitated the savage harvester with the very sickle that Herakles had been given by his murderous host.[99] Theocritus repeats what he claimed to be a version of the Lityerses song. He notes that to keep the rhythmic chanting of the harvesters in synchrony with the swinging of their sickles, a girl flautist played for them while they worked and sang.[100] Athenaeus comments on the song in a long passage on various kinds of work songs where he notes that 'the song of the reapers is called Lityerses,' and he connects it to another type of song 'sung by hired workers who laboured in the fields.'[101] The dirge recalled the association with violence and death in a prefigured rhythmic pattern. These dirges, sung by reapers, remembered disappearance and loss. The reapers in Bithynia were said to have chanted a song called the Bormos or Borimos. Bormos was reputed to have been a handsome young man of royal lineage who, one hot summer day, while he watched the reapers labouring in the fields, brought water to them to drink and then went away and was never seen again. Reapers, so it was said, are searching for him, chanting his name as they advance through the fields.[102]

Death Song

Songs and dirges like this are somehow linked to stories and songs connected with a plaintive youth named Linos.[103] Which is interesting, since 'the Linos' appears in close connection with the reaping scene on the Shield of Achilles with which we began our investigation. The verbal picture of the grain harvest is immediately followed by one of the vintage.[104] There is nothing unusual in this. The same sequencing is found in many such evocative passages, including the Book of Revelation. It is in this sequence of harvesting that Linos makes his appearance.

> Next Hephaistos placed on it a vineyard heavily laden
> with bunches of grapes in resplendent gold, the grapes dark purple,
> the orchard laid out with silver poles rising through the vines.
> Around it he fashioned a ditch of bluish enamel and
> around that a fence of tin – a single path led in where
> the grape pickers went in and out at harvest time.
> In childish joy, young girls and boys carry off
> the honey sweet crop in their wicker baskets.
> In the middle of them all, a young boy plays beautifully on his
> singing lyre and in his delicate fine voice he sings
> the lovely Linos song. His companions keep time,
> beating the ground together, leaping, shouting and dancing.

Both the picture and the metaphors inherent in it bring us back to a creative strand in poetics that constantly drew on these ideas. But in a later and different epoch, the deliberative and creative spirit was not drawn to these similitudes. The shield that is forged by Vulcan for the Roman hero Aeneas as described by the

4.20: Harvesters marching on a Minoan vase. Archaeological Museum,
Herakleion, Crete; ArtResource

poet Vergil contains no such mundane points of reference to the work of daily life.
Instead, high-flown historical and symbolic analogies drawn from the traditions of
the political elite are redrawn for their benefit.[105]

The connections between reaping and rhythmic chanting and, as in the
Homeric harvesting scene, beating the ground with feet in time, accompanied
by the flute and other instruments, had a long history. On the famous Harvester
Vase of Minoan vintage, the harvesters, carrying their haying forks, can be seen
marching in line, with at least one of them portrayed in the act of singing or
chanting. The harvesters are divided into two groups. They follow each other
in sequence, with each group headed by an elaborately costumed gang leader. A
group of fourteen men in the back of the line are led by three singers or chant-
ers, one of whom is shaking a sistrum to keep time, while the remaining eight
harvesters in front of them are escorted by their leader as if in a parade.[106] A musi-

4.21: Hoplites marching in formation on the Chigi Vase, c. 650 BCE, Protocorinthian vase. Museo Nazionale Etrusco di Villa Giulia, Rome; ArtResource

cal instrument – either a percussion instrument like a drum or tambourine, or a wind instrument like a flute – was used to keep the rhythmic time of the work, just as the playing of the flautist in the canonical picture of hoplites on the Chigi Vase kept the march time of the phalanx in order. Marching in rhythm to a musical beat points to another analogue between the work of reaping and marching in battle. The same behaviour is also found in the organization of traditional agricultural labour in the modern-day Maghrib. As expected, the social practice is rapidly fading before the impact of machines and the modernization of media.[107] One of the most important features of these field songs is not their lyrical content or their narrative lines. It is the distinctive sequences of words that are matched to rhythms so that the reapers can vary the beat with their work by drawing on different sets of lines or by improvising on set ones as the mode of the different work tasks requires. As important yet are the connections between the work regimen and belief.

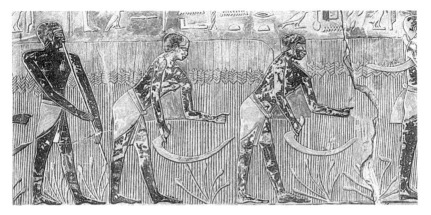

4.22: Flute-player timing the reapers: tomb of the Vizier Mereruka, Chamber A.13: East Wall Scene 2; c. 2300 BCE, Saqqara, Egypt. *The Mastaba of Mereruka by the Sakkarah Expedition*, vol. 2 (Chicago: University of Chicago Press, 1938), pl. 169; permission courtesy of the Oriental Institute, University of Chicago

These songs are very advantageous because they induce a trance-like effect in the workers and help them to endure and to speed along the hard work. This effect can be explained in many ways. First, many verses in these songs are religious, and since religion is one of the main sources of relief in Moroccan society, the worker derives great confidence and courage from anything related to religion. Second, the songs are very rhythmical and by superimposing this rhythm on that of the monotonous work, the harvester becomes intoxicated and forgets about the hardship. Third, given the dual structure of the songs – each verse is made up of two inseparable halves, each sung by a group – each worker has to follow the singing attentively in order to think of the suitable half of the verse in time.[108]

That is to say, they work according to a dyadic system of call and response. Each set of chants and songs is different, modulated according to the different aspects of harvest work, whether that of reaping (trochaic shouts), threshing (rhymed couplets urging animals along), or winnowing.

The rhythmic organization of work, whether of war or of reaping, is, of course, far more ancient than the world of the Maktar Harvester. In a funerary painting from the tomb of an Old Kingdom noble, the vizier Mereruka, at Saqqara in Egypt, we see a line of reapers working in rhythm. They are accompanied at the end of their line by a man playing a long flute who is keeping them in time.[109] These were the same ways that order and direction were maintained in the fields

4.23: Reaper clapping hands in rhythm with the work: tomb of the Vizier Mereruka, Chamber A.13: East Wall Scene 2; c. 2300 BCE, Saqqara, Egypt. *The Mastaba of Mereruka by the Sakkarah Expedition*, vol. 2 (Chicago: University of Chicago Press, 1938), pl. 169; permission courtesy of the Oriental Institute, University of Chicago

of late antique Africa in the age of the Maktar Harvester. Perhaps his choice of verse as the mode with which to celebrate his own life had more than just the provocation of high culture. Augustine says as much of harvesters in his own day when he speaks of the 'strange rhythmic chants of the workers in the fields.' It is this chanting that reminded and provided him with an image of the fullness of the vision of God: 'So men who sing like this – in the harvest ... or in any task that wholly absorbs them – may begin by showing their contentment with songs in words. But soon they become filled with such a joy that they can no longer express it in mere words. And so, leaving aside regular syllables, they strike up a wordless chant of jubilation.'[110] That sort of jubilation is also seen in the colourful reliefs from the mastaba of Mereruka at Saqqara. In the same line of reapers timed by the flute-player is a man clapping his hands in rhythm with the work. Many types of rural labour elicited the same sing-song response in late antiquity, according to Christian versions of them: 'the ploughman guiding the handle of his plough sings an alleluia, the sweating harvester calls out with the psalms, and, wielding his hooked pruning knife and trimming the vine, the worker in the vineyard sings something Davidic.'[111] These songs were presented as Christian analogues of existing reaping rituals.

Harvest of Death

Raucous voices shouting out in unison hint at elements of strife and violence. The rhythmic shouts of the workers and the exhortations by martial-like field leaders were needed because reaping sometimes developed into a competition that was likened to the conflict of battle. The other harvest scene described in Homer is also linked to a war shield, the shield carried by Hektor, and it vividly reflects this strife.

> In the front ranks, Hektor carried his perfectly shaped shield,
> and just as the Dog Star blazes out from behind the clouds
> with its brilliant light, then fades again behind the shadowing haze,
> so Hektor would sometimes be shining in the front ranks,
> and sometimes would be shouting orders to men in the rear. All in bronze,
> he flashed like the thunderbolt of Father Zeus, the Aegis Bearer.
> And the men, like lines of reapers working for some great man
> who, facing each other, cut their way through swaths
> of wheat or barley, and the cut sheaves fall in lines,
> so the Trojans and Akhaians, driving in against one another,
> cut men down, neither of them giving a thought to disastrous panic.[112]

The reference to the reapers working for some great man evokes the earlier scene of harvest in Homer with which we began, but here its martial dimensions are filled out for the listener. The metaphor forges the link between the work of the reaper and the work of the warrior, as men, bloodied and mortally wounded, fall and tumble like cut sheaves in a harvest field. The same metaphor was used by Catullus in his mini-epic of the marriage of Peleus and Thetis, and the future life of their son Achilles. Here the imagery of the reaper signals the ending of life with blood and violence.

> For just as the reaper cutting the dense sheaves
> under the burning sun reaps the golden fields,
> he [Achilles] will cut down the bodies of the
> Trojan born with his harmful steel.[113]

We have already seen the way in which Richard Jefferies reported the advent of the harvest in nineteenth-century England: 'The next day the village sent forth its army with their crooked weapons to cut and slay.'[114] The metaphor works with what I would call a mirror-like replication that permitted a ready transition from one image and idea to the other and then back again: REAPING = WAR = REAPING. Not just peasants, but aristocratic elites, modern as well as ancient, were well acquainted with the metaphor and used it, just as when Field Marshal Erich von Manstein helped put together the plan for the great sweeping movement of Blitzkrieg that was, in the spring of 1940, to cut through the defences of France – a plan nicknamed *Der Sichelschnitt*: the Cut of the Sickle.[115]

4.24: Mathew Brady: 'The Harvest of Death' at Gettsyburg, July 1863.
Library of Congress, Public Access: LC-B8184-7964-A

This flip-flop device produced imagery of great antiquity. It could be reversed one way or the other and exploited to picture vividly either human action. In Sumer, the god Ninurta waded into combat 'reaping like grain the necks of the insubordinate.' And the Old Babylonian god Papulegarra was sung of as 'the harvester in battle.'[116] We find the same common motif of a violent harvest of men shared by Zeus in Greek lands and by Saturn in Roman Africa. All of these supremely potent gods regulate the final harvest of men, a harvest that will be bloody. Just as the blade cuts sheaves of wheat, so men cut each other down under his aegis.

> When there is battle, men suddenly have their fill of it, for
> although the bronze blade scatters straw on the ground in abundance,
> what is reaped is very little when Zeus tilts his balance to war,
> Zeus, the dispenser of men in combat.[117]

So too, the machinery of war was sometimes connected with the reality of reaping tools, as warriors stood in their dangerous scythe-mounted chariots, lopping off limbs as they drove their way through the carnage of battle.[118] Employing a technical innovation, they too reaped another bloody harvest. The connection between mowing and being mown down in battle is not incompatible with modernity. It is just that the mower's scythe has been replaced by the machine gun, as when, in 1893, in the Matabele War, in what is now Zimbabwe, British forces used their new Maxim guns against the Ndebele. As reported by Gordon Rattray, one of the gunners, the Ndebele rebels 'were mown down just as if with a scythe.'[119] No doubt, Gordon Rattray, raised in later nineteenth-century Surrey, could have been recollecting the 'as if' from some real-life experience. Or, as when British troops went over the top at the Somme, to be witnessed by a lance corporal who watched his friends 'mown down like meadow grass.'[120]

The Regal Reaper

If the ordinary human reaper personified a sense of power and violence, it is hardly surprising that these same traits were also embodied in a supreme deity. And if this powerful image was available, one would expect it to be mapped onto the image of the ruler: the king or monarch who was responsible for the full granaries of his land and who wielded the cutting force of the armed might of his army. This mapping is found in the cases of many ancient Near Eastern states. In pharaonic Egypt, there are descriptions and images of the pharaoh as a reaper. But for the great dominant figures of democratic Greek city states, for the big men of the late Roman Republic, or even for the autocratic emperors of the Principate and Dominate, this was not so.[121] Well, almost not. We might consider an impressive relief of the Roman emperor Caracalla. Appearing to contradict our rule of thumb, it appears on the wall of the impressive Ptolemaic temple at Esna (ancient Ta-Senet, Graeco-Roman Latopolis) located about fifty miles south of Luxor. The contradiction, however, is only apparent. The depiction of the emperor as a reaper exploits a peculiar regional significance of cutting cereal crops in framing the emperor of Rome within a local political ideology and iconography. It is this that explains the unusual translation of the Roman Caracalla into a Pharaonic reaper.

What this representation of Caracalla as reaper does *not* explain is why this mapping does not occur elsewhere. As far as I can determine, nowhere in numerous relief depictions of the Roman emperor in other places of the empire or on the mass production of the coinage meant to celebrate his image does this same identification occur. Apparent cross-identifications do sometimes happen, but care must be taken to understand that they are not direct harvesting metaphors. A coin, an antoninianus of Valerian, for example, portrays the emperor with a radiate crown on the obverse and the god Saturn wielding an Italian-style long-handled sickle on the reverse.[122] In these icons, the identification has less to do with reaping or with suggesting that the ruler is a reaper than it does with an identification of the ruler

4.25: The Emperor Caracalla as a reaper: temple at Esna, Upper Egypt. Hölbl, *Altägypten im Römischen Reich*, fig. 1, p. 4; permission courtesy of Dr Günther Hölbl

4.26: Coin of Caracalla: four youths as the seasons, Summer wielding a sickle. ANS 1944.100.51405.rev; permission courtesy of the American Numismatic Society, New York

with a god who brandishes a sickle as one of his attributes. In this case, the identification is with Saturn, who represents the theme advertised in the legend on the obverse of the coin: the *Aeternitas Augustorum*, the Eternity of the Emperors.[123] Similarly, a coin of Caracalla featuring a sickle hints at the broader theme of time and not specifically that of reaping. The obverse of this coin features a laureate head of the emperor, and the reverse a series of four youths, one of whom wields a sickle, who represent the cycle of the seasons. The youths also illustrate the main theme of the legend that is explicitly spelled out on the obverse: *Felicia Tempora*. These were Happy Times.[124]

The role of the emperor as a war leader, a function expected of him, might have led to this type of iconographic representation since, in both antiquity and more modern times, there has been a thematic comparison of harvest workers and warriors. Grain harvesters in nineteenth-century East Anglia, armed with the new scythe, were said to be engaged in 'a quasi military operation ... an attack to beat an ancient enemy: the weather.' In the previous century, the Netherlandish poet Lucas Rotgans said of mowers that they were 'Westphalian heroes who wield the scythe like a spear; grass knights, intrepidly swinging their arms.'[125] From these images, one might expect a near-automatic and natural transference of the imagery to the king. But the mapping of the figure of the reaper onto that of the ruler was culturally limited and determined. Even in the great Near Eastern monarchies of Pharaonic Egypt and Mesopotamia, the image, where it is used, is greatly inferior to other dominant metaphors for rulership, such as THE KING IS A SHEPHERD, THE THE KING IS A GREAT HUNTER, or even THE KING IS A GREAT BUILDER. Which is to say that even where the agricultural cycle was so pronounced, intense, concentrated, and direct as it was in these great riverine civilizations, the identification of the monarch with such a hard quotidian labour activity as taking in the harvest was still cast in a minor key.

The more common transfer by far was among less exalted persons, and it appealed neither to the image of the warrior nor to the good farmer, but to the common everyday experience of dying. The connections with death and disappearance are surely not accidental. Rather, they have a ritual significance grounded, as Sir James Frazer and Ernesto de Martino saw, in human ecology and social behaviour. With the harshness of cutting off life and the end of the season of growth, the harvest signalled death and acts of violence: cutting, shearing, beating, and locking away. We are told that reapers in Egypt struck their breasts and sang laments over the first sheaf of grain that they cut down with their sickles, calling on the goddess Isis and thanking her for the earth's bounty.[126] The taking of life was sometimes seen so literally that the stalks of grain being reaped bled red blood, as in the prodigy reported by Livy of the reapers at Antium who had bleeding stalks of grain fall into the harvesters' transport baskets.[127] The scene of reapers singing a lament and reaping blood returns us to the primal evidence of Homer. The continuation of the grain harvesting scene to which I referred at the beginning of this book features a second harvesting scene: that of the vintage. In the midst of the harvesters, as we have seen, 'a young boy plays beautifully on his singing lyre and in his delicate fine voice he sings the lovely Linos song,' a song which was almost certainly the dirge identified with death in later sources.[128] The matter is complex and double-edged. Linos sang a song that was happy and joyous, and which was associated with the dances danced at the completion of harvest, but it was also sad and mournful, since the last of the living crops had been cut and the deathliness of the winter season was at hand.

Christian Death

For many Africans in the age of the Maktar Harvester, specifically for the Christians of the time, the same metaphoric connection was at the heart of their thinking. Mental pictures of harvesting and its connections with death were found throughout their sacred writings and were expounded upon by their preachers. The images were heavily conditioned by the oral stories told by Jesus to the crowds of listeners who gathered by the shores of Lake Kinneret. He was attempting to explain the future Kingdom of Heaven to them in terms that they would understand. When he first attempted to tell the story to the people who had come to hear him, the crowds became so large and pressing that (so it is said) he had to get into a boat and move a little offshore to get away from the crush of humanity and to make himself heard. Understandably, for a rural society, his stories concerned sowing and reaping. There were several of them, of which the following one is particularly significant.

The kingdom of heaven is like a man who sowed good seed in his field. But while everyone was asleep, his enemy came and sowed weeds through the wheat, and then went away. When the new wheat had sprouted and began to ripen, the weeds also appeared. The farmer's slaves went to their master and said: 'Lord, didn't you sow good seed in the field? So where have all these weeds come from?' 'Some hostile person has done this,' he replied. 'Well then,' the slaves said to him, 'in that case do you want us to go to pull out the weeds?' 'No,' he answered, 'in pulling out the weeds you might pull out the wheat at the same time. Let them grow together until the harvest. At harvest time I will tell the reapers: "Pull out the weeds first and tie them in bundles to be burned. Then collect the wheat and put it in my granary."'[129]

From their everyday experience with agricultural work, the people in the crowd listening might well have understood what he was saying. Some of his students, however, were said to have been confused. What did he mean? They demanded an explanation and he gave it.

The sower of the good seed is the son of man. The field is the world. The good seed stands for the sons of the kingdom. The weeds for the sons of the evil-doer. The enemy who sowed the weeds is the Devil. The harvest is the end of time. The reapers are the angels. The gathering up and burning of the weeds in the fire will be at the end of time. The son of man will dispatch his angels, who will take out of his kingdom all snares and those things creating disorder, and these will be thrown into the blazing furnace. At that time, there will be wailing and grinding of teeth. And then the just will shine like the sun in the kingdom of their father. If you have ears, then listen.[130]

A selection of images such as those cited over the whole first part of this chapter can be assembled from the entire range of Greek and Latin writings from antiquity. They are sufficient to show that there was a general cognizance of the trope, and that it was accessed now and then by poets and writers in both languages, most often by those who wished to evoke bucolic fantasies. Otherwise, they were rare things. Only when the tradition of the Jesus stories and the explications of his students reached their acme in late antiquity, with the advent of the Christian priest and bishop as preacher, did the metaphoric connections with reaping become common in written sources. It is the Christian writers and sermonizers who constantly gloss the significance of reaping for their readers and listeners. Among the many thousands of such uses, we might consider the following passage from the letter of Paulinus of Nola to Sulpicius Severus as typical.

For you are the field to Him [the Lord] who, in turn, is the field for us. For we sow our seed in Him and we are reaped by Him. You are certainly the field – and not one with horrid spiny growths, or dry with sandy soil, or barren and hard with rocks, in which seed once it has been sown either withers away or is neglected or burns up in the heat. Rather you are that one *which God blessed with the dew of the sky and the richness of the earth* [cf. Mt. 13:4–7; Gn. 27:28]. Your tongue is whetted with the Word of God, and your heart with God's abundance, and your seed multiplies with spiritual growth, so that from your fruits *the harvester fills his hand and collects the cut sheaves in his lap* [cf. Ps. 128 (129):7]. That is to say, God Himself, whose Word is in us, is both our sower and our reaper: it is God Himself and his right hand, which hand we fill with our good works. Likewise, the lap is the bosom of Abraham, in which we shall rest as the pay for our hard work.[131]

Reaping as death and the rewards of harvest labour as a final repose in the bosom of Abraham: this was the harvest scene that was being fixed in the mind of every Christian believer. A strong connection was being struck between a text that reflected the tropes of everyday life and which connected the preacher's words with the daily experiences of the person hearing them. The message systematically connected this life as a field, one's life as a growth, and one's coming death, God's reaping, to expectations of a divine payback. This much was sufficiently clear to all who heard the message because it extended the elements of the harvesting process, including the hiring of reapers for pay, to produce the image of another thing.[132] When his students asked: 'Rabbi, do we have something to eat?' they were faced with the following reply from Jesus:

Do you not have a saying: 'Four months and then the harvest'? Well, I tell you: Look around you, look at the fields: already they are white, ready to be reaped. Already the reaper is being paid his wages, already he is bringing in the grain for eternal life, and so the sower and the reaper will rejoice together. For here the saying is true: one sows, another reaps. I sent you to reap a harvest that you had not worked for. Others worked for it, and you will come into the rewards of their hard work.[133]

In his reply to the question, the experiential elements of the harvest, some of them encapsulated in popular sayings, are replayed and extended as a figure for the forthcoming reaping of humans and the storage of these persons in which they will reap the rewards of a new and eternal life.

Apocalyptic Expectations

Some of the reactions of the living to death were personal passions – ritualistic displays of grief. But others were more aggressive and violent: protesting and striking out against loss. Images of the reaper connected the anger and the violence. For the purpose of understanding harvest violence in late antique Africa in the age of the Maktar Harvester, we might begin with the words of the writer of the Apocalypse, a core text of African Christianity provided with magnificent commentaries by the greatest African exegetes, from Tyconius to Primasius.

Then, as I looked, there appeared a white cloud and on the cloud sat one like the Son of Man. He had on his head a crown of gold and in his hand a sharp sickle. Another angel came out of the temple and cried out in a loud voice to him who sat on the cloud: 'Stretch out your sickle and begin reaping. For the harvest time has come and the crop of the earth is overripe.' So he who sat on the cloud put his sickle to the earth and its harvest was reaped.[134]

The author of the Apocalypse of John goes on to consider other harvests, including the vintage, in which the harvesting angel throws the grapes into the great winepress of God's wrath and human blood flows from the press to a distance of two hundred miles round about.[135] He was not the only one to revel in this gory vision. As one of the most effective of metaphors, it was repeatedly emphasized by a whole range of Christian writers of late antiquity that the harvest signalled the End of the Age or the End of Time, in which the violence of reaping was to have a special place. This was particularly true of African Christian writers like Tyconius and Augustine who lived in the age of our harvester, as well as others who wrote immediately afterwards, like Primasius in his monumental commentary on the Apocalypse.[136] In his vivid replaying of the End of Time, Primasius reruns the picture of the angels as the Harvesters of the Lord who will come with their sharp sickles to ply the ripe stalks of humanity. He sees Christ as crowned, seated on the white cloud, menacing, and armed with the grain harvester's sickle.[137] These more forceful visions of the Apocalypse had been prefigured, as when Jerome glossed the process of metaphor in his commentary on the Book of Isaiah:

... those grains bursting forth before maturity perish quickly, and those which come before the completion of time are useless growths. Thus, he said, as useless branches the Egyptian peoples are cut off with sickles [i.e., pruning blades] and all the plantings will be laid bare. And you should not think that he is speaking about vines and not about men, but he is turning the metaphor to the truth of history.[138]

Elsewhere he spelled out the nature of the equivalencies as they were to be understood by the reader or the listener.

And in reply He said: The one who sows the good seed is the Son of Man. He [Jesus] sets out his argument very clearly: the field is the world, the sower is the son of man, the good seed are the sons of the kingdom, the weeds are the evil sons [i.e., the worst possible ones], the sower of the weeds is the Devil, the harvest is the end of the world, the reapers are the angels.[139]

But the sudden appearance or manifestation of the divine, a parousia that was threatening – a terrible being demanding retribution – was not something entirely new. Divine arrivals had often been signalled by just such instruments of the harvest. The wonderworker Alexander of Abonoteichos arose in the later part of the second century CE in remote Paphlagonia. He staged his first appearance: 'wearing his hair long in a cascade of curls, he donned a purple tunic with a white band in the middle and he put a shining cloak over it. And he wielded a sickle, like that of Perseus, from whom he claimed descent on his mother's side.'[140] Alexander knew how to present himself because the picture of how such a figure was to appear was already a common thing in his world.

The image of an angry and avenging deity armed with a sickle or similar cutting blade, so vividly envisaged by the author of the Apocalypse, and assumed by the writers of the Sibylline oracles, would not have struck Africans, like our man from Mactaris, as at all unusual, even if they were not Christians. The supreme deity of traditional pre-Christian cult in Africa, the god Saturn, was frequently pictured in just this manner: armed with a sickle or a reaping hook.[141] One of the god's most common epithets was *falcifer*: 'he who wields the sickle.' No less than the Christian god of the Apocalypse, Saturn was a stern and vengeful deity who demanded living sacrifices. In our later age, the sacrifices were lambs who substituted as vicars for human beings, some of whom – actual living humans, that is – were still being sacrificed to the savage god in the age of Tertullian at the end of the second century[142] The African Saturn had also come to be identified with the Greek *Urgott* Kronos, who consumed his own children, and by a similarity of the sound of the name, with the concept deity of Chronos or Time. And Kronos was also linked to the practice of ritual human sacrifice.[143] In this dual identification, Saturn appeared as the Lord of the Seasons, the deity overseeing the progression of the zodiac. This identity, in turn, was connected with the special place that this same deity had in the season of harvesting in Africa, which was connected with

4.27: Saturn stele from Nicivibus, Algeria: the vicarious sacrifice.
Leglay, *SAM* 2, pl. xxxi.2

the intensity of ritual practice and the focus of devotion, and therefore thinking.[144]

The parallels might excite speculation on the nature of Saturn's wielding of the harvester's sickle.[145] Who was reaping what? 'Some think that the sickle is given to him because Time reaps, severs, and then cuts short everything.'[146] This draws our attention back to the sharp instrument itself. The cutting tool of reaping, the sickle, was so thoroughly indentified with particular divine actions and deities, and so borne along in various types of mythos, that its shape and function could be seen as written in the landscape. By a further metaphoric shift, the sickle – the *drepanon* or *falx* – could be transferred from its mental container in a story about the creation of the world order to various specific places in the Mediterranean that *looked as if* they were embodiments of the instrument, and therefore places identified with Kronos. These successive places, as they move in Greek forms of designation from east to west across the middle sea, have been argued to be fossil tracers, as it were, of the real movements of peoples as they travelled from east to

west, and back, over the same waters for commerce, agriculture, and war.[147] The
basic concepts underlying both Saturn and his cutting instrument were themselves readily transferrable to a new and different system of belief that had an
analogous relationship to reaping and death.

A similar matrix of ideas that embedded the cutting of crops in a larger symbolic system of cosmic meaning is found in the African bishop Cyprian's letter
addressed in 250 CE to priests and confessors held in prison at Carthage. They
were defendants who had been caught up in the dragnet initiated by the emperor
Decius. To sense the larger frame of Cyprian's interpretation, consider the passage in which he lays down the foundation of its meaning in a letter addressed to
martyrs in prison at Carthage.

Now let the magistrates parade forth, the consuls and the proconsuls, let them pride themselves in the regalia of their annual office and their twelve bundles of rods. Be assured that
in your own case, your heavenly office has been invested with all the brilliance of a year's
honours. And already, by the long continuance of its victorious glory, the year has traversed
beyond the revolution of the annual cycle ... Winter passed by with the changing months,
but imprisoned as you all were, you exchanged the season of winter for the winter of perse-
cution. Winter was succeeded by the mildness of spring, glad with roses and crowned with
flowers, but as for you, you have the roses and blossoms from the delights of paradise and
heavenly wreaths have crowned your heads. And then summer came, fertile with its abundant harvests and the threshing floor was filled with the reaped crops, but you who have
sown glory have reaped a harvest of glory. Standing, as you now do, on the threshing floor of
the Lord, you can witness the chaff being burned in unquenchable fire while you yourself,
already inspected and stored like the winnowed wheat and the valuable grain, can regard
your residence in prison as your granary. In autumn, too, for discharging these seasonal
tasks, spiritual grace does not fail you. Outside, the vintage is being pressed and the grape,
later to be drunk in cups, is being extorted by heavy screw presses. Likewise you, like the
rich clusters of the Lord's vineyard, bunches of fruit now ripe, are being pressed under the
violence of the pressures of this world. Prison is our wine press. You feel its crushing force as
it contorts you, but instead of wine it is your blood that pours forth. Courageous in the face
of the suffering you must endure, you freely drain the cup of martyrdom. Such is the cycle of
the year for the slaves of God. Such are the spiritual merits and heavenly rewards for which
the changing seasons are made famous.[148]

What Cyprian offers is a cosmic interpretation of the zodiacal revolution of the
seasons. He places Christian men and women in prison and condemned to death
in counterpoint to the consuls and magistrates who inaugurated the beginning of
the New Year in Rome and vicariously, through their ritual action, in the municipalities of the empire. At the centre of this agricultural year is the reaping of the
crops, the burning of the chaff, the valuation of the worth of the grain, and its

storage in granaries. The seasonal shifts within the zodiacal cycle, the agricultural tasks associated with them, and the standard imagery used for them were now reoriented by Christian exegetes to a new cosmic system in which death signalled a new meaning of the reborn life that will come from the grain that has been reaped and the wine that has been pressed. This was not just a series of metaphorical figures, but a new symbolic system that bore a conclusive message to the men and women who were awaiting imminent death in a dark prison.

Birth, growth, death, and the great seasonal cycle of nature, in which real day-to-day reapers were involved, set the context for interpretation and the extension of meaning. The identification of the harvester with a god or part-god, a hero, was pervasive. With this extension, there was an overlap with the salvation of body parts and even the whole corpse. At least part of this phenomenon also went back to real in-the-field experiences. If the figure of the harvester was thought to be sufficient to represent the sufferings of back and leg pains, there was probably more to the magical amulets that were meant to ward off the worst effects of such afflictions (see figs. 1.9 and 1.10). It has been argued that the figure of the reaper represented on the amulets, as with other apotropaic divinities found on other amulets, must be a powerful god who is identified with these afflictions and that this deity is none other than Kronos.[149] The case seems convincing. But the argument does not refute the idea that the figure on the amulet is also a human reaper doing double duty in a complex metaphoric representation. The equations are triangulated between a human reality (the reaper), the divine power (Kronos), and ordinary human suffering. The amulets are most heavily documented in Roman Egypt, but they are found throughout the Roman world, including Gaul. Indeed, they have been found in the very area, the lands of the Mediomatrici along the Meuse, that was the northern region noted for the celebration of the use of the scythe and the Gallic harvesting machine.[150]

On the one hand, the harvest was a symbol of good and plenty; on the other, it was associated with feelings of sorrow and loss. In post-Roman Europe the figure of death assumed various forms. In sixteenth-century Europe, it has been argued, 'the harvest had become a symbol of death and destruction,' and the dominant picture that emerged was that of the evil harvester.[151] It is further asserted that it was in this same age that the figure of Death came to be pictured with a scythe rather than a noble spear. The final harvester had come to be associated with the threatening figure of the violent peasant.[152] Both ideas, even if they bear a partial truth for this specific time and age, are in need of serious modification. There had been occasional shifts in the grain harvest from the sickle to the scythe in real practice. In particular, we have seen this effect in the aftermath of the Black Death, and the effect was therefore reflected in both representation and in metaphor.[153] But a general shift of this nature is at best a debatable proposition. The shift was much less from a spear than simply from the less powerful sickle to the more powerful scythe: from an instrument that was gendered male and female, to one that was resolutely more virile. This did not have much to do with any special or novel connection with a new apparition of threatening peasants. The figure of the harvester as a messenger of death was not new at all, but part of a continuity or, at least, a consistent association of ideas and symbols. The mental connection with violent rural men who were seen as particularly threatening was not new either. All of these concepts were connected with back-and-forth shifts in technology – but within limits. It is not only with humorous point that Mr Eddie Izzard has suggested that in our day the Grim Reaper ought to be armed not with a scythe but with a lawnmower.[154]

All of these convergences point to changing interpretations of the same labour process by those who contemplate it. Within these changes, it is perhaps easy to forget that Pieter Bruegel's *The Harvest* was part of a larger unified work of six pieces, each of which reflected a particular time of the year. The whole was therefore connected to existing representations of the agrarian cycle and a calendrical tradition that extended far back in time before Bruegel's early modern period through high and low medievalism back to Graeco-Roman antiquity. Of course, modern interpreters and spectators can concentrate on the painting *The Harvest* as such. They need not be drawn into the larger metaphor of life and death, but rather they can be attracted to the dominant individual of the resting reaper as a figure embodying a kind of work, repose, and a satisfying rest: an image of personal and private well-being.[155] Bruegel's paintings, and especially those akin to them that followed later in the long nineteenth century, tended to evoke a more 'realistic' picture of rural life in peasant Europe of the time. The figure of the reaper was more closely attached to the then current fascinations (one might even say romantic ideals) with farming not as a symbol of an annual cycle of necessary production that was a battle against lethal threats, but as a reflection of life, with all of its attendant hardships to be sure, but at least of life.

Until the end of antiquity, however, the reaper bearing his sickle, taking in the harvest, remained an avatar of death, a grim metaphor. In the Byzantine lives or sacred biographies of the holy man Ioannikos by Sabas and Peter, when the harvester wielded his sickle the hour of the harvest, the *therous hora*, had come. It was a way in which the death of the saint was predicted.[156] There was always a potentially darker side to the men who did the reaping. The continuity in basic economic forms ensured that the fundamental metaphors survived cultural transitions, even severe ones, from the late Byzantine to the early Arabic Maghrib for example. In the local premodern lore of the Maghrib, the image of the harvester was sometimes assimilated to that of the Holy Warrior: 'All harvesters are considered especially pure because they are, in a sense, authorized by God. The harvest is a holy war. The one who dies with the reaping sickle in his hand goes directly to Paradise.'[157] These identifications raise powerful images of the *mujahid*, the *jihad*,

4.28: Violence and power: the reaper at work. Internet Image

and the *shahîd*, the holy witness or martyr. The constant overlaps and exchanges between late antique Christian metaphors and those of early Islam formed porous frontiers through which not just ideas of martyrdom and sacred war became shared tropes, but so did the metaphors in which they were expressed. In the late antique Maghrib, Augustine spoke in an attacking mode against the heretical African Christians of his own time: 'Observe the branch that has been pruned, like the martyr Cyprian; observe the branches that have been cut off, like the heretics and the Donatists. Why do you people say that you belong to this man who bore the fruit of peace and unity, who was reaped with the sickle of martyrdom, to obtain the crown of eternal salvation?'[158] Similarly, in the explication of the parable of harvesting in the evangelist Matthew, the bundles of weeds that are taken out at the time of the harvest and that are thrown into piles to be burned are the bad growths that have been sown by the Devil and that are straightforwardly identified with heretics.[159]

These Christian tropes were so well known and so frequently repeated in the early modern period in western Europe that they were often cobbled together in confections that were a little overdone in tone and fervour, as in John Flavel's *Husbandry Spiritualized* in the mid-seventeenth century.

When the fields are white to harvest, then husbandmen walk through them, rub the ears, and finding the grain full and solid, they presently prepare their scythes and sickles, send for their harvest-men, who quickly reap and mow them down; and after these follow the binders, who tie it up ... How bare and naked do the fields look after the harvest, which before were pleasant to behold; when the harvest-men enter into the field, it is ... before them, like the garden of Eden, and behind them a desolate wilderness ...[160]

Then, after quoting the words of Jesus that 'the harvest is the end of the world; the reapers are the angels,' Flavel adds by way of his own comment:

The field is the world; there both the godly and the ungodly live and grow together, till they both be ripe, and then they shall both be reaped down by death; death is the sickle that reaps down both ... Neither the corn nor tares can possibly resist the sharp and keen sickle when it is applied to them by the reaper's hand; neither can the godly or ungodly resist the stroke of death when God inflicts it ... The frail body of man is as unable to withstand that stroke, as the weak reeds, or feeble stalks of the corn, are able to resist the keen scythe and sharp sickle.

Except for the novel appearance of the scythe, Flavel's words echo tropes that are found in Augustine. They are replete with images of violence that connect the reaper's cutting with the 'stroke of death.' And men who cut and inflict death could be identified with the armed warrior.

The connections between reapers and warriors, the harvest and warfare, remained constant to the advent of modern times. Even in the most peaceful of circumstances, such as those found in the American West of the 1870s and 1880s, the 'great armies of harvesters,' as one reporter described the gangs of men, evoked the same combination of awe and fear. Another reporter, writing in 1880 about the harvest on the immense Dalrymple farm in the Dakotas, described the long line of reapers harvesting the wheat as a line of war chariots, denying the violent power of the image in favour of the apparent good being done.

Not such as once swept over the Delta of the Nile in pursuit of an army of fugitive Israelites, not such as the warriors of Rome were wont to drive, with glittering knives projecting from the axles to mow a swath through the ranks of the enemy, to drench the ground with blood, to cut down the human race, as if men were noxious weeds, but chariots of peace, doing the work of human hands for the sustenance of men.[161]

The connection of the harvest reaper with the soldier taking life on the battlefield was a commonplace in all ages. So here, at least, is a consistent linkage between a work regime, its tools, its successes and failures, and the formation of ideas. But just how necessary are these tropes and the parts of which they are made?

Making a Metaphor

It would be convenient to claim that the connection of the technology of reaping, the cutting of plant life, and the onset of the winter season is so generalized in the premodern world that it invariably generated the peculiar kinds of metaphoric thought found here. But it is not so. We might continue to focus on the figure of the Grim Reaper. This image is widespread in Western culture, but it is not found everywhere. The fictional scene of reaping with which we began our investigation (see chap. 1, p. 4) that illustrated the transition from economic life to novelistic creation was Tolstoy's famous scene of mowing in his *Anya Karenin*. So far, so good. But if it exists at all, the figure of the Grim Reaper is singularly absent from figurations of death and dying in premodern Russia.[162] Here, if anywhere, one might think, the metaphor ought to have taken root in the human mind. But it did not, and often, as in our own time, other metaphors did not either. Eddie Izzard's idea that in our day the Grim Reaper ought to be armed with a lawnmower just doesn't work. We all sense that it won't. That's why everyone, including myself, laughs with him at the mere thought. It's funny, not scary. The lawnmower is a pathetic emblem of middle-class drudgery and aesthetics. Mowing the lawn just ain't reaping. Even Canadianizing the metaphor and arming Grim Death with a combine harvester doesn't improve things much. All of which raises the fact of a pattern that has been observed. Not just any set of real-life things is transportable

4.29: A stereotype of the figure of the Grim Reaper. Internet image

in any form into metaphor. And once a metaphor exists, it cannot be put to every immediate use in turn.[163] There are limits on what is ordinarily thought by masses of humans in given social networks, and some parameters on how this thought can be imagined.[164] In this context, my remarks about Canadianizing are no longer so funny or so flippant, since it was precisely this type of metaphoric shift that did take place in the Gauls and Germanies, where, as we have seen, a harvesting machine replaced reapers and their sickles, to signal death on the tombstones of provincial Romans of the time.[165]

The traditional modern metaphoric construction of the Grim Reaper is interesting in itself, but it is historically determined and it involves a number of changes in a more general field of thinking and representation.[166] The changes were from the many to the one: from the Christian reapers of Roman times as angels of the Lord to *the* singular Grim Reaper; from full flesh-and-blood men to a skeletal figure; from lightly clothed or semi-nude reapers with their sun hats to a figure wearing a dark hooded cloak; and from many men wielding sickles to one man wielding a scythe. This dark figure is the one that we commonly think of when the Grim Reaper is mentioned today. It is the same one that is found in a wide range of media.[167] But there are different streams of cultural development that feed into the picture of the death reaper.[168] The changes are several, they are linked in a pattern, and they are fundamental in type. Each of them points to more than a simple shift from a spear-bearing noble to a threatening scythe-bearing peasant.

What specific inputs went into the formation of the latter metaphoric image of death? An explanation and a diagram of the process have been repeatedly presented in detailed analyses of the formation of metaphoric thought.[169] The argument about the process of the blend by which this particular metaphor arises includes the following assumptions. I quote the argument in detail for the sake of clarity.

Stereotypical reapers are subject to persuasion and argument. But the blending of the abstract story of causal tautology and event-story of individual dying gives a Death that is beyond persuasion. The Grim Reaper is inhuman.

The individual authority of any actual reaper is unknown: perhaps he takes his orders from others; perhaps he is a slave. But Death has authority that is blended with the reaper to create an absolutely transcendent authority completely incompatible with that of normal reapers.

Actual reapers are numerous and essentially interchangeable. But Death is conceived of as a single abstract cause, which is projected into the blend, making Death-the-Reaper single and definite. This explains the appropriateness of the definite article: *the* Grim Reaper.

Actual reapers are mortal and are replaced by other reapers. But Death is neither. Projecting these features of Death into the blend creates a Death-the-Reaper who is immortal: the same Grim Reaper who cut our ancestors down will cut us down.

Stereotypical reapers are strong, productive, healthy, and attractive. But the killer is destructive, unhealthy, and works on *us*, so the Grim Reaper must be unattractive or 'Grim.'

Stereotypical reapers perform heavy labor for long intervals and wear clothing suited to these conditions of labor. But the killer acts only once, on the person who dies, so Death-the-Reaper can wear clothing suited to repose; this clothing can further carry connotations of the killer as grim and isolated.

Stereotypical reapers use their scythes, but the Grim Reaper is often thought of as doing his work merely by appearing … In the blend, the Grim Reaper has aspects of the reaper and the killer, but his effective action comes from the input story of the herald rather than the input story of the reaper or killer.

Stereotypical reapers work in daylight, reaping the entire field indiscriminately, ignorant of the individual existence of plants or wheat, and they harvest rather than kill. But Death and the killer have an entirely different set of meanings, so the Grim Reaper comes for a specific person at a specific time and he kills. He can stalk you like a killer.[170]

And so on. The list of affinities and of necessary conditions includes other characteristics of this system of metaphoric thought production. The analysis concludes with the claim that the metaphor of '*the* Reaper *must* [my italics] therefore have

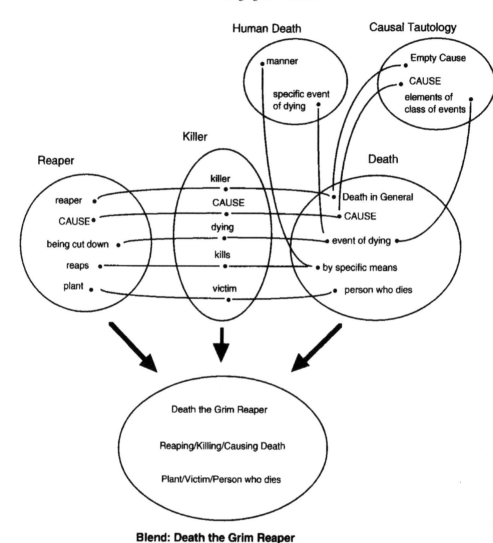

4.30: Creating of the metaphor of the Grim Reaper. Kövecses, *Metaphor in Culture*, fig. 11.7, p. 280; permission courtesy of the author

these features.' The definite article in the designation of *the* Reaper, for example, is said to come from a causal tautology.

In light of the evidence on the work of reaping cereal crops that we have presented so far, it is necessary to challenge the central points in the set of assumptions outlined above and to argue that this particular metaphor of death is a historical production of mind that depends on specific economic and cultural conditions in western Europe in post-Roman times. First, the claim that harvesters or reapers are healthy, good, and attractive is surely a point of view. And it is one that is gainsaid by not inconsiderable amounts of evidence, from times ancient and modern, in which reapers are presented as barbaric aliens, prone to drink and disorder, poor, dirty, and dangerous. A good argument could be made, surely, that there is not any clash here, but rather an extension of an existing experience or, perhaps more compellingly, of existing popular images of reapers. Typical reapers might well have used scythes, but they did so only in precisely limited cultural, historical, and temporal contexts. There is no special need for the 'death reaper' to be armed with a scythe. For considerable stretches of time and space he was not. Nor is it necessary for him to be male. For long periods of past time this was not necessary either. It was only the use of the scythe rather than the sickle that made this particular selection of gender far more probable. Which brings us to another point. There is no need, despite the claim about the causal singularity of Death, for the reaper to be one. This, too, was a specific historical development.

The points of objection to necessary connections between real reapers and the metaphor extend to matters as simple as clothing. The figure of the Grim Reaper is clothed in a hooded cloak. An appeal is made to a specific historical instance that is suggested to be more general in impact: 'Priests, monks, mourners, and members of lay brotherhoods that are associated with dying, funerals, burial, and afterlife are metonymically associated with Death. They are not counterparts of Death, but in the blend, the attire we associate with them – robe and cowl – can be the attire of the Grim Reaper.'[171] The new clothing, including the dark hoodie, is nothing unusual. The hooded cloak indicates a rural northwest European environment in which peasants were normally clothed in a hooded cloak or *cucullus* – as we have already seen them figured, for example, in the realistic portraiture of the peasant workers on the Montauban-Buzenol reliefs.[172] The use of the scythe as the eminent and, literally, the most striking instrument for the reaping of grasses for cattle fodder took place in this same region in combination with the shift to the use of the stripping machine for the harvesting of cereal grains. This picture, too, was always in the agenda of possible mental images that could be selected and emphasized as the circumstances encouraged. There remains the problem of the shift to a single dominant figure.

As for the change from the many to one, part of this transformation was con-

4.31: Peasant wearing a cowled cucullus. Bronze statuette: Rheinisches Landesmuseum, Trier; permission courtesy of the Rheinisches Landesmuseum

nected with the relative balance of the sickle and the scythe in the economy of reaping different cereal and forage crops. The harvesters who are the angels of death that are repeatedly referred to by Augustine and other late antique Christian writers from Africa – indeed, ubiquitously, by all writers in the late Roman world – wielded reaping sickles. So did Saturn, the great near-monotheistic god of traditional pre-Christian cult in Africa, the linear successor to the lordly, singular Punic deity Ba'al Hammon. He also wielded a harvester's sickle or a reaping hook. And he was not many, but resolutely one.[173] At some point, outside Africa the iconography and mental associations of Saturn changed on the basis of an already existing difference. In these more northerly Mediterranean lands, he came to be identified with the mowing of hay rather than the cutting of cereal grains. This northern, sometimes Italian, version of Saturn came to wield not a sickle but the long-bladed Italian scythe.[174] In conventional aetiologies that explained his appearance, the god Janus specifically added the sickle to his identity in order to use this symbol of the harvest to signal Saturn's beneficent power.[175] This alternative version presents *in nuce* in the image of Saturn-Kronos; Death was on his way to becoming the Grim Reaper. The sheer striking power required by the longer

4.32: Peasant wearing a cowled cucullus. Rheinisches Landesmuseum,
Trier; permission courtesy of the Rheinisches Landesmuseum

blade also signalled a close ecological connection with the importance of mowing meadowlands and with the strong men required to do the cutting.

This history points to two analogous developments. One was a geographic shift in the gravitational centres of the new technologies and ecologies of western European reaping. The other was a shift in the locus of the main writers who came from more northerly regions: from the Po Valley region of Italy and further north. These men were composing out of a different living background that emphasized the greater significance of the move to the mowing of fodder for the maintenance of cattle through their long winters.[176] The shift was a fundamental ecological one in which the viewer's eyes moved from an emphasis on the reapers of cereal grains with their sickles to the mower of meadows armed with his scythe. The temporal move was a cosmic one. It was a visual and mental change in focal point taken by viewers in more northerly ecologies, shunting the images of harvest and reaping expected for the month of July in the Mediterranean to the later month of August.[177] The change highlighted the greater and growing significance in the northern Gallic and Germanic lands of the mower of fodder crops armed with his large threatening scythe.

4.33: Saturn with his reaping sickle, first century CE, Rusicade, Algeria. Leglay, *Saturne africain*, pl. 1.1; ArtResource

4.34: Saturn-Kronos wielding reaping blade, Pompeii, Italy. Wall fresco: Museo Nazionale, Naples, Italy; ArtResource

The image of the grim reapers that prevailed in the minds and messages of the Christian writers of Graeco-Roman antiquity who were Mediterranean men was not so grim and it was of a plurality of men, the *messores* or reapers who worked in gangs armed with sickles and not with scythes. These reapers were following the orders of a divine Lord who worked through his agents to send the harvesters down to earth to reap his fields, fields that he himself had sown with the souls of men. The claim made by some literary and linguistic proponents concerned with the forming of the Grim Reaper metaphor that the metaphoric thought is imperfect in the blend because plants, unlike humans, are not being reaped at the end of their life cycle seems to be modestly misleading.[178] If one accepts a secular twenty-first-century conception of human death which is indeed final and absolute – it is *the* end of our life – then the analogy is reasonably good. But for most humans in the ancient societies that we are considering, including most of their religious writers and thinkers, it is manifest that this death was not final and not the end. The person was being reaped, like the crop, to be stored and preserved for an ongoing life-after-death. In the cases of the wall paintings of reaping on the tombs of the nobles of Pharaonic Egypt, the entire metaphor is a mirror-like reflection of life-after-death being the same as life-before-death. The nobleman and his spouse will sow and reap in those fields just as they do now. And they will have lots of sex, just as they do now (they hoped). All of this was barely, if at all, metaphoric in our sense. It was more like a real transformation enabled by magical means. Furthermore, in the sequence of metaphoric representations that we have already discussed – the fuller or complete sequence in which individual scenes of reaping are embedded – the reaping scene is usually followed by ones of transportation, storage, and sometimes winnowing. The latter scenes were included, as in the *Tomba della Mietitura* mosaics at Ostia, precisely because they were figurations of further steps in the continuation of an existence after the reaping of death.

These objections prompt other questions. Was the Christian figural presentation of death, from Cyprian to Augustine, and beyond, the thought world which the Maktar Harvester shared, part of a wider Mediterranean field of thinking? Was the picture evoked by the patristic writers of the grim reapers as angels sent by the Lord to reap his earthly crop, as many in number, wielding sickles, and coming in a group or at least portrayed as more than a single figure, the norm of the time? And was this thinking just as ecologically conditioned as the scythe-bearing, cowl-hooded, darkly cloaked skeletal figure of Death that was generated in western European lands in post-Roman times? These questions are pertinent because they call for a systematic cataloguing of metaphors and their deployment in different types and cultural contexts of communication. A rough survey of the various species of Latin literatures not composed by Christian writers, especially by authors in the mainstream of the Roman literary elites, reveals a startling absence of the reaper metaphor. Nothing in biographical writers like Suetonius, where elements of personal values are everywhere assessed and judged. And nothing at all in a historian like Tacitus, where concerns with vengeance, retribution, and the violent evening of scores are ever present. Nothing in Seneca's rhetorical and philosophical texts, where the same incentives are present. And nothing in the large corpus of Livy's historical writings. There is nothing in the rhetorical works of Quintilian, where discussion of the use of striking, appropriate, and commonplace metaphors is part of his program for the training of the Roman orator.[179] But perhaps what is most telling of all: nothing in the massive corpus of Ciceronian writings with their deployment of rhetorical tropes in public speeches, their use of current allusions and language in letters, their references to allegorical types and symbols in philosophical treatises, and so on.[180] Nothing. Of course, such rough surveys are always open to the discovery of this or that individual item hidden in the entire corpora of Latin texts composed by upper class literary writers, but the general aura of absence is striking when compared with the profusion of reapers in the literary productions of Christian writers.

Representing Reaping

Most representations of reapers that are fuller in nature and which are not meant to be simple one-to-one symbols, like the totems of a given month or a season of the year in the calendrical tradition, conform to the ancient pattern indicated in the texts of the patristic writers. Whether it is a relief sculpture in the architrave friezes from the impressive tomb of a grandee from the Tripolitanian predesert (see fig. 4.9), a graceful mosaic that is part of the funerary complex at Ostia (see fig. 4.8), or a relief sculpture on the sarcophagus of a Roman nobleman of late antiquity (see fig. 4.6), the pictorial attachment to death is represented by multiple reapers wielding sickles, working as part of a group. None of them is portrayed in attire that would be identified as anything other than the normal light clothing and sun hats that were worn by reapers in the ancient Mediterranean. This is precisely how they, and the death with which they are associated, were imagined.

Although the huge waves of human activity involved in harvesting left little of their detail in either the literary or the iconic productions from Africa of the high Roman empire, later Christian writings (those contemporary with the Maktar Harvester) are replete with references to this quotidian activity. Recourse to these common scenes of everyday life was provoked by the need to develop a medium of mass communication. The audiences of the preachers and bishops were easily able to identify with recurrent rural work tasks which could then be used to illustrate a point of doctrine. We might expect that patristic writings, as the great common literature of the age, would be a mine of information on the daily work activities of the countryside. And agricultural metaphors *do* figure prominently in their texts. Even so, the data that are pertinent to our inquiry are more meagre than one might expect. The connection between metaphor and the lived reality of the time is less direct than expected, since many of the metaphors were derived from existing biblical prototypes. These were then redeployed, remorselessly, for metaphoric and symbolic ends that sometimes had no immediate connection with the contemporary economic experiences of the preacher's listeners.[181] The field was now open not just to preaching, but also to other popular modes of conveying meaning – like the Christian hymn. It is to these forms of communication, like the chant and the song, that we should look to understand the impact of images of reaping on the mind.

If the harvest was like a war or a sacred battle, and the harvesters its foot-soldiers, the comparison was not entirely inapt. Singing and chanting in unison hyped group aggression, as it did among soldiers. Both this behaviour and the adrenaline needed to propel backbreaking work, were found here. And the sacred element was here too. We are told that the following words were 'the stuff for men that work in the sun to sing.' They were verses of the divine Lityerses:

> Demeter, rich in fruits, rich in grains, allow that this
> crop be easily harvested and be abundant. And you binders: keep binding the
> sheaves, unless someone passing by says: 'See these good-for-nothings. Just more
> wages wasted.'
> Cut the end of your swaths facing to the north wind
> or to the west, so the heads of wheat will then grow full.
> When you thresh the wheat, don't siesta at midday:
> it's then that the head is most easily separated from the stalk.
> And when you reap, get to your work when the lark wakens
> and stop when he goes to sleep. But rest out the heat.
> Hey guys: the frog has a happy life. He doesn't have to worry who'll pour *his* drink:
> he has an unending supply!
> Hey you tight-fisted foreman: boil the beans better for us …[182]

And so on, expatiating, it is imagined, on the driving and disciplinary foreman, the hard work, the long day, the heat, and the need for drink. Singing of this sort by harvesters is referred to in the biblical Psalms; songs about songs, so to say. Theophrastus's poem just quoted, of course, is not an actual work song, but rather a literary-aesthetic representation of one. But real work songs and chants of this kind were common among harvest gangs in the premodern Maghrib.[183] And also in the Roman Maghrib. When the violent circumcellion reapers who accompanied a dissident Christian bishop Proculeianus into Hippo in the year 409 chanted rhythmically, it was surely because this behaviour was one of their normal modes of cohesion. They would have sung comparable rhythmic lines as part of their daily work in the fields.[184] They marched and sang, like soldiers. Being armed was also a normal part of the harvest process. As indicated in the song sung by Theocritus's Greek reapers, sheaves and piles of grain were sometimes left lying on the ground in the fields to dry, and they were only later transferred to granaries by means of baskets or carts. During the waiting period, the reaped grain was vulnerable to theft.[185] Sometimes the grain was left in piles on the *area* or threshing floor waiting to be processed. In this critical time, the cut sheaves and grain had to be guarded by men who were drawn from the harvesters themselves or by armed men known as *custodes fructuum* who were sometimes hired outsiders.[186] Harvest guards like these are attested for all well-documented instances of grain harvesting in the premodern Mediterranean, Near East, and Europe.[187]

Despite usages like these, metaphors of reaping, as we have already emphasized, even if a tolerable pastiche-history of them could be assembled, are rare in the writings from classical antiquity. An obvious cause for this huge gap between Homer and the quasi-oral Christian writings of late antiquity, like the written versions of the sermons of its leading preachers, is that almost all of the literate productions of the intervening social formations were adjusted to a steeply attenuated social order. In this order, creative writings were constrained by known boundaries of representation. Metaphors could be redacted within a set range of aesthetically acceptable tropes and genres. It was only with the sudden efflorescence of the sermon and sermon-like compositions of Christian preachers that we begin to see reflections of what was happening in everyday speech in an alternative part of the oral spectrum that included the song and the Psalm. It would be a mistake to take the apparent rarity of reaping metaphors in the wide range of literary texts of pre-Christian writers as an indication that a massive and constantly recurrent labour process that involved large numbers of people every year had little or no effect on their modes of thinking. It seems more probable by far that this absence is just another case of the 'dark figure' at work in the history of Roman antiquity, another instance of a very frequent social practice that has left almost no imprint in our literary sources, which is to say, in our *written* ones.

Vis et iniuria

If potential dangers, and images and fears of injury and death, were present, it was not just because the taking of the plant growth symbolized the end of life. The arrival of swarms of outsiders, armed with dangerous implements, who were to assist in taking off the harvest, provoked the spectre of real violence in this time and in this earthly place. The annual invasions of large numbers of young men for the purpose of harvesting cereal grains were structurally conducive to violence. The factors that fed tendencies to miscreant and violent behaviour were many. They included elements of mobility and homelessness, pay disputes and mal-treatment, and the insecurity and uncertainty of employment during the harvest season.[188] This last circumstance meant that in some seasons far more men turned up than could be employed. And the plain fact is that the alcoholic drink normally given to harvesters as part of their pay, usually wine or beer, was conducive to drunkenness, which further exacerbated loutish and violent behaviour.[189]

Perhaps more dangerous was the autonomy of the harvesting gangs. The wandering harvest workers shared their own mobile culture of young men on the move. They were normally alien to the regions into which they came to work and on this score alone they were liberated from normal local constraints. In the American and Canadian West, the workers were often perceived as unwanted outsiders who were grouped together under similar terms of disapprobation. Migrants, tramps, hoboes, bums, and vagrants were some of the negative terms that were used indiscriminately to describe the wage drifters.[190] In any case, when they were no longer required and their labour was no longer wanted, a base sentiment of antipathy towards them soon surfaced.[191] There was always a profound ambivalence towards seasonal workers. They were needed and tolerated as long as their work was required, but they were not wanted and even feared as soon as the demands of the harvest had been met. In almost every salient aspect, they represented values and styles of living that were not respected by respectable society. Not infrequently, violent scuffles broke out between the locals and the incoming outsiders. When necessary, or as felt, laws on vagrancy were harshly enforced against them. On other occasions, vigilante parties were formed to expel the dangerous men, as they were perceived to be.[192]

But we do not have to dilate on the field record of such harvesting gangs in Canada and the United States in the twentieth century to document the antipathies. Such behaviour was equally true of German lands and England in the eighteenth and nineteenth centuries. As gangs of Irish harvesters, nicknamed Mickies, worked their way through the nineteenth-century English countryside, the drinking, the aggression, and the hostility of the locals towards them led to recurrent episodes of violence which were usually blamed on the itinerant harvesters. The editor of the *Courier* in East Anglia, when speaking of these 'Milesian disturbances,' noted the following:

The attention of the constables should be drawn to the doings of these emeralders who appear to be stragglers from the main hordes that have ravaged England like another eruption of the Huns of Attila ... the vagrant labourers and beggars we meet with wandering through the country are about the worst specimens of barbarism we could desire to meet.[193]

The itinerant Irish labourers, so critical to taking off the harvest, were variously labelled as Mickies, Emeralders, Milesians, Goths, or Vandals, none of which signified anything positive or peaceful. But in an age long before the Irish were the typical harvesters, the same negative characteristics are found in a detailed survey of vagrants in sixteenth- and seventeenth-century England, about a quarter of whom served as itinerant harvesters. This observation matches contemporary evidence from German lands in this period, where the same negative attitudes are also found.[194] As commercial agriculture took hold and the effects of the agricultural revolution were felt, control of vagrants became a major theme of the age.

It is therefore hardly surprising that the African society in which the Maktar Harvester staged his successful rise was characterized by the same structural problems posed by movements of seasonal labourers. The widespread concern of both the imperial and local municipal authorities with the control of undesired men and women on the move, threatening drifters as they were seen to be, is well attested.[195] The Africans had their own Latin slang that they used to designate seasonal harvesters. They called them *circumcelliones* or 'men who hang out around *cellae*.' What were these *cellae* or cellars, and why were these men so noted for 'hanging out' around them? The question has occasioned much scholarly speculation, but given the absolutely consistent use of the Latin term in the one body of literature that tells us the most about these men – the writings of Augustine of Hippo – there is no doubt that the cellars were normally used to store wine. It made sense for these men to 'hang out' around such places. Issuances of wine (or of beer in the northern provinces of the empire) were a normal part of their pay.[196] In one of his sermons, Augustine reports on the drinking and violent behaviour, the mayhem fuelled by much drinking and festivity, that marked the harvest season. Not a little of which, one must suspect, was caused by the hard men who gathered in the town to reap the crops in the surrounding fields.[197] It was the same in nineteenth-century England where 'beer money' was part of the salary remitted as wages to harvesters. Although everyone knew that violence frequently resulted from the combination of alcohol, the temperament of the workers, and the nature of the work, few intervened to correct the situation because beer and cider were staples of the harvesters' diet.[198] These drinks 'provided the necessary fluid in the hot and hard work, and there was no cheap substitute that was available. And from the farmers' perspective, it was part payment of wages.'[199]

The connection between work and reward makes good sense of one of the constant condemnations directed against the circumcellions in numerous polemical writings. Drunkenness was the single vice that was consistently connected with their violence. Modern historians have usually interpreted this bad behaviour either as a loutishness characteristic of the inferior classes in Africa in general or as something connected with a practice of sacred inebriation. The explanation, surely, is less celestial and more mundane. Harvesters were habitually paid with a range of remittances: some money, food and lodging, and, almost invariably, an alcoholic beverage: beer in Pharaonic Egypt (though wine in the Roman period) and in the more northerly climes of the Roman empire, and wine everywhere else. The work was compulsive and intense, and the drinking no less so. In these conditions, alcohol was everywhere associated with a greater propensity to violence. Reports from nineteenth-century England, often focused on the Irish harvesting gangs and drunkenness, are so prolific as not to require detailed repetition. Both employers and hired hands accepted that part payment in alcoholic drink, 'beer money' as we have said, was an expected perquisite of the job. The customary payment was such a deeply embedded part of the social system of harvest work that attempts to ban the practice in England by formal legislation in 1887 met with general disregard and non-compliance on all sides.[200] Violence and mayhem were the expected results. It was the controlling of the resulting violent disorders that alarmed both local officials and magistrates of the central government.

All of these problems must have been confronted by the Maktar Harvester in his role as a contractor and a manager of harvesting gangs. In this, as in other matters, the contractors – the *procuratores, conductores,* or *mancipes* – were held liable by imperial law for the behaviour, or the misbehaviour, of the men under their control.[201] The fact that the so-called circumcellions were the core of the harvesting gangs in the Africa of our man from Maktar is confirmed by Augustine. On two occasions, he indulges in agricultural metaphors in which it is clear that he and his readers (the formal addressees here are his Donatist rivals, but many Catholic parishioners would also hear a public letter like this) assume that the circumcellions principally worked as harvesters. It is a metaphor in which Augustine interprets injunctions of the Lord:

He himself said: Allow them to grow to be harvested. He did not say: let them grow weeds, let the harvests decrease. He said: This field is beautiful, He did not say: This field is Africa. He said: The harvest is the end of the age. He did not say: The harvest is the age of Donatus. He said: The harvesters [*messores*] are angels; he did not say: The harvesters are the leaders [*principes*] of the circumcellions.[202]

In a sermon delivered some seven years later, Augustine repeated much this same description of the circumcellions as gangs of harvesters.

One also finds God saying this in the story about the weeds in the field. *The field is this world.* He does not say that the field is Africa, but rather that it is this world. Grain is found throughout the world, weeds are found throughout the world. Nevertheless: *The field is the world, the sower is the Son of Man, the harvesters [messores] are the angels.* They are *not* the leaders [*principes*] of the circumcelliones … And what is the harvest? Listen to what He says: *The harvest is the end of the world.* [The quotations by Augustine are from Mt. 13:37–9.][203]

Delivered to everyday listeners in the church at Hippo in a homely agricultural metaphor the sermon presents images that Augustine's parishioners would understand from their own experience.

Harvesters of Men

These same harvesters, especially the reapers, chanted and sang to provide cohesion for their hard work and, when required, for other kinds of collective tasks, including the acts of sectarian violence fronted by circumcellions that so concerned Augustine. The idea was a popular expression of the fact that one could be a reaper of moral judgments.[204] One could therefore reap those who had been morally judged.[205] Christian ideas linked reapers and the harvesting of men (or, in another metaphor, the fishing of them). Also integral to this process was the second line of workers behind the reapers who, as Homer had already vividly described many generations earlier, would do the picking up and binding of the sheaves, and the stacking of them for transport. They, too, echoed the chanting of the reapers, but in their own mode. It seems that one of the rhythms used by the binders who followed in the track of the reapers ran as follows.

TOLLE! LEGE!
TOLLE! LEGE!
TOLLE! LEGE!

PICK IT UP / GATHER IT UP!
PICK IT UP / GATHER IT UP!
PICK IT UP / GATHER IT UP![206]

Although he cautiously pretends otherwise, Augustine had surely heard this refrain chanted during the harvesting of the fields around his home at Thagaste.[207] His father Patricius, the landowner, employed his own slaves, called on his neighbours, and hired seasonal workers to take off the harvest in his fields, and they chanted refrains like this as they worked. It was just that, amid the real violence in late Roman Africa that called for the mobilizing of hard men from reaping gangs for purposes of sectarian enforcement, Augustine's harvest and his sheaves were to be ideas and words, men and their souls.

CHAPTER FIVE

Blade of Vengeance

He would use all possible weapons of thought, other than metaphor ...[1]

Amid the terrors of the late summer of 1941, Ukrainians in villages south of Gomel faced two grim prospects. One was the onrush of the heavy armour of Heinz Guderian's Second Panzer Group. The other was a threatening order from the Stalinist state to join a forced evacuation to a safe haven in a remote place to the east of the Volga. The catastrophe of the Holodomor, the harvest of sorrow, had embedded in Ukrainians a pervasive fear and an angry rejection of deadly solutions imposed on them by outsiders. The women in the fields began to resist the demand that they evacuate their villages, nor would they suffer themselves to be forced from their homes by the vile foreign enemy.

Out in the fields. Wind, wind, wind. Cold. Nature is waiting for snow. Women, cold, in sackcloths. They are rebelling. They don't want to leave this place ... They raise their sickles. Their eyes are crying. The next moment, the women laugh and swear, but then their anger and grief returns ... 'We won't leave, we'd rather die here. If any lousy snake comes to force us out of our homes, we'll meet him with our sickles!'[2]

This was not death and mourning. At a time towards the end of summer and the beginning of autumn, harvest implements of cutting and reaping, already in hand for work, were taken up and brandished in a gesture of manifest defiance, including the promise to decapitate the snake, the embodiment of evil. It was in their tradition. Ukrainian peasants had long used the sickle as a weapon of retribution.[3] This threatening use of the sickle was part of a long use of metaphor in Slavic culture in which the cutting tools of harvesting were symbolically loaded. More than a century earlier, the poet Fedor Nikolaivich Glinka, reflecting on another invasion of Russia, compared the resolute resistance of Russian serfs, 'ready to defend their motherland with their scythes,' to (in his eyes) the dissolute and

5.1: Hammer and sickle motifs of the Soviet Union. Internet images

listless aristocracy.[4] There was nothing unusual in this. In the vast sweep of European peasant culture, from the rural French revindicators of the Vendée to Polish peasant rebels, the sickle was a weapon of choice.[5] But by the time the Ukrainian women brandished their sickles at Nazi invaders, the symbolism had become doubly sharp. Everywhere in their world, the hammer had come to represent the city and industry, the sickle the countryside and agriculture – the two foundations of the New State in which they had to live. In antiquity, things had been different. It was the sickle alone that had to bear the symbolic weight of the foundations of community and state. As Augustine noted of the African deity Saturn: his sickle represented all agriculture.[6] In his age, indeed, there was nothing else for the greatest of all deities to embody.

Before turning to the world of antiquity, we might reflect on a more modern (well, early modern) story about the relationship between the figure of the reaper, the sickle, and the theme of revindication. The bloody revolt of the Catalans in the mid-seventeenth century was known as *La Guerra dels Segadors* – 'The War of the Reapers.'[7] As with Ukraine in the early 1940s, the threatening situation that provoked reaction was an armed foreign occupation. In this case, the military forces of Castile had occupied the lands of Catalonia. The Corpus of Blood, as the rising of June 1640 later came to be known, was centred on the grisly killing of the Spanish Viceroy, the Count of Santa Columba.[8] The reapers or *segadors* were scheduled to enter Barcelona on 7 June, the day of Corpus Christi. The outbreak in the city was signalled by the death of a reaper, whose murder by stabbing initiated a series of events that led to widespread violence. In the next year, on 16 January 1641, Pau Cleris declared the autonomous Generalitat. The violence dragged on until 1659. Although apparently resolved in favour of the national state centred at Madrid, the resistance permanently marked Catalan autonomy and identity. As the modern phase of nationalism took hold in the late nineteenth century, music and lyrics were composed for a Catalan national anthem entitled *Els Segadors* or *The Reapers*.[9] The music and especially the lyrics catch the close connection between reaping, the dangerous sickle, the demands for justice and fairness, and the threats of vengeance directed against one's enemies.

> Catalonia triumphant
> shall once again be rich and bountiful.
> Drive them back, those people
> so conceited and so arrogant!
>
> A good blow with the sickle!
> A good blow with the sickle!
> Defenders of the land!
> A good blow with the sickle!
>
> Now is the time, you reapers,
> now is the time to be alert.
> For when another June comes,
> let us sharpen our tools well!
>
> A good blow with the sickle!
> A good blow with the sickle!
> Defenders of the land!
> A good blow with the sickle!
>
> Let the enemy tremble
> On seeing our banner.
> Just as we cut down the golden stalks of wheat
> when the time is right, we shall reap our chains!
>
> A good blow with the sickle!
> A good blow with the sickle!
> Defenders of the land!
> A good blow with the sickle!
>
> Catalunya triomfant
> tornarà a ser rica i plena.
> Endarrera aquesta gent
> tan ufana i tan superba.

Bon cop de falç.
Bon cop de falç.
Defensors de la terra!
Bon cop de falç!

Ara és hora, segadors.
Ara és hora d'estar alerta.
Per quan vingui un altre juny
esmolem ben bé les eines.

Bon cop de falç.
Bon cop de falç.
Defensors de la terra!
Bon cop de falç!

Que tremoli l'enemic
en veient la nostra ensenya.
Come fem caure esipgues d'or,
quan convé seguem cadenes.

Bon cop de falç.
Bon cop de falç.
Defensors de la terra!
Bon cop de falç![10]

In the emblematic national song of an entire people, the symbol of the sickle as a tool of labour and as a weapon the theme of reaping as the taking of crops, and the cutting of the chains of servitude are all connected. The image of the reaper is of a dangerous vindicator who comes both to inflict harm and to liberate. The sickle becomes the means of striking back. But *how* is it that these ideas are linked? First, as in the Ukrainian case, the imagery is founded in a historical reality and in daily experience. In Catalonia itinerant reapers were at the heart of the outbreak of the rebellion in 1640. Some additional clues might be found in other representations of the same mode of thinking, such as those on display in the pavilion of the nascent Spanish Republic in the International Exposition of Arts and Technology at the Paris World's Fair of 1937. It was the place of the exhibition of Picasso's *Guernica*. Other large pieces on display included the mural entitled 'The Reaper,' *El Segador*, painted by Joan Miró on six masonite panels.[11] An angry peasant farmer gestures defiantly with one hand holding a sickle and with the other clenched into a fist moving out of a chaotic sharded explosion of fragments of paint. A metallic sculpture named 'Our Lady of Montserrat,' *La Montserrat*, forged and welded into a solid creation by his fellow Catalan, Juli González, stood at the entrance to the same pavilion, dominating the way into the building. It was the sculpture of a strong iron-clad body of a peasant woman wielding a sickle, while she carries a baby with her left arm in a defensive posture, like a shield. The paint and the metal of González's creation indicate a common language of imagery that was shared by the words of the national song.

The proximity of reapers and soldiers as takers of life, and of swords and sickles as instruments that ended life, was so close that the transformation from one into the other was thought to be almost natural. The same mapping can be found in Latin speech as well. In his *Georgics*, Vergil lamented the terrible fratricide of civil wars that had forced good farmers to bend and reshape their sickles into swords.[12] Much later, the poet Claudian spoke in the same vein, comparing the behaviour of two conquered, defeated, and domesticated Gallic peoples. Instead of making war, the Salii were busy cultivating their fields and the Sygambri were bending their swords into curved sickles.[13] Like a mathematical equation, the process, and therefore the identity, was conceived as reversible. Both the modern creations in paint and metal, and the ancient literary evocations of work and tools in words, play on obvious connections with work, cutting, and harm, connections that are assumed and the dynamic nature of which is not manifest. One possible way to analyse the relationship between the tools and work of reaping in scenes like these is to see the thinking as screened by a series of existing symbols which are then deployed in creative representation, writing, and speaking. These are artfully interpreted or glossed by learned scholars as similitudes or metaphors that reveal various types of literary referentiality and the skill of the speaker, the writer, or the artist in manipulating them.[14] But the function, indeed the very presence of metaphors, is deeper and more fundamental than this kind of artfulness.

Ricoeur observed that the reduction of the metaphor to a literary type diminished its value and impoverished our understanding of its greater significance.[15] It is this larger field of meaning that we are embracing, in which metaphors are containers and extensions that are central to the most basic processes of human thought and communication.[16] Unlike the Tsarist minister Speransky, both admired and detested by Prince Andrey Bolkonsky, whose judgment of the man is quoted at the head of this chapter, we cannot decide to do otherwise. All of us have to think in metaphors all of the time, and we wield metaphoric weapons all of the time. That the great majority of all human speech is littered with so-called dead metaphors is something of which Borges has reminded us. The existence of these verbal and conceptual corpses is a long-observed fact that argues in favour of the more universal approach to metaphor.[17] This is surely a better way for the problem of the relationship between reaping and thinking to be pursued. For the task of reaping, the focus should be on how a strongly recurrent human action in common labour, like women's work in weaving cloth, produces categories and extensions of thinking.[18] Our problem is that there is, as yet, no systematic cataloguing of dominant metaphors in the patterns of thinking in the Latin-speaking societies of the western Roman empire. Even disregarding this huge deficit, big problems remain within the ancient field of the metaphor. The mapping of reaping onto death is everywhere manifest, but this hardly begins to encompass the extensions and entailments of the idea that enabled other important work to be done with it.

The mental and biological connections in the case of the reaping of cereal crops are fundamental. The relationships between humans and plants can be conceived as a one-way process by which we control and mutate them. A better argument has been made that the relationship has always been a reciprocal process, and that plants domesticate us as much as we tame them.[19] In reaping cereals this is particularly significant as types of grains adapted to the means used to harvest them. In turn, the tools used to cut the grains also went through complex sequences of adaptation: witness the successive responsive modifications of the sickle (see figs. 3.13a and b). As the cereal crops changed in their physical nature and the designs of sickles gradually mutated, each in response to the other, they affected matters as fundamental as human body position, movement, gesture, and work organization.[20] As the tools of reaping, like the sickle and the scythe, gradually adapted, so did the cereal grains that were being domesticated in response to them and so, consequently, did the humans and their ideas that were caught up in this nexus. Modes of thought were not immune to the ecological changes that were producing them, that excited, encouraged, and enabled extensions and mutations of existing mental concepts. With this observation in mind, let us reconsider the Ukrainian peasant women brandishing their reaping sickles in mid-air. By using an instrument and a gesture connected with death, their message went beyond death to suggest a more active threat. In embracing the identification with death, the reaper and her sickle could further exploit the violence that produced the death.

The symbol or, better, the concept employed by the Ukrainian women was analogous to similar ones found in Roman antiquity. Extensions of the pattern are found in the dream of the Christian martyr, Perpetua. While she was imprisoned at Roman Carthage in the year 203, she had a vision in her sleep in which she sought refuge from impending death. She saw a ladder ascending into the sky. The problem was that by the foot of the ladder by which she might ascend to Paradise a dangerous serpent was coiled. Hanging on the rungs of the ladder were common implements, sharp and pointed, ready for her to use in her own defence.[21] In dreaming this dream while she was still alive, Perpetua was seeing what lay beyond her death. There would be a Final Judgment in which she and her fellow Christians would win. They would then help their god wreak vengeance on their persecutors. This function of divine justice as a final payback or punishment is still embodied in popular and commercial images of reaping today. Christian preachers in Africa in the age of the Maktar Harvester made this much clear too: it was with a sickle or a reaping blade that God would come for vengeance. He would come armed with the sickle of His Law.[22] Beyond the simplicity and the finality of death, beyond the recurring cycle of the seasons, and beyond the divine grim reaper was the murkier and greyer world of an extraordinary human reaper who would come to enforce his own law and order. He would bring with him a kind of divine justice or violence.[23]

The Threat

The not-too-covert threat of this harvest is that you will, as the new and the old songs say, reap what you sow. The threat could move peasants in their fields and kings on their thrones. Henry I of England in the early twelfth century had a nightmare apparently so frightening that it was vividly pictured in a contemporary chronicle. Enraged peasant farmers crowd around his bed at night, menacing him with their pitchforks and reaping scythes. The harvesting tools no doubt represented being pitched out and terminated.[24] A worry for any monarch. The instruments of reaping, like the sickle and the scythe, were not just harvest implements; they were potential weapons. If the sickle could be a weapon, by this same account the reaper armed with his sickle could be an avenging soldier, a threatening bringer of death and destruction and also of just punishment. It is no accident that the most advanced, most heavily armed, and most lethal hunter-killer drone developed by GAA Systems for the United States Airforce, the MQ-9, is called The Reaper.[25] It is coming and it will get you. In many not-so-modern societies where a harvesting sickle has been used, one finds the same connection between the harvesting tool and bladed weapons used for cutting in a spirit of vengeance. In the Tamil lands of Sri Lanka, the sickle is knitted into a divine cosmology of justice on the one hand, and into a threatening ideology of revindication on the other.[26] With this language, the downtrodden demand a more just social order.

If for Roman soldiers the sickle was supplemental and analogous to their sword, for rebel peasants and other servile insurrectionists it was another one of their tools ready to hand to be picked up for use as a weapon. So regular Roman soldiers who wished to enter the dangerous depths of the Ciminian Forest in Etruria in 310 BCE could manipulate the same understood symbols in reverse. They could pretend to be the real thing. They disguised themselves as peasants and armed themselves with sickles and rural spears, the normal weaponry, one assumes, of the dangerous locals.[27] The rebellious slaves who laboured in the wheat fields and mountain pasturelands of Sicily in the second century BCE, and who rose against their masters in two great wars, were not alone in this respect.[28] If the slave 'king' Eunus had managed to arm some of his followers with formal weapons, the vast majority of them took up axes, hatchets, slings, fire-hardened sticks, cooking spits, and harvesting sickles for their millenarian struggle: that is, just about the same range of ordinary, potentially threatening tools hanging from the ladder that Perpetua climbed in her ascent to Paradise in her predictive dream. Regular soldiers, like the legionaries in the service of Antonius Primus in the manoeuvres before the second battle at Cremona in October of 69, could do the same. They were sent out into nearby farm fields to gather ropes, axes, and sickles that were to serve as weapons of war.[29]

The monarchical anxieties that focused on the peasant sickle and the reaping blade were ancient as well as medieval. They were known and could be consciously made part of a Machiavellian advice literature. After seizing power in a *coup d'état* in the latter years of the seventh century BCE, Kypselos, the tyrant of Corinth, proceeded, we are told, to make himself very unpopular with his subjects. He was succeeded by his son Periander, who was 'even bloodier' and for good reason. Periander had sought advice on how better to govern his city from a more experienced despot, Thrasyboulos, the tyrant of Miletos.[30] Thrasyboulos invited the messenger whom Periander had sent to Miletos to collect his advice to take a walk with him through the wheat fields outside the city. The story continues.

As they walked through the wheat field, Thrasyboulos kept asking questions about why the messenger had come to him from Corinth. While doing this, Thrasyboulos kept cutting off the highest stalks of wheat that he could see, and he then threw away the cut stalks. He continued doing this until he had destroyed the best and most valuable part of the crop. Having walked through the countryside and not having added so much as a word, he sent the messenger away. When the messenger returned to Corinth, Periander was eager to hear Thrasyboulos' advice. The messenger replied that Thrasyboulos had given no advice, and added that he was surprised at having been sent to a man who was manifestly deranged and who was a destroyer of his own property. He then described what he had seen Thrasyboulos do. Periander immediately realized what had happened. In his mind, it was manifest that Thrasyboulos was recommending killing all the outstanding men in Corinth. From that time onward, he displayed every kind of evil to his fellow citizens. Whatever acts of murder and exile Kypselos had left undone, Periander completed.

No words were needed. The wielding of a sickle or a blade to cut off heads that were too eminent produced a meaning that was readily understood then, as it has also been in more modern times. The cutting function was so obvious that it was

5.2: The tyrant reaps: 'Jeff Davis Reaping the Harvest.' *Harper's Weekly*,
26 October 1861, p. 688: LC –US Z62-115352: Library of Congress, Public Access

the fodder of popular jokes.[31] The subject of tyrants and sickles is useful, since it
raises the question of power that was perceived to be based more on violent force
than on the legitimacy of tradition. The two images could be combined, as when
Xenophon makes the despotic king Hieron of Syracuse say in dialogue with his
poet guest and advisor Simonides: 'tyrants do not have ordinary sentries or guards
as in armies; rather they hire their guards, like reapers.'[32] The image of hiring for
protection, the employment of men whose demeanour was threatening, was connected with a typical instance of hiring for work that in itself contained an aura
of threat.

Part of the cause, surely, goes back to the metaphoric extension inherent in the
description of the cutting instrument itself, the *falx*. The ordinary *falx* of the high
and later Roman empire was indeed the harvesting sickle, which was a normal
part of the tool kit of every Roman farm. It is also typically found in the inven-

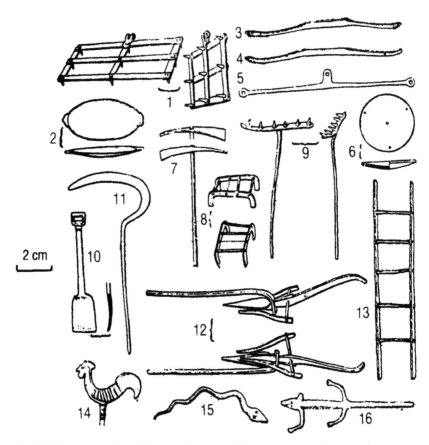

5.3: Tool implement kit of a Roman farm near Cologne, Roman Colonia Agrippinensis.
Mainzer Zeitschrift 34 (1939), fig. 5, p. 9

tories of farm equipment from Egypt.[33] Even those with a modest knowledge of rural life would know what a sickle was and how it was used. Nevertheless, the term *falx* contained its own internal extensions. Given the normal context of its use in the taking off of cereal crops, without further modification the word most often meant a grain-harvesting sickle. But not always.[34] There was flexibility within the word itself. Absent the context of reaping cereal grains, the word signified something more general like 'a bladed agricultural tool for cutting.' To specify a particular use, its meaning had to be refined by an adjective – *falx messoria, falx faenaria, falx vinitoria* – signifying, respectively, a harvesting sickle, a mowing blade, and a pruning hook. The addition of the descriptive modifier made clear the nature of the blade and its precise function.[35] But *falx* could mean any of these things. The same applied to the general term *messor* or harvester. A harvester of what? Normally the word signified a cutter of cereal grains, but given other different contexts it could signify a cutter and picker of grapes or a beater and collector of olives. Because it was an extension of the right hand, the hand that dealt blows and that delivered punishment, the hand that held weapons and that punished, the sickle was vicariously identified with more than just the specific violence of reaping.[36] This sentiment, in turn, was connected with basal brain functions that are both moved by and produce responses connected with power and control, and emotions of apprehension and fear. Since the word *falx* evoked wider and more complex mental images of cutting and harming, the mind could easily extend a term which was itself already elastic and flexible.

The logical extensions of this violence are things that we have already seen, but perhaps they deserve repeated emphasis here. The most important of these was the taking of life, the violent separation of two things, in which the most basic agricultural activities are seen as doing the same acts at a primordial level. As Bourdieu has noted, 'there is the separation of reunited contraries, with, for example, the sacrifice of the ox and the act of reaping, enacted as denied murders.'[37] A host of performed activities in the rural societies of the Kabylie in north-central Algeria that he observed re-enacted these homologies as basic rituals. It is 'the ploughshare, the sickle, the carding-comb and the dagger (and also the blacksmith's fire and poker) – which are used to cut and sever (especially the throats of sacrificial animals, and of men), to pierce, burn and bleed, and also to drive away the evil forces of the kingdom of the wet, such as *djnun*.'[38] He powerfully argued that the forced and violent separation inflicted on nature is somehow undone, rescued, and restored by a reverse act of violence: the sacrifice.

When these acts have to be committed by those who are responsible for and benefit from them, like the defloration of the bride, turning the first furrow, cutting the last thread in weaving, or harvesting the last sheaf, they are transfigured by a collective dramatization intended to give them a collectively proclaimed meaning, that of a sacrifice, which is the exact opposite of their socially recognized, and therefore no less objective reality, which is that of murder.[39]

Note the last word. Murder. All of this came directly out of experience. I can do no better than to quote Bourdieu, again, on the nature of the denial involved in reaping cereal grains, with specific reference to indigenous north African practices.

In the case of the harvest, the social truth to be collectively denied, is unambiguous: harvesting (*thamergra*) is a murder (*thamgert'* designates the throat, violent death, revenge;

and *amgar*, the sickle), through which the earth, fertilized by ploughing, is stripped of the fruits it has brought to maturity ... As in weaving where the sacrifice preceding the cutting of the cloth is justified by explicitly stating the principle 'a life for a life,' the logic adopted is that of blood vengeance (*thamgert'*), a 'throat' for a 'throat,' and the 'master of the field' risks paying this with his life for the life he takes from the field by cutting the throat of the last sheaf ...[40]

A whole series of threads that lead from the violence inherent in the action of reaping was carried forward and extended into a concatenated series of meanings that associated the violence with murder and its compensation, sacrifice. It is no surprise that Christian preachers in the age of the Maktar Harvester joined the images of the cutting of reaping, the sickle, and the sacrifice of the martyr. In Africa, Augustine could speak of the Lord cutting unwanted things off the saint, especially, as here, in his example of the blessed Cyprian, 'with the sickle of the martyr's passion' or 'with the sickle of martyrdom.'[41] There are so many evocations of this connection with sacrifice in the modern Maghrib that it is difficult not to see them as replications of some kind. In Morocco the ritual Master of the Field turns to face east when he cuts the last sheaf of grain. He lays it on the ground with its head also facing east and he simulates the cutting of its throat. In other cases, as he cuts the last sheaf, he recites the *shahada*, the prayer of 'the witness' or the martyr, the ritual prayer of dying with the hope of resurrection.[42]

Another cause of elasticity in meaning was the possessive power that flowed from the reaping of grain, since it marked the acquisition of the basic annual resource on which the entire community depended. The appropriation was effected by the violence of cutting that involved deprivation in the process of taking and possessing. The act suggested the possibility of the decapitation of excess power. This was not a passive dying but the active inflicting of harm and death. In a consideration of the power of kings, a prophetic speaker in ancient Israel argued that 'those who are not soldiers, but who reap and bring in the crops' are emblematic of the opposite of regal power which finds its quintessential instance in the ability to order men to kill and to be killed.[43] In this light, it is hardly surprising that these images worked their way into the sleeping mind, and into the rhetoric of visions, even of kings, as in the dreams of Henry I. Not only did the cutting of cereal grains portend social violence, the cut sheaves themselves signalled a language and imagery of political power. The dream interpreter, Joseph, had an important vision that marked the beginning of his career and his ascent to power.

Joseph had a dream, and he repeated it to his brothers. 'Listen,' he said, 'to this dream that I have had. We were binding sheaves in the countryside. And my sheaf, it seemed, rose up and stood upright. Then I saw your sheaves gather round and bow to my sheaf.' 'So ... you want to be king over us?' his brothers retorted, 'Or to lord it over us?' And they hated him even more, on account of his dreams and what he had said.[44]

The sheaf, made up of cereal grain that had been cut, was understood to signal something potentially subversive.[45] The sheaf was identified with the reaper, and there was always a potential overlap with the cutting instrument itself. So there was some confusion as to whether *mergae*, the reaping tools, signified the instrument or the sheaves.[46] Just so, the reaping tool entered pop entertainment for violence, as in Plautus's *Rudens* when Daemones threatens: 'If you so much as touch that door, by god I'll harvest your face with my *mergae*-armed fists.'[47] Likewise, in the not-quite-conscious unwaking world of dreaming, the reaper and his sickle were thought to be a signal, a *semeion*, of deliberate deprivation. The sickle took away the inherent power of life. So Artemidorus, the great dream interpreter, stated explicitly that the sickle was a sign of taking away, of robbery, loss, and damage, because it divides and cuts in two and never makes anything into one.[48] Dreaming in terms of harvesting and sheaving was unusual in written documents, but still significant. In the case of Joseph's dream, the sheaves embodied the position of eminent brothers or potential power holders. The idea seems to be connected with the power inherent in cutting the sheaves, since the reaper came not just to cut, but also to possess: to lord it over others and therefore to put everything in his own order.

The Power

In a similar fashion, in the formal law of Rome the cutting and the gathering of grain signalled the potential transfer of possession and ownership. It is against this background that the Augustan jurist Labeo discussed the position of the usufructuary who harvests a crop and then dies.

Labeo says that the grains which are lying on the ground harvested belongs to his [i.e., the usufructuary's] heir, but that the grain still attached to the soil belongs to the owner of the land. For the crop is considered to be gathered only when the heads of grain or the meadow grasses … have been cut.[49]

The work of cutting helped to create possession and ownership. The action of harvesting made one the master. If the reaper was a hired man, he cut for the lord who would own the cut grains. The idea was one that was capable of transfers between different kinds of cutting and empowerment. It was said that Hybrias of Crete, an island famed for its hired killers, composed a drinking song that made the point.

My spear and my sword are my great wealth,
my wild-hided shield, the defence of my skin.
With this one I plough, with the other I reap;
with this one I work the sweet wine from the vine,
with this one I am called the master of my peasants.
Those who don't dare to hold a spear or a sword
and the good-hided shield, defence of the body,
they all throw themselves at my knees, cringing,
hailing me as Master and Great Lord.[50]

Reaping with the sword paid off: it made one lord and master. The assertion of ownership required an act of violence or the threat of it. This was generally true of reaping and taking in the Roman Mediterranean. The violent man reaped, the gleaner cleaned up the remnants left on the field of battle for his lord. The conqueror reaped the spoils of victory, his underlings and successors mopped up for him. Antigonos Gonatas boasted: 'Alexander harvested Asia, I cleaned it up.'[51] This secondary operation of picking up leftover grain was a vital economic cleaning-up operation in which more of the harvested grains were appropriated for the owner. In the world of the Greek city-states and that of the Roman empire, this secondary collecting operation did *not* have, as it would in later post-Roman times, overtones of the leaving of modest leftovers for the general benefit of the poor and the indigent as a form of alms giving.[52] It was just another gathering operation that was conducted by the landowner or his surrogates and which also denoted possession.[53] If there was anything analogous to gleaning, it was the picking up of uncollected stalks of grain, the *stipula illecta*, left in the fields by the main reaping operations.[54] But this was *not* gleaning in the Christian sense. Antigonos Gonatas was not a poor mendicant.

The collecting of the grains that had fallen on the ground and the sprigs of straw that were left behind in the field, either through natural wastage or as a result of the reaping operation itself, was done by family members and other permanent household labourers who followed in the wake of the reapers. Those who took what the landlord's reapers had cut were, as his surrogates, possessing in his or her stead. In this world, gleaning was just another way of taking possession or ownership for the true owner, the *dominus* or the landlord. In the Roman Mediterranean, there are few or no signs of gleaning in the sense of a popular or folk right granted to the poor or to the indigent who themselves would acquire ownership of left-over grains that had fallen in the fields during the harvest.[55] It appears that this social practice *was* followed in the communities of the Near East, including those of the Kingdom of Judah, where the traditional gleaning of the fields by the poor is richly attested in biblical sources, especially in the Book of Ruth of the Hebrew Bible. It is no simple effect produced by the literary and theological repetition of typologies that the story in the Book of Ruth involving its female protagonist and the lordly Boaz came to be heavily commented on in Latin texts of the early medieval West.[56] In Israel and Judah, the practice was enshrined in what was known as the ancestral constitution or *politeia*, the laws of Moses, which held: 'when reaping and gathering in the crops at the height of summer you shall not clean up the remnants, but rather you shall leave them as well as some of the sheaves for the destitute.'[57] This perspective of community, and hence of poverty, was alien to the Greek and Roman Mediterranean world in which the harvester from Maktar and his gangs went reaping. There is nothing in the whole mainstream Greek and Latin literary tradition that is as central as the discussions and deliberations on gleaning found in the Tractate Peah in the Mishnah and in the Talmud, the latter more or less contemporary with our harvester.[58]

The vivid visuals of reaping in wide-awake imaginations or dreams, such as those seen by Joseph and interpreted by Artemidorus, were bound up with how the process of reaping, the cynosure of harvesting, was depicted, and of how it was visualized. It could be seen as pleasant and anodyne, or even quite pleasing. Or not. Which raises the problem of by whom and for whom pictures or images are made or interpreted. From what point of view did they construe meaning? In the medieval calendrical tradition, painters and illuminators portrayed figures of peasant workers, including those of mowers and reapers, in a far more aesthetically pleasing way than the real-life day-to-day sordid workers were ordinarily viewed; certainly more pleasantly than the actual peasants were viewed by the elite patrons for whom the art works were being created. As has been acutely observed, the hard work depicted in the illustrated scenes of the main agricultural labour associated with each month of the year 'may be back-breaking, but it is never heart-breaking.' The emotional tone of the paintings and illustrations is calm, serene, and not marked by suffering and sin, or harbingers of disaster. Here 'no sudden hailstorm flattens the harvest.'[59] In short, it is a world of ornament.

These are the accessories of the rich. In a common scene in this tradition, the labour of harvesting is 'all bright gold against a bright blue sky.'[60] And why not? We are in the made-up world of the well-off. Why should they have to live with a distasteful world of sweat, back-breaking work, and few rewards if they did not have to? They were paying the painter and they deserved to get what they were paying for: their view of their world. The resulting tone is a strange combination of elegance and lightness in the picturing of what would otherwise be wearying, dirty work. Analogues from Roman antiquity are the scenes of cute little *putti* play-harvesting the grapes and other fruits of the season.[61] A brilliant mosaic from late antique Antioch that features the Earth, *Ge*, and gay little *putti* as cute cherubic reapers, or *karpoi*, who playfully cut the wheat crop and bring the sheaves to

5.4: Putti/Erotes as miniature grape harvesters. Marble sarcophagus, Museo Nazionale Romano, Terme di Diocleziano, Rome; Antonine Date; ArtResource

5.5: Putti/Erotes as harvesters: Palazzo dei Conservatori, Rome. H. Stuart-Jones, *The Sculptures of the Palazzo Conservatori* (Oxford: Clarendon Press, 1926), p. 265

her, is part of this same aesthetic.[62] There is no heavy religiosity here – just more ornamentation. The Antioch mosaic found its literary counterpart in an artistic ekphrasis of a mosaic that the author, John of Gaza, claims to have viewed as a decoration, not in a temple or a shrine, but in the winter baths, perhaps of his own town, but perhaps at Antioch.[63] In either case, the lord vicariously controls all that he sees, including the beautiful men and women, or pretty cherub-like miniature humans, who do the heavy trampling of the grapes and the arduous cutting of the harvest for him.[64] Seen in another way, the *putti* are cute, cuddly, and embraceable versions of slaves, who are also usually pictured as pint-sized beings, although meaner in appearance. It was the same with the context of the symbols of the harvest as they were embedded in numerous brilliant mosaics in Africa. They were meant to decorate the private spaces in the grand homes of the social elite of the time.[65] This specific modification of a fundamental mode of cutting and separation is an indication of the obvious: there are strong cultural screens or veils that effect some of the fundamental work of artful metaphoric thinking.[66]

The same point is made by the brilliant sets of 'the cycle of labours' paintings that graced western European medieval manuscripts of the seasons. One of the best known and most beautiful is the manuscript conventionally known as the *Très Riches Heures*.[67] It was produced between 1412 and 1415 by the Limbourg brothers from Flanders for the Duc de Berry. One of the highest-ranking members of the French nobility of his age, the Duke of Berry's wealth was marvellous in its extent, as is illustrated by the 1,500 pet dogs, the pet ostriches, the pet bears, and the pet camels that he kept on his estates. It goes without saying that the Duke was someone who could barely stand the sight and smell of real peasant workers. Yet the representation of the mowers in the month of June (see fig. 1.5) and the reapers of grain in the month of July, dressed much like their Roman counterparts, with the lord's great castle as the scenic backdrop, configures peace, order, cleanliness, and prosperity. They exude an air of tranquillity and, more powerfully, of beauty. So many ornaments. After all, this is one of the functions of ornamentation, in this case of the Duke's exquisite handbooks to his daily liturgical practice (he had at least fifteen of them of which we know) aesthetically guiding his religious rituals. Could it be that we are facing not only the use of humans as accessories, but also as ideological props? It has been imagined. 'The calendar pictures he enjoyed as he turned the pages of the Book of Hours must have woven a beautiful *veil* of illusion, perhaps to mask the ugly reality of the world outside his castle walls.'[68] Perhaps. The appeal to the metaphor of ideology as a veil or mask that hides and obscures is hardly novel.[69]

It is probably true that the workers on the Duke's great domains, treated with the usual careless brutality and disdain, did not mirror the sentiments evoked in the panoramas of the calendrical scenes, but rather resentment, which is to say, something short of vengeance.[70] There was this other cultural experience and construction of the front end of the harvest: reapers could be threatening. They could be transfixed with anger and hatred. They were potentially dangerous men. The problem is that *these* reapers do not make it into the fine world of visual art, by definition an expensive and exclusive world of costly accoutrement. This

5.6: *Les Très Riches Heures* of the Duc de Berry: reaping in the month of July.
Musée Condé at Chantilly, France: ms. 65, f. 7 v.; Art Resource

seems as true of Roman antiquity as it was of the aristocratic traditions of later medieval and early modern western Europe. The tradition of the calendrical representations of the seasons and months aside, the standard icons of reaping in antiquity are mostly found in funereal contexts where they represent something rather different from the luxuriant arcadias of the *Très Riches Heures*. This function of the reaper has mostly escaped the written and printed word. To find this other representational world of the reaper, it is necessary to look to writings that have been inflected in more manifest and direct ways by oral communications and by everyday talk. The lyric song, the ritual chant, the folk tale, the popular stage, the world of the parable and the fable, and the Christian sermon are as good examples as any. Here the harvest was found frequently and it was explicitly recognized as a metaphor.[71] It was more directly identified with threats of personal violence: a harvest of knuckles in your face.[72] This reaper existed in a daily regime where he was caught between his own marginal existence and the frights and dangers that threatened, every year, to destroy and to eradicate the basis of his life and that of others. These malign forces passing through him and his work were transmitted by images of the reaper and his reaping into thought and belief. The keynotes were apprehension, fear, and the impending sense of a threat.

At precisely the same time in the year, not only the harvest workers, but also the enforcers, the men who came to collect what was owed, whether to the tax-collector or to the landlord, threatened violence. Not infrequently in the age of the Maktar Harvester, they were one and the same person. The peasants who took off the harvest might plead, often in vain, against excessive exaction, such as the hard enforcement of dues insisted upon by the fourth-century notable Letoios from Antioch.[73] He came out into the countryside to inspect 'his villages' and to have the sheaves of grain that the peasants had reaped stacked on carts and transported to the city, all over the protests of the locals. We only happen to know about this episode because of the narrative of a late antique holy man, Maisymas. In the same mode, the taking of the crop by the landlord was replicated in another view that we have already seen: the illustration on the Boglio Stele. On it the landowner takes the sheaves that the workers have cut by the law of possession and ownership, a legal structure backed by a combination of violence and thought (see fig. 1.13). All of this happens under the watchful and potentially vengeful eye of the supreme deity Saturn, who wields a cosmic cutting instrument (variously, a reaping hook or a sickle) as a reminder that he had reaped from his own father.

Day of the Torches

The divine Lord's oversight brought a special edginess to the process of reaping and harvesting, since it signalled a peculiar convergence of interests. In modern-day Tunisia, in the same region of the Great Plains where the large imperial domains

5.7: The measurement of the field and the collection of the grain: tomb of Mennah, Thebes, c. 1395 BCE; Art Resource

of the high Roman empire were located, the critical significance of getting the harvest in quickly, even in an age of mechanization, is tied to the pressing need for the peasant cultivator to acquire money to pay off his debts. These include the taxes claimed by the state.[74] It is therefore no accident that one sees pictured on the walls of the tombs of the nobles and functionaries of pharaonic Egypt the sudden descent of the tax man, the state's tributary collector, and, later, the private landlord and his agents, at this critical time in the annual cycle of production, measuring the fields before the reapers appear. In Africa, the idea worked its way laterally into poetic celebration in the verses of Dracontius in the Vandal age. In his poem on 'The Months,' he marked the month of June in the following manner.

The golden heads of grain are waving their spikes;
the farmer accounts for his expenses, the sailor for his sailings.

Messibus armatis flavae crispantur aristae;
Rusticus expensas et fluctus nauta reposcit.[75]

Expectations and hopes were reflected in visual representations of the seasons and the months. They portrayed the summer and the month of harvest (usually June in the case of the Mediterranean) with the symbols of the sickle and the torch (see fig. 4.14). Reaping was attached to a day of social ritual that signalled the season of reaping: the great Day of the Torches. The eighth day before the kalends of July, the 24th of June in our computation, or the time of the summer solstice, demarcated the ritual time of the harvest. It was the *dies lampadarum*. It is probably the reason why an error crept into the poem attached to the representation of the Codex Calendar of 354 for the month of June.

> June, his limbs bare, looks intently at the solar dial
>   and indicates that the Sun has changed his course.
> The torch shows that the heads of Ceres [i.e., grain] are now ripe
>   and the lilies strewn about that the flowers are gone.

> Nudus membra dehinc solares respicit horas
>   Iunius ac Phoebum flectere monstrat iter.
> Lampas maturas Cereris designat aristas
>   florialisque fugas lilia fusa docent.[76]

The alternative reading of *iam falx* ('and now the sickle') was suggested by Baehrens for the beginning of the third line: *Iam falx maturas Cereris designat aristas.*[77] He wished to have a reference to the sign of the sickle in the illustration and he was perplexed by the meaning of the torch. A series of scholarly investigations, however, have confirmed that the reading of *lampas* referring to the torch must be correct.

We know that the Day of the Torches was the most important social ritual that marked the time of the harvest, not only in Africa but in the later empire at large.[78] A panel from the seasons and months mosaic from Thysdrus (modern El-Djem) for the month of June looks very much like a pavilion set up for the sale of torches to celebrants.[79] An anonymous African preacher from the age of Dracontius, known as the pseudo-Fulgentius, makes clear how the Day of the Torches and its rituals had been claimed by the Christians under the rubric of the day of John the Baptist.[80] The classic concern with the zodiacal cycle of months and seasons was now read in a Christian mode. The new perspective connected a critical turning point in the year, the season of reaping and cutting, with the anniversary of the martyrdom of John the Baptist, who lost his head, severed by a blade and displayed on a plate.[81] The day was identified with him, states an African preacher

5.8: Jules Breton, the Day of the Torches: *Fête de Jean le Baptiste/Le Jour de Torches*, c. 1875. Philadelphia, Philadelphia Museum of Art; ArtResource

of the age, 'because it was on this day that he was born and he was decapitated just like reaped grain.'[82] This tradition then became embedded in practice in which new Christian meanings were attached to the display of the sickle and the torch. In rural regions of medieval France, the carrying of torches in a procession at harvest had the following significance attached to it as an explanation: 'It is the custom to carry burning torches on this night because John the Baptist was a burning light, the light which prepared the way of the Lord.'[83] This memory of his death became part of the conventions of the artists who painted realist pictures of peasant life in nineteenth-century France. Although the death of John the Baptist was technically marked on 29 August, the fact that 24 June, the time of the summer solstice, was regarded as his *natalis* purposefully confused the distinction between his natural birth and his 'birthday' as a pre-martyr of the faith.

The God of Justice

The threats that existed with the sudden profusion of seasonal labour bursting into local time and into the local social order were the cause of deep-seated fears on the side of both the reapers and their employers. Consequently, there was a need for a deterrent enforcement that might have to be swift, sudden, and final. The annual turn of the seasons brought not only a natural progression of cosmic order, but also a final accounting within that order. If the tax man showed up in this earthly existence, just so in the greater order of things the divine collector would appear. The basic nature of the enforcer is his threat. He presents a vivid picture of what will happen to you should you transgress. Saturn, in whatever regional manifestation, was not the only god to wield a threatening sickle. Many important Mediterranean and Near Eastern deities and heroes, at one point or another in their life stories, picked up and wielded a cutting instrument of the harvest. Mithras is another example, although he is hardly alone.[84] He is sometimes portrayed as a reaper of arboreal fruits armed with a *harpê*, a bill-hook or curved pruning knife. At other times, he is seen as a harvester of cereal grains armed with a reaper's sickle.[85] The equivalencies make the back-and-forth shifts between different types of reaping blades understandable. In texts and visual images, Mithras is pictured wielding a cutting instrument of the harvest and is identified with Kronos and Chronos, and in turn with Saturn, marking the connection of particular concern to Africans in the age of the Maktar Harvester.[86] The cutting and reaping tools also had a vital connection with death, as is found on the tombstone of an anonymous burial near Akmonia in southern Lykia. On the stone was inscribed a warning against anyone who dared to violate the grave. The miscreant would have to face the punishing vengeance of the 'God of the Highest and the Reaping Sickle of his Curse.'[87] Now, that is a threat.

The god Mars in the early Roman Republic and the Italian deity Saturn, gods of enforcement and retribution, both used a form of reaping or cutting instrument sometimes known as a *harpê*, with which they were identified.[88] The *harpê* was also the sharp tool with which Hermes cut off the head of the monster Argos.[89] According to another variant of the story, Jupiter himself wounded the monster Tryphon with a *harpê*. Once again, we see the identification of this attribute with the greatest of the gods, and therefore with the African Saturn.[90] Sometimes, however, the divine reaper was less than one of these great and august gods. All of these figures assumed the aura of threat and violence that was signalled by the action of reaping and the armament of the sickle. The instrument of the harvest symbolized aggression as much as did that other male tool.[91] Sometimes the deity was a vengeful and menacing little creature, an evil dwarf. Priapus, for example, the guardian of the garden, wielded his harvester's sickle as a weapon.

Let the gardens breathing the scent of saffron flowers invite *them* in [the bees], but let the guardianship of Hellespontine Priapus, on guard against thieves and birds, armed with his willowy sickle, protect them ...[92]

Priapus was a guardian, a *custos*, just like the hard-working harvest guards, *custodes fructuum*, armed with their own reaping tools as weapons.[93] There is no doubt that this vicious little garden gnome, armed with his sickle, would cut down the intruders. The threat was plain. You do this to me and I will do this to you.

> Enclose the garden with walls and close set fences so that
> it won't be exposed to cattle and to thieves. And
> don't go looking for a work created by the finely skilled
> hand of a Daedalus or wrought by a Polyclitus, a Phradmon or an
> Ageladas ... Get the trunk of some rough-hewn ancient tree
> to worship as the divine spirit of Priapus of the awe-inspiring
> prick, always on guard in the middle of your garden, threatening
> young boys with his crotch and robbers with his sickle.[94]

The equation was clear, and so another metaphor was produced and drawn upon: the equation of the threat of rape with the threat of the reaping sickle that would cut off genitalia. The equation of THE PENIS IS A TOOL is a metaphor that is found everywhere, of which THE PENIS IS A WEAPON is a refinement or variation. The words on Priapus in the last line from Columella quoted above had already been penned by Ovid (and perhaps even he had acquired them) and were cautionary: Priapus was 'the god who threatened thieves with his sickle or his prick.'[95] As another of the *Priapea* makes clear, the farm manager or *vilicus* who wanted a handy weapon to ward off thieves could break off the distended and turgid *membrum virile* of the wooden statue and use it as a club.[96] That is to say, the two were equivalent kinds of armament.[97] The metaphor is embedded in contexts that linked both with the equation of the tool with a weapon, and of sex with war, like the ritual chanting of Marines in training on Parris Island. 'This is my dick / this is my gun // This one's for killing / this one's for fun.' All the time being encouraged by the DI to touch each instrument so as physically to make the point. The training is to kill, the ritual shouting embodies the threat that they *will* do so. Roman legionaries, one can be sure, did not miss the connection and didn't need to read lyric poets on love as a form of combat to get the point: 'Are you ready for war?' their officer shouted. 'Yes, we are!' the men shouted back three times, punching the air with their fists in unison.[98]

In Africa, the power of Priapus, his *membrum virile* and his sickle, was much needed. It was directed against another threat to the crops. A statue of Priapus found at a place called 'Aïn Jelloula, about fifty kilometres directly east of Mactaris, not only features his dangerous tool, but also, nested neatly in the fold of his tunic, atop the fruits that illustrated agrarian fertility, a locust.[99] That he had to guard against a real local danger by threatening punishment, a sanction that the other sickle-bearing deity of the land, Saturn, also threatened, is made clear by other equivalencies. On a votive stele set up to the god Saturn at Thamugadi,

5.9: Priapus statuette with locust, 'Aïn Djelloula, Tunisia, third century CE.
Foucher, 'Priape ithyphallique,' p. 1, figs. 2–3

modern Timgad, in southern Numidia, the devotee himself is pictured, accompanied by a large image of the dangerous locust.[100] The location is not accidental. Thamugadi, and the nearby town of Lambaesis, lay at the head of one of the major defiles that ran from the periphery of the Sahara northward into the grain-producing high plains of Numidia.[101] In its positional ecology, this pass, the Bab al-Biskra, parallels that of the Cilician Gates in southeastern Anatolia. There, too, a god was similarly implored to help keep the airborne clouds of destructive insects at bay.

> Mercury of the Powerful Staff, Slayer of Argos,
> Messenger of the Gods
> ward off the clouds of locusts from these places
> with your sacrosanct rod.
> Your likeness stands on this place to help the increase of crops

5.10: Saturn stele: dedicant with locust, Thamugadi, Algeria. Leglay, SAM 2, pl. xxvii. 9

and for the health of these places and these peoples.
Be kind and well disposed to all men
and give increase to the crops and all things.[102]

The images and the threats were directed against one of the greatest perils to bringing off the cereal harvest each year. Invasions of locusts created an additional sense of the urgency to get the harvesters out into the field. One locust attack had been powerful enough to drive all the inhabitants of an African town from their homes.[103] Since the conflict was seen as a war, soldiers of the regular army were mobilized for the fight.[104] Clouds of locusts could be a truly frightening apparition. Sweeping up from Africa towards Italy, they created panic and provoked consultation of the Sibylline Books, and, we are told, such consultations happened often.[105] Fear seized the Italian peninsula. In 173 BCE, great threatening clouds of locusts suddenly swept in from the sea and invaded Apulia, devastating crops far and wide. The response was to take the praetor designate, Gnaeus Sicinius, and to invest him with a military command in Apulia. He was armed with formal *imperium*, no less, to go to war with the hoppers. It took him some time, and the draft of a large number of men, to defeat the locusts.[106] The connection between soldiers, reapers, and the dangers of the harvest was a usual and an intimate one.

Africa was particularly susceptible to locust invasions coming out of the northern fringe areas of the Sahara. One of the more vivid reports of these attacks describes a hopper invasion that swept over Africa in the mid-120s BCE.

It was the year when Marcus Plautius Hypsaeus and Marcus Fulvius Flaccus were consuls [125 BCE], when, hardly having gained rest from the destruction of war, Africa was struck with a terrible and unexpected disaster. Boundless multitudes of locusts massed over the whole of Africa. They not only extinguished all hope of crops, they razed all the plants right down to their roots. They consumed the leaves of the trees and the tender parts of the branches. They even gnawed away at the bitter bark and the wood itself. A great wind swept them up from the land and carried them for a long time through the air, collecting them in great masses and dumping them near the sea where the pushing waves spread them far and wide along the shore; their putrefying bodies, decomposing, emitted a terrible stench.[107]

The ravages of the locusts were followed by a plague that inflicted death on huge numbers of people. To the end of Roman times in Africa, the threat of locust invasions remained one of the looming fears that hovered over the taking of the cereal crops on which the wealth and prosperity of the empire depended. The Byzantine court poet Corippus, an African himself, could readily evoke the horrors of a hopper attack.

Who is able to conceive in mind so many thousands of men? It was *as if* locusts, darkening the sky with the South Wind blowing, scattering through African fields, suddenly struck … they cause horror in fearful farmers, lest the horrid pests grind their crops to nothing, lay waste tender growths and verdant gardens, and harm the olive flourishing on supple limbs.[108]

The use of the image of the locust engaged the mind of the reader or listener with a metaphor that suggested countless numbers and a truly frightening danger.

The element of threat and the harvest was not something that was grounded solely in nature. The danger did not involve only harmful pests and destructive weather. Even if the crops managed to survive these dangers, there remained threats posed by human agents. Human intruders intending harm were also part of this danger to the harvest. The crops had to be guarded, since they were sometimes the object of attacks that intended either theft or the infliction of damage.

In each region of the empire, these attacks were handled with a different level of seriousness. We are told that the same crimes were more severely punished in some regions of the empire than they were in others: 'as, for example, in Africa, those who burn cereal crops' were dealt with more seriously.[109] Not surprisingly (note, again, the link with war), military men like the Byzantine general Solomon on the high plains of Numidia in 539 knew that the burning of crops was a real threat to the enemy's power.[110] If the resource was general and valuable, elements of criminality and vengeful getbacks – 'I'll burn your crops' – were an ever-present threat. It is in this sense that the reaping of cereal crops was linked in a logical sequence with acts that caused the crops to come into being in the first place.

Reaping was therefore vitally and integrally connected with the whole ecological process of promises, urgencies, and threats that began each year with the sowing of the seed. Everyone understood the threatening metaphors that were logically entailed by connecting the beginning with the end. You would reap what you had sown. The conclusions were embedded in popular sayings about reaping found in the plays of Plautus, as when a father opined to his miscreant son about hard work down on the farm: 'You plough for yourself, you harrow and you hoe for yourself, you sow for yourself and, yes, in the same way you reap for yourself.'[111] In another play, a nefarious character who is offering up an evil plot remarks: 'I'm not sowing this crop or reaping it for myself.'[112] This is tied to the mental concept that one tended to reap what one had earlier sown: the same crop and the quality of the return. So there were large numbers of popular sayings that you would reap a harvest of evils, or whatever other bad things, if you deserved them.[113] The meaning of the work of reaping acquired its wider significance from its connection with the other parts of the agrarian cycle as it was understood by the audiences of these plays and the purveyors of these pop sayings. Their understanding made the metaphor possible.

It was precisely in the context of discussing the figure of *translatio* or metaphor that Cicero was content to repeat the popular remark: *ut sementem feceris, ita metes*, 'as you have sown, so shall you reap.'[114] Cicero did not mean to mark an inventive moment in Latin rhetoric. He was repeating a near-universal metaphor found in the Mediterranean and Near East. The predictive futurity in the words 'you shall ...' was intended to be threatening. The dire predictions about future consequences assumed political significance with the alarming words of the seer, as when the seventh-century BCE Hebrew prophet Hosea warned when he repeated, through his own voice, threats originating with the Almighty Himself.

> Because they will sow the wind,
> they will reap the whirlwind.
> Their wheat will yield no head,

the head will yield no flour …
Why have you sown unfairness
and why do you reap injustice?[115]

In this case, a mundane logical extension is added. Since there will be no grain that will sprout (that is, one will only have more wind to reap), no one will be able to eat. It will be an appropriate death world. The reverse of this 'death equals lack of growth' equation was later to be part of the basis of Christian martyrdom. Here, too, there was an implicit threat, carefully noted by the African exegete Tertullian in his explication of Christianity addressed to the rulers of his world: 'Whenever we are cut down [i.e., reaped] by you, our numbers only increase: the blood of Christians is just more seed.'[116]

The threatening words packed power because of two material connections: the image of the reaper and the cutting weapon of the harvester were joined with the great divinity who himself would come reaping and would exact just retribution. This divine harvest was connected with night and with the underworld. It arrived in the twilight of time with avenging spirits and deities. And with retribution came the image of a kind of vengeance or payback signalled by the cutting of the sickle. Just so, Vergil has Queen Dido, the woman in his *Aeneid* so loved by Augustine, boast of her pretended use of magical powers of the underworld to inflict terminal damage on a traitorous lover: 'The priestess sprinkles waters [around the altars] like those of Avernian spring, and new growth grasses, reaped with bronze sickles under the moonlight, dripping their milky black poison.'[117] Africans in the age of our harvester and earlier, who gloried in their Vergil, knew these lines and their power.[118] This is not death itself, although Dido's self-inflicted death was soon to come, but rather a curse that will be played out in the future when the amorous betrayer will be made to pay back. The cutting sickle refers to this promise.

> I hope that if the divine spirits of good faith still have any power,
> wrecked on the rocks in mid-sea you'll drink your fill
> of punishment, crying out the name of Dido over and over again
> and, even if no longer here, I'll hound you with pitch black flames,
> and when icy death has severed my body from its breath,
> then my death shadow will stalk you through the world.
> You – you depraved man – you *will* pay the price![119]

As the old song says, you will reap what you sow. If you've mistreated someone, eventually, further on up the road (or over the sea) you *will* pay the price. My ghost will stalk you. Such vengeance is beyond death. It is a threat about what *will* be reaped.

Apocalyptic Visions

The reaper and the sickle were not just embedded in a vision of death, but in a longer and more complex narrative of a particular kind of death that had to do with what we might call payback. Let's begin by harking back to Eliphaz of Teman, the friend of the long-suffering Job:

> I speak of what I know: those who plough
> iniquity and sow the seeds of grief,
> they reap a harvest of the same kind.[120]

The prophets who enunciated sentiments like these were not so much inventing the images as they were drawing on a long-established wisdom literature cast in proverbial and oral form. These common forms of communication were created out of connections made by persons in the field: experiences produced brief sayings that quickly encapsulated the core idea of a reciprocal harvest pay-off that was a kind of balance or justice.

> He who sows injustice reaps evil,
> and he shall be done in by the rod of His wrath.[121]

The prophet drew on an agrarian language that in turn drew on rural images attached to the land to assert a restorationist justice.[122] From these sayings, already canonized in written collections that were easily accessed, and which were continually reinforced by present conditions and experience, we can move to the admonitions of the early Christian communities in the Roman empire. Their writers exploited these same bodies of sayings, as when Paul wrote a letter that was filled with moral warnings to the church in Galatia.

Don't make the mistake of thinking that God can be deceived. What a man sows, that is what he reaps. If he sows his seeds in the flesh, he will reap from this flesh a harvest of corruption. If he sows in the Spirit, he will reap from the Spirit a harvest of eternal life. Let's never weary of doing good, and in due time we shall reap our harvest.[123]

The apostolic cue was picked up and played upon for explication by the preachers of late African antiquity. In a wonderful disquisition on sin and its wages, Fulgentius of Ruspe repeatedly emphasizes the element of retribution, of paying back, and the reaping of the crop that one has sown.[124] He begins by laying down the basic fact for the sinner about the Time of Vengeance.

The Divine Word shows that when the Time of Vengeance arrives, conversion will no longer enable the evil person to evade punishment. Rather, the Wrathful Avenger will destroy him with the damnation that is owed to him. For that time will be a time not of remission but of revenge, not of forgiveness but of retribution ... The blessed John in his Apocalypse recalls that it is the saints who asked for this vengeance in these words: 'How long will it be, Lord, holy and true, before You sit in judgment and avenge our blood on those who live on the earth?'[125]

Warning about this future time-to-come, Fulgentius cautions more than once: 'For that will not be a time of forgiveness but rather one of retribution.' In all of this, he emphasizes the initial work of one's life, the *opera* of sowing, and the payback of the reaping, in which it is justice or *iustitia* that is gained. The two essential elements, he preaches to the listener, are the good sowing and the good reaping which will result in the third element, the promised pay, the *promissio mercedis*. It is in the hope of this future harvest that we work. We put in time for the payback or what we have earned: our wage, the *retributio mercedis*. For the fellowship of men who reap, the *consortium messorum*, the reward comes when the angels who are the reapers collect their sheaves in bundles and throw the unwanted growths into an eternally burning conflagration. The metaphors play on the equation that justice is the reaping of the crop that one has sown and that the two are in a perfect balance. The payback, good or bad, is directly related to the good or bad seed that one has sown. This much was naturally understood by Fulgentius's listeners from their experiences with the farming of cereal grains and other crops.[126] This could be seen as a rather anodyne equation: outputs (should) equal inputs. But in harsh reality it was never quite so anodyne, since in a world of pressing and sometimes dangerous inequalities, justice suggested the opposite: that there was a balance owing for which you, the bad person, would have to pay.

A more powerful version of this justice was reflected in the metaphor that gave expression to a greater spirit of revenge, one that called upon the divinity in images of reaping to wreak destruction not just on individuals but on whole communities.[127] Both the weaker and the more powerful versions depended on a sense of justice as balanced payback. The violence and levelling inherent in reaping were potentially threatening to any social order that was vertiginously unequal. The underlying assumption was that my enemies must have sown bad seed, and they therefore deserved to reap the evil that they had carefully cultivated against me and my people.

> Let all the enemies of Zion
> be thrown back in shame;

> let them be like grass growing on the roof
>> which withers before it can shoot;
> which will never fill a mower's hand
>> nor yield an armful for the harvester …

The Christian preachers in Africa in the age of our harvester were heirs to these images. Augustine frequently refers to precisely this one.[128] They did not speak simply of reapers, of harvest day-workers, but rather they used a series of images that linked the growth of crops and their reaping with death as the end of human experience. This death might not be just a personal natural experience. It could be purposeful: a cutting down inflicted on someone who deserved it as their reward. So Augustine went well beyond the point of natural death, emphasizing instead particular kinds of sacrificial deaths that were oriented towards the future and that would happen at a forthcoming time of accounting.[129] In the body of his sermons, the consistent line of development of these tropes generally tied the harvest and its reaping to present and past Christian deaths that were sacrifices for the faith: to the deaths of the martyrs. Then he went to a point beyond these deaths where the harvest, and especially the task of reaping, indicated the Final Judgment at the End of Time.

The Harvest of the Lord was to be the time when the final separation would be made by the winnowing of the grain and the straw.[130] The idea of the Lord of Justice was also integrally part of real experience. In this sense, the real-life social practices of ownership, management, agency, and the need to acquire reapers for the harvest were reconfigured in thought into a template of power relationships. The same words used by a foreman every year could be repeated, but with apocalyptic meanings.

Then he said to his students: 'The harvest is rich, but the workers are few, so ask the Lord of the Harvest to send labourers to his own harvest.'[131]

Here we have the nexus between the observed phenomena of the too abundant bumper harvest, the urgent need for more workers, and the figure of the Lord of the Harvest, the *kyrios therismou*, whom we have already seen strutting about, lording it over workers and the process of reaping.[132] This harvest metaphor is one of the most important ones found in Augustine's sermons and treatises, especially through the first part of his episcopacy when he was mainly concerned with attacking his sectarian enemies in Africa, the so-called Donatists.[133] The whole picture went beyond the harvest itself, in which the reapers, the angels of the Lord, played a particularly powerful role, to the subsequent steps in a narrative whose driving force was mainly enabled by metaphor.[134] The first was the winnowing by which the harvested grain was separated, the good from the bad, the grain from the straw. The former was to be stored in the barn, the latter was to be burned in a fiery conflagration. Beyond the cutting of the cereal grains that signified a temporal or secular death, there was a bigger final accounting that signified a larger, more cosmic, life and death. In this judgmental process the Lord is the great landowner who sends his hired day labourers, the reapers, the *operarii*, out to the field to cut the human crop.

The lordly commanding figure is also pictured as the great winnower who will preside over the separation of the good and the bad.[135] The winnowing metaphor was not as innocuous as it might at first seem – nothing more, say, than pleasant assisting breezes blowing away unwanted chaff and straw. Since the chaff and straw represented those who were evil or, at least, not good, this metaphor was shaped by a powerful sense of retribution.[136] The chaff represented heretics and the unrighteous, a fact that was embedded in popular use of the metaphor as early as Augustine's pop song against the Donatists.[137] Even in his earliest use of the metaphor, the point is made that they are bad persons, chaff who will be weeded out at the End of Time when The Winnower will come and rid the threshing floor of these unwanted persons in the Final Harvest.[138] The later stronger versions of the harvesting metaphor that concentrate on the back-end threshing and storage operations draw on prophetic writings, like those of Jeremiah, to show how, in the harvest of the End Time, the tares will be separated from the good grain. The weeds and chaff, the bad persons who will pay the price for their badness, will be burned in a final conflagration.[139] The chaff will be burned in 'an unquenchable fire.'[140] The metaphors were presented to listeners in sermons where the reaping and storing of the good grain in the granary are contrasted with the bundling of weeds by the reapers and the separation of the bad chaff from the good grain by the winnowers. The weeds and the chaff will burn, and it will be a time of weeping and sorrow.[141] The reaping will be a time of reckoning for the unjust and the unrighteous, the heretics, who will now face payback for the evil that they have done.[142]

The Sign of the Sickle

The harvester and his sickle therefore embodied not just death, but also more powerful forces of divine vengeance, retribution, and justice. The two sides fed into each other. Out of a metaphor of sowing and reaping, the cutting instrument, the sickle, symbolized the sense of justice and fairness. It remains so even to the present day, as when a protester in South Africa joins an outraged crowd and brandishes his sickle in a gesture that is at once threatening and a symbolic demand for justice.[143] At its best, personal vengeance was the righting of a grievous wrong. It

5.11: The sickle as an emblem of protest: demonstrators in South Africa. *New York Times,* 7 September 2009, A4; permission Siphiwe Sibeko and Reuters

therefore often involved moral writing of a sacred kind. One of the holy monks from the settlement of Sketis in upper Egypt, Abba David, who each year engaged in harvesting for hire, had such a story told of him.[144] In the scorching midday heat of the harvest, David sought shelter in a makeshift hut beside the field. The farmer who had hired him found him resting and erupted in anger. 'Why aren't you working, old man!' he shouted. David tried to explain that in the overpowering heat of the day many of the grains of cereal were being lost in the reaping process, falling from the heads as the stalks were cut. He replied that he was just waiting a little so that the farmer wouldn't suffer such needless losses. The farmer was furious and simply would not listen. 'Get up and get back to work, even if all the crop is burned up.' 'Surely you don't want it all burned, do you?' David interjected. 'Sure!' the farmer angrily retorted, 'Just get back to work and do what I've told you to do!' We are informed that the old man got up to do as he was ordered and immediately the whole field of grain caught fire. In a panic, the farmer ran and begged the other men to intercede with David, but David said: 'He himself said that the crop should be burned up.' With charity in his heart, however, David gave in to the men's pleas and went and stood in prayer by the field of burning wheat, and the fire was quenched.

This kind of sacred retribution referred to foundational events and cosmic forces. The primal divine *coup d'état* happened when Kronos castrated his father Ouranos with the reaper's sickle: 'In his right hand he grasped the giant long sickle with its jagged teeth and he quickly reaped the genitals of his father.'[145] The act might well have been a primal one, but the transition from Near Eastern (in this case, Hittite) versions to Greek ones required the retooling of the teeth from those of a human jaw, like Bond's Mr Jaws, to those serrating the metal blade of a sickle.[146] A plethora of sad and violent cases demonstrates that in stories like these the sickle was understood to be the usual reaper's instrument and that it was 'the normal weapon in Greek mythology for the amputation of monsters, and a very suitable one for the job.'[147] A jagged saw-toothed sickle was wielded by Iolaus when he helped Herakles to decapitate the heads of the monstrous Hydra of Lernaea.[148] The sickle was also used by Perseus to behead Medusa, and it remained a potent symbol of his power.[149] Like the cutting or stripping of the heads of wheat or barley, all these cases are stories of decapitation. What is involved is not the sacrifice of the object, but rather, a little more brutishly, its reaping. The point is made not only in verbal descriptions, but also in pictorial representations. The large number of pictures of Perseus decapitating Medusa on Athenian Red and Black Figure wares, for example, highlight not just the decapitated head, but the blade that was used as the weapon brandished by Perseus.[150] The death or rather the execution of Orpheus has a similar background, although the precise reasons for the assassination are hidden from us. Here, too, the pictorial representations indicate much the same range of agricultural weapons in the hands of the Thracian Bakhai who attack him as was found on Perpetua's ladder: spits, lances, knives, and the harvester's sickle.[151] This was so, I think, because of the close analogy between the sickle and regular weapons: the sickle is an 'almost weapon.' For various reasons that have been well expressed by others, sacrifice requires the flow of real blood.[152] Swords, knives, and cleavers perform this task. The sickle also takes life, although hardly in as dramatic a fashion and in a context not of execution or of the imposition of a death sentence. It is rather an extension to another kind of life and context, and so, by a further extension, it can be seen as the agent of a sacrificial ritual.[153]

Not a few of these mythic narratives have earlier Near Eastern versions where the power inherent in the violent and punitive aspects of the agricultural instrument, the sickle, were adopted by fearsome monarchs: 'It is a popular weapon for a god attacking a foe in Babylonian-Assyrian art, and a common royal attribute in the ancient Near East.'[154] All of this killing was not just normal violence or the use of a weapon in war, but a more special kind of moral violence that was revindicative in quality. The difference is clear in the direct inheritor of Ba'al and Kronos in Africa in the age of our harvester: the great god Saturn. Although he shared many agricultural attributes with other deities, like wheat sheaves with Ceres and the Cereres, these others were not conventionally armed with the sickle.[155] As the African writer Arnobius says, in recognizing Saturn's central role as *frugifer* or the deity who caused the growth and ripening of crops, mainly cereal grains, the reaping sickle was his particular attribute: *falx messoria… quae est attributa Saturno.*[156] In addition to its function of cutting the harvest, the sickle carried with it a more threatening meaning of the rural enforcer or guard: As a rural guard, *custos ruris*, Saturn is armed with an *obunca falx.*[157] Whether as himself, or in the guise of Jupiter, in Africa Saturn was not only the protector of the cereal crops in the fields as they were being taken off; he was also the guardian spirit of the the floor or *area* where they were being threshed.[158] Exactly the same word, *area*, was used to designate a burial ground, a cemetery. The *area* was the place where humans were brought after they had been reaped, so it is no accident that reapers are normally portrayed in connection with the tombs where the bodies were kept. The tombs, after all, were *like* granaries.

We end here, again, with the sentiments and feelings that motivated the killer, the soldier, the holy warrior, and the martyr, from whom the powerful image of reaping was never far away. We have already witnessed the constant association of the harvest with war, and the action of reaping with violence. The question is: How much did this image affect behaviour? The plain fact is that sickle-like devices were used as weapons, as they were (poetically at least) among the Geleni from the periphery of the Black Sea.[159] Among the Gauls, says Cicero in a piece of quasi-ethnological reportage, it was deemed to be shameful to engage in harvesting with their own hands, and so the they went armed into the fields belonging other men in order to reap. The stigma of manual labour for the warrior was replaced by the use of weapons to gain the same end. The one more or less substituted for the other.[160] Christian preachers in late Roman Africa had inherited a rich panoply of literary tropes along these same lines, not only from their 'pagan' predecessors, but also from their more specific Jewish background – tropes that configured reaping as more than just death. In his note to the Christians of Corinth encouraging them to engage in a traditional but innovative type of generosity to their religious leaders, Paul called on a line from the prophet Hosea.

> Sow integrity for yourselves
> and reap a harvest of kindness[161]

This advice correspondence and preaching constantly played upon the metaphor of 'as you sow, so shall you reap.' Even today, the trope has lost none of its metaphoric power. It can be used to describe 'good' things. But it is astonishing, in post-2008 circumstances, to see that it was used in the mid-1990s to justify the celestial bonuses paid to elite executives of highly profitable American business corporations.[162] But this blade has two sides. If the line on sowing and reaping was being used to justify the fairness of 'inputs should equal outputs,' the writers of the news report on the inflated payouts, even at that time, hinted at social distress and tension. The same metaphor could be used in a blunter fashion to indicate a fearful retribution. At the beginning of June 2009, the anti-abortion activist Terry Randall announced in public regarding the killing of Dr George Tiller that he 'was a mass murderer and, horrorifically [sic], he reaped what he sowed.'[163] The blade was double-edged in another sense. There is little doubt that Mr Randall considered the murder of the doctor to be 'justice,' whereas many others did not.

The use of the reaping metaphor also appeals to the significance of the harvest in the divine order of things. This time, however, the end is not the bountiful harvest reaped by the joyful giver. Rather, the metaphor can set the stage for a prolonged description of the vengeance of Jahweh, as is made manifest in the declaration of the prophet Hosea.

> Why have you ploughed iniquity and
> reaped injustice, and why have you eaten the produce,
> namely lies? … Turmoil is going to break out in your towns,
> and all your fortresses will be laid waste
> as Shalman laid Beth-Arbal waste on the day of battle,
> when mothers fell on their children, dashed to pieces.
> This is what I mean to do to you, House of Israel,
> because of your great wickedness … [164]

The divine vengeance is for disloyalty, and the payoff that will be reaped will not be pleasant.

> I mean to destroy you, Israel …
> Samaria must atone for rebelling against her God.
> They shall fall by the sword,
> their little children shall be dashed to pieces,
> their pregnant women disembowelled.[165]

Note the emphasis on infants and women about to give birth. The connection of the harvest and reapers with figures of violence and death, indeed apocalyptic figures, was an old one in circum-Mediterranean lands. The prophets in the Kingdom of Judah of the late seventh and early sixth centuries BCE used the image of the harvest as a threat, as a marker for a final accounting that was soon to come. In consequence, Jeremiah was prompted to make a prophetic utterance concerning the impending doom of Babylon.

> For the Lord of Hosts, the God of Israel, has spoken:
> 'Daughter Babylon is like a threshing floor when it is trodden. And soon the harvest time will come.'[166]

The words of the prophet signal that the harvest, by which he more specifically meant the actions of the reapers, is soon to come, and the threat of their violence is directed at the daughter of Babylon. She is construed, metaphorically, as a threshing floor that will soon be 'trampled' by soldiers.[167] Sexual violence is imputed, and the equivalence of reapers and soldiers is found once again. The same transformation also occurs in the equally dark warning issued by the prophet Joel to his own people.

> Warriors advance!
> Quick march!
> Hammer your ploughshares into swords,
> Your sickles into spears ...
> March your warriors down, Yahweh ...
> Get ready to use the sickle, for the harvest is ripe;
> and come – tread the grapes,
> for the press is full and the vats overflowing;
> great is the wickedness of the nations.
> The roar of the multitudes, the multitudes,
> in the Valley of Decision!
> The Day of the Lord is at hand.
> In the Valley of Decision,
> the sun and moon are darkened,
> and the stars refuse to shine.[168]

This harvest will be in the ominous darkness. The language was part of a discourse of threat in which the overtones of judgment and vengeance were mixed. In a dire warning delivered to the kingdom of Israel, the prophet Isaiah foretells of its demise.

> On that day, the glory of Jacob will be brought low
> and the fat of his flesh will grow lean.
> And it will be like the time when
> the reapers gather the standing grain,

> and when their arms cut the heads of grain,
> and as when one gleans the heads of grain
> in the Valley of Rephaim ... [169]

The metaphors in this prophetic discourse are drawn from everyday rural life in a fashion that suggests that the writers, even if they themselves were from a literate elite, were deliberately casting their messages in forms that were thought to be common or popular, and which were therefore set against dominant images of royalty and priesthood. In order to mobilize large numbers of minds, the appeal was couched in terms of well-known proverbial and common knowledge that emerged from experiences in reaping real harvests.

It is no surprise, then, that this same mode of forging prophetic warnings was also employed in millenarian warnings of the Roman period. Similar harvest imagery is employed in the Sibylline oracles, in which the balance and reversibility of the earthly harvest with the final divine one is construed in such a fashion that the advent of the one cues the demise of the other.

> But the wicked men who sent heavenward their lawless talk will cease their nattering against each other, and they will hide themselves until the cosmos is changed.
> And there will be a rain of glowing fire from the clouds,
> and no more will mortal men reap the golden grain from the earth. [170]

This last age will be brought on by an unbearable wickedness. At that time, earthly cataclysms will signal the coming reaping of the last surviving generation of humans, the final crop.

> And the wickedness upon the earth will sink into the vastness of the sea. And at that time, which is now near, there will be the harvesting of mortal men. [171]

The end time will be a harvest in a double sense: a season of finality and death will have arrived. Plants will no longer procreate, and neither will humans.

> ... You miserable men
> of the last generation: you evil doers, you terrible men;
> you are like children who do not know
> that when womankind no longer bears children
> then will come the time of the harvesting of mortal men. [172]

All of these claims and prognostications point to a connection between reapers and the technologies of harvesting and things that stand beyond death. These things *will* happen. The dying is only part of the justice that will result. The statements connect fear and violence with a retributive and a redistributive sense of putting things right and with the reasserting of a just order of things. Death is not the end, but only the means: it is the divine punishment. No wonder that kings feared the images of harvesters armed with sickles, scythes, and pitchforks in their nightmares and that prophets and seers warned these same monarchs about the coming thunderbolt of justice. The appeal to divine power summoned up the threats and fears that the words were meant to cause.

The connections were sometimes more mundane. They were linked to the potential violence of the harvest that was created not by the mental impressions made by the violence inhering in the cutting instruments and the cut plants, but by the animated hostilities that the hiring and labour processes threatened. Since the majority of the work was done by freely negotiated labour, once every year disputes over pay, rewards, and fair treatment were sharpened and brought into high relief. There are reports on the proclivities of landlords and their agents not to pay the harvesters whom they had hired. The distress was part of the inequality that marked the weak position and near-servile dependence of the hired worker.[173] The chronic problem was the ground of prophetic calls for a just order that noted the propensity of the powerful to defraud the harvesters of their rightful wages, arbitrarily to pay them less, and to break the reaping agreements that concerned their recompense.[174] For Africa in the age of our harvester, Augustine similarly notes this tendency of wealthy employers not to pay or to short-change their hired workers.[175] The anger and the violence of the day labourers in response to this unfairness suggested the apocalyptic threat of action now.

Now you rich men, now start crying, wailing for the miseries that are coming to you. Your wealth is rotting and your clothes are all eaten by moths. All your gold and silver are rusting away. This same corrosion will be a witness against you. It will eat into your body. It is a burning fire that you have stored up as your treasure for the Last Days. The wages of the day labourers who mowed your fields and which you withheld from them cry out. Know that the shouts of the reapers have reached the ears of the Lord of Hosts. On earth you have been nourished on luxury and excess. On the Day of Slaughter, you went on eating to your heart's content. It was you who condemned the innocent and killed them. They offered you no resistance.[176]

The writer of the letter of James in the New Testament cautions 'the brothers' to be patient. Wait. Wait like the farmer who waits for the fruit of the ground to mature, who waits for the autumn rains, who waits for the spring rains. The Lord is coming soon. The Judge is waiting at the gates.[177] Soon there will be vindication. This was the threat. It was embodied in the instrument of reaping. The shouts of the reapers, well practised from their chanting in the fields, had reached the ears of their Lord – the divine one, that is.

The Human Apocalypse

The number of connections that are felt, heard, or seen depends on the media that are used to convey them. The same applies to our understanding of the drawing power or the weight of individual metaphors in the past. The proportional power of any metaphor was defined and limited in specific modes. As long as elite producers of written texts determined the field of metaphoric images in writing, this is what readers in later ages get to see. The range of acceptable metaphors was a reflection of the hierarchies of speech of the learned and literate elites. Harvesting and reaping metaphors proliferate in the writings of the late Latin Church Fathers, but they were surely not inventing much about their use except for the fact that they were recording them in script. But sometimes the same written sources allow us to glimpse what was widespread in the everyday speech of the ordinary people with whom they were trying to communicate. Although transfers from daily manual work to metaphor were constant among most people, they were not much in evidence in the upper-class writers. This screening of acceptable and unacceptable figures of speech parallels the tacit barriers that social elites had erected against detailed descriptions of labour, as can be witnessed in the writers of agricultural manuals.[178] They preferred not to see or discuss hard work as part of their reality. The apparent chasm separating Homer and the later Christian letters, treatises, and sermons has very little to do with either the bulk or the weight of the use of metaphors by most speakers but rather with the selectivity of who gets to use what metaphors, why, how often, and in what circumstances.

Elite inhibitions and popular attractions that configured the metaphor and its use can be seen coalescing around a social phenomenon, a threatening one, in the Maktar Harvester's Africa. A sizeable and variable portion of all harvest labour in premodern societies, even in periods close to full modernity, was done by underemployed or unemployed persons on the move who were labelled vagrants, vandals, goths, bums, or tramps.[179] They were felt to be a social danger.[180] The same pejorative epithets extended over a range of similar unwanted persons. The mobility of their existence provoked recourse to a host of nasty adjectives. To counter this tendency, people who approved of the seasonal workers attempted to draw a distinction between good professional harvesters and bad migrants who were not of this approved class.[181] Just so, in the American West in the decades leading up to the First World War pejorative terms like drifters, hoboes, tramps, gypsies, floaters, transients, and migrants were commonly used to describe mobile harvest workers.[182] A similar and extraordinary range of despicable epithets was attached to wandering workers in the Kingdom of Naples in the eighteenth century.[183] Much of this had to do with an attitude, an old attitude. As was noted by Olivier de Serres in France of the sixteenth and seventeenth centuries: 'we find it agreeable to have our harvests taken off by whores and bandits.'[184]

Unlike the hired workers who were 'compelled to labour at usual wage levels because of family responsibilities and community pressures, migratory labourers often exhibited an exasperatingly carefree attitude toward employment.'[185] Faced with this poor attitude and the sometimes raucous independence of the migratory workers, angry locals responded by marshalling responsible persons like students, militia personnel, women's leagues, and even local businessmen. They moved these surrogates out into the fields to 'save the harvest.' The tension between the huge need and desire for seasonal workers and the attitudes about the men on the move generated a strange response that vacillated between attempts to attract and to fix such labourers and outraged condemnations of layabouts, loafers, and bums.[186] The problem of the disparity between the need for labour and the actual numbers who turned up for work, a well-documented problem that plagued even modern harvest employment, was probably worse in antiquity when there were no newspapers, no telegraph companies, no private agencies, no railroads or government institutions that took a direct interest in the smooth transit of seasonal labour.[187] The potential violence inherent in the harvest and in the figures of the reapers meant that there was often an association of the image of harvesting and reaping with things that were violent or retributive in nature. It is not without a feeling of normality that Cicero could refer to the 'harvest reaped in the time of Sulla' as if it were almost an apocalyptic thing.[188]

In the Africa of the Maktar Harvester, similar fearful sentiments coalesced around the figure of the migrant labourer who was known as a 'circumcellion.' The word had a nasty and threatening edge to it. Without doubt, it was used by some people to name the men in our harvester's own gangs as they traversed the fields of Numidia in the later fourth century, especially when the itinerant reapers were unwanted or not behaving. The term also had the popular connotation of vagrant or tramp, with an air of distaste and fear attached to it. The gangs of men and women who roamed the high plains of Africa and Numidia each year seeking employment in the harvest had to face being labelled as nasty and unwanted, and as volatile and potentially violent upsetters of local communities. They also had to assume the normal stigma of persons who were stained with the servile poison of having to work not as free men should, that is, for themselves and at their own behest, but for wages at the whim and command of others. Some of the same loathings and fears that were attached to masterless slaves doubtless attached to them. Being constantly on the move, they were like *fugitivi*. An astrological interpretation manual of the age grouped wanderers (*erratici, errabandes, errones, peregrinantes*), exiles (*exules*), fugitive slaves (*fugitivi*), the indigent and impoverished (*pauperes, mendici*), vagrants (*vagi, vagabundi*) and day labourers (*laboriosi, operae*) all under the same sign[189] In addition to the incidents of violence in which the reapers were actually involved, there were always apprehensions about what they *might* do.

Given that large numbers of itinerant young men were involved, there can be no surprise, as is hinted at in the story of Ruth and Boaz, that violence against women, including rape, was a common result.[190] The sudden appearance of large numbers of men on the high plains of Numidia must also have had something strange and unpredictable to it. So it has been in all ages, and so it was imagined, as in the sudden arrival of harvesters in the Pontine Marsh areas west and south of Rome in the early nineteenth century. It is just that a less happy image of them than Leopold Robert's joyful evocation is needed. Many attempts were made to control and to organize the movement of seasonal harvest labour onto and off of the Great Plains of North America before 1914, but exactly how the whole thing happened was perplexing.

In spite of the efforts to control the labor supply, the flow of harvesters into and throughout the wheat lands continued each year as a response to the quiet workings of the law of supply and demand and the highly individualized peripatetic habits and longings of the migrants themselves. When the wheat ripened, the men appeared with a regularity that continued to be as mysterious to observers as it was in the 1870's. After the grain was cut and threshed, the men 'mysteriously disappeared' and little thought was given to them as the villages and farmlands settled again into another winter of quiet.[191]

What was the possibility of tapping into the strength of men who gathered together in numbers and who, by the nature of their work, were hard to control and to repress because of their functional independence? Freedom, after all, was one of the main motives for young men to go on the move.[192] At least labour organizers in the modern world thought so. Of such men, one of them optimistically opined:

His cheerful cynicism, his rank and outspoken contempt for most of the conventions of bourgeois society ... make him an admirable example of the iconoclastic doctrines of revolutionary unionism. His anomalous position, half industrial slave, half vagabond adventurer, leaves him infinitely less servile than his fellow worker of the East ... Nowhere else can a section of the working class be found so admirably suited to serve as scouts and advance guards of the labor army. Rather, they may become the guerrillas of the revolution – the *franc tireurs* of the class struggle.[193]

If a modicum of organization could be brought to such men, then the apparition of fear that they brought to the regions in which they suddenly appeared in large numbers would be considerable. Take the brief but ultimately unsuccessful

5.12: Arrival of harvesters in the Pontine marshes. Leopold Robert, *L'arrivée des moissoneurs dans les marais Pontins*, 1833. Pushkin Museum, Moscow; ArtResource

attempt by the IWW to organize seasonal labourers in the American West at the time of the First World War. The movement was attended by sporadic episodes of violent behaviour that evoked attitudes from the authorities not much different from the ones displayed by Augustine towards the circumcellions. A reporter from Sioux City, Iowa, in August of 1916 is worth quoting at length to get a sense of the similarity of the rhetoric.

... thousands of these migratory mendicants have thronged the Middle West this year creating a reign of terror throughout the rural communities and intimidating all who do not join their organization ... in order to compel farmers to grant their demands ... I.W.W. gangs have taken possession of trains, clubbing off all who could not show a membership in their organization. In most cases, they have driven trainmen from their trains ... Often they travel in mobs of 300 to 400 ... Great camps are established not only by the I.W.W. but by those who are not members of that organization. The men congregate at these 'jungles,' cook their food, often pilfered from nearby farms, wash their clothes, bathe, and not infrequently stage drunken orgies. This year the I.W.W.'s have posted signs at their 'jungles' reading, 'For I.W.W.'s only,' and any man who dares wander into their camp without proper credentials is due for a beating ... This year they have been more numerous than ever ... All methods of handling the situation have proven unavailing ... One method suggested is for each state to employ forces of mounted police similar to the famous Northwest Mounted Police of Canada to keep the bands from congregating, to break up their 'jungles' and otherwise deal with them. Power seems the only force they recognize and they laugh at the county sheriffs and town constables.[194]

One need not belabour the similarities too much. The individual elements of this discourse with its references to migratory mendicants, intimidation, mobs, a reign of terror, drunken orgies, beatings, the use of clubs, the numbers – 'more numerous than ever' – power being the only force that they recognize, the laughing at normal authority, and so on, can easily be replicated in the conventions of the anti-circumcellion discourse broadcast in late antiquity by Augustine.

It is not accidental that there is an almost linear connection of cause and effect that led Augustine to develop the larger metaphor of the harvest and reaping for polemical purpose in late Roman Africa. In doing so, he systematically connected a series of existing pictures and texts together so as to produce an image of the coming of the Day of the Lord on which there would be a final accounting of the good and the bad. The rhetoric and the ideas were all in aid of his tendentious, though adventitious idea that good and bad men would live together in this world until the coming of the Lord at the End of Time. It was only then that there would be a true final accounting. In forming this idea, he could knit together biblical texts, especially from the evangelist Matthew (13:24–30), with references to the circumcellions, to produce a counterfactual metaphor. The basic sequence is the initial claim that it is only at the end of time that the Lord will send his reapers. These divine harvesters are the angels of the Lord and *not* the dissident circumcellions. It is only in this final reaping of human lives that the good and the bad will be separated, and the bad will be judged and held responsible for their misdeeds.[195]

Once this picture had been formed, it could be turned to again and again in the same work, as it was for example in Augustine's *Letter against Parmenian*, written in 404, to shape a threatening narrative about the future.[196] Almost all such references to reaping and to the harvesting gangs of the Lord contained in the same treatise are further connected with the idea of martyrdom. A second work by Augustine, *Against the Letter of Petilian*, composed in the years 400–2, makes frequent and repeated recourse to this metaphor from the beginning to the end of his polemic. The purpose of the metaphor was to contrast the good with the bad, and to liken the angels of the Lord as reapers to circumcellions as reapers.[197] The metaphor worked because it appealed to images that were well known to contemporary Africans from their experiences with crops in the fields and with seasonal harvest workers. The metaphor enabled the writer to play with morality: the good reapers, the angels of the Lord, are consistently contrasted with the bad men, the evil reapers, the circumcellions.[198] The core characteristic that is identified with the bad reapers is specifically that of actual violence or the threat of it.[199] Much more important is the extensive use of the reaping metaphor within discussions of the harvest in oral contexts, especially in preaching. It is in preaching that the revindicative and judgmental elements of the divine harvesters are brought into full play. The final harvest is the time when the good will be rewarded and the bad will be punished. The good grain that is reaped will be stored in a granary while the bad chaff will be burned in a fire that will never be extinguished.[200]

The uses of the images of the reaper and the harvest in Augustine are of direct significance to us since they are contemporary with our African harvester from Maktar, and they connect with his story. The use of the metaphor in Augustine's treatises and sermons, however, is an exceedingly small sample of this imagery in the writings of a large range of Christian writers in the Latin West over the whole of the third to seventh centuries CE. A picture that was used and developed poetically in Homer, became a prolific image again and for many centuries. It now appears in an almost embarrassing abundance: a profusion of images, statements, and explanations, all of them orbiting around ideas of violence, a final judgment, the condemnation of bad people, and the coming of divine retribution or vengeance. The obvious filter that connects the two is a heavy oral interface, the domination of the sermon and the potential for the use of homiletic materials in the case of the Christian preacher. This mode suggests that the apparent absence of the metaphor, which is found only sporadically in the literature of the Greek city-state and in the Latin writings of the Roman empire, is to be linked not just to cultural screens that allowed or permitted the expression of basic metaphors of thought, but also to class distinctions. The most obvious explanation for the profusion of the metaphor in the thinking of later Christian writers was not just its availability in biblical texts that they often used as points of reference. The existence of these metaphoric and potentially metaphoric materials in the New Testament texts that were heavily exploited by Augustine, or in the story of Ruth and Boaz in the Hebrew Bible, indicates an oral milieu of simple language in which they already circulated as popular stories. Both literary and artistic invention played into the mix, as when a Christian artisan could picture the primal human couple, Adam and Eve, working at the primordial harvest: he reaping and she sheaving. Surely the reason that these stories were drawn on by preachers like Augustine was because they connected with the mass of their parishioners, who already sensed from their personal experiences the parameters of meaning embedded in them.

On occasion, the potential threats, perceived and real, coalesced into social insurgence, and the reapers came to collect what they felt was their just due. In the mid-340s CE on the high plains of Numidia, the same region to which our man led his reaping gangs, two African religious leaders, Commanders of the Saints as they were called, Axido and Fasir, led a movement of revindication that was fronted by circumcellion reapers. We happen to have the following account because the Catholic bishop Optatus of Milevis reported the relations between these men and his religious opponents, the bishops of the Donatist Church in Numidia.

At that time a gathering of those men was whipped up whose madness had apparently been condemned by these very same bishops [i.e., Optatus's sectarian enemies] only a brief time before. For in the time before Unity [i.e., before the year 347], when men of this kind were accustomed to wander through small hamlets in the countryside, at the time when Axido and Fasir were being called Commanders of the Saints by these same madmen, no one could be secure in his own possessions. Records of debts had lost their force. At that time no creditor was at liberty to enforce payment. Everyone was terrified by the letters issued by men who boasted that they were Commanders of the Saints. And if there was any delay in obeying their orders, a demented mob suddenly flew to their side. As the terror advanced before them, creditors were besieged with threats. In fear of death, persons who deserved to demand repayment of what was owed to them were forced to grovelling supplications. Each of them hurried to write off the debts owed to him, even if these were enormous, and reckoned it a profit if he escaped injury at the hands of these men. Even the safest road could not be travelled because masters, thrown out of their vehicles, scampered like slaves

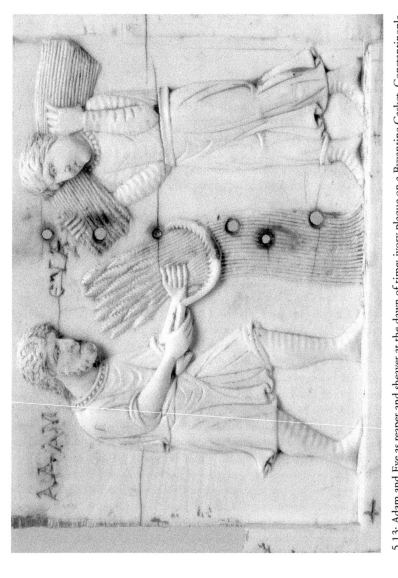

5.13: Adam and Eve as reaper and sheaver at the dawn of time; ivory plaque on a Byzantine Casket, Constantinople, tenth–eleventh century. Metropolitan Museum of Art, New York; ArtResource

before their own slaves who were now ensconced in the seats of their masters. At the behest and command of such men, the positions of masters and slaves were reversed.[201]

It was a world turned upside down, a violent carnivalesque in which masters and slaves were made to trade places. Angry gangs were summoned and they quickly assembled in large and frightening numbers. Market criers were used to bring messages to the seasonal workers, who were known to hang out at rural centres and at periodic markets in the countryside.

From their names alone, it is surmised, surely correctly, that these men emerged from local African social ranks that were not fully integrated with the Romano-Latin culture of the towns. Although Axido and Fasir were not Christian bishops, it is important to note that their strength was rooted in religious power. They were popularly known and represented themselves as *duces sanctorum* or Commanders of the Saints.[202] The parallels with certain institutions known from Berber society in modern-day Morocco are perhaps too suggestive to ignore.[203] What strands of holiness or sanctity in local society were being tapped is unknown, but a skein of Christian ideas and beliefs is strongly suggested by the fate of the men who followed them into battle. The incident discloses problematic aspects of the Christian status of the reapers, even in the eyes of the leaders of the Donatist Christian church. As far as Optatus was concerned, the reaction of the Donatist bishops to the violent men associated with Axido and Fasir exhibited a hypocrisy that was a source of malicious joy for the Catholic bishop.

Because of these events, real hostility arose towards the bishops of your party. So it is reported that they composed a petition to Taurinus, then the Count of Africa, in which they stated that it was not possible to discipline men of this kind within the confines of their church. So it came about that it was *your* bishops who demanded that these men be punished by this same *Comes* [i.e., the Count of Africa, Taurinus]. In response to their letter, Taurinus ordered armed soldiers to sweep through all of the periodic marketplaces where the demented gangs of the circumcellions were accustomed to wander. At the place known as Locus Octavensis, large numbers of them were killed and many were decapitated. The number of their dead bodies can still be calculated today by counting the whitewashed altars and [martyr] tables set up at the place. When they had begun to bury some of the dead inside the local basilicas, Clarus, who was priest at the village known as the Locus Subbulensis, was forced by his bishop to undo the burials. Following this incident, an express order was issued as to what was to be done – and it was done – since it was expressly forbidden [i.e., by the Donatist bishops] for such men to be buried in the House of God.[204]

The civil authorities and the Christian bishops knew where it was that such men normally congregated. They collected at the periodic market centres scattered throughout the countryside of Numidia in search of seasonal work. Two of these rural villages or *loca* are named in the account: the *locus Subbullensis* and the *locus Octavensis*. It is likely that the latter place was so named because it was the eighth place on the round of eight market days that made up a single cycle linking different locales into a single network of communication.[205] The fact that the burial places of these men were marked by tables or *mensae*, and that the local priest of the *locus Subbullensis* began burying some of the dead inside his basilica, signalled that the men cut down by the Count of Africa's soldiers had achieved a special and exalted status. They were martyrs.

In seeking both to control the status of these martyrs and to persuade millions of ordinary, illiterate, hard-working men and women in a rural life of antiquity, it is hardly surprising that Christian preachers mobilized with metaphor. In reaping they had a metaphor that signalled precise understandings and empathies, and with which they were able to move their congregations. This was a cutting instrument that individual Christians witnessed being used, and which many of them had actually handled, sharpened, and worked with every harvest season. The Final Days were to be like this. The Catholic preacher might fulminate that the Angels of the Lord were *not* circumcellions, and that the Leaders of the Angels were *not* the foremen and contractors of itinerant reaping gangs. But the denials were deeply rooted in potent metaphoric images that were widely shared by the people of the time. They would readily understand that the preacher's words were a prefiguration of the Final Harvest in which the Harvesters of the Lord would come and reap the crop of humans. The Christian preacher worked with metaphor to persuade. He colonized the minds of his people and moved them to a new ethic of internal discipline. And what better to implant in those minds than the same first order mental extensions and transfers that were derived from their daily life? In mobilizing the gangs of reapers armed with their sickles in southern Numidia in the 340s, the Commanders of the Saints, Axido and Fasir, no doubt did the same, probably employing many of the same metaphors of harvesting and reaping. After all, the circumcellion reapers whom they were inciting were in the vanguard of the insurgent violence of the time. But Axido and Fasir saw things differently than the bishops. They had a different agenda. It was not with death and the beyond. It was right here, right now.

Harvesting Contracts from Roman Egypt and Italy

A. Harvesting Contracts for the Reaping of Cereal Grain Crops: Roman Egypt (Hermopolite Nome)

1: P. Flor. 80 (*RIL*, ser. 5, 13 [1904], no. 4, pp. 134–5) = WChr 145 = Montevecchi, *Contratti di lavoro*, no. 9, pp. 44–5: Hermopolite Nome (first/second century CE)

Ἁρπαῆσις Φθόναρος τῶν ἀπὸ κώμης Ἰβίωνος
Τατκελμεως κ(αὶ) Τοθήους Πολεῖτος τῶν
ἀπὸ Σεσιοὶ κ(αὶ) Ἰναρῶυς Πανεχώτου τῶν ἀπὸ Σιλα-
μόγθα κ(αὶ) Θέων Σαραπίωνος Ἑρμοπολίτης
κ(αὶ) Πεουῆς Τοθέους κ(αὶ) Σαραπίων Θέωνος Ἑρμοπ(όλιται)
οἳ ἔξ θερισταὶ Πολυδεύκει Κάστορος χ(αί)ρειν.
ὁμολογοῦμ[ε]ν παρέξειν ἡμᾶς
θερίζοντες οὓς ἔχεις [π]υρίνους σπόρους ἐν κώμῃ
Θνῆφι κ(αὶ) Βῶ[υ] κ(αὶ) ἐν Ἰβίωνι Τατκέλμεως
ἀρούρας πεν[τ]ηκοντατέσσαρες μισθοῦ
ἑκάστης ἀρούρης τῆς ἐν σπόρῳ φανησομένης πυροῦ ἀρτάβης ἥμισυ ἀρξόμεθα δὲ
τ[οῦ] θερισμ[ο]ῦ ὁ[πό]τε .[.]..ε ἐὰν κελευσθῶμεν ὑπό σου
[...].εξο...[.5]ερ..[c ?]

Harpaêsis, son of Phthonar, from the village of Ibiôn Tatkelmeôs, from Tothês son of Poleis, from the village of Sesis, and from Inaros son of Panechôtes, from the village of Silamontha, and from Theon, son of Sarapion, from Hermopolis, and from Peouês, son of Tothês and from Sarapion son of

Theon, both from Hermopolis – the six reapers – to Polydeukês, son of Kastor. Greetings!

We agree to make ourselves available as harvesters to reap the wheat fields which you have around the village of Thnêphis and Bôu and around Ibiôn Tatkelmeôs, 54 arourai in extent, at the rate of pay for each aroura which has been been seeded to wheat of half an artaba [of wheat reaped per aroura]. We will begin the reaping when shall be ordered to do so by you [...]

2: P. Flor. 101 (*RIL*, ser. 5, 13 [1904], no. 2, pp. 131–3 = Montevecchi, *Contratti di lavoro*, no. 7, pp. 39–41): Hermopolite Nome (21 April 91 CE ?)

[c 14].[c 4].ει..[c 20]
Καίσαρ[ος τ]οῦ κυρίου ἀρούρας πεντηκοντατέσσαρας·
(γίνονται) (ἄρουραι) ν[δ], ἑκάστῳ (ἀρούραι) ϛ· καὶ δώσεις ἡμῖν ὑπὲρ μισθοῦ
θερισμο[ῦ ἑ]κάστης ἀρούρης πυροῦ ἥμισυ τρίτον · (γίνεται) ἑκ(άστης) (ἀρούρης)
(πυροῦ) ἥμισυ τρίτον · καὶ μετρή[ϛ]εις ἡμῖν μετὰ τὸν θερισμὸν τῶν προκειμένων
ἀρ[ουρῶν] τοὺς προκείμενο(υς) μισθο(ύς), ἐφ' ᾧ ἀναλέξῃς
σὺ ὁ Εὐδ[αίμων τὰ] δράγματα· καὶ χορηγήσεις ἡμῖν ὕδωρ
εἰς πιεῖν ἄχ[ρι] οὗ ἐκβῶμεν τοῦ θερισμο(ῦ) τῶν α(ὐτῶν) ἀρουρῶ(ν)· ἐφ' ᾧ, ἐὰν
ἀργήσῃ[ται ?] εἶς ἐξ ἡμῶν, ἐπάναγκο(ν) στήσωμεν ἀντ' αὐτο(ῦ) ἐν τῇ αὐτῇ [ἡμέ]
ρα. τὸν δὲ προκ(είμενον) πυρὸ(ν) μετρήσεις ἡμῖν μέτρωι [Ἀ]θηναίῳ ἑ[κτημ]όρωι,
καὶ [δ]ώσεις ἡμ[ῖν] τῇ ἐσχάτῃ ἡμέρᾳ ζύτου κερ[άμιον ἕ]ν ἀρξώμεθα δὲ το[ῦ]
θερισμοῦ ἐπάναγκο(ν) τῇ τριακά[δι τοῦ] ἐνεστῶτο(ς) μηνὸ(ς) Φαρμοῦθι τοῦ
ἐνεστῶ-τος δεκά[του (ἔτους)]. ὑπ(ὲρ) δὲ τῆς εὑρεθησομέν(ης) ἐν σπόρωι μετρήσεις [ἡμῖ]ν, καθὼ[ς πρόκειται, ἐκ(άστης) (ἀρούρης) (πυροῦ). [(ἔτους) δε]
κάτου [Αὐ]τοκράτορος Κα[ίσαρος c. 15 μη(νὸς) Νερωνείο(υ)]
[σεβας]το(ῦ) κε. Θέω[ν c ?]

[about 20 missing letters ...] in the year of our Lord Caesar: 54 arourai, making 54 arourai in total, 6 arourai to each. As the wages for reaping, you will give to [each of] us, five-sixths of an artaba of wheat for each aroura (reaped), making five-sixths of an artaba for each aroura of grain; and after the harvest you will measure out the above-mentioned wage for the above-mentioned aroura, on condition that you, Eudaimon, are responsible for gathering the sheaves of wheat. You will also supply us with drinking water until we finish the harvesting of the said arourai of land. If any one of us is idle at any time, we shall be required, without fail, to substitute another man in his place for the same day. The above-mentioned wheat you will pay to us in the Athenian sixth-part measure, and in addition you will give us a *keramion* of beer on the last day. We shall be required to begin harvesting on the 30th of the present month, Pharmouthi, in the current 10th year [i.e., of the emperor Domitian]. For each aroura in wheat that is reaped you will pay us the stated five-sixths of an artaba of wheat. The 10th year of the Emperor Caesar [Domitianus Augustus. Month Neroneus Augustus] 25. Theon [about 25 missing letters]

3:     P. S. I. 789 = Montevecchi, *Contratti di lavoro*, no. 10, pp. 46–7: Hermopolite Nome (first–second century CE)

[c ?]ν[c ? o]ἵ δ θερισταὶ Τ̣[.]
[c ? καὶ] Μητόκωι ἀμφ[οτέ]ροις Εὐδήμου χα(ίρειν). ὁμ̣ο-
[λογοῦμεν c ?] τε πυρίνους σπόρους ἐν τῶι Πα-
[c ?] ἐκ τοῦ Πτολεμαίου κλήρου ἀρούρας
[c ? τῆς ἐν σπόρωι] φανησομένης γενήματος τοῦ
[c ? (ἔτους) c ?]υ Καίσαρο[ς το]ῦ κυρίου μισθοῦ τοῦ
[θερισμοῦ ? ἑκά]στης ἀρούρης πυροῦ ἀρτάβης δι-
[μοίρου (γίνεται)] (πυροῦ) (ἀρτάβης) β̄ αὐτόθι δὲ ἐσχήκαμεν παρ' ὑμῶ̣ν
[c ? ἀργυρίου] δραχμὰς δεκαέξ, (γίνονται) ἀργ(υρίου) (δραχμαὶ) ις. ἀρξό-
[μεθα] αρξω[μεθα] [δὲ ἀπὸ δε]κάτης ἡμ(έρας) τ[οῦ] Παχὼν καὶ οὐκ ἀποστη-
[σόμεθα c ?] καὶ τῇ ἐσχάτῃ ἡμέρᾳ ὁμοίως θερίσομ[ε]ν
[c ?] περὶ Νεκοσὺ ἀρούρας τρ[ε]ῖς ο.<.>.τη.εν
[c ?]ης συμφονειάς . [τ]οὺς [δὲ] μισθοὺς με-
[τρήσεις ἐν τοῖς Παῦνι] καὶἘπεὶφ μησὶ το[ῦ] αὐ[το]ῦ ἔτους μετρησι
[πρώτῃ c ?].η.α..[c ?]ωντα.[c ?]
[c ?]μῳγ[c ?]

[… …] the 4 reapers to [T… /… and] to Metokos, both sons of Eudemos. Greetings! We a[gree…] (to reap) the wheat fields seeded in (the district of) Pa[… / …] the arourai on the kleros of Ptolemaios [of those arourai where the crops] have grown ripe, in the [year … x … of Our] Lord Caesar. The pay of two-thirds of an artaba [… the reaping? For ea]ch aroura of wheat, making two-thirds of an artaba […] per aroura of grain reaped. When we finish there we will receive from you sixteen [silver] drachmai making a total of 16 silver drachmai. We will begin [from the] first day of Pachon and we will not stop [from working … until we finish] and on the last day we will likewise reap [… / …] the three arourai belonging to you […] on [the same conditions… of contract?] The pay will be measured out in [… the months of Pauni] and Epeiph of the same year, with the (same) measures […]

The following four contracts with harvesters are for the reaping of crops on the lands of the Sarapion family near Hermopolis in Upper Egypt. Records from the managerial archives of the family have survived for a span of years between 90 and 133 CE. From this archive, we have contracts made with gangs of harvesters for the three successive harvest seasons in the years 123, 124, and 125 CE (P. Sarap. 49, 50 and 51), demonstrating the tralaticious and standard nature of the annual contract agreements.

4:    P. Sarap. 49 [P. gr. 247]: Hermopolite Nome (27 March–25 April, 123 CE)

[The earliest of the series, this contract is better preserved in its first parts]

[παρὰ „„]εθιςʾΙναρώουτος .[.6]ρουʿΕρμαίου Κορνηλίου Σύρου καὶ Ἰούστος Ἑρμαίου τῶν δ [καὶ Σαβο]υρίων Τοθήους καὶʿΕρμᾶιςʾΙναρώουτος η β τῶν ἀπὸ κώμης Σινκερὴ η ξ [θεριστῶ]ν Ε[ὐτυ]χίδη Σαραπίωνος Ἑρμοπ(ολίτη) χ(αίρειν). μεμισθώκαμεν παρὰ σοῦ πρὸς θερισμὸν [τοῦ ἐνεστῶτος] ἑβδόμου (ἔτους) Ἀδριανοῦ Καίσαρο[ς] τοῦ κυρίου οὓς ἔχει[ς] πυρίνου σπόρους [c ? τ]ῷ Περὶ πόλ(ιν) κάτωι ἀρούρας ἑκατόν {τεσσαρακον} τεσσαρ[ά]κοντα καὶ ἐν [ὁ]μοίως ἀρούρας ὀγδοήκοντ[α] (γίνονται) (ἄρουραι), μισθοῦ τῶν ἐν Πασκὼ (ἀρουρῶν) [(πυροῦ) (ἀρτάβης) . μετρη]μένου ὑπὸ …… νος ἑκά[στης] (ἀρούρης) καὶ τῶν ἐν τῶι Περὶ πόλ(ιν) κάτω [ἐν σπόρωι φα] νησομενου ὑπὸ ..ε[.].τορ [Σινκ]ερὴ καὶ Μαγδώλων Μιρὴ ἐφ᾽ ᾧ τωι ἡμῖν ὕδωρ καὶ τρ.[.]..ο.[.. καὶ] τοὺς ἀναλέγοντας τὰ <δράγ>ματα. [τοὺς δὲ μις]θοὺς μετρησι ε.. [c 9 ἐ]φ᾽ αλανον [Μαγ]δώλων [μαγ]δωλον Μιρὴ [c ?] νέου …[.].αρ.[c ?]ριως ε..[c 4]το.του καὶ α..<κ>( ) [c ?]..[c ?]

From […]ethis son of Inarôos [and from …]ros of Hermais, from Cornelius Syrus and Ioustos of Hermais, total 4 men; and from Sabourios of Totheos and Hermais of Inarôos, total 2 men, from the village of Sinkerê – for total of 6 harvesters – to Eutychides son of Sarapion, citizen of Hermopolis. Greetings! We shall be paid by you [i.e., Eutychides] for the harvest in the [current] seventh year of the Lord Hadrian Caesar which 140 arourai seeded to wheat which you have in the 'Around-the-Village' area and likewise the 80 arourai in Paschon to be paid per artaba for the arourai (reaped), for a total of 220 arourai … Measured by […] for each aroura both of those in the 'Around-the-Village' area below Phanesomenos … and [those below] … in Sikerê and Magdôla Mirê. For which [work you will provide] water for us and [dried fruits? and persons to collect the sheaves …]

[the remainder of the text is difficult to decipher]

5: P. Sarap. 50 [P. gr. 216 + two fragments of P. gr. 271]: Hermopolite Nome (27 March–25 April, 124 CE)

[This papyrus is considerably more fragmentary than the contract of 125 CE, but it can be seen that most of its employment provisions were, as one would expect, typical.]

[c ?]. υμειν [.8].ο[...].[c ?]
[c ?]δι[.]δ..[c 10]αι...[c ?]
[c ? ἀρούρας δια]κοσίας τρ[ιάκοντα] ...ῳς.[c ?]
.[c 14].....[.9]...[c ?]
τον[.4]..ι ι[...].[.]της[..]...οι[.]....ο( ) θ[.4].. δὲ
ἐπάν[α]γκον ἀπο...[.]ής[ω] ἄγδ[ρ]ας δέκ[α] καὶ παραστήσω
ὑμῖν ὕδωρ καὶ {κᾳὶ} τοὺς δεσμοὺς καὶ τ[ο]ὺς ἀναλέγοντᾳς τὰ
δράγματα καὶ δώσω υμε[ι]ν τῆι ἐσχάτῃ ἡμέρα
οἴνου [κ]εράμια δύο τοὺς δὲ ..αμις[..].. δ[ρ]ᾳ[χμὰ]ς κ̄
ἐν τῶι Ἐπεὶφ μηνί. ἔτους ὀγδόου Ἀὐτοκράτορ[ο]ς Καίσ[αρ]ος
Τραιανοῦ Ἀδριανοῦ [Σεβ]αστοῦ Φαρμοῡ̄θ̄[ι)

Ε[ὐ]τυχ(ίδης) Σα[ρα]π(ίωνος) [μεμίσ]θ(ωκα) καθ(ὼς)

… for us … the 230 [arourai] … we must provide 10 men. You must provide water and the ties and the collectors of the sheaves, and I will give to you on the last day (of the harvest) two jugs (*keramia*) of wine and … 20 drachmai … in the month of Epeiph. In the eighth year of the Imperator Caesar Trajan Hadrian Augustus.

Pharmouthi

[Second hand: that of Eutychides]: Paid in full by Eutychides son of Sarapion.

6: P. Sarap. 51 [P. gr. 183]: Hermopolite Nome (12 April 125 CE)

[c ?]..λ[.6].. Τοθήους

[c 8 ο]υ Ἀπολλωνίου θεριστῶν
τῶν [ἀφ''Ἑρμο]υπόλ(εως). βουλόμ[ε]θα ἑκουσίως
ἐκ..[c 4 πα]ρὰ σοῦ πρὸς θερισμὸν οὓς
ἔχεις πυρίνους σπόρους ἐν τῶι Περὶ πόλ(ιν)
κάτω (ἀρούρας) ἑκατὸν τριάκοντα μισθοῦ
ἑκάς[τη]ς (ἀρούρης) πυροῦ αρταβην ημις[υ] δωδεκατον
αὐτ[ό]θεν τε ἐσχήκαμεν παρὰ [ς]οῦ ἐν προχ(ρείᾳ)
ἀργυρίου δραχμὰς τεσσαράκοντα ἃσ ἀποδώσομ(εν)
ἀπολαμβάνοντες τὸν π[υ]ρὸν .....( ) ἄδολ(ον)
μέτρῳ Αθηναιω ἑκτημόρῳ ἐν Ἑρ[μ]ουπόλ(ει).
ἐπάν[αγ]κον δὲ παρεξόμεθά ς[ο]ι θερ[ις]τὰς
δέκα σοῦ παρέχοντος ἄλλους τρεῖ[ς] ε[ἰ]σ πλή-
ρωσι[ν] θεριστῶν δέκα τ[ρι]ῶν. ἀρξόμ[ε]θα
δὲ ἀπὸ τριακάδος τοῦ ἐνεστῶτος μη[νὸ]ς Φαρμ(οῦθι)
κ̣αὶ οὐκ ἀποστησόμεθα α[c 5]...[.]...
ὄντε[ς] ἀλλήλων ἔγγυοι κ̣αὶ θεριοῦμέν σοι
αμις[θ]ει ἡμέραν μίαν σοῦ παρέχοντος ἡμεῖν
<ὕδωρ> καὶ δεσμοὺς καὶ τὸν ἀναλέγοντα τὰ δράγματα
τῆς α̣ἱρέσεως οὔσης περὶ ἡμᾶς περὶ τοῦ ἀνα-
μετρη[θ]ῆ̣ν̣α̣ι τρὺς σπόρους ἢ λάβειν ὑπὲρ
τῶν π[ρ]οκ(ειμένων) (ἀρουρῶν) τοὺς μισθοὺ[ς] ἀποτάκτου
καὶ δώσε[ις] ἡμεῖν φακοῦ ἀρτά[β]ην μίαν καὶ παρ-
έξῃ τὸ π[α]λάνσιον καὶ δώσεις ἡμεῖν δράγματα
δύο τοὺς δὲ μισθ[ο]ὺς ἀποδώσεις ἡμεῖν τῶι
Ἐπεὶφ τ̣οῦ ἐνες[τῶ]τος (ἔτους). (ἔτους) θ Αὐτοκράτορος
[Κ]αίσαρ[ος] Τραιανο̣ῦ Ἁδρι[ανοῦ] Σεβασ̣τ̣[οῦ] Φαρμοῦθι.

[Εὐ]τ[υ]χ̣ίδ(ης) [Σ]αραπ(ίωνος) με[μ]ίσθ(ωκα) (c 6) ας θερίσαι ἀπὸ Φαρμ[ουθ]ι
κς (c 12) καθὼς πρόκειται (c 4) βα [c 9] ε δὲ ὑπεσχ (c 4) τ[ὰ]ς προ[κ]είμεας
δρ[αχμ]ὰς τεσσε[ράκ]οντα

[The names of the individual reapers were on the now-lost top part of the papyrus.]

[from ...] of Tothêos [and ...] from Apollonios ... reapers from Hermoupolis. We ask, without compulsion, to obtain from you for the harvest, the 130 arourai of wheat land which you have in the lower part of the district Around-the-Village. The pay for the reaping of each aroura is one-half plus one-twelfth [i.e., seven-twelfths] of an artaba [of wheat]. We have also received from you, as an advance, 40 drachmai which we will pay back to you once we have received our wheat ... without fraud, measured according to the Athenian sixth-part measure, at Hermoupolis. On our part, we are obliged to provide 10 harvesters and you will provide 3 others to make up a total of 13 harvesters. We will begin work on the 30th of the current month of Pharmouthi [about 25 April] and we will not stop working [until the harvest is completed,] each of us supporting the others [in the work.] We will also provide one day's work free for you. You will provide us with water, ties, and someone to collect the sheaves. We will have the choice between making a check on the fields that have been seeded and of accepting [or rejecting] the job on the basis of the number of arourai that have been declared and on the pay that has been set. You will provide an artaba of beans, you will provide dried fruits, and you will give two sheaves as a gift. You will pay us our salary in the month of Epeiph of the current year. In the ninth year of the emperor Caesar Trajan Hadrian Augustus. 17 Pharmouthi.

(Second hand: that of Eutychides): Paid in full by Eutychides son of Sarapion [...] the harvesters [...] on 27 Pharmouthi and [...] correctly according to the agreement [...] having received back the aforementioned 40 drachmai.

B. Standard Contract Forms for the Harvesting of Olives in Central Italy Preserved in the Text of the Elder Cato (Second Century BCE)

The following contract is the first in a series of formulaic or model agricultural labour and sales contracts found in Cato the Elder's *De agricultura*. The other model contracts are those for the processing of olives (145), for the selling of the olive crop (146), for the sale of grapes on the vine (147), for the sale of wine in jars (148), for the leasing of winter pastures (149), and for the commercial use of flocks of sheep (150). Since the 'John Doe' general name used for the landowner in them is one 'Lucius Manlius,' some have speculated that these model contracts were later insertions into Cato's text made by a landowner, Lucius Manlius, who edited his own contents into the *De agricultura*. Although this is possible, it seems more probable (to me, at least) that Cato drew on existing model contracts and inserted them into his text. Supporting one or the other of these propositions, however, does not affect our use of the standard contract in the context of this inquiry.

> Cato, *De agricultura*, 144: Labour Contract for the Harvesting/Picking of Olives.
> LEX OLEAE LEGENDAE.
> OLEAM LEGENDAM HOC MODO LOCARE OPORTET.
> Oleam cogito recte omnem arbitratu domini aut quem custodem fecerit aut cui olea venierit; oleam ne stringito neve verberato iniussu domini aut custo-

dis; si adversus ea quis fecerit, quod ipse hodie delegerit, pro eo nemo solvet neque debebitur. [2] Qui oleam legerint omnes iuranto ad dominum aut ad custodem sese oleam non subripuisse neque quemquam suo dolo malo ea oleitate ex fundo L. Manli; qui eorum non ita iuraverit, quod is legerit omne, pro eo argentum nemo dabit neque debebitur. Oleam cogi recte satis dato arbitratu L. Manli. Scalae ita uti datae erunt, ita reddito, nisi quae vestustate fractae erunt; si non erunt redditae, aeque <viri boni> arbitratu deducetur. [3] Si quid redemptoris opera domino damni datum erit, resoluito: id viri boni arbitratu deducetur. Legulos quot opus erunt praebeto et strictores; si non praebuerit, quanti conductum erit aut locatum erit deducetur, tanto minus debebitur. De fundo ligna et oleam ne deportato; qui oleam legerit, qui deportarit, in singulas deportationes HS n. II deducentur neque id debebitur. [4] Omnem oleam puram metietur modio oleario. Adsiduos homines L praebeto, duas partes strictorum praebeto; ne quis concedat quo olea legunda et faciunda carius locetur, extra quam si quem socium in praesentiarum dixerit; si quis adversum ea fecerit, si dominus aut custos volent, iurent omnes socii; [5] si non ita iuraverint, pro ea olea legunda et faciunda nemo dabit neque debebitur ei qui non iuraverit. Accessiones: in M ∞ CC accedit oleae salsae M V, olei puri p. VIIII; in tota oleitate HS V; aceite q. V; quod oleae salsae non acceperint, dum oleam legent, in modios singulos HS s(estertii) s(inguli) dabuntur

[Cato, *De Agricultura*, ed. Goujard, pp. 93–4]

AGREEMENT FOR THE HARVESTING OF OLIVES:
THE HARVESTING OF OLIVES SHOULD BE HIRED OUT AS
FOLLOWS:

Let him [i.e., the contractor] keep in mind that the whole olive harvest ought to be done according to the decision of the owner or the one whom he will have appointed to be the guardian of the crop, or the one to whom he will have sold the olive crop. He shall not pick or beat down the olives except at the express order of the owner or the guardian. If he does anything against this agreement, no one shall pay him for what he picked that day, nor will he be owed anything. All those men who pick the olive crop shall swear an oath in the presence of the owner or the owner's guardian that they have not taken any olives, and that no one by any act of deceit or fraud has taken olives from the farm of Lucius Manlius ['John Doe'] during the olive harvest. If any one of them does not so swear, no one shall give that man any money nor shall he be owed anything for all which he has picked. He [the contractor] must provide surety [bond] that the olive harvest is done to the satisfaction of

Lucius Manlius. The ladders which have been provided are to be returned in the same condition in which they were provided, unless some have broken because of old age. If they are not returned, a fair amount will be deducted according to the decision of a fair man [i.e., an arbitrator]. If the owner suffers from any damage caused by the contractor, let compensation be made. This amount will also be deducted following the terms decided by a fair man. [The contractor] shall provide collectors and pickers as required. If he will not have provided the number [as required], a deduction will be made from the amount that was set by the contract for hire: that much less will be owed to him. No wood [rods] or olives are to be taken off the farm. The man who picks olives and has then carried them off will have two sesterces deducted [from his pay] for each [incident], and this amount will not be owed to him. All cleaned olives are to be measured in a *modius* measurer for olives. He shall provide 50 men in good physical condition, two-thirds of them being pickers. No person shall form agreements whereby the harvesting and processing of the olive crop has to be let out at a higher price – unless, that is, the contractor declares his partner openly at the time. If anyone acts contrary to these agreements and if the owner or his guardian so wish, all the partners shall swear an oath. If they do not so swear, he will not give pay for the harvesting of that olive crop nor shall anything be owed to the one who will not have sworn the oath. Bonuses [*accessio*: an additional charge or payment: see, e.g., Cic. 2 *Verr.* 3.116]: for the whole harvest: let the bonus be 1200 modii [of harvested olives], five *modii* of salted olives, 9 pounds of clean olive oil, and five quintals of vinegar. For that part of the salted olives which they did not receive while they were engaged in the picking of the olive crop, for each individual *modius* they will receive one sesterius.

Note

The contract is called a *lex*, which is a common term for the contractual conditions under which a given piece or type of work was to be done. The terms bound the contract labourers, whether they were urban undertakers (as in the famous municipal contract from Puteoli, for example) or rural tenant farmers or *coloni*, to the conditions under which they performed their tasks. This type of rural contracting is well attested for Africa in the terms of the *Lex Manciana*, also known as the *consuetudo Manciana*, the Mancian 'law' or 'customary arrangement' by which sharecropping arrangements were made (see Kehoe, *Economics of Agriculture*, pp. 47–55, for analysis of the modern debates and disputes). Some have argued that the agricultural labour contracts in Cato are copies of actual contracts. I would rather tend to see them as general model arrangements that the landlord could use as a basis for making his own specific contract. The contract foresees potential conflicts between the landlord, the *dominus*, and the contractor and his men. Throughout, these disputes were ordinarily to be resolved *b.v.a.* or *boni viri arbitratu*: by the arbitration of a good or an honest man.

The Maktar Harvester Inscription: Text and Commentary

As it now survives, the stone stele on which the harvester's autobiography was inscribed measures approximately 1.09 m. in height, 0.54 m. in width, and 0.23 in thickness. These are the present dimensions of the stone, however. It suffered minor damage in transportation in 1886 from the Régence of Tunis to the Louvre, where it is now stored. At some point, the stone suffered more substantial breakage across the whole of its top end, although the precise extent of the loss is uncertain. Charles-Picard has argued that the stone must have extended another 70 cm. in height.[1] But his estimate of the amount of the loss at the top of the stele is based on his assumption that the stone was originally topped by a special garland decoration typical of some other funerary stones at Mactaris. His claim is biased to the extent that it is important to his argument on the dating of the text on the stone. As for the form of the stone, it has been claimed that it is of the *arula*-pillar type of stele and that it is therefore to be included in a category of similar kinds of funerary monuments found at Maktar.[2] As it survives, however, our stone bears no resemblance to the altarettes that are part of the design of these other gravestones. It is therefore a simple postulate that the portion of the stone now missing from its top end would have contained all the required decorative and structural elements of the *arula* type and that the size of the loss is therefore considerable.[3] The present condition of the stone, including the use of an existing blank stele, does not suggest the existence of the pedestal feature that is typical of the garlanded funerary stelae found at Maktar. Although we can agree that some of the top of the stone has been lost, unless we accept Charles-Picard's hypothesis, precisely how much is difficult to say.

Further light might be shed on the inscription if the history of the use of the stone on which the poem was inscribed is considered first. The stone contains traces of other inscriptions. At the top of the gravestone are the remnants of four separate but brief funerary notices of at least two women and one man (and one person of unknown gender), not bearing the classic *tria nomina*, that feature a formula – *pius/pia vixit annis* – that is typically Christian.[4] They are inscribed in a quite different script from that of the harvester inscription. Furthermore, their carving on the stone must date to a time later than the harvester inscription since they have been incised in a rough and ready fashion, and at a slant, over the existing top lines of the harvester's poem. The texts of these four funerary epitaphs are as follows.

> Caeselia Nam[...] / pia vixit annis /
> [......]/lianus pius [vix]it annis
> [...] pia vixit annis [....]
> [......] annis

The *gentilicium* Caesel(l)ius is relatively rare in Africa: only two other possible examples are known.[5] The number of possibilities for restoring Caeselia's cognomen are simply too great to designate any one of them. They include, among other permutations: Namgidde, Namgabe, Namp(h)amo, Namp(h)ame, Namp(h)amina, Nampulus, Nampulosa, and so on – all of Punic derivation.[6] What the other names in the list were is beyond rescue. The relationship of these additional epitaphs (and still others to be mentioned below) to the harvester inscription stele is a problem that must be faced. But they are not in the same script, and it is most improbable that they have any direct relationship to it. Therefore, those who have taken the Caeselia of the first of these inscriptions to be the name of the spouse of our man must be mistaken. She is surely some other person wholly unrelated to him.[7]

Additionally, on the left and right sides of the stele, are further funerary epitaphs that feature the standard DMS formula. These could be 'pagan' and earlier in date, but since use of the DMS formula continues through the later Christian period (a practice that is widely attested at Mactaris) this is hardly necessary.[8] The standard abbreviation *can* be found on Christian epitaphs, but the formulaic nature of these inscriptions with a brief *vixit annis*, in addition to the use of the full *tria nomina*, would normally point to an earlier use of the stone. The epitaph on the left side of the stone (fig. A.2.2) is:

> [D] M S / Mulceius / [M]aximus / [vix(it) ?] an(nis) XXX

On the right side of the stone, there is a similar epitaph (fig. A.2.3):

> [D M S] / S. Au[re/li]us F[. . .]/anus / [vix(it) ?] an(nis) XL

Aurelius is far too common a *gentilicium* in Africa for much to be deduced from it. From the number of missing letters, and the limited number of possibilities of the cognomen, however, Flavianus would seem to be a probable restoration, and that combination of names suggests a late fourth-century date.[9] At the other end of the spectrum of possibilities, the name Mulceius, rather frustratingly, is as rare as Aurelius is common. It appears to be unique among *nomina* attested in Africa, and is of little help in shedding more light on the context of persons bearing the nomen.[10] The formula *vixit annis/os*, however, is generally late in appearance in African funerary epigraphy, hardly appearing in inscriptions to the end of the Severan period.[11]

Another important technical matter must be taken into consideration. It is one that is manifest from any inspection of the stone itself, though it has not received sufficient attention in the existing scholarship. It is the simple fact that an existing prepared stone has been used for our inscription. In raking light one can clearly see the large rectangular field that had been prepared for an earlier inscription or for some other purpose (see fig. A.2.1). The lower horizontal edge of the indented border that marks the flat field of this earlier preparation of the stone cuts through lines 22–3 of the our inscription. Lines 24–8 of the inscription are carved onto the rough part of the stone that lies below the smooth rectangular surface that had been prepared to received an inscribed text. In other words, the harvester's long poem substantially exceeded the space available on the existing prepared field and so the stonecutter had to continue to incise six or seven verses on the stone beneath the bottom edge of the rectangular prepared field. It has been claimed that another verse inscription from Maktar, the epitaph of the young woman named Beccut, reveals this same use of a stone with a pre-carved field, where the cutter similarly exceeded the field in cutting the inscription.[12] But there is no valid comparison between the two cases (see fig. 2.7). In the Beccut inscription, there is no overrun of the field that is discernible: not a single whole line in it goes beyond the prepared part of the stone. There is nothing as dramatic as the many lines of overrun found in the harvester inscription.[13] In addition, quite unlike the Beccut epitaph, the *ordinatio* in our inscription is less than exacting, with the result that the lines in the latter half of the poem begin to drift a little to the right of the vertical line of the left margin. All that can reasonably be deduced is that the inscription dated to a time when the stone was re-used, and that it was inscribed on a stone that had been prepared to receive a shorter text.

Among the possibilities that would account for the presence of these three sets of inscriptions on the same stone, some are more convincing than others. The stone itself was manifestly a ready-made one. It could have been selected by the relatives or friends of the deceased for his poem, perhaps in explicit obedience to his testamentary dispositions. In which case, the tight-fisted heir or heirs, wishing to preserve as much as possible of the harvester's hard-won patrimony for themselves, simply took what was available, a prepared stone lying around in the stonecutter's shop. But this would mean that other inscriptions which do not seem as though they were much later in date (if not indeed earlier) than the harvester's epitaph were carved into it for no apparent reason. They were certainly not funerary epitaphs for all the various persons so named, carved at off-kilter angles on the sides and top of the existing stone. A different scenario seems more much probable than this odd hypothetical, especially since there is little evidence that *this stone* was itself actually used as a funerary stone. Moreover, the funerary inscriptions cut on the edges and along the top of the stone were clearly *not* meant for this stone either, but rather for other separate stones that in reality bore the individual funerary epitaphs of the particular persons concerned. The presence of these funerary epitaphs on this larger stone is explained by the fact that they are manifestly the results of sessions in which the cutter practised carving the epitaphs that he would later place on each individual proper funerary stone. These other inscriptions, appearing haphazardly around its edges, are practice sessions and nothing more. This suggests something about the harvester inscription itself which, although much longer and in a much more elaborate script, is nonetheless laid out in a less than finished fashion.

To review the main points: Despite the careful and elaborate cutting of the script for the harvester inscription, and its length, it was set out on an already prepared stone. Furthermore, the cutter deliberately, if carelessly, overran the available prepared field by such a significant number of lines that he could not have been unaware of the fact that he was going to use much more than the prepared field on the stone when he began cutting the lines of the poem on it. Not only that, as he rushed along, transferring the written text of the poet to the field of the stone, he was careless enough to omit two lines from the poem – one following line 17 and the other following line 24 – two lapses that would indicate, once again, that his concern was not so much to take the necessary care to get the complete poem onto the stone, but rather to test the feel of the whole in its unusual script on a prepared stone that lay to hand. Haste probably also accounts for cutting errors where letters were dropped out and spacing was misjudged: line 17 has *conta* for *contenta* (a patent error of compression); in line 21, he caught himself in another error of cutting a word too fast and had to add the 'ip' in *conscriptos*, originally dropped out, above the line (given the nature of the script, it is a similar type of error to the 'conta'). And in lines 23 and 24, the stonecutter, facing a rough blemish in the stone, was forced to do crude work-arounds. One is therefore left with the impression that this inscription is perhaps not the finished verse epitaph as it appeared on our man's funerary monument. As we have it, the inscription seems much more like the result of a practice run. If so, then the stone that we have was never meant to be the actual funerary monument itself. The poem was surely carved more properly onto another monument which has not survived, if it was ever made (or it has not yet been discovered).

As for the verse form of the inscription, we can note that in most verse epitaphs in Africa the dactylic hexameter was the ruling form – or, sometimes, the best approximation to it that the novice or talentless poet could make.[14] In fact, hexameters, including those of elegiac couplets, were by far the generally preferred metrical forms for the *carmina epigraphica* found in Africa.[15] Our poem is composed in elegaic couplets that scan reasonably well. Bianchi, 'Carmina,' p. 64, noted a 'fault' in lines 4: neque; 5: vixi (note the oddity of the shortened final 'i'); 6: pausa; 9: falcifera; 14: opere; 15 undecim et (note the failure of elision between '-cim' and 'et'); 17: vita; 19: opibus; 20: nostra vita; 26 lingua. More specific comments on the diction and individual items of poetic expression will be dealt with in the comments that follow.

The Text

```
[ . . . . .        c. 40          . . . . . ]
      ve [ . . . ] sp [ . . . . . . .] on [ . . ] fui
pau[p]ere progenitus lare sum parvoq(ue) parente,
      cuius nec census neque domus fuerat.
ex quo sum genitus, ruri mea vixi colendo:                              5
      nec ruri pausa nec mihi semper erat,
et cum maturas segetes produxerat annus,
      demessor calami tu(n)c ego primus eram,
falcifera cum turma virum processerat arvis,
      seu Cirtae Nomados seu Iovis arva petens,                         10
demessor cunctos ante ibam primus in arvis,
      pos tergus linquens densa meum gremia.
bis senas messes rabido sub sole totondi
      ductor ex opere postea factus eram.
undecim et turmas messorum duximus annis.                               15
      et Numidae campos nostra manus secuit.
hic labor et vita parvo con<ten>ta valere
      [missing line...]
et dominum fecere domus, et villa paratast
      et nullis opibus indiget ipsa domus.
et nostra vita fructus percepit honorum,                                20
      inter conscr<ip>tos scribtus et ipse fui.
ordinis in templo delectus ab ordine sedi
      et de rusticulo censor et ip[vac. 3]se [vac. 2] fui.
```

et genui et vidi iuvenes caro[vac. 2]sq(ue) [vac. 2] nepotes.

    [*missing line…*]

Vitae pro meritis claros transegimus annos,   25

    quos nullo lingua crimine laedit atrox.

Discite mortales sine crimine degere vitam;

    sic meruit, vixit qui sine fraude, mori.

l. 21: <…>: letters added as a suprascript correction

Commentary

1–2:   Early editors of the text claimed to be able to see more of the first two lines. Cholodniak, for example, claimed to see the following.[16]

    [D]emessor, pra[t]is [su]a grami[n]a [f]alce re[tondens],
        verni[li] o[ff]icio [dedictus?] s[p]on[te] fui:

    No later readers have been able to discern much except scattered letters in the second line, which might or might not admit of the restorations guessed at by this editor and by others. The letters on the stone as it now exists do not support these speculative readings.

3:    *paupere progenitus lare*: compare Varro, who explicitly derives *pauper* from *paulus lar* (*LL*, 5.92). The term *lar* was a traditional metonymy for a home: *familiaeque Lar pater*. Plaut. *Merc.* 5.1.5 (Bianchi, 'Carmina,' p. 63); shared by African writers, cf. Apul. *Met.* 11.19: *larem temporalium*; cf. 9.24, 9.31.

3:    *progenitus*: never found in Tertullian or Cyprian; it is astonishingly rare in classical Latin: only once in Aulus Gellius and once in Statius. There are, however, about two dozen instances instances in the writings of Augustine; epigraphically, another instance is found in CIL 13.5657 (Germania Superior) in a family inscription bearing analogies to ours, dated to the late fifth century CE. Almost all usages are post-classical and are late fourth-century in date, or later: see TLL 10.2: 1765.13–25.

3:    *parvo(que) parente*: *parens*: the parent should be his father, but it could equally well refer to his 'parentage' in general. The singular is rare in African funerary epigraphy: see Söderstrom, 'Vocabula necessitudinis ceteraque appellativa et epitheta,' in *Epigraphica Latina Africana*, pp. 60–114, at p. 62. The connotation of *parvus* here, where it means not literal smallness but 'of small means,' is echoed again in l. 17: *hic labor et vita parvo contenta*, indicating that our man had inherited his parents' status. In connection with *domus*, it is reminiscent of the kind of traditional phrasing used by Ovid, *Met.* 6.13: in demeaning the low social origins of Arachne, and remarking on the plebeian occupation of her father and background of mother, he says: 'orta domo parva parvis habitabat Hypaepis.'

4:    *census*: Used both for wealth that counted socially (i.e., that placed one above the level of the propertyless who were the 'proletarians' of the small towns and cities in the North African provinces) and for the formal levels of wealth needed to participate in the life of the town council and to run for election to town office (or to be acclaimed to such). The ability of a person or town to be able to boast of their 'census' was a mark of liberty and status continued through later periods: Modéran, 'La renaissance,' = AE 1996: 1704 ('Aïn Jelloula, anc. Cululis, Tunisia): censuram, statum, cives, ius, moenia, fastus – listed as the principal elements of a town's restored status under Justinian. The word here surely prefigures the later acme of our man's career, noted in the second part of the poem (l. 23), as *duumvir quinquennalis*, the municipal equivalent of the Roman censor who performed duties analogous to those of censors: see l. 23 below.

4:    *domus*: meaning not literally any house, but rather one that would be counted as such. This word, too, is echoed later, twice, in ll. 18–19, where the acquisition of a real house and its appurtenances signals, publicly, our man's changed social status. For the identification of *domus* with status see R. Saller, '*Familia, domus* and the Roman Conception of the Family,' *Phoenix* 38 (1984), 336–55, and the bibliography cited there.

5:    *genitus*: picking up the *progenitus* of l. 3, it is also echoed in the second part of the poem, in l. 24: 'et genui … iuvenes carosq(ue) nepotes': whereas our man was born to poverty, his sons and grandsons were born into a house with wealth and status; cf. Apul. *Apol.* 36.

5:    *ruri*: repeated in the following line (6): *rus* is used, often poetically, for a farmstead: OLD, s.v. 'rus'; but also in technical prose descriptions: see Pliny, *NH*, 14.5.52: 'sedulum ruris larem'; (2) it is never so used, however, by Apuleius, for whom it always means 'the countryside,' whereas Tertullian does use it for a rural domain: *De cult. fem.* 2.4.

6:    *semper*: see Bianchi, 'Carmina,' p. 63 and Courtney, *Musa Lapidaria*, p. 318 = CLE 1095 = CIL 5.3415 [Verona], ll. 1 and 4: 'Quaerere consuevi semper neque perdere … et labor a puero qui mihi semper erat.'

7:    *produxerat*: see Bianchi, 'Carmina,' p. 63: Ov. *Trist.* 4.6.11: 'tempus et in canas semen produxit aristas' and Tib. 1.25: 'quodcumque mihi pomum novus educat annus' for some parallels.

8:    *tuc*: for tu(n)c: a foreshortened form sometimes found in epigraphical texts: see Courtney, *Musa Lapidaria*, p. 318, referring to his no. 94b.1.

8:    *demessor*: repeated in l. 11: *hapax*: an occupational noun derived from the verb *demeto, demessui* meaning to cut grain or to harvest (for which the verbal form is common), but found as a substantive only in this inscription: *TLL*, 5.1: 483.21–4 (citing the spurious line 1, alas). It does not occur in any classical Latin text of the first two and a half centuries CE; as Bianchi, 'Carmina,' p. 63, already noted: 'deest lexicis.'

8:    *calami: calamus* is used for the stalks of cereal grains: Verg. *Georg.*, 1.76; Pliny, *NH*, 18.7.10/61: 'calamus altior frumento quam hordeo'; Nemesianus, *Cynegeticon* (*Poetae latini minores*, 290–2): 'Inde ubi pubentes calamos duraverit aestas / lactentesque urens herbas siccaverit omnem / messibus humorem' (see Billiard, *L'agriculture dans l'antiquité*, p. 123). The verses are of some interest, since Nemesianus is supposedly from Carthage (with caution: the source is the *HA*) and dates to the end of the third century.

8:    *ego primus eram*: The *primus* theme is part of the epic presentation of the harvester's life: like the heroes of martial achievements, the protagonist is 'the first,' a boast that is repeated in l. 11: 'cunctos ante ibam *primus* in arvis,' and which is further emphasized by the repeated emphasis that 'even I' (*et ipse*) was able to achieve these personal victories: see ll. 21 and 23 below. The author mimics the claims normally reserved for the great officials and military men of the Roman state, going back at least to the time of the middle Republic: compare the case of Gaius Duil(l)ius: 'Enque eodem mac[istradud bene / r]em navebos primos c[eset copiasque /c]lasesque navales primos ornavet pa[ravetque]' (CIL I² 25, Rome, c. 260 BCE); or the magistrate of the famous 'Polla Elogium': 'eidemque / primus fecei ut de agro poplico / aratoribus cederent paastores' (CIL I² 638, Polla, c. 134–33 BCE).

9:    *falcifera*: see Ovid, *Met.* 13.929–30: '… neque umquam / falciferae secuere manus'; Ovid, *Ib.* 218: 'falciferique senis'; Mart. *Ep.* 5.16.5: '… nam si falciferi defendere templa Tonantis' (i.e., Saturn). Cf. Bianchi, 'Carmina,' p. 63: '*falcifer* inter scriptores aetatis aureae habet tantum Ovidius, posteriore aetate hoc vocabulo usi sunt Sil. Mart. Macrob.' It was a common epithet of the god Saturn. The reaping hook is sometimes displayed as a symbol in relief sculptures on the stelae that were part of the cult in north Africa; see, e.g., Leglay, *SAM*, 1, pl. xi.4–5 (Sbeïtla), xviii, 1–4 (Hippo Regius); *SAM*, 2, pl. xxxvi.5 (Sillège).

9:    *turma* (cf. *turmas*, l. 15): *turma* and its derivatives are usually used in a military context to designate a small band or unit, for example of cavalry (usually of about 30 horsemen), but they are also used of gangs of workers, and specifically of harvest labourers, probably of the same general order of size, or, or more generally, just to designate a 'crowd' of something.

9:    *processerat*: from *procedo*: see OLD s.v. (p. 1466): with military overtones of marching out on campaign.

10: *Cirtae Nomados (arva)*: equivalent to the Greek Νομάδας: the word must be used adjectivally to mean something like 'the fields of nomad Cirta,' surely meaning those plains areas both southeast and southwest of Cirta that were the habitual annual summer pasturelands of the pastoral nomadic groups coming north from the Saharan periphery. See Courtney, *Musa Lapidaria*, p. 318, who is uncertain whether the *Nomados* goes with the Cirtae or Iovis. The adjective *Numidus* appears twice elsewhere in epigraphical poems (CLE 1554.1 and 1525A.2) while *Nomas* appears only in this poem.

10: *Iovis arva*: the 'fields of Jupiter': the consensus of most studies has identified the 'Iovis' with a spectacular feature such as a mountain. Early on, Tissot noted the identification of just such a mountain named by Ptolemy, which seemed to be a peak in the extreme southeastern part of Tunisia (Tissot, *Géographie comparée*, 1, pp. 23–4). He noted that Ptolemy (4.3) placed 'the mountain called Jupiter' (τὸ καλούμενον Διῶς ὄρος) one degree to the south-southeast of Thysdrus and about the same distance west of Macomades on the coast. Victor Vitensis, however, offers the most explicit parallel in the *Mons Domini*, which is to be identified with Djebel Zaghwân about fifty kilometres south of Carthage, at a height of 1343 metres, precisely in the centre of a triangle of towns indicated by Ptolemy: Uthina (Oudna), Thuburbo Maius (Hr. Qasbat), and Medicerra ('Aïn Medker). Most authorities, however, have opted for the Mons Balcarnensis, the mountain of *Iuppiter Balcarnensis*, close to Carthage, which in turn most scholars have tended to identify with the modern Jebel Zaghwân. A voice of dissent has been offered by A. Deman, 'Notes de lecture 62. CIL VIII, 1184, v. 8,' *Latomus* 17 (1958), p. 543, who has proposed the location of the 'mountain of Jupiter' in the environs of Cirta (modern Constantine). That the Cirta here is to be identified with Sicca Veneria – an old warhorse ridden by A. Berthier in *La Numidie* (Paris: Picard, 1981), p. 150 – should be rejected.

11: *demessor*: see comment under l. 8 above.

12: *pos*: used for *post*, see *TLL* 10.2: 156–7; see Courtney, *Musa Lapidaria*, p. 318–19 on *tergus*.

12: *densa*: typical poetic usage for cut sheaves: see Catull. *Carm.*, 64.353: 'namque velut densas praecerpens messor aristas'; see ch. 4, p. 189 above.

12: *gremia* ('sheaves'): The word was first reported in the *Bulletin épigraphique de la Gaule* 5 (1885), p. 137, although many of the first editors sought to insert other words at this point, since this was a singularly odd usage for classical Latin. A consideration of the word *gremia* by Louis Havet, however, confirmed that this word was the correct reading (*Archiv für lateinische Lexicographie* 2 [1887], p. 135). B. Kübler, 'Die lateinische Sprache aus afrikanischen Inschriften' *Archiv für lateinische Lexicographie* 8 (1893), 161–202, at p. 191 f., argued that this use of the word was African in origin, noting occurrences in the Vetus Latina at Genesis 37:4 and Leviticus 23:15 (as quoted by Augustine); as did Paul Capelle, *Le texte du Psautier latin en Afrique* (Rome: F. Pustet, 1913), p. 108n125, who in a consideration of the variant early texts of the Psalms (of Psalm 125:6), notes the translation as 'tollentes sua gremia' from the time of Cyprian (cf. p. 30), and remarks that this usage, 'qui est très original,' was very probably African in origin. He further noted that H. Rönsch in *Zeitschrift für österreichisches Gymnasiums* (1884), 402, pointed to two passages in Optatus (3.10 and 4.6); cf. the Jurist Ofilius as quoted in Dig. 32.1.55.4 (Ulpian; where Mommsen and Krueger, not understanding the term, suggested the correction *cremia*); and Columella, *RR*, 12.19.3, where he is speaking of the process of wine-making: '... lenique primum igne et tenuibus admodum lignis, quae gremia rustici appellant, fornacem incendemus ...' (again, the real meaning of 'gremia' in this passage was often misunderstood and editors mistakenly corrected it to *cremia*). It is used in the common Latin of the so-called *Itala* and the Vulgate to mean sheaves of cereal grains: so the Itala, Genesis 37:7 (as quoted by Quodvultdeus, *Liber promissionum*, 1.25.34 [CCL 60: 42]): 'putabam nos ... ligare gremia in campo surrexit gremium meum et erectum est; conversa autem gremia vestra adoraverunt gremium meum' (for which the word is δράγμα in the LXX, and *manipulus* in the Vulgate). Not only is the African preference for this usage apparent in the surviving uses of the word, but they tend to be later: late fourth- and early fifth-century uses: so Augustine, *Serm.* 313D (MiAg. 1, 534) and *Serm.* 358A (MiAg. 1, 607). But not invariably, so the usage alone is no sure guide: see, e.g., Cassiodorus, *In Psalm.* 125.6 (CCL 98: 1171); and the title of *Lex Burgundionum*, 63: 'De his qui messem in gremiis furati fuerint.' But it is clear that the word was in common use in Africa for a sheaf of grain. Thus, as Capelle noted, when Cyprian twice quotes Psalms 125:6 [126:6 Vulg.] (*Ad Quir.* 3.16 = CCL 3: 108; *Ad Fort.* 12 = CCL 3: 212), the difference between the Italian and the African Latin text is manifest. The text of the Vulgate reads: 'Euntes ibant et flebant, mittentes semina sua. Venientes autem venient cum exultatione, portantes *manipulos* suos.' The African text used by Cyprian reads: 'Ambulantes ambulant et plorabant mittentes semina sua, venientes autem venient in exultatione tollentes *gremia* sua.'

13: *rabido*: 'furious' or 'raging,' sometimes used of the sun: *Laus Pisonis*, 80: 'rabido ... sole'; Aul. Gell. *NA*, 5.14.18: 'sole medio ... rabido et flagranti.' Also Catull. *Carm.*, 64.353–4: 'namque velut densas praecerpens messor aristas / sole sub ardenti flaventia demetit arva.' Close parallels are part of the normal description of reaping in poetics, cf. Ps.-Verg. *Priapea* 2.7: 'mihi rubens arista sole fervido.'

13:   *sub sole*: Working under the scorching heat of the sun: *laborat sub sole* is frequently found in Augustine: at least 14 examples, although most are derived from Eccl. 1:3: 'What does a man gain from all the work at which he toils under the sun?': e.g., Aug. *Enarr. in Ps.* 4.3 (CCL 38: 14) in the context of hard labour: 'Quand abundantia homini in omni labore suo, quo ipse laborat sub sole?'; 38.10 (CCL 38: 411); 141.17 (CCL 40: 2057); *Serm.* 61.11 (CCL 41Aa: 273, quoting Eccl. 1:2–3) and many other cases; once in Cyprian (*Ad Quir.* 3.11 [CCL 3: 99], quoting his version of the book of Ecclesiastes) and never in Tertullian.

13:   *totondi*: from *tondere*: to cut (of hair), but usually in a poetic sense of crops: Verg., *Georg.*, 1.290: 'tondeturque seges maturos annua partus'; compare our poem: 'cum maturas segetes produxerat annus' (l. 7) ; of shearing sheep: Aug. *Enarr. in Ps.* 94.11 (CCl 39: 1339); cf. Bianchi, 'Carmina,' pp. 63–4: 'totondi pro messui,' citing Tibull. 4.1.172: 'tondeturque seges maturos annua partus,' and Sen. *Phoen.* 130: 'colonos agros uberis tondes soli'; cf. Tib. 1.7.34: 'Hic viridem dura caedere falce comam.'

14:   *ductor*: 'leader' or 'commander', most often of a military unit: Suet. *Tib.* 6.4: 'ductor turmae puerorum'; but also in agricultural contexts of persons driving herd animals, significantly in Apul. *Met.* 7.25: '… deierans nullum semet vidisse ductorem'; 8.16: 'ductores … onustos nos ad viam propellunt'; 8.18: 'ubi placuit illis ductoribus nostris …' It is also possible, as MacMullen has suggested in his translation of the poem, that the word here might be poetic for *conductor*, or the man who 'leased' the work of the labourers in the gang that he led, with a contract of *locatio-conductio operae*. Another alternative is to see *ductor* as a shortened form of *ducator*, a word that indicates someone who is in charge of others and who is leading them along: Possid. *Vita Aug.* 12.2 (Bastiaensen, p. 156: *ducator*). Ten instances are found in Augustine; none in earlier patristic authors from Africa (although the word is frequently found in other late fourth-century Christian writers like Ambrose and Jerome). There is a similar hint in Verg. *Georg.* 1.316–17: 'Saepe ego, cum flavis messorem induceret arvis / agricola et fragili iam stringeret hordea culmo …' In this case, the verb *inducere* might contain the suggestion of more than just the owner or farmer 'leading' the harvester to the fields; cf. Paul in *Dig.* 33.7.19: 'mancipia colendi agri causa inducta.' 'Ductor' *DE* 2 (1922), p. 2072, cites this as the only known case in epigraphical texts.

14:   *ex opere*: *opera* would be the usual classical term for such a day labourer (L&S, B.2): for 'a day labourer, a journeyman,' citing Plaut. *Amphit.* 1.1.16: 'plures operas conducere'; Columella, *RR*, 3.21: 'nona opera': a ninth hired labourer on his farm; 'ex' is used to designate the post or rank 'out of which' one has been promoted: Suet. *Galb.* 14.2: 'Cornelius Laco ex assessore praefectus praetorii'; *AE* 1942–3: 84.9: 'ex gregale M. Antonio ... Maximo Syro' (as very commonly on military diplomata); CIL 6.31142 (cf. CIL 13.646): 'M. Ulpius Candidus ex signifero.' More usually, however, the usage is 'post-classical' (L&S, IIA2): 'With the names of office or calling, to denote one who has completed his term of office, or has relinquished his vocation,' especially in inscriptions; see also 'ex' TLL 5.2: col. 1101.80–1102.9: 'spec. de munere post aliud munus subeundo'; cf. CJ 1.17.2.9: 'magistratum ex quaestore et ex consule,' and Amm. Marc. 14.7.7: 'ex duce'; 14.7.9: 'ex comite,' for instances that offer near-contemporary examples.

14: *postea*: see Courtney, *Musa Lapidaria*, p. 319; basing his comments on TLL 10.2: 186.22, he notes that the word was not used in this fashion until the fourth century and later.

16: *Numidae campos*: *Numida, -ae* is used of the people or ethnic group, but is used here, poetically, for the region 'Numidia,' hence 'Numidian' or 'of Numidia.' The name for the region or province is usually Numidia: Apul. *Apol.* 24.1.

16: *nostra manus*: possibly 'our hand,' used poetically for the harvester's own hands engaged in the act of cutting the crop. But it is probably better read as equivalent to *nostra turma* or such, since *manus* is frequently used in the sense of a 'gang' or a group of men engaged in some forceful, collective activity; it may usefully be interpreted as a play on words.

16: *secuit*: see Bianchi, 'Carmina,' p. 64: 'secare aristas': Sen. *Troad.* 76.

17: *vita parvo con[ten]ta valere*: the stonecutter obviously carelessly cut *conta* for *con[ten]ta*, his eye passing over the two 'n's'; Courtney, *Musa Lapidaria*, wishes to construe this as a life 'content with a little' rather than a life 'content to thrive on a little,' which he regards, however, as 'possible.'

17: I presume, along with Courtney, *Musa Lapidaria*, p. 319, and many others, that a pentameter line is missing following this verse; it was an error or lapse of the cutter as he practised his writing. For those who love solving crossword puzzles, consider a suggested restoration that was offered by Cholodniak, *Carmina sepulcralia latina*, p. 477: 'et fecere deis nomina nostra satis.'

18: *dominum fecere domus*: His success here answers to the position of his father, who did not have a 'domus' (l. 2); our harvester thereby becomes at once an 'owner' and a 'lord' or *dominus* (with word play on both *dominus* and *domus*), which 'title' carried with it a sense of independence and honour. In some clear sense the harvester is contrasting this property-owning with the land or *rus* that he had to cultivate when he was a young man (ll. 5–6). The distinction *seems* to be one between owning one's own property and not, between being a proprietor and merely a labourer.

18: *villa*: As in the agricultural writers of a homestead, the main farm and its building complex: *OLD*, s.v. 1a–b.

21: The stonecutter later inserted the 'ip' of 'conscriptos' above the line in order to rectify an error of cutting, probably mistaking the capital 'R' and 'P' in his paper copy. For *conscripti* as those 'enrolled' formally in the local ordo, see ILS 6093, 878; and with the spelling 'conscribti': ILS 9106 (Apulum): 'conscribti et c(ives) R(omani) consist(entes) kan(abis) leg(ionis).' 'Conscriptos' is unusual. The word is very common in Augustine, often with the precise technical meaning found here, of being registered in a local senate or curia; earlier uses in Tertullian (six times) and in Cyprian are prosaic, meaning simply 'written down' or 'recorded.' On the form *scribtus*, see the literature cited by Courtney, *Musa Lapidaria*, p. 319.

22: *ordinis in templo*: see CIL 8.757: 'aedes curialis'; but the closest parallel is found in an inscription from Lambaesis (CIL 8.18328 = ILS 5520 = Eph. epigr. 5 [1884], 766): 'curia igitur ordinis, quam maiores nostri merito templum eiusdem ordinis vocitari voluerunt,' which dates, rather significantly, to the later fourth century (379–83 CE); for some useful comment, see Lepelley, *Cités de l'Afrique romaine*, 2, no. 8, pp. 420–1, who draws specific attention (421n20) to the parallel in the Maktar inscription. For the *ordo* itself called *sanctissimus* see: CIL 10.410 = ILS 2071 (Volcei in Lucania), CIL 8.1921 = ILS 7024 (Lugdunum); and CIL 13.1900 = ILS 7025 (also Lugdunum); local town senates often met, as did the Senate at Rome, in a temple (see ILS, p. 677 for examples); Apul. *Flor.* 16.150: 'Quid quod et Karthaginienses omnes, qui in illa sanctissima curia aderant'; so, too, in later literary Christian sources from Africa: *Passio Dativi, Saturnini presbyteri et aliorum*, 3 (J.-L. Maier, *Le dossier du Donatisme, 1: Des origines à la morte de Constance II (303–61)* [Berlin: Akademie Verlag, 1987], p. 63): 'Adhuc in primum certaminis campum prior Dativus ibat quem sancti parentes candidum senatorem caelesti curiae genuerunt.'

22: *delectus ab ordine*: that is to say, he was adlected by the members of the local town council into their ordo. The choice of *delectus* is odd; the usual term was *adlectus*: see 'Allectio,' *DE* 1: 411–22, at pp. 415–16 for adlection into municipal *curiae*, where CIL 12.1585 (Lugdunum) offers a close parallel: *allectus in curiam*. See Courtney, *Musa Lapidaria*, p. 319, who cites C. Lepelley, *Cités de l'Afrique romaine*, 1, p. 141 and Jacques, *Privilège de liberté*, pp. 448–9; more classically, see Cic. *Rosc.* 8: 'qui ... ex senatu in hoc consilium delecti estis.'

23:   *rusticulus*: unusual: not very widely used as a substantive, but see Cic. *Sest.* 38.82; not, for example, in Apuleius, who prefers *rusticanus* or *rusticus*.

23:   *censor*: Echoing the 'nec census' of l. 4, thereby, once again, contrasting his changed status by balancing his improved condition in the second half of the poem with his origins in the first half. Every fifth year the *duoviri* of the town in a Roman colony or municipality acted as *duoviri quinquennales* or 'censors' who oversaw the *lustrum* of the town's citizens, including the head count and the valuation of their property. The position was important not only for purposes of the internal politics of the town, but also because of the responsibilities for central-state tribute collection; see CIL 8.686 for a *duumvir quinquennalis* at Mactaris. See Modéran, 'La renaissance,' pp. 96–8 on the role of the *census* and the *IIvir qq.* at this time; and also, Jacques, *Privilège de liberté*, p. 576.

23:   *ipse*: Because of a rough blemish in the stone, around which the stonecutter had to work, there is a gap between the 'ip' and the 'se' of the 'ipse.'

24:   *et genui*: Echoing the *progenitus* of l. 3 and the *genitus* of l. 8; a not unusual statement to make in an epitaph, but the strong claim of family continuity through three generations of male descendants has a modestly epic and aristocratic ring to it, going back at least to the middle Republic: compare the claims on one of the Scipionic *elogia*: 'progeniem genui' (CIL I², 15, Rome: the epitaph of Cn. Cornelius Scipio Hispanus, c. 135 BCE (?); notably in the verse *elogium* in elegiacs that follows the prose epitaph); our man could not and did not wish to boast of ancestry as this Scipio did – the words immediately following in the Scipionic *elogium* are: 'facta patris petiei / maiorum optenui laudem, ut sibei me esse creatum / laetentur; stirpem nobilitavit honor' – but our man could attempt the same effect by stressing his self-made status.

24:   *carosq(ue) nepotes*: Verg. *Aen.* 6.682: 'carosque nepotes'; for a similar rejoicing in being able to see descendants and what one has given to them, see the great verse inscription to Titus Flavius Secundus the elder at Cillium (Kasserine, CIL 8.212, lines 60–1): '[adsi]due patrias hinc cernere dulciter arces / quosq(ue) dedit natis prope semper habere penates.' The word *nepotes* has been lost because of damage caused in the transport of the stone to the Louvre; it is no longer visible. Because of the same blemish in the stone that caused a work-around by the stonecutter in line 23 (see 'ipse' above), there is a space between the 'caro' and the 'sq' of carosq(ue), and another space before 'nepotes.'

24:   I presume, with others, that there is another pentameter verse missing after this line, caused by the same reasons for the slip following l. 17; for a suggested restoration, see Cholodniak, *Carmina sepulcralia latina*, p. 477: 'et qui post obitum nostra sepulcra colant.'

25: Sentiments similar to those in these lines seem to be found in a Christian epitaph from Mactaris: 'Si quis honos vitae est testis post munera fati ... Namque egomet, quod pio semper in corpore vixi ...' (Prévot, *Recherches archéologiques*, p. 232 and no. II.18), although the sentiment of having lived *in pio corpore* does mark a watershed of sorts.

25–6: *Vitae pro meritis claros transegimus annos, / quos nullo lingua crimine laedit atrox*: Pikhaus and others see a direct Vergilian influence: *Aen.*, 4.550–1 from the Dido and Aeneas episode, which was very popular in Africa: 'Non licuit thalami expertem sine crimine vitam / degere more ferae, talis nec tangere curas.' Since the theme was widespread in Africa, and the part hemistich 'sine crimine vitam / degere' is often found in the funerary poetry of both 'pagans' and Christians, I find it difficult to see the precise influence on the poetic diction here. For l. 25 closer parallels are later ones: Tac. *Agr.* 4.3: 'pueritiam adulescentiamque transegit'; SHA, *Vita Clod. Alb.* 5.1: 'omnem pueritiam in Africa transegit.'

26: *laesit*: See Masqueray, *Bulletin du correspondance africaine* (1885), p. 361; *laesit* was restored by some early editors, but Mommsen (CIL) says that the stonecutter clearly carved a 'd,' and his views (naturally) have held the day. But in comparing the letter with similar letters in the text, the letter on the stone clearly looks like an 's' not a 'd.'

27. *sine crimine degere vitam*: see the discussion at l. 25–6 above, and Phaedr. 1.3.2; Cholodniak, *Carmina sepulcralia latina*, p. 477, long ago pointed out that 'vixit sine crimine vitae' was a standard sentiment in funerary verse.

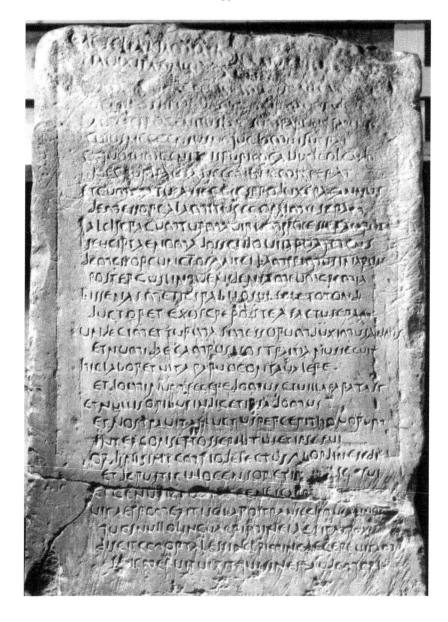

A.2.1: Maktar Harvester inscription. The Louvre, Paris;
permission courtesy of the Louvre

A.2.2: Maktar Harvester inscription: left side of the stele. The Louvre, Paris; permission courtesy of the Louvre

A.2.3: Maktar Harvester inscription: right side of the stele. The Louvre, Paris; permission courtesy of the Louvre

The Gallo-Roman Reaping Machines: Iconographic Data

1: The Bas-Relief from Montauban-Buzenol

Place: Buzenol, in the extreme southeastern corner of Belgium, in the Belgian province of Luxembourg, just west of the border with the state of Luxembourg, about 75 km west-southwest of Trier. Discovered on 16 June 1958.

Reference and illustrations: Bloc Inv. No. 58 Bu 19; Musée Gaumais, Virton: MGV 1254; Raepsaet and Lambeau, *La moissonneuse*, fig. p. 40; Lambert, *Luxembourg romain*, p. 52, fig. 87.

Material: Limestone.

Date: The funerary structure of which the reliefs were originally part probably dated to the end of second or the beginning of the third century (Mertens, 'Sculptures romaines de Buzenol,' p. 51).

Description: Fragment of an agricultural scene, 155 cm. in length, 58 cm. in width, 55 cm. in height; with a border of 3 cm. and a depth of carving of about 3 cm. in relief. To the left is a peasant in a short tunic wielding a stick; there are spiggots of grain in a box that is the front end of the machine; the catcher of the machine, fronted by teeth, is mounted on two wheels. To the right is a long pole to which a mule or an ass has been harnessed; the head of the animal alone is preserved.

Bibliography: Mertens, 'Sculptures romaines de Buzenol,' pp. 17–53, block 19 of the series of 46 discovered at the site: see pp. 31–2 and fig. 6, p. 32, and plate xiv; 'Le *vallus*,' pp. 217–20 and plates xliii–xlvii; 'Eine antike Mähmaschine,' pp. 1–3; 'Römische Skulpturen,' pp. 386–92; 'La moissonneuse de Buzenol,' pp. 59–63, figs. 46 and 47; 'Nouveaux monuments funéraires,' pp. 35–47 and plates i–vii; Fouss, 'Le *vallus*,' pp. 125–36; White, *Agricultural Implements*, pp. 159, 162–4, and 172; Breyel, Coessens, and Walschot 'Essai d'analyse,' plate p. 40.

2: The Bas-Relief from Arlon

Place: Arlon, Luxembourg, Roman *Orolaunum Vicus*, located at the crossroads of the main west-east road from Reims to Trier, Roman *Augusta Treverorum*, and the main north-south route from Tongeren (Belgium), Roman *Atuatuca Tungrorum*, to Metz, Roman *Divodurum*. First discovered in 1854, at the Maison Gérard, Grand'rue, Arlon. Now located in the Musée Luxembourgeois, Arlon.

Reference and illustrations: J.-B. Sibenaler, *Guide illustré du Musée lapidaire d'Arlon* (Arlon, 1905), p. 88, no. 50; Espérandieu, *Recueil général*, 5, no. 4036; A. Bertrang, *Le Musée Luxembourgeois* (Arlon, 1954), p. 84, no. 34; Raepsaet and Lambeau, *La moissonneuse*, fig. p. 39; Ardhuin, ed., *La moissonneuse gauloise*, p. 6; L. Lefèbvre, *Le Musée luxembourgois Arlon* (Brussels: Ludion, 1990); Lambert, *Luxembourg romain*, p. 53, fig. 88; Lejeune, *Musée archéologique luxembourgeois Arlon*, fig. 200, p. 162.

Material: Limestone.

Date: Probably to be dated to the same general time period as the Buzenol relief sculptures (no. 1 above) – that is, approximately between the end of the second and the mid-third century CE – although there is no surviving archaeological context to confirm the date.

Description: A heavily worn relief sculpture, 79 cm. in width, 62 cm. in height, 115 cm. in length. Its state of preservation is so bad that it is difficult to make out the main lineaments of the figures. At the bottom of the stone are the tops of the sprigs of wheat. In front of the man, one can still see the mane, tail, and hoof of a horse or mule that was harnessed to poles that run on either side of the peasant cultivator who stands between them.

Bibliography: Rostovtzeff, *SEHRE* (Oxford, 1926), plate 29, fig. 4, first identified it as a pictorial representation of the mechanical reaper; cf. *SEHRE*² (Oxford, 1957), plate 37.4; A. Bertrang, 'Un mystère dissipé. Le Musée d'Arlon possède depuis plus d'un siècle un fragment de la moissonneuse gauloise,' *Bulletin trimestriel de l'Institut archéologique de Luxembourg* no. 4 (1958), 73–7; White, *Agricultural Implements*, pp. 159, 162 and 172; Breyel, Coessens, and Walschot, 'Essai d'analyse,' plate, p. 39.

3: The Bas-Relief from Trier

Place: Trier, Roman *Augusta Treverorum*, on the middle Rhine, where the relief was first correctly identified as the fragment of a representation of an ancient mechanical reaper in 1964. First discovered in a field behind the Landesmuseum in 1890.

Reference and illustrations: Landesmuseum Trier, Inv. No. 19093; Raepsaet and Lambeau, *La moissonneuse*, fig. p. 43; Ardhuin, ed., *La moissonneuse gauloise*, p. 9.

Material: Local limestone.

Date: From design and type, the relief derives from much the same workshops, and period, that produced nos. 1 and 2 above.

Description: A small limestone fragment, 46–51 cm. in length, 19 cm. in width, and 25 cm. in height; the relief shows one side of lower part of the harvesting machine, including one wheel and part of the *vallus* or catcher, the lower part of the harnessing pole, and the forepart of the horse or mule that is pushing the machine.

Bibliography: Stern, *Calendrier de 354*, p. 208 and plate 38, fig. 4; Cüppers 'Gallo-römische Mähmaschine,' 151–3 and plate 32, top; Renard '*Vallus* de Trèves,' 486–97 and plate 23; White, *Agricultural Implements*, pp. 159–60, 164–5, and 172; Breyel, Coessens, and Walschot, 'Essai d'analyse,' plate, p. 43.

4: The Bas-Relief from Koblenz

Place: Koblenz (Coblenz) Germany, Roman *Castellum ad Confluentes*, on the middle Rhine. Discovered in 1969.

Reference and illustrations: Mittelrhein-Museum, Koblenz, no. 2.10; P. Noelke, 'Quader mit Ernteszene von der Koblenser Moselbrücke,' *Kölner Römer Illustrierte* 2 (1975), fig. 238; H. von Petrikovits, *Die Rheinland in Römischerzeit: mit einem Uberblick die rheinische Urgeschichte*, 2 vols. (Dusseldorf: Schwann, 1980), fig. p. 55; Raepsaet-Lambeau, *La moissonneuse*, fig. p. 42; Ardhuin, ed., *La moissonneuse gauloise*, p. 10.

Material: Limestone from the Upper Moselle.

Date: The style and design would indicate that it was produced out of the same material, by much the same craftsmen and in the same cultural environment as nos. 1–3 above.

Description: 55 cm. in height, 74 cm. in length, 37 cm. in width.

Bibliography: P. Noelke, 'Quader mit Ernteszene von der Koblenzer Moselbrücke,' *Kölner Römer Illustrierte* 2 (1975), pl. 238, p. 182; Heinen, 'Grundzüge,' pp. 89–91.

5: The Bas-Relief from Reims

Place: Located in the vault of the central arch in the so-called Gate of Mars, the 'Porte de Mars,' in the Place de la République, Reims, Roman *Durocortorum*. The papers of the architect Auguste Caristie (most dating to about 1827), found in the Bibliothèque Municipal de Reims, show that he already recognized that this panel pictured the kind of mechanical reaper described by the Elder Pliny and Palladius.

Reference and illustration: A. Caristie, 'Description de la voûte du grand arc du monument de Reims,' manuscript in the Bibliothèque municipale de Reims, 20 pp., 1 plan and 1 line drawing. A first series of drawings were made by Jean Colin at some point between 1660 and 1695 at Reims; these are archived in the Bibliothèque National (AA3, Cabinet des Estampes); the one for the central arch reliefs is reproduced by Stern, 'Les calendriers romains illustrés,' pl. XIII.64. The most accurate reproduction remains the drawing of Jacques-Martin-Silvestre Bence in A.L.J. [Comte] de Laborde, *Les monuments de la France: classés chronologiquement ete considérés sous le rapport des faits historiques et de l'étude des arts*, 2 vols. (Paris: P. Didot l'Aîné, 1816–36), vol. 1 (1816), pl. cxiii, p. 91, reproduced by Stern, 'Le cycle des mois,' pl. cclxxxix (between pp. 1442 and 1443) and 'Les calendriers romains illustrés,' pl. XXIII.65.

Material: Lutatian limestone (from a quarry near Reims).

Date: Given the developmental patterns of the city, the arches, including this one, probably date to the the late second or to early third century CE. Based on the design and stylistic decoration of the arch, Charles-Picard 'La "Porte de Mars" à Reims,' pp. 67–8, contends that the arch is Caracallan, or slightly later, in date.

Description: Approximately 120 cm. in height by 150 cm. in width. Only the drawings made in the late seventeenth century and in the mid-eighteenth survive as good indications of the original. The right panels of the central arch contain a program of relief sculptures of agricultural production based on months of the year, including two scenes of harvesting. The first scene is of three harvesters who are wielding scythes. The neighbouring panel shows a scene of harvesting featuring the harvesting machine. Only the front teeth of the *vallus* are portrayed (the box itself is not shown on the surviving drawings); one wheel is shown, since the machine is seen in profile, along with a horse that is driving the machine, and one of the harnessing poles. In front is a peasant wielding a long pole of the sort used to control the entry of the grain stalks into the teeth of the machine.

Bibliography: Specific studies, apart from general treatments of the architecture and iconography of the arch: N. Brunette, *Projet de restauration de l'arc de triomphe antique de Mars à Reims d'après les dsssins exposés au Musée du Louvre* (Reims: Bibliothèque de Reims, 1860); Y. Burnand, 'La première identification de la moissonneuse gallo-romaine sur la "Porte de Mars" à Reims par l'architecte Auguste Caristie (vers 1829),' in *Actes du 95e Congrès national des Sociétés savantes, Reims, 1980: Section d'archéologie et d'histoire de l'art* (Paris, 1974), pp. 85–92; S. Reinach, *Répertoire de reliefs grecs et romains*, vol. 1 (Paris: E. Leroux, 1909), fig. 2, p. 231; Raepsaet and Lambeau, *La moissonneuse*, fig. p. 41; Ardhuin, ed., *La moissonneuse gauloise*, pp. 7–8; Espérandieu, *Recueil générale*, vol. 5, no. 3681; White, *Agricultural Implements*, pp. 159, 162, and 172; Legros, 'Ordre romain,' pp. 696–702 and plate xii, fig. 3; Stern, 'Le cycle des mois,' p. 1442; and Breyel, Coessens, and Walschot, 'Essai d'analyse,' plate, p. 41.

Further Information

Further items of bibliography, other than those above here, can be found in Kolendo, 'La mietitura,' pp. 158–68; Renard, 'Technique et agriculture,' pp. 89–94 and in his *Technique et agriculture*, passim. I suspect that there might well be other Roman monuments that have not been 'seen' simply because no one at the time seriously considered the reaping machine as a possible candidate for the representation. For example, a relief from Arlon in Gaul (the same findspot as in no. 2 above) that features a ploughing scene (used, symbolically, to signify sowing and the beginning of life) shows a container on wheels with two long bars attached to it that might not be a simple two-wheeled cart (as it is often taken to be) but a reaping machine that represented the 'reaping' or the end of life (see Prat, *Histoire d'Arlon*, vol. 1, pl. 64; cf. Gow, 'The Ancient Plough,' p. 258, fig. 9). Consider, for example, how the Arlon scene, now recognized as the representation of the reaping machine (no. 2 above), was completely misapprehended from the time of its discovery onwards until the mid-1920s when Rostovtzeff had the perspicacity to see what it really was: Prat, *Histoire d'Arlon*, vol. 1, 2e sér., facing p. 151. Ploughing and reaping scenes, when paired, appear as a foreshortened version of the sequence that normally runs through hoeing and weeding, to reaping, and then to storage in order to represent the course of life: see Ferdi, *Corpus des mosaïques de Cherchel*, pl. LXXXVII.94, for the well-known agricultural scene from Caesarea in Mauretania Caesariensis, where only the ploughing and hoeing sequences have survived.

Abbreviations of Sources

AAT	E. Babelon, R. Cagnat, and S. Reinach, eds., *Atlas archéologique de la Tunisie: édition spéciale des cartes topographiques publiées par le ministère de la guerre, accompagnée d'un texte explicatif* (Paris: E. Leroux, 1893–1932)
AE	*L'année épigraphique* (Paris: Presses Universitaires de France, 1888 to present)
AfrRom	*L'Africa romana* (Sassari: Gallizzi, 1984 to present)
AtlArch	S. Gsell, *Atlas archéologique de l'Algérie* (Algiers: Gouvernement générale de l'Algérie: Service géographique de l'Armée, A. Jourdan, 1911; reprint Osnabrück: O. Zeller, 1973)
BA	*Bibliothèque Augustinienne: Oeuvres de saint Augustin* (Paris: Desclée de Brouwer, 1948 to present)
BMCRE	*British Museum Catalogue: Coins of the Roman Empire*, vols. 1–29 (London: British Museum, 1923–74)
CCL	*Corpus christianorum, series Latina* (Turnhout: Brepols, 1954 to present)
CIL	*Corpus Inscriptionum Latinarum*, vols. 1–17 (Berlin: G. Reimer, 1863 to present)
CIMRM	M.J. Vermaseren, *Corpus Inscriptionum et Monumentorum Religionis Mithriacae*, 2 vols. (The Hague: Nijhoff, 1956–60)
CJ	*Codex Justinianus*: P. Krueger, ed., *Codex Iustinianus*, vol. 2 in *Corpus Iuris Civilis*, 9th ed. (Berlin, 1915; reprint pref. W. Kunkel, Zürich: Weidmann, 1967)
CLE	F. Buecheler, ed., *Carmina Latina Epigraphica*, 2 vols. (Leipzig, 1895–7; E. Lommatzsch, ed., *Supplementum*, Leipzig, 1926)
Corp. Gloss.	G. Goetz, ed., *Corpus Glossariorum Latinorum*, 7 vols. (Leipzig: Teubner, 1888–1923)
CSEL	*Corpus Scriptorum Ecclesiasticorum Latinorum* (Vienna: Tempsky, 1866 to present)

CTh   *Codex Theodosianus*: Th. Mommsen and P. Krueger, eds., *Theodosiani libri xvi cum Constitutionibus Sirmondianis et Leges Novellae ad Theodosianum pertinentes*, 2 vols. (Berlin: Weidmann, 1905; reprint Zürich: Weidmann, 1971)

DE   E. di Ruggiero, ed., *Dizionario epigrafico di antichità romane* (Rome: Pasqualucci, 1886 to present)

Dig.   *Digesta*: Th. Mommsen and P. Krueger, eds., *Digesta*, vol. 1 in *Corpus Iuris Civilis*, 9th ed. (Berlin: Weidmann, 1915; reprint pref. W. Kunkel, Zürich: Weidmann, 1967)

Eph. Epig.   *Ephemeris epigraphica: Corporis inscriptionum Latinarum supplementum*, 9 vols. (Berlin: Berlin Academy–G. Reimer, 1872–1913)

FIRA, 1   S. Riccobono, ed., *Fontes Iuris Romani antejustiniani, vol. 1: Leges*, 2nd ed. (Florence: Barbèra, 1968)

FIRA, 3   V. Arangio-Ruiz, ed., *Fontes Iuris Romani antejustiniani, vol. 3: Negotia*, 2nd ed. (Florence: Barbèra, 1972)

ILAfr.   R. Cagnat, A. Merlin, and L. Chatelain, eds., *Inscriptions latines d'Afrique (Tripolitaine, Tunisie, Maroc)* (Paris: E. Leroux, 1923)

ILAlg.   *Inscriptions latines de l'Algérie* (Paris: Champion; Algiers: République algérienne démocratique et populaire; and Paris: de Boccard, 1922 to present)

ILCV   E. Diehl, ed., *Inscriptiones Latinae Christianae Veteres* (Berlin: Weidmann, 1925–31; reprint 1961–7)

ILMB   Z. B. Ben Abdullah, *Catalogue des inscriptions latines païennes du Musée du Bardo* (Rome: Ecole française de Rome, 1986)

ILS   H. Dessau, ed., *Inscriptiones Latinae Selectae*, 3 vols. in 5 (Berlin: Weidmann, 1892–1916; reprint Berlin, 1954–5; 1962)

ILTun.   A. Merlin, ed., *Inscriptions latines de la Tunisie* (Paris: Presses Universitaires de France, 1944)

InscrItal   *Inscriptiones Italiae* (Rome: Libreria dello Stato, 1931 to present)

MGH AA   *Monumenta Germaniae Historica: auctores antiquissimi* (Berlin: Weidmann, 1877 to present)

MGH SRG   *Monumenta Germaniae Historica: scriptores rerum Germanicarum* (Hannover-Leipzig: Hahn, 1871 to present)

MGH SRM   *Monumenta Germaniae Historica: scriptores rerum Merovingicarum* (Hannover: Hahn, 1937 to present; reprint 1969)

MiAg   *Miscellanea Agostiniana: testi e studi pubblicati a cura dell'ordine Eremitano di S. Agostino nel XV centenario dalla morte del santo dottore*, 2 vols. (Rome: Tipografia Poliglotta Vaticana, 1930–1)

PG   J.-P. Migne, ed., *Patrologiae cursus completus, series graeca*, 161 vols. in 166 (Paris: Editions Garnier Frères, 1857–66)

PIR²   E. Groag, A. Stein, and L. Petersen, eds., *Prosopographia Imperii Romani saec I.II.III*, 2nd ed. (Berlin: de Gruyter, 1933 to present)

PL   J.-P. Migne, ed., *Patrologiae cursus completus, series latina*, 222 vols. (Paris: Editions Garnier Frères, 1844–66; 2nd ed., 1878–90)

PLS   A.-G. Hamman et al., eds., *Patrologiae Latinae Supplementum*, 5 vols. (Paris: Editions Garnier Frères, 1958–74)

RAC   *Reallexikon für Antike und Christentum* (Stuttgart: A. Hiersemann, 1941 to present)

RIC   *The Roman Imperial Coinage*, vols. 1–10 (London: Spink, 1923–94)

RMR   R.O. Fink, ed., *Roman Military Records on Papyrus* (Cleveland: American Philological Association, 1971)

RRC   M.H. Crawford, *Roman Republican Coinage*, 2 vols. (Cambridge: Cambridge University Press, 1974; reprint, with corrections, Cambridge, 2001)

SC   *Sources chrétiennes* (Paris: Editions du Cerf, 1942 to present)

TLL   *Thesaurus Linguae Latinae* (Munich–Stuttgart: Teubner, 1900 to present)

VG   The Latin 'Vulgate' translation of the Bible: R. Weber et al., eds., *Biblia Sacra iuxta vulgatam versionem*, 4th ed. (Stuttgart: Deutsche Bibelgesellschaft, 1994)

Table A. Survey of modern/post–Second World War land use patterns in the Maghrib (excluding Morocco)

Year	1948	1954	1958	1961	1968	1974	1979
ALGERIA							
Total land	220,486	220,486	238,174	238,174	238,174	238,174	238,174
Arable	5,676	6,878	6,985	7,066	6,787	6,981	7,485
Pasture	41,311	40,176	38,511	38,405	37,416	38,452	36,258
Woodland	3,000	3,070	3,050	3,045	3,045	2,424	4,122
Unusable	170,499	170,362	189,628	189,658	191,547	190,317	190,309
TUNISIA							
Total land	15,583	12,500	12,518	12,518	15,590	15,536	15,536
Arable	3,766	4,265	4,912	4,334	4,570	4,360	4,415
Pasture	4,225	–	–	5,652	3,250	3,250	3,250
Woodland	1,009	900	980	1,376	1,240	576	510
Unusable	6,583	7,230	6,251	–	7,415	8,175	7,361
TRIPOLITANIA							
Total land	35,304	–	35,000	35,300	–	–	–
Arable	2,260	–	2,500	1,724	–	–	–
Pasture	6,542	–	6,452	8,276	–	–	–
Woodland	17	–	12	35	–	–	–
Unusable	21,759	–	14,988	25,265	–	–	–

Land areas: in thousands of hectares

Source: *FAO Annual Production Yearbooks*, United Nations, 1948–80 (Rome: Società Grafica Romana): reports for 1950, 1955, 1960, 1965, 1970, 1975, and 1980.

Table B. Pre–Second World War cereal grain production in the Maghrib (Algeria and Tunisia only)

	Area sown ha/000	iug/000	Yields q/ha	mod/iug	Total production q/000	mod/000
WHEAT						
Algeria						
Bad year (1931/1936)	1,250	5,000	4.2	15	5,230	74,800
Good year (1934)	1,200	4,800	6.6	23.6	7,930	113,440
Tunisia						
Bad year (1936)	360	1,440	3.4	12.3	1,235	17,640
Good year (1932)	848	3,392	4.1	14.7	3,494	49,960
BARLEY						
Algeria						
Bad year (1938)	1,145	4,580	6.5	23.3	7,450	106,560
Good year (1934)	1,270	5,080	9.9	35.4	12,587	180,000
Tunisia						
Bad year (1936/1938)	300	1,200	4.3	15.3	1,285	18,372
Good year (1932)	610	2,440	7.2	25.6	4,370	64,472
AVERAGES						
Wheat						
Algeria		4,900		19.2		94,120
Tunisia		2,415		13.9		33,800
Barley						
Algeria		4,830		29.7		143,280
Tunisia		1,820		22.2		40,422
TOTAL						
Wheat						127,920
Barley						183,702
Both cereals						311,622

Abbreviations: ha: hectares; iug: iugera; mod: modii; q: quintals

Source: *Algeria*, vol. 2, tables 1 and 2, pp. 434–45; *Tunisia*, table 1, p. 461; these figures are within the range of those for the first years of the twentieth century attested for Tunisia: see Decker-David, *Agriculture indigène*, p. 322; Rivière and Lecq, *Traité pratique*, pp. 308–10.

Table C. Survey of modern/post–Second World War cereal grain production in the Maghrib: 1945–80

	Area sown			Yields			Total		
	High	Low	Av.	High	Low	Av.	High	Low	Av.
WHEAT									
Algeria	2,403	1,482	1,900	8.0	5.1	6.5	1,580	630	1,150
	[1972]	[1966]		[1979]	[1969]		[1963]	[1966]	
Tunisia	1,358	800	1,075	7.1	3.7	5.5	714	330	525
	[1954]	[1969]		[1953]	[1964]		[1965]	[1967]	
Libya-T	67	23	45	5.3	1.9	3.5	23	7	15
	[1963]	[1950]		[1958]	[1964]		[1958]	[1950]	
Morocco	1,953	1,220	1,565	13.2	4.7	9	669	1,700	1,150
	[1969]	[1950]		[1968]	[1958]		[1958]	[1970]	
BARLEY									
Algeria	1,412	394	900	8.2	3.3	5.5	950	130	530
	[1954]	[1966]		[1963]	[1966]		[1964]	[1970]	
Tunisia	882	319	600	4.6	1.9	3.5	282	70	175
	[1954]	[1963]		[1970]	1954]		[1959]	[1967]	
Libya-T	309	177	225	3.6	1.4	2.5	84	37	60
	[1964]	[1963]		[1958]	[1959]		[1958]	[1959]	
Morocco	2,135	1,535	1,800	15.1	3.4	8.5	3,217	612	1,900
	[1968]	[1963]		[1968]	[1966]		[1968]	[1966]	
TOTALS									
Algeria	3,815	1,874	2,800	8.1	4.2	6.0	2,530	760	1,680
Tunisia	2,240	1,119	1,650	5.9	2.8	4.5	996	400	700
Libya-T	376	200	270	4.5	1.6	3.0	107	44	75
TOTALS	6,431	3,193	4,750	6.2	2.9	4.5	3,633	1,204	2,455

Area sown: in thousands of hectares

Yields: hundreds of kilograms per hectare

Total Production: in thousands of metric tonnes

Abbreviations: Av. = Average; Libya-T: Tripolitania

Source: *FAO Annual Production Yearbooks*, United Nations, 1948–80 (Rome: Società Grafica Romana)

Table D. Pre–First World War indigenous cereal grain production in Algeria: 1872–1914

Year	Area sown ha/000	Hard wheat q/000	Yields q/ha	mod iug	Barley q/000	Yields q/ha	mod iug	Total q/000	Yields q/ha	mod iug	Total
1872	1,573	3,277	4.8	17.1	5,595	7.3	26.1	8,972	6.1	21.8	128.3
1874	2,433	4,825	4.7	16.8	7,311	5.8	20.7	12,136	5.3	18.9	173.5
1877	–	2,428	2.1	7.5	4,502	3.4	12.1	6,930	2.8	10.0	99.1
1878	2,315	3,333	3.4	12.1	5,157	4.3	15.4	8,490	3.9	13.9	121.4
1882	2,517	4,149	4.4	15.7	6,695	4.0	14.3	10,844	4.2	15.0	155.1
1884	2,523	5,689	5.6	20.0	9,685	7.1	25.3	15,374	6.4	22.8	219.8
1886	2,400	4,622	4.9	17.5	8,443	6.4	22.8	13,065	5.7	20.3	186.8
1890	2,443	4,280	5.4	19.3	8,808	6.7	23.9	14,088	6.1	21.8	201.5
1902	2,244	6,096	6.8	24.3	9,056	6.9	24.6	15,152	6.9	24.6	216.7
1906	2,203	5,584	6.2	22.1	8,875	7.5	26.8	10,658	6.9	24.6	152.4
1910	2,248	5,491	6.0	21.4	8,699	7.3	26.1	14,190	6.6	23.6	199.7
1914	2,216	4,313	4.9	17.5	6,824	5.8	20.7	11,137	5.4	19.3	159.3

Sources: Agéron, *Les Algériens musulmans et la France*, vol. 1: 378–81; vol. 2: 794–801;

Statistique générale de l'Algérie: every fourth year, 1872–90, 1902–14; plus the worst year: 1877; and the best year: 1884.

Abbreviations: ha = hectares; iug = iugera; mod = modii; q = quintals

Notes

1. Under the Burning Sun

1 Hom. *Il.* 18.550–60; my English translations of Homer have obviously benefited in different ways from the existing translations by Lattimore, Fagles, and Lombardo; cf. Gow, *Theocritus*, 2, p. 204: 'This seems to be the only detailed description of the proceedings that survives.'

2 For the special 'kingly' figure represented here, see Guizzi, 'Ho visto un re,' pp. 83–5, and pp. 85–8 on the meaning of the *temenos*.

3 On the ἔριθοι see Guizzi, 'Ho visto un re,' p. 88, and the works cited in 88n32, especially A. Mele, *Società e lavoro nei poemi omerici* (Naples: Università degli Studi di Napoli: Istituto di storia e antichità greche e romane, 1968), p. 38.

4 Even with the mechanization of American and English agriculture in the last decades of the nineteenth century, the need for hand labour remained massive in scale: Morgan, *Harvesters and Harvesting*, pp. 9–10.

5 Leo Tolstoy, *Anna Karenina*, trans. R. Pevear and L. Volokonsky (London: Penguin, 2000), pp. 247–56.

6 A.E. Astin, *Cato the Censor* (Oxford: Clarendon Press, 1978), p. 8, expresses the point nicely: 'The "rustic" virtues of a robust physique, hard work, endurance, and indifference to material advantage were emphasized by a calculated and largely consistent display of austerity, by an oft-proclaimed scorn of ostentatious luxuries.'

7 For some contextual background on Venetsianov, see O. Figes, *Natasha's Dance: A Cultural History of Russia* (London: Allen Lane, 2002), pp. 116–18.

8 Morgan, 'The Place of Harvesters,' p. 29.

9 Cherwinski, '"Misfits," "Malingerers," and "Malcontents,"' p. 273.

10 For example, at the end of the Second World War, early in 1945, units of the Red Army that were advancing into the homelands of the Third Reich were warned that they would be required to work to take off the harvest in German lands that they

occupied: M. Hastings, *Armageddon: The Battle for Germany, 1944–1945* (New York: Vintage, 2005), p. 243. In America, the situation was no different: Atkinson, *Army at Dawn*, p. 53.

11 P. Yale 33 (= P. Hibeh 44; Hibeh, 5 April 253 BCE): the letter of one Deion ordering the toparch Harimouthes to send a detachment of indigenous soldiers – *machimoi* – along with a group of reapers, according to the instructions of the Dioiketes Apollonios. Were the reapers somehow connected with the soldiers in the sense of doing reaping for them? Or were they simply recruited and moved around in the same manner as the soldiers? It is unclear.

12 CIL 8.4322 = 18547 (Casae, modern al-Madher or 'Aïn Kerma): a dedication to Jupiter Optimus Maximus and the Nymphs on behalf of the well-being of the emperor Septimius Severus, Caracalla, Julia Domna, and the whole divine household (c. 208–10 CE) by the soldiers of the Third Augustan legion who were *morantes ad fenum sec(andum)*. Either the labour of the soldiers was requisitioned for the local harvest or, more likely, they were mowing fodder from the *prata legionis*, on which see Mócsy, 'Zu den *prata legionis*,' pp. 211 f. For possible instances of soldiers hiring themselves out for seasonal agriculture labour, such as the harvest, see, e.g., Xen. *Hell.* 2.1.1; 6.2.37.

13 Caes. *BG*, 4.32.4–5: 'Nam quod omni ex reliquis partibus demesso frumento pars una erat reliqua, suspicati hostes huc nostros esse venturos noctu in silvis delituerant; tum dispersos, depositis armis in metendo occupatos subito adorti, paucis interfectis reliquos incertis ordinibus perturbaverant …'

14 Joseph. *BJ*, 1.323–4, seems to me to be one of these cases: five cohorts of men taken on a raid to carry off the wheat at midsummer. Note that the site of an army camp might be selected precisely because the nearby crops were ready for reaping, with the implication that the soldiers themselves would do the reaping: Livy 31.2.7 (201 BCE).

15 Roth, *Logistics of the Roman Army*, pp. 131–2, who notes the case of the 7,000 unarmed men lost to an attack of the Boii in northern Italy in 201 BCE while engaged in a reaping operation: Livy 31.2.7–8; as Roth says, these *inermes* could be 'non-combatant military servants,' although in this case they were most probably the soldiers who had put down their arms in order to reap.

16 Ps.-Caes. *Bell. Afr.* 20.4: 'Etiam animum advertebat frumento se in Africa nisi importaticio uti non posse: priore anno enim propter adversariorum dilectus, quod stipendiarii aratores milites essent facti, messem non esse factus.'

17 Livy 42.64.2–3: 'Ubi cum audisset raptim Romanos circa ex agris demessum frumentum convehere, deinde ante sua quemque tentoria spicas falcibus desecantem, quo purius frumentum tereret, ingentes acervos per tota castra stramentorum fecisse …'

18 Livy 42.64.7: 'Demessis circa segetibus, Romani ad Crannona, intactum agrum, castra movent.' And then, later: 'Inde offensus longuinquitate itineris, res ad Mopscium

castra movit; et Roman demessis Crannonis segetibus in Phalannaeum agrum transeunt. ibi cum ex transfuga cognosset rex sine ullo armato praesidio passim vagantis per agros Romanos metere …' Perseus then strikes. The word for the waggons that he captures is *vehiculum* – the same word later used to designate the Gallic reaping machine (see chap. 3, p. 108).

19 Cichorius, *Traianssäule*, Tafel lxxxi, scene cix–cx, 291–92; *Dritter Textband: Commentar zu den Reliefs des zweiten dakischen Krieges* (Berlin: Georg Reimer, 1900), pp. 199–202, on Bild CX, Tafel lxxxi, scene 292–3; see Koeppel, 'Die historischen Reliefs der römischen Kaiserzeit, IX,' pp. 88–9, fig. 24.

20 Eugippius, *Vita S. Severini*, 12, 22.4 (CSEL 9.2: 28–30, 40–1).

21 On foraging for fodder, see Roth, *Logistics of the Roman Army*, pp. 125–30, with several examples of soldiers engaged in cutting and mowing operations; and on foraging for grain, see pp. 130–4; for similar instances of Roman soldiers engaged in reaping, see, e.g., Livy 31.36.7; 38.41.8; 42.64.2–3; 42.65.1; and Tac. *Ann.* 14.24.

22 Already recognized as such in Roman antiquity: Cic. *De Or.* 3.43.167, in speaking of the metaphor of substitution or *traductio*: 'campum' pro comitiis.

23 P. Giss. Bibl. 1.5 (132–31 BCE), lines 9–10 … καὶ ἐπὶ τοῦ καιροῦ τοῦ θερισμῷ / [σ]τρατευομένων αὐτῶν καὶ μὴ / [ὑ]πομενόντων μισθοῦσθαι θεριστὰς / ἀκ[ο] λούθ[ω]ς τοῖς διὰ τῆς / μισθώσεως διηγορευμένοις ἠναγκάσθην.

24 Joseph. *BJ*, 3.95; as Roth, *Logistics of the Roman Army*, p. 131, states, the instrument might well have been a more general cutting instrument; but it is called a δρέπανον and the engagement of legionary soldiers in reaping is well attested.

25 Roth, *Logistics of the Roman Army*, p. 132.

26 The similes are not just ancient. Consider a description of migrant seasonal harvesting labour in the late nineteenth-century United States: 'In no other area of the national economy was the use of military terminology to describe the labor forces involved quite as appropriate as it was in the highly specialized agriculture that developed in the midwestern Wheat Belt. The success of much of this agriculture depended on the movement of large numbers of people from crop to crop and area to area in rhythm with the seasons.' Similarly, a report from a correpondent of *The Times* of London, who visited the great wheat fields of North Dakota in 1879, evoked a comment from the editor that the men who worked the fields 'are soldiers of agriculture, fighting a battle and treated accordingly'; see Applen, 'Migratory Harvest Labor,' pp. 52–3.

27 Applen, 'Migratory Harvest Labor,' p. 121, referring to the *World's Work* magazine of 1904.

28 Both from Applen, 'Migratory Harvest Labor,' p. 107.

29 Cherwinski, 'The Incredible Harvest Excursion of 1908,' p. 57; 'it was a crusade because,' he continues, then follows this with a remark on the necessity of such myths.

30 Consider De Ste Croix, 'Hired Labour,' chap. 3.6 in *Class Struggle*, pp. 179–204, one

of the few consistent efforts to tackle the legalistic nature of the source materials on labour, perhaps because the author had such a fine appreciation of the limitations of the evidence ordinarily used to resolve the question; he notes: 'In the whole of Rostovzteff, *SEHRE²*, there are hardly any references to hired labour which are supported by the production of evidence. And I know of nothing at all to compare with the Mactar inscription' (p. 576n19).

31 Standard textbooks on the subject of labour in the ancient world ordinarily have nothing on the subject; so, for example, Heitland, *Agricola*, despite its detailed subtitle with specific reference to labour, oddly enough has rather little about the subject, no doubt reflecting the quality of the literary texts that were the main sources that the author used for his study. Standard works like those of Claude Mossé, *The Ancient World at Work*, trans. J. Lloyd (London: Chatto and Windus, 1969) (*Le travail en Grèce et à Rome* [Paris: Presses Universitaires de France, 1966]), and J.M. Frayn, *Subsistence Farming in Roman Italy* (Fontwell: Centaur Press, 1979), have nothing at all on harvesting. A significant exception, and one to which reference will be made in what follows, is Spurr, 'Harvest, Storage and Yields,' chap. 4 in *Arable Cultivation*, pp. 66–88. The sparse references in Burford, *Land and Labour*, for example, would seem to justify the view that there is not much than *can* be known from Greek sources of the classical period.

32 The parallel example of seaborne traders and shippers in the Mediterranean might be offered for consideration. These men were critical to the ancient economy, very numerous, and at least some of them were rather well off. But the numbers who actually set up memorials of themselves or their careers is so exiguous as to be almost non-existent: see A. Giardina, 'The Merchant,' chap. 9 in A. Giardina, ed., *The Romans*, trans. L.G. Cochrane (Chicago: University of Chicago Press, 1993), pp. 245–71; and note the contrast with A.J. Gourevitch, 'Il mercante,' chap. 7 in J. Le Goff, ed., *L'uomo medievale* (Bari: Laterza, 1988), pp. 273–317 (= chap. 7 in *Medieval Callings*, trans. L.G. Cochrane [Chicago: University of Chicago Press, 1990], pp. 243–83). Some of the extent of the imbalance in evidence, even from literary sources, can be discerned from F. Meijer and O. van Nif, eds., *Trade, Transport and Society in the Ancient World: A Sourcebook* (London–New York: Routledge, 1992): they are able to collate numerous texts *about* trade, commodities, laws governing exchange, but exiguously little on the merchants themselves.

33 The sum total of studies known, for example, to De Ste Croix. *Class Struggle*, p. 577n19, included MacMullen, *Roman Social Relations*, p. 42, p. 162nn43–8; White, *Roman Farming*, pp. 347–50, with the review by P.A. Brunt, *JRS* 62 (1972), 158; and A.H.M. Jones, *Later Roman Empire*, vol. 2, p. 792–3; to which must be added the general study by Brunt ('Free Labour and Public Works at Rome') and the disappointing collection of texts specifically devoted to harvest labour assembled by Krenkel, 'Zu den Taglöhnen bei der Ernte.' The range and number have not expanded substantially since.

34 De Ste Croix, *Class Struggle*, p. 186: 'Hired labour at the peak periods of agricultural activity (harvesting, vintage, olive-picking) must have been quite common everywhere; but I have come across surprisingly few passages in Greek literature which mention the employment of hired labour in any form of agricultural work in the Classical period.'

35 R. Porter, *English Society in the Eighteenth Century* (Harmondsworth: Penguin, 1982), p. 25: 'The harvest was still, in 1700, the heartbeat of the economy. Would there be enough to eat? And how much would it cost? The weather would hold the answer.' Compare Thomas Tooke's observation in the mid-nineteenth century for England in his *History of Prices* (London, 1838) that the harvest was the most important guide to the economic fortunes of the country from year to year: see E.A. Wrigley, *Population and History* (London: Weidenfeld and Nicolson, 1969), p. 76.

36 Olivier de Serres, seigneur du Pradel, *Le théâtre d'agriculture et mesnage des champs, dans lequel est représenté toute qui est requis et nécessaire pour bien dresser, gouverner, enrichir et embellir la maison rustique* (Paris: I. Métayer, imprimeur ordinaire du Roy, 1600, and many subsequent editions; reprint: Arles: Actes Sud, 1996), as quoted by Comet, *Le paysan et son outil*, p. 172: 'La moisson est la couronne de l'agriculture, la récompense des dépenses et des sueurs du labourer, l'espérance de sa famille, la sûreté du maître, la vie et la richesse de tout l'Etat.'

37 For seventeenth- to nineteenth-century England, see Snell, 'Agricultural Seasonal Unemployment, the Standard of Living, and Women's Work, 1690–1860,' chap. 1 in *Annals of the Labouring Poor*, pp. 15–66, esp. 18–22, and figs. 1.1 and 1.2. Women, notably, were more erratically affected by the seasonal fluctuations in rural labour demand. The test tranches of the data, divided into five different periods over this time, show the same seasonal patterns of highs and lows in rural employment over the whole period.

38 In this work of reconstruction, some the following modern works were particularly useful: Homans, *English Villagers*; Weber-Kellerman, *Erntbrauch in der ländlichen Arbeitswelt des 19. Jahrhunderts*; Thirsk, *The Agrarian History of England and Wales, Vol. 4*: chap. 7, 'Farm Labourers,' pp. 396–465; P. Jones, 'Italy'; Horn, *Labouring Life*; Morgan, *Harvesters and Harvesting*; and Goubert, *The French Peasantry*.

39 See, for example, the classic work of Le Roy Ladurie, *Peasants of Languedoc*; Rasmussen, 'Grain Harvesting and Threshing in Calabria'; Davis, *Land and Family in Pisticci*; and Bell, *Fate and Honor*, chap. 6, 'Work,' pp. 113–50.

40 The work involved in the production and processing of wine is not much studied for north Africa; for olives and the processing of olive oil, however, there is now an immense literature on both production and processing, including labour requirements: see, *inter alia*, Mattingly, 'Maximum Figures and Maximizing Strategies of Oil Production?' with detailed references to earlier studies.

41 It is a somewhat arbitrary choice, since other elements of harvesting operations, like

threshing and winnowing, were just as necessary, seasonally repetitive, involved as large numbers of people, and also had a large impact on the social organization of work, and therefore on thinking: see Rikoon, *Threshing in the Midwest*, esp. chaps. 6 and 7.

42 Grantham, 'Divisions of Labour,' pp. 481–2.

43 For more detail, see chap. 3, pp. 102–3.

44 Grantham 'Divisions of Labour,'pp. 482–4, and tables 1 and 2 in his article; (1999), pp. 107–9.

45 Grantham 'Divisions of Labour,' p. 491.

46 Grantham 'Divisions of Labour,' p. 493; the percentage is applied to an 'optimistic' estimate of the population of the high and later empire of about eighty million.

47 Pliny, *NH*, 18.67.258: 'Prata circa kal. Iun. caeduntur …' this fact is noted, however, in the context of zodiacal discussions, and it is surely based on an earlier type of approximation that was to be replaced by the summer solstitium as the approximate time marker; cf. Columella, *RR*, 11.2.54: 'His diebus locis temperatis et maritimis messis conficitur, et intra dies triginta quam desecta est, stramenta praecisa in acervum congeruntur. Iugerum stramentorum opera una desecat.'

48 Columella, *RR*, 11.2.40: 'Per hos dies runcandae segetes sunt, faenisciae instituendae. Bonus operarius prati iugerum desecat, nec minus mille ducentos manipulos unus alligat, qui sint singuli quaternarum librarum.' The Elder Pliny is either copying Columella or they are using a common source: *NH*, 18.67.262: 'Italus fenisex dextra una manu secat. Iustum est una opera in die iugerum desecari, alligarique manipulos CC quaterna pondo.' Rackham reasonably suggested that the correct reading for the number of *manipuli* in Pliny should be MCC or 1,200. Binders in Egypt were thought to be able to tie about 400 sheaves a day, but these might have been larger and heavier than their Italian equivalents: P. Flor. 3.322.31–2; cf. Rathbone, *Economic Rationalism*, p. 160.

49 Columella, *RR*, 2.12.1 [= fr. 4 of Saserna], for wheat: 'messoris unam et dimidiam'; 2.12.2 for barley or *hordeum*: 'messoriam unam.'

50 Varro, *RR*, 1.50.3: 'Cum est matura seges, metendum, cum in ea <in> iugerum fere una opera propemodum in facili agro satis esse dicatur. Messas spicas corbibus in aream deferre debent.' These carrying baskets are portrayed on reliefs depicting the harvesting process, as on the calendrical-seasonal reliefs from the 'Gate of Mars' at Reims: see chap. 3, pp. 117–18, and fig. 3.11, p. 119.

51 Palladius, *Opus agr.* 7.1 (under the month of June and the heading 'de messibus'): 'Quinque modios recidere potest pleni agri opera una messoris experti, mediocris vero tres, ultimi etiam minus.'

52 Kolendo, *L'Agricoltura nell'Italia romana*, pp. 155–6: Palladius himself (*Opus agr.* 2.4) says that one iugerum was usually sown to 8 modii of barley (*hordeum_Galaticum*, see Pliny below); these seem to be the conditions obtaining in northern Italy; elsewhere

in Italy, the amounts were less, usually in the range of 5 to 6 modii: Columella, *RR*, 2.12.2, 2.12.5, 11.3.75; Pliny, *NH*, 2.9.16 (6 modii per iugerum for Gaulish or Galatian barley, presumably the same as that recorded by Palladius above); 18.55.198: 5 modii per iugerum for triticum and siligo wheat; barley 6 modii per iugerum; in *NH* 18.55.199–200, however, he notes that for chalky and damp soils, this should be 6 modii per iugerum for triticum and siligo wheat, but only 4 modii per iugerum in looser less fertile soil. In calculating the labour in this fashion, however, Kolendo is taking Palladius to refer to the amount of land *sown to*, say, 5 modii of barley, but this is not what Palladius says; he states that a man is able to reap 5 modii of barley. If one iugerum was sown to 8 modii of barley, then with yields at 4–6 to one, that is 30 to 50 modii per iugerum, the part of a iugerum reaped by one man would be very small, indeed too small to be realistic. Somehow, therefore, Palladius must have meant the former.

53 See appendix 1 for a selection of reaping contracts; cf. Schwartz, *Archives de Sarapion*, p. 111.

54 Collins, 'Migrant Labour in British Agriculture in the Nineteenth Century,' p. 39.

55 Halstead and Jones, 'Agrarian Ecology in the Greek Islands,' p. 47; note that Grantham, 'La faucille et la faux,' p. 105, is rather sceptical of these rates.

56 Osborne, 'The Economics and Politics of Slavery at Athens,' p. 40n34, notes that 'early modern English figures for reaping and binding are considerably lower than even the lowest of Halstead and Jones's figures: compare L. Meagre, *The Mystery of Husbandry*, London, W. Olney for H. Nelme, 1697, p. 66 and J. Mortimer, *The Whole Art of Husbandry*, London, J.B. for R. Robinson and G. Mortlock, 1707, both reckoning that a reaper and a binder can manage 1 acre a day (i.e. 5 man-days a hectare for reaping and binding).' He then refers to Columella's estimates in *RR* 2.12.1 (see n. 49 above).

57 See White, 'Wheat Farming in Roman Times,' citing, inter alia, E.C. Curwen, *Antiquity* 17 (1942), p. 196; cf. Spurr, *Arable Cultivation*, p. 183.

58 Collins, 'Harvest Technology,' p. 460, for nineteenth-century England, and our table 1.2.

59 For another comparable estimate, see Jardé, *Les céréales*, p. 160n1: an experienced harvester with a hand-held sickle can cut at most 18 ares per day, which, as he remarks, is close to Columella's estimate of 4–5 work-days for a reaper to cut one hectare of cereal grains (citing the entry 'moisson' in L. Moll and E. Gayot, *Encyclopédie pratique de l'agriculture*, 13 vols. [Paris: Firmin Didot et frères, 1859–71]; vol. 2 [1859]: 18 ares = 0.45 acres or about two-thirds of a iugerum. Quick and Buchele, *The Grain Harvesters*, fig. p. 10, estimate the labour of reaping with hand-held balanced sickles at 48 hours of work per man per acre to be reaped (that is, about three 16-hour days, working from sun-up to sundown).

60 Rivière and Lecq, *Traité pratique*, vol. 1, p. 414.

61 Collins, 'Migrant Labour in British Agriculture in the Nineteenth Century,' p. 41: 'The extent of seasonal migration and its contribution to agricultural work output cannot be measured or even guessed at because, apart from the Irish who were enumerated in 1841 and annually from 1880 to 1914, there is no reliable statistical information about numbers of migrants, or their deployment.'

62 J.H. Johnson, 'Harvest Migration from Nineteenth-Century Ireland,' p. 97: that is, by the 1830s and 1840s. One of the censuses, that of 1841, shows that over 57,000 Irish harvest workers journeyed to Britain that year, 'and there is reason to believe that this figure is an underestimate.' Even after a late-century downturn in numbers, it is generally estimated that Irish migrant labourers still numbered in the range of 40,000–50,000 every year: see Morgan, *Harvesters and Harvesting*, p. 82; there were, however, marked flucuations and a long-term downturn between the early 1880s and c. 1900: see Johnson, 'Harvest Migration from Nineteenth-Century Ireland,' pp. 97–8 and fig. 1.

63 Wyman, *Hoboes, Bindlestiffs, Fruit Tramps*, p. 3: 12,000–15,000 for Oklahoma; 30,000 for Missouri, 40,000 for Kansas, all in 1914; p. 30, for the total (in the 1890s).

64 Cherwinski, 'The Incredible Harvest Excursion of 1908,' pp. 57 and 64; '"Misfits," "Malingerers," and "Malcontents,"' p. 276; cf. Lumsden, *Through Canada in Harvest Time*.

65 Collins, 'Migrant Labour in British Agriculture in the Nineteenth Century,' p. 39, quoting the study by W.H. Kirkpatrick, *The Seasonal Distribution of Farm Labour Requirements* (Cambridge: University of Cambridge, Department of Agriculture, Farm Economics Branch, 1930); for Canada, see Thompson, 'Bringing In the Sheaves,' p. 468: 'More than 50 per cent of the labour required annually on a grain farm was needed in August, September, and October,' citing the study by R.W. Murchie, W.H. Carter, and F.J. Dixon, *Seasonal Unemployment in Manitoba* (Winnipeg: King's Printer, 1928), pp. 34–5: a wheat crop of 160 acres required 2,785 man hours of labour, of which 1,430 were required in the months specified.

66 Grantham 'Divisions of Labour,' pp. 478–9.

67 Wyman, *Hoboes, Bindlestiffs, Fruit Tramps*, p. 30: in the mechanized agriculture of the American West, this self-sufficient unit tended to settle in at an average of a family farm of about 320 acres; above that more than just friends and neighbours would be needed to bring off the harvest.

68 Lescohier, *Conditions Affecting the Demand for Harvest Labor*, pp. 19–23; Wyman, *Hoboes, Bindlestiffs, Fruit Tramps*, p. 30: for the 1921 harvest in the American West, about 40 per cent of harvest labour was drawn from family or immediate neighbours; about 44 per cent had to be hired from outside seasonal supplies.

69 By comparison, the high plains of western Canada, a comparable area, in a good year, yielded about 120,000,000 bushels or 480,000,000 modii equivalent of wheat per

annum in the decades before the Second World War: Cherwinski, 'The Incredible Harvest Excursion of 1908,' p. 63.

70 See the figures in tables C and D. The annual average wheat production for Algeria and Tunisia amounts to 1,680,000 metric tonnes or about 255,000,000 modii equivalent (the modius being calculated at roughly 6.6 kilograms); the total barley harvest at 700,000 metric tonnes or 106,000,000 modii for a total of c. 360,000,000 modii. Tripolitanian production would add to this average, but only slightly, by about 11,630,000 modii on average.

71 Average crop yields are difficult to estimate since there was so much variation from one year to the next. In central Italy in Roman antiquity, Varro, Columella, and Pliny the Elder all report the same general sowing quantities of 5 modii per iugerum; yields are generally estimated to be four- to sixfold on average, therefore between 20 and 30 modii per iugerum: see White, 'Wheat Farming in Roman Times,' Spurr, *Arable Cultivation*, pp. 82–8, and Duncan-Jones, *The Economy of the Roman Empire: Quantitative Studies*, p. 49 and 49nn3–5, with full references to the primary sources. It must be borne in mind that the average for any annual or decadal production in a large territory is a figure that reduces the extreme highs and lows to a median figure. Pre–First World War cereal production statistics for indigenous agriculture in north Africa produces average results of about 5–6 quintals per hectare for hard and soft wheats, and about 6 quintals per hectare for barley: see Rivière and Lecq, *Traité pratique*, vol. 2, pp. 308–9. These figures translate to average production figures of about 21–5 modii per iugerum, which fit reasonably well within the general estimates given by the Roman agricultural writers. For the problems of reportage on yields, and the extremes of reportage, see Valensi, *Fellahs tunisiens*, pp. 195–200, who accepts that cereal yields produced in the period of 'precolonial' agriculture probably averaged about 5 quintals, or slightly more, per hectare (pp. 198–9), although with significant regional and seasonal variations.

72 See tables B, C, and D.

73 See, e.g., Cherwinski, '"Misfits," "Malingerers," and "Malcontents,"' p. 277 (60 days).

74 Rathbone, 'Prices and Price Formation in Roman Egypt,' p. 191.

75 For the scale of the barley crop in Roman Egypt see Bagnall, *Egypt in Late Antiquity*, p. 25, who estimates barley at one-fifth of the whole crop, based largely on the figures in Schnebel, *Die Landwirtschaft*, p. 97 f. The estimate seems a little low to me, but might well be correct.

76 Rathbone, 'The Proportion of Casual Labour,' chap. 4B in *Economic Rationalism*, pp. 148–54, and table 11, p. 153, where the redacted figures for the two estates of Euhemia and Theadelphia are provided. Because of the nature of the records, he regards these proportions as minima (p. 152).

77 CTh 11.28.13 (issued at Ravenna on 20 February 422): 'Breves, quod spectabiles ac probatissimi nobis viri ad palatinorum sacrarum vel ad praetoriana scrinia detulerunt,

et professionis modum eum, qui brevibus sedit, scribi volumus, eum vero qui recisus est de chartis publicis iubemus auferri. Unde secundum fidem polyptychorum per provinciam proconsularem novem milia duas centurias iugera centum quadraginta unum in solvendo et quinque milia septingentas centurias iugera centum quadraginta quattuor semis in removendis, per provinciam vero Byzacenam in praestanda functione septem milia quadringentas sexaginta centurias iugera centum octoginta, septem milia sescentas quindecim vero centurias iugera tria semis in auferenda constat adscribta, ut circa eos, quibus conlocata ac relevata sunt praedia, ad securitatem perpetuae proprietatis intermina possint aetate servari. De his vero, quae edictis pendentibus nondum sunt certis adsignata personis, rectores provinciarum decernimus providere, ut manentibus remediis, quae fides supra dicta adtribuit, idoneis conlocentur.'

78 Lepelley, 'Décline ou stabilité de l'agriculture africain au Bas-Empire?' p. 229: of 91,000 km² of arable lands, about 50,000 km² were in cereal crops or in fruit tree or vines, about a 5:9 ratio; similarly, in the law of 422, there were about 8,322 km² out of a total of 15,052 km² in cultivation: again, approximately the same 5:9 ratio.

79 In general, see table A. For Tunisia in the 1930s, for example, the total amount of potentially useful land was estimated at roughly 3,000,000 hectares; of this total, about 1,500,000 hectares were sown to wheat and barley crops: see *Tunisia*, Naval Intelligence Division, p. 280 and map, p. 282, for the geographical distribution of lands sown to cereals; and see appendix H, table 1, 'Area and Production of Cereal Crops, 1929–1938' (oats, a modern European introduction, can be ignored, since the amount of land sown to it was negligible). The local non-European farm lands devoted to cereal grain cultivation varied between two-thirds to three-quarters of all cereal grain production. For the decades immediately preceding the First World War, see Decker-David, *Agriculture indigène*, vol. 2, pp. 741 f.: between 800,000 and 950,000 hectares in wheat and barley for Tunisia. For the lands of eastern Algeria, see *Algeria*, Naval Intelligence Division, vol. 2, pp. 193 f. Of about 20 million acres of cultivable land (8 million hectares) – about 40 per cent of the land of the northern departments – about 7.5 million acres were sown to cereal crops, or about 38–40 per cent of the total; and see appendix A, table 1: 'Area and Production of Cereal Crops, 1929–1938,' p. 434. These figures indicate that out of the total of arable lands – located roughly in modern-day Tunisia and eastern parts of Algeria – about half, more or less, were normally sown to cereal crops in the interwar period. Rivière and Lecq, *Traité pratique*, vol. 1, p. 379, similarly estimate the land in indigenous farms sown to cereals (nine-tenths of it to wheat and barley) in Algeria in this period at 2,900,000 hectares and in Tunisia at about 900,000 hectares, for a total of 3,900,000 hectares or 14,450,000 iugera. For what it is worth, this is roughly the same as the 15,000,000 iugera that we have postulated as the average for the Roman period.

80 Public and private horrea or grain-storage buildings are a partial exception to this observation: see, e.g., G. Rickman, *Roman Granaries and Store Buildings* (Cambridge: Cambridge University Press, 1971), pp. 132–6 and 140–3.

81 By the terms of the so-called *lex* or *consuetudo* Manciana (CIL 8.25902 = *FIRA²*, 100 = *ILMB* 388, with photograph; Henchir Mettich, reign of Hadrian) § 4, ll. 22–7; see Kehoe, *Economics of Agriculture*, pp. 32–3, 36; Flach, 'Inschriftenuntersuchungen,' pp. 480, 483: 'Ne quis conductor vilicusv[e colonu]m in[q]uilinu[m eius]/ f(undi) <amplius quam ter binas operas praestare praecipiat>: coloni / qui intra f(undum) Vill(a)e Magn(a)e[e / sive Mapp]ali(a)e Sig(a)e ha[bit]/abunt, dominis aut conduct[oribus vilicisve eorum] in assem [q]/[u]o<t>annis in hominibus [singulis in aratio]nes oper/as n(umero) II et in messem op[eras n(umero) II et cuiusqu]e generi[s / s]ingulas operas bin[as] pr[(a)estare debebun]t.'
Flach wishes to read line 22: 'Ne quis conductor vilicus[ve {eoru]m} in[q]uilinu[m eius]' etc. One can compare the procurators' letter for the Saltus Burunitanus (CIL 8.10570 = FIRA², 102; Souk el-Khemis, reign of Commodus), § 3, ll. 11–13; see Kehoe, *Economics of Agriculture*, pp. 65–6, 67; and Flach, 'Inschriftenuntersuchungen,' pp. 490, 492: '… non amplius annuas quam binas / aratorias, binas sartorias, binas messo/rias operas debeamus …' These are the limits established in the letter of the procurators governing the domain, a copy of which was filed in the record office of the Tractus Karthaginiensis at Carthage.

82 Duby, *Rural Economy*, pp. 210–11: 1185, on demesnes cultivated by the Templars in Gloucestershire: villein tenancies provided 'two man-days per week during the slack season from Martinmas to haymaking […] but] they had to give four days a week as long as hay-making lasted, and then two again until 1st August. When harvest began and the need for manpower became more pressing than at any other time of the year, six man-days were required from them each week.'

83 Thompson, 'Bringing In the Sheaves,' p. 467; Cherwinksi, 'The Incredible Harvest Excursion of 1908,' pp. 278–9, for the heavy harvest of 1928, estimates were made of a requirement of 75,000 harvesters, of whom about 25,000 were locally available – the rest of the demand had to be met by itinerant workers.

84 See Lepelley, 'Décline ou stabilité,' who argues, correctly in my opinion, that the land-tax figures in the constitution only refer to imperial lands held by the emperor in in the provinces of Proconsularis and Byzacena. Translated into square kilometres, the figures produce totals (4,551 km² cultivated + 2,881 km² uncultivated) of 7,432 km² in Proconsularis and (3,771 km² cultivated + 3,849 km² uncultivated) of 7,620 km² in Byzacena, for a grand total of 15,052 km² of imperial lands in both provinces. The total of arable lands in both provinces was probably in the range of 90–100,000 km². Imperial estates were about one-sixth of this total.

85 One must bear in mind Finley's caution, *Ancient Slavery and Modern Ideology*, pp. 133–6, that units of legal ownership were not the same as operational units, and it is the latter that concern us here. The assumption, however, is that units of larger ownership would be manned in a fashion that would require a minimum of *permanent* labour in place and that a majority of them would therefore require additional season harvest workers.

86 Pliny, *NH*, 18.258: 'Prata circa kal. Iun. caeduntur'; Olck, 'Ernte,' pp. 477–8, cites evidence from late nineteenth-century Italy.

87 See Palladius, *Op. Agr.* 7.2.1: 'Nunc [sc. Mensis Iunius] primo hordei messis incipitur' (barley); 7.2.2: 'Nunc etiam mense postremo locis maritimis et calidioribus ac siccis tritici messis absciditur'; and 8.1.1: 'Mensis Iulius: De iterandis agris, de messe triticea; and Varro'; *RR*. 1.32.1: 'Quarto intervallo inter solstitium et caniculum [24 June to 24 July] plerique messem faciunt, quod frumentum dicunt …'; Columella, *RR*, 9.14.5: 'Tumque peracto solstitio usque ad ortem Caniculae [24 June to 24 July], qui fere dies triginta sunt, pariter frumenta et favi demetuntur.' Again, Olck, 'Ernte,' pp. 479–80, cites comparative and supporting evidence from late nineteenth-century Italy.

88 Menologium Rusticum Colotianum: CIL 1² 280 = 6.2305 = Inscr. Ital. 13.2: 47: p. 288: Mensis Iunius: Faenisicium; p. 289: Mensis Iulius: Messes hordiar(iae); Mensis August(us): Messes frumentar(iae), item triticar(iae), stupulae incendunt(ur). And the Menologium Rusticum Vallense: CIL 1².281 = 6.2306 = Inscr. Ital. 13.2: 48: p. 295: Mes(is) Iun(ius): Faenisic(ium); Me(n)s(is) Iul(ius): Messes hodiar(iae); Me(n)s(is) Aug(ustus): messes frumentar(iae) stuplae incendunt(ur). Both calendars seem to come from findspots close to Rome.

89 Broughton, 'The *Menologia Rustica*,' remains a useful discussion. She was the first to note the critical fact, against Georg Wissowa, that the months to which mowing of hay (July) and the reaping of wheat (August) were assigned could not possibly reflect conditions in the plains regions of central Italy. Her answer was to suspect that the texts reflected in the menologia must have a different ecology, perhaps one much further to the north, like the Po Valley. This is possible. An alternative explanation might be that although the calendars as they stand are at least Augustan in date (i.e., the names of the months July and August), the drafting of the text on which they are based and which they copied might have been done in the late Republic when the calendrical months had wandered off true course by a month and more: see Shaw, 'Seasonal Mortality,' pp. 98–101, for some remarks and references.

90 For the details, see chap. 2, pp. 70–1.

91 Rivière and Lecq, *Traité pratique*, pp. 419–23.

92 Rivière and Lecq, *Traité pratique*, pp. 425–6.

93 Columella, *RR*, 2.20.1–2: 'Sed cum matura fuerit seges, ante quam torreatur vaporibus aestivi sideris, qui sunt vastissimi per exortum Caniculae, celeriter demetatur; nam dispendiosa est cunctatio, primum quod avibus praedam ceterisque animalibus praebet, deinde quod grana et ipsae spicae culmis arentibus et aristis celeriter decidunt.'

94 Columella, *RR*, 2.9.15: '… idque ubi paulum maturuerit, festinantius quam ullum aliud frumentum demetendum erit; nam et fragili culmo et nulla vestitum palea granum eius celeriter decidit, isdemque de causis facilius teritur quam cetera.'

95 Dig. 9.2.27.25 (Ulpian on the Edict): 'Si olivam inmaturam decerpserit vel segetem desecuerit inmaturam vel vineas crudas, Aquilia tenebitur; quod si iam maturas, cessat Aquilia: nulla enim iniuria est, cum tibi etiam impensas donaverit, quae in collectionem huiusmodi fructuum impenduntur; sed si collecta haec interceperit, furti tenetur.'

96 App. *BC*, 2.14, with Plut. *Ti. Gracch.* 16.2; the involvement and recruiting of reapers for violent political activities in the city is confirmed by Plut. *G. Gracch.* 13.2, where Cornelia, the mother, is said to have hired men from outside the city who were to come to Rome 'like reapers' to provide 'muscle' for the forthcoming campaign.

97 CTh 2.8.19 (Valentinian, Theodosius, and Arcadius, from Rome, to Albinus, Praefectus Urbi; 7 August 389): '… autumnis fetibus decerpendis …' In the commentary, the emperors note that the time-off for harvest was customary and that they were reaffirming traditional practice. Nevertheless, they try to define the time, allowing that the holidays must be established according to he nature of the province, but that they were generally set from the eighth day before the kalends of July (24 June) up to the kalends of August (1 August). In their interpretation, they add the Lord's Birthday (Christmas), Epiphany, and the emperor's own birthday to the list: 'Et licet lex quattuor menses ad fructus colligendos indulserit, sed ita pro provinciarum qualitate et pro praesentia dominorum credidimus faciendum, ut die viii kal. Iul. usque in kal. Aug. messivae feriae concedantur …'

98 CTh 11.16.4 (cf. CJ 11.48.1): Constantine to Aemilianus PP (Rome, 9 May 328): 'Neque umquam sationibus [CJ: rationibus] vel colligendis frugibus insistens agricola ad extraordinaria onera trahatur, cum providentiae sit opportuno tempore his necessitatibus satisfacere' (Pharr's translation, with modifications).

99 CJ 11.47.1: same text as above.

100 See the Lex Irnitana, § K (*JRS* 76 [1986]: 161-2): 'R(ubrica). De rebus proferendis. Duumviri qui in eo municipio nunc sunt quive postea erunt … per quos dies res prolata intra suum h[on]orem mes[sis vin]demiae causa placeat esse … dum ne amplius quam bis neve pluribus quam bis XXX diebus uno anno res probatas [sunto] … nisi [de] i(i)s rebus de quibus Romae mes[sis] vindemiaeve causa rebus prolatis ius dici solet … <repeated again> nisi de iis reibus de quibus Romae messis v[indem]iaeque causa rebus prolatis ius dici solet …'

101 Dig. 7.1.13.6 (Ulpian): '… sed nec aedificium quidem positurum in fundo, nisi quod ad fructum percipiendum necessarium sit.' The allowance was a marginal one, however, since the same passage makes clear that permanent constructions for large numbers of workers or pickers (i.e., of olives) were ordinarily not permitted.

102 Dig. 7.8.12.pr (Ulpian): 'Venire plane proprietarium ad fructus percipiendos magis dicendum est, et per tempora fructuum colligendorum etiam habitare illic posse admittendum est.'

103 Dig. 2.12.1 (Ulpian): 'Ne quis messium vendemiarumque tempore adversarium cogat ad iudicium venire, oratione divi Marci exprimitur, quia occupati circa rem rusticam in forum compellendi non sunt.' For the exceptions, however, see Dig. 2.12.2 and 3 (Ulpian)

104 Dig. 2.12.4 (Paulus): 'Praesides provinciarum ex consuetudine cuiusque loci solent messis vindemiarumque causa tempus statuere.' From the tone of the wording, I take it that the governor was to do this each year, although it is possible that it was a single tralatician declaration made at the beginning of his governorship.

105 Pliny, *NH*, 18.78.341: 'Tradunt eundem Democritum metente fratre eius Damaso ardentissimo aestu orasse ut reliquiae segeti parceret raperetque desecta sub tectum, paucis mox horis saevo imbre vaticinatione adprobata.'

106 Dig. 19.2.25.6 (Gaius): 'Vis maior, quam Graeci θεοῦ βίαν appellant, non debet conductori damnosa esse, si plus, quam tolerabile esse, laesi fuerint fructus: alioquin modicum damnum aequo animo ferre debet colonus, cui immodicum lucrum non aufertur.' There were limitations, however. *Vis maior* did not include *normal* storms or weather conditions which any tenant was expected to foresee: see Frier, 'Law, Economics, and Disasters,' pp. 243, 249–51, and Kehoe, *Investment, Profit and Tenancy*, pp. 226–7: 'The principle of granting a remission of rent on the basis of *vis maior*, then, did not relieve the tenant of any of the risk that he bore for the greatest danger affecting Mediterranean agriculture, namely, the severe variations in weather, especially rainfall, that made droughts a regular part of life.' The storm would have to be extraordinary – an *unaccustomed* freeze or heat wave, for example: see Dig. 19.2.15.2 (Ulpian).

107 Verg. *Georg.* 1.311–40 (although all of the passage to line 350 is relevant).

108 Nicely picked out by R.F. Thomas, 'The Great Storm,' in *Virgil, Georgics, Volume I, Books i–ii* (Cambridge: Cambridge University Press, 1998), pp. 120–7.

109 Palladius, *Op. Agr.* 7.2.1: 'Nunc primo hordei messis incipitur. Quae consummanda est antequam grana refractis spicis lapsa decurrant, quia nullis sicut triticum folliculis vestiuntur ... Sed hordei culmos iacere in agris aliquantum sinamus, quia fertur hoc more grandescere'; cf. Columella, *RR*, 20.20.2: '... propter quod quae recrastinari non debet.'

110 Hall, *Harvest Wobblies*, p. 25: 'Farmers needed their grain harvested and threshed as quickly as possible. Poor weather, such as a heavy rain, could damage the crop, causing it to rot. Also, if farmers did not cut the grain fast enough, wheat heads would shatter, scattering seed on the ground.'

111 Smith, *Europe after Rome*, p. 55, citing *Annals of St-Bertin*, trans. Janet L. Nelson (Manchester: Manchester University Press, 1991; *Annales de Saint-Bertin*, ed. F. Grat, J. Vielliard, and J. Clémencet [Paris: Klinksieck, 1964], p. 28), p. 42.

112 For background, see Bitel, 'Ekphrasis at Kildare,' chap. 6 in *Landscape with Two Saints*, pp.137–62.

113 Cogitosus, *Sanctae Brigidae Virginis Vita* (PL 72: 779): 'Et eadem messores ac operarios convocat in messem suam; et facta illa messorum conventione, nebulosa ac pluviales dies illa accidit conventionis. Et pluviis largiter ex nubibus effusis, per totam illam in circuitu provinciam, ac rivulis guttarum effluentia per convalles et rimas terrarum currentibus, sola messis sua arida sine pluviarum impedimento et perturbatione perstitit; et cum omnes messores undique ipsius regionis prohibiti pluviali die, sui, sine ulla umbra caliginis pluviae, illa die tota, ab ortu usque ad occasum, messores, Dei potentia opus exercebant.' The following translation has been offered by Seán Connolly and Jean-Michel Picard, 'Cogitosus's *Life of St Brigit*,' pp. 14–15, based on a new text that they are preparing [their numbering 4.1–2]: '[4.1] Again, she summoned the reapers and labourers to help with the harvest and, when the reapers had assembled, the day of the gathering turned out cloudy and wet; the rain poured down from the sky in torrents all over the whole surrounding province and overflowing streams of waters coursed in spate through the glens and fissures of the land, whereas her harvest alone remained dry, without hindrance or damage from the rain. [4.2} And while all the reapers of the surrouding area had been hampered by the rainy day, her reapers, by God's power, carried on with their work that whole day from dawn until sunset without the lowering shadow of rain.' The event is noted in the later 'First Life' of St Brigita (AASS Februarius I, where five Latin lives are preserved). The following is the translation by Seán Connolly, 'Vita Prima Sanctae Brigitae'(44): '[98.1]: Another day, saint Brigit called reapers into her harvest [cf. Mt. 9:38; Lk. 10:2]. It was a rainy day and whereas the rain poured down in torrents all over the province, her harvest alone remained dry and was not adversely affected by the rain. [98.2] And whereas all the reapers of the area were hampered by the rain that day, her reapers, by God's power, carried on their work in fine weather without interruption or any lowering clouds all day long from dawn until sunset.'

114 See Dutton, 'Thunder and Hail,' esp. pp. 122 f. on the *tempestarii*, who had the power deliberately to create storms to harm others by the use of incantations.

115 See the introduction to the following passage by B. Krusch in MGH SRM, 3: 176–9. As a boy, Aridius had left his home town to serve in the court of King Theudobert (regn. 533–48). But when his father died, he returned to Limoges to take care of his mother. He died in 591 of dysentery.

116 *Vita Aridii Abbatis Lemovicini*, 15 (MGH SRM, 3: 587): 'Quodam tempore eum ad maturitatem se segetes aristas armassent et iam se adgravatae meti poscerent a cultore, inormitas erupit pluviae, ne quisquam fruges colligeret, ut in suis spicis grana lactantia germinarent. Interea suggeritur ipsi a populo; facit vigilias intercessor. Sequenti igitur die, reliquiis sanctorum adprehensis opportune et venerabiliter coopertis de palleolo serico, diacones in albis exeunt ad processum; plebs clamat non posse ire pro nimborum incursu. Quibus vir sanctus respondit: "Qui iussit aquam creari, potens est hunc imbrem sedari." Tunc mox de templo progressi sunt: subito

nubes excissae sunt, sol in claritate reducitur, serenitas caeli mundo redditur, ad opera cultor trahitur, et ad manipulos colligendos messor frugibus invitatur.'

117 Jonas of Bobbio, *Vita Columbani*, 1.13 (MGH SRG 37: 173–4): 'Interea tempus evenerat, ut copia segetum horreis conderentur, nec prorsus vis ventorum nubes compilare cessabat. Urguebat sane necessitas, ne maturae messis spica in stipulam, germine emisso, periret. Eratque vir Dei apud Fontanas coenobium, ubi et messium copiam novus ager locupletem dederat. Irruebant ventorum flabra cum vehementia imbrium nec omnino nubila caeli dare terris pluviam quiescebant. Quid inter haec vir Dei ageret, anxio corde pensabat; armavit mentem fides, docuit impetrare oportuna, accersivitque omnes, ac segetem praecidi iubet. Mirantur illi patris imperium nec tamen quisquam patri cogitatum depromit. Venerunt omnes falceque inter diffusionem imbrium secant segetem, patremque, quid agat, conspiciunt. Ille quattuor plenos religione viros per quattuor angulos messis praeponit, Comininum et Eunocum ac Equonanum ex Scottorum genere quartumque Gurganum genere Brittonem. His ordinatis, ipse cum reliquis medius messem praecidebat. Mira virtus! Fugebat imber a segete et undique pluvia diffundebatur; medios tantum messores solis ardor torrebat aestusque vehemens quousque messem conderent afflavit. Sic fides et oratio meruit, ut, pulsa pluvia, aestum inter imbres haberet.'

118 It is also of interest that these stories come out of monastic contexts, in which agricultural work was part of the regimen of the community and in which there emerged a different valuation of manual labour.

119 Aug. *Civ. Dei*, 22.22 (CCL 48: 844): 'Agricolae, immo vero omnes homines, quot et quantos a caelo et terra vel a perniciosis animalibus casus metuunt agrorum fructibus! Solent tamen de frumentis tandem collectis et reconditis esse securi. Sed quibusdam, quod novimus, proventum optimum frumentorum fluvius inprovisus fugientibus hominibus de horreis eiecit atque abstulit.'

120 Aug. *En. 1 in Ps.* 68.10 (CCL 39: 911): 'Labore magno metitur, portatur ad aream, trituratur, ventilatur; post tanta pericula caeli et tempestatum, et labores rusticanorum curamque dominorum, mittitur in horreum frumentum purgatum. Venit hiems, et quod purgatum erat, profertur et proicitur; imprudentia videtur; sed ut non sit imprudentia, spes facit.'

121 Collins, 'Migrant Labour,' for England in the nineteenth century, although note his caution (p. 43): 'The evidence is too thin to permit the identification of all migrant labour flows, still less their changes in volume and direction.'

122 See Erdkamp, 'Agriculture,' for the concept of 'the externalization of labour costs.'

123 The conclusions reached by Donald Lescohier were derived from his survey of 36,000 harvest workers in the American wheat belt in 1919, 1920, and 1921 conducted by Lescohier and his assistants; see the initial reports in Lescohier, 'The Farm Labor Problem,' and *Harvest Labor Problems*.

124 See Isern, 'Hands,' chap. 5 in *Bull Threshers and Bindlestiffs*, for an analysis of these

data; his figure, p. 143, provides a nice visual of the different sources of seasonal labour.

125 J.H. Johnson 'Harvest Migration,' pp. 98–9 and table 1, 102–3, 108 and fig. 6.

126 These results are reported in Lescohier, 'Harvesters and Hoboes,' and 'Hands and Tools,' and summarized in *Sources of Supply* and *Conditions Affecting the Demand*; for another detailed analysis of these sources, see Applen, 'Migratory Harvest Labor,' pp. 77–87, at pp. 86–7: in the 1919 survey, about one-third of all harvest labour was permanently migrant and in search of work.

127 J.H. Johnson, 'Harvest Migration,' p. 103 for Ireland and England in the nineteenth century.

128 See Shaw, 'Soldiers and Society,' pp. 143–8, tables 1–3, and maps 1 and 2.

129 When the Persian monarch Kawad (Cavades) had the Lakhmid chief al-Nu'mân (II) invade Mesopotamia, attacking the lands of Edessa in October (Teshri) of 502 CE, the incursion took place in the vinting season. As a result, he captured a large number of itinerant harvesters coming out of the towns and cities in the region: Ps.-Joshua Stylites, *Chron.* 52 (W. Wright, Cambridge, 1882) = 53 in P. Martin, ed., 'Chronique de Joshué le Stylite, écrite vers 515,' *Abhandlungen für die Kunde des Morganlandes* 6 (Leipzig, 1878), p. 44 (p. xlvi), as noted by Jones, *LRE*, 2, p. 792 and 1325n51.

130 Kaplan, *Les hommes et la terre*, pp. 58 and 274, with references.

131 P. Brem. 54. 3–4: ἀπὸ τοῦ θερισμοῦ; see Braunert, *Die Binnenwanderung*, p. 140n149.

132 Braunert, *Die Binnenwanderung*, p. 180, citing the case of harvest labourers on the move: P. Flor. 1.180; cf. O. Montevecchi, 'Contributi per una storia sociale ed economica della famiglia nell'Egitto greco-romano,' in *Actes du Ve Congrès International de Papyrologie* (Oxford, 1938), pp. 300–13; see Braunert, *Die Binnenwanderung*, pp. 44–5, for seasonal workers involved in the wine and olive harvest who were coming out of cities like Memphis and Heliopolis for work. These kinds of movements are ones that Braunert (pp. 18–19) categorizes as his 'beta/alpha' type: 'den persönlichen Wunsch der Wandernden nach Sicherung des Erwerbs (Wanderarbeiter).'

133 Certainly true in modern times: see Servier, *Tradition et civilisation*, p. 305; for Roman antiquity, see the arguments and evidence in Shaw, 'Pastoralists, Peasants and Politics,' pp. 326 ff.

134 See Grantham, 'Divisions of Labour,' p. 494, for early modern France.

135 Everitt, 'Farm Labourers,' pp. 433–4, cites cases of farmers in lowland areas of Yorkshire and Kent who liked to go to adjacent hill or forest lands to find additional labour at harvest time.

136 Shaw, 'Pastoralists, Peasants and Politics,' pp. 274 f.

137 Hall, *Harvest Wobblies*, pp. 16–17; cf. Applen, 'Migratory Harvest Labor,' pp. 77 f. on the extent of the migration and the proportion of the labour that was migrant at

the end of the nineteenth century and the beginning of the twentieth in the wheat belt of the United States.

138 Hall, *Harvest Wobblies*, p. 18

139 See the discussion of Salvemini, 'Migrants saisonniers,' pp. 162–3. On 'Brownian motion' use of human movements, see M. Bloch, *Feudal Society, 1: The Growth of the Ties of Dependence*, trans. L.A. Manyon (London: RKP, 1965), p. 64; and the specific references in Horden and Purcell, *The Corrupting Sea*, pp. 142 and 150.

140 Salvemini, 'Migrants saisonniers,' pp. 163–4, pointing, for example, to the advances marked by Horden and Purcell, *The Corrupting Sea*, pp. 377–80: 'The question at any moment in Mediterranean history must be: where are the people?' (p. 378).

141 See Applen, 'Migratory Harvest Labor,' pp. 108–10, quotation from p. 109.

142 Cherwinksi, '"Misfits," "Malingerers," and "Malcontents,"' p. 274.

143 Wyman, *Hoboes, Bindlestiffs, Fruit Tramps*, p. 5.

144 AE 1984: 933 (Aradi). Ferchiou and Gabillon, 'Une inscription grecque magique,' provide commentary.

145 Valensi, *Fellahs tunisiens*, p. 194: invasions of locusts, frequent in the seventeenth century, were less numerous in the eighteenth. In the 1840s they appeared frequently again, and in force.

146 Pliny, *NH*, 11.35.101 ff. in general on locusts; 11.35.105 on this passage in particular.

147 Varro as reported by Pliny, *NH*, 8.43.104; on the locust attack see Livy, *Per.* 60 (126–25 BCE); Julius Obsequens, *Prodigiorum Liber*, 30 (125 BCE).

148 Pliny, *NH*, 11.35.105.

149 CIL 8.26517 (Thugga, 48–9 CE); see Desanges, 'Un curateur de la sauterelle sur la *pertica* de Carthage en 48/49 de notre ère,' *Eos* 64 (1976), pp. 281 ff. and 'Un curateur de la sauterelle sur la pertica de Carthage en 48/49 de notre ère,' *BCTH* 10B (1974), pp. 135 ff.

150 See, e.g., CJ 4.65.18 (Diocletian and Maximianus to Annius Ursinus; 21 September 290): 'Excepto tempore, quo edaci lucustarum pernicie sterilitatis vitium incessit, sequentis temporis fructus, quos tibi iuxta praeteritam consuetudinem deberi constituerit, reddi tibi praeses provinciae iubebit.' Note that it was an established custom, surely because this kind of damage to crops was a recurrent problem. In this case, the locusts are only an example of a type of more general condition that justified a landlord's remission of rents. On the line of arguments from Papinian ap. Dig. 19.2.15.4 (Ulpian) to CJ 4.65.8 (Alexander Severus), however, that was rather strict on what counted as such a bad harvest that it justified such remssions, see Frier, 'Law, Economics, and Disasters,' pp. 247–8 and 253–4, and Kehoe, *Investment, Profit, and Tenancy*, pp. 214–15.

151 Hall, *Harvest Wobblies*, pp. 18–19

152 So in the American West in the decades leading up to the First World War: Applen,

'Migratory Harvest Labor,' p. 109: 'Criticism of migratory wheat harvesters often stemmed from real grievances related to matters such as labour supply and wages. The flow of labour within the Wheat Belt during harvests was erratic, resulting in an abundance or oversupply in some areas and shortages in others.'

153 Horn, *Labouring Life*, p. 75: 'It was hard, hot work.' For records of men commonly passing out from heat exhaustion – 'though incidents of men and horses dying of heat exhaustion were rare, they did occur' – see Hall, *Harvest Wobblies*, p. 26.

154 Orenstein, *Pieter Bruegel the Elder*, pp. 243–5, nos. 109–10 (now in the Kunsthalle, Hamburg); and see Silver, *Peasant Scenes and Landscapes*, fig. 6.19, p. 125 and p. 123: originally part of a series of four drawings (this one dating to 1568).

155 Again, as in the well-documented modern cases: Wyman, *Hoboes, Bindlestiffs, Fruit Tramps*, pp. 49–50.

156 Parrish, *Season Mosaics*, p. 31n93, notes the broad-brimmed hat worn by the harvester pictured on the fresco in the Catacomb of San Ponziano (Rome); citing the description in J. Wilpert, *Roma sotterranea: le pitture delle catacombe romane*, 1 (Rome: Desclée-Lefebvre, 1903), p. 34, no. 6; and the drawing reproduced in Hanfmann, *Season Sarcophagus*, vol. 2, no. 543, fig. 147; Parrish, *Season Mosaics*, p. 37, cites more cases, including his Cat. no. 53, a pavement from Lixus in Tingitana. Sometimes, it seems, a more bowl-shaped (perhaps basket-weave) hat was worn: see Spiro, *Critical Corpus of the Mosaic Pavements*, vol. 2, fig. 117: a late antique mosaic floor from Thebes.

157 On small bronze coins of Alexandria of the Antonine period: Dattari, *Monete Imperiali Greche: Numi Augg. Alexandrini*, vol. 1 (description) nos. 2986–9; and vol. 2 (illustrations), tav. xxvi, nos. 2989 (conical hat) and 2987 (broad brim) – perhaps most easily seen in the clear illustration in *Roman Provincial Coins Online*, nos. 13958 and 16142 (141–2 CE); on magical amulets: Bonner, *Studies in Magical Amulets*, plate v, nos. 115–17; plate vi, nos. 119, 121–2 for the conical shape, nos. 118, 120, 124–5 for the broader brim. It might well be possible that the two sun hats are the same – with the brim folded up (when not needed) and folded down (in the full glare of the sun).

158 See Weiss, *Sepphoris Synagogue*, fig. 69, p. 128, and his discussion on p. 127–9 and n. 370, who draws attention to the passage in John of Gaza, noting that Summer wore such a hat (*pilos*) to protect her from the sun's heat: see also Hanfmann, 'The Seasons,' pp. 113–18.

159 Compare the mowers with scythes on Worcester Cathedral: E.G. Tasker, *Encyclopedia of Medieval Church Art* (London: Batsford, 1993), p. 280, figs. 8.68 and 8.69; the scene of a reaper in a Book of Hours illustration of the month of June (France for English markets; ca. 1440–50); an illustration of mowing from a Book of Hours illustrating the month of June (same source); and the illustration of a 'harvest picnic' in a Book of Hours for the month of August (Flemish early sixteenth century): note

the broad-brimmed hats in all instances: see Henisch, 'In Due Season,' fig. 58, p. 311, fig. 62, p. 318, and fig. 65, p. 323.

160 See, e.g., Vignet-Zunz, 'La moisson à faucille,' p. 231 (listing the usual equipment of reapers) and the illustrations on pp. 233–4.

161 Parrish, *Season Mosaics*, p. 38, noting the *flabella* (his Cat. nos. 9, 16, and 48), including one from Djebel Oust. For the water vases or *gillones*, see his Cat. nos. 12, 16, and 56.

162 For the θερίστρον, see LXX Gen 24:65; P. Petr. 1.37; Philo Mech. 1.666; Acta Philipp. 8.3; and for the θερίστριον, see Theocr. 13.69; Aristaenet. 1.27; therefore, not just the flimsy garment worn by reapers, but also a young woman's summer attire. Most mosaics and other illustrations show this type of light dress: e.g., Spiro, *Critical Corpus of the Mosaic Pavements*, 2, fig. 117 (Thebes; personification of the month of July).

163 Jerome, *Comment. in Esaiam*, 5.18.4 (CCL 73: 190): '"Et considerabo," inquit, "qui rerum finis adveniat." *Sicut meridiana lux clara est, et sicut nubes roris in die messi.* Sicut in toto die nihil est clarius meridie, quando sol de medio caelo rutilat et omnem orbem pariter illustrat, et sicut in aestu et calore torrente, quando nudus messor excoquitur, et operis magnitudinem anhelitu probat, gratissima est roris temperies, si arentes stipulas matutinus umor secabiles faciat.' The text here is modified according to the text established by R. Gryson and J. Coulie, eds., *Commentaires de Jérôme sur le prophète Isaïe: Livres V–VII* (Freiburg: Herder, 1994), pp. 612–13. For the rest of the metaphor, see chap. 4, pp. 197–8.

164 Greg. Tur. *Vitae Patrum* 10.1 [De sancto Friardo recluso], 2 (MGH SRM 1.2: B. Krusch ed., *Gregorii Episcopi Turonensis Miracula et Opera Minora*, 256): 'Quodam vero die dum cum reliquis in segitem, culmis incisis, manipulos colligaret, examen miserabilium atque saevarum muscarum, quas vulgo vespes vocant, repperiunt. Cumque acerrime messores, emissis aculeis, lacerarent, undique circumeuntes messem, locum illum in quo haec adunatae erant transiliunt atque inridendum beatum Friardum adloquuntur dolosae, dicentes … Tunc [ille] quasi ad confusionem dominicae virtutis haec verba suscipiens, provolutus terrae, orationem fudit ad Dominum; et accedens, facto desuper signo crucis, ait: *Adiutorium nostrum in nomine Domini, qui fecit caelum et terram.* Ad hanc eius orationem confestim omnes vespae se infra antrum, unde egressae fuerant, abdiderunt. Ille vero ad spectaculum omnium messem desuper inlaesus expediit.'

165 Hall, *Harvest Wobblies*, p. 25

166 Jefferies, *Field and Hedgerow*, pp. 131–2; cf. Morgan, 'The Place of Harvesters,' p. 30, and *Harvesters and Harvesting*, p. 26 (slightly different versions).

167 Hesiod, *W&D*, 573: ἀλλ' ἅρπας τε χαρασσέμεναι καὶ δμῶας ἐγείρειν; Apoll. Rhod. *Argonaut.* 3.1388: ἅρπην εὐκαμπῆ νεοθηγέα χερσὶ μεμαρπώς; Columella, *RR*, 2.21; the whetstones were special sharpening stones acquired from Crete and

were kept, with the olive oil or water the reaper used, in a container of animal horn tied to his waist: Pliny, *NH*, 18.67.261: 'Fuit hoc quoque maioris impendii apud priores, Creticis tantum transmarinisque cotibus notis nec nisi oleo aciem falcis excitantibus: igitur cornu propter oleum ad crus ligato fenisex incedebat.'

168 Bonner, *Studies in Magical Amulets*, plate v, figs. 115–17; and plate vi, figs. 118–27; cf. Festugière, 'Amulettes magiques,' pp. 84–5; Seyrig, 'Invidiae Medicus,' pt. 5 in 'Notes archéologiques,' p. 50.

169 Victor Vitensis, *Hist. Pers. Vand.*, 2.10 (MGH AA 3.1: 15; ed. Helm): '... cogitat ut nostrae religionis homines in aula eius constituti neque annonas neque stipendia solita potirentur. Addidit quoque et laboribus eos conterere rusticanis. Dirigit viros ingenuos et admodum delicatos ad campum Uticensem, ut sub ardentis solis incendio *caespites* messium desecarent ...'

170 Evidence from antiquity is hard to come by. Based on the records of the Heroninos archive from mid-third-century Roman Egypt, Rathbone, *Economic Rationalism*, p. 164, can say that there is no known case of the employment of women as temporary seasonal labourers. Since such workers are almost never named, but treated as anonymous units of labour (p. 148), the explicit data that would resolve the problem are missing even in this otherwise well-documented case.

171 H. Michell, *The Economics of Ancient Greece*, 2nd ed. (Cambridge: Cambridge University Press, 1940; reprint New York: Barnes and Noble, 1957), p. 137, claims evidence for women's involvement in the harvesting process, including reaping, citing Hesiod, *W&D*, 602; Theocritus, *Idyll.* 15.80, but neither of the references has anything to say on the subject. He also refers to Pollux, 7.148 (actually 7.150), who notes a feminine word for 'harvester' (θεριστήρ) that apparently existed in Aristophanes (θεριστερία) [Kock, *Frag. Att. Com.* Aristophanes, frag. 788]. Given the comic context, perhaps not too much should be made of this single instance as evidence of anything in real life. Women are referred to as 'collectors' or *kalametrides*: Hesychios, s.v.; see *Anth. Pal.* 9.89 for the verb ἀκρολογεῖν used in a clear instance of the collecting of stalks of grain, notably by a starving woman, Niko, and other young girls. She dies in the overbearing heat. On what was meant by gleaning in the Roman world, see chap. 5, pp. 234–5, below; cf. Lerche, 'Observations on Harvesting,' p. 36, fig. 6 and p. 37 (Iran in the mid-1960s).

172 Morgan, 'The Place of Harvesters,' pp. 32–5, for some examples; also true in modern Greece, although under the exceptional condition where many of the men had gone off the islands to take up work elsewhere. The same applies in other times and places. In England, in the late eighteenth and early nineteenth century, given the huge deflection of young men into the forces fighting the French and Napoleonic wars, there was a considerable escalation of female workers in the task of reaping, in some cases outnumbering men by three to one in years that were later remembered as the 'petticoat harvests': see G.E. Mingay, ed., *The Agrarian History of England and*

Wales, 6: 1750–1850 (Cambridge: Cambridge University Press, 1989), pp. 684–5; see also Hostettler, 'Gourlay Steell,' pp. 95–6, indicating the common involvement of women in reaping with sickles, although, again, in a northern European context. The involvement of women in the front line of reaping seems to have depended heavily on cultural constraints: see Isern, *Bull Threshers and Bindlestiffs*, p. 25: Doukhobor women harvesting with sickles in western Canada around 1900, bringing to their new home gendered conventions in fieldwork from old Russia; see Salvemini, 'Migrants saisonniers,' p. 167, for early modern Italy.

173 See Rathbone, *Economic Rationalism*, p. 164, and the evidence cited by him; they are instanced in the back end operations, such as winnowing: P. Fay. 102 (Euhemeria, 106 CE), see A.C. Johnson, *Roman Egypt*, pp. 208–9.

174 See the evidence collated by Vignet-Zunz, 'La moisson à faucille,' where women are sometimes found involved in reaping (in the Moroccan Jbala, for example) and sometimes they are not (in the Ourasenis of western Algeria, for example); and see the illustrations, pp. 233–4.

175 Accepted, for example, as fact by Sigaut, 'L'évolution des techniques,' p. 9, but doubted by others.

176 Mane, 'Qui moissone?,' in *L'outil et le geste*, 1, pp. 424–8; for the Mediterranean as part of a larger global pattern, see Sigaut, 'Les techniques de récolte des grains,' pp. 41–2, and map 2, p. 40. He sees the preceding simpler modes of harvesting (his nos. 1–7) as being 'female.' 'Avec la faucille [no. 8] s'introduit une opposition tout à fait remarquable ... dans presque toute la zone semi-aride qui va du Maroc et de l'Espagne à l'Asie centrale, et peut-être jusqu'en Chine du Nord, la faucille est un outile masculin; les femmes interviennent peu ou pas dans la récolte proprement dit, seulement pour glaner ... dans presque toute l'Europe non méditerranéenne au contraire ... la faucille et un outil principalement féminin; les hommes interviennent pour aiguiser les outiles, pour faire et lier les gerbes, et pour le transport, main la récolte proprement dite est fait par les femmes.' However attractive this structural polarity might be, I must say that it seems to contradict almost every piece of evidence, pictorial and literary, that I have encountered on harvesting in non-Mediterranean Europe (see, for example, Mane, cited above). Moreover, to make the connection between women's work and the sickle as strong as he does, Sigaut has to claim that historians have mistakenly attributed men reaping with the sickle with their actual use of the 'volant,' which he accepts is a 'male' tool.

177 Bonner, *Studies in Magical Amulets*, p. 72: leggings: plate vi, figs. 124–5; Seyrig, 'Notes archéologiques,' p. 50; also visible on some of the bronze coins issued in 141–2 CE at Alexandria in the reign of Antoninus Pius: see *Roman Provincial Coinage Online*, no. 13958.

178 The holy man was Columbanus, who at the time was engaged in reaping with these men: Jonas of Bobbio, *Vita Columbani*, 1.15 (MGH SRG 37: 177): 'Quadam

etenim die cum vir egregius ad praecidendam messem cum fratribus poenes calmen quam Baniaritiam vocant venissent et blando commodoque austro flante, falce segetem secarent, evenit, ut unus eorum Theudegisilus nomine digitum falce praeciderit, nec prorsus hereret preter pellis parvae retentaculo. Itaque stantem vir Dei Theudegisilum a longe cernens, imperat, ut cum sodalibus coeptum opus perficiat. At ille rei gestae causam promit. Celer ille ad ipsum properat digitumque inlitum salivo pristine statim sospitati reddit; imperat, ut celer ad coeptum opus, vires augeat. Coepit cum gaudio geminare laborem ac pre ceteris ad praecidendam stipulam uberius urguere, qui dudum de praeciso membro animum meroris subderat. Haec nobis ipse Theudegisilus narravit digitumque monstravit. Et in supradicto monasterio Luxovio tale quiddam vice alia simile gessit.' Since Columbanus seems not infrequently to have served as a reaper, he (c. 15 fin) conventionally wore hardened work gloves known as *wanti*. As the end of the text informs us, this was not the only case of a sickle cutting off a digit; a similar incident had also happened in reaping the lands of the monastery at Luxeuil.

179 Bryer, 'Byzantine Agricultural Implements,' p. 76 and fig. 20, p. 77, who notes: 'The present distribution of these devices in former Byzantine lands is so widespread as to suggest that it has a history, yet I find no pictorial or literary reference to this essential gadget, so transitory and insignificant that it has left no archaeological or documentary trace.'

180 Mane, *L'outil et le geste*, p. 446 and n. 1619.

181 Lerche, 'Observations on Harvesting,' p. 38, fig. 9, for the tin finger extensions (southeastern Iran, mid-1960s).

182 See Vignet-Zunz, 'La moisson à faucille,' p. 231, and illustration, p. 233.

183 Meurers-Balke and Leonnecken, 'Zu Schutzgeräten,' for the studies and the evidence; cf. Comet, *Le paysan et son outil*, p. 183; the problem, also, is that degradable substances like wood, bamboo, or cane (Avitsur, *Implements for Harvesting*, p. xvii), leather (Lerche, 'Observations on Harvesting,' p. 38 and fig. 9, fig. 38), or even cloth (see Lerche 'Observations on Harvesting,' p. 34 and p. 35, fig. 3) were sometimes used.

184 Ps.-Aug. *Sermo*, 227 (PL 39: 2163–4): 'Quando enim messorum manibus gremia defecta bene cinguntur, manipuli non solvuuntur, sed integri iactantur ad carrum. Sic et corpora sanctorum gremia integra ad carrucam carnis Christi levantur …'

185 Ps.-Aug. *Breviarium in Psalmos*, 128 (PL 26: 1286–7): '"De quo non implevit manum suum qui metit": Qui retributionem dignam operis sui mercedem non recepti; "Nec sinum suum qui manipulos colliget": Qui per conscientiae puritatem, et si minus habet, voluntatem tamen bonam adhibuit. Ideoque a Deo, tamquam si multum dedisset, manipulos refert, sicut vidua de duobus minutis' (referring to Mk. 12:42–4); '"Benedicimus vobis in nomine Domini": Ut, relictis infructuosis

aridisque operibus, ea seratis, quae et messorum manum et colligentium manipulos repleant sinum.'

186 Ps.-Aug. *Sermo*, 13.5 (PL 39: 1766); the original biblical incident on which Augustine is commenting is found at Genesis 37:7: 'Putabam ligare nos manipulos in agro et quasi consurgere manipulum meum et stare vestroque manipulos circumstantes adorare manipulum meum.' [VG]

187 Paulinus Nolanus, *Ep.* 23.1 (CSEL 29: 158): '… ut de fructibus tuis impleat manum suam messor, et sinum suum qui manipulos colligit, hoc est, ipse Deus, qui verbi in nobis sui et seminator et messor est.' Note that the 'ut' cues the simile and the metaphoric usage.

188 Aug. *En. in Ps.* 128.12–13 (CCL 40: 1888). 'Et venient messores, sed non de illis implent manipulos. Venturi sunt enim messores, et collecturi sunt triticum in horreum, et zizania alligabunt et mittent in ignem … Non inde implet messor manus. Sequitur enim et dixit: *Non replevit manum suam messor, et sinum suum qui manipulos colligit. Messores autem angelos sunt*, Dominus dixit. … Alii sunt qui manipulos colligunt, non de illis replent manus, alii sunt transeuntes viam. Qui manipulos colligunt, non de illis replent manus, quia non colligitur ad horreum fenum tectorum? Qui sunt qui manipulos colligunt? Messores. Qui sunt messores? Dominus dixit: *Messores autem angeli sunt*.' In saying that the angels are the harvesters, Augustine was commenting on Matthew 13:39–41: '… messis vero consummatio saeculi est, messores autem angeli sunt, sicut ergo colliguntur zizania et igni conburuntur. Sic erit in consummatio saeculi; mittet Filius hominis angelos suos et colligent de regno eius omnia scandala …'[VG]

189 Bérard, 'Mosaïques inédites de Cherchel,' pl. i–iv, for the brilliant agricultural mosaic from Cherchel (anc. Iol-Caesarea): save for the grape harvest, however, all the other harvesting scenes have been lost; only the ones on ploughing and seeding remain; see Ferdi, *Corpus des mosaïquess de Cherchel*, 'Maison des travaux aux champêtres,' pp. 113–22 (nos. 94–8) and pl. LXXXVII.94; Précheur-Canonge, 'La moisson,' pt. IIA3 in *La vie rurale*, pp. 46–53, summarizes the evidence as of 1950s; cf. Romanelli, 'La vita agricola tripolitana,' p. 62, fig. 6 (Ghirza reliefs).

190 Cypr. *Ad Quir.* 3.16 (CSEL 3: 108); *Ad Fortunat.* 12 (CSEL 3: 212); Augustine has a slight variant: 'venientes autem venient in exultatione, portantes gremia sua' (*Serm.* 313D = MiAg 1: 534).

191 Spiro, *Critical Corpus of the Mosaic Pavements*, 2, no. 227; for comment, see vol. 1, 207–14.

192 Leglay, *SAM*, 1, pp. 224–8.

193 Leglay, *Saturne africain*, pl. III: dated, purely on stylistic grounds, to the 'tetrarchic period' (*Saturne africain*, p. 29: 'datable par le décor, le style et les portraits de l'époque tétrarchique'); *SAM*, 1, pl. ix.4; 'Tunisie centrale' no. 9; see Charles-Picard, 'La collection Boglio à Siliana,' pp. 37–78 (nos. 13 and 13a); and (1946–49), pp. 121–2.

194 AE 1946: 46; cf. 1966: 513 (Siliana Region), suggesting P(ublius) N(—) for the name of Cuttinus.

195 The name Cuttinus is not directly attested elsewhere in Africa, although there are analogues: Cuttu[…] (CIL 8.1071: Carthage: but doubtful), Cutula (CIL 8.19809: Castellum Celtianum = El Meraba), Cutteus (CIL 8. 21671, two cases: Albulae = Aïn Temouchent), and the Cuttilulenses of late antiquity (AE 2003: 1977, Aïn Zouza; 290–4 CE) – all manifestly of Punic derivation; see Leglay, *Saturne africain: histoire*, pp. 362–3, for the expression *bonis bene*.

196 De Ste Croix, *The Class Struggle*, pp. 183–4: 'in what follows, most of the details come from the world of the Greek *poleis*, and not much of it on harvesting. Some of the following items are relevant: Demosthenes (57.45) takes that fact that many citizen women in a time of crisis were forced to become wet-nurses, woolen workers and grape-harvesters to show the way in which poverty made free men perform "many servile and base acts" (δουλικα καὶ ταπεινα πραγματα).'

197 The claim was made in a lengthy, detailed, and influential study by Bürge, 'Der *mercennarius* und die Lohnarbeit.'

198 Heitland, *Agricola*, p. 108; citing [Dem.] *Nikostr.* 21 (p. 1253): ὁπότε γὰρ οἱ ἄνθρωποι οὗτοι ἢ ὀπώραν πρίαιντο ἢ θέρος μισθοῖντο ἐκθερίσαι ἢ ἄλλο τι τῶν περὶ γεωργίαν ἔργων ἀναιροῖντο, Ἀρεθούσιος ἦν ὁ ὠνούμενος καὶ μισθούμενος ὑπὲρ αὐτῶν.

199 Heitland, *Agricola*, p. 109, referring to Dem. *Coron.* 51–2, where the speaker clearly suggests that harvest workers were usually hired men who were paid a wage (and with whom one never could be said to have relations of *xenia* or *philia*): … εἰ μὴ καὶ τοὺς θεριστὰς καὶ τοὺς ἄλλο τι μισθοῦ πράττοντας φίλους καὶ ξένους δεῖ καλεῖν τῶν μισθωσαμένων.

200 Convincing arguments against Bürge's somewhat extreme views have been made by Möller, 'Die *mercenarii* in der römischen Arbeitswelt,', who demonstrates that *mercenarii* were not always slaves let out by owners on hire.

2. Primus in Arvis/First in the Fields

1 Atkinson, *Army at Dawn*, chap. 8, 'A Bits and Pieces War,' pp. 301–37 (cemetery at Maktar: p. 301).

2 M'Charek, 'Un itinéraire inédit,' and esp. maps A and B.

3 Prévot, *Recherches archéologiques*, p. 3n31 with bibliography; Beschaouch, 'Mactaris (Makthar, Mactar),' p. 201; Lepelley, *Cités de l'Afrique romaine*, 2, pp. 289–95; for the location, see AAT, f. 30 (Maktar), no. 186.

4 Charles-Picard, 'Le temple du Musée à Mactar.'

5 T. Hardy, *The Mayor of Casterbridge*, ed. M. Seymour-Smith (Harmondsworth: Penguin, 1978), p. 94.

6 CIL 8.11824 = *Eph. Epigr.* 5 (1884), no. 279, pp. 276–8 = *Eph. Epigr.* 7 (1892), no. 64, pp. 22–3 = ILTun 528 = ILS 7457; cf. *CRAI* (1884), p. 64; and additional comment in AE 1946: 62; 1987: 1025 and 1988: 1118; see Héron de Villefosse, 'Note sur l'inscription,' for the first report of the find by the discoverer, Joseph Letaille; Héron de Villefosse, *Ant. Afric.* (1885), pp. 239–41; Tissot, 'Les missions' and 'Quatrième rapport,' with a good photographic reproduction. A good reproduction can be found in *Bulletin épigraphique de la Gaule* 5 (1885), plate 5 (between pp. 292 and 293); and another in Leclercq, 'Moissonneur,' fig. 8279; further good reproductions are offered by Bond, Thompson, and Warner, *Facsimiles of Manuscripts and Inscriptions* (1886), plate II.49 (part of the inscription and only from a cast), and by E.A. Lowe, *CLA*, pl. 7.b.

7 Charles-Picard, Le Bonniec, and Mallon, 'Le cippe de Beccut,' pp. 157–64, figs. 20–3.

8 As categorized by Remigius of Auxerre in the ninth century: '*Untiales* sunt litterae magnae quae in initiis librorum ad ornatum fiunt … Sunt etiam et alia genera litterarum. Quedam enim *Virgilianae* dicuntur quibus initia versuum frequenter in metro scribuntur. Sunt et *Affricanae* quae tunse appellantur … Sunt praeterea et *Longariae* … scriptura quibus cartulae et edicta atque praecepta scribuntur.' B. Bischoff, *Mittelalterliche Studien: Ausgewählte Aufsätze zur Schriftkunde und Literaturgeschichte*, 3 vols. (Stuttgart: A. Hiersemann, 1966–81), vol. 1, p. 2. As Lowe, *CLA*, viii, noted, the forms of writing are, respectively, uncials, rustic capitals, semi-uncials, and cursives (although the equation in the case of the *Litterae Africanae* is only approximate).

9 On the metrical quality, see the early study of Bianchi, 'Carmina latina,' at pp. 63 f., who noted that the poem is not perfectly regular in its construction. Some of his objections relate to perceived irregulaties in the metrical structure of the couplets. These observations, however, do not carry conviction as judgments about the poet's skills and talents. The lapses of the so-called aberrant lines are the cutter's errors and not those of the poet (see my remarks in appendix 2).

10 See the general study, *Flavii de Cillum*, esp. D. Pikhaus, 'Le carmen de Cillium et l'épigraphie versifiée de l'Afrique romaine,' pp. 131–52; and J. Peyras, 'Le coq du Mausolée,' pp. 235–50, on the misunderstandings of between the commissioned poet and the heirs.

11 CIL 8.11824 (Berlin, 1891) = Bücheler, *CLE*, 1238 [vol. 2, 1897] = Cholodniak, *Carmina Sepulchralia Latina*, no. 1142 = Pikhaus, *Inscriptions latines versifées*, B74 = Courtney, *Musa Lapidaria*, no. 109, pp. 108–9. For the Latin text and analysis, see appendix 2. I have benefited from a wide range of existing translations, of which the following are only a selection: in French, G. Boissier, *L'Afrique romaine* (Paris: Hachette, 1895; 6th ed., Hachette, 1912), p. 146; J. Toutain, *L'économie antique* (Paris: La Renaissance du livre, 1927), p. 360, reprinted by J. Lassère, 'Sentiments

et culture d'après les épitaphes latines d'Afrique,' *BAGB* (1965), pp. 209–27, at pp. 212–13; Charles Picard, *Civilisation*, p. 120, reprinted in G. Charles Picard and J. Rougé, eds., *Textes et documents relatifs à la vie économique et sociale dans l'empire romain* (Paris: Société d'édition d'enseignement supérieur, 1969), pp. 224–7; C. Saumagne, 'Les circoncellions d'Afrique,' *AHES* 6 (1934), 360; Macqueron, *Travail des hommes libres*, p. 225; in German, H. Geist, *Römische Grabinschriften: Gesammelte und in Deutsche übertragen* (Munich: Heimeran, 1969), no. 236; and Lukits, 'Die Schnitterinschrift von Maktar,' pp. 77–8; in English: MacMullen, *Roman Social Relations*, p. 43; and Courtney, *Musa Lapidaria*, p. 109.

12 The following are merely a selection: MacMullen, *Roman Social Relations*, pp. 42–3; Gagé, *Classes sociales*, p. 289; De Ste Croix, *Class Struggle*, p. 187: 'this man was probably a very rare exception'; J.-M. Carrié and A. Rousselle, *L'Empire romain en mutation des Sévères à Constantin, 192–337* (Paris: Editions du Seuil, 1999), p. 698.

13 Rostovtzeff, *SEHRE²*, p. 331; the label 'conservative' is used in the way we have defined it for our purposes; in his own terms, Rostovtzeff was a liberal.

14 Charles-Picard, *Civilisation*, p. 121: 'Cette carrière exemplaire, datable *sans doute* de la première moitié du IIIe siècle [m.i.] … Le cas du moissonneur n'est d'ailleurs pas isolé.'

15 De Ste Croix, *Class Struggle*, p. 187, at the end of a lengthy discussion of the status of hired labour in the Greek and Roman worlds; the reference to the Christian bishop comes from John Moschus: a bishop who helped in the exceptional circumstances of the rebuilding of Antioch after the great earthquake of 526.

16 Finley, *Ancient Economy*, p. 274n28; the words quoted by Finley refer to G. Steiner, 'Farming,' in C. Roebuck, ed., *The Muses at Work: Arts, Crafts and Professions in Ancient Greece and Rome* (Cambridge, MA: MIT Press, 1969), pp. 248–70, at pp. 169–70.

17 The following items are no more than an illustrative selection: J. Toutain, *Les cités romaines de la Tunisie: Essai sur l'histoire de la colonisation romaine dans l'Afrique du Nord* (Paris: A. Fontemoing, 1896), pp. 355–6; Raven, 'The Harvester of Mactar,' in *Rome in Africa*, pp. 84–6; Charles-Picard, *Civilisation*, pp. 67, 120–4; (rev. ed., 1990), p. 224; Lepelley, *Cités de l'Afrique romaine*, vol. 2, p. 291; A. Berthier, *La Numidie. Rome et le Maghreb* (Paris: Picard, 1981), pp. 150–2; Février, *Approches*, vol. 1, pp. 77 and 139–40; M. Brett and E. Fentress, *The Berbers* (Oxford: Blackwell, 1996), p. 61; and C. Hugoniot, *Rome en Afrique: de la chute de Carthage aux débuts de la conquête arabe* (Paris: Flammarion, 2000), pp. 107–8, who repeats all of the usual verities, including the canonical date of the 260s CE.

18 Desideri, 'L'iscrizione,' pp. 137–49, is one of the few. His study derives from a seminar held by Professor Italo Lana at the University of Turin to which the author contributed. Desideri is principally interested in the autobiographical elements of the inscription. Another has been offered by Pikhaus, 'Littérature latine,' a study which

naturally concentrates on the inscription as an exemplary piece of verse epigraphy; her conclusions are ones with which this author disagrees in almost every respect.

19 Thompson, 'Bringing In the Sheaves,' p. 467.

20 Charles-Picard, *Civitas Mactaritana*, pp. 6–67; Prévot, *Recherches archéologiques*, pp. 1–2.

21 Until the reign of Trajan, the town was administered by a board of three *sufetes*, after which Latino-Roman *triumviri* take their place: Gascou, *Politique municipale*, pp. 150–1; there was a fundamental shift in municipal organization under Trajan when numbers of citizens belonging to the *tribu Papiria* suddenly appear: see Gascou, *Politique municipale*, p. 149 and Charles-Picard, *Civitas Mactaritana*, p. 148.

22 Charles-Picard, 'Le *conventus civium Romanorum*' (1963–4) and 'Le *conventus civium Romanorum*' (1966); cf. his *Civitas Mactaritana*, pp. 21–4.

23 In the Punic and African periods, it was the centre of a district named *Thuska* containing 'fifty' towns (obviously a round number, a guess): see Appian, *Libyka*, 62: οὐ πολὺ δὲ ὕστερον ὁ Μασσανάσσης ἠμφισβήτει καὶ τῶν λεγομένων μεγάλων πεδίων καὶ χώρας πεντήκοντα πόλεων, ἣν Τύσκαν προσαγορεύουσιν. It was the centre of the *Pagus Thuscae et Gunzuzi*, a region that administered 64 tribute-paying cities or *civitates stipendiariae*: later reduced to 62 by 158 CE: CIL 8.23599 and AE 1963: 96 (Mactaris): see Charles-Picard, Mahjoubi, and Beschaouch, '*Pagus Thuscae et Gunzuzi*,' pp. 124–30; cf. Pflaum, 'La romanisation,' p. 80, Beschaouch, 'Mactaris (Makthar, Mactar),' pp. 198–9; then, under Trajan, it began to function as a centre of the four major imperial taxes for Africa, the *IIII Publica Africae*: Charles-Picard, *Civitas Mactaritana*, pp. 21–4; see AE 1949: 30 (Mactaris): Titus Flavius Symphorus, an Augustal freedman procurator of the *IIII Publica Africae*, and AE 1900: 126: a slave of the same service.

24 AE 1983: 976 (Mactaris): Sextus Iulius Possessor, whose equestrian career took him there as adiutor Praefecti Annonae ad horrea Ost(i)ensia et Portuensia.

25 Pflaum, 'La romanisation,' does not seem to include the *pagus Thuscae*, which Mactaris administered, as within the pertica of Carthage, as seems likely.

26 CIL 8.11801 and 11802; cf. 11910, ad. 677 (Mactaris), perhaps as early as 176–80 under Marcus Aurelius and Commodus, so Charles-Picard, *Civitas Mactaritana*, p. 153, and 'Le statut politique de Mactar'; and Gascou, *Politique municipale*, pp. 147–8 and 'La politique municipale,' p. 197; but perhaps rather later in 191 or 192, in the last years of Commodus's reign: see H.-G. Pflaum, *Athenaeum* 54 (1976), p. 158 = *Scripta Varia, I: Afrique romaine* (Paris: L'Editions Harmattan, 1978), p. 399; Mastino, 'La ricerca epigrafia,' p. 94; Lepelley, *Cités de l'Afrique romaine*, 2, p. 290n8; and Beschaouch, 'Mactaris (Makthar, Mactar),' p. 201.

27 Lancel, *Actes de la Conférence de Carthage en 411*, vol. 4 (Paris: Le Cerf, 1991) = SC 373, s.v. 'Mactaritana plebs,' p. 1413.

28 Ben Baaziz, 'Les fermes fortifiées de la Dorsale méridionale,' pp. 51–8, indicating conditions of growing insecurity.

29 Prévot, *Recherches archéologiques*, p. 4: nos. II.18, X.28, XI.4, X.6, and XII.1; cf. Beschaouch, 'Mactaris (Makthar, Mactar),' p. 201.

30 In the late fourth and early fifth century, the dissident 'Donatist' church had a bishop in the town; he appears to have been unopposed by a Catholic bishop: see *Gesta Conlationis Carthaginis anno 411*, 1: 202 = Lancel, *Actes de la conférence*, vol. 2 (SC 195: 872) and vol. 4 (SC 373: 1413); for the churches in the town, see Duval, *Églises africaines à deux absides*, 2, pp. 107–54.

31 Martyrs: Dasius, Abdasius, and Iacobus: AE 1960: 111 (Mactaris), and probably others: see AE 1946: 115 and 1949: 25; clergy or *cleri*: AE 1953: 46a–b (Mactaris); presbyteri: AE 1960: 112–13 (Mactaris); a castimonialis: AE 1946: 114 (Mactaris).

32 See Mesnage, *L'Afrique chrétienne: évêchés*, pp. 103–4 – if, as seems likely, the Victor 'Mattaritanus,' dating to c. 500–50, is understood to be 'Mactaritanus': Cassiod. *Inst.* 1.29.2 (ed. Mynors): 'Cuius dicta Victor Mattaritanus, episcopus Afer, ita Domino iuvante purgavit, et quae minus erant addidit, ut ei rerum istarum palma merito conferatur …'

33 Dated to the age of the Antonines: Rostovtzeff, *SEHRE*, p. 382; Charles-Picard, *Civilisation*, p. 224; M'charek, *Aspects de l'évolution démographique*, pp. 208–9; to the age of the Severi: Tissot, *Géographie comparée*, p. 65. Dated to the mid-third century: Courtney, *Musa Lapidaria*, p. 318; to the second half of the third century: Charles-Picard and Rougé, 'Le "moissonneur de Mactar,"' pp. 224–7, at p. 225: 'En faite, la comparaison avec les autres monuments funéraires de Mactar permet de dater le cippe autour de 260–270 ap. J.C.,' a judgment that is accepted by, among others, Desideri, 'L'iscrizione,' p. 140 and Lukits, 'Die Schnitterschrift von Maktar,' p. 81. Charles-Picard, *Les Religions de l'Afrique antique* (Paris: Plon, 1954), pp. 120–2, oddly enough, connects the typical Saturn stelae of the Siliana region (including the Boglio stele, see chap. 1, pp. 43–6) with the world of the Maktar Harvester, but dates the stelae to the fourth century, reflecting the confidence of a class of agricultural proprietors who had made it through the third-century crisis. For dating to the third century, see Warmington, *North African Provinces*, p. 87, again using it as an illustration of social mobility; Février, *Approches*, 1, p. 196, also places our man in the mid-third century. These earlier dates have worked their way into more popular presentations: Raven, *Rome in Africa*, p. 84: 'the second century.'

34 Tissot, 'Quatrième rapport,' p. 65: 'nous inclinerions à considerer cette inscription comme contemporaine des Sévères et de la grande prospérité industrielle et agricole dont l'Afrique jouit sous ces empereurs.'

35 Charles-Picard, Le Bonniec, and Mallon, 'Le cippe de Beccut,' at p. 148: 'si'il est mort vers 270, il a fort bien pu naître vers 190; son enrichissement s'est situerait dans la période 210–235, alors que l'Afrique était encore en pleine prosperité.' Charles-Picard's reasoning is made a little more explicit in *Civilisation*, p. 381n28: 'Le texte, maintes fois commenté et reproduit, a été daté parfois du IVe siècle et même du VIe siècle pour des raisons paléographiques … *En fait la situation sociale décrite* (non

moins que la langue et la forme du poème) interdisaient de le faire descendre plus bas que la [première] moitié du IIIe siècle' (my italics). The statement is followed by an appeal to the inscriptions of Pinarius Mustulus and Beccut Euthesia. Not a few have accepted the date and for these same reasons, e.g., Pikhaus, 'Littérature latine,' pp. 83–4 and Lukits, 'Die Schnitterinschrift von Maktar,' pp. 85.

36 Gagé, *Classes sociales*, p. 289.

37 In one of the first reports in the *Bulletin épigraphique de la Gaule* 3 (1883), p. 151, in which de la Blanchère first reported the existence of the inscription (at the meeting of 20 April): 'Il a communique aussi une inscription métrique *de basse époque*, trouvée à Mactar par M. Letaille' (my italics).

38 J.-P. Brisson, *Autonomisme et christianisme dans l'Afrique romaine de Septime-Sévère à l'invasion Vandale* (Paris: E. de Boccard, 1958), p. 338, esp. p. 338n6, where he connects this man with the circumcellions of the late fourth century, but he then dates the inscription to the third century, noting (p. 339) that the circumcellions must be tied to an Africa in decline and characterized by rural immiseration, constrasting the social milieux that he expected of of the two.

39 G. Charles-Picard, *BCTH* (1955–6), p. 179 = *AE* 1960: 116 (Mactaris): '[et genui] feliciter et rem non [modicam / a mini]mo quaestui fraude [sine ulla / atque m] eis propriis natorum [et honoribus auctus / aeternam mo]riens famam claramq[ue reliquis] / [...]Pinarius Mustulus / [...]h LXXV h. s. e. / est inferre longis / [...]iae morumque / [...p]ercepi iu[... / ...]heptae.'

40 Charles-Picard, Le Bonniec, and Mallon, 'Le cippe de Beccut,' p.148n2: citing the case of Lucustio Colonicus (CIL 8.11828) and arguing that the man's cognomen reflects his occupation; he also draws attention to Cuttinus, a rich proprietor in the Siliana region and patron of the so-called Boglio stele, who still bears a Punic name, significantly, in the age of the Tetrarchs or later: see Leglay, *SAM* 1, pp. 227–8, on the dating.

41 For *colonus* in the sense of a larger landowning farmer, especially in a provincial context, see Cic. *Pro Font.* 12 and discussion by Guido Clemente in *I Romani nella Gallia meridionale, II – I sec. a. C.* (Bologna: Patron, 1974), p. 114 f.; cf. Kehoe, *Economics of Agriculture*, pp. 97–100, in his discussion of the 'great domain' inscriptions of the middle Bagrada valley.

42 *AE* 1960: 116 (Mactaris): '[Et genui] feliciter et rem non [modicam] / [---e mini]mo quaestui fraude [sine ulla] / [--- atque m]eis propriis natorum [et honoribus auctus / --- aeternam mo]riens famam claramq[ue reliquis] ...'

43 Charles-Picard, Le Bonniec, and Mallon, 'Le cippe de Beccut,' pp. 148–9: in the first group are: (i) the four texts of the mausoleum of the Julii (CIL 8.645, 647, 648, 650); (ii) the epitaph of Lucustio Colonicus (see n. 40 above); (iii) the epitaph of Pinarius Mustulus and his wife; (iv) the cippus of Beccut, and (v) the narrative of our harvester. In his second group are: (i) epitaph of Julia Benenata: see now Prévot,

Recherches archéologiques, 36–40, and fig. 27; (ii) the three poems on the mosaic of the 'Church of the Iuvenes' (*CRAI* [1945], pp. 109–10: the Greek cross on the mosaics permits a Byzantine date, he thinks); and (iii) the epitaph of Alurius Geminus (*BCTH* [1950], p. 160): the monogram cross appears c. 425 CE.

44 The trend is thoroughly documented by Lepelley in *Cités de l'Afrique romaine*, and in many individual studies published subsequently.

45 Just one striking example of the continued strength of at least some traditional cult in the town is the restoration of the temple of the Punic goddess Hoter Miskar at the end of the fourth century. Some of the accumulated wealth of the time was therefore devoted to this project. Another is the so-called *schola* of the *iuvenes* at Mactaris which Noël Duval (unlike Charles-Picard) identifies as a wealthy house restored and re-embellished in the fourth century; he dates its transformation into a Christian church to a rather later date: see Lepelley, *Cités de l'Afrique romaine*, 2, pp. 291–2.

46 Prévot, *Recherches archéologiques*, p. 233: 'On est frappé par l'importance de l'héritage païen, non seulement dans l'expression … mais surtout dans les thèmes développés, dont la plupart n'ont rien de chrétien.'

47 On Calama and Sufes see the notorious episodes involving the so-called pagan populations of these towns reported by Augustine, *Ep.* 90–1 (CCL 31A: 153–9), see Lepelley, *Cités de l'Afrique romaine*, 2, pp. 97–101 (Calama); and Aug. *Ep.* 50 (CCL 30: 214) on Sufes; on which, see Lepelley, *Cités de l'Afrique romaine*, 2, pp. 305–7.

48 Prévot, *Recherches archéologiques*, p. 211: 'L'épigraphie mactaroise se caracterise donc par une survivance exceptionnelle de formulles païennes'; and p. 236: 'On ne s'étonnera donc pas de la faible présence du christianisme dans ces épitaphes.'

49 Courtois et al., *Tablettes Albertini*, p. 16n5fin: 'cette question, qui serait entièrement à reprendre.' Their project to reproduce and to offer a detailed study of the epigraphical texts containing the unusual script of the harvester inscription from Mactaris (p. 16n1), to the best of my knowledge, was never actually undertaken or completed.

50 I use the term 'cursive' throughout in a general sense of a writing that shares some distinctive characteristics of 'longhand' handwriting, but I do not suggest that it must be categorized as one of the 'types' that have canonically been used to label late antique and medieval Latin manuscript hands. Mallon has rightly objected that it is mistaken to categorize this writing precisely as 'uncial,' 'quasi-uncial,' or 'cursive' according to one of the standards proffered by handbooks on scripts: see Mallon in Charles-Picard, Le Bonniec, and Mallon, 'Le cippe de Beccut,' p. 157.

51 Hübner, *Exempla*, p. xxxviii, § 10: 'Scriptura uncialis'; for what followed in terms of comparative materials from north Africa, by far the best guide to mid-century was the reconsideration of all examples of writing by the editors of the 'Tablettes Albertini': Courtois et al., *Tablettes Albertini*, chap. 2, 'L'écriture et la langue: 1. Étude paléographique: les documents paléographiques africains,' pp. 15–20, p. 16n5 for specifics on the 'Maktar Harvester' inscription.

52 The earliest example, CIL 5.2781 (Patavinum), dates to 314 CE; the earliest dated examples for the use of verse were above the city gate and on an obelisk in Constantinople in honour of Theodosius and Eudoxia (CIL 3.734–7: 388/403 CE); the base of a column to Tatian, Praefectus Urbi (CIL 3.738, 451 CE); above the city gate of Pusaei (CIL 3.739: 465/67 CE); and a carmen of eight distichs carved into living rock near a spring at a coastal site in Dalmatia (CIL 3.1894: 446/74 CE).

53 Hübner, *Exempla*, p. 271, nos. 794–6: the examples are as follows: no. 794 = CIL 8.5353 (Calama; 540 CE); no. 795 = CIL 8.8483 (Sitifis) mentioning Solomon, and so of Byzantine date; no. 796 = CIL 8.2245 = ILS 9350 (Mascula; 578/79 CE); in addition, see Courtois et al., *Tablettes Albertini*, p. 16n1.

54 Hübner, *Exempla*, pp. 411–12, no. 1149 = CIL 8.2368 (Lambaesis): where the DMS formula might suggest a pre-Christian date, but not necessarily: see Lassère, 'Recherches chronologiques,' pp. 96–106; no. 1150 = CIL 8.257 (Sufes); no. 1151 = CIL 8.653 (Mactaris); no. 1152 = CIL 8.1152 (Mactaris). Both the Mactaris examples are from the so-called Mausoleum of the Iulii. The scripts in these inscriptions, however, are not close in style to the writing in our inscription.

55 Vocontius Publius Flavius Pudens Pomponianus: Hübner, *Exempla*, p. 410, no. 1147 = CIL 8.2391 = 17910 = ILS 2937 = E. Boeswillwald, R. Cagnat, and A. Ballu, *Timgad, une cité africaine sous l'empire romain* (Paris: E. Léroux, 1905), pp. 74–6, fig. 3 = René Cagnat, *Cours de l'épigraphie latine*, 4th ed. (Paris: Fontemoing, 1914), pl. xv.4 (Thamugadi); cf. Courtois et al., *Tablettes Albertini*, p. 16n1 (Thamugadi): 'Vocontio / P(ublio) Fl(avio) Pudenti Pompo/niano c(larissimo) v(iro), erga civeis patriamque / prolixe cultori, ex//ercitiis militaribus /effecto, multifari/am loquente lit//teras ampliant, At/ticam facundiam ad//aequanti Romano / nitori / ordo incola fontis, / patrono oris uberis / et fluentis, nostr[o] / alteri fonti.' A dedication to his wife, Caelia Procilla, was also found at Timgad (west of the Great Baths in the northern part of the city): J. Carcopino and H. Focillon, 'Inscriptions latines d'Afrique,' *BCTH* (1904), pp. 212–14, no. 39. Then L. Leschi, 'Découvertes récentes à Timgad: *Aqua Septimiana Felix*,' *CRAI* (1947), pp. 95–7 = *Etudes d'épigraphie, d'archéologie et d'histoire africaines* (Paris: Arts et métiers graphiques, 1957), pp. 240–5: an inscribed base found in the Byzantine fortress: dedicated to Caracalla and his mother, dated to between 10 December 214 and 9 December 215, by P. Flavius Pudens Pomponianus c(larissimus) v(ir). The senator's career (PIR² F 346) would seem to place him somewhere in the mid-third century. This is one of the closest to our inscription in type of writing; cf. CIL VIII 2400 = 17911; 17912; AE 1895: 111; AE 1909: 156 (all from Thamugadi). See Fentress, 'Frontier Culture,' pp. 403–4, for a possible social significance of the use of the script: the senator as a highly educated man of cosmopolitan culture, with equal facility in Greek and Latin, who remained resident 'at home' in Thamugadi, used the script as a special form of self-advertisement.

56 AE 1895: 111 = ILS 8981 (Thamugadi), as Dessau noted: 'litteris q. d. uncialibus';

see R. Cagnat, 'Nouvelle inscription latine en lettres onciales,' *RPh* 19 (1895), pp. 214–17, and *BSAF* (1895), p. 135, with photograph.

57 Hübner, *Exempla*, p. 411, no. 1148 = CIL 8.2409 = 17909 (Thamugadi): 'M(arco) Virrio M(arci) fil(io) / Pap(iria tribu) Flavio Iugur/thae eq(uiti) R(omano) fl(amini) p(er)p(etuo) decu/rioni spendidissi/mae Coloniae // Carthaginiensium, /Curatori Rei P(ublicae) / tan/tum diserto quan/tum bono, splendidis/simus ordo col(oniae) Thamu//gadensium ...'; cf. M.S. Bassignano, *Il flaminato nelle province Romane dell'Africa* (Rome: L''Erma' di Bretschneider, 1974), p. 113, no. 29 (Carthage); cf. no. 30 (AE 1909: 156: Carthage: his daughter), cf. p. 291, no. 19 and who dates him (p. 115) to the third or to the fourth century; R. Duncan-Jones, 'Equestrian Rank in the Cities of the African Provinces under the Principate: An Epigraphic Survey,' *PBSR* 35 (1967), 147–86, at p. 172, no. 85 thinks that he was *flamen* not at Carthage but at Thamugadi; cf. C. Lucas, 'Notes on the *curatores rei publicae* of Roman Africa,' *JRS* 30 (1940), pp. 56–74, at p. 59, who dates his career to the first half of the third century, whereas Ballu, *Ruines de Timgad*, p. 124 dates him to the first half of the fourth; see Lepelley, *Cités de l'Afrique romaine*, 1, pp. 168 f. with table.

58 AE 1969–70: 658 (Mactaris).

59 J. Mallon, 'L'écriture,' an appendix to Charles-Picard, Le Bonniec, and Mallon, 'Le cippe de Beccut,' pp. 157–64: of the writing of the Maktar Harvester inscription (p. 162), and the similar body of scripts found on stone from north Africa, he says, 'qui ont été qualifiées improprement d'"oncials", voire de "cursives", et aussi, assez confusément, de "minuscules."' He considers the first manuscript version of the script to be exemplified on an Egyptian papyrus containing the *Epitome* of Livy.

60 E. Chatelain, *L'inscription du moissoneur* (Paris, 1889): a small dedicatory booklet produced by Chatelain to celebrate the occasion of Héron de Villefosse's marriage ('au mariage de M. Antoine Héron de Villefosse et de Mlle Lucie de Thomassin, 24 avril 1889') [non vidi].

61 Février, 'Evolution,' p. 213.

62 Charles-Picard, Bonniec, and Mallon, 'Le cippe de Beccut,' p. 140.

63 Pikhaus, 'Les origines sociales'; placed in a wider context by the same author in 'La poésie épigraphique latine.' And, finally, for the context of such poetic production in its north African context, her valuable studies 'Les carmina latina epigraphica' and 'Literary Activity in the Provinces.'

64 Desideri, 'L'iscrizione,' pp. 148–9, although admitting that he knows of no good epigraphical parallels to the life of our man: p. 141.

65 For these and related matters, see the more detailed comments in appendix 2.

66 CIL 8.212–13 = CLE 1552 = Pickhaus B25 = Courtney, *Musa Lapidaria*, no. 199A and B, pp. 186–93 (commentary, pp. 399–406); *Flavii de Cillium* is the standard synoptic treatment.

67 For the constant laudation of the acquisiton of wealth, see CIL 8.212 (Cillium), lines

13–20, and what follows; for agricultural investments: 'dum munera Bacchi / multa creat primasq(ue) cupit componere vites / et nemus exornat revocatis saepius undis?' (ll. 51–3): obviously viticulture and the use of irrigation.

68 See, e.g., Tissot, 'Quatrième rapport,' 65; for the judgment.

69 *ILTun.* 243 (Uppenna; Henchir Chigarnia): 'P(ius) v(ir) Dion bixsit annos octaginta et instituit arbores quatuor milia' (a Christian farmer: the head of the funerary inscription is marked with a chi-rho symbol: dated to the later fourth century, or even later). The region saw extensive development in late antiquity, and real wealth: it became a *colonia*, probably under Constantine (CIL 8.11157) and boasted two basilicas and, later, a Byzantine fortress: see C. Saumagne, 'Copie et description de quelques textes épigraphiques,' *BCTH* (1932–3), pp. 40–52; and, more recently, Stone, 'Culture and Investment,' p. 107.

70 Peyras, 'Le *Fundus Aufidianus,*' p. 198 = AE 1983: 975 (Biha Bilta?): '... agricolae in [spl(endidissima)?] / re p(ublica) Bihensi Bilt[a] / conductori pari/atori restitutori / fundi Aufidiani et, / praeter cetera bona q[uae] / in eodem f(undo) fecit, steriles / qu[o]que oleastri surcul[os] / inserendo plurimas o[leas] / instituit; puteum iux[ta] / viam, pomarium cum tri[chilis] / post collectarium, vin[eas] / novellas sub silva aequ[e in]/stituit. Uxor mar[ito] / incomparabili fe[cit].'

71 ILAlg. 1.2195 (Madauros, forum): 'Hoc est sepultus L(ucius?) Aelius [or, Laelius] Timminus / loco patiens laborum, frugi, vigilans, sobrius, / qui rem paravit haud mediocrem familiae // domumque tenuem ad equestrem promovit gradum.' See de Robertis, *Lavoro e lavoratori,* p. 32n38.

72 Stone, 'Culture and Investment,' studies six of these accounts, only one of which, however, that of the Maktar Harvester, is a first-person verse celebration.

73 Aur. Vict. *Caes.* 20.5: 'Quo bonis omnibus ac mihi fidendum magis, qui rure ortus tenui atque indocto patre in haec tempora vitam praestiti studiis tantis honestiorem'; cf. Lepelley, 'Quelques parvenus,' pp. 582–5, with analysis of other educated parvenues of the age. Note that Aurelius Victor was also a scion of pagan culture.

74 On the location of the 'Nomadic plains of Cirta' see Lancel, 'Suburbures et Nicibes.'

75 On the Fields of Jupiter (Saturn): see appendix 2, commentary on l. 10.

76 See Wyman, *Hoboes, Bindlestiffs, Fruit Tramps,* p. 30, for the dominant south-to-north pattern in reaping the wheat fields of the American and Canadian West.

77 Morgan, 'The Place of Harvesters,' p. 50; cf. his *Harvesters and Harvesting,* pp. 48 and 77–9 for more reports of these typical rounds and circuits.

78 Valensi, *Fellahs tunisiens,* p. 183.

79 Applen, 'Migratory Harvest Labor,' pp. 121–2; see his cautions at pp. 122–4, however, about the factors that militated against most seasonal labourers completing the full circuit.

80 Billiard, *L'agriculture dans l'antiquité,* pp. 126–7.

81 Schnebel, *Die Landwirtschaft,* pp. 162–3.

82 Schnebel, *Die Landwirtschaft*, p. 166, citing the literary sources Pliny, *NH*, 18.60 and Theophr. *Hist. pl.* 8.2.7, who place the barley harvest in Egypt in the sixth month and the wheat harvest in the seventh.

83 See Shaw, 'Soldiers and Society,' pp. 144–7; table 2a, p. 145, and maps, pp. 158–9.

84 Adelman, *Frontier Development*, pp. 119–20; cf. MacKenzie, *Harvest Train*, for one part of the east-to-west movement in Canada.

85 See Erdkamp, 'Agriculture, Underemployment,' 566–7 on the scale; for the use of legal forms, see ibid., p. 568, who draws attention to S. Von Bolla-Kotek, *Untersuchungen zur Tiermiete und Viehpacht im Altertum*, 2nd ed. (Munich: Beck, 1969), 7 f. and S. Martin, '*Servum meum mulionem conduxisti.* Mules, Muleteers and Transportation in Classical Roman Law,' *TAPhA* 120 (1990), 301–14.

86 Pliny, *NH*, 7.42.135, quoting Cicero to the effect that he was a 'mulionem castrensis furnariae fuisse'; and Cic. *Ad fam.* 10.18.3, quoting Munatius Plancus: 'Ventidiique mulionis castra despicio.'

87 Aul. Gell. *NA* 15.4.3, provides the basic information on how Ventidius acquired his wealth, rising from 'the most ignoble of ranks' and 'humble origins,' by purchasing mules and vehicles which he then leased to officials as they departed for their provinces.

88 Suet. *Aug.* 2.3: 'M. Antonius libertinum et proavum exprobrat, restionem e pago Thurino, avo argentarium.' As Suetonius notes, the elevated ancestry was reported by others; Augustus himself claimed nothing more than that he came from an 'old and wealthy equestrian family' and that his father was the first to enter the senate. The Thurian origins and location of the family make sense of the fact that Augustus's father was sent, as praetor, to deal with remnants of Spartacus's and Catilina's supporters in the deep south of Italy. Syme accepts the grandfather 'banker' (noting Münzer's reference to a tessera supposedly connected with him), but seems to suggest that the rest was 'hostile slander': *The Roman Revolution* (Oxford, 1939), p. 112n1. I cannot see why.

89 The process is hinted at in a famous statement in Tacitus, *Ann.* 13.27.1: 'et plurimis equitum, plerisque senatoribus non aliunde originem trahi.' Its purport is denied by Syme, *Tacitus* (Oxford: Clarendon Press, 1958), pp. 612–13: 'To believe it does less than justice to the art of the historian, who, employing speeches to dramatize a person or expand a theme, claims his full liberty and achieves plausibility by adding what speeches normally contain: that is to say, distortion and deceit.' Full belief is not required; and rhetorical exaggeration is one thing, outright falsification quite another. The phenomenon was surely more frequent than the rejection of it made by Syme, who ignores some of the evidence in support and finesses the rest in support of his own view which (for example, nomenclature) was was just as open to 'distortion and deceit.'

90 See Isern, *Bull Threshers and Bindlestiffs*, pp. 104–26, who reports the costs and net incomes of men who organized threshing gangs in the late nineteenth and early twentieth centuries in the western United States and Canada. He documents several cases

of the rise of such men from manual labour to real wealth: 'W.G. McGill of Boisse-vain, Manitoba, retired in 1914, before he was thirty-five, rich from harvesting – and all of this was in western Canada, where rates ran low, and before the wartime boom' (p. 108). Even if not common, such cases surely existed.

91 Suet. *Vesp.* 1.4. It was a rumour, and one that Suetonius says that he could not confirm in any reliable source, despite assiduous inquiries of his own: 'Non negaverim iactatum a quibusdam Petronis patrem e regione Transpadana fuisse mancipem oper-arum, quae ex Umbria in Sabinos ad culturam agrorum quotannis commeare soleant. Subsidisse autem in oppido Reatino uxore ibidem ducta. Ipse ne vestigium quidem de hoc, quamvis satis curiose inquirerem, inveni.' In many ways, the story, if true, would offer a case of upward mobility similar to that of the Maktar Harvester. Petro's father made his fortune, then settled down at Reate, where he made a good marriage, and the family began its rise, first as municipal *domi nobiles*: see B. Levick, *Vespasian* (London: Routledge, 1999), pp. 6–8, who notes that the cognomen Petro is Gallic in origin; she seems agnostic on the truth of the story, however. The existence of Ves-pasian's maternal grandfather, Vespasius Pollio, at Nursia has now been confirmed by epigraphy: *Suppl. Ital.* 13, no. 16; see Alföldy, 'Epigraphische Notizen.' Spurr, *Arable Cultivation*, p. 67n2, expresses some doubt that harvesting was necessarily the main work done by the gangs managed by Flavius Petro's father, suggesting the clearing of fallow land as an alternative.

92 Not necessarily, of course, but there are parallels: Collins, 'Migrant Labour,' p. 52: 'An increasingly popular arrangement after 1870 was for the same groups of Irish to be employed from year to year on the one farm, the "gangers" being sometimes notified by letter as to when they were required.'

93 Rositani, *Harvest Texts*, pp. 16–20.

94 For the text and comment, see appendix 1.B; for reasons that are not entirely clear, no contracts for the harvesting of cereal grains are contained in Cato's sample model contracts.

95 For the standard provisions of some of these contracts, see the examples in appen-dix 1.A.1–7; there are others that exist only in more fragmentary form. See, e.g., P. Hamb. 107 (253–52 BCE).

96 As they often were, still, for reaping, in nineteenth-century England; see Morgan, 'The Place of Harvesters,' p. 48.

97 See Rositani, *Harvest Texts*, p. 18, on these oral assumptions.

98 See Hengstl, *Private Arbeitsverhältnisse*, pp. 36–62, for a study of some of these labour contracts; cf. MacMullen, *Roman Social Relations*, p. 42, citing P. Flor. 101 (see above) and P. Oxy. 1631 (grape harvest).

99 See appendix. 1.A.2; cf. P. Flor. 101, 'Locazione d'opera (mietitori)' (Hermopolite Nome, 91 CE); cf. A.C. Johnson, *Roman Egypt*, p. 207, no. 106; dated to 20 April (on the restoration of the editors) of the year 91 CE.

100 Schwartz, *Archives de Sarapion*, pp. 111–12; cf. P. Sarap. 49–51, appendix 1.A.4–6; in addition to the contracts, the account books also have line items showing that reapers employed by them were paid in kind: see, e.g., P. Sarap. 75, lines 6 (36 artaba), 9 (66 artaba), and 16 (9 artaba); on historical significance, see Kehoe, *Management and Investment*, pp. 30–2, 67–72.

101 For wheat prices in Egypt from the end of the first century CE to the mid-third century CE, with all the necessary caveats, see Rathbone, *Economic Rationalism*, appendix 2, pp. 464–6; (1997), pp. 191–2; fig. 7, p. 213, and table 1, pp. 217–20.

102 See, e.g., P. Lond. 7, no. 1194, col. 3, line 66 (pay for reapers); no. 1195, col. 6, line 113 (pay for reapers of barley crop) from the so-called Zenon archive; P. Mil. Volg. 7, no. 5, col. 8, line 188: pay for reapers (about 40 obols); line 191 (pay for reapers, amount lost); col. 9, line 210 (pay for reapers, both numbers of reapers and pay lost) – Tebtunis, second century CE; the same is found in the payment of wages to vineyard workers: see Kloppenborg, *Tenants in the Vineyard*, pp. 528, citing P. Oxy. 11, no. 3354 (Oxyrhynchus, 257 CE), as well as similar cases reported in P. Oxy 14, no. 1631, 1692; PSI 13, no. 1338; P. Ross. Georg. 2, no. 19; and P. Vind. Sal. 8.

103 See CPR 7.52 (first century CE; Oxyrhynchite nome); for the *misthos* of *theristai*.

104 Athenaeus, 14.618d, refers to handfuls or δράγματα of barley, which, when gathered separately, were called ἄμαλλαι or *amallai*; cf. Theocr. *Id.* 10.40, who refers to the binders or sheavers as ἀμαλλοδέται. When they were gathered and then several of them were made into a single bundle, they were referred to as *ouloi* or *iouloi*; in Egypt, a *dragma* or sheaf was also known as an *angkalê* (ἀγκάλη). Reekmans, *A Sixth-Century Account of Hay*, p. 20: a load of these hauled by an ass or a mule was called a *gomos* (γόμος) and consisted of 50 *angkalai*.

105 See P. Cair. Preis. 31.21 (second century CE) for another case of one of these 'gifts' given in addition to wages.

106 See, e.g., P. Lond. 2.414 = P. Abinn. 5 (c. 346 CE; Hermopolis or Theoxenis in the Arsinoite nome): from the Abinnaeus archive.

107 De Robertis, *Lavoro e lavoratori*, pp. 340, 351, and 368; this arrangement was also standard in the contracts known from Egypt, where most of the hiring was done by agents or managers of the landowner, even down to the level of tenant farmers, such as those in P. Giss. 5 (132–31 BCE; Euhemeria, Arsinoite nome), where the landowner, Antimachos, holds his two indigenous Egyptian tenants responsible for the hiring of reapers to take off crops on his lands near the village of Dionysias at the time of harvest.

108 Rositani, *Harvest Texts*, pp. 20–3, 27: the money (silver) or barley retainers were given in the form of a contract of 'debt' that condemned the receiver to subsequent performance. Compare the advance of 40 drachmai given to reapers by the landowner Eutychides at Hermopolis, Egypt, in the early second century CE; it was

a bond that was returned to the landowner when the harvesters arrived to do the reaping (see appendix 1.A.6).

109 Braunert, *Die Binnenwanderung*, p. 369: see his references under the category II.1.a: 'fluktuierende Landarbeiter.'

110 Jones, *Later Roman Empire*, vol. 2, p. 792, and 1325n51: Rufinus, *Hist. Mon.* 18: A.J. Festugière, ed., *Historia Monachorum in Aegypto* (Brussels: Société de Bollandistes, 1961): *Subsidia Hagiographica*, no. 34, pp. 114–15 (Greek text); Eva Schulz-Flügel, ed., *Tyrannius Rufinus: Historia Monachorum sive de Vita Sanctorum Patrum* (Berlin–New York: de Gruyter, 1990): *Patristiche Texte und Studien*, Bd. 34, pp. 349–50 (Latin text): the Latin version gives 80 modii; the Greek text gives 12 artabas, 'which is equivalent to what we call 40 modii'; as Jones says, this was a full year's rations in normal circumstances, and one presumes that monks could live on much less; cf. John Moschus, *Pratum Spirituale*, 183 (PG 87.3: 3053–6).

111 Horn, *Labouring Life*, p. 72, quoting Arthur Randell; for an example of a contract redacted in writing in Cambridgeshire in 1891, see ibid. pp. 74–5.

112 Horn, *Labouring Life*, p. 72.

113 Ps.-Fulgentius, *Serm.* 68, De Martyribus (PL 65: 940): 'Delectat videre campos segetum aureis maturatis calamis aristarum … Segetes enim sunt passiones martyrum … Nam sic modo beatus David martyrum purpurata germina, et ante messores gaudiorum tanquam manceps secantia messoria cithara decantabat.'

114 Applen, 'Migratory Harvest Labor,' p. 53.

115 Verlinden, *Les statuettes anthropomorphes*, pp. 78–9 and pls. 14–15: cat. 30 (from Tylissos) and cat. 31 (provenience unknown); Younger (1998), pp. 6–7 and pl. 2.

116 Verg. *Georg.* 1.252–3: 'Hinc tempestates dubio praediscere caelo / possumus, hinc messisque diem tempusque serendi …'; and see also 1.316–17: 'Saepe ego, cum flavis messorem induceret arvis / agricola …' (for the rest, and the military-like context, see chap. 1, pp. 16–17).

117 Morgan, 'The Place of Harvesters,' pp. 46–50, and his fig. 2, p. 49 from which our figure 1.1 is taken.

118 Cic. 2 *Verr.* 5.12.29: 'Cum vero aestas summa esse coeperat, quod tempus omnes Siciliae semper praetores in itineribus consumere sonsuerunt … cum in areis frumenta sunt, quod et familiae congregantur et magnitudo servitii perspicitur et labor operis maxime offendit'; see Billiard, *L'agriculture dans l'antiquité*, p. 126; for the use of neighbours, see Cato, *Agr.* 4.1; Cic. *De off.* 1.18.59: 'Ut vicinum citius adiuvaris in fructibus percipiendis.'

119 Varro, *RR*, 1.17.2: '… aut mercenariis, cum conducticiis liberorum operis res maiores, ut vindemias ac faenisicia, administrant'; see Heitland, *Agricola*, p. 180.

120 Lk. 15:17–19, prompting remarks, for example, by Ambr. *Ep.* 36.12 (CSEL 82: 10), one of the first to proffer the idea of Christians as *mercenarii* and *operarii*: see P. Garnsey, *Ideas of Slavery from Aristotle to Augustine* (Cambridge: Cambridge University Press, 1997), p. 201.

121 Aug. *Serm.* 198.12 (Mainz 62): F. Dolbeau, *Vingt-six sermons au peuple d'Afrique,* rev. and corr. ed. (Paris: Revue des études augustiniennes, 2009), pp. 375–6.

122 Dig. 34.1.15.1–2 (Scaevola): 'Testator concubinae mancipia rustica numero octo legavit et his cibaria praestari iussit in haec verba: "eisque mancipiis, quae supra legavi, cibarii nomine ab heredibus meis praestari volo, quae me vivo accipiebant." Quaesitum est, cum vivo testatore semper mancipia rustica tempore messium et arearum delegata fuerint et eo tempore cibaria ex ratione domini sui numquam acceperint excepto custode praedii, an heres eius quoque temporis, id est messi et arearum, et cibaria concubinae pro mancipiis rusticis praestare deberet.'

123 That seems to be the sense of the verb 'delego' here, i.e. 'to assign a task to': see, e.g., Caelius Rufus apud Cic. *Ad fam.* 8.1.1: 'Quod hunc laborem alteri delegavi …'; and the use of the ass in Apul. *Met.* 7.17: 'Delegor enim ligno monte devehundo.'

124 For some reason, however, the *custos praedii* among them (*excepto custode praedii*) was still fed from the master's account.

125 P. Lips. 97.III.6 (338 CE, Hermonthis).

126 P. Lips. 111 (place unknown; dated to the fourth century CE by handwriting) = M. Naldini, *Il cristianesimo in Egitto: Lettere private nei papiri dei secoli II–IV* (Fiesole: Nardini Editore, 1998), no. 57, pp. 245–8; line 9 should not be read ἀλλὰ σὺν Διδύμῳ ὅτι δούλους μισθώσῃ as in Mitteis, but rather ἀλλὰ εἶπον Διδύμῳ ὅτι δὸς τοὺς μισθο[ὺς] (as corrected by Wilcken).

127 See appendix 1; the reaping gangs in these contracts number 4, 6 [two cases], 9, and 10+ (two cases); see Schwartz, *Archives de Sarapion*, p. 111; at least one of the land-owners involved, one Eutychides, possessed 230 arourai (about the same in iugera) of land (Schwartz, *Archives de Sarapion*, p. 115), but the operational unit that the men were brought in to reap, the 'Peri Polin Katô' or 'Around the Lower City' fields, were about 120–130 arourai, which suggests that a consolidated working holding of about 100 iugera represented a threshold of sorts.

128 Rositani, *Harvest Texts*, p. 17.

129 Gregorius Turonesis, *Liber in gloria confessorum*, 1 (MGH SRM 1.2: 299; ed. Krusch): 'iam operariis in segite collocatis circiter septuaginta …'

130 As is suggested by Cato, *Agr.*, 6.4: 'Vicinis bonus esto … si te libenter vicinitas videbit, facilius tua vendes, opera facilius locabis, operarios facilius conduces.' Notably, even in cultivating good relations with neighbours, Cato is still speaking about letting out and hiring day labourers for money wages. For some of the factors involved in provoking recourse to additional migrant labour in a modern case, see Applen, 'Migratory Harvest Labor,' p. 70: 'By the end of the nineteenth century the migration of laborers into the midwestern wheat growing areas was essential for the successful harvesting of grain on all but the smaller and more diversified farms.' (He goes on to describe the main factors; in modern conditions, with machinery, the upper limit that could be coped with by one family was about 300 acres.) As Applen (pp. 71 f.) points out, the more a given region was devoted to a cereal monocul-

ture, the less extra labour was built into the system and the more outside help was needed at harvest time; the more crop diversification there is (probably more typical of Mediterranean conditions), the less the demand for extra labour. Family labour varied between one-third and two-thirds of the total at harvest, depending on these different regimes (pp. 72–3; see his charts 1–2, pp. 75–6, depending on the research of Lescohier, *Sources of Supply*).

131 For this calculation in modern conditions, see Lescohier, *Harvest Labor Problems*, pp. 205–6; *Conditions Affecting the Demand for Harvest Labor*, pp. 2–3, who made the initial calcuations and refined the formula for determining the amount of excess seasonal labour that would be required in any given region of the harvest. Most of the variables in the equation are not available to us for any one given cereal grain producing region in Africa of the Roman period; see Isern, *Bull Threshers and Bindlestiffs*, pp. 150–2.

132 For variations in a modern instance, see the study of 'threshing rings' or just such sharing arrangements made between neighbouring farms: Rikoon, *Threshing in the Midwest*, pp. 83–8, and all of chapter 5.

133 A. Jones, 'Harvest Customs,' p. 14, noting other cases, however, where manors awarded as much as three to four sheaves an acre. He goes on to discuss the various customary modes, usually using parts of the harvester's own body, by which the standard 'harvester's sheaf' was measured.

134 Hall, *Harvest Wobblies*, p. 25; for more evidence on the difference between normal wages and those for harvest labour, see Wyman, *Hoboes, Bindlestiffs, Fruit Tramps*, pp. 31, 50, with important caveats on how many days were lost in terms of wages while the men searched for the next job.

135 Everitt, 'Farm Labourers,' p. 435 (derived from figures offered by Bowden in the same volume), for England and Wales in the sixteenth and early seventeenth century, speaks of ranges from 4 pence to 1 shilling per diem, apart from food and drink. Malcolmson, *Life and Labour*, p. 37, states that wages for harvesting in eighteenth-century England varied between 10 pence and 1 shilling threepence per day, apart from additional allowances in beer and cider, and notes that wages for harvesting were normally at least 50 per cent higher than normal seasonal daywork for other agricultural tasks; Thompson, 'Bringing In the Sheaves,' p. 471: for Canada in the late nineteenth and early twentieth century, the rates rose to double those for normal manual agricultural labour, about one and a half times that for skilled construction workers.

136 Morgan, 'The Place of Harvesters,' pp. 38–40, with figures and graphs.

137 Rivière and Lecq, *Traité pratique*, p. 345.

138 And it has nothing to do with Africa being a 'modern' or a 'premodern' economy: see the case of England in the thirteenth and fourteenth centuries: Stone, *Decision-Making*, pp. 103–8, 203 and fig. 7.4.

139 See appendix 1, and Schwartz, *Archives de Sarapion*, p. 111; on the value of wheat prices, see Rathbone, 'Prices and Price Formation'; on day-labourers' wages in Egypt, see Rathbone, *Economic Rationalism*, pp. 155–66, and table 12; Drexhage, *Preise, Mieten/Pachten, Kosten und Löhne*, pp. 405, 412–25; and K. Harl, *Coinage in the Roman Economy, 300 BC to AD 700* (Baltimore: Johns Hopkins University Press, 1996), pp. 225, 276–82: running at about 3–7 obols per diem over the first century, then, from 125 CE onwards, at about 8–16 obols per diem.

140 For the wheat equivalents of day-workers' wages over the long term in Egypt, see Scheidel, 'In Search of Roman Economic Growth,' p. 58, fig. 5: 'Daily Wheat Wages for Unskilled Rural Labour in Egypt, 260 B.C.–A.D. 1050 (in litres of wheat)'; and Scheidel, 'Real Wages,' table 4. As he points out, the comparison should be valid, since, over the long term reflected in his data, day-rates remained amazingly stable, with a significant real rise in wages only in the aftermath of the Justinianic plague, much as one would expect, given the comparable rise in rural wage rates in western Europe in the later fourteenth century in the aftermath of the Black Death.

141 Fiensey, *Social History of Palestine*, pp. 86–7: the denarius per diem is based on Mt. 20:2; the higher rates for harvest labour are attested in the Tosephta and the Babylonian Talmud.

142 Aug. *Serm.* 56.10 (PL 38: 380): in discussing the famous passage in the gospel of Matthew concerning the hiring of day labourers, Augustine notes: 'It is absolutely necessary for us now, as workers in the vineyard: it's our food, not our wages. Whoever hires a worker for his vineyard, you see, owes him two things: food so that he doesn't faint and wages for him to enjoy …': 'Panis noster quotidianus est: inde vivunt non ventres, sed mentes. Necessarius est nobis etiam nunc operariis in vinea; cibus est, non merces. Operario enim duas res debet, qui illum conducit ad vineam, cibum, ne deficiat; et mercedem, unde gaudeat.' For Roman Egypt, see, e.g., P. Lond 131V, col.xii (Harmopolis, 78/79 CE; A.C. Johnson, *Roman Egypt*, p. 195)

143 Goubert, *The French Peasantry*, p. 100: even in early modern France, the drink was rarely as good as an acceptable table wine, but rather a vinegary *buvande*. For beer as the dominant drink in Egypt and in northwestern Europe, and wine in the central Mediterranean, see Nelson, *The Barbarian's Beverage*, passim, and esp. chap. 5, 'The Celts and the Great Beer Decline,' pp. 45–66, with reference to the production centres for beer that were concentrated along the Moselle (pp. 56–63). In the modern American and Canadian West, more puritanical by far, drinking of alcoholic beverages was off work time and off the job; on it, water was the mainstay: see Rikoon, *Threshing in the Midwest*, p. 133, and Isern, *Bull Threshers and Bindlestiffs*, p. 164.

144 E.g. Dig. 25.1.16 (Neratius): 'Et ante omnia quaecumque inpensae quaerendorum fructuum causa factae erunt, quamquam eaedem etiam colendi causa fiant ideoque non solum ad percipiendos fructus …' in a discussion of counterclaims in the case

of divorce; Dig. 36.1.46.1 (Marcellus) '… scilicet quia suo periculo faeneravit colendove fundo vel in cogendis fructibus insumpsit operam …'

145 Joseph. *AJ*, 5.325: … ὁπότε σιτίζοι τοὺς θερίζοντας.

146 *Bel and the Dragon*, l. 33–4 (LXX version): καὶ ἐγένετο τῇ ἡμέρᾳ τῇ ἕκτῃ καὶ ἦν Αμβακουμ ἔχων ἄρτους ἐντεθρυμμένους ἐν σκάφῃ ἐν ἑψήματι καὶ στάμνον οἴνου κεκερασμένου καὶ ἐπορεύετο εἰς τὸ πεδίον πρὸς τοὺς θεριστάς. It is notable that the non-LXX versions, probably reflecting Near Eastern mises-en-scène, mention the pot of gruel but not the jug of wine.

147 Gregorius Turonensis, *Liber in gloria confessorum*, 1 (MGH SRM 1.2: 298–9; ed. Krusch): 'Igitur dum in Arverno territorio commorarer, vir mihi fidelis retulit, et scio, quia vera narravit, quia evidenter cognovi gestum fuisse, quae dixit. Iubet, inquid, fieri, ex annonis aqua infusis atque decoctis, messoribus poculum praeparari. Hanc autem coctionem Orosius a coquendo ceriam (*vel* caeliam) vocari narravit. Quod eum praeparatum fuisset et in vase reconditum, atque ille apud urbem moras innecteret, ut mos servorum est, maximam partem exhaustam, exiguam dominicis usibus reliquerunt. Ille quoque fidus de iussione invitare messores iubet, ut, eo ab urbe redeunte, hos segitem decidere repperiret. Quo facto, iam operariis in segite collocatis circiter septuaginta, advenit dominus fundi, perscrutansque qualitatem quantitatemque potus, perparum repperit. Tunc pudore confusus et sibi factum ad verecundiam reputans, ne potum deficeret operariis, quod, ut ipse arbitrabatur, super quinque modiorum mensuram non erat, quid ageret, quo se verteret, in ambiguo dependebat. Tandem, inspirante Domino, conversus ad vasculum, nomina angelorum sanctorum, quae sacrae docent lectiones, super aditum eius devote invocat, orans, ut virtus eorum parvitatem hanc in abundantiam convertere dignaretur, ne operariis defeceret quod haurirent. Mirum dictu! Tota die ab hoc extractum nunquam defuit bibentibus, sed, usque quod nox finem operandi fecit, omnibus fuit in abundantia ministratum.' For a translation and some background, see Nelson, *Barbarian's Beverage*, pp. 91–2 (he uses the cleaned-up text in MGH, SRM 1.2: 748–9).

148 See Nelson, *Barbarian's Beverage*, pp. 76–7.

149 Goubert, *The French Peasantry*, p. 100, emphasizes this admixture of money wages, food, and drink, parts of the crop, and IOUs for the borrowing of other resources during the year; pay ran at between 5 and 10 sous a day.

150 Xen. *Hier.* 6.10; see chap. 5, p. 229.

151 See n. 147 above.

152 Jn. 4:35–8, at 36: ὁ θερίζων μισθὸν λαμβάνει καὶ συνάγει καρπὸν εἰς ζωὴν αἰώνιον, ἵνα ὁ σπείρων ὁμοῦ χαίρῃ καὶ ὁ θερίζων. Jerusalem Bible translation (with modifications).

153 We must remember, again, that this *misthos* or pay (or 'wages') could be either in coin or in kind (or a mixture of both); for the evidence from Egypt, see Rathbone,

Economic Rationalism, p. 148n1, where he notes the cases of *misthos* where it is paid in money and others where it is paid in kind.

154 De Ste Croix, *Class Struggle*, p. 186, who cites the only two cases from the classical period known to him. At Athens men offering their labour for hire congregated at the *Kolonos Agoraeios* (or 'Ergatikos' or 'Misthios Agora') 'apparently at the west end of the Athenian agora': see Fuks, Ἀκολονὸς μισθιὸς,' pp. 171–3; and the reference in the New Testament book of Matthew: *vide infra*. It is interesting to note that such hired workers were named colloquially after their place of employment, in this case Κολωνεταί: Fuks, Ἀκολονὸς μισθιὸς,' p. 173/303n41 citing Hypereides, fr. 8; Harpokration, s.v. Ἀκολωνεύτας' (cf. Suidas, s.v. and Pollux).

155 Mt. 20:1–16: The owner (οἰκοδεσπότη) came early in the morning (πρωΐ) to hire labourers for pay to work in his vineyard (μισθώσασθαι ἐργάτας εἰς τὸν ἀμπελῶνα αὐτοῦ). He discussed the contract (that is, he bargained orally) with them, including the rate of pay: one *denarius* per diem was settled on (Συμφωνήσας δὲ μετὰ τῶν ἐργατῶν ἐκ δηναρίου τὴν ἡμέραν ἀπέστειλεν αὐτοὺς εἰς τὸν ἀμπελῶνα αὐτοῦ.). After having sent these men off to work, the owner returned periodically to the marketplace (at the third, seventh, ninth hours, etc.) to find more men there loitering around (ἑστῶτας ἐν τῇ ἀγορᾷ ἀργούς) waiting to be picked up. He kept going there to the end of the day and found men milling around who had not yet been picked up for hire.

156 Ioh. Chrysos. *Hom. in Matth.* 61.3 (PG 57–8: 591–2)

157 Implied by Optatus, *Contra Parm.* 3.4.2 and 3.4.6 (SC 413: 38 and 40); cf. Shaw, 'Rural Markets,' pp. 70–1.

158 Rivière and Lecq, *Traité pratique*, 2, p. 345: 'Les ouvriers indigènes étaient payés à la journée; à l'époque des grands travaux, ils arrivaient par bandes nombreuses, souvent de fort loin; non logés, ils couchaient sur la dure, le plus souvent à la belle étoile. Dans certaines régions, les femmes indigènes travaillant aux champs dans les exploitations européennes …'

159 Servier, *Tradition et civilisation*, p. 305: 'Les ouvriers sont, le cas échéant, recrutés sur les marchés où ils se groupent par équipes de même origine. L'employeur s'entendra avec eux sur le salaire qui est en générale fixé tacitement par région chaque année, en fonction de la physiognomie du marché de la main-d'oeuvre, et qui varie tout au long du saison. Le salaire est fixé en argent, l'abri et la nourriture viennent s'y ajouter …'

160 Gregorius Turonensis, *Liber in gloria confessorum*, 1 (MGH SRM 1.2: 298–9); see n. 147 above.

161 Everitt, 'Farm Labourers,' pp. 433–4.

162 See Gaddis, '"The Monks Commit Many Crimes": Holy Violence Contested,' chap. 6 in *There Is No Crime*, pp. 208–50, who documents both the recruitment of monks as agricultural labourers and their parallel use as sectarian enforcers in the religious battles of late antiquity in the Eastern Empire.

163 Chitty, *The Desert a City*, p. 34, with reference to the sources.

164 *Vita Pachomii: vita graeca prima*, 106 = F. Halkin, ed., *Sancti Pachomii Vitae Graecae* (Brussels: Société des Bollandistes, 1932), p. 70; on the first Greek life, see L.T. Lefort, *Les vies coptes de saint Pachôme* (Louvain: Muséon, 1943), pp. xxiii ff.; and Chitty, *The Desert a City*, p. 24 and 40n35.

165 John Moschus, *Pratum spirituale*, 183 (PG 87.3: 3053–6); cf. Chitty, *The Desert a City*, p. 145.

166 E. Schulz-Flügel, ed., *Tyrannus Rufinus Historia Monachorum sive de Vita Sanctorum Patrum*, 18 (De Serapione) 1–3 (Berlin–New York: Walter de Gruyter, 1990), pp. 349–50: 'Sed et in regione Arsenoites Serapionem quendam presbyterum vidimus, multorum monasteriorum patrem, sub cuius cura plura et dispersa monasteria quasi decem milium habebantur monachorum, qui omnes ex laboribus propriis, quos praecipue messis tempore mercede manuum conquirebant, partem plurimam ad supradictam patrem conferentes in usus pauperum destinabant. Hoc autem moris est non solum ipsis, sed et omnibus paene Aegypti monachis, ut messis tempore elocent ad metendum operam suam. Atque ex ea mercede octogenos unusquisque modios frumenti plus minusve conquirit et horum partem plurimam pauperum usibus offerunt, unde non solum regionis ipsius indigentes alantur, sed et Alexandriam naves frumento onustae diriguntur vel in carcere conclusis vel reliquis peregrinis atque egentibus prorogandae.'

   For the Greek text, see A.-J. Festugière, ed., *Historia Monachorum in Aegypto* (Brussels: Société des Bollandistes, 1961), pp. 114–15. Whether or not the text was actually written by Rufinus himself, it surely reflects a situation in Egypt in the last decades of the fourth century.

167 For wheat prices see Jones, *Later Roman Empire*, 1, pp. 445–6; Rathbone, 'Prices and Price Formation,' fig. 2; and the run of twenty wheat prices found in papyrus documents from Egypt in the fifth and sixth centuries in Johnson and West, *Byzantine Egypt*, pp. 176–8, averaging about 12 artabas or about 40 modii to the solidus; this appears to a 'normal' figure: in the sixth century, under normal non-famine, non-shortage conditions, one solidus usually bought about 10 artabas of grain. Other price runs indicate wheat prices in Egypt ranging from 40 modii per solidus (early sixth century) to 45–60 modii per solidus (in the latter half of the century): see K.W. Harl, *Coinage in the Roman Economy, 300 B.C. to A.D. 700* (Baltimore: Johns Hopkins University Press, 1996), pp. 286–7.

168 See Duncan-Jones, *The Economy of the Roman Empire*, pp. 63–4, 242; and appendix 16: 'Wheat and Land Prices in Egypt,' pp. 365–6.

169 A collection of the basic sources can be found in Fink, *RMR*, nos. 68–72; for one of the better discussions of pay records, see Cotton and Geiger, 'Legionary Pay Record,' commenting on Latin Papyrus 722 from Masada in *Masada II*, pp. 35–56, who cite much of the relevant literature. From the other pay receipts, including P. Gen. Lat. 1 (c. 80 CE) from Egypt, it is clear that although footsoldiers were receiving

about 100 denarii per stipendium (three stipendia per year), the deductions from pay left them with much less in cash. In P. Gen. Lat. 1, the soldiers are left with only about a quarter of their pay in cash (i.e., about 25 denarii per stipendium or about 75 denarii [= 300 HS] per annum). The Masada pay deductions, if made from a standard legionary of the time, would suggest something more like half of his pay remained in cash, or about 600 HS per annum. Of course, a legionary soldier was receiving a gross per diem pay that was superior to that of a reaper, but such comparisons usually do not take into consideration the mandatory deductions from the soldier's pay: N. Lewis, 'The Prices of Goods and Services,' appendix in *Life in Egypt under Roman Rule* (Oxford, 1983), pp. 208–9.

170 Thompson, 'Bringing In the Sheaves,' pp. 482–6, and table III, p. 482.

171 Roberts, 'Sickles and Scythes Revisited,' citing the study by Gregory Clark on farm wages and living standards in England at the time of the Industrial Revolution.

172 Charles-Picard, *Civitas Mactaritana*; M'charek, 'Documentation épigraphique,' plus site map.

173 Arch, *Joseph Arch*, pp. 39–41; cf. Morgan, *Harvesters and Harvesting*, p. 48, who quotes part of the passage.

174 Aug. *Contra ep. Parm.* 1.11.18 (CSEL 51: 40): 'Unde merito constitutionibus iustis graviora patiuntur circumcellionum mancipes …'

175 Aug. *Op. monach.* 15 (PL 40: 561): '… corporis labore pecuniae, sicut sunt vel negotiatores, vel procuratores, vel conductores: cura enim praesunt, non manibus operantur, ideoque …'

176 See Aug. *Serm.* 308A (MiAg 1: 48): 'Missus est enim filius ad malos illos colonos, ad malos conductores nolentes reddere mercedem, et lapidantes servos missos ad se …'

177 Xen. *Oec.* 18.1: Where, for example, Socrates as the interlocutor assumes in discussion with the young landowner, Ischomachos, that he himself will be part of the reaping process, asking whether or not Ischomachos usually stands with his back to the wind when he cuts the grain.

178 Mt. 9:37–8: Then he said to his students: 'The crop is heavy, but workers are scarce. You must therefore beg the owner to send workers to harvest his crop.' τότε λέγει τοῖς μαθηταῖς αὐτοῦ, Ὁ μὲν θερισμὸς πολύς, οἱ δὲ ἐργάται ὀλίγοι· δεήθητε οὖν τοῦ κυρίου τοῦ θερισμοῦ ὅπως ἐκβάλῃ ἐργάτας εἰς τὸν θερισμὸν αὐτοῦ.

179 Musonius Rufus, *Dissertationum reliquiae*, 11.13–15: πῶς μὲν γὰρ οὐ καλὸν τὸ φυτεύειν; πῶς δὲ τὸ ἀροῦν; πῶς δὲ τὸ ἀμπελουργεῖν; τὸ δὲ σπείρειν, τὸ δὲ θερίζειν, τὸ δὲ ἀλοᾶν, οὐ πάντ' ἐλευθέρια ταῦτα καὶ ἀνδράσιν ἀγαθοῖς πρέποντα; see Heitland, *Agricola*, pp. 278–80.

180 Although even here there are sufficient warnings of what we do and do not see. The whole institution of the *Augustales*, for example, one of the critical public self-representational aspects of elite freedmen in the western empire, would be almost wholly unknown, apart from the single literary reference in Petronius's *Satyrica*, were it not for the epigraphical texts that they produced.

3. Sickle and Scythe/Man and Machine

1 J. Spence, *The Memory Palace of Matteo Ricci* (New York: Viking, 1984), p. 162.
2 In 1831, the year of McCormick's invention of his mechanical reaper, at least 90 per cent of the population of the United States were directly involved in agricultural production; today the figure is less than 2 per cent.
3 This is the general argument of 'Why Not Then?,' chap. 2 in Schiavone, *The End of the Past*, pp. 16–32; the quotation is from p. 27 (slightly modified in sequence).
4 Steward, 'Early Machines,' chap. 2 in *The Reaper*, pp. 16–55, and Ardrey, 'The Reaper,' chap. 6 in *American Agricultural Implements*, esp. pp. 40–5, outline some of these early developments. For the human story behind these inventions retold in a rather engaging manner, see Canine, 'Romance of the Reaper,' chap. 2 in *Dream Reaper*, pp. 19–52.
5 For an exemplary handbook treatment, see Schneider, *Antike Technikgeschichte*, pp. 60–2.
6 Finley, 'Technical Innovation,' pp. 30/177, quoted *inter alios* by White, 'Gallo-Roman Harvesting Machines,' p. 634 (down to the words 'in other branches of agriculture'), and by Kolendo, 'Pourquoi la moissonneuse antique' and 'La mietitura,' pp. 165–6; and Andrea Carandini in his preface to Kolendo, *Agricoltura nell'Italia romana*, pp. xliii–xliv, embedded in what is, in effect, a wider attack on Finley's ideas. For the reaper, Finley refers to the studies of Kolendo, 'Techniques rurales,' and Renard, *Technique et agriculture*. For the Australian story, he refers to E.A. Thompson, *A Roman Reformer and Inventor* (Oxford: Clarendon Press, 1952 [reprint New York: Arno, 1979)], pp. 80–1.
7 Greene, 'Perspectives' and especially 'Technology and Innovation' is good and catches most of the objections; cf. Raepsaet, 'The Development,' p. 63; on milling technology, see Amouretti and Comet, 'La meunerie,' who substantially revise the easy assumptions.
8 Lefebvre des Noëttes, *L'attelage*; see Carandini, 'Le Commandant Lefebvre des Noëttes,' in his preface to Kolendo, *L'Agricoltura nell'Italia Romana*, pp. xii–xiv.
9 Beginning with Burford, 'Heavy Transport,' who showed that oxen, not horses or mules, provided the normal heavy draft power in Mediterranean antiquity; but the main riposte is now found, more thoroughly, in the work of Raepsaet, 'The Development,' pp. 55–7, and Rommelaere and Raepsaet, 'Les techniques,' who concentrate on the problems of harnessing. Water mills, of course, are another such case: Sigaut, 'L'évolution,' p. 8.
10 Schiavone, *The End of the Past*, pp. 135–6, for one of the more passionate and complex of these statements.
11 Heitland, *Agricola*, p. 398: all of this was published in 1920, with no knowledge of the not insignificant number of monuments that attested the actual use of the

instrument. The rest of the passage must be read to sense the pervasive pessimism engendered by images of slavery and serfdom as a general explanation of the supposed growing technological backwardness of the empire.

12 Finley, 'Technical Innovation,' pp. 192–3, where his position on the effects of the pervasive presence of slaves and other forms of dependent labour on technological innovation is rather complex. On the one hand, he seems to argue for a general impedance to incentives created by the common availability of slave labour; on the other hand, slavery did not necessarily stop innovation; in fact, in some spheres (he singles out mining and farm machinery on latifundia), he argues that slavery was part of the more intensified economic forces that provoked development.

13 Lloyd, *Ambitions of Curiosity*, pp. 85–6, offers some other cautions based on the comparison with the regimes in China contemporary with the Roman empire.

14 See Greeno, *Obed Hussey*; Steward, 'Obed Hussey,' chap. 3 in *The Reaper*, pp. 56–81; and Swift, *Who Invented the Reaper?* for some of the early controversy; cf. Gladwell, 'In the Air,' who provides other similar examples. The mechanical reaper is only one example among many (the steam engine, the electric telegraph, and the railway are others) where it is almost impossible to state categorically who was the inventor, given the production of similar advances on that technological advance at more or less the same time: see Weightman, *Industrial Revolutionaries*, pp. 48 f. (the steam engine), and pp. 197 f. (the electric telegraph), for some cases among many.

15 For some of this story, see Steward, *The Reaper*, chaps. 5–7; Stabler, *A Brief Narrative*, p. 6, who mentions a number of other possible competitors; and, again, Gladwell, 'In the Air,' who notes other close-run cases, including Alexander Graham Bell and Elisha Gray and the invention of the telephone, that likewise led to proceedings before the courts and lawsuits. As for the invention of the mechanical reaper, the matter was disputed even within the McCormick family itself: see Weightman, *Industrial Revolutionaries*, p. 226.

16 Stabler, *A Brief Narrative*, p. 3, and throughout the whole work.

17 John Ridley, born in Durham, England, in 1806, came from a milling family; he was always interested in innovation. At age eighteen, he became a Wesleyan preacher. His great financial successes in South Australia, in fact, enabled him to return to England in 1853 to engage in his true interests in missionary and evangelical work. A true Weberian exemplum.

18 McCormick, *Century of the Reaper*, pp. 1–2; the story is told by his grandson, Cyrus Hall McCormick III, the sucessor as head of International Harvester Company.

19 McCormick, *Century of the Reaper*, p. 11. Colonel William Massie, it might be noted, was a large-scale slave owner who owned four plantations in the Virginia Piedmont. He provided financial support to Cyrus Hall McCormick for the production of his mechanical reaper. The McDowell family was one of the most eminent in Virginia. Colonel James McDowell was father of his namesake who was later governor of

Virginia in 1843. He, too, was one of the first of the early big financial backers of McCormick.

20 For background to the Wyeth painting, see Allen and Allen, *N.C. Wyeth*, p. 294, s.v. '1931': the picture was painted for the International Harvester corporation; it was used to celebrate the historical image of the company in the *Saturday Evening Post*, *Maclean's*, and similar mass-circulation glossy magazines of the time.

21 See Weightman, *Industrial Revolutionaries*, pp. 225–6.

22 Moneyed interests in Savannah, Georgia, financed the building of the first steamship to cross the Atlantic, named, appropriately, the *Savannah*. It crossed the ocean in November 1819. Admittedly only with the partial aid of a steam engine, but the basic point about innovation stands. And the same slave South produced the first iron-clad battleship, and so on.

23 Weightman, *Industrial Revolutionaries*, pp. 101–3: the first extensive use of the steamboat and the economy of the Mississippi River; see pp. 105–10, on the invention of the cotton 'gin by Eli Whitney – on a plantation just upriver from Savannah: 'Paradoxically, the labour-saving device Whitney had invented vastly increased the demand for slave labour as the acreage under cotton spread over thousands of square miles.'

24 For what little is known of his background, see Greeno, *Obed Hussey*, pp. 5–11.

25 Grantham's work is one of the best in delimiting these factors, especially 'Divisions of Labour' and 'La faucille et la faux,' which will be referred to in detail in what follows.

26 For example, P. Jones, 'Italy,' p. 376, notes that the harvesting of cereal grains in most regions of Italy into the 'middle ages' continued to be done with the sickle.

27 Dig. 33.7.8.pr (Ulpian), in a standard list for legal purposes: 'Cogendi, quemadmodum torcularia corbes falcesque messoriae falces fenariae quali vindemiatorii exceptoriique'; repeated in a practical guide for late antiquity that lists the standard *instrumenta agrestium*: Palladius, *Op. agr.* 42: 'falces … item messorias vel fenarias …' Whether or not owners were expected to provide this 'standard equipment' for farms on lease is uncertain, since in the main Digest text (Dig. 19.2.19.2) Ulpian uses a letter of Neratius Priscus as his main example, but the letter deals only with the specific case of fitting out a *fundus* dedicated to olive production: see Frier, 'Law, Technology, and Social Change,' pp. 204–12.

28 For the continuity of the hand-held sickle as the main instrument for the harvesting of cereal grains throughout Graeco-Roman antiquity, see White, *Agricultural Implements*, on the *falx, falces*: pp. 72–85 on the *falx messoria* or the main reaping sickle for cereal grains, as well as on the different types and regional variations. For comment on the later Byzantine illustrations, see Kaplan, *Les hommes et la terre*, pp. 52–3, and Bryer, 'Byzantine Agricultural Implements,' figs. 7, 10, 11, 13 and 14, and pp. 75–8.

29 For example, Morgan, 'The Place of Harvesters,' p. 29, notes that the methods and tools for reaping in England had changed very little between 1750 and 1850; and the

four basic tools – the sickle, the reaping hook, the fagging hook, and the scythe – as he notes, were all hand-held tools.

30 Morgan, 'The Place of Harvesters,' pp. 61 ff. The mechanical reaper first came into general use from the 1870s but was 'by no means universal even at the turn of the century'; see Quick and Buchele, *The Grain Harvesters*, chaps. 4–7 for the history of this transition in terms of technical developments in the machinery.

31 See Sigaut, 'L'évolution,' pp. 9–10, with references; the division is strongly assumed by all male writers: e.g., Lib. *Or.* 53.19: neither free nor slave women could leave the grain mills in order to participate in communal festivals, so critical were they to the milling process.

32 Aug. *Ep.* 185.15 (CSEL 57: 14–15).

33 The scenes on sarcophagi, for example, Kranz, *Jahreszeiten-Sarkophage*, Kat. 585 and tafel 126, nos. 2 and 3 (Tipasa); Kat. 590, Taf. 124, nos. 1, 2, and 4 (Tunis); and Kat. 5. These might well be stereotypes, but they are confirmed by other iconographic evidence such as on the 'Boglio stele' (see fig. 1.13).

34 Varro, *RR*, 1.49.1–2: 'Primum de pratis summissis herba, cum crescere desiit et aestu arescit, subsecari falcibus debet et, quaad perarescat, furcillis versari; cum peraruit, de his manipulos fieri ac vehi ad villam; tum de pratis stipulam rastellis eradi atque addere faenisiciae cumulum. Quo facto, sicilienda prata, id est falcibus consectanda quae faenisices praeterierunt ac quasi herba tuberosum reliquerunt campum.'

35 Varro, *RR*, 1.50.1 and 3: 'Messis proprio nomine dicitur in iis quae metimur, maxime in frumento, et ab eo esse vocabulo declinata …'

36 Columella, *RR*, 2.20.

37 Varro, *RR*, 1.50.1: 'Frumenti tria genera sunt messionis, unum, ut in Umbria, ubi falce secundum terram succidunt stramentum et manipulum, ut quemque subsicuerunt, ponunt in terra. Ubi eos fecerunt multos, iterum eos percensent ac de singulis secant inter spicas et stramentum. Spicas coiciunt in corbem atque in aream mittunt, stramenta relincunt in segete, unde tollantur in acervum.' See Gow, *Theocritus*, 2, p. 205 (on Theoc. *Id.* 10.46: *korthmos*): 'Corn was cut near the ground only when the straw was short; otherwise in the middle of the stem, in order to save trouble both to the reaper working with a sickle and to the threshers [citing Xen. *Oec.* 18.2; cf. Hes. *W&D.* 480, on which see more, below]. Consequently when gathered it formed heaps rather than the sheaves and stooks familiar to us.'

38 Varro, *RR*, 1.50.2: 'Altero modo metunt ut in Piceno, ubi ligneum habent incurvum bacillum, in quo sit extremo serrula ferrea. Haec, cum comprendit fascem spicarum, desecat et stramenta stantia in segeti relinquit, ut postea subsecentur.'

39 See the account books from Egypt, e.g., P. Lond 131V, col. xxiii.25; and col. xxvi.1 (Harmopolis, 79/79 CE; A.C. Johnson, *Roman Egypt*, pp. 203 and 205): the pay for the reapers of the straw was only 2 obols per diem, quite a bit below the normal pay rates for the reapers of cereal grains.

40 Varro, *RR*, 1.50.2–3: 'Tertio modo metitur, ut sub urbe Roma et locis plerisque, ut stramentum medium subsicent, quod manu sinistra summum prendunt; a quo medio messem dictam puto. Infra manum stramentum quod terra haeret, postea subsecatur; contra quod cum spica stramentum haeret, corbibus in aream defertur.' For an illustration of the process, see, e.g., Brandt, *Schaffende Arbeit: Altertum*, p. 131, fig. 169 (a funerary relief from Mainz).

41 In Greek manuals for landowners, for example, high cutting seems to have had a technical term, the verb *akrotomeo -ein* (ἀκροτομέω, -ειν), as did mid-cutting, where the verb *mesotomeo –ein* (μεσοτομέω –ειν) was used, as opposed to low cutting, which was simply described as 'cutting close to the ground' (παρὰ γῆν τέμνειν): see, for example, the discussion between Socrates and Ischomachus on reaping in Xen. *Oec.* 18.2; cf. Pomeroy, *Xenophon Oeconomicus*, p. 331.

42 Ovid, *Met.* 14. 642–3: 'O quotiens habitu duri messoris aristas / corbe tulit verique fuit messoris imago.'

43 Cic. *Pro Sest.* 38.82, where Quintus Numerius's head was covered with such a basket: 'messoria se corbe contexit.' It is often misleadingly translated as a reaper's basket; but it was technically only a harvester's basket since reapers themselves did not (normally) do the collecting and carrying. So, correctly, R.A. Kaster, *Cicero, Speech on Behalf of Publius Sestius* (Oxford: Clarendon Press, 2006), p. 77. For further reference to these baskets, in addition to the *Pro Sestio* passage, see Kolendo, *L'Agricoltura nell'Italia Romana*, p. 156n9, citing Cato, *Agr.* 136; Varro, *LL*, 5.139; Livy, 2.5.3., 22.10.10; Ovid, *Met.* 14.644; Prop. 4.2.28 and Dig. 33.7.8; and Baldassare, 'Tomba della Mietitura,' p. 102; cf. chap. 1 n. 50.

44 Diod. Sic. 5.21.5 and Strabo 4.5.5 provide descriptions for the practice from Roman Britain.

45 See the illustrations in *Roman Provincial Coinage Online*, nos. 13958, 14838, and 16142 (141–2 CE); for an account book, see P. Lond. 141V, col. xxiii.25 (Harmopolis, 78/79 CE; A.C. Johnson, *Roman Egypt*, p. 203).

46 White, *Agricultural Implements*, pp. 114–15.

47 Schnebel, *Die Landwirtschaft*, pp. 169–70; Bagnall, *Egypt in Late Antiquity*, pp. 38–40, citing some of the specific studies; see also C. Adams, *Land Transport in Roman Egypt*, pp. 52–8, 71–2, 160–1; 172–80: donkeys were the common mode; and see also Reekmans, *A Sixth-Century Account of Hay*, pp. 28–30, who calculates the normal transport capacity of a donkey at 200 bundles (*angkalai*) of reaped hay.

48 Pliny, *NH*, 18.67.260–1: 'Quaedam partes Italiae post messem secant. Fuit hoc quoque maioris inpendii apud priores, Creticis tantum transmarinisque cotibus notis nec nisi oleo aciem falcis excitantibus; igitur cornu propter oleam ad crus ligato fenisex incedebat. Italia aquarias cotes dedit limae vice imperantes ferro, set aqua protinus virentes.'

49 Pliny, *NH*, 18.67.259: '... praeterea quotiens secta sint siciliri, hoc est quae feniseces praeterierunt secari ...'

50 Pliny, *NH*, 18.67.262: 'Iustum est una opera in die iugerum desecari, alligarique manipulos CC [Rackham: MCC] quaterna pondo'; see chap. 1, pp. 13–14 and n. 48.

51 M. van der Veen, A. Grant, and G. Barker, 'Romano-Libyan Agriculture: Crops and Animals,' chap. 8 in Barker et al., *Farming the Desert*, 1, pp. 227–63, at pp. 243–5, 254–6.

52 The carrying capacity of mules, donkeys, and asses is specified in Egyptian documents as being 4 *gomoi* (bundles) or 200 *angkalai* (sheaves), which works out to about 80 kg. See Reekmans, *A Sixth-Century Account of Hay*, pp. 10 and 28–30.

53 The bibliography is rather large. Basic treatments can be found in White, 'Gallo-Roman Harvesting Machines' and 'Reaping Machines,' chap. 10 in *Agricultural Implements*, pp. 157–73; and Kolendo, 'La mietitura,' pp. 158–62, who cite most of the earlier studies; see appendix 3 for a list of the five relief sculptures, their location and content.

54 The text used here is fundamentally that of Henri Le Bonniec for the Budé series. For a discussion of some of the problems with the text, see Poelaert, Puissant, and Vander Linden, 'Le témoignage,' pp. 5–6. They note that the mss reading of *infestis* does not make much sense and was corrected by Urlichs to *insertis* (the error is palaeographically understandable); they also note that *direptae* is found in the best ms (F²), but *dereptae* is found in the rest and seems preferable. I have followed these readings.

55 On Palladius's chronology and background, see Frézouls, 'La vie rurale,' pp. 193–4, and Morgenstern, 'Die Auswertung,' pp. 180: a *vir illustris* with knowledge of lands in northern Italy, Spain, and Sardinia, but most of whose personal connections place him in Gaul, in the years circa 400–60 CE..

56 This is how I read the text. However, the weight of the *praeter* in the phrase *praeter hominum labores*, and the relationship of these words to the words *unius bovis opera* that follow, is a little unclear. For a different interpretation, see Clouner, Grès, and Lambeau, 'Nouvelles lectures,' p. 13. In addition, they understand the *spatium* to refer literally to space, whereas I understand Palladius to mean something like *spatium (temporis)*, such that the *spatium totius messis absumit* at the beginning of the text is equivalent to the *brevi horarum spatio tota messis inpletur* at its end.

57 The Latin text I have used is basically the Teubner edition by Rodgers, with minor modifications. For additional comment, see Clouner, Grès, and Lambeau, 'Nouvelles lectures,' pp. 9–10; Renard, *Technique et agriculture*, pp. 32–3; and Lebel, 'Moisson et fenaison en Gaul,' p. 72, who prefer the existing reading *ac rari* over the suggested *aptati*, seeing no need for emendation – as both say (and I accept their argument) the author clearly intended to say that the teeth on the machine were somehow separated or spaced apart. Instead of *rari*, Thaer, accepted by Blümner, suggested the reading *a<pt>a<t>i* . But the emendation seems strained and unnecessary. Note that Ovid uses precisely the same adjective, *rarus*, to describe the teeth of the reaping comb or *pecten* that is surely a strict analogue to the teeth mounted on the edge of the *vallus*: see p. 139 below.

58 Syme, 'Pliny the Procurator,' pp. 746–8. Between 47 and 58 CE, Pliny served his equestrian *tres militiae* in the Germanies. One of these stints, probably in 47, found him in Germania Inferior, as shown, possibly, by a phalera from Xanten (Castris Veteribus) inscribed *Plinio praef(ecto) eq(uitum)* (CIL 13.10026, no. 22), see PIR² P 493. If his *tres militiae* were served in posts along the Rhine, it is possible that the machine would have attracted his curiosity at this earlier date. More likely, I think, is a time during his procuratorship of Belgica, which Syme admits as possible (offering the dates of 74–6), albeit with little enthusiasm. In the list of items in support of his personal knowledge of Belgica (p. 753), our notice about the mechanical harvester is missing in Syme's accounting. It should be added.

59 Pliny, *NH*, 18.183: '… cum hieme praegelida captae segetes essent, reserverunt etiam campos mense martio uberrimasque messes habuerunt'; see Mertens, 'Le *vallus*,' p. 218n5.

60 As has been noted, Palladius reflects a different type of agriculture from that outlined by the classical agronomists: Morgenstern, 'Die Auswertung,' pp. 181 and 186. He has no discussions of *vilici* managers and slave *ergastula*; and he shows a real interest, unlike them, in devices like the reaping machine and the water mill (*Op. agr.* 1.41).

61 See Varro, *LL*, 5.140, for this earlier agricultural usage: 'Vehiculum in quo faba aliudve quid vehitur, quod ex viminibus vietur aut eo vehitur. Brevius vehiculum dictum est aliis vel "arcera," quae etiam in duodecim tabulis appellatur; quod ex tabulis vehiculum erat factum, ut arca, arcera dictum. Plaustrum ab eo quod non ut in his quae supra dixi, sed ex omni parte palam est, quae in eo vehuntur, quod perlucet, ut lapides, asseres, lignum.'

62 So, correctly, Poelaert, Puissant, and Vander Linden, 'Le témoignage,' p. 6, with other reasons added. But the meaning attributed by most modern scholars is still accepted by Glare, *OLD*, 2009; as White, 'Gallo-Roman Harvesting Machines,' p. 636, noted, the *vallus* in Pliny refers to the basket and the whole machine took its name from this container.

63 Verg. *Georg.* 1.166, cf. Billiard, *L'agriculture dans l'antiquité*, p. 139.

64 Again, in agreement with Poelaert, Puissant, and Vander Linden, 'Le témoignage,' p. 6. They rightly reject connections that have been proposed with supposed Celtic words.

65 See appendix 3.1 for a basic description and bibliography.

66 The dating is a little speculative; some would date it as early as the early third century: see Ardhuin, ed., *La moissonneuse gauloise*, p. 7.

67 See appendix 3.2 for a basic description and bibliography.

68 Anon. 'Gallic Harvester,' *Time* (30 June 1958), p. 47; Anon. 'Oldest Mechanical Reaper,' *Life* 45.6 (11 August 1958), p. 46.

69 Fouss, 'Le *vallus*,' p. 125 and fig. 3; part of the reason for the interest was that Fouss, director of the Musée Gaumais, had acquired a substantial sum from the government of

Belgium, in connection with the World Fair held at Brussels in 1958, to transform the site at Montauban-Buzenol into a museum. The fortuitous discovery made on 16 May of the same year nicely converged with these other projects.

70 Mertens, 'Sculptures romaines de Buzenol,', pp. 17–19, and fig. 2, p. 20; and plan A for a general plan of the site; see also his first detailed report and mapping of the site in Mertens 'Le refuge antique'; and E.P. Fouss, 'Images de Montauban,' *Le pays Gaumais* 3 (1942), pp. 116–23, for earlier studies.

71 For the arrangement of the blocks, see Mertens, 'Le *vallus*,' plans B and C; for reportage, see Renard, 'Technique et agriculture,' p. 77.

72 Mertens, 'Sculptures romaines de Buzenol,' pl. xii.

73 Mertens, 'Sculptures romaines de Buzenol,' p. 43 provides reference to well-known examples from Neumagen, Arlon, and Igel; CIL 13.7128 (Mainz) confirms the funerary symbolism; see Hatt, *La tombe gallo-romaine*, pp. 73, 190–1.

74 Mertens, 'Sculptures romaines de Buzenol,' p. 34, my translation.

75 See Drinkwater, 'Die Secundinier von Igel' and 'The Gallo-Roman Woollen Industry'; Marcone, 'Tra archeologia e storia economica,' and Mehl, 'Wirtschaft, Gesellschaft, Totenglauben,' who cite the earlier relevant bibliography on the monument.

76 See appendix 3.2 for the basic description and bibliography.

77 Rostovtzeff, *SEHRE*, 1st ed. (1926), pl. xxix, fig. 4; cf. 2nd ed. (1957), pl. xxxvii, fig. 4, and the author's comments: 'A man and two animals (oxen?) in a cornfield. The operation represented is probably reaping by means of a machine drawn by a team of oxen.' It took the further insight of Alfred Bertrang, director of the Museum of Luxembourg at Arlon, to connect the object in his museum and Rostovtzeff's insight with the newly discovered relief at Buzenol.

78 For example, White consistently argued – see 'Gallo-Roman Harvesting Machines,' pp. 641–3 and *Agricultural Implements*, pp. 165–6 – that the machines described by Palladius and Pliny are different machines, as are some of the depictions on the reliefs. Without going into his arguments in detail here, I shall dissent. In my view, the differences are not so great as to constitute anything more than modest local variations of a common type.

79 See appendix 3.4 for the basic description and bibliography.

80 That this was one good way of providing the motor power for the machine is shown by the fact that one of the earliest praticable reaping machines, invented by the Reverend Patrick Bell of Scotland in the late 1820s, was powered in exactly this fashion; see Steward, *The Reaper*, pp. 32–43, and fig. p. 38. In explaining the mode of traction, Bell explained that the horses drove his device from the rear so that they wouldn't trample the grain before it could be reaped. Surely the same logic applied to the Roman-period machine.

81 As Charles Picard, 'La "Porte de Mars" à Reims,' p. 60, notes, there is no reason for associating it with the god Mars, nor is it a triumphal arch; Legros, 'Ordre romain,'

p. 44, provides useful background; for the basic bibliography, see appendix 3.5; it is important to note the analysis in Stern, *Calendrier de 354*, pp. 207–10.

82 On the dating of the Reims arch, see appendix 3.5.

83 And the drawing of Auguste Caristie, 'Description de la voûte du grand arc du monument de Reims' – manuscript in the Bibliothèque municipale de Reims, 20 pages, 1 plan, 1 wash drawing.

84 In the early 1960s, Stern, 'Le cycle des mois,' p. 1442, had new detailed photographs made of the reliefs: 'Il résulte d'une comparaison de ces photographies avec la gravure de Bence que celle-ci est fidèle pour l'essentiel et même pour la plupart des détails, mais que le relief est actuellement dans un état de détérioration beaucoup plus avancé qu'il y a 150 ans.'

85 Importantly, Stern, 'Le cycle des mois,' p. 1443n2, could make out the detail of the whetstone on his close inspection of the photographs (see above) that he had taken of the monument: 'Le geste n'est pas clair sur la lithographie, mais je crois discerner sur la photographie un aiguisoir dans la main droit de l'homme.'

86 Legros, 'Ordre romain,' pl. xii, top right.

87 See Stern, 'Le cycle des mois,' p. 1445, who charts several Carolingian sources.

88 Calendars and calendrical mosaics and reliefs in the Mediterranean tradition usually feature June for mowing and July for reaping: Webster, *Labors of the Months*, pl. XV.31 (Rome), XVI.32 (Florence: as early as May–June), XXII.36 (Beneventum), XXIV.38 (Cremona), XXXI.50 (Piacenza), whereas the fairly consistent record of the western European illustrated medieval manuscripts is to picture July as the month of mowing and August as the month of the reaping of cereal grains: see, e.g., Webster, *Labors of the Months*, pl. X.24 (Vienna), XI.25 (Rome: Martyology of Wandelbert), XVIII.33b (London), LVIII.92 (Cambridge), LIX.93 (Cambridge), LX.94 (Glasgow), LXI.95 (Leiden), LXII.96 (London).

89 See Gladwell, 'In the Air,' for an introduction to the problem, referring to important early works by Dorothy Swaine Thomas and William F. Ogburn; the latter in his chapter on 'Inventions, Mental Ability and Culture,' chap. II.5 in *Social Change with Respect to Culture and Original Nature* (New York: Viking Press, 1928), pp. 80–90, early on saw the problem. He appended to this chapter 'A List of Some Inventions and Discoveries Made Independently by Two or More Persons' (pp. 90–102) – some 148 such cases, of which no. 139 is 'Reapers. By Hussey (1833) and McCormick (1834).' Merton, 'Singletons and Multiples,' studied the same phenomenon, and offered a similar list.

90 Roberts, 'Sickles and Scythes Revisited,' p. 79, notes 'the neighbouring parish of Eckington, where twenty-five out of thirty-one sickle manufacturers in the 1787 Sheffield Directory were living.'

91 Roberts, 'Sickles and Scythes Revisited,' p. 79.

92 The economic effect is usually argued to be a result of path dependence.

93 Cic. *Cat.* 1.4.8: 'Dico te priore nocte venisse inter falcarios'; cf. *Sull.* 18.52: '… cum inter falcarios ad M. Laecam nocte ea quae consecuta est …'

94 Sigaut, 'Les spécificités,' p. 29.

95 Sigaut, 'Les spécificités,' pp. 29–30, stating that his hypothesis is part of a larger project of matching crops with technologies of harvesting; it is difficult, however, to understand his claim that the disappearance of the machine and its location in a specific region of Gaul 'are certainly not reducible to an economic explanation.'

96 Raepsaet, 'Les prémices de la mécanisation agricole,' p. 912.

97 For what follows, the classic works by Wightman, *Roman Trier* and *Gallia Belgica*, and Heinen, 'Grundzüge' and *2000 Jahre Trier, 1: Trier und der Trevererland*, remain fundamental.

98 Wightman, *Gallia Belgica*, p. 121, with a guess at a rise in population from about 12–15 persons per km² to perhaps 20 per km² (a level not attained again until the eighteenth century).

99 On this and what that follows, see Raepsaet, 'Les prémices de la mécanisation agricole,' pp. 918–19 ff.

100 Pliny, *NH*, 18.172: 'Latior haec quarto generi et acutior in mucronem fastigata eodemque gladio scindens solum et acie laterum radices herbarum secans. Non pridem inventum in Raetia Galliae ut duas addiderent tali rotulas, quod genus vocant plauromati. Cuspis effigiem palae habet.' The term 'enigmatic' is rightly used by Wightman, *Gallia Belgica*, p. 123, of Pliny's description.

101 Deroy, 'La racine étrusque,' Martin, *Recherches sur les agronomes*, pp. 76–7, and Kolendo, 'Origine et diffusion,' among others for antiquity; for an overview of the newer views, see Comet, 'Technology and Agricultural Expansion,' pp. 21–4; Raepsaet, 'The Development of Farming Implements,' pp. 43–5; and Sigaut, 'L'évolution,' pp. 12–16.

102 Pliny, *NH*, 18.173: 'Serunt ita non nisi culta terra et fere nova. Latitudo vomeris caespites versat. Semen protinus iniciunt cratesque dentatas supertrahunt. Nec sarienda sunt hoc modo sata, sed protelis binis ternisque sic arant. Uno boum iugo censeri anno facilis soli quadragena iugera, difficilis tricena iustum est.'

103 See the typical study of Kolendo, 'Origine et diffusion,' who refers to the long line of works, and eminent researchers, including Marc Bloch and Georges Duby, going back to the fundamental study of the whole phenomenon in Haudricourt and Delamare, *L'homme et la charrue*, esp. pp. 108–18. Ferdière, 'La charrue gauloise,' has denounced the whole as a myth.

104 P. Jones, 'Italy,' pp. 373–4; disputed by the studies in Comba and Panero, *Il seme, l'aratro, la messe*, who also postulate a north Italian origin for the wheeled plough, although on evidence that seems to me to be too weak to sustain the claim.

105 White, 'Ploughs,' chap. 7 in *Agricultural Implements*, pp. 123–44; Spurr, 'Plough Types,' in chap. 2 in *Arable Cultivation*, pp. 27–35, and fig. 1, p. 31; for north Africa:

Camps, 'L'araire en Afrique du Nord,' chap. I.B.ii in *Massinissa*, pp. 81–6; still of considerable use, despite its age, on the ard plough is Gow, 'The Ancient Plough.'

106 See Marbach, *Les instruments aratoires des Gaules et Germanie Superieure*, but especially, *Recherches sur les instruments aratoires*, pp. 74 f. and his general conclusions at pp. 110–14; it seems to me that Marbach's work clearly refutes Ferdière's claim, 'La charrue gauloise,' that the appearance of a new type of 'Gallic plough' (that is to say a true plough as opposed to a simple 'ard' cutter) is nothing but a myth. To relegate the novelty to the status of a myth, for example, Ferdière has to claim that Pliny's notice on the *plauromatum* found in Raetia and Gaul, unlike the Gallic reaper, refers to a purely localized curiosity. He does admit, however, that the elements that went into the true plough were indeed developed over the Late Iron Age and Roman period (p. 170).

107 So the fact that Ferdière, 'La charrue gauloise,' p. 179, does not accept a modified ard plough armed with 'ears' and drawn by wheels as a 'true plough' is, in some sense, a bit of a semantical argument. Such a different type of 'plough' manifestly existed, and the literary references to it – for example, in the commentators on Vergil – cannot simply be dismissed (pp. 172–3).

108 See Brunner, 'Continuity and Discontinuity,' pp. 23, 25–6; cf. Henning, 'Zur Datierung' for a description of the finds in the hoard and the new dating.

109 As is attested by Servius, a rough contemporary of Palladius, in his commentary on Vergil's *Georgics*, 1.174: '"currus" autem dixit propter morem provinciae suae, in qua aratra habent rotas, quibus iuvantur.' Where ploughing, notably, is also construed as a military activity.

110 Ferdière, 'La charrue gauloise,' seems to be undecided as to the epicentre of this device, preferring instead to place the origins of the 'true plough' in Danubian regions; Kolendo, 'Origine et diffusion,' puts the canonical case for a northern Gallic origin and point of dispersal; Forni, 'Aratra des types,' attempts to make a case for the Po Valley region of northern Italy.

111 That it did not concerned Wightman, *Gallia Belgica*, p. 123, who found the absence 'surprising.'

112 See White, *Agricultural Implements*, p. 72(b): *falces faenariae* (Cato, *RR*, 10.2: inventory of equipment for a farmyard); 73(e): *falces faenariae* (Ulpian, Dig. 33.7.8.pr: against, a list of necessary equipment that must be transferred with a rural property); 74 no.2.

113 The agricultural tool replicated the same hybridity of design that the attachment of a 'sickle' blade to the end of a spear did in producing a weapon – called the *dorudrepanon* in Greek: *Anth. Graec.* 11.89.

114 See Joseph. *BJ*, 3.20.225: witnessed by Josephus in the siege of Jotopata: to reach and cut down sacks buffering the attack of a siege engine, the soldiers make a makeshift long cutter by attaching their sickles to the ends of long poles.

115 The middle part of this text, as it stands, reads: 'Galliarum latifundia maioribus *** conpendia, quippe.' In his Teubner text, Mayhoff conjectured 'latifundiis' for 'latifundia' and 'maiores' for 'maioribus.' The existing mss seem corrupt or deficient in some fashion. However one restores the text, there must be some balance in this part of it for the earlier 'brevius' that would indicate (surely) that there was a Gallic blade that was 'bigger' or 'longer.'

116 Legros, 'Ordre romain,' plate xii, fig. 3; cf. Stern, 'Le cycle des mois,' esp. pl. lxxxix, reproducing the most accurate surviving replication of the relief made by J.M.S. Bence and reprinted by A.L.J. de Laborde (see appendix 3.5) and in the fine detail by Ardhuin, *La moissonneuse gauloise*, pp. 12–13. In the century and a half since Bence made his drawing, the monument has suffered severe deterioration.

117 Henning, 'Fortleben und Weiterentwicklung,' p. 154, figs. 6.a–d, provides some good illustrative examples, as does Ferdière, *Les campagnes en Gaule romaine*, vol. 2, figs. 52 and 55 (Francalmont).

118 See Ardhuin, *La moissonneuse gauloise*, fig. p. 12, immediately above the lower left corner. In this case, the *falx* is probably a large pruning and trimming instrument used to cut away scrub and brush, and so useful in late spring activities; the figure to the right is carrying away a bundle of the material, presumably to be burnt.

119 Brunner, 'Continuity and Discontinuity,' pp. 26–7.

120 Rees, 'The Harvest,' pp. 22–5 and fig. 29e.

121 On the short scythe, see Rees, 'The Harvest,' p. 27: blade about 84–120 cm (33–7 inches) in length; on the long scythe, see p. 27, plates 15–16, fig. 29: blade about 130–60 cm (51–63 inches) in length.

122 The data were compiled, laboriously, by the author himself by a systematic reading through and culling the evidence catalogued in the many volumes of the *Carte archéologique de la Gaule*.

123 See Fussell, 'The Hainault Scythe,' on its origins and spread to England; Roberts, 'Sickles and Scythes,' p. 15; and Henning, 'Fortleben und Weiterentwicklung,' p. 153, with fig. 5.

124 Raepsaet, 'The Development,' p. 58, appearing in Flanders before the end of the thirteenth century; for early illustrations, see Mane, *L'outil et le geste*, 1, pp. 448–52.

125 Comet, *Le paysan et son outil*, pp. 186–8; 'Technology and Agricultural Expansion,' p. 25: invented at the end of the thirteenth century, it spread throughout Flanders, the Artois, and Hainault; see Fussell, 'The Hainault Scythe,' for its move to south-eastern England.

126 Steensberg, *Ancient Harvesting Implements*, p. 232.

127 Collins, 'Labour Supply and Demand in European Agriculture 1800–1880,' p. 85; the rest of the analysis that follows, at pp. 85–92, is a detailed investigation of the modes by which the use of the scythe for reaping cereal crops spread eastwards through Slavic lands and through the Balkans. This is by now an older classic expres-

sion of the problem, but I know of no subsequent studies that would substantially alter its central point.

128 See Henning, 'Fortleben und Weiterentwicklung,' p. 155, figs. 7a and b; Webster, *Labors of the Months*, pl. XI.25; the Kalendarium dates to 818 precisely. I hasten to add that Henning himself does not interpret this evidence in the manner indicated.

129 Stern, 'Le cycle des mois,' p. 1444, ad n6: information conveyed to him by M.E. Panofsky at the IAS; citing the 1933 OED entry for 'scythe': J.H. Hesseling, *An Eighth-Century Latin-Saxon Glossary presented in the Library of Corpus Christi College, Cambridge* (Cambridge: Cambridge University Press, 1890).

130 For the recognition of the element of 'savings' or *conpendium* in assessing the use of different tools or work regimens, see Kolendo, 'I progressi tecnici nell'agricoltura e il *conpendium operae*,' chap. 8 in *L'Agricoltura nell'Italia Romana*, pp. 179–91.

131 Finley, 'Technical Innovation,' p. 193: 'When we read, therefore, in Pliny's *Natural History* (18.300) in the sentence immediately following the description of the Gallic reaper, that "the diversity of methods employed depends upon the quantity of the crops and the scarcity of labour," the implication, the consequence, ought to be self-evident. Unfortunately, the facts belie the logic.'

132 Albanese Procelli, 'Greeks and Indigenous People,' p. 175.

133 See White, *Agricultural Implements*, p. 80, with bibliography; several of Steensberg's 'type B' of this kind of sickle have been found, for example, at Pompeii; see *Ancient Harvesting Implements*, p. 211, fig. 8; see pp. 209–23 on the development of the balanced sickle.

134 Steensberg, *Ancient Harvesting Implements*, pp. 209–11.

135 Steensberg, *Ancient Harvesting Implements*, pp. 111 f., 116 f., 190–209 and 225–32, and fig. pl. 13 (in end pocket), which is reproduced here.

136 See, e.g., Roberts, 'Sickles and Scythes,' p. 4, referring to Singer et al., *History of Technology*, 2, p. 95 and Steensberg, *Ancient Harvesting Implements*, p. 191.

137 Grantham, 'La faucille et la faux,' p. 104.

138 Rivière and Lecq, *Traité pratique*, 1, p. 414.

139 Comet, 'Technology and Agricultural Expansion,' p. 24, estimates these losses as significant – at about 10 per cent of the whole crop.

140 The factors are laid out so well by Grantham, 'Divisions of Labour,' p. 495, that I have simply quoted his words.

141 The survey of Roberts, 'Sickles and Scythes,' p. 5, if modestly constrained in the body of data consulted, is surely a sufficient sample to indicate the main trend.

142 Hostettler, 'Gourlay Steell,' pp. 97–8, for the effect of the adoption of the scythe on women's work in reaping.

143 Roberts, 'Sickles and Scythes,' pp. 6–8 (quotation from p. 8); a further defence of the conclusion is offered in 'Sickles and Scythes Revisited.'

144 Cherwinski, '"Misfits," "Malingerers," and "Malcontents,"' p. 296.

145 White, *Agricultural Implements*, p. 169: i.e. to reap one iugerum would take the equivalent of twelve man-hours; even with two men operating it (White strongly doubts that this is sustained by the evidence), it would take the machine about four man-hours. It would be six times as efficient if the whole contraption was – as White believes – worked by one man. But there are other problems that must be factored in (as White details), including the use of a draft animal (which he does not).

146 Legros, 'Ordre romain,' p. 699; my translation.

147 Renard, 'Technique et agriculture' (1959a), pp. 106–8, places special emphasis on existing technological advantages; as does Raepsaet, 'The Development,' esp. pp. 49–51 on carriage and harnessing technology.

148 For example, the relief on Block 45a of this same monumental series features a small wheeled vehicle, a *cissium*, and its harnessing: see Mertens, 'Sculptures romaines,' pp. 43–5, and plate xxxii, p. 117.

149 Mercer Museum, *Catalogue*, vol. 2, no. 10010: 'clover header'; the following notes are on this machine. There was, however, another one of the type that was acquired by Henry Mercer: *Catalogue*, vol. 1, no. 881, also called a 'clover header' (acquired from O.J. Frantz in Hilltown). There is no further information available on the latter.

150 Henry Mercer's notes are interesting (*Catalogue*, vol. 2, p. 513): 'used to gather heads from standing clover *in order to get seed* [my italics]. Bought from Henry Rinker near Coopersburg by Wm. A. Labs for 10.00 [dollars]. Mr. Rinker bought this machine many years ago. It was hand made and home made and was the *only machine of its kind known in upper Bucks County* [my italics] It was said by Mr. Chas. H. Dieterly, who assisted in getting this machine, and by Mr. Rinker that this machine was used by many farmers in upper Bucks Co. *on account of no other there* [sic, my italics] and was often loan[e]d to farmers in Coopersburg, Springto[w]n, Pleasant Valley, etc. [all these towns are in northern Bucks County, just south of Allentown-Bethlehem line] Mr. Lab first heard of it in June 1916 [couldn't get it because Rinker thought he was an antiques speculator – later secured through the efforts of Mr. Chas. H. Dieterly of Springtown]. Extra pair of small wheels used when the crop of clover was very short.'

151 An important observation made by Sigaut, 'Les spécificités,' which has found some acceptance: see Raepsaet, 'The Development,' pp. 46–7, and Honée, Lesseux, and Vassart, 'Les céréales,' in their thorough study of the archaeology of cereal culture in the region, especially in their conclusion at pp. 57–8.

152 See White, *Agricultural Implements*, who sees them as different tools: the *mergae* (no. 6, pp. 110–13) and the *pecten* (no. 7, pp. 112–15). Pliny, *NH*, 18.296.5–297.2: 'Stipulae alibi mediae falce praeciduntur, atque inter duas mergites spica distringitur, alibi ab radice caeduntur, alibi cum radice velluntur … Differentia haec: ubi stipula domos contegunt, quam longissimam servant; ubi feni inopia, e stramento paleam quaerunt … Panicum et milium singillatim pectine manuali legunt Galliae.'

153 Columella, *RR*, 2.20.3: 'Multi falcibus veruculatis atque iis vel rostratis vel denticu-
     latis medium culmum secant, multi mergis, alii pectinibus spicam ipsam legunt,
     idque in rara segete facillimum, in densa difficillimum est.' This seems to be the
     same instrument described by Varro, *RR*, 1.50.2, for the harvest in Picenum: 'Altero
     modo metunt, ut in Piceno, ubi ligneum habent incurvum bacillum, in quo sit
     extremo serrula ferrea. Haec cum comprendit fascem spicarum, desecat et stramenta
     stantia in segeti relinquit, ut postea subsecentur.'

154 Sigaut, 'Identification des techniques,' p. 151, 'Les spécificités,' pp. 30–1, 'Les tech-
     niques de récolte,' p. 35, and 'L'évolution,' pp. 10–11: although he sees that these
     comb-like tools, called *mesorias* in some modern cases, might have been a provo-
     cation for the development of the Roman *vallus*, he seems to leap to the unwar-
     ranted conclusion that *vallus* was no improvement over the sickle, but was over the
     mesorias; see, especially, Barris and Totelin, 'Un peigne pour des épis,' who present
     a full historical and ethnographic analysis, with special attention to the relationship
     between actual fork- or comb-like reapers and the *mesorias*.

155 Festus, *De verb. signif.* 111 (L): 'Mergae: furculae quibus acervi frugum fiunt, dictae
     a volucribus mergis, quia, ut illi se in aquam mergunt, dum pisces persequuntur, sic
     messores eas in fruge demergunt, ut elevare possint manipulos.'

156 Ovid, *Remed. Am.* 191–2; see Renard, 'Technique et agriculture' (1959a), pp.
     99–100, who correctly discerned what was happening in these verses.

157 Isid. *Etym.* 20.14.6: 'Rastra quoque aut a radendo terram aut a raritate dentium
     dicta.' Again, rightly seen by Renard, 'Technique et agriculture' (1959a), pp. 99–100
     (although he has oddly substituted 'humum' for the correct 'terram').

158 Pliny, *NH*, 18.72.296: 'Panicum et milium singillatim pectine manuali legunt Gal-
     liae.'

159 Comet, *Le paysan et son outil*, p. 175, drawing attention to the uses recorded in Du
     Cange.

160 See White, *Agricultural Implements*, p.115n1, citing L.C. Gray, *A History of Agri-
     culture in the Southern United States to 1860*, vol. 2 (Washington, DC, 1933), pp.
     798–9, referring specifically to Virginia and South Carolina.

161 Stabler, *A Brief Narrative*, p. 3.

162 Chuksin, 'The Revival of the Gallic Harvester.'

163 See Steward, 'Headers and Strippers and Mowing Machines,' chap. 14 in *The
     Reaper*, pp. 257–64, who notes (p. 257) that the Gallic machine was basically a
     type of 'header' and (p. 264) that the similar Ridley stripper was manufactured for
     harvesting in dry conditions and was useful only 'in semi-arid regions.'

164 Isern, *Bull Threshers and Bindlestiffs*, pp. 27–31; in particular the distribution maps
     on pp. 28–9, notably fig. 2.2: Areas Where Wheat Was Cut with a Header in 1919,
     drawing on data from J.H. Arnold and R.R. Spafford, 'Farm Practices in Growing
     Wheat: A Geographical Presentation,' *Yearbook of the [U.S.] Department of Agricul-*

ture (Washington, DC: GPO, 1919), pp. 123–50; the quotation on the ecological conditions required by the header is taken from p. 145 of this publication.

165 The literature on the European Wet Phase or 'Little Ice Age' is immense and can only be alluded to here. Its existence was first made widely known by E. Le Roy Ladurie, *Histoire du climat depuis l'an mil* (Paris: Flammarion, 1967; trans. B. Bray, *Time of Feast, Time of Famine: A History of Climate Since the Year 1000* [Garden City, NY: Doubleday, 1971]). The phase lasted, generally speaking, from the mid-thirteenth to the mid-seventeenth centuries. In general, see H.H. Lamb, 'Decline Again in the Late Middle Ages,' chap. 11, pp. 187–209; and 'The Little Ice Age: Background to the History of the Sixteenth and Seventeenth Centuries,' chap. 12 in *Climate, History and the Modern World*, 2nd ed. (London: Routledge, 1995), pp. 211–41.

166 Comet, 'Technology and Agricultural Expansion,' p. 16, which goes some way to explaining the geographic shift in regions devoted to the planting of spelt apparent in the map in Sigaut, 'Les spécificités,' p. 47, map. 1.

167 See Comet, *Le paysan et son outil*, p. 183, citing the work of Amouretti.

168 There is no sign of any special vocabulary for the scythe through the end of the seventeenth century: see E. Kriaras, *Λεξικό της Μεσαιωνικής Ελληνικής Δημώδους Γραμματείας, 1100–1669*, vol. 5 (Thessalonike, 1977), pp. 210–11. No distinction is made in the modern tongue, in which δρέπανι suffices for both tools.

169 Overton, *Agricultural Revolution*, pp. 121–8.

170 Roberts, 'Sickles and Scythes Revisited,' pp. 82–3.

171 Grantham, 'La faucille et la faux,' p. 106.

172 Grantham, 'La faucille et la faux,' p. 106: reapers' strikes in the case of the big farms in northern France, and the withdrawal of the women's labour force in England.

173 Stone, *Decision-Making*, pp. 249–50 and 275.

174 Roberts, 'Sickles and Scythes Revisited,' p. 84; in the 1830s and 1840s, most cereal crops were still being harvested with sickles: Grantham, 'La faucille et la faux,' p. 107.

175 Grantham, 'La faucille et la faux,' p. 107.

176 In refuting Bull's claim to the invention, Ridley, in a letter to the Adelaide patent office in 1886, states that it was an article in Loudon's encyclopedia on the Gallic reaper (see n. 178) that incited the idea of the machine reaper in his mind: see the personal memoir by Annie E. Ridley, *A Backward Glance: The Story of John Ridley, a Pioneer* (London: J. Clarke, 1904), pp. 380 ff. and fig. p. 94.

177 For a summary, see Renard, 'Technique et agriculture' (1959a), pp. 79–81; de Crescenzi's work, also known as *Ruralia Commoda*, was probably originally written about 1305–6, but print editions only begin in 1471, and it was only in the next century that print editions became common.

178 John Claudius Loudon, *An Encyclopaedia of Agriculture: comprising the theory and practice of the valuation, transfer, laying out, improvement, and management of landed*

property; and the cultivation and economy of the animal and vegetable productions of
agriculture, including all the latest improvements; a general history of agriculture in all
countries; and a statistical view of its present state, with suggestions for its future progress
in the British Isles, 1st ed. (London: Longman, Rees, Orme, Brown and Green,
1825), p. 26 and fig. 16; the same illustration and account appear in the second,
1831, and subsequent editions.

179 See Chuksin, 'The Revival of the Gallic Harvester,' for some of the background; the
increase was from about 1,000 acres to about 168,000 in 1856.

180 As early as the 1970s, Heinen, 'Grundzüge,' argued that the region of the Moselle
represented a special zone of economic development in Roman times. It is a precursor of the argument that I shall be making here.

181 Renard, 'Technique et agriculture' (1959b) assembled much of the basic data; then
Wightman, *Roman Trier,* pp. 48–52, 58–62, 83–92, and the map of regional settlement at pp. 158–9.

182 For more detail on what follows, see Heinen, *2000 Jahre Trier, 1: Trier und das*
Trevererland, passim, but esp. 'Wirtschaft,' pp. 141–64.

183 Wickham, *Framing the Early Middle Ages,* p. 476, noting the work of Van Oussel,
Ouzoulias, and Van Ossel – and noting that the concentrations of Roman-style rural
villas seem to have disappeared by the late fifth century.

184 Wickham, *Framing the Early Middle Ages,* pp. 284–7

185 Lebel, 'Moisson et fenaison en Gaul,' p. 74; Hobi, *Die Benennungen von Sichel*
und Sense, offered a fundamental study of the way in which the terms for the two
instruments developed out of Latin and Germanic languages; cf. Lebel, 'Moisson et
fenaison en Gaul,' p. 74, and Sigaut, 'L'évolution,' pp. 5–6.

186 Lebel, 'Moisson et fenaison en Gaul,' p. 74.

187 Raepsaet, 'Les prémices de la mécanisation agricole,' p. 916.

188 White, *Roman Farming,* p. 183; noted by Raepsaet, 'Les prémices de la mécanisation
agricole,' p. 912n7.

189 Noted by Kolendo, 'La mietitura,' p. 163

190 Leglay, 'La Gaule romanisée,' pp. 212–18: the northwest is the zone of 'villas verita-
bles.'

191 Leglay, 'La Gaule romanisée,' p. 212: 'on est frappé par l'homogénéité et la régularité
des "plans rationnels, orthogonaux, parfaitement ordonnés et d'une étonnante
similitude."'

192 Leglay, 'La Gaule romanisée,' p. 228: 'Mais il est clair que l'implantation des villae,
centres moteurs des domaines ruraux, se trouve surtout en relation étroite avec les
conditions naturelles, topographiques et climatiques.'

193 Leglay, 'La Gaule romanisée,' p. 231: 'Il est donc une exigence qui l'emporte sur
toutes les autres, c'est la fertilité du sol. En Gaule, les villae sont systématiquement
installées au milieu des terres les plus riches. C'est la règle d'or. Car la villa est avant

tout – répétons le – une exploitation agricole, liée à un domaine rural dont elle dirige l'activité et commande la vie.'

194 Finley, 'Technical Innovation,' p. 189: 'The objection will be raised that I have looked in the wrong place, among the landed magnates. I accept that, though I cannot refrain from noting that the two centuries covered by Cato, Varro, and Columella were the most fertile in the invention of agricultural machinery – the Gallic reaper, the screw press, and the water mill – and that all three manuals seem totally ignorant of what was happening in this field.' He adds that 'there is no other place in which to look.'

195 For Pliny's procuratorship in Africa, see H.-G. Pflaum, *Les carrières procuratoriennes équestres sous le Haut-Empire romain*, 4 vols. (Paris: Geuthner, 1960–1), no. 45, pp. 106–11, based on personal testimonia such as *NH* 7.36 and 17.41, probably in 71–2 CE.

196 Lloyd, *Ambitions of Curiosity*, pp. 81–5, cf. p. 97.

197 Frézouls, 'La vie rurale,' pp. 196–7, drawing attention, for example, to *Opus agr.* 3.17.8: 'Hispanus quidam mihi hoc genus novae insitionis ostendit: ex persico se adserebat expertum'; and 12.15.3: 'Cui contra celerem putredinem conperi in Sardinia hoc generi provideri ...'

198 Some of the main points are summarized for Graeco-Roman antiquity by Schneider, *Antike Technikgeschichte*, pp. 1–7.

199 Well analysed, with important cautions and nuances for our instances, by Grantham, 'La faucille et la faux,' pp. 103–4; see a good description and analysis by Paul A. David, one of its progenitors, in David 'Path Dependence, Its Critics and the Quest for "Historical Economics,"' which also contains a bibliography of his own work up to that date; Mahoney, 'Path Dependence in Historical Sociology,' offers one of the better summations.

4. The Grim Reapers

1 Dialogue from Todd Browning (director), *Dracula*, Universal Films (USA, 1931); see R.T. McNally and R. Florescu, *The Essential Dracula: A Completely Illustrated and Annotated Edition of Bram Stoker's Classic Novel* (New York: Mayflower Books, 1979), p. 320

2 Ps. 126:5–6: 'Qui seminant in lacrimis in exultatione metent / euntes ibant et flebant portantes semina sua, venientes autem venient in exultatione portantes manipulos suos [VG]'; for reference in the African tradition, see, e.g., Tert. *Adv. Marc.* 4.14.12; 4.15.13 (CCL 1: 576, 580); Cypr. *Ad Quir.* 3.16 (CCL 3: 107–8, note that it is used in connection with martyrdom); Aug. *En. in Ps.* 125.11–14 (CCL 40: 1852–5), *Sermo* 313D (MiAg 1: 534), and Quodvult. *Liber Promiss.* 1.29.41 (CCL 60: 48), for a few citations among many.

3 Aug. *Sermo*, 31.1 (CCL 41: 391): his African text of the the Psalm is slightly different from that of the VG. His own comments follow: 'Quo euntes et unde venientes? Quid seminantes in lacrymis? Quae sunt semina? Qui manipuli? Euntes in mortem, venientes a morte. Euntes a nascendo, venientes resurgendo. Seminantes opera bona, metentes mercedem aeternam. Semina ergo sunt nostra, quidquid boni fecerimus; manipuli nostri, quod in fine recipiemus. Si ergo bona sunt semina, bona opera, quare cum lacrymis, cum hilarem datorem diligat Deus?'

4 Spiro, *Critical Corpus of the Mosaic Pavements*, 2, fig. 227; for comment on the Christian era building of which it was part, see vol. 1, pp. 207–9. See our fig. 1.12.

5 Paul, 2 Cor. 9:6–7 and 10–11. In the italicized passages, Paul is 'quoting' Ps. 22:8 (LXX) and Hos. 10:12.

6 Aug. *En. 3 in Ps.* 136.7 (CCL 38: 373); the quotations in the sermon are from Gal. 6:9–10; 2 Cor. 9:6; and Ps. 125 (126):6, respectively.

7 Abrams, 'Bringing In the Sheaves'; lyrics by Knowles Shaw (1874), a prolific composer of popular evangelical hymns, who noted, in the second stanza: 'Fearing neither clouds nor winter's chilling breeze.'

8 One of the insightful referees of this work called on the author to declare his position. So here it is. Although I am interested in and concede the utility of understanding the conscious and deliberate employment and creation of metaphors by talented writers, this is not the focus of my interest in metaphor here. It is rather with the lineage of studies in metaphor from Lakoff and Turner to Kövecses and Pinker that have focused on the nature of metaphor as a core element in human cognition. As Steven Pinker has described it, this latter approach has come to abjure the idea of the innate presence of a Deep or a Universal Grammar as espoused by Chomsky, in favour of seeing the human mind as having certain experiential sensations – like space, time, movement – that form the basic categories out of which spoken language is formed, and hence also the primal operative place of metaphor: Pinker, 'Down the Rabbit Hole,' chap. 2 in *Stuff of Thought*, 25–87. This perspective on metaphor also concurs with Donald Davidson's argument that even metaphors of literary artifice have no special structure that gives them meaning; they work just like all the rest: see Davidson, 'What Metaphors Mean.'

9 R. Lewontin, 'Why Darwin?,' *NYRB* 56.9 (28 May 2009), 19–22, at p. 20.

10 Or, it might be the other way around: our minds produce narratives which then serve as explanations. See Gazzaniga, 'Humans: The Party Animal,' who surveys some of the recent studies, especially in the case of split-brain patients in whom, as a last-ditch attempt to deal with severe epilepsy, the two spheres of the brain are severed. The right hemisphere can be commanded to do something which the left does not understand (not hearing or processing the initial command) – so it does not know why, for example, the patient has picked up an apple. Even so, the left hemisphere simply

makes up the appropriate reason or 'story' of 'why' this happened. This 'interpreter function' in the left hemisphere makes order out of potential chaos, understanding out of ignorance.

11 See, e.g., *Anth. Graec.* 6.36; 6.41; 6.95; and 6.104, for a series of such dedications to Demeter that feature the reaped sheaves of grain and the sickles themselves 'that cut the heads of grain.'

12 Apul. *Met.* 6.1: 'Et ilico dirigit gradum, quem defectum prorsus assiduis laboribus spes incitabat et votum. Iamque naviter emensis celsioribus iugis pulvinaribus sese proximam intulit. Videt spicas frumentarias in acervo et alias flexiles in corona et spicas hordei videt. Erant et falces et operae messoriae mundus omnis, sed cuncta passim iacentia et incuria confusa et, ut solet aestu laborantium manibus proiecta.'

13 For the parallel with other basic metaphors, such as LIFE IS A DAY: see Kövecses, *Metaphor*, pp. 44–9.

14 See, e.g., *Anth. Graec.* 7.225: Time wears stones down and does not spare even iron, but with its sickle destroys everything. The trope is exploited to reinforce another: that it is only the fame of imperishable words that preserves the memory of heroic figures (in this case, of Laertes).

15 Emile Zola, *La Terre* (Paris: Charpentier, 1887); *The Earth*, trans. Douglas Parmée (Harmondsworth: Penguin, 1980), pp. 239–40.

16 Kosinski, *Van Gogh's Sheaves of Wheat*, pp. 11 and 17.

17 Vincent Van Gogh to Theo Van Gogh (5–6 September 1889), *Vincent Van Gogh: The Letters*, vol. 5, no. 800, pp. 80 and 85, with slight modifications to their translation. In the same letter, Van Gogh expresses the wish to make a copy for 'Mother,' having been persuaded that she would understand it. See Kosinski, *Van Gogh's Sheaves of Wheat*, p. 17 and Fratello, 'Standing on Holy Ground,' p. 51.

18 Robert Fagles, *I, Vincent*, p. 77, a poem on 'The Wheat Field behind St. Paul's Hospital at the Fall of Day with a Reaper.'

19 Cato, *Agr.* 91 and 129 (preparing the threshing floor), 134 (a brief notice of the sacrifices to be made before the harvest begins, apparently, though not necessarily, for the grain harvest). That is it. He does discuss the olive harvest, and the contracting for picking and milling of olives at greater length (144–5); Varro, *RR*, 1.49–53, is practically the sum of the whole, in which there is the great virtue that he does at least discuss different kinds of reaping. Palladius has one brief reference to the grain harvest in his entry for the month of June but almost nothing on the organization and mobilization of the labour.

20 For example, Mane, *L'outile et le geste*, 1, p. 420, after noting the lavish illustration of harvest scenes in medieval calendars and such: 'Il est, par contre, surprenant de constater un relatif désintérêt de la part de l'agronome Pietro de' Crescenzi; dans son traité, il ne s'attarde guère que sur la moissonneuse décrite par Pline et ne dit rien sur

les faucilles.' In the fourteenth and fifteenth centuries, as she notes, by contrast, the illuminators of this same treatise show some considerable interest in the the the mechanics of the harvest and of reaping.

21 Fussell, *The Classical Tradition*, p. 86: even of these, there were 'relatively few copies scattered over western Europe in the fourteenth and fifteeth centuries'; it was not until the eighteenth century that western European agricultural writers began to break with this tradition (p. 147). For de' Crescenzi's text and its background, see W. Richter, ed., *Petrus de Cresecentiis (Pier de' Crescenzi): Ruralia Commoda: Das Wissen des vollkommenen Landwirts um 1300*, 4 vols. (Heidelberg: Winter, 1995–2002).

22 Frézouls, 'La vie rurale,' p. 199, citing *Palladius, Traité de l'agriculture*, ed. Martin, vol. 1, p. xxx.

23 See Fussell, *The Classical Tradition*, pp. 64–72, 96–104.

24 Harvesting operations are almost entirely missing, for example, from the *Georgics* of Vergil. *Georg.* 1.316–17 (cf. 1.298), lines that were rather influential with seventeenth-century western European poets (see Vardi, 'Imagining the Harvest,' 1386 f.), are just about the sum of the whole: 'Saepe ego, cum flavis messorem induceret arvis / agricola et fragili iam stringeret hordea culmo': cf. chap. 2, p. 79. Hesiod, *Op.* ll. 382–4 refers briefly to the harvest; 573–7 and 597–608 refer to the cereal harvest and to the mowing of hay; cf. *Sc.* l. 288.

25 There is a similar absence in late medieval and early modern handbooks and guidebooks on agriculture, but they are so heavily under the influence of their ancient models, from Cato to Palladius, that it is perhaps too much to expect that they would have developed a new concern with labour that was wholly alien to the tradition that they were copying.

26 M.A. Sullivan, *Bruegel's Peasants*, pp. 43–4, points out that the pictures of peasants in the seasonal paintings are less obviously 'satyric' and somewhat more 'realistic' than his portrayal of peasants in the rest of his work; cf. Vardi, 'Imagining the Harvest,' pp. 1364–6.

27 Vardi, 'Imagining the Harvest,' p. 1360.

28 This conclusion is based, admittedly, on nothing other than several years of leafing through art-sale, auction, and museum catalogues and inspecting collections. Even so, I feel confident in stating that such scenes (e.g., reaping) are virtually non-existent in formal painting, drawing, and decoration of ceramics of the period – as compared, for example, with the limited theme of hunting – even, specifically, that of fox hunting. The odd example can be found – e.g., 'The Reaper's Return' produced by the Staffordshire pottery in the 1820s, notably for a child's use – but they are exceedingly rare: see http://www.rubylane.com/shops/childhoodantiques /item/AA558.

29 So, for example, it is not found anywhere in the large repertoire of the popular realist American illustrator Norman Rockwell, who was drawn, on occasion, to painting populist scenes of rural life in the United State of his time. The theme of the harvest

and therefore of reaping cereal crops would seem an obvious choice of subject, but the latter does not appear. The closest that I have been able to find is the painting for the *Saturday Evening Post* (19 August 1923) entitled *Farmer and Bird* (the farmer is holding a scythe), although even here most of the reaping instrument is outside the frame of the painting.

30 Kranz, 'Nordafrikanische Jahreszeiten-Sarkophage und Jahreszeiten-Deckel,' II.4 in *Jahreszeiten-Sarkophage*, pp. 285–8 (nos. 579–90): a mere handful of known examples as compared to the much greater numbers from Rome and Italy, for example; the same gross imbalance is manifest in Dresken-Weiland's count in her *Sarkophagbestattungen*, Katalog G, 'Africa,' pp. 396–411 (42 cases only, as opposed to hundreds elsewhere).

31 See Dresken-Weiland, 'Recherches sur les sépultures paléochrétiennes,' table 3, p. 310: the proportion of 'seasons' reliefs remains about the same for the period 270–300 as opposed to 300–30. There are 161/788 cases or 20 per cent of all in the former period, and 53/317 cases or 17 per cent in the latter period (from the data in Kranz, *Jahreszeiten-Sarkophage*). The same trend is also apparent for scenes of vintage: 44/788 or 7 per cent for the former period, as opposed to 17/317 or 5 per cent in the latter period (from the data in Bielefeld, *Die Stadtrömischen Eroten-Sarkophage*).

32 See Dresken-Weiland, 'Recherches sur les sépultures paléochrétiennes,' pp. 306–8, and *Sarkophagbestattungen*, pp. 199–200.

33 Silver, *Peasant Scenes and Landscapes*, pp. 123–4: the panel for 'Wheat Harvest' is one of five that survive out of (probably) an original six panels, entitled *The Months*, that pictured the different months and the labour associated with them based on the medieval calendrical tradition.

34 Buchanan, 'The Collection of Niclaes Jongelinck,' provides the necessary details.

35 J. Renault, *Cahiers d'archéologie tunisienne*, vol. 3 (Tunis: Picard-Danguin, 1910), fig. 6, p. 127, provides an example of the picture of a reaper, turned to the viewer's right, on a lamp.

36 Baldassare, 'Tomba della Mietitura,' esp. fig. 45, p. 97 and fig. 49, p. 101; it is guessed (p. 94) that the tomb and the mosaics date to the Antonine period.

37 Brogan and Smith, *Ghirza*, pl. 57a (tomb NB = north group, tomb B); pl. 64a (ploughing scene).

38 Brogan and Smith, *Ghirza*, pl. 67a.

39 Brogan and Smith, *Ghirza*, pl. 66b and c; for the scene of the local chieftain on his throne, see pl. 63a. They appeal to Cumont, *Recherches sur le symbolisme funéraire*, pp. 422, 431–2, for the idea that these scenes represent the idea that hard work earns a place in the afterlife. I would tend to see the meaning as more symbolic in terms of birth, growth, and death cycles.

40 R.S. Poole, *British Museum: Catalogue of the Coins of Alexandria and the Nomes* (London: British Museum Department of Coins and Medals, 1892; reprint Bologna:

Arnaldo Forni editore, 1964), p. 128, nos. 1090 and 1091; plate XII, nos. 1091 and 1092 (141–2 CE). Strangely misrepresented by Brandt, *Schaffende Arbeit, Altertum*, p. 148 (and figs. 189–90) as coins of Marc Antony.

41 BMC, Poole, *British Museum*, no. 1078–90; plate XII, nos. 1078–80, 1082, 1084, 1086–8, and 1090 (144–5 CE).

42 Prat, *Histoire d'Arlon*, vol. 1, pl. 64; cf. the complete misunderstanding of the relief now known to contain a mechanical harvester (appendix 3.2): Prat, ibid., vol. 1, sér. 2, facing illustration for p. 131.

43 As Kolendo, 'La mietitura,' p. 162, noted of the harvesting machines, all of them, with the sole exception of the one portrayed on the calendrical theme on the arch at Reims, are on funerary monuments.

44 For what follows, the analysis and the translation of the texts offered by Lesko, 'The Field of Hetep,' are basic.

45 CT 464: 'Coming to Be as Hetep, Lord of the Two Fields of Offerings': Lesko, 'The Field of Hetep,' p. 92. Note that many of the texts come from coffins from al Barsh, a necropolis of Hermopolis, the same village that is the source of several of our reaping contracts from the Roman period: see appendix 1.

46 CT 466: xiv: 'Plowing and reaping barley and emmer of the God's district, with no snake therein': Lesko, 'The Field of Hetep,' p. 94.

47 CT 467: Lesko, 'The Field of Hetep,' pp. 95–6. CT 468 provides further variants of these same themes.

48 See Assmann, *Tod und Jenseits*, pp. 299–318, on the different context of this Egyptian view of 'Elysium.' Cf. M. Smith, *Traversing Eternity: Texts for the Afterlife from Ptolemaic and Roman Egypt* (Oxford–New York: Oxford University Press, 2009), for continuities and development, where the different nature of this life beyond life is seen as a rather joyful and exuberant replica of present life.

49 Budge, 'The Harvest and the Reapers in the Kingdom of Osiris,' in *The Egyptian Heaven and Hell*, vol. 2, pp. 175–89, which is, in fact, a pastiche of different source materials. It is interesting, however, that the number of reapers, that is twelve, more or less approximates the number of reapers found in actual harvesting gangs later in Ptolemaic and Roman Egypt (although caution must be exercised: such assistants of deities and spirits are frequently found in twelves). The translation (p. 189) is one of which there are several variants (e.g., pp. 180, 181).

50 Budge, *The Egyptian Heaven and Hell*, vol. 2, pp. 181–6.

51 Assmann, 'Nachwort,' in *Tod und Jenseits*, pp. 526–33; see also the afterword in the English version, 'Egypt and the History of Death,' in *Death and Salvation*, pp. 407–17. Assmann offers a clear summation in 'Todesbilder und Totenriten im Alten Agypten,' in J. Assman and T. Macho, *Der Tod als Thema der Kulturtheorie* (Frankfurt: Suhrkamp Verlag, 2000), pp. 9–88.

52 Budge, *The Egyptian Heaven and Hell*, vol. 3, pp. 42–3, appealing also to illustrations

in the Papyrus of Nebseni (p. 43, BM) and in the Papyrus of Ani (p. 45, BM). But the iconography continues much the same into later periods, as shown in the Papryus of Anhai of the 22nd Dynasty (p. 60) and the Turin Papyrus of Auf-ankh (p. 61).

53 See, e.g., Sontag, *Illness as Metaphor*, passim.

54 Sullivan, *Weaving the Word*, for example, offers a study of some of the metaphors based on women's involvement in weaving; for the connection between action and thought, see Scheid and Svenbro, *Craft of Zeus*, pp. 9–10.

55 See Seaford, *Money and the Early Greek Mind*, for the argument that coined money created new conceptions of the universal and impersonal commonness in a mental view of the cosmos that could, in turn, be explained by uniform and individual common denominators of causation.

56 Valenze, *The Social Life of Money*, and Poovey, *Genres of the Credit Economy*, present model studies of its impact on thinking in seventeenth- to nineteenth-century thinking in British society.

57 Cic. *De Or.* 3.38.154–5: 'Tertius ille modus transferendi verbi late patet quem necessitas genuit inopia coacta et angustiis, post autem iucunditasque delectatio celebravit … sic verbi translatio instituta est inopiae causa, frequentata delectationis. Nam gemmare vites, luxuriem esse in herbis, laetas esse segetes etiam rustici dicunt.' See Guidorizzi and Beta, *La metaphora*, T. 36, pp. 84–7.

58 Quintil. *Inst. Or.* 8.6.6: 'Necessitate rustici "gemmam" in vitibus (quid enim dicerent aliud?) et "sitire" segetes et fructus "laborare"'; cf. Guidorizzi and Beta, *La metaphora*, T. 38, pp. 92–5.

59 Isid. *Etym.* 1.37, in referring to the case of 'fluctuere segetes,' is probably noting another one of these: cf. Guidorizzi and Beta, *La metaphora*, T. 53, pp. 120–3.

60 Stern, 'Les calendriers romains illustrés,' is still the most dependable survey for the calendars; other bibliography will be noted as necessary.

61 The so-called *menologia rustica* are probably the best Roman examples of this tendency: *Inscr. Ital.* 13.2, 47–8; cf. Degrassi, *Fasti anni Numani et Iuliani*, 284–98.

62 Stern, 'Un calendrier romain illustré,' pp. 195–6; cf. Foucher, 'Terrains Salah Abdallah et Hadj Ferdjani Kacem' and 'Le calendrier de Thysdrus.'

63 Palladius, ed. Martin, *Palladius, Traité de l'agriculture*, vol. 1, pp. xxv–xvii; Frézouls, 'La vie rurale,' p. 195.

64 Rebuffat, 'Comme les moissons,' esp. pp. 115–17, in a discussion of the labour involved in fortifying cities and drawing attention to the Panegyric of Eumenius on the rebuilding of the schools of Gaul: *Pan. Lat.* 9.18.4: 'Qua veris autumnive clementia tot manu positae arbores convalescunt, quo calore solis tot depressae imbribus segetes resurgunt, quot ubique muri vix repertis veterum fundamentorum vestigiis excitantur. Adeo, ut res est, aurea illa saecula, quae non diu quondam Saturno rege viguerunt …' See C.E.V. Nixon and B.S. Rogers, *In Praise of Later Roman Emperors: The Panegyrici Latini* (Berkeley–Los Angeles: University of California Press, 1994),

pp. 170 and 562. Note that the passage ends with a reference to Saturn as the king of the gods.

65 Bourdieu, *Logic of Practice*, p. 201, at Aïn Aghbel: 'When the ears of grain are ripe, the senior men get together and fix the day of the harvest. It will be a feast-day. They come to an agreement. Everyone begins [work] on the same day.'

66 Trousset, 'Les centuriations romaines,' pp. 74–5, based on the work of A. Carrier and J. Lenne; he speculates about a connection with Caelestis and Tinnit at Carthage.

67 As Stern, *Calendrier de 354*, pp. 254–5, notes, in most plains regions in central Italy both then and now the grain harvest tended to begin around mid-June and was completed in early July.

68 There might be some indication of this in the celebrations of Demeter and Korê with whom African preachers, like the pseudo-Fulgentius (see chap. 5, p. 241), associated the 'day of the torches.' Diodorus Siculus knew of a harvest festival in his home town connected with the 'return of Korê': Diod. Sic. 5.4.5–7: τῆς μὲν γὰρ Κόρης τὴν καταγωγὴν ἐποιήσαντο περὶ τὸν καιρὸν ἐν ᾧ τὸν τοῦ σίτου καρπὸν τελεσιουργεῖσθαι συνέβαινε, καὶ ταύτην τὴν θυσίαν καὶ πανήγυριν μετὰ τοσαύτης ἁγνείας καὶ σπουδῆς ἐπιτελοῦσιν ὅσης εἰκός ἐστι τοὺς τῇ κρατίστῃ δωρεᾷ προκριθέντας τῶν ἄλλων ἀνθρώπων ἀποδιδόναι τὰς χάριτας. The problem is with the significance of the verb *telesiourgeisthai*. Martin Nilsson took it to mean when the harvest was completed or 'ended'; Stern, on the other hand, wanted to read the verb as meaning that the wheat crop was completed or 'ripe' (*Calendrier de 354*, p. 256, with reference to Nilsson's work). If the former, which I would tend to think, then the harvest festival of which Diodorus knew and which was associated with the 'day of the torches' was celebrated at the completion of the harvest.

69 See Bourdieu, *Logic of Practice*, p. 209: 'By the last day of *iquranen*, known as "a fiery ember has fallen in the water," an expression that alludes to the quenching of iron by the blacksmith, everyone should have started harvest (*essaïf*), which is completed around *insla*, the day of the summer solstice (24 June), when fires are lit everywhere.'

70 For example, the great Council of Cebarsussi was called to meet on 24 June of the year 393, and the same council set the precise dates marking the period of grace for Christians whom it was judging as extending from the eighth day before the Kalends of July (i.e., 24 June) to the eighth day before the Kalends of January (i.e., 25 December). The former was the day of the Sun, the latter was the day of Saturn; both were now marked by the Christian church as the Day of John the Baptist and Christmas, the nativity of Christ. For the text, see J.-L. Maier, *Le Dossier du Donatisme, t. 2: De Julien l'Apostat à Saint Jean Damascene (361–750)* (Berlin: Akademie Verlag, 1989), no. 54, pp. 73–82, at § 8, p. 80.

71 Fulgentius, *Mitologiae* (CPL 849), ed. R. Helm (Leipzig, 1898), 22–3:
'Ceres enim Graece *gaudium* dicitur, et ideo illem frumenti deam esse voluerunt, quod ubi plenitudo sit fructuum gaudia superabundaent necesse est. Proserpinam

vero quasi *segetem* voluerunt, id est terram radicibus proserpentem … Hanc etiam mater cum lampadibus raptam inquirere dicitur, unde et lampadarum dies Cereri dedicatus est, illa videlicet ratione quod hoc tempore cum lampadibus, id est cum solis fervore, seges ad metendum cum *gaudio* requiratur.' See L.G. Whitbread, ed. and trans., *Fulgentius the Mythographer* (Columbus: Ohio University Press, 1971), p. 53 (with an odd translation, however).

72 Bourdieu, *Logic of Practice*, p. 208: The changing appearance of the wheat fields is indicated by the names of the ten- or seven-day periods into which the month is divided: the yellow days (*iwraghen*) are followed by the white days (*imellalen*).

73 For what follows, see Stern, *Calendrier de 354*, pp. 256–7.

74 See, especially, Rives, *Religion and Authority*, pp. 157–61, who distinguishes this 'indigenous' cult developed as a result of Carthaginian-Sicilian connections at the end of the fourth century BCE from the later cult of the Roman Ceres established in conjunction with the colony at Carthage.

75 Parrish, *Season Mosaics*, is the standard study; 'Two Mosaics from Roman Tunisia,' p. 279n3, as of the end of the 1970s counted no less than seventy-six known examples.

76 Foucher, 'Terrains Salah Abdallah et Hadj Ferdjani Kacem'; Stern, 'Un calendrier romain illustré,' and 'Les calendriers romains illustrés,' p. 436 and pl. III, pl. IV.8. The placing of this primary image in the 'season' elements of the mosaic left space to depict minor and more specific elements of the summer in its 'months' elements; of the latter, June and July highlight the annual rural labour cycle, while the rest symbolically reference religious and civic rituals.

77 Leglay, *SAM* 1, p. 292, no. 5; and pl. vii.4 (region of Béja-Le Kef; now in the Rijksmuseum van Oudheden): in the upper register, the god Saturn with two assistants; in the lower register, figures of the four seasons: Winter, Spring, Summer (with a sickle and a sheaf of grain), Autumn.

78 Stern, 'Les calendriers romains illustrés,' pp. 445–9 (the mosaic is now in the museum at Saint Germain-en-Laye); as at Thysdrus, by making 'harvest' the prime theme of the 'season' representation for summer, the artist could devote the pictures in the 'months' panels to more specific rural occupations.

79 Anthologia Latina 490a: 7 (Riese); cf. Courtney, 'The Roman Months,' p. 50.

80 For one of many examples, although a striking one, see Spiro, *Critical Corpus of the Mosaic Pavements*, 2, no. 227: Ioulios, from Thebes, Greece.

81 Anthologia Latina 490A: 8 (Riese); cf. Courtney, 'The Roman Months,' p. 51.

82 Tert. *De spect.* 8.3 (CCL 1: 234): '… columnae Seias a sementationibus, Messias a messibus, Tutulinas a tutela fructuum sustinent.'

83 See A. Cameron, 'The Colours in Corippus (*Laud. Just.* I, 319-29),' appendix E in *Circus Factions: Blues and Greens at Rome and Byzantium* (Oxford: Clarendon Press, 1976), pp. 336–8, for analysis; the Blues and Greens dominate in our sources, however, since the most avid fans tended to be polarized into these two oppositional groups.

84 Apul. *Met.* 11.26: 'Ecce transcurso signifero circulo Sol magnus annum compleverat, et quietem meam rursus interpellat numinis benefici cura pervigilis, et rursus teletae, rursus sacrorum commonet.' He is referring to the time after the Ides of December, approaching the great festival of Saturn that would mark this transformation. In late antiquity, a shift would made forward to the first of January as the great turning point.

85 Bourdieu, *Logic of Practice*, is the English translation that will be used here, particularly because of the diagrams. The book begins, notably, with a critique of 'theoretical reason.' The term Kabylie here is used more generally, as Bourdieu does, to cover not just the Lesser Qabiliyya mountains, but also adjacent areas in which he did his research, including the Greater Qabaliyya, and the Warsenis mountains to the south; this fieldwork and its analysis were also encapsulated in his theoretical summa, *Outline* (see next note).

86 Bourdieu, 'Irresistible Analogy,' chap. 2.3 in *Logic of Practice*, pp. 200–70; most of which is repeated, including the diagrams, in the more theoretical framework of 'Generative Schemes and Practical Logic: Invention within Limits,' chap. 3 in *Outline*, pp. 96–158.

87 On the gendering of space and work in this context, and for the work regimens – for example, men's work is reaping grain while women's work (like weaving) is transporting the grain – see *Logic of Practice*, pp. 216–21, and fig. 4, p. 220 = *Outline*, fig. 3, p. 134; and, especially, pp. 248–9, and fig. 5 = *Outline*, fig. 5, p. 147, based on the work of Henri Basset. For discussion of the context of weaving and metaphor in antiquity, see Scheid and Svenbro, *Craft of Zeus*, pp. 5, 13; and chaps. 3–4, on the gendering of the activity and of the warp and woof for lovers' congress and marriage.

88 Stern, *Calendrier de 354*; Salzman, *On Roman Time*, pp. 25–6, 43–5; cf. Stern, 'Un calendrier romain illustré,' pp. 168–9, and, 'Les calendriers romains illustrés,' pp. 458–61.

89 Salzman, *On Roman Time*, pp. 42–3.

90 Stern, 'Les calendriers romains illustrés,' pl. XXXII, fig. 86; cf. Salzman, *On Roman Time*, pp. 91–3 and fig. 37.

91 See Alexiou, *Ritual Lament*, pp. 56–60, on funerary lamentation in modern Greece, with reference to ancient precedents; Danforth and Tsiaris, *Death Rituals*, pp. 96–9, 104–6.

92 Danforth and Tsiaris, *Death Rituals*, p. 96.

93 Weiss, 'The Synagogue Mosaics,' chap. 3 in *The Sepphoris Synagogue*, pp. 55–198, retails most of cases in addition to the one from the synagogue at Zippori; cf. Weiss and Netzer, *Promise and Redemption*, esp. pp. 26–9, for a more general introduction. The Sepphoris synagogue mosaic probably dates to the first half of the fifth century CE, close in time to the age of our harvester in Africa. See Levine, *The Ancient Synagogue*, pp. 160–224 for these later Late Roman and Byzantine era synagogues.

94 Similar figures of summer are found in the synagogue mosaic at Hammat Tiberias, as well as in a church mosaic from Petra, where they obviously have the same general signification: see Weiss, *The Sepphoris Synagogue*, fig. 70, p. 129 and fig. 71, p. 130.

95 De Martino, 'Raccolto e passione dei cereali,' chap. 6.4 in *Morte e pianto rituale*, pp. 249–62, who cites Liungman, *Traditionswanderungen*, vol. 1, pp. 261 f. for examples and bibliography. The reason? (p. 250): ' il mietere è sperimentato come violenza mortale recata ad un nume, ma al tempo stesso – con un comportamento che si sarebbe tentati di definire ipocrita – se ne piange cerimonialemente la morte *come se* non fosse stato il contadino stesso a procurarla mercé il gesto inesorabile compiuto con la falce messoria.'

96 West, *Ancient Greek Music*, p. 28, who cites Telecleides, fr. 8; Menander, *Carchedonius*, fr. 3 (Sandbach) in addition to Theocr. *Id.* 10.16.41, as the principal sources; see also Athenaeus, 10.415b, who notes that Lityerses is an illegitimate son of Midas, and a renowned glutton; see also De Martino, *Morte e pianto rituale*, p. 253.

97 *Schol. In Theocr.* 10.42. It is this aspect of the song that drew the attention of Sir James Frazer, 'Lityerses: Songs of the Corn Reapers,' chap. 7 in *The Golden Bough*, 5.1, pp. 214 f., accompanied by a long list of not always terribly relevant north-western European 'parallels' at pp. 218 f. As Frazer notes, at p. 217n1, the story was told by Sositheus in his play *Daphnis* (citing A. Westermann, ed., *Scriptores rerum mirabilium Graeci* [Brunswick: private; London: Black and Armstrong, 1839], pp. 220 f.); Apostolius, *Centur.* 10.74.

98 Athenaeus, 14.619a; and see Photios, Hesychios, and the Suda, s.v. 'Lityerses.'

99 See Serv. *Ad Verg. Ecl.* 8.10–15: '... per totum orbem quaesisset, invenit in Phrygia apud Lityersem regem servientem, qui hac lege in advenas saeviebat, ut cum multas segetes haberet, peregrinos advenientes secum metere faceret victosque iuberet occidi. Sed Hercules, miseratus Daphnidis, venit ad regiam et audita condicione certaminis, falcem ad metendum accepit eaque regi ferali sopito metendi carmine caput amputavit.'

100 West, *Ancient Greek Music*, p. 28, citing Theocr. *Id.* 10.16, 41 (see n. 96 above).

101 Athenaeus 14.619f–620a: ἡ δὲ τῶν θεριστῶν ᾠδὴ Λιτυέρσες καλεῖται. καὶ τῶν μισθωτῶν δ1ε τις ἦν ᾠδὴ τῶν ἐς τοὺς ἀγροὺς φοιτώντων, ὡς Τηλεικλείδης φησὶν ἐν Ἀμφικτύοσιν.

102 See Julius Pollux, 4.54; and Hesychios, s.v. Βῶρμον and Μαριανδυνὸς θρῆνος; and Barynos: Σ Apoll. Rhod. 2.780; for additional comment, see Fraser, *The Golden Bough*, 5.1, p. 216, and Alexiou, *Ritual Lament*, pp. 58–60.

103 Alexiou, *Ritual Lament*, pp. 57–8.

104 Hom. *Il.* 18.561–72.

105 Verg. *Aen.* 8.370–453 (Vulcan at his forge, by way of introduction) and 626–731 (the detailed description or 'ekphrasis' of the shield). See K.W. Grandsen, ed., *Virgil: Aeneid, Book VIII* (Cambridge: Cambridge University Press, 1976), pp. 161–84.

106 Verlinden, *Statuettes anthropomorphes*, pp. 78–9, pls. 14–15; cat. 30 (from Tylissos) and 31 (provenience unknown); Younger, *Music in the Aegean Bronze Age*, pp. 6–7, pl. 1 (sistrum player and three singers/chanters) and fig. 2 (line drawing of the line of harvesters).

107 Mou, 'Amazigh Harvest Izlan (Songs),' from which much of the following is taken.

108 Mou, 'Amazigh Harvest Izlan (Songs),' p. 1 (e-version).

109 *The Mastaba of Mereruka, the Sakkarah Expedition*, 2 vols. (Chicago: University of Chicago Press, 1938), vol. 2, pl. 169.

110 Aug. *Enarr. 2 in Ps.* 32.8 (CCL 38: 253–4); cf. Peter Brown, *Augustine of Hippo: A Biography* (Berkeley: University of California Press, 2000*)*, p. 255.

111 Jerome, *Ep.* 46.12 (CSEL 54: 342–3): 'Quocumque te verteris, arator stivam tenens alleluia decantat, sudans messor psalmis se avocat et curva adtondens vitem falce vinitor aliquid Daviticum canit. Haec sunt in hac provincia carmina, hae, ut vulgo dicitur, amatoriae cantiones, hic pastorum sibilius, haec arma culturae.'

112 Hom. *Il.* 11.61–71.

113 Cat. 64, ll. 353–55: 'Namque velut densas praecerpens messor aristas / sole sub ardenti flaventia demetit arva, / Troiugenum infesto prosternet corpora ferro.' Not a few commentators have seen these lines as an echo of the Homeric ones just quoted.

114 See chap. 1, p. 37, above.

115 A. Horne, 'The Sickle and the Reaper,' chap. 7 in *To Lose a Battle: France 1940* (London: Macmillan, 1969; reprint London: Penguin, 1990), pp. 184–213; the operation was actually code-named *Fall Gelb* or 'Case Yellow': see K.-H. Frieser, 'The Struggle over the Sickle Cut Plan,' chap. 3 in *The Blitzkrieg Legend: The 1940 Campaign in the West*, trans. J.T. Greenwood (Annapolis, MD: Naval Institute Press, 2005), pp. 60–99; original title *Blitzkrieg-Legende. Der Westfeldzug 1940*, 2nd ed. (Munich: Oldenbourg, 1996).

116 Both instances highlighted by M.L. West, *The East Face of Helicon: West Asiatic Elements in Greek Poetry and Myth* (Oxford: Clarendon Press, 1997), pp. 228–9.

117 Hom. *Il.*, 19.221–4.

118 So, rather vividly, Lucr. *Nat.* 3.642–5: 'Faciferos memorant currus abscidere membra / saepe ita de subito permixta caede calentis / ut tremere in terra videatur ab artubus id quod / decidit abscisum …' cf. 5.1300–1; see also Xen. *Hell.* 4.1.17; *Anab.* 1.7.11–12, 1.8.10, 6.1.50; *Cyr.* 6.2.7, 7.1.47, 8.6.19; Diod. Sic. 2.5; 17.53; Polyb. 5.53; Aul. Gell. *NA*, 5.5; 2 Macc. 13.2; Livy, 37.41.7 (on Antiochus); Quintus Curtius, *Hist. Alex.* 4.9.5; Veg. *Mil.* 3.24.

119 C.J. Chivers, *The Gun* (New York–Toronto: Simon and Schuster, 2010), p. 87.

120 Chivers, ibid., p. 134, quoting from M. Middlebrook, *The First Day on the Somme, 1 July 1916* (London: Allen Lane, 1971*)*.

121 Verg. *Aen.* 10.513–15: 'Proxima quaeque metit gladio latumque per agmen / ardens limitem agit ferro, te, Turne, superbum / caede nova quaerens.' This offers one

instance where the metaphor was transferred to a Roman mythic prototype in the age of Augustus. But note how very unusual the application was: as Harrison, *Vergil, Aeneid 10*, p. 202, at ll. 513–14, notes: '*meto*, "harvest", occurs only here in the *Aeneid*,' adding that 'Its metaphorical use ... and the comparison of mass slaying to reaping is an epic topos.' Its use here is not as much part of a metaphor of kingliness as it is of another kind of behaviour: 'it is the *proxima quaeque* which expresses the lack of discrimination in Aeneas' passion for *revenge*' (my italics).

122 RIC 5: 210

123 The association of Aeternitas Augustorum with the representation of Saturn as the symbol of the age is also found on antoniniani of Gallienus of 267 CE on which Saturn is shown wielding the harpa-sickle with which he had mutilated his father Uranus.

124 RIC 4: 126 (206 CE, Caracalla); the bearer of the sickle represents 'Summer.'

125 Both quoted by Roberts, 'Sickles and Scythes Revisited,' p. 78.

126 Diod. Sic. 1.14.2: ἔτι γὰρ καὶ νῦν κατὰ τὸν θερισμὸν τοὺς πρώτους ἀμηθέντας στάχυς θέντας τοὺς ἀνθρώπους κόπτεσθαι πλησίον τοῦ δράγματος καὶ τὴν Ἶσιν ἀνακαλεῖσθαι ... On this text and those that follow, see the glosses offered by Frazer, *The Golden Bough*, 4.2, pp. 45 f.

127 The poor folk of Antium seem to have experienced this same prodigy repeatedly: Livy 22.1.10–11 (217 BCE): 'Et Antii metentibus cruentas in corbem spicas cecidisse'; 28.11.2 (206 BCE): 'Antio nuntiatum est cruentas spicas metentibus visas esse.' Or is this a case of annalistic duplication?

128 Hom. *Il.* 18, 569–71 (this time of harvesters of grapes rather than reapers of cereal grains); see West, *Orphic Poems*, pp. 56–61, with various fragmenta at pp. 62–7; Stephens, 'Linus Song,' notes that the song is variously happy and sad in different accounts, and seems unsettled by this duality of the singer, but it is probably inherent in the transitional time of the harvest. For our purposes, it is noteworthy that he was known to Augustine: *Civ. Dei*, 18.14.

129 The whole mise-en-scène is Mt. 13:1–52; the story here is 13:24–30. The text as in the African tradition (von Soden, *Das Lateinische Neue Testament*, pp. 394–5): 'Similitum est regnum caelorum homini seminanti bonum semen in agro suo. Et cum dormiunt homines, venit inimicus et seminavit zizania inter frumentum et abiit. Cum autem crevit herba et fructum fecit, tunc adparuerunt zizania. Accesserunt autem servi ad patrem familias et dixerunt: domine, non bonum semen seminasti in agro tuo; unde ergo habet zizania? Ait illis: inimicus homo hoc fecit. Dicunt ad eum servi: vis, eamus et colligamus ea? Dicit illis: non, ne forte dum colligitis zizania, eradicetis simul et frumentum cum eis. Sinite ambos crescere usque ad messem, et in tempore messis dicam messoribus: colligite primo zizania et alligate fasciculos ad exurendum ea, frumentum autem colligite in horreum meum.'

130 Mt. 13:37–43. with no parallels in the synoptics; the text as in the African tradi-

tion (von Soden, *Das Lateinische Neue Testament*, pp. 395–6): 'Qui seminat bonum semen, filius est hominis: ager autem est mundus; bonum autem semen hi sunt filii regni; zizania autem sunt filii mali: inimicus autem, qui ea seminat, diabolus est; messis autem consummatio saeculi est; messores autem angeli sunt. Quommodo ergo colliguntur zizania et igni exuruntur, ita exit in consummatione saeculi. Mittet filius hominis angelos suos, et colligunt de regno illius amnia scandala et eos, qui faciunt iniustitiam, et mittent illos in fornacem ignis, illic erit ploratio et stridor dentium. Tunc iusti fulgebunt sicut sol in regno patris sui. Qui habet aures, audiat.'

131 Paul. Nol. *Ep.* 23.1 (CSEL 29: 158): 'Nam et ager tu illi es, qui vicissim ager nobis est. In ipso enim serimus, et ab ipso metimus. Ager vero tu, non ille spinis horridus aut harenis aridus aut petrosis asper et nudus, in quo semen datum aut subfocatur, aut destituitur aut uritur; se ille, *quam benedixit Deus a rore caeli et ubertate terrae*. Unde et lingua tua verbo Dei rorat, et cor tuum fertile Deo, semen exceptum spiritali fruge multiplicat ut de fructibus *suis inpleat manum suam messor et sinum suum qui manipulos conligit*. Hoc est, ipse Deus, qui verbi in nobis sui et seminator et messor est. Ipse, et manus qui dextera Dei, quam bonis operibus implemus. Idem et ille Abraham sinus est, in quo operum mercede requiescimus.'

132 Indeed, it is in this context, of the hiring of reapers for pay, that I originally referred to it: chap. 1, p. 86 above.

133 Jo. 4:35–38: οὐχ ὑμεῖς λέγετε ὅτιἜτι τετράμηνός ἐστιν καὶ ὁ θερισμὸς ἔρχεται; ἰδοὺ λέγω ὑμῖν, ἐπάρατε τοὺς ὀφθαλμοὺς ὑμῶν καὶ θεάσασθε τὰς χώρας ὅτι λευκαί εἰσιν πρὸς θερισμόν. ἤδη ὁ θερίζων μισθὸν λαμβάνει καὶ συνάγει καρπὸν εἰς ζωὴν αἰώνιον, ἵνα ὁ σπείρων ὁμοῦ χαίρῃ καὶ ὁ θερίζων. ἐν γὰρ τούτῳ ὁ λόγος ἐστὶν ἀληθινὸς ὅτι Ἄλλος ἐστὶν ὁ σπείρων καὶ ἄλλος ὁ θερίζων. ἐγὼ ἀπέστειλα ὑμᾶς θερίζειν ὃ οὐχ ὑμεῖς κεκοπιάκατε· ἄλλοι κεκοπιάκασιν, καὶ ὑμεῖς εἰς τὸν κόπον αὐτῶν εἰσεληλύθατε. Jerusalem Bible translation (with minor modifications).

134 Rev. 14:14–16; what is left of this in the African tradition (von Soden, *Das Lateinische Neuetestament*, p. 584): '… super nubem: mette falcem tuam et mete, [quoniam] venti hora metendi; quia iam arida est messis terrae. Et misit ille sedens super nubem falcem suam in terram, et demessus est terram': … καὶ ἐν χειρὶ αὐτοῦ δρέπανον ὀξύ … Πέμψον τὸ δρέπανόν σου καὶ θέρισον, ὅτι ἦλθεν ἡ ὥρα θερίσαι, ὅτι ἐξηράνθη ὁ θερισμὸς τῆς γῆς … τὸ δρέπανον αὐτοῦ ἐπὶ τὴν γῆν, καὶ ἐθερίσθη ἡ γῆ. The modern bibliography, as might be expected for anything Biblical, is overwhelming; for a beginning, see Aune, 'Visions of Eschatalogical Salvation,' pp. 781–2, and esp. pp. 839–45 on these particular verses.

135 Rev. 14:17–20: the text as in the African tradition (von Soden, *Das Lateinische Neue Testament*, pp. 584–5): 'Et alius angelus e[xivit de] templo, quod est in caelo, et ipse habens falcem acutam. Et alius angelus exivit de ara Dei habens potestatem ignem et clamavit voce magnam ad illum, qui habebat falcem acutam dicens: mitte falcem

tuam acutam et vindemia botruos vinearum terrae, [quoniam] adulate factae sunt uvae eius. Et misit angelus falcem suam in terram et vendemiavit vineam terrae et misit in torcula irae Dei magnum, et calciatum est in torculari extra civitatem et manavit inde sanguis usque ad frenos equorum per stadia mille sexcenta.' Again, see Aune, 'Visions of Eschatalogical Salvation,' pp. 845–8 on these verses.

136 For *messis est finis saeculi, veniet tempus messis, veniet finis saeculi, messis est consumma-tio saeculi, saeculi finis*, or similar expressions, see Aug. *Ep.* 76.2 (CSEL 34.2: 326); *Tract. in Ioh.* 115.2 (CCL 36: 644); *En. in Ps.* 128.7 (CSEL 40: 1885); *Ep. ad Cath. de Donat.* 18.47 (CSEL 52: 293); *Serm.* 73A.1 (MiAg. 1: 248); *Civ. Dei*, 20.5 (CCL 48: 704); *Contra ep. Parm.* 1.14.21 and 2.2.5 (CSEL 51: 42–3 and 48); quoted at the great Conference of Carthage in 411 by the dissident bishop Habetdeum (3.258 = SC 224: 1198).

137 See the rich and compelling description in Primasius, *Comm. in Apocalyps.* 4.14 (CCL 92: 218–19); and the recapitution in the *Recapitulatio*, 14 (CCL 92: 314): 'Item Christum diverso scemate super nubem albam sedentem adserit coronatum cum falce messoria.'

138 Hieron. *Comment. in Esaiam*, 5.18.4 (CSEL 73: 190): for the first part of this pas-sage, see chap. 1, p. 37 above: 'Quomodo enim ante maturitatem segetes erumpentes cito pereunt, et antequam perfectio temporis veniat, germinantes inutiles sunt, sic, inquite, Aegyptii populi quasi rami inutiles falcibus praecidentur et cunctae propagines nudabuntur. Ac ne putares eum de vinea dicere, et non de hominibus, vertit metaphoram in historiae veritatem.' The text here has been modified to follow the text established by R. Gryson and J. Coulie, eds., *Commentaires de Jérôme sur le prophète Isaïe: Livres VI–VII* (Freiburg: Herder, 1994), pp. 613–14.

139 Hieron. *Comm. in Matt.* 2.37 (CCL 77: 111 = SC 242: 286): '*Qui respondens ait: Qui seminat bonum semen est filius hominis*: Perspicue exposuit quod ager mundus sit, sator filius hominis, bonum semen filii regni, zizania filii pessimi, zizaniorum sator Diabolus, messis consummatio seculi, messores angeli.'

140 Lucian, *Alex.* 11: ἅρπην ἔχων κατὰ τὸν Περσέα … The precise type of the cutting instrument, as with other heroes and dieties, varies according to the text and con-text.

141 Versnel, *Tradition and Reversal*, pp. 140–1 and 164, seems both to admit the connec-tion with the harvest and to query the identity of the *falx* as a harvester's sickle, saying that it is 'primarily a mythical attribute.' But the latter concession is sufficient for my purposes.

142 For the continuation of human sacrifice in Africa, see the bibliography and refer-ences, and discussion, in Shaw, 'Cult and Belief.'

143 Versnel, *Transition and Reversal*, pp. 100–2.

144 See Schörner, 'Neue Bilder für alte Rituale,' abb. 6, p. 206: 'Verteilung von Satur-nopfern im Jahresablauf,' who demonstrates that most sacrifices connected with the

cult were made in May–June and again in September–October, that is, just before the grain harvest and the olive harvest.

145 Or is it? Versnel, *Transition and Reversal*, pp. 100 and 114, has his doubts and says that the 'so-called "sickle" cannot prove this' (i.e., a connection with the harvest). I agree, but I do not take the sign of the 'sickle' (i.e., a cutting instrument) as fixed in its significance – the meaning of these signs could shift given time and place. Again, it is sufficient for my purpose that more than a few persons in late antiquity definitely thought of Saturn as armed with a reaper's *falx* (see Macrobius in the note following). And, as Versnel later notes (p. 140), the sickle was one of Time's 'emblems' that was shared by Saturn, citing Fest. 202.17 (Lindsay); 423.12 (Lindsay), Plut, *Quaest. Rom.* 42; Servius *ad Georg.* 2.406, in addition to the Macrobius cited below.

146 Macrobr. *Sat.* 1.8.9: 'Falcem ei quidam aestimant attributam quod tempus omnia metat exsecet et incidat.' At the end of a passage in which Saturn is identified with Kronos and Khronos (Time); and also with a penis because, as Macrobius states, the Greek word σάθη denotes the penis – so the god was once called Sathurn (pointing a similar origin for satyrs, who were once called 'sathyrs')

147 Brilliantly evoked, and documented, by Lane Fox, *Travelling Heroes*, pp. 269–77, with maps 7 and 8.

148 Cyprian, *Ep.* 37.2.1–2 (CCL 3B: 178–80). The translation offered here is basically that of G.W. Clarke, *The Letters of St. Cyprian of Carthage, 2: Letters 28–54* (New York: Newman Press, 1984), pp. 49–50, with minor modifications throughout.

149 See chap. 1, pp. 38–9; Festugière, 'Amulettes magiques,' pp. 84–6, in rejecting Bonner's more straightforward interpertation of the significance of the reaper on the amulets in *Studies in Magical Amulets*, pp. 71–5.

150 See the six examples listed and illustrated in F. Mourot, ed., *La Meuse*, vol. 55 in *Carte archéologique* (2002), p. 434, nos. 175–80, from the region around Naix, Roman Nasium.

151 Vardi, 'Imagining the Harvest,' pp. 1381–6, quotations from p. 1381.

152 Vardi, 'Imagining the Harvest,' pp. 1383–4: it is central to her argument that in common earlier figurations, Death was armed with a nobleman's spear. Despite much searching in evidence from earlier periods, however, I have not found much evidence to show that this was usually the case.

153 See chap. 3, pp. 142–3 above.

154 Eddie Izzard, *Glorious*, EPITAPH/WEA, 1997 (DVD release, 2004).

155 William Carlos Williams, 'The Corn Harvest,' no. 7 in *Pictures from Brueghel*, p. 9; compare his 'Haymaking,' no. 6, ibid., p. 8, with the same deflection to (or reflection of?) more modern sensibilities.

156 *Ioannikos, Vita Sabae* (BHG 935; AASS Nov. II.1 332–4 at p. 361C and the *Ioannikos, Vita Petri* (BHG 936; AASS Nov II.1 384–1435, at p. 423A: the saint lived

between 752/54 and 846. *Theristai* or reapers are actually referred to in the latter passage.

157 Servier, *Tradition et civilisation*, p. 307.

158 Aug. *Serm.* 313E.6 (= Guelferbytanus 29 = PLS 2: 620 = MiAg 1: 541): 'Attendite sarmentum purgatum, martyrem Cyprianum: attendite sarmenta amputata, haeretici et Donatistae. Quid vos ad istum dicitis pertinere, ad istum ferentem fructum pacis et unitatis, purgatum falce martyrii ad percipiendum coronam aeternae salutis.'

159 See, e.g., Hieron, *Comment. in Matt.* 2.37 (CCL 77: 112 = SC 242: 286–7): 'Quod autem dixit zizaniorum fasciculos ignibus tradi et triticum congregari in horrea, manifestum est hereticos quosque et hypocritas fidei gehennae ignibus concremandos ...'

160 J. Flavel, 'Upon the Harvest Season,' chap. 15 in *Husbandry Spiritualized; or, The Heavenly Use of Earthly Things* (London: Rober Boulter, 1669, with many subsequent reprints); as cited from the 1824 edition, pp. 163–4; Flavel deals with the following chapters, e.g., chap. 17, 'Upon Reaping the Same We Sow' (pp. 179–85), and chap. 18, 'The Joy of the Harvest-Men' (pp. 186–91).

161 Applen, 'Migratory Harvest Labor,' p. 53.

162 The trope and the image, at least, are singularly absent from works like Merridale, *Night of Stone*, which are fairly comprehensive in coverage; and oral sources seem to confirm to the author the absence.

163 See Scheid and Svenbro, *Craft of Zeus*, esp. pp. 131 ff. on the metaphor of weaving and *textus* in Latin, and the variable valencies of speaking and writing in Greek and Latin.

164 See Turner, *Death is the Mother*, esp. pp. 11–12, for one critique of so-called postmodernism; for this problem, as for so many others, it just does not work. As for what extensions are possible, one cannot rule out the possibilities suggested by imagination. In passing through Pearson International Airport on 10 March 2011 and picking up a discarded *Globe and Mail*, I saw, to my amazement, that the newspaper's cartoonist (A24) had armed the Grim Reaper with a chain saw.

165 See Breyel, Coessens, and Walschot, 'Essai d'analyse,' for an analysis.

166 Discussions of the image have used this commonplace test case in general analyses of the problem of metaphoric thinking: see Lakoff and Turner, *More Than Cool Reason*, pp. 73–9; Kövecses, *Metaphor in Culture*, pp. 279–82; and Fauconnier and Turner, *The Way We Think*, pp. 291–5. The same diagram (our fig. 4.25) is used in all of these discussions.

167 Several interesting cases are studied by Moore, 'The Grim Reaper.'

168 Studies that try to integrate the so-called *danse macabre* figures into the stream, I believe, are mistaken. The separate French case of 'La Grande Faucheuse' is one of these parallel developments: see Card and Wilson, 'Death-Defining Personifications.'

169 See note 166 above for more of the continued replication and use of the paradigm;

in this case, I shall fix on the two most detailed expositions in Turner, *Literary Mind*, pp. 76–84, and Fauconnier and Turner, *The Way We Think*, pp. 291–5.

170 Turner, *Literary Mind*, p. 79; the same basic points are repeated in later works.

171 Turner, *Literary Mind*, p. 80.

172 For conveniently accessible illustrations of the *cucullus* or hooded coat, see, e.g., T.J. Cornell and J. Matthews, *Atlas of the Roman World* (New York: Facts on File, 1981), p. 128: statue from Trier of a peasant dressed in a *cucullus*; pp. 132–3: a wall fresco, also from Trier, of rural workers outside a country house, one of whom wears the hooded cloak. Notably, it is also pictured on the season reliefs on the Reims arch: Stern, 'Les calendriers romains illustrés,' p. 65, fig. XXIII: October shown as a hooded peasant engaged in ploughing. For the Buzenol relief, see chap. 3, pp. 112–13 above.

173 See Shaw, 'Cult and Belief,' on the near-monotheistic position of the African Saturn.

174 See White, *Agricultural Implements*, p. 98; and Leglay, *Saturne africain: Histoire*, pl. viii: a painting from Pompeii where Saturn is armed with the long 'Italian' reaping blade.

175 Macrob. *Sat.* 1.7.24: 'Observari igitur eum [sc. Ianus] iussit maiestate religionis quasi vitae melioris auctorem: simulacrum eius indicio est, cui falcem, insigne messis, adiecit.'

176 See Sigaut, 'L'évolution des techniques,' pp. 16–20, who goes even further and co-ordinates the appearance of the first true scythes with this much enhanced importance of cattle and forage crops in the economy of the region.

177 For the manner in which human minds responded to different ecological conditions by shifting the representations of harvest months for mowing and reaping in the illustrated calendar tradition, see the charts redacted by Stern, 'Les calendriers romains illustrés,' between pp. 468 and 469. In almost all Mediterranean cases, the cereal grain harvest is placed in the month of July (with the assumption that the mowing of fodder would be a month earlier).

178 Turner, *Literary Mind*, p. 81.

179 See Carter, *Quintilian's Didactic Metaphors*, pp. 24, 31, 36–7, 43, 58–9: all on agriculture but with nothing on harvesting or, much less, reaping; and the more detailed study by Assfahl, *Vergleich und Metapher bei Quintilian*, esp. III.A, 'Landwirtschaft,' pp. 44–5, where nothing pertaining to reaping appears.

180 One possible case is his use of the time of harvest for old age and death: Cic. *De Senect.* 70; but it is a truly lonely one.

181 Taking one of the biblical passages so central to our analysis here – Mt. 13:24–43; ¶ Lk. 3:17; Straw, 'Augustine as Pastoral Theologian,' shows in what ingenious and complex ways Augustine interprets and re-interprets these primarily for exegetical and theological ends.

182 Theocr. *Id.* 10.42–56; see Gow, *Theocritus*, vol. 1, pp. 83–5, with useful annotation:

vol. 2, pp. 204–7. The last line of the song, which I have left out, seems to be a kind of threat to the foreman about cutting his own hand, the significance of which I do not clearly understand.

183 Servier, *Tradition et civilisation*, pp. 311–18.

184 Aug. *Confess.* 1.16.26 (CCL 27: 14); cf. Brown, *Augustine of Hippo*, p. 23.

185 Later post-Roman law codes make this clear: *Lex Burgund. Const.* 64: (ed. De Salis, *MGHLegesBurgundionum*, 1.2.1, Hanover, 1892): 'Of those who have stolen grain standing in sheaves [*in gremiis*]': 'If a native freeman has taken grain standing in sheaves, let him pay threefold, and let the fine be according to the rank of the person. If a slave has done so, let his master pay in simple for him, and let the slave receive three hundred blows' (trans. K. Drew)

186 Publicola apud Aug. *Ep.* 46.2 (CCL 31: 198), c. 396/9 CE, on the Roman military officials, tribunes and decurions, who supervised the crossing of the frontier in Tripolitania by men hired *ad servandas fruges ipsas*: 'Singuli possessores vel conductores solent ad custodiendas fruges suscipere quasi fideles epistulam decurione mittente, vel singuli transeuntes quibus necesse est per ipsos transire.' For fears of theft and fraud of grain from the threshing floor, see Pallad, *Opus agr.* 1.36. Guards were conventionally hired, not just for harvested grains, but also for a wide variety of vulnerable agricultural produce: see, e.g., P. Fay. 101, col. 1R and col. 1V (Euhemera, c. 18 BCE: A.C. Johnson, *Roman Egypt*, p. 175); P. Lond. 131V, col. xii (Harmopolis, 78/9 CE; A.C. Johnson, *Roman Egypt*, p. 195).

187 For some examples, see Fiensey, *Social History of Palestine*, p. 86; Adams, *Land Transport in Roman Egypt*, p. 161n9, and Kloppenborg, *Tenants in the Vineyard*, p. 384: PSI 4, no. 345 (Philadelphia, Arsinoite Nome; 256 BCE: Zenon Archive); p. 403: P. Cair. Zen. III, no. 59329 (Philadelphia, Arsinoite Nome; 256 BCE; Zenon Archive); and p. 455: P. Gur. 8 (Apollonias, Fayum; 210 BCE); for modern instances, see Vardi, 'Construing the Harvest,' p. 1433 and n. 36, for arrangements concerning the posting of *gardes messiers* in documents, legal and otherwise, from fifteenth- to eighteenth-century France.

188 See James 5:4 (on which see chap. 5, pp. 260–1), a violent attack on the rich who keep earned pay from reapers whom they have hired; it was a typical problem.

189 Morgan, 'The Place of Harvesters,' p. 37.

190 Hall, *Harvest Wobblies*, p. 27.

191 A constant theme: see Wyman, *Hoboes, Bindlestiffs, Fruit Tramps*, pp. 3–5, 7, 40–1, 43, and 48; the control of unwanted hangers-on often required coercion and sometimes led to violence.

192 Hall, *Harvest Wobblies*, pp. 27–8.

193 Morgan, *Harvesters and Harvesting*, p. 78.

194 R. Jütte, *Poverty and Deviance in Early Modern Europe* (Cambridge: Cambridge University Press, 1994), p. 150.

195 E.g., Braunert, *Die Binnenwanderung*, pp. 44–5, 60–1 and 192–3; Moatti, 'Le contrôle de la mobilité,' passim; cf. Salvemini, 'Migrants saisonniers,' pp. 172–3 for early modern southern Italy.

196 For a more detailed argument, see Shaw, 'Bad Boys,' chap. 14 in *Sacred Violence*, pp. 630–74.

197 Aug. *Serm.* 230.1 (PL 38: 1104): 'Quid enim cantatis, vos estis, si bene vivatis. Quam multi per hos dies inebriantur? Quam multi per hos dies, parum est quia inebriantur, insuper etiam turpiter et crudeliterque rixantur?' In the sermon, it is to be noted that he quotes the same verse (Romans 13:13–14) that he read on hearing the chant 'tolle lege' (see n. 206 below).

198 Morgan, 'The Place of Harvesters,' pp. 43–4, for #6 in his elements of the harvester's pay; *Harvesters and Harvesting*, pp. 88 f., 108 on beer as wages; p. 142 on drinking and violence.

199 Morgan, *Harvesters and Harvesting*, p. 142.

200 Horn, *Labouring Life*, p. 152: largely because of the widespread episodes of violence associated with gangs of harvesters, the Truck Act of 1887 finally made it illegal for employers to pay their workers in any form of alcoholic liquor.

201 As the edict issued by the *cognitor* or president of the legal hearing at Carthage in 411 (CCL 149A: 179) makes clear; his aim was to control violent acts or the maintenance of circumcellions on lands of landowners, but it is manifest who the personnel were who were liable for the men's behaviour – which is my point here.

202 Aug. *Ep.* 76.2 (CCL 31A: 78–9), dated to c. 403. Augustine is saying that no one would be so silly as to say 'cultivate weeds'; for the zizania (Gk. ζιζάνιον) see Mt. 13:25, part of the 'parable of the weeds among the wheat' (Mt. 13:24–30; kept as 'zizania' in the Vulgate).

203 Aug. *Serm.* 47.18 (CCL 41: 590), dated to mid-410.

204 See Plaut. *Capt.* 660–1: 'Rogas, / sator sartorque scelerum, et messor maxume?'

205 Mt. 13:30–9.

206 Aug. *Confess.* 8.12.29 (CCL 27: 131): 'Et ecce audio vocem de vicina domo cum cantu dicentis et crebro repetentis quasi pueri an puellae, nescio: "tolle lege, tolle lege." Statimque mutato vultu intentissimus cogitare coepi, utrumnam solerent pueri in aliquo genere ludendi cantitare tale aliquid.' For comment, especially on Courcelle's famously provocative interpretation of the passage, see J. O'Donnell, *Augustine, Confessions*, 3 vols. (Oxford: Clarendon Press, 1992; reprint 2000), vol. 3, pp. 59–65.

207 That is to say, he claims that it was *like* the voice of a child (and therefore one of the normal channels for direct divine communication) but he then admits that these were not the words of any child's game he knew; cf. Brown, *Augustine of Hippo*, p. 101.

5. Blade of Vengenance

1 Leo Tolstoy, *War and Peace*, trans. A. Briggs (Harmondsworth: Penguin, 2005), p. 460.

2 V. Grossman, *A Writer at War: A Soviet Journalist with the Red Army, 1941–1945*, ed. A. Beevor, trans. L. Vinogradova (New York: Vintage, 2007), pp. 36–7. Gomel is in the extreme south of the modern state of Belarus; the villages and peasants described by Vasily Grossman, however, were ethnically Ukrainian.

3 It was a tradition remembered. 'Sickles, scythes and hoes were important to peasants with tiny plots to look after. When they weren't used in the fields, these tools were readily adapted as weapons during the peasant uprisings': William Kurelek, *To My Father's Village* (Montreal: Tundra Books, 1988), facing p. 3.

4 F. Glinka, *Letters of a Russian Officer* (Moscow, 1815), as quoted by O. Figes, *Natasha's Dance: A Cultural History of Russia* (New York: Metropolitan Books, 2002), p. 74.

5 As pointed out by Le Gall, 'Les *falces* et la faux,' p. 56; for a specific case, see the peasant anarchists at Jerez de la Frontera in southern Spain in 1892, armed with sickles and scythes in their attacks on local landlords: B.W. Tuchman, *The Proud Tower: A Portrait of the World before the War, 1890–1914* (New York: Macmillan, 1966), p. 85.

6 Aug. *Civ. Dei*, 7.19 (CCL 47: 201): '"Falcem habet," inquit, "propter agriculturam." … An falcem sceptro perdito accepit, ut, qui primis temporibus rex fuerat otiosus, filio regnante fieret operarius laboriosus?'

7 Elliott, *Revolt of the Catalans*, passim for the revolt in general; for the specific role of the itinerant reapers or *segadors*, see pp. 144–51; these were itinerant harvesters and reapers who usually worked their way northwards from Barcelona in June and July of each year (see p. 64).

8 As Elliott, *Revolt of the Catalans*, p. 446n3, points out, the name given to the day, *Corpus de Sang*, was not used by the people of the time, but was later popularized by a novel in the nineteenth century.

9 The music, composed in 1892 by Francese Alió, was based on a traditional popular song; the lyrics by Emili Guanyavents were written at the end of the same decade, in 1899. It became the official national anthem of the Catalan government exactly a century later, in 1993, although it had already been accepted as a national anthem of the Catalans by the Generalitat at the time of the Republic.

10 Lyrics widely available: here from Wikipedia entry: http://en.wikipedia.org/wiki/Els_Segadors.

11 The painting was later dismantled and shipped to Valencia, the capital of the Republic, but was lost and never recovered; for a series of truly evocative pictures of Miró doing the painting itself, see M. Daniel and M. Gale, eds., *Joan Miró: The Ladder of Escape* (London: Thames and Hudson, 2011), pp. 118–21. For some of the

background, see A. Beevor, *The Battle for Spain: The Spanish Civil War 1936–1939* (Harmondsworth: Penguin, 2001), pp. 248 ff.

12 Verg. *Georg.* 1.506–8: '... non ullus aratro / dignus honos, squalent abductis arva colonis / et curvae rigidum falces conflantur in ensem'; see L.P. Wilkinson, *The Georgics of Virgil: A Critical Survey* (Cambridge: Cambridge University Press, 1969), p. 175, for comment; and R.F. Thomas, *Virgil, Georgics, Volume 1, Books i–ii* (Cambridge: Cambridge University Press, 1998), p. 153, who notes Page's insightful glossing of the vocabulary of death and mourning. In this passage, Vergil reflects the same zero-sum manpower game to which we have alluded already (see chap. 1, pp. 6–7 above): the military recruitment for killing meant that the fields were left untilled or unharvested.

13 Claud. *De consulat. Stilich.* 1.222–3: 'Salvius iam rura colat flexosque Sygambrus / in falcem curvat gladios ...'

14 This is the only significance, for example, that Guidorizzi and Beta, editors of *La metaphora*, contemplate; they list none of the works on cognitive scientific interpretations of metaphor to which I refer in what follows.

15 One of the basic arguments of Ricoeur, esp. 'The Decline of Rhetoric: Tropology,' chap. 2 in *The Rule of Metaphor*, pp. 44–64.

16 Pinker, 'The Metaphor Metaphor,' chap. 5 in *The Stuff of Thought*, pp. 235–78, a scintillating introduction from the perspective of the cognitive sciences.

17 J.L. Borges, 'The Metaphor,' chap. 2 in *This Craft of Verse* (Cambridge, MA: Harvard University Press, 2000), pp. 21–41, at p. 22: 'The Argentine poet Lugones ... said, in the foreword to a book called *Lunario sentimental*, that every word is a dead metaphor. This statement is, of course, a metaphor.'

18 See Sullivan, *Weaving the Word*, for a parallel study of the phenomenon drawn from the world of women's weaving. Of particular relevance to our argument is the violence inherent in the cutting of cloth, an action that is woven into this series of metaphoric extensions emerging from rural work; for the Maghrib, see Bourdieu, *Logic of Practice*, pp. 224, 234–5.

19 See Grantham, 'La faucille et la faux,' pp. 111 f., for a compelling exposition.

20 See Helmer, 'Les faucilles et les gestes.'

21 *Pass. Perp.* 4.3–4 (SC 417: 112–14).

22 Anon. *De Natali Sancti Iohannis Baptistae* = *Sermo Mai* 48: 1 (PLS 2: 1152): 'Non illa falcem legis senserat, non ibi vomer caelestis agricolae sulcos semitae rectionis induxerat ...'

23 Žižek, 'Divine Violence,' chap. 6 in *Violence*, pp. 178–95.

24 Henisch, 'In Due Season,' p. 324, with reference to the Chronicle of John of Worcester (England, c. 1130–40), Oxford, Bodleian Library MS Corpus Christi Coll. 157, f. 382.

25 See 'General Atomics MQ-9 Reaper,' *Wikipedia* (citation of 21 April 2011).

26 See Daniel, *Charred Lullabies*, in a general argument on the nature of violence found throughout the work, but see, e.g., pp. 39–42, 81–3, 97–100, and fig. 1, p. 41.

27 Livy 9.36.6: 'Iere pastorali habitu, agrestibus telis, falcibus gaesisque binis armati.'

28 Diod. Sic. 34/35.2.16 [= Photios, *Bibliotheka*, 385]: stating that in three days, Eunus had armed, as best he could, six thousand men, besides the others among his followers who had only axes, hatchets, slings, *sickles*, or fire-hardened sticks.

29 Tac. *Hist.* 3.27: 'Paulum inde morae, dum ex proximis agris ligones, dolabras, et alii falcis scalasque convectant.'

30 Hdt. 5.92e–f: … καὶ ἐκόλουε αἰεὶ ὅκως τινὰ ἴδοι τῶν ἀσταχύων ὑπερέχοντα, κολούων δὲ ἔρριπτε, ἐς ὃ τοῦ ληίου τὸ κάλλιστόν τε καὶ βαθύτατον διέφθειρε τρόπῳ τοιούτῳ.

31 As, for example, when a man's beard was said to be so thick that it should be reaped with a sickle rather than cut with a barber's shears: *Anth. Graec.* 11.368.

32 Xen. *Hier.* 6.10: οἱ δὲ τύραννοι μισθοῦ φύλακας ἔχουσιν ὥσπερ θεριστάς.

33 See, e.g., P. Enteux 29 (in a petition for the restoration of property): a harvesting sickle, δρέπανον θεριστικόν, valued at 2 drachmai; P. Giss. 10, col. 2, line 6 (second century BCE): two harvesting sickles: δρέπανα θεριστικά.

34 Hobi, *Die Benennungen von Sichel und Sense*, traces the development of the terms, both in Latin and in Germanic languages, out of which the terms for sickle and scythe emerge. Note that the words for these tools, as they were used in their northwestern European environment, have local linguistic origins.

35 These are just a few examples; for at least a dozen more, see Le Gall, 'Les *falces* et la faux,' pp. 55–60. Similarly, in Greek *drepanon* often signified a harvesting sickle, but not always. In general, it signified a cutting blade, larger than a small knife but smaller than, say, a sword: like a pruning hook: see, e.g., *Anth. Graec.* 6.3, 6.21, and 11.37.

36 Just as, for example, the winnowing fork was said to be 'the hand' or 'the five-fingered hand' of the farmer – and so, another example of 'extension': see, e.g., *Anth. Graec.* 6.104.

37 Bourdieu, *Logic of Practice*, p. 223, cf. p. 224, where he adds 'the cutting of cloth' to these homologies.

38 Bourdieu, *Logic of Practice*, pp. 226–7.

39 Bourdieu, *Logic of Practice*, p. 234.

40 Bourdieu, *Logic of Practice*, pp. 234–5, going on to note the ritual of the 'first sheaf' and studies of it since Frazer.

41 See, e.g., Aug. *Ep.* 93.10.40 (CCL 31A: 196): 'purgavit pater falce passionis'; repeated in *De Bapt.* 1.18.28 (BA 51: 173): 'et passionis falce purgatum'; *Ep.* 108.9 (CCL 31B: 73): 'etiam gloriosa martyrii falce purgatum est'; repeated in *Contra Cresc.* 2.38.49 (CSEL 52: 409): 'certe falce martyrii purgaretur'; and in *Serm.* 313E (MiAg 1: 541): 'purgatum falce martyrii ad percipiendam coronam aeternae salutis?'

42 Bourdieu, *Logic of Practice*, p. 235, citing the work of Bourilly, *Eléments d'ethnographie marocaine*, pp. 126–8, and Servier, *Tradition et civilisation*, pp. 227–30. These references are only *exempli gratia*; there is much more detail here that deserves consideration.

43 *1 Esdras*, 4.1–12; see Joseph. *AJ*, 11.43–8, at 46: in a typical prophetic discourse on the power of kings, where the stereotype is that of a farmer who ploughs the soil and reaps as the typical subject of royal power.

44 Gen. 37:5–9 (the New Jerusalem Bible translation, with minor modifications); cf. Joseph. *AJ*, 2.11: Joseph and his brothers have been sent out into their father's fields to reap. There he has the dream of the sheaves who bow to his sheaf 'like slaves to their master': τὰ δὲ ἐκείνων προστρέχοντα προσκυνεῖν αὐτὸ καθάπερ οἱ δοῦλοι τοὺς δεσπότας. Note the ritualistic gesture of proskynesis. In the later age of our harvester from Maktar, Joseph's dream was commented on by Quodvultdeus, the Christian bishop of Carthage, as the sign of a divine promise that was actually later made real: Quodvultdeus, *Liber promiss.* 1.25.34 (CCL 60: 42), another example of a *promissio facta et figurata*: 'Somniavit Ioseph somnium narravitque fratribus suis: *Putabam nos*, ait, *ligare gremia in campo surrexitque gremium meum et erectum est; conversa autem gremia vestra adoraverunt gremium meum.*' The importance is that the VG has a different version: '*Putabam ligare nos manipulos in agro et quasi consurgere manipulum meum et stare vestrosque manipulos circumstantes adorare manipulum meum.*' Note that, throughout, the non-African word *manipulus* is used for sheaf instead of *gremium*.

45 M.A. Sullivan, *Bruegel's Peasants*, p. 204, reports the use of the wheat sheaf in precisely this manner in the 1560s, to indicate rebellious opponents of the Church.

46 Verg. *Georg.* 2.516–17 and Servius, ad loc. and Corp. Gloss. 4.258 and 5.222.18; cf. White, *Agricultural Implements*, p. 111.h–j.

47 Plaut. *Rudens*, 762–3: 'Daem.: Si attigeris ostium, / iam hercle tibi messis in ore fiet mergis pugneis.'

48 Artemid. *Oneir.* 2.24: δρέπανον δὲ ἀφαιρέσεως καὶ βλάβης ἐστὶ σημεῖον διὰ τὸ πάντα διχάζειν καὶ μηδὲν ἐνοῦν.

49 Dig. 7.4.13 (Paul on Sabinus): 'Si fructuarius messem fecit et decessit, stipulam, quae in messe iacet, heredis eius esse Labeo ait, spicam, quae terra teneatur, domini fundi esse fructumque percipi spica aut faeno caeso ... quamvis nondum tritum frumentum ... coacta sit.'

50 Apud Athenaeus, *Deipn.* 15.25.695i–696a = PLG 3.651.

51 Plut. *Regum et Imp. Apophtheg.*182a: 'ἀλλ' οὐκ Ἀλέξανδρος ἦν τοιοῦτος' 'εἰκότως' εἶπεν, 'ἐκεῖνος μὲν γὰρ ἐθέριζε τὴν Ἀσίαν, ἐγὼ δὲ καλαμῶμαι.; for mopping up after the battle equated to gleaning, see Septuagint: Jd. 20.45, and Is. 3.12: οἱ πράκτορες ὑμῶν καλαμῶνται ὑμᾶς.

52 Vardi, 'Construing the Harvest,' p. 1436: later medieval and early modern European justifications for gleaning as a right of the poor were based on biblical injunctions –

especially the model of the Book of Ruth; jurists and administrators of these times founded their decisions on these sources and not on classical precedents or, notably, on the legal opinions of the Roman jurists.

53 Varro, *RR*, 1.53: 'Messi facta spicilegium venire oportet aut domi legere stipulam aut, si sunt spicae rare et operae carae, compasci. Summa enim spectanda, ne in ea re sumptus fructum superet.' That is to say, this is the final operation of the harvest to be conducted by the owner: he collects the remaining grains for himself in a process called *spicilegium* or, if it is not worth the labour to do the collecting, he uses the leftovers for grazing. In any event, it is not 'free stuff' – Varro cautions that the owner should not let the costs of doing the collecting exceed the value of the grains collected. See White, *Roman Farming*, p. 183; and Vardi, 'Construing the Harvest,' throughout, who notes that it was not a Roman practice or, indeed, one found in the post-Roman 'barbarian' law codes.

54 Dig. 50.16.30.1: '"Stipula illecta" est spicae in messe deiectae necdum lectae, quas rustici cum vacaverint colligunt.'

55 See Billiard, *L'agriculture dans l'antiquité*, p. 134, who cites only Theoc. *Id.*, but, alas, citing no specific verses; and nothing in Theocritus hints at a right of gleaning. See Lerche, 'Observations on Harvesting,' p. 37 for Iran in the mid-1960s: noting the social-relief function in the Hebrew Bible, he states: 'The gleaning near Sirjan can hardly be explained in this way.'

56 Whereas there is relatively little in the way of detailed reference and analysis to the end of Graeco-Roman antiquity, there is a huge profusion of commentaries beginning in the early medieval period in the West.

57 Joseph. *AJ*, 4.231: Ἀμῶντας δὲ καὶ συναιροῦντας τὰ θέρη μὴ καλαμᾶσθαι, καταλιπεῖν δὲ τινα καὶ τῶν δραγμάτων τοῖς βίου σπανίζουσιν ἕρμαιον εἶναι πρὸς διατροφήν.

58 For the texts, see R. Brooks, 'Peah,' in *The Mishnah*, ed. and trans. Neusner, pp. 14–35; and in Neusner, *The Talmud of the Land of Israel, 2: Peah* (Chicago: University of Chicago Press), pp. 202–20: *Y. Peah* 4: 7 (*M. Peah* 4: 10) and *Y. Peah* 5.2 (*M. Peah* 5: 2); for some interpretation, see Instone-Brewer, 'Tractate *Peah*: Harvest Leftovers for the Poor,' in *TRENT*, 1, pp. 121–67.

59 Henisch, 'In Due Season,' pp. 313–14.

60 Henisch, 'In Due Season,' p. 319, who notes that the 'calendar scenes are small. They are ornaments ... There is a doll's house air to many examples, and, even in the medium of stone, the little figures often look more like pixies than real people.'

61 Among the many cases for Africa alone, see Ferdi, *Corpus des mosaïques de Cherchel*, 'Maison des noces de Thétis et Pélée,' pp. 65–73: 'C: Mosaïque des vendages,' pp. 69–70 and pl. XX; for (still) useful comment, see Brandt, *Schaffende Arbeit: Altertum*, pp. 90–7; for a large dossier of such representations, see Bielefeld, *Die Stadtrömischen Eroten-Sarkophage*, passim.

62 S. Campbell, *The Mosaics of Antioch* (Toronto: Pontifical Institute of Mediaeval Studies, University of Toronto Press, 1988), pp. 7–8, pls. 9–11; cf. Hanfmann, 'The Seasons in John of Gaza's *Tabula Mundi*,' p. 111.

63 John of Gaza, *Ekphrasis tou kosmikou pinakos tou ontos en toi cheimerioi loutroi*, esp. 2.23–44, on Gê, the harvest, and the *karpoi*. For scholarly concerns about the date and the place see, especially, A. Cameron, 'On the Date of John of Gaza,' *CQ* 43 (1993), 348–51, also discussing the location of the baths.

64 For African examples, see Parrish, *Season Mosaics*, p. 25 (see his Cat. 13, for a fourth-century example from Carthage); with further reference to vinting *putti* on other mosaics, including one from the domain of the Liberii at Uthina; cf. Parrish, 'Two Mosaics from Roman Tunisia,' p. 281, for more detail.

65 Parrish, *Season Mosaics*, p. 69, provides the evidence and the figures: in his catalogue, of the 62 pavements whose location is known, 52 'adorned' (his word) private buildings; only 8 *might* have been in public structures. See Stern, 'Un calendrier romain illustré,' and Foucher, 'Terrains Salah Abdallah et Hadj Ferdjani Kacem' and 'Le calendrier de Thysdrus' for a typical instance from Thysdrus, part of a 'grande maison.'

66 The work of Kövecses – see 'The Basis of Metaphor,' chap. 6 in *Metaphor*, pp. 67–77, and *Metaphor in Culture* – is, in this respect, important in its modifying of the original claims of Lakoff and Johnson in *Metaphors We Live By*.

67 For what follows see, in part, Longnon, Cazelles, and Meiss, *The Très Riches Heures of Jean, Duke of Berry*, pp. 15–28.

68 So Henisch, 'In Due Season,' p. 333.

69 See above n. 60; cf. J.G. Merquior, ed. E. Gellner, *The Veil and the Mask: Essays on Culture and Ideology* (Boston–London: Routledge, 1979), where the metaphor is explicit and pervasive.

70 Meiss, *French Painting in the Time of Jean de Berry*, vol. 1, p. 32; see Henisch, 'In Due Season,' p. 333.

71 E.g. Plaut. *Mostell.* 159–61: 'Scapha: Eventus rebus omnibus, *velut* horno messis magna / fuit. Philematium: Quid ea messis attinet ad meam lavationem? / Scapha: Nihilo plus quam lavatio tua ad messim.'

72 Cf. Plaut. *Rudens*, 761–2: 'Si attigeris ostium, / iam hercule tibi messis in ore fiet mergis pugneis.'

73 Theodoret, *Historia Religiosa*, 14 (PG 82: 1412C–1413B); cf. P. Brown, *Power and Persuasion in Late Antiquity: Towards a Christian Empire* (Madison: University of Wisconsin Press, 1992), p. 27.

74 Bardin, *Vie d'un douar*, pp. 68–9: 'Chaque année ceux-ci [the peasant cultivators] attendant avec impatience l'époque des récoltes. Avec l'argent frais provenant de la vente de blé et d'orge, ils espérent pouvoir payer les impôts, se libérer de leurs dettes, procéder aux achats indispensables à la famille.'

75 Dracontius, *De mensibus*, 11–12 (ed. E. Vollmer, MGH AA 14, Berlin, 1905), 227

= *Anthologia Latina* 487a: 11–12 (ed. Riese); Courtney, 'The Roman Months,' p. 49, notes that Stern would prefer to connect this with the illustration for the month of July, with its large sack of coins that represented the pay-off of the harvest for the farmer; cf. Levi, 'The Allegories of the Months,' p. 262, for more comment. For the same imagery of the beards on the heads of grain being like spears, see Verg. *Georg.* 1.314–15, chap. 1, p. 27 above.

76 *Anthologia Latina* 395, ll. 21–4 (ed. Shackleton-Bailey, no. 391, p. 206), where, however, I do not accept his emendation of *Iam falx* at the beginning of line 3; cf. Levi, 'The Allegories of the Months,' p. 262 for comment; he, too, accepts the emendation of *Iam falx* at the beginning of the third line.

77 I agree with Courtney, 'The Roman Months,' pp. 48–9, that the adoption by Shackleton-Bailey of the reading *Iam falx* is in error. *Lampas* is in all of the manuscripts, and makes perfectly good sense. Also with Courtney, I cannot make much sense of the final line beginning 'florialisque' – but, *faute de mieux*, have offered a standard translation. Stern, *Calendrier de 354*, pp. 253 and 257, also accepts the last line as it stands, connecting it with 'the end of the season of flowers'; cf. Levi, 'The Allegories of the Months,' p. 262.

78 See Dolbeau and Etaix, 'Le "jour des torches,"' and Scheid, 'Les réjouissances.'

79 Foucher, 'Terrains Salah Abdallah et Hadj Ferdjani Kacem,' p. 38, fig. 9; Stern, 'Les calendriers romains illustrés,' pl. vi.16.

80 Ps.-Fulgentius, *Serm.* 56 'De natali S. Joannis Baptistae' (PL 65: 925–7, at 926): 'Si vultis recta lingua vocare diem lampadarum, diligite Spiritum sanctum: sed hoc dolemus, quia sunt multi qui diem vocant lampadam, et sunt in medio tenebrarum.' Another unknown African preacher, from about this same time, noted this same connection: *De Solstit. et Aequinoct.* ll. 256–61; 414–18 (ed. Botte, 100 and 104): 'Nam Moyses manifeste declaravit menses scilicet cum dicat initium mensis frumentariae. Tunc ergo repertum est esse primum solstitium mundi quando Ioannes natus est, quem diem lampadem appellant. Lampada enim erat luminis Christi a quo lumen acceperat cum esset adhuc in utero matris ... Unam [sc. diem] quidem diximus Iohannis esse mense Iunio id est octavo kalendas Iulias quem lampadem appellant quo tempore messis tritici caeditur.' See Stern, *Le Calendrier de 354*, pp. 253–4, and Dolbeau and Etaix, 'Le "jour des torches,"' for further comment.

81 Mt. 14:6–10; see Poque, 'La prédication des deux solstices,' chap. 15.2 in *Langue symbolique*, pp. 383–7, for some of the celestial imagery in Augustine's preaching. Poque does not note, however, the significance of the day in Africa as the Day of the Torches.

82 *De Solstit. et Aequinoct.* ll. 417–18 (ed. Botte, 104): 'Ostenditur quod et Iohannes qui eo tempore natus est et ipse velut messis decollatus est.'

83 Stern, *Le Calendrier de 354*, p. 255, citing work by Van Gennep, documenting this ritual as late as the nineteenth and earlier twentieth century in some rural regions of

France; the quotation (noted by Sir James Frazer) is from Durandus in his *Rationale divinorum officiorum* (Lyon, 1584), p. 556: 'Consuetum item est hac vigilia ardentes deferri faculas quod Johannes fuerit lucerna et qua viam Domini praeparavit.'

84 The *harpê* cutting instrument was a symbol of the fifth rank in the Mithraic hierarchy, the rank of the 'Persian' (cross-identified with Perseus); and a larger curved cutting instrument, a type of *falx*, was the symbol of the seventh grade of the *Pater*, god 'the Father': see Ulansey, *Origins of the Mithraic Mysteries*, pp. 37–9, and fig. 3.9; and CIMRM, no. 299; also of Herakles, even if only in one tale that was part of his cycle (above chap. 4, pp. 183–4).

85 See H. Strohm, *Mithra, oder: Warum 'Gott Vertrag' beim Aufgang der Sonne in Wehmut zurückblickte* (Munich: Wilhelm Fink, 2008), p. 201, fig. 52: Mithras reaping a grain crop (relief from the Dieburg Museum).

86 See Vermaseren, *Mithriaca*, I, pl. xix, and his comments on p. 22; for other such harvesting scenes, see CIMRM, nos. 241a, 1292–4b, 1421, and 1771.

87 CIJ 764 (Acmonia, third century CE); L. Robert, *Hellenica*, 11–12 (Paris: Adrien-Maisonneuve, 1960), p. 407; cf. Mitchell, 'The Cult of Theos Hypsistos,' pp. 112–13, who notes (p. 113n92) that the phrase 'sickle of the curse' is 'a cryptic reference' to a passage in the LXX version of Zechariah 5:2–4.

88 See a republican aes litra minted at Rome: on the obverse, the helmeted head of Mars; on the reverse, a horse's head with the *harpê* to the left (c. 241–235 BCE): Sydenham, *The Coinage of the Roman Republic* (London: Spink, 1952), no. 26; a denarius of Lucius Appuleius Saturninus, 104 BCE (Crawford, *RRC*, I, nos. 317.2–3b, p. 323): the obverse features a helmeted Roma (on 3a only); the reverse pictures Saturn in a quadriga wielding a *harpê*/sickle in his right hand, obviously reflecting the cognomen of the revolutionary tribune; and a denarius of Lucius Papius, 79 BCE (Crawford, *RRC*, I, no. 384.1, pp. 398–9; pl. xlix; symbols, no. 150): Juno Sospita on the reverse, with the *harpê* symbol to the left.

89 Ov. *Met.* 1.718: falcato ense; Luc. *BC*, 9.662–7: 'harpen Cyllenida.'

90 Apollod. *Bibl.* 1.6.3: Ζεὺς δὲ πόρρω μὲν ὄντα Τυφῶνα ἔβαλλε κεραυνοῖς, πλησίον δὲ γενόμενον ἀδαμαντίνῃ κατέπληπεν ἅρπῃ…; Hermes against Argos is another case: Ov. *Met.* 1.717; Lucian, 9.662; see West, *Hesiod, Theogony*, p. 217

91 For the more general background on what follows, see Richlin, *Garden of Priapus*, esp. pp. 58–9, where she lays out the field in which the threatening figure of Priapus dominates, and where the phallus (as much as the sickle) is his weapon '*militat omnis amans*, with a big gun.' The difference is that what I have to say here does not have much to do with humour, even aggressive humour.

92 Verg. *Georg.* 4.109–11: 'Invitent croceis halantes floribus horti / et custos furum atque avium cum falce saligna / Hellespontiaci servet tutela Priapi'; see Billiard, *L'agriculture dans l'antiquité*, p. 132; more extensively, and analytically, Fantham, 'Gods in a Man-Made Landscape: Priapus,' chap. 5 in *Latin Poets and Italian Gods*, 133–59 (for the

following two items, see esp. pp. 139–40). For other references to his armament with a sickle, see Tib. 1.1.17–18; 1.4.7–8; Proper. 4.2.25–6; and for the context of the poetry, and its function as an aggressive, threatening genre of poetics, see Richlin, 'Priapic Poetry,' in *Garden of Priapus*, pp. 116–27.

93 Ps.-Verg. *Priapea*, 2.4–5: 'erique villulam hortulumque pauperis / tueor, malasque furis arceo manus'; for the *custodes fructuum*, see chap. 4, p. 216 above.

94 Columella, *RR*, 10.27–34: 'Talis humus vel parietibus vel saeptibus hirtis / claudantur, ne sit pecori neu pervia furi. / Neu tibi Daedaliae quaerantur munera dextrae, / nec Polyclitea nec Phradmonis, aut Ageladae / arte laboretur, sed truncum forte dolatum / arboris antiquae numen venerare Priapi / terribilis membri, medio qui semper in horto / inguinibus puero, praedoni falce minetur.'

95 Ovid, *Met.* 14.640: 'Quique deus fures vel falce vel inguine terret'; cf. Fantham, *Latin Poets and Italian Gods*, p. 147.

96 Ps.-Verg. *Priapea* 2.19–21: '... at pol ecce vilicus / venit, valente cui revulsa bracchio / fit ista mentula apta claus dexterae.'

97 As is assumed even in personal action: cf. Ps.-Verg. *Priapea* 33.5–6: 'Turpe quidem factu, sed ne tentigine rumpar. / Falce mihi posita fiet amica manus.' See Richlin, *Garden of Priapus*, pp. 118–19, for further comment.

98 Noted by the same Josephus who noted the sickle as part of the legionaries' kit: Joseph. *BJ*, 3.5.92.

99 Foucher, 'Priape ithyphallique,' and figs. 1–3.

100 Leglay, *SAM*, 2, no. 24, pp. 140–1; plate xxvii, fig. 9

101 Strabo, 17.3.10 (sourcing Poseidonios): the arid zone, and marginal wetlands, of the northern Sahara and 'Aithiopia' tended to produce large numbers of locusts.

102 Horden and Purcell, *The Corrupting Sea*, pp. 417–18, citing the inscription as published in Varilioglu, 'Une inscription de Mercure,' p. 59 = AE 1988: 1048, cf. 1991: 1557: 'Mercuri sceptripotens, Argifonta, deorum angele / abige lucustarum nubis de his locis sacrosancta / virga tua, tuum enim similacrum hoc in loco stat / ponendum ad proventum frugum et ad salutare / remedium locorum et nationum harum. / Sis propitius et placatus hominibus cun/ctis et des proventus frugum omnium rerum.'

103 Pliny, *NH*, 8.29.104: (sourcing Varro).

104 Pliny, *NH*, 11.29.105: '... et in Syria militare imperio coguntur.'

105 Pliny, *NH*, 11.29.105: 'Italiam ex Africa maxime coortae infestant, saepe populo Romano ad Sibyllina coacto remedia confugere inopiae metu.'

106 Livy, 42.10.7–8: 'Lucustarum tantae nubes a mari repente in Apuliam inlatae sunt ut examinibus suis agros late operirent. Ad quam pestem frugum tollendam, Cn. Sicinius, praetor designatus cum imperio <in> Apuliam missus, ingente agmine hominum ad colligendas eas coacto, aliquantum temporis absumpsit.' He might well have been press-ganging seasonal harvesters in addition to regular soldiers, as was done in early modern Italy: Salvemini, 'Migrants saisonniers,' p. 170.

107 Oros. *Adv. pagan.* 5.11.1–3: 'M. Plautio Hypsaeo, M. Fulvio Flacco consulibus, vixdum Africam a bellorum excidiis quiescentem horribilis et inusitata perditio consecuta est. Namque cum per totam Africam inmensae lucustarum multitudines coaluissent et non modo iam cunctam spem frugum abrasissent herbasque omnes cum parte radicum. Folia arborum cum teneritudine ramorum consumpsissent, verum etiam amaras cortices atque arida ligna praeroderent, repentino abreptae vento atque in globos coactae portataeque diu per aerem, Africano pelago inmersae sunt. Harum cum inmenses acervos longe undis urguentibus fluctus per extenta late litora propulissent, taetrum nimis atque ultra opinionem pestiferum odorem tabida et putrefacta congeries exhalavit.'

108 Corippus, *Ioh.* 2: 195–203 (ed. Diggle and Goodyear): '… Quis cernere posset / milia tanta virum? Sic si lucusta sub astris / Austro flante cadit Libycos diffusa per agros / vere sub extremo, vel cum Notus aethere ab alto / in mare praecipitem magnoque a turbine raptam / ire iubet: dubiis horrescunt corda pavore / agricolis, segetes ne conterat horrida pestis, / neu vastet fructus teneros hortosque virentes, / mollibus aut ramis florentem laedat olivam.'

109 *Dig.* 48.19.16.9 (Claudius Saturninus): 'Evenit, ut eadem scelera in quibusdam provinciis gravius plectantur, ut in Africa messium incensores, in Mysia vitium, ubi metalla sunt adulteratores monetae.'

110 Procop. *Bell. Vand.* 2.19.20.

111 Plaut. *Merc.* 71: 'Tibi aras, tibi occas, tibi seris, tibi idem metis …'

112 Plaut. *Epidic.* 265: 'Mihi istic nec seritur nec metitur …'

113 Plaut. *Rud.* 637: 'et tibi eventuram hoc anno uberem messem mali …'; *Trinumm.* 32–3: 'eorum licet iam metere messsem maximam, / neque quicquam hic nunc est vile nisi mores mali.'

114 Cic. *De orat.* 2.65.261: for earlier examples, see Arist. *Rhet.* 3.3.4 (also in the context of metaphor).

115 Ho. 8:7: 'Quia ventum seminabunt et turbinem metent, culmus stans non est in eis, germen non faciet farinam' (VG); cf. 10:12–13: 'Seminate vobis in iustitia, metite in ore misericordiae, innovate vobis novale tempus autem requirendi Dominum cum venerit qui docebit vos iustitiam. Arastis impietatem iniquitatem messuistis comedistis frugem mendacii' (VG). Francis I. Andersen and David Noel Freedman, *Hosea*, The Anchor Bible, vol. 24 (New York–Garden City, NJ: Doubleday, 1980), pp. 496–9, suggest that the metaphors in the standard translation do not work as intended, and so they translate: 'They will sow when it is windy. They will reap in a whirlwind.'

116 Tert. *Apol.* 50.13 (CCL 1: 171): 'Etiam plures efficimur quotiens metimur a vobis; semen est sanguis Christianorum.'

117 Verg. *Aen.* 4.512–14: 'Sparserat et latices simulatos fontis Averni, / falcibus et messae ad lunam quaeruntur aenis / pubentes herbae nigri cum lacte veneni.' For the

use of *bronze* sickles for magical purpose, see also Ovid. *Met.* 7.226; Macrob. Sat. 5.19.6–10 (citing Sophokles).

118 For example, Apuleius quoted and then commented on these lines in his defence speech on the charge of black magic: *Apol.* 30, lines 19–37.

119 Verg. *Aen.* 4.382–6: 'Spero equidem mediis, si quid pia numina possunt, / supplicia hausurum scopulis et nomine Dido / saepe vocaturum. Sequar atris ignibus absens / et, cum frigida mors anima seduxerit artus, / omnibus umbra locis adero. Dabis, improbe, poenas' (translation by Robert Fagles, with minor alterations).

120 Jb. 4:7: (4:8 VG): 'quin potius vidi eos qui operantur iniquitatem et seminant dolores et metunt eos …' (VG). M.H. Pope, *Job*, The Anchor Bible, vol. 5 (New York–Garden City, NJ: Doubleday, 1973), p. 34: 'I have observed that they who plow evil / And sow trouble reap the same. / At a breath of God they perish, / A blast of His anger, and they vanish.'

121 Pr. 22:8 (cf. 12:14): 'Qui seminat iniquitatem metet mala et virga irae suae consummabitur' (VG).

122 Davis, 'Running on Poetry: The Agrarian Prophets,' chap. 7 in *Scripture, Culture, and Agriculture*, pp. 120–38, esp. pp. 122–4; 129–31.

123 Gal. 6:7–9: 'Nolite errare Deus non inridetur. Quae enim seminaverit homo haec et metet. Quoniam qui seminat in carne sua de carne et metet corruptionem. Qui autem seminat in spiritu, de spiritu metet vitam aeternam. Bonum autem facientes non deficiamus, tempore enim suo metemus' (VG).

124 Fulgent. *De remiss. peccat.* 2.7.4, 2.8.2–6 (CCL 91A: 686–9), beginning by quoting Paul: 'Quae enim seminaverit homo, haec et metet' (Galat. 6:8–9).

125 Fulgent. *De remiss. peccat.* 2.5.2 (CCL 91A: 683).

126 Indeed, Fulgentius, *De remiss. pecat.* 2.18.2–2.19.4 (CCL 91A: 702–4), later advances to an extended use of the metaphor of the workers in the vineyard and their pay, only to morph back into the wheat harvest.

127 Ps. 129:5–7 (NEB)

128 See, e.g., Aug. *En. in Ps.* 128.12–13 (CCL 40: 1888).

129 Poque, 'Ventilabrum,' chap. 2.6 in *Langue symbolique*, 1, pp. 151–6, catches a small part of this symbolism of language, on the specific action of winnowing the harvested cereal grains.

130 Aug. *Contra ep. Parm.* 1.7.12 (CSEL 51: 33): 'Quod utique si esses, cum videres in scripturis sanctis messem domini tui ante ultimam segregationem et ventilationem a zizaniis et palea non posses separari …'

131 Mt. 9:37–8; ¶ Lk. 10:2–3: τότε λέγει τοῖς μαθηταῖς αὐτοῦ, Ὁ μὲν θερισμὸς πολύς, οἱ δὲ ἐργάται ὀλίγοι· δεήθητε οὖν τοῦ κυρίου τοῦ θερισμοῦ ὅπως ἐκβάλῃ ἐργάτας εἰς τὸν θερισμὸν αὐτοῦ.

132 That is to say, although the writer is configuring the Lord of the Harvest as the supreme deity Himself, he is using an analogy based on realities such as the Aramaic

rab hesâdâ, which signified the person responsible for hiring and releasing the reapers: see W.F. Albright and C.S. Mann, *Matthew*, The Anchor Bible, vol. 26 (New York–Garden City, NJ: Doubleday, 1971), p. 114.

133 There is an African connection, since in discussion of the 'end of times' with non-African audiences and readerships in the years when he is mainly concerned with the Priscillianist controversy, he does not resort to this metaphor. See, e.g., *Ep.* 197–9 (CSEL 57: 231–92), three letters written to Hesychius bishop of Salona; *Ep.* 199, in particular, is a huge letter verging on a treatise, that discusses the end of the world, with Greek concerns related to the calculation of time, but without any recourse to the harvest metaphor.

134 For reapers as 'the angels of the Lord,' see, e.g., Aug. *Tract in Ioh.* 15.32; 115.2 (CCL 36: 163–4 and 644); *En. in Ps.* 128.7; 128.12–13 (CCL 40: 1185, 1888); *Sermo* 73 (PL 38: 472); 73A (MiAg 1: 248, 250), 79A (PLS 2: 808); 88 (RB 94: 95); *Civ. Dei* 20.9 (CCL 48: 715–16); *Contra ep. Parm.* 1.14.21; 2.1.3–2.2.4 (CSEL 51: 42–3, 46–7).

135 Aug. *Psalmus contra partem Donati*, vv. 179–80 (BA 28: 174): 'Quod hos tamquam aream suam / posset Christus ventilare. / Misit in messem operarios / discipulos praedicare ...'; the Lord as the paterfamilias who makes the decision on the winnowing, who oversees the separation: Aug. *Contra ep. Parm.* 3.3.19 (CSEL 51: 123): 'Veniet enim ille pater familias ferens ventilabrum in manu sua, mundabit aream suam, frumenta recondet in horreum, paleam vero comburet igni inextinguibili, name per aliam similitudinem omne triticum ovium nomine et omnis palea haedorum nomine significatur, quo duo pecorum genera interim permixta sub uno pastore pascuntur.'

136 Poque, *Langue symbolique*, 154–6.

137 *Psalmus contra partem Donati*, vv. 185–8 (BA 28: 176); see Shaw, *Sacred Violence*, chap. 11 for a more detailed exposition.

138 See *Psalmus contra partem Donati*, vv. 181–3, 185–7, 190, 199, 203, 213–14 (BA 28: 176, 178, 180) amongst others: 'Misit in messem operarios discipulos praedicare / per quos area collecta est et ventilata de cruce. / Tunc isti tamquam frumentum ecclesiam impleverunt caste /... ut alia surgeret messis quae ventilanda est in fine, / et crescit inter zizania quia sunt haereses ubique; / huius palea sunt iniusti, qui non sunt in unitate, /... Pone in corde areas duas... / Iniusti iniustos sufferebant venturo ventilatore, ... / Quid vobis ad haec videtur? / Secunda messis ecclesiae, / quae per orbem totum crescit ... / Sed palea quasi aristarum quidam <sunt> superbi valde / quos antequam ventilentur, / tempestas rapit de messe.'

139 Among many references, see Aug. *Contra ep. Parm.* 1.13.20–1.14.21 (CSEL 51: 42–3), developing Mt. 13:23; 3.2.18 (CSEL 51: 122–3), appealing to the prophet Jeremiah; *Ep. ad Cath. contra Donatist.* 19.52–2 (CSEL 52: 301–2); *Contra litt. Petil.* 3.2.3 (CSEL 52: 164); *En. in Ps.* 92.5; 100.12 (CCL 39: 1295, 1416).

140 All of this developing ideas in Mt. 3:12; see the note above, and, further Aug. *En. in Ps.* 128.7–8, 12 (CCL 40: 1885–6; 1888).

141 Again, in addition to all of the above, Aug. *Serm.* 31.6 (CCL 41: 395–6).

142 Aug. *Sermo*, 73A = Caillau 2.5 (PLS 2: 421–4; MiAg 1: 248–51) in extenso, naming the heretics who are represented in the tied-up bundles of weeds that will be thrown into the unquenchable fire.

143 B. Bearak, 'Renewing a Tradition of Protest, South Africa's Poor Demand Basic Services,' *New York Times* (Monday, 7 September 2009), p. A4: the picture features protesters from the township of Siyathemba who were chanting slogans in late July of that year. Their demand was that government should begin providing basic human services.

144 See John Moschus, *Pratum spirituale*, 183 (PG 87.3: 3053–6); cf. Chitty, *Desert a City*, p. 145, where the story is retold.

145 Hes. *Theog.* 179–81: δεξιτερῇ δὲ πελώριον ἔλλαβεν ἅρπην, μακρὴν καρχαρόδοντα, φίλου δ' ἀπὸ μήδεα πατρὸς ἐσσυμένως ἤμησε…; see West, *Hesiod, Theogony*, pp. 217–19; Brown, 'The Ritual Sickle,' chap. 2.5 in *Israel and Hellas*, pp. 78–9; and Burkert, *Homo necans*, pp. 290–1, for comment. Some have doubted that the *harpê* here is a harvester's sickle. I do not dispute that mention of the instrument could have been derived from Near Eastern contexts where it might have been a different kind of cutting instrument, even a sword; but here, there is little doubt about its significance: see Nilsson, 'The Sickle of Kronos.'

146 On the transition from the Hittite Kumarbi and his bite to the Greek Kronos, see Lane Fox, 'The Great Castrator,' chap. 16 in *Travelling Heroes*, pp. 259–79, at p. 265, with the interesting suggestion (p. 267) that the epithet *ankulomêtês* ('of crooked counsels') for Kronos is a later misapprehension of an original *ankulamêtês* ('crooked reaper').

147 West, *Hesiod, Theogony*, p. 218.

148 Quintus Smyrnaeus, 6.215–19, and Eur. *Ion*, 191: Λερναῖον ὕδραν ἀναίρει / χρυσέαις ἅρπαις ὁ Διὸς παῖς.; cf. West, *Hesiod, Theogony*, p. 217.

149 For example, Apollod. *Bibl.* 2.4.2; Lykophron, 840; Nonnius, *Dionys.*, 47.503–4; Eratosth. *Kataster.* 22; Ov. *Met.* 4.666, 720–7; 5.69.

150 For example, see 'The Beazley Archive,' no. 42079: Bonn, Akademisches Kunst-museum, 62d = *AA* (1935), p. 482, fig. 58; no. 44584: Berlin, Antikensammlung, F 2344 = Schefold and Jung, *Die Urkönige*, p. 113, fig. 136A; no. 46075: Palermo, Mormino Collection, 4691; 214131: Tubingen, Eberhard-karis-univ. Arch. Inst. E134 = J. D. Beazley, *Attic Red-Figure Vase-Painters*, 2nd ed. (Oxford: Clarendon Press, 1963), 1009.8; no. 207172: Madrid, Museo Arqueologico Nacional, L169 = Beazley, *Attic Red-Figure Vase-Painters*, 619.19.

151 For example, see 'The Beazley Archive,' no. 207002: Boston, Museum of Fine Arts, 90.156 = Beazley, *Attic Red-Figure Vase-Painters,*, 605.62; Schefold and Jung,

Die Urkönige, p. 85, fig. 96; *LIMC*, pl. 60 (Orpheus, 28); 204533: Cincinnati, Art Musuem, 1979.1 = Beazley, *Attic Red-Figure Vase-Painters*, 416.2; Schefold and Jung, *Die Urkönige*, pp. 82–3, figs. 93–5.

152 Burkert, 'The Function and Transformation of Ritual Killing,' chap. 5 in *Homo necans*, p. 40: 'The most thrilling and impressive combination of these elements [terror, bliss, recognition of authority] occurs in sacrificial ritual: the shock of the deadly blow and flowing of blood, the bodily and spiritual rapture of festive eating, the restrictive order surrounding the whole process.'

153 Burkert, *Homo necans*, pp. 44 f., argues that the extension took place historically with the supersession of agriculture over hunting. The argument that blood sacrifice *must* accompany harvest or harvest festivals, however, seems to be as dubious as the claim that the death penalty was an extension of 'seriousness' into the state sphere and that it was aimed mainly at sacral violations (pp. 46–7).

154 West, *Hesiod, Theogony*, p. 218.

155 Leglay, *Saturne africain*, pp. 191–5; for Ceres and the Cereres, see p. 192n3.

156 Arnob. *Adv. nat.* 6.25 (CSEL 4: 236): 'Falx messoria scilicet, quae est attributa Saturno, metum fuerat iniectura mortalibus, vitam vellent ut pacificam degere ac malitiosa, abicere voluntates …'; on Saturn as *frugifer*, see Leglay, *Saturne africain*, pp. 120–4; oddly enough, he nowhere seems to refer to the passage in Arnobius.

157 Arnob. *Adv. nat.* 6.12 (CSEL 4: 223): 'Itaque Hammon cum cornibus iam formatur et fingitur arietinis, Saturnus cum obunca falce custos ruris …'; cf. Leglay, *Saturne africain*, pp. 7–8.

158 At Uzelis in the hinterland of Cirta, for example, Jupiter Optimus Maximus was the *Genius areae frumentariae*: CIL 8.6339 = ILS 3669; cf. Février, 'Religion et domination dans l'Afrique romaine,' p. 313 = *La Méditerranée de Paul-Albert Février*, p. 797.

159 Claud. *De Consul. Stilich.* 1.110: 'non falce Gelonus …' in a list of armaments of Black Sea barbarians.

160 An opinion ascribed to Lucius Furius Philus (via L. Furius Rufus) by Cic. *De Rep.* 3.9.15–16: 'Galli turpe esse ducunt frumentum manu quaerere, itaque armati alienos agros demetunt.'

161 Hos. 10:12 (JB version).

162 J. Smolowe and B. Baumohl, 'Reap As Ye Shall Sow,' *Time Magazine* (5 February 1996).

163 P. Rucker, 'Pro-Life Activist Says Doctor "Reaped What He Sowed,"' *Washington Post* (1 June 2009).

164 Hos. 10:13–15; 11:1–9 continues the same theme.

165 Hos. 13:9 and 14:1.

166 Jer. 51:33 (JB version)

167 D. Bourguet, 'Métaphore de l'aire,' in *Des Métaphores de Jérémie* (Paris: Librairie Lecoffre, 1987), pp. 408–14, at pp. 411–12.

168 Jl. 3:9–10, 13–14 (JB version); although retailing much earlier events, the book as it stands was probably composed at the end of the fifth or the beginning of the fourth century BCE.

169 Is. 17:4–5 (NEB, with modifications).

170 *Orac. Sibyll.* 5.271–75: οἱ δὲ κακοὶ στείλαντες ἐπ᾽ αἰθέρα γλῶσσαν ἄθεσμον / παύσονται λαλέοντες ἐναντίον ἀλλήλοισιν, /αὐτοὺς δὲ κρύψουσιν, ἕως *κόσμος ἀλλαγῇ; / ἔσται δ᾽ ἐκ νεφέων ὄμβρος πυρὸς αἰθομένοιο· / κοὐκέτι καρπεύσουσι βροτοὶ στάχυν ἀγλαὸν ἐκ γῆς·

171 *Orac. Sibyll.* 14.355–56: ἐν γαίῃ κακίη καταδύσεται εἰς ἅλα δῖαν. / καὶ τότε δ᾽ ἐγγὺς ἔην τὸ θέρος μερόπων ἀνθρώπων.

172 *Orac. Sibyll.* 2.161–64· ὦ μέγα δειλοί / ὑστατίης γενεῆς φῶτες κακοεργέες αἰνοί / νήπιοι οὐδὲ νοοῦντες, ὅθ᾽, ἡνίκα φῦλα γυναικῶν / μὴ τίκτωσιν, ἔφυ τὸ θέρος μερόπων ἀνθρώπων. (Lightfoot, *Sibylline Oracles*, p. 296; for comment, see pp. 470–71); cf. Clement, *Stromateis*, 3.6.45.

173 See some of the striking cases described by de Ste Croix, *Class Struggle*, pp. 185–8, 198–201.

174 Fiensey, *Social History of Palestine*, p. 87, with sources.

175 Aug. *Ep.* 153.23 (CSEL 44: 423): '… nam plerique ne medico volunt reddere honorem suum nec operario mercedem': 'For many people do not want to give the doctor his honorarium or pay the worker his wage'; on *operarii*, see ch. 4, n. 120 above.

176 Jm. 5:1–6 (NT: Jerusalem Bible, with modifications): 'Age nunc divites plorate ululantes in miserii quae advenient vobis. Divitiae vestrae putrefactae sunt et vestimenta vestra a tineis comesta sunt. Aurum et argentum vestrum eruginavit. Et erugo eorum in testimoniam vobis erit et manducabit carnes vestras sicut ignis thesaurizastis in novissimis diebus. Ecce merces operariorum qui messuerunt regiones vestras qui fraudatus est a vobis clamant. Et clamor ipsorum in aures Domini Sabaoth introiit. Epulati super terram et in luxuriis enutristis corda vestra. In die occasionis addixistis occidistis iustum non resistit vobis' [VG]. Cf. the Greek version at 5:4: ἰδοὺ ὁ μισθὸς τῶν ἐργατῶν τῶν ἀμησάντων τὰς χώρας ὑμῶν ὁ ἀφυστερημένος ἀφ᾽ ὑμῶν κράζει, καὶ αἱ βοαὶ τῶν θερισάντων εἰς τὰ ὦτα κυρίου Σαβαὼθ εἰσελήλυθαν.

177 Jm. 5:7–9: Μακροθυμήσατε οὖν, ἀδελφοί, ἕως τῆς παρουσίας τοῦ κυρίου. ἰδοὺ ὁ γεωργὸς ἐκδέχεται τὸν τίμιον καρπὸν τῆς γῆς, μακροθυμῶν ἐπ᾽ αὐτῷ ἕως λάβῃ πρόϊμον καὶ ὄψιμον. μακροθυμήσατε καὶ ὑμεῖς, στηρίξατε τὰς καρδίας ὑμῶν, ὅτι ἡ παρουσία τοῦ κυρίου ἤγγικεν. μὴ στενάζετε, ἀδελφοί, κατ᾽ ἀλλήλων, ἵνα μὴ κριθῆτε· ἰδοὺ ὁ κριτὴς πρὸ τῶν θυρῶν ἕστηκεν. And in the VG version: 'Patienter igitur estote fratres ad adventum Domini … patienter ferens … Ecce Iudex ante ianuam adsistit.' For the significance of the town gates in north Africa, see W. Seston, 'Des "Portes" de Thugga à la "constitution" de Carthage,' *RH* 237 (1967), pp. 277–94.

178 What I am suggesting is a pattern similar to that long ago argued by Erich Auerbach, *Mimesis: The Representation of Reality in Western Literature* (Princeton: Princeton University Press, 1953; reprint 2003), although not in such an almost law-like fashion.

179 Applen, 'Migratory Harvest Labor,' pp. 89–92: 'as with other categories of wheat harvesters, they were freely showered with the epithets of "bum" and "tramp" by the residents of the wheat growing regions, although beyond appearance they bore little resemblance to those chronically unemployable vagabonds who occasionally entered the wheatlands' (p. 92).

180 One of the more striking of these reports was made by the novelist Jack London in a perhaps less well known work of his entitled *The War of the Classes* (New York: Macmillan, 1905), pp. 66 ff. under the entry on 'The Tramp.'

181 Applen, 'Migratory Harvest Labor,' p. 108; see also Salvemini, 'Migrants saisonniers,' pp. 170–1: roughly, the distinction between his despised 'compagnies volantes' and the more acceptable 'compagnies des moissonneurs' in southern Italy.

182 Wyman, *Hoboes, Bindlestiffs, Fruit Tramps*, p. 6.

183 Salvemini, 'Migrants saisonniers,' p. 171, in which the mobile reapers were identified with 'fugitifs des régions les plus éloignées du Royaume, en raison des dettes ou de délits … tuent les boeufs, volent les arrhes et les semailles, mettent le feu aux meules et exercent … l'art infâme des bandits de grands chemins.'

184 Quoted by Comet, *Le paysan et son outil*, pref.: 'Avec putains et larrons convient faire nos moissons.'

185 Applen, 'Migratory Harvest Labor,' p. 110.

186 Applen, 'Migratory Harvest Labor,' pp. 110–12.

187 Applen, 'Migratory Harvest Labor,' pp. 116–17, 124–7 on examples of the disparity in labour available as opposed to demand, all of it causing much distress in the American West in the last decades of the nineteenth century.

188 Cic. *Paradox. Stoic.* 46, following a long litany of terrible crimes of that age: 'qui illam Sullani temporis messem recordetur.'

189 See, e.g., Firm. Mat. *Math.* 3.7.14; 4.10.5; 4.13.12; 4.14.15; 4.15.6; 5.6.4; 6.15.9; 6.17.2; 8.76.18; 8.83.1; all this from a learned man in the elite who made the transition from traditional cult to Christianity. Notably, our man from Maktar rose from being a day labourer in the fields, *ex opere*, to his position as manager of a gang of reapers.

190 On the Ruth and Boaz story, see chap. 2, p. 83; on violence of men against women, see Morgan, 'The Place of Harvesters,' pp. 36–7 (surely a very small hint of a much larger problem).

191 Applen, 'Migratory Harvest Labor,' p. 149.

192 Thompson, 'Bringing In the Sheaves,' p. 471, for Canada: 'the dream of independence'; cf. Cherwinski, 'The Incredible Harvest Excursion of 1908,' p. 58, for the same motive.

193 Applen, 'Migratory Harvest Labor,' pp. 152–3, citing Frank S. Hamilton, an IWW pamphleteer, writing in November of 1914.

194 Applen, 'Migratory Harvest Labor,' p. 157, citing the report from the *New York World* (13 August 1916, p. 11; dated Sioux City, Iowa, 12 August 1916).

195 Aug. *Contra ep. Parm.* 1.13.20–1.14.21 (CSEL 51: 42–3) is the first sequence like this in this polemical work against Parmenian, the dissident bishop of Carthage and Primate of Africa.

196 For example, Aug. *Contra ep. Parm.* 2.1.1–2.3.6 (CSEL 51: 43–50) is another use of the metaphor that leads off the second book (ending with reference to circumcellions); 2.2.5 repeats it (again with specific reference to the circumcellions); 2.4.9–6.11 again repeats the metaphor, as do 2.11.25 and 2.15.34–6; the next book leads off with the same metaphor: 3.1.2–11; 3.2.13–3.2.18, repeats the metaphor, and it leads to a direction discussion of the circumcellions; and 3.4.25–3.5.28 (CSEL 51: 131–6) towards the end of the work uses the harvest metaphor again, with further reference to the gangs of circumcellions; cf. *Contra Cresc.* 3.31–5 (CSEL 51: 442–3): the metaphor of the wheat and tares with the allied metaphor of the good and the bad; *Tract. in Ioh.* 10.9 (CCL 36: 105–6) ties the harvest metaphor to the storehouse for the grain that is reaped.

197 Aug. *Contra litt. Petil.* 1.18.20–22.24; 1.25.27; 2.20.45–6; 2.31.72–32.73; 2.39.93; 2.45.106–47.110; 2.73.174; 3.2.3–3.4.5; 3.9.10, and 3.37.43, provide similar linked sequences.

198 For example, Aug. *Ep. ad Cath. contra Donatist.* 14.35, 15.38–16.41 (CSEL 52: 277, 280–6): extensive use of the reaping metaphor with the notation of the circumcellions as a prize example of the 'bad men' whom his sectarian enemies tolerate in their church.

199 For example, Aug. *Ep. ad Cath. contra Donatist.* 19.51–2 (CSEL 52: 298–301).

200 For example, Aug. *De mor. eccl. Cath. et Man.* 1.34.76 (CSEL 90: 81–2); *En. in Ps.* 92.5 (CCL 39: 1294–5); *Ep.* 43.8 (CCL 34.2: 103); 93.10 (CSEL 34.2: 481); 105.5 (CSEL 34.2: 609); 108.3 (CSEL 35.2: 624); *Quaestiones XVI in Matthaeum: Quaestio XI* (all); *Tract. in Ioh.* 68.2; 115.2 (CCL 36: 498, 644), among dozens and dozens of such references.

201 Optatus, *Contra Parm.* 3.4.3–5 (SC 413: 38–40): 'Et eorum illo tempore concursus est flagitatus quorum dementia paulo ante ab ipsis episcopis impie videbatur esse succensa. Nam cum huiusmodi hominum genus ante unitatem per loca singula vagarentur, cum Axido et Fasir ab ipsis insanientibus sanctorum duces appellarentur, nulli licuit securum esse in possessionibus suis. Debitorum chirographa amiserant vires, nullus creditor illo tempore exigendi habuit libertatem, terrebantur omnes litteris eorum qui se sanctorum duces fuisse iactabant, et si in obtemperando eorum iussionibus tardaretur, advolabat subito multitudo insana et praecedente terrore creditores periculis vallabantur ut qui pro praestitis suis rogari meruerant, metu mor-

tis humiles impellerentur in preces. Festinabat unusquisque debita etiam maxima perdere et lucrum computabatur evasisse ab eorum iniuriis. Etiam itinera non poterant esse tutissima quod domini de vehiculis suis excussi ante mancipia sua dominorum locis sedentia serviliter cucurrerent. Illorum iudicio et imperio inter dominos et servos condicio mutabatur …'

202 Some, like Vannier, 'Les circoncellions,' p. 17, have thought that Optatus was anachronistically transferring a later religious element of the circumcellions to this earlier case. I see no reason why this should be so, and take the argument to repose mainly on Vannier's desire to secularize the phenomena.

203 On the 'Commander of the Faithful' or Amir al-Muslimîn in the Maghrib al-Aqsa in more modern times, see J. Waterbury, *Commander of the Faithful* (New York: Columbia University Press, 1970), with caveats by E. Gellner, *Muslim Society* (Cambridge: Cambridge University Press, 1981), p. 72.

204 Optatus, *Contra Parm.* 3.4.5–7 (SC 413: 40–3): '… unde cum vestrae partis episcopis tunc invidia fieret, Taurino tunc comiti scripsisse dicuntur huiusmodi homines in ecclesia corrigi non posse. Mandaverunt ut a supra dicto comite acciperent disciplinam. Tunc Taurinus ad eorum litteras ire militem iussit armatum per nundinas ubi circumcellionum furor vagari consueverat. In Loco Octavensi occisi sunt plurimi et detruncati sunt multi quorum corpora usque in hodiernum per dealbatas aras aut mensas potuerunt numerari. Ex quorum numero cum aliqui in basilicis sepeliri coepissent, Clarus, presbyter in Loco Subbullensi ab episcopo suo coactus est ut insepultam faceret sepulturam. Unde proditum est mandatum fuisse fieri quod factum est quando nec sepultura in domo Dei exhiberi concessa est.'

205 Shaw, 'Rural Markets in North Africa,' offers an analysis of these peculiar African periodic markets or *nundinae*, and their role in the management of labour by domanial landowners.

Appendix 2

1 Charles-Picard, Le Bonniec, and Mallon, 'Le cippe de Beccut,' p. 148.

2 Charles-Picard, Le Bonniec, and Mallon, 'Le cippe de Beccut,' pp. 144–6 on the types, and p. 148 for the claim with respect to the stele of the Maktar Harvester.

3 Charles-Picard, Le Bonniec, and Mallon, 'Le cippe de Beccut,' p. 148: 'En effet, tandis que l'autel de Beccut possède une base largement débordante, qui assurait bien sa stabilité, celui du moissonneur était fiché en terre, et toute la partie inférieure, striée de coups d'aiguille, n'était pas visible … La hauteur de la partie supérieure manquante devait donc atteindre environ 70 cm: il y avait ainsi place, au dessus de l'inscription, pour un décor consistant probablement en une guirlande.' And so on.

4 On the *pius vixit annis* formula, and on *pius* and *pietas* in this context, see Shaw, *Anc-Soc* 32 (2002), 212–16; H. Sigismund-Nielsen in B. Rawson and P. Weaver, eds., *The Roman Family in Italy* (Oxford: Clarendon Press, 1997), pp. 169–204, at pp. 193–8.

5 CIL 8.13531 (C(e)es[ellia?], Carthage) – which seems rather questionable to me; and 4270 (C. Florius Cesellianus, Verecunda); cf. J.-M. Lassère, *Ubique Populus* (Paris: CNRS, 1977), pp. 90 and 460, for its possible gubernatorial origins.

6 See J. Stroux, ed., CIL 8.7: *Inscriptiones Latinae Africae, Indicum: Nomina virorum et mulierum* (suppl. vol. 5.1) and *Cognomina virorum et mulierum* (suppl. vol. 5.2) (Berlin: G. Reimer, 1942), p. 102.

7 Mastino, 'La ricerca epigrafia,' p. 107, citing M'Charek, *Aspects de l'évolution démographique*, p. 186, p. 81n25; and also suggested by Lukits, 'Die Schnitterinschrift,' p. 90.

8 For the continuity of DMS on Christian inscriptions at Mactaris, see Prévot, *Recherches archéologiques*, pp. 207–8, who notes 57 instances in a total of 221 inscriptions. Even if, as he shows (see map, p. 209), Mactaris is somewhat exceptional in this practice, this exceptionality applies to our inscription. Where it can be dated, the formula at Mactaris appears always to postdate 180 CE: Mastino, 'La ricerca epigrafia,' p. 98, 101 f. For its use in general in different north African contexts, see Lassère, 'Recherches chronologiques,'passim, and chart, pp. 120–1.

9 Lukits, 'Die Schnitterinschrift,' p. 80, suggests 'Faustinus' – but the letters 'anus' are clearly visible on the stone, and five letters seem too many for the gap.

10 It is the only case noted in Stroux (see n. 6), p. 49; it must be admitted, however, that the lettering on the stone is less than decisive for this reading of the name.

11 Lassère, 'Recherches chronologiques,' p. 127.

12 Charles-Picard, Le Bonniec, and Mallon, 'Le cippe de Beccut,' p. 148.

13 See the excellent photographs of the Beccut inscription in Charles-Picard, Le Bonniec, and Mallon, 'Le cippe de Beccut,' figs. 21 and 23.

14 Prévot, *Recherches archéologiques*, p. 231 f.

15 As was already clear from Bianchi's survey, 'Carmina,' p. 42 (based on Buecheler and CIL 8): dactylica 166 (hexametri 99, disticha 67) quibus addas commatica 20; iambica 18 (all others 7).

16 Cholodniak, *Carmina sepulcralia latina*, no. 1142, p. 476.

Bibliography

Periodicals and journals are cited according to the abbreviations in *L'Année philologique*; standard abbreviations of collections of literary, epigraphical, and papyrological texts are cited according to standards in the *Oxford Classical Dictionary* (3rd edition), with minor modifications. For patristic texts, the standard abbreviations are those found in H.J. Frede, *Kirchenschriftsteller, Verzeichnis und Sigel: Repertorium scriptorum ecclesiasticorum latinorum saeculo nono antiquiorum*, 4th revised edition (Freiburg: Verlag Herder, 1995) (with R. Gryson, *Aktualisierungshefte = compléments*, 1999 and 2004); and for papyri, those in J.F. Oates et al., *Checklist of Editions of Greek, Latin, Demotic and Coptic Papyri, Ostraca and Tablets*, 5th edition, BASP Supplement no. 9, 2001; and the continually updated list at http://scriptorium.lib.duke.edu/papyrus/texts/clist.html.

Selected Primary Sources

St Aridius, Life:
- B. Krusch, ed. *Vita Aridii Abbatis Lemovicini*. MGH SRM, 3 (Hannover, 1896), 581–609

Carthage Council of 411:
- S. Lancel, ed. *Actes de la conférence de Carthage*. 4 vols. Paris: Editions du Cerf, 1972–91 (SC 194–5, 274, 373)

Cato the Elder:
- R. Goujard, trans. and comm. *Caton: De l'agriculture*. Paris: Les Belles Lettres, 2002
- A. Mazzarino, ed. *M. Porci Catonis De Agri Cultura*. Leipzig: Teubner, 1982
- G. Purnelle. *Cato, de agricultura. Fragmenta omnia servata*. Liège: Faculté de philosophie et lettres, 1988

St Columbanus, Life:
– B. Krusch, ed. Abbas Jonas, *Vita Columbani*, MGH SRM 4 (1902) 1–156 and 7.2 (1920) 822–7 = MGH SRG, 38 (Hannover–Leipzig, 1919–20; reprint 1997), 1–294

Columella:
– W. Richter, ed. and trans. *Lucius Iunius Moderatus Columella, De re rustica libri duo-decim.* 3 vols. Munich: Artemis Verlag, 1981–3
– R. Goujard, ed. *Les Arbres.* Paris: Les Belles Lettres, 1986
– J.C. Dumont, ed. *De l'agriculture: Livre III.* Paris: Les Belles Lettres, 1993
– E. de Saint-Denis, ed. *De l'agriculture: Livre X.* Paris: Les Belles Lettres, 1969
– J. André, ed. *De l'agriculture: Livre XII.* Paris: Les Belles Lettres, 1988

Corippus:
– J. Diggle and F.R.D. Goodyear, eds. *Flavii Cresconii Corippi Iohannidos Libri VIII*, Cambridge: Cambridge University Press, 1970

De Solstitiis et Aequinoctiis:
– B. Botte. 'Le traité *De Solstitiis et Aequinoctiis*.' Append. in *Les Origines de la Noël et de l'Epiphanie: étude historique.* Louvain: Abbaye de Saint César, 1932, 88–105, at pp. 93–105

Gregory of Tours:
– *Gregorii Turnonensis Opera*, ed. W. Arndt and B. Krusch. MGH SRM, Hanover, 1884–5

John of Gaza:
– P. Friedländer, ed. *Johannes von Gaza und Paulus Silentiarius: Kunstbeschreibungen Justinianischer Zeit.* Leipzig–Berlin: Teubner, 1912

Mishnah:
– J. Neusner, ed. and trans. *The Mishnah: A New Translation.* New Haven: Yale University Press, 1988

New Testament:
– Greek: B. Aland, K. Aland, I. Karavidopoulos, C.M. Martini, and B.M. Metzger, eds. *The Greek New Testament.* 4th ed. Stuttgart: Deutsche Bibelgesellschaft, 1994.
– Latin: H. Freiherr von Soden. *Das Lateinische Neue Testament in Afrika zur Zeit Cyprians nach Bibelhandschriften und Väterzeugnissen.* Leipzig: J.C. Hinrichs'sche Buchhandlung, 1909

Palladius:
– R.H. Rodgers, ed. *Palladius: Opus Agriculturae, De Veterinaria Medicina, De Insitione.* Leipzig: Teubner, 1975.
– R. Martin, ed. *Palladius, Traité de l'agriculture: Livres 1 et II.* 2 vols. Paris: Les Belles Lettres, 1976 and 2003.
– E. Di Lorenzo, B. Pellegrino, and S. Lanzaro, eds. *Palladio Rutilio Tauro Emiliano: Opus Agriculturae.* Salerno: Cues, 2006

Pliny the Elder:
– H. Le Bonniec and A. Le Boeuffle, eds. *Pline l'Ancien Histoire Naturelle, Livre XVIII.* Paris: Les Belles Lettres, 1972

Rabbinic Sources:
– D. Instone-Brewer (*TRENT*, 1). *Traditions of the Rabbis from the Era of the New Testament, 1: Prayer and Agriculture.* Grand Rapids, MI: Eerdmans, 2004

Sibylline Oracles:
– J. Geffcken, ed. *Die Oracula Sibyllina.* Leipzig: Hinrichs, 1902 (Die griechische christlichen Schriftsteller der ersten drei Jahrhunderte, Bd. 17)

Talmud:
– The Talmud Yerushalmi: J. Neusner. *The Talmud of the Land of Israel: A Preliminary Translation and Explanation.* 35 vols. Chicago: University of Chicago Press, 1972–93

Varro:
– D. Flach, ed. *Marcus Terentius Varro Gespräche über die Landwirtschaft, Buch 1.* Darmstadt: Wissenschaftlische Buchgesellschaft, 1996. Text republished in D. Flach, ed., *Varro: Uber die Landwirtschaft.* Darmstadt: Wissenschaftliche Buchgesellschaft, 2006
– J. Heurgon, ed. *Varro, L'économie rurale, I.* Paris: Les Belles Lettres, 1978
– C. Guiraud, ed. *Varro, L'économie rurale, II.* Paris: Les Belles Lettres, 1985

Vergil:
– E. de Saint-Denis, ed. *Géorgiques.* Paris: Les Belles Lettres, 2003
– R.A.B. Mynors. *Virgil, Georgics,* edited with a commentary. Oxford–New York: Clarendon Press, 1990

Modern Primary Sources

Annuaire statistique de l'Algérie, République française de l'Algérie, Direction de l'agriculture, du commerce et de la colonisation, Service de la statistique générale. Algiers: Emile Pfister, 1928–63/4

Statistique générale de l'Algérie. République française, Gouvernement générale de l'Algérie, Algiers: Giralt, 1867–1927

Statistique générale de la Tunisie. Tunis: Société anonyme de l'Imprimerie rapide, 1913–34

United Nations: Food and Agriculture Organization, Production Yearbook. Rome: Food and Agriculture Organization of the United Nations, 1948 to present

Secondary Studies

Abrams, W.A. 'Bringing In the Sheaves.' In J.W. Williamson, ed., *An Appalachian Symposium: Essays Written in Honor of Cratis D. Williams.* Boone, NC: Appalachian State University Press, 1977, 169–85

Adams, C. *Land Transport in Roman Egypt: A Study of Economics and Administration in a Roman Province.* Oxford–New York: Oxford University Press, 2007

Adelman, J. *Frontier Development: Land, Labour, and Capital on the Wheatlands of Argentina and Canada.* Oxford–New York: Clarendon Press, 1994

Agéron, C.R. *Les Algériens musulmanes et la France (1871–1919).* 2 vols. Paris: Presses Universitaires de France, 1968 (Publications de la Faculté des Lettres et sciences humaines de Paris-Sorbonne, série 'Recherches,' 44–5)

Ainsworth, M.W., and K. Christiansen, eds. *From Van Eyck to Bruegel: Early Netherlandish Painting in the Metropolitan Museum of Art.* Exhibition Catalogue. New York: Metropolitan Museum of Art, 1998

Albanese Procelli, R.M. 'Greeks and Indigenous People in Eastern Sicily: Forms of Interaction and Acculturation.' In R. Leighton, ed., *Early Societies in Sicily: New Developments in Archaeological Research.* London, 1996, 167–75

Alexander, J.S. 'A Note on the Interpretation of the Parable of the Threshing Floor at the Conference of Carthage of A.D. 411.' *JThS* 24 (1973), 512–19

Alexiou, M. *The Ritual Lament in Greek Tradition.* 2nd ed., rev. D. Yatromanolakis and P. Roilos. Lanham, MD: Rowman and Littlefield, 2002

Alföldy, G. 'Epigraphische Notizen aus Italien, III: Inschriften aus Nursia (Norcia), pt. I: Vespasius Pollio, der Großvater Vespasians.' *ZPE* 77 (1989), 155–60

Algeria. Vol. 2. Naval Intelligence Division, Geographical Handbook Series, no. 505A, 1944

Allen, D., and D. Allen Jr. *N.C. Wyeth: The Collected Paintings, Illustrations and Murals.* New York: Bonanza Books, 1984

Alpers, S. 'Bruegel's Festive Peasants.' *Simiolus: Netherlands Quarterly for the History of Art* 6 (1972–3), 163–76

Amouretti, M.-C. 'Les instruments aratoires dans la Grèce archaïque.' *DHA* 2 (1976), 25–52

Amouretti, M.-C., and G. Comet. 'La meunerie antique et médiévale.' *Archives internationales d'histoire des sciences* 20 (2000), 18–29

Amouretti, M.-C., and G. Comet, eds. *L'evolution des techniques est-elle autonome?* Aix-en-Provence: Colloque d'Aix-en-Provence, Espace Méjanes, 17 nov. 1989: états généraux de la culture scientifique, technique et industrielle, Université de Provence, 1991 (Cahier d'histoire des techniques, 1)

– *Hommes et techniques de l'Antiquité à la Renaissance*. Paris: A. Colin, 1993– *La transmission des connaissances techniques*. Aix-en-Provence: Tables rondes d'Aix-en-Provence, avril 1993–mai 1994, Université de Provence, 1995 (Cahier d'histoire des techniques, 3)

Anderson, J.H. *Translating Investments: Metaphor and the Dynamics of Cultural Change in Tudor-Stuart England*. New York: Fordham University Press, 2005

Angelucci, S., I. Baldassare, I. Bragantini, M.G. Lauro, V. Mannucci, A. Mazzoleni, C. Morselli, and F. Taglietti. 'Sepolture e riti nella necropoli dell'Isola Sacra.' *Bollettino di archeologia* 5–6 (1990), 49–113

Applen, A.G. 'Migratory Harvest Labor in the Midwestern Wheat Belt, 1870–1940.' PhD Dissertation, Kansas State University, 1974

Aravantinos, V.L. *The Archaeological Museum of Thebes*. Athens: John S. Latsis Public Benefit Foundation, 2010

Arch, J. *Joseph Arch: The Story of His Life Told by Himself; edited with a preface by the Countess of Warwick*. 2nd ed. London: Hutchinson, 1898; reprint New York–London: Garland, 1984

Ardhuin, M., ed. *La moissonneuse gauloise (des rêmes aux trévires)*. Reims: Group d'Etudes Archéologiques Champagne Ardenne, 1982

Ardrey, R.L. *American Agricultural Implements: A Review of Invention and Development in the Agricultural Implement Industry of the United States*. Chicago: Apud Auctorem, 1894; reprint New York: Arno, 1972

Artaud, A. *Van Gogh, le suicide de la société*. Paris: K Editeur, 1947; reprint Paris: Gallimard, 1990

Ashabranner, B.K. *Dark Harvest: Migrant Farmworkers in America*. Photographs by Paul Conklin. New York: Dodd, Mead and Co., 1985

Assfahl, G. *Vergleich und Metapher bei Quintilian*. Stuttgart: Kohlhammer, 1932 (Tübinger Beiträge zur Altertumswissenschaft, no. 5)

Assmann, J. *Tod und Jenseits im alten Agypten*. Munich: Beck, 2001; Engl. trans. by D. Lorton, *Death and Salvation in Ancient Egypt*, abridged and updated by the author. Ithaca–London: Cornell University Press, 2005

Astill, G., and J. Langdon, eds. *Medieval Farming and Technology: The Impact of Agricultural Change in Northwest Europe*. Leiden–New York: Brill, 1997

Astolfi, R. 'Riflessioni in tema di *instrumentum fundi*.' *SHDI* 63 (1997), 521–46

Atkinson, R. *An Army at Dawn: The War in North Africa, 1942–1943*. New York: Henry Holt, 2002

Aune, D.E. 'Visions of Eschatalogical Salvation and Judgment (14:1–20).' Chap. III.D.4 in *Revelation 6-16: World Biblical Commentary*, vol. 52B. Nashville: Nelson, 1998, 781–849

Avitsur, S. *Implements for Harvesting and Similar Purposes Used in the Traditional Agricultue of Eretz Israel = Kele h-asif ba-hakla 'ut ha-mesoratit shel Erets Yisra'el, katsir ve-dayish, asif perot.* Tel Aviv: Ha-Histadrut ha-kelalit shel ha 'ovdim be-Eretz Yisra'el, 1966

Bagnall, R. *Egypt in Late Antiquity.* Princeton: Princeton University Press, 1993

Baldassare, I. 'Tomba della Mietitura.' *Bollettino di archeologia* 5–6 (1990), 90–106

Ballu, A. *Les ruines de Timgad (antique Thamugadi).* 2 vols. Paris: Leroux, 1897–1903

Bang, P.F. *The Roman Bazaar: A Comparative Study of Trade and Markets in a Tributary Empire.* Cambridge: Cambridge University Press, 2008

Barceló, M., and F. Sigaut, eds. *The Making of Feudal Agriculture.* Leiden–Boston: Brill, 2004

Bardin, P. *La vie d'un douar: essai sur la vie rurale dans les Grandes Plaines de la Haute Medjerda, Tunisie.* Paris–La Haye: Mouton, 1965

Barker, G., et al., eds. *Farming the Desert: The UNESCO Libyan Valleys Archaeological Survey.* 2 vols. Paris: UNESCO Publishing; Tripoli: Department of Antiquities of tthe Socialist People's Libyan Arab Jamahiriya; London: Society for Libyan Studies, 1996

Barris, S., and L. Totelin. 'Un peigne pour des épis: approches ethnographiques des outils de la récolte.' In Raepsaet and Lambeau, eds., *La moissonneuse*, 63–71

Battye, K.M. 'Sickle-Makers and Other Metal Workers in Ecklington, 1534–1750.' *Tools and Trades* 12 (2000), 26–38

Bell, R. *Fate and Honor, Family and Village: Demographic and Cultural Change in Rural Italy since 1800.* Chicago–London: University of Chicago Press, 1979

Ben Baaziz, S. 'Les fermes fortifiées de la Dorsale méridionale à l'époque romaine.' In F. Bejaoui, ed., *Histoire des Hautes Steppes: Antiquité-Moyen Age.* Tunis, 2003, 49–80

Bérard, J. 'Mosaïques inédites de Cherchel.' *MEFR* 52 (1935), 113–42

Bertrang, A. 'Une mystère dissipé: le musée d'Arlon possède depuis plus d'un siècle un fragment de la moissonneuse gauloise.' *Bulletin trimestriel de l'Institut archéologique du Luxembourg* (1958), 73–7

Beschmakoff, A. 'L'évolution de la charrue à travers les siècles au point de vue ethnographique.' *L'Anthropologie* 42 (1932), 82–90

Beschaouch, A. 'Mactaris (Makthar, Mactar).' *DE* 5.7 (1991), 198–204

Bianchi, H. 'Carmina latina epigraphica Africana.' *Studi Italiani di Filologia Classica* 18 (1910), 41–75

Bielefeld, D. *Die Stadtrömischen Eroten-Sarkophage, fasc. 2: Weinlese- und Ernteszenen.* Berlin: Mann Verlag, 1997 (Die Antiken Sarkophagreliefs, Bd. 5.2)

Billiard, R. *L'agriculture dans l'antiquité d'après les Géorgiques de Virgile.* Paris: E. de Boccard, 1928

Binnie-Clark, G. *Wheat and Woman.* London: Heinemann; Toronto: Bell and Cockburn, 1914; reprint intro. S. Jackel, Toronto: University of Toronto Press, 1979

Bitel, L.M. *Landscape with Two Saints: How Genovefa of Paris and Brigit of Kildare Built Christianity in Barbarian Europe*. New York: Oxford University Press, 2009

Blazquez, J.M. 'Tecnicas agrícolas representadas en los mosaicos del Norte de Africa.' *Afr-Rom* 11 (1996), 517–28

Blum, J. *Our Forgotten Past: Seven Centuries of Life on the Land*. London: Thames and Hudson, 1982

Boak, A.E.R. 'An Overseer's Day-Book from the Fayoum.' *JHS* 41 (1921), 217–21

Bond, E.A., E.M. Thompson, and G.F. Warner. *Facsimiles of Manuscripts and Inscriptions*. Second series, vol. 1. London: Palaeographical Society, 1884–94

Bonner, C. *Studies in Magical Amulets, Chiefly Graeco-Egyptian*. Ann Arbor: University of Michigan Press; London: Geoffrey Cumberlege; Oxford University Press, 1950

Boserup, E. *The Conditions of Agricultural Growth under Population Pressure*. New York: Aldine, 1965

Bouard, V., N. Demaison, and L. Maurin. 'CIL, VIII, 26580 et l'écriture "africaine."' In M. Khanoussi and L. Maurin, eds., *Dougga (Thugga): études épigraphiques*. Paris: de Boccard, 1997, 209–36

Bourdieu, P. *The Logic of Practice*. Trans. R. Nice. Cambridge: Polity, 1990; Engl. trans. of *Le sens pratique*. Paris: Editions du Minuit, 1980

– *Outline of a Theory of Practice*. Trans. R. Nice. Cambridge: Cambridge University Press, 1977; Engl. trans. of *Esquisse d'une théorie de la pratique, précédé des trois études d'éthnologie kabylie*. Geneva: Librairie Droz, 1972

Bourgeois, A. 'Les lampes en céramique de Mactar.' *Karthago* 19 (1977–8), 33–85

Bourrilly, J. *Eléments d'ethnographie marocaine*. Ed. E. Laoust. Paris: Librairie coloniale et orientaliste Larose, 1932

Brandt, P. (*Schaffende Arbeit: Altertum*) *Schaffende Arbeit und bildende Kunst im Altertum und Mittelalter*. Leipzig: A. Kröner Verlag, 1927

– (*Schaffende Arbeit: Mittelalter*) *Schaffende Arbeit und bildende Kunst vom Mittelalter biz zum Gegenwart*. Leipzig: A. Kröner Verlag, 1928

Braunert, H. *Die Binnenwanderung: Studien zur Sozialgeschichte Agyptens in der Ptole-mäer- und Kaiserzeit*. Bonn: L. Röhrscheid, 1964 (Bonner Historische Forschungen, no. 16)

Breyel, C., B. Coessens, and J. Walschot. 'Essai d'analyse de l'image du *vallus* dans l'iconographie funéraire.' In Raepsaet and Lambeau, eds., *La moissonneuse*, 33–43

Brogan, O., and D.J. Smith. *Ghirza: A Libyan Settlement in the Roman Period*. Tripoli: Department of Antiquities of the People's Republic of Libya, 1984

Broughton, A.L. 'The *Menologia Rustica*.' *CPh* 31 (1936), 353–6

Brown, J.P. *Israel and Hellas*. 3 vols. Berlin–New York: de Gruyter, 1995–2001

Brun, J.P., and P. Jockey, eds. *Techniques et sociétés en Méditerranée*. Paris: Maison méditer-ranéenne des sciences de l'homme, Maisonneuve et Larose, 2001

Brunner, K. 'Continuity and Discontinuity of Roman Agricultural Knowledge in the Early Middle Ages.' Chap. 2 in Sweeney, ed., *Agriculture in the Middle Ages*, 21–39

Brunt, P.A. 'Free Labour and Public Works at Rome.' *JRS* 70 (1980), 81–100

Bryer, A. 'Byzantine Agricultural Implements: The Evidence of Mediaeval Illustrations of Hesiod's *Works and Days*.' *ABSA* 81 (1986), 45–80

– 'The Means of Agricultural Production: Muscle and Tools.' In A.E. Laiou, ed., *The Economic History of Byzantium from the Seventh through the Fifteenth Century*, vol. 1. Washington, DC: Dumbarton Oaks, 2002, 101–13

Buchanan, I. 'The Collection of Niclaes Jongelinck, II: The "Months" by Pieter Bruegel the Elder.' *Burlington Magazine* 132 (1990), 541–50

Buck, J.E., ed., G.A. Kratzner, ill., M.R.D. Owings, dir. *Harvest Scenes of the World*. Chicago: International Harvester Company Service Bureau, 1913

Budge, E.A.W. *The Egyptian Heaven and Hell, Being the Book of Am-Tuat, the Shorter Book of the Am-Tuat, the Book of the Gates*. 2 vols. in 1. London: Martin Hopkinson, 1925

Burford, A. 'Heavy Transport in Classical Antiquity.' *EcHR* 13 (1960), 1–18

– *Land and Labor in the Greek World*. Baltimore–London: Johns Hopkins University Press, 1993

Bürge, A. 'Der *mercennarius* und die Lohnarbeit.' *ZRG* 107 (1990), 80–136

Burkert, W. *Homo necans: Interpretationen altgriechischer Opferriten und Mythen*. 2nd ed. with afterword. Berlin–New York: de Gruyter, 1997; Engl. trans. by P. Bing, *Homo Necans: The Anthropology of Ancient Greek Sacrificial Ritual and Myth*. Berkeley–Los Angeles: University of California Press, 1983

Burnand, Y. 'La première identification de la moissonneuse gallo-romaine sur la "Porte de Mars" de Reims par l'architecte Caristie.' In *Actes du 95ème Congrès National des Sociétés Savantes, Reims, 1970*. Paris, 1975, 85–92

Camps, G. *Massinissa ou les débuts de l'histoire = Libyca, archéologie-épigraphie* 8 (1960)

Camps-Fabrer, H., and J. Courtin. 'Essai d'approche technologique des faucilles préhistoriques dans le Bassin méditerranéen.' In *Histoire des techniques et sources documentaires* = Cahier du G.I.S. no. 7, CNRS. Aix-en-Provence, 1985, 179–92

Canine, C. *Dream Reaper: The Story of an Old-Fashioned Inventor in the Hi-Tech, High-Stakes World of Modern Agriculture*. New York: Knopf, 1995

Card, L., and F. Wilson. 'Death-Defining Personifications: The Grim Reaper vs. La Grande Faucheuse.' *LACUS Forum* 33 (2007), 83–92

Carte archéologique de la Gaule. 95 vols. Sous la dir. de M. Provost. Paris: Académie des Inscriptions et Belles-Lettres – Maison des sciences de l'Homme, 1988 to present

Carter, J.G. *Quintilian's Didactic Metaphors*. New York: G.P. Putnams, 1910

Carter, J.M.T., and R.T. Cross. 'Mills, Millers and Millwrights: How the Machine Age Came to South Australia.' *Electronic Journal of Australian and New Zealand History* (2001): http://www.jcu.au/aff/history/articles/carter_cross.htm

Charles-Picard, G. 'La basilique funéraire de Iulius Piso à Mactar.' *CRAI* (1945), 185–212

– 'La chronologie et l'évolution stylistique des monuments funéraires de Mactar (Tunisie).' *BCTH* n.s. 1–2 (1965–6), 159–60
– 'La collection Boglio à Siliana.' *BCTH* (1943–5), 475–81
– 'Le *conventus civium Romanorum* de Mactar.' *BCTH* (1963–4), 197
– 'Le *conventus civium Romanorum* de Mactar.' *Africa* 1 (1966), 65–83
– 'Le démographie de Mactar.' In *Acts of the V International Congress of Greek and Latin Epigraphy, Cambridge, 1967*. Oxford, 1971, 269–75
– 'Nouveaux fragments épigraphiques trouvées à Mactar.' *CRAI* (1945), 489–90
– *Civitas Mactaritana*. Paris: de Boccard, 1957 = *Karthago* 8 (1957)
– *La civilisation de l'Afrique romaine*. 1st ed. Paris: Plon, 1959; 2nd ed. Paris: Etudes Augustiniennes, 1990: cited from the latter edition
– 'La "Porte de Mars" à Reims.' In *95e Congrès national des sociétés savantes, Reims, 1970*. Paris, 1974, 59–73
– 'Le statut politique de Mactar de Trajan à Marc Aurèle,' *AfrRom* 4 (1987), 461–7
– 'Le temple du Musée à Mactar,' *RA* (1984), 13–28
– 'Tombeaux des prêtresses de Cérès à Mactar.' *BCTH* 6 (1970), 195–97
Charles-Picard, G., A. Bourgeois, and C. Bourgeois. *Recherches archéologiques franco-tunisiennes à Mactar*. Rome: Ecole française de Rome, 1977
Charles-Picard, G., H. Le Bonniec, and J. Mallon. 'Le cippe de Beccut.' *AntAfr* 4 (1970), 125–64
Charles-Picard, G., A. Mahjoubi, and A. Beschaouch. '*Pagus Thuscae et Gunzuzi*.' *CRAI* (1963), 124–30
Charles-Picard, G., and J. Rougé. 'Le moissonneur de Mactar.' No. 3 in *Textes et documents relatifs à la vie économique et sociale dans l'empire romain, 31 avant J.C.–225 après J.C.* Paris: Société d'édition d'enseignment supérieur, 1969, 224–7
Cherwinski, W.J.C. 'The Incredible Harvest Excursion of 1908.' *Labour/Le Travailleur* 5 (Spring 1980), 57–79
– '"Misfits," "Malingerers," and "Malcontents": The British Harvester Movement of 1928.' In J.E. Foster, ed., *The Developing West: Essays on Canadian History in Honor of Lewis H. Thomas*. Edmonton: University of Alberta Press, 1983, 271–302
Chitty, D.J. *The Desert a City: An Introduction to the Study of Egyptian and Palestinian Monasticism under the Christian Empire*. London–Oxford: Mowbrays, 1966
Cholodniak, J. *Carmina sepulcralia latina*. St Petersburg: Typis Academicis, 1897; 2nd ed., 1904
Chuksin, P. 'The Revival of the Gallic Harvester.' *TRIZ* (April 2008): http://www.triz-journal.com/archives/2008/04/02
Cichorius, C. *Die Reliefs des Traianssäule, Tafelband*, 2 vols. and *Textband*. 3 vols. Berlin: G. Reimer, 1896–1900
Clouner, P., G. Grès, and F. Lambeau. 'Nouvelles lectures de Palladius 7, 2.' In Raepsaet and Lambeau, eds., *La moissonneuse*, 9–16

Collins, E.J.T. 'Harvest Technology and Labour Supply in Britain, 1790–1870.' *EcHR* 22 (1969), 453–73

– 'Labour Supply and Demand in European Agriculture 1800-1880.' Chap. 3 in E.L. Jones and S.J. Woolf, eds., *Agrarian Change and Economic Development: The Historical Problems.* London, 1969, 61–94

– 'Migrant Labour in British Agriculture in the Nineteenth Century.' *EcHR* 29 (1976), 38–59

Comba, R., and F. Panero, eds. *Il seme, l'aratro, la messe: le coltivazioni frumentarie in Piemonte dalla preistoria alla meccanizzazione agricola.* Cuneo: Roccoi de'Baldi, 1996

Comet, G. 'Les céréales du Bas-Empire au Moyen Age.' In Barceló and Sigaut, eds., *Making of Feudal Agriculture,* 131–76

– *Le paysan et son outil: essai d'histoire technique des céréales (France, VIIIe–XVe siècle).* Rome–Paris: Ecole française de Rome, 1992 (CEFAR no. 165)

– 'Technology and Agricultural Expansion in the Middle Ages: The Example of France North of the Loire.' Chap. 2 in Astill and Langdon, eds., *Medieval Farming and Technology,* 11–39

Connolly, S. 'Vita Prima Sanctae Brigitae: Background and Historical Value.' *Journal of the Royal Society of Antiquaries of Ireland* 119 (1989), 5–49

Connolly, S., and J.-M. Picard. 'Cogitosus's *Life of St Brigit.*' *Journal of the Royal Society of Antiquaries of Ireland* 117 (1987), 5–27

Corbin, A. *The Life of an Unknown: The Rediscovered World of a Clog Maker in Nineteenth-Century France.* Trans. A. Goldhammer. New York: Columbia University Press, 2001; Engl. trans. of *Le monde retrouvé de Louis-François Pinagot: sur les traces d'un inconnu, 1798–1876.* Paris: Flammarion, 1998

Cotton, H., and J. Geiger. *Masada II: The Yigael Yadin Excavations, 1963–1965.* Jerusalem: Hebrew University of Jerusalem, 1989

Courcelle, P. 'Note sur le *Tolle, lege.*' *Année Théologique* (1951), 233–60

– 'Source chrétienne et allusions païennes de l'épisode de "Tolle, lege" (Saint Augustin, *Confessions,* VIII, 12, 29).' *Revue d'histoire et de philosophie religieuses* 32 (1952), 171–200

Courtney, E. *Musa Lapidaria: A Selection of Latin Verse Inscriptions.* Atlanta: Scholars Press, 1995

– 'The Roman Months in Art and Literature.' *MH* 45 (1988), 33–57

Courtois, C., L. Leschi, C. Perrat, and C. Saumagne. *Tablettes Albertini: actes privés de l'époque Vandale (fin du Ve siècle).* Paris: Arts et métier graphiques, 1952

Cumont, F. *Recherches sur le symbolisme funéraire des Romains.* Paris: P. Geuthner, 1942

Cuomo, S. *Technology and Culture in Greek and Roman Antiquity.* Cambridge: Cambridge University Press, 2007

Cüppers, H. 'Gallo-römische Mähmaschine auf einem Relief in Trier.' *Trierer Zeitschrift* 27 (1964), 151–3

Danforth, L.M., and A. Tsiaras. *The Death Rituals of Rural Greece*. Princeton: Princeton University Press, 1982

Daniel, E.V. *Charred Lullabies: Chapters in an Anthropology of Violence*. Princeton: Princeton University Press, 1996

Dattari, G. *Monete Imperiali Greche: Numi Augg. Alexandrini catalogo della collezione G. Dattari*. 2 vols. Cairo: Tipografia dell'Instituto Francese d'Archaeologia Orientale, 1901

David, P.A. 'Path Dependence, Its Critics and the Quest for "Historical Economics."' In P. Garrouste and S. Ioannides, eds., *Evolution and Path Dependence in Economic Ideas: Past and Present*. Cheltenham: Edward Elgar, 2001, 15–40

Davidson, D. 'What Metaphors Mean.' Chap. 17 in *Inquiries into Truth and Investigation*. Oxford: Clarendon Press, 1984, 245–64

Davies, N.M., and N. de G. Davies. 'Harvest Rites in a Theban Tomb.' *JEA* 25 (1939), 154–6

Davis, E.F. *Scripture, Culture, and Agriculture: An Agrarian Reading of the Bible*. Cambridge: Cambridge University Press, 2009

Davis, J. *Land and Family in Pisticci*. London: Athlone; New York: Humanities Press, 1973

De Martino, E. *Morte e pianto rituale nel mondo antico: dal lamento pagano al pianto di Maria*. Turin: Einaudi, 1958

De Robertis, F.M. 'I lavoratori liberi nelle *familiae* aziendali romane.' *SDHI* 24 (1958), 269–78

– *Lavoro e lavoratori nel mondo romano*. Bari: Adiatrice editore, 1963; reprint New York: Arno, 1979

De Ste Croix, G.E.M. *The Class Struggle in the Ancient Greek World*. London: Duckworth, 1981

Decker, M. *Tilling the Hateful Earth: Agricultural Production and Trade in the Late Antique East*. Oxford: Oxford University Press, 2009

Decker-David, M.P. *L'agriculture indigène en Tunisie: rapport général*. 2 vols. Tunis: Saliba et fils, 1912

Degrassi, A. *Fasti anni Numani et Iuliani, accedunt Feralia, Menologia Rustica, Parapegmata = Inscriptiones Italiae*, vol. 13: *Fasti et elogia*, fasc. 2. Rome: Academiae Italicae, Libreria dello Stato, 1963

Demelenne, M., E. Glibert, and C. Reveillon. 'Moissonneuse et machinisme agricole.' In Raepsaet and Lambeau, eds., *La moissonneuse*, 89–93

Denison, M. *Harvest Triumphant: The Story of Massey-Harris*. New York: Dodd, Mead and Co., 1949

Deroy, L. 'La racine étrusque "plau-, plu-" et l'origine rhétique de la charrue à roues.' *Studi Etruschi* 31 (1963), 99–120

Desanges, J. 'Un curateur de la sauterelle sur la pertica de Carthage en 48/49 de notre ère.' *BCTH* 10B (1974), 135–42

- 'Un curateur de la sauterelle sur la *pertica* de Carthage en 48/49 de notre ère.' *Eos* 64 (1976), 281–6

Desideri, P. 'L'iscrizione del mietitore (C.I.L. VIII 11824): un aspetto della cultura mactaritana del III secolo.' *AfrRom* 4 (Sassari, 1986), 137–49

Dieter, L. *Der lateinische Begriff Labor.* Munich: Fink, 1975

Dolbeau, F., and R. Etaix. 'Le "jour des torches" (24 juin), d'après un sermon inédit d'origine africaine.' *Archiv für Religionsgeschichte* 5 (2003), 243–59

Dresken-Weiland, J. 'Recherches sur les sépultures paléochrétiennes en sarcophage (Occident, IVe–VIe siècles).' *AntTard* 11 (2003), 305–19

- *Sarkophagbestattungen des 4.–6. Jahrhunderts im Westen des römischen Reiches.* Rome–Freiburg–Vienna: Herder, 2003 (Römische Quartalschrift für Christliche Altertumskunde und Kirchengeschichte, Supplementband, no. 55)

Drexhage, H.-J. *Preise, Mieten/Pachten, Kosten und Löhne im römischen Agypten bis zum Regierungsantritt Diokletians. Vorarbeiten zu einer Wirtschaftsgeschichte des römischen Agypten.* Münster: Scripta Mercaturae, 1991

Drinkwater, J.F. 'The Gallo-Roman Woollen Industry and the Great Debate: The Igel Column Revisited.' Chap. 13 in D.J. Mattingly and J. Salmon, eds., *Economies beyond Agriculture in the Ancient World.* London–New York: Routledge, 2001, 297–308

- 'Die Secundinier von Igel und die Woll- und Textilindustrie in Gallia Belgica: Fragen und Hypothesen.' *Trierer Zeitschrift* 40–1 (1977–8), 107–25 = 'The Wool Industry in Gallia Belgica and the Secundinii of Igel.' *Textile History* 13 (1982), 111–28

Duby, G. *Rural Economy and Country Life in the Medieval West.* Trans. Cynthia Postan. London: Edward Arnold, 1968; Engl. trans. of *L'Economie rurale et la vie des campagnes dans l'Occident médiéval: France, Angleterre, Empire, IX–XV siècles: essai de synthèse et perspectives de recherches.* Paris: Aubier, 1962

Duncan-Jones, R. *The Economy of the Roman Empire: Quantitative Studies.* 2nd ed. Cambridge: Cambridge University Press, 1982

- 'The Price of Wheat in Roman Egypt under the Principate.' *Chiron* 6 (1976), 241–62 = revised version, 'The Price of Wheat in Roman Egypt.' Chap. 9 in *Structure and Scale in the Roman Economy.* Cambridge: Cambridge University Press, 1990, 143–55

Durand, A., and P. Leveau. 'Farming in Mediterranean France and Rural Settlement in the Late Roman and Early Medieval Periods.' In Barceló and Sigaut, eds., *Making of Feudal Agriculture,* 177–254

Dutton, P.E. 'Thunder and Hail over the Carolingian Countryside.' Chap. 6 in Sweeney, ed., *Agriculture in the Middle Ages,* 111–37

Duval, N. *Les eglises africaines à deux absides, 2: Inventaire des monuments, interpretation.* Paris: de Boccard, 1973

Edwards, M.W. *The Iliad: A Commentary, Volume V: Books 17–20.* Cambridge: Cambridge University Press, 1991

Eitrem, S. 'A Few Remarks on *spondê, thallos,* and Other Extra Payments in Papyri.' *SO* 17 (1937), 26–48

Elliott, J.H. *The Revolt of the Catalans: A Study in the Decline of Spain, 1598–1640*. Cambridge: Cambridge University Press, 1963

Erdkamp, P. 'Agriculture, Underemployment, and the Cost of Rural Labour in the Roman World.' *CQ* 49 (1999), 556–72

Espérandieu, E. *Recueil général des bas-reliefs, statues et bustes de la Gaule romaine*. Vols. 1–16. Paris: Imprimerie nationale, 1907–81

Everitt, A. 'Farm Labourers.' Chap. 7 in J. Thirsk, ed., *The Agrarian History of England and Wales, 4: 1500–1640*. Cambridge, 1967, 396–465

Fagles, R. *I, Vincent: Poems from the Pictures of Van Gogh*. Princeton: Princeton University Press, 1978

– *Homer: The Iliad*. Trans. Robert Fagles. New York: Viking, 1990

Fantham, E. *Latin Poets and Italian Gods*. Toronto–Buffalo–London: University of Toronto Press, 2009

Farmer, D.L. 'Prices and Wages, 1350–1500.' Chap. 5 in E. Miller, ed., *The Agrarian History of England and Wales, 3: 1348–1500*. Cambridge, 1991, 431–525

Fauconnier, G., and M. Turner. *The Way We Think: Conceptual Blending and the Mind's Hidden Complexities*. New York: Basic Books, 2002

Fentress, E. 'Frontier Culture and Politics at Timgad.' In *Actes du 1er colloque international sur l'histoire et l'archéologie de l'Afrique du Nord (Perpignan, 14–18 avril 1981)* = *BCTH* 17B (1981), 399–408

Ferchiou, Naïdé, and A. Gabillon. 'Une inscription grecque magique de la région de Bou Arada (Tunisie), ou les quatre plaies de l'agriculture antique en Proconsulaire.' In S. Lancel, ed., *Actes du IIe colloque international sur l'histoire et l'archéologie de l'Afrique du Nord (Grenoble, 5–9 avril 1983)* = *BCTH* 19B (1985), 109–23

Ferdi, S. *Corpus des mosaïques de Cherchel*. Paris: CNRS, 2005

Ferdière, A. 'A propos du vallus: propos libres sur les techniques et l'outillage agricole en Gaule romaine.' In Raepsaet and Lambeau, eds., *La moissonneuse*, 103–5

– *Les campagnes en Gaule Romaine, 1: Les hommes et l'environnement en Gaule rurale (52 av. J.-C.–486 ap. J.-C.)*; 1: *Les techniques et les productions rurales en Gaule (52 av. J.-C.–486 ap. J.-C.)*. Paris: Editions Errance, 1988

– 'La charrue gauloise: histoire d'un mythe.' In J.-P. Brun and P. Jockey, eds., *Techniques et sociétés en Méditerranée*. Paris: Maisonneuve et Larose, 2001, 169–89

Festugière, A.J. 'Amulettes magiques: à propos d'un ouvrage récent.' *CPh* 56 (1951), 81–92

Février, P.-A. *Approches du Maghreb romain*. 2 vols. Aix-en-Provence: Edisud, 1989–90

– 'Evolution des formes de l'écrit en Afrique du Nord à la fin de l'Antiquité et durant le Haut Moyen-Age.' In *Atti del Convegno internazionale sul tema: Tardo Antico et Alto Medievale. La forma artistica sul passaggio dall'Antichità al medioevo* = *Accademia nazionale dei Lincei, Quaderni* 105 (1968), 201–17

– 'Religion et domination dans l'Afrique romaine,' *DHA* 2 (1976), 305–36 = *La Méditerranée de Paul-Albert Février*, 2. Rome: Ecole française de Rome, 1996, 789–812

Fiensey, D.A. *The Social History of Palestine in the Herodian Period: The Land Is Mine.* Lewiston: Edwin Mellen Press, 1991

Finley, M.I. *The Ancient Economy.* London, 1974; rev. ed., 1985; 2nd rev. ed., 1999 (cited from the second edition)

– *Ancient Slavery and Modern Ideology.* New York: Viking Press, 1980; reprint Princeton: Markus Wiener, 1998

– *Economy and Society in Ancient Greece.* Ed. B.D. Shaw and R.P. Saller. London: Chatto and Windus; New York: Viking, 1982

– 'Technical Innovation and Economic Progress in the Ancient World.' *Economic History Review* 18 (1965), 29–45 = chap. 11 in *Economy and Society,* 176–95

– 'Technology in the Ancient World.' *Economic History Review* 12 (1959), 120–5

Fitzgerald, W. 'Labor and Laborer in Latin Poetry: The Case of the *Moretum.*' *Arethusa* 29 (1996), 389–418

Flach, D. 'Inschriftenuntersuchungen zum römischen Kolonat in Nordafrika.' *Chiron* 8 (1978), 441–92

– *Römische Agrargeschichte.* Munich: Beck, 1990 (Handbuch der Altertumswissenschaft, III.9)

Les Flavii de Cillum: étude architecturale, épigraphique, historique et littéraire du mausolée de Kasserine (CIL VIII, 211–216). Rome: Ecole française de Rome, 1993

Flynn, M. *Harvest: A History of Grain Growing, Harvesting and Milling in Ireland from the Earliest Times to the Twentieth Century.* Gorteenroe-Macroum, Co. Cork: Heritage House, 1996

Foraboschi, D. *La Contabilità di un'azienda agricola nel II sec. d. C. = Papiri della Università degli Studi di Milano.* Vol. 7. Milan: La Goliardica, 1981

Forni, G. 'Aratra des types *currus, plaum, versorium* dans le nord de l'Italie romaine.' In J.-P. Brun and P. Jockey, eds., *Techniques et sociétés en Méditerranée.* Paris: Maisonneuve et Larose, 2001, 191–205

Foucher, L. 'Le calendrier de Thysdrus.' *AntAfr* 36 (2000), 63–108

– 'Priape ithyphallique.' *Karthago* 7 (1956), 173–7

– 'Terrains Salah Abdallah et Hadj Ferdjani Kacem.' In *Découvertes archéologiques à Thysdrus en 1961 = Notes et Documents de l'Université de Tunis* 5 (1961), 27–59

Fouss, E.P. 'Le *vallus* ou la moissonneuse des Trévires.' *Le Pays Gaumais* 19 (1958), 125–36

Fratello, B. 'Standing on Holy Ground: Van Gogh, Millet, Symbolism, and Suicide.' In Kosinski, *Sheaves of Wheat,* 43–55

Frazer, J. *The Golden Bough, 4.2: Adonis, Attis, Osiris: Studies in the History of Oriental Religion.* 3rd ed. London: Macmillan, 1914

– *The Golden Bough, 5.1: Spirits of the Corn and of the Wild.* 3rd ed. London: Macmillan, 1912

Frézouls, E. 'La vie rurale au Bas-Empire d'après l'oeuvre de Palladius.' *Ktèma* 5 (1980), 193–210

Friedrich, W.-H. *Wounding and Death in the Iliad: Techniques of Description.* Trans. P. Jones and G. Wright. London: Duckworth, 2003

Frier, B.W. 'Law, Economics, and Disasters Down on the Farm: "Remissio Mercedis" Revisited.' *BIDR* 31–2 (1989–90), 237–70

– 'Law, Technology, and Social Change. The Equipping of Italian Farm Tenancies.' *ZRG* 96 (1979), 204–29

Fuks, A. Ἀκολονὸς μισθιὸς: Labour Exchange in Classical Athens.' *Eranos* 49 (1951), 171–3; reprinted in *Social Conflict in Ancient Greece.* Jerusalem–Leiden, 1984, 303–5

Fussell, G.E. *The Classical Tradition in West European Farming.* Rutherford, NJ: Fairleigh Dickinson University Press, 1972

– *The Farmer's Tools, 1500–1900. The History of British Farm Implements, Tools and Machinery before the Tractor Came.* London: A. Melrose, 1952

– 'The Hainault Scythe in England.' *Man* 60 (1960), 105–8

– *Landscape Painting and the Agricultural Revolution.* London: Pindar Press, 1984

Gaddis, M. *There Is No Crime for Those Who Have Christ: Religious Violence in the Christian Roman Empire.* Berkeley: University of California Press, 2005

Gagé, J. *Les classes sociales dans l'empire romain.* Paris: Payot, 1959; 2nd ed. 1971

Gallant, T.W. *Risk and Survival in Ancient Greece: Reconstructing the Rural Domestic Economy.* Stanford: Stanford University Press, 1991

García-Gelabert, María Paz. 'El carro como transporte agricola en mosaicos y otras figuraciones plásticas de Roma y sus provincias del ámbito mediterráneo.' *AfrRom* 11 (1996), 529–54

Gascou, J. *La politique municipale de l'empire romain en Afrique proconsulaire de Trajan à Septime Sévère.* Rome: Ecole française de Rome, 1972

– 'La politique municipale de Rome en Afrique du Nord. I. De la mort d'Auguste au début du IIIe siècle.' *ANRW* 2.10.2 (1982), 136–229

– 'Les status des villes africaines: quelques apports dus à des recherches récentes.' In J.-P. Bost, J.-M. Roddaz, and F. Tassaux, eds., *Itinéraire des Saintes à Dougga. Mélanges offerts à Louis Maurin.* Bordeaux, 2003, 231–46

Gazzaniga, M.S. 'Humans: The Party Animal.' *Daedalus* (Summer 2009), 21–34

Genelle, G. *La vie économique et sociale dans l'Afrique romaine tardive d'après les sermons de saint Augustin.* Lille: ANRT, 2005

Gibbs, R.W. *The Poetics of Mind: Figurative Thought, Language, and Understanding.* Cambridge: Cambridge University Press, 1994

Gibson, W.S. *Mirror of the Earth: The World Landscape in Sixteenth-Century Flemish Painting.* Princeton: Princeton University Press, 1989

Girard, R. *Violence and the Sacred.* Trans. P. Gregory. London–New York: Continuum, 2005; Engl. trans. of *La violence et le sacré.* Paris: B. Grasset, 1972

Gladwell, M. 'In the Air.' *New Yorker* 84.13 (12 May 2008), 50–60

Goody, J. *Capitalism and Modernity: The Great Debate.* Cambridge: Polity Press, 2004

– *The Theft of History*. Cambridge: Cambridge University Press, 2006

Goubert, P. *The French Peasantry in the Seventeenth Century*. Trans. I. Patterson. Cambridge: Cambridge University Press, 1986; Engl. trans. of *La vie quotidienne des paysans français au XVIIe siècle*. Paris: Hachette, 1982

Gow, A.S.F. 'The Ancient Plough.' *JHS* 34 (1914), 249–75

– *Theocritus*. 2 vols. Cambridge: Cambridge University Press, 1965

Grantham, G. 'Divisions of Labour: Agricultural Productivity and Occupational Specialization in Pre-Industrial France.' *EcHR* 46 (1993), 478–502

– 'La faucille et la faux. Un exemple de dépendence temporelle.' *Etudes rurales* 151–2 (1999), 103–31

Greene, K. 'How Was Technology Transferred in the Western Provinces?' In M. Wood and F. Queiroga, eds., *Current Research in the Romanization of the Western Provinces*. Oxford: Tempus Reparatum, 1992, 101–5

– 'Perspectives on Roman Technology.' *OJA* 9 (1990), 209–19

– 'Technology and Innovation in Context: The Roman Background to Medieval and Later Developments.' *JRA* 7 (1994), 22–33

– 'The Study of Roman Technology: Some Theoretical Constraints.' In E. Scott, ed., *Theoretical Roman Archaeology: First Conference Proceedings*. Aldershot: Avebury, 1994, 39–47

– 'Technological Innovation and Economic Progress in the Ancient World: M.I. Finley Reconsidered.' *EcHR* 53 (2000), 29–59

Greeno, F. L., ed. *Obed Hussey, who, of all inventors, made bread cheap; being a true record of his life and struggles to introduce his greatest invention, the reaper, and its success, as gathered from pamphlets published heretofore by some of his friends and associates*. Rochester, NY: Rochester Herald Publishing Company, 1912

Grey, C. 'Letters of Recommendation and the Circulation of Rural Laborers in the Late Roman West.' Chap. 3 in L. Ellis and F.L. Kidner, eds., *Travel, Communication and Geography in Late Antiquity: Sacred and Profane*. Aldershot: Ashgate, 2004, 25–40

Griffin, J. *Homer on Life and Death*. Oxford: Clarendon Press, 1980

Grossmann, F. *Bruegel: The Paintings: Complete Edition*. 3rd rev. ed. New York: Phaidon, 1973

Guidorizzi, G., and S. Beta, eds. *La metaphora: testi greci e latini*. Edizioni ETS, 2000

Guizzi, F. 'Ho visto un re… La regalità nello Scudo di Achille.' In M. D'Acunto and R. Palmiscinano, eds., *Lo Scudo di Achille nell'Iliade: esperienze ermeneutiche a confronto* = *Aion* 31 (2009), 83–96. Pisa–Rome: Fabrizio Serra, 2010

Gundel, H.-G., *Zodiakos: Tierkreisbilder im Altertum: kosmische Bezüge und Jenseitsvorstellungen im antiken Alltagsleben*. Mainz: P. von Zabern, 1992

Hall, G. *Harvest Wobblies: The Industrial Workers of the World and Agricultural Laborers in the American West, 1905–1930*. Corvallis: Oregon State University Press, 2001

Halstead, P.L.J., and G. Jones. 'Agrarian Ecology in the Greek Islands: Time, Stress, Scale and Risk.' *JHS* 109 (1989), 25–40

Hamblenne, P. 'Le *vallus* de Pline et la moissonneuse "lourde" palladienne: relectures.' *Ollodagos* 11 (1998), 155–94

Hanfmann, G.M.A. *The Season Sarcophagus in Dumbarton Oaks.* 2 vols. Cambridge, MA: Harvard University Press, 1951

– 'The Seasons in John of Gaza's *Tabula Mundi.*' *Latomus* 3 (1939), 111–18

Harlan, J.R. (1967), 'A Wild Wheat Harvest in Turkey.' *Archaeology* 20 (1967), 197–201

Harrison, S.J. *Vergil, Aeneid 10: Introduction, Translation and Commentary.* Oxford: Clarendon Press, 1991

Hatt, J.-J. *La tombe gallo-romaine: recherches sur les inscriptions et les monuments funéraires gallo-romains des trois premiers siècles de notre ère.* Paris: Presses universitaires de France, 1951; reprint Paris: Picard, 1986

Haudricourt, A.G., and M. Jean-Bruhnes Delamare. *L'homme et la charrue à travers le monde.* Paris: Gallimard, 1955

Haversath, J.-B. *Die Agrarlandschaft im römischen Deutschland der Kaiserzeit (1.–4. Jh. n. Chr.).* Passau: Passavia Universitätsverlag, 1984

Heimberg, U. 'Römische Villen an Rhein und Maas.' *BJ* 202–3 (2002–3), 57–148

Heinen, H. 'Grundzüge der wirtschaftliche Entwicklung des Moselraumes zur Römerzeit.' *Trierer Zeitschrift* 39 (1976), 75–118

– *2000 Jahre Trier, 1: Trier und das Trevererland in römischer Zeit.* Trier: Spee Verlag, 1985

Heitland, W.E. *Agricola: A Study of Agriculture and Rustic Life in the Greco-Roman World from the Point of View of Labour.* Cambridge: Cambridge University Press, 1921; reprint Westport, CT: Greenwood Press, 1970

Helmer, D. 'Les faucilles et les gestes de la moisson.' In M.C. Cauvin, ed., *Traces d'utilisation sur les outils néolithiques du Proche Orient* = Table Ronde CNRS. Lyon: GIS Maison de l'Orient, 1983, 189–98

Hengstl, J. *Private Arbeitsverhältnisse freier Personen in den hellenistischen Papyri bis Diokletian.* Bonn: Habelt, 1972

Henisch, B.A. 'In Due Season: Farm Work in the Medieval Calendar Tradition.' Chap. 14 in Sweeney, ed., *Agriculture in the Middle Ages,* 309–36

Henning, J. 'Fortleben und Weiterentwicklung spätrömischer Agrargerätetraditionen in Nordgallien: Eine Mähsense der Merowingerzeit aus Kerkhove (Belgien).' *Acta Archaeologica Lovaniensis* 30 (1991), 49–59

– 'Zur Datierung von Werkzeug- und Agrargerätefunden im germanischen Landnahmegebiet zwischen Rhein und oberer Donau (Der Hortfund von Osterburken).' *Jahrbuch des römisch-germanischen Zentralmuseums Mainz* 32 (1985), 570–94

Héron de Villefosse, A. 'Note sure l'inscription de Makteur [*sic*] dite du Moissonneur, conservée au Musée du Louvre.' *BCTH* (1885), 529–31

Hobsbawm, E.J., and G. Rudé. *Captain Swing.* Harmondsworth: Penguin; New York: Pantheon, 1968; reprint London: Phoenix, 2001

Hobi, F. *Die Benennungen von Sichel und Sense in den Mundarten der romanischen*

Schweiz. Heidelberg: Winter, 1926 (Wörter und Sachen: Kulturhistorische Zeitschrift für Sprach- und Sachforschung, Beiheft 5)

Hölbl, G. *Altägypten im Römischen Reich: Der römische Pharao und seine Tempel, 1: Römische Politik und altägyptische Ideologie von Augustus bis Diocletian, Tempelbau in Oberägypten*. Mainz: Verlag Philipp von Zabern, 2000

Homans, G.C. *English Villagers of the Thirteenth Century*. Harvard University Press, 1941; reprint New York: Norton, 1975

Honée, A., N. Lesseux, and J. Vassart. 'Les céréales et la moissonneuse gauloise.' In Raepsaet and Lambeau, eds., *La moissonneuse*, 45–61

Hoppenbrouwers, P., and J.L. van Zanden, eds. *Peasants into Farmers? The Transformation of Rural Economy and Society in the Low Countries (Middle Ages–19th Century) in Light of the Brenner Debate*. Turnhout: Brepols, 2001

Horden, P., and N. Purcell. *The Corrupting Sea: A Study of Mediterranean History*. Oxford: Blackwell, 2000

Horn, P. *Labouring Life in the Victorian Countryside*. Dublin: Gill and Macmillan, 1976
– *Life and Labour in Rural England, 1760–1850*. Houndmills–Basingstoke, Macmillan, 1987

Hostettler, E. 'Gourlay Steell and the Sexual Division of Labour.' *History Workshop* 4 (1977), 95–101

Hübner, E. *Exempla scripturae epigraphicae Latinae a Caesaris dictatoris morte ad aetatem Iustiniani*. Berlin: G. Reimer, 1885

Hugoniot, C. *Rome en Afrique: de la chute de Carthage aux débuts de la conquête arabe*. Paris: Flammarion, 2000

L'ideologica dell'arricchimento e l'ideologia dell'ascesa sociale a Roma e nel mondo romano: II sec. a. C. – II sec. d. C. = Index, vol. 13 (1985)

Instone-Brewer, D. (TRENT, 1). *Traditions of the Rabbis from the Era of the New Testament, 1: Prayer and Agriculture*. Grand Rapids, MI: Eerdmans, 2004

Isager, S., and J.E. Skydsgaard. *Ancient Greek Agriculture*. London–New York: Routledge, 1992

Isern, T.D. *Bull Threshers and Bindlestiffs: Harvesting and Threshing on the North American Plains*. Lawrence: University of Kansas Press, 1990

Jacques, F. *La privilège de liberté. Politique impériale et autonomie municipale dans les cités de l'occident romain (161–244)*. Rome: Ecole française de Rome, 1984

Jardé, A. *Les céréales dans l'Antiquité grecque: la production*. Paris: Editions de Boccard, 1925; reprint 1979

Jefferies, R. *Field and Hedgerow, being the last essays of Richard Jefferies collected by his widow*. London–New York: Longmans, Green and Co., 1889; reprint Oxford–New York: Oxford University Press, 1982

Johnson, A.C. *Roman Egypt to the Reign of Diocletian*. Baltimore: Johns Hopkins University Press, 1936. Vol. 4 in T. Frank ed., *An Economic Survey of Ancient Rome*, vol. 2; reprint New York: Octagon Books, 1975

Johnson, A.C., and L.C. West. *Byzantine Egypt: Economic Studies*. Princeton: Princeton University Press, 1949 (Princeton Studies in Papyrology, no. 6)

Johnson, J.H. 'Harvest Migration from Nineteenth-Century Ireland.' *Transactions of the Institute of British Geographers* 41 (1967), 97–112

Jones, A. (1977a). 'Harvest Customs and Labourers' Perquisites in Southern England, 1150–1350: The Corn Harvest.' *Agricultural History Review* 25.1 (1977), 14–22

– (1977b). 'Harvest Customs and Labourers' Perquisites in Southern England, 1150–1350: The Hay Harvest.' *Agricultural History Review* 25.2 (1977), 98–107

Jones, A.H.M. *The Later Roman Empire: A Social, Economic and Administrative Survey*. 3 vols. Oxford: Blackwell, 1964; reprint 2 vols., Baltimore: Johns Hopkins University Press, 1986

Jones, P. 'Italy.' Chap. 7.2 in M. Postan, ed., *The Cambridge Economic History of Europe, 1: The Agrarian Life of the Middle Ages*. 2nd ed. Cambridge: Cambridge University Press, 1971, 340–431

Josserand, C. 'Les dents de la moissonneuse gauloise (Palladius, *Agric.* VII 2,3).' *AC* 44 (1975), 664–7

Kadra, K. Fatima. 'Nécropoles tardives de l'antique Theveste: mosaïques funéraires et mensae.' *AfrRom* 6 (1989), 265–82

Kaplan, M. *Les hommes et la terre à Byzance du VIe au XIe siècle: propriété et exploitation du sol*. Paris: Publications de la Sorbonnne, 1992

Kehoe, D. *The Economics of Agriculture on Roman Imperial Estates in North Africa*. Göttingen: Vandenhoeck and Ruprecht, 1988

– *Investment, Profit, and Tenancy: The Jurists and the Roman Agrarian Economy*. Ann Arbor: University of Michigan Press, 1997

– *Management and Investment on Estates in Roman Egypt during the Early Empire*. Bonn: Habelt, 1992

Kenney, E.J. *The Ploughman's Lunch: Moretum*. Bristol: Bristol University Press, 1984

Kiechle, F. *Sklavenarbeit und technischer Fortschritt im römischen Reich*. Wiesbaden: Steiner, 1969

King, P.W. 'The North Worcestershire Scythe Industry.' *Historical Metallurgy* 41 (2007), 124–47

Kloppenborg, J.S. *The Tenants in the Vineyard: Ideology, Economics and Agrarian Conflict in Jewish Palestine*. Tübingen: Mohr Siebeck, 2006 (Wissenschaftliche Untersuchungen zum Neuen Testament, no. 195)

Koeppel, G.M. 'Die historischen Reliefs der römischen Kaiserzeit, IX: Der Fries der Trajanssäule in Rom, Teil 2: Der Zweite Dakische Krieg, Szenen LXXIX–CLV.' *BJ* 192 (1992), 61–122

Kolendo, J. *L'Agricoltura nell'Italia romana: tecniche agrarie e progresso economico nell tarda repubblica al principato*. Pref. A. Carandini; trans. Celeste Zawadska. Rome: Riuniti, 1980

– 'Origine et diffusion de l'araire à avant-train en Gaule et en Bretagne.' *Cahiers d'Histoire* 24 (1979), 61–73

– 'La mietitura e la mietitrice gallica.' Chap. 8 in *L'Agricoltura nell'Italia romana*, 155–78
– 'Pourquoi la moissonneuse antique était-elle utilisée seulement en Gaule?' In *Sozialökonomische Verhältnisse im Alten Orient und im Klassischen Altertum*. Berlin: Akademie Verlag, 1961, 187–90
– 'Techniques rurales. La moissonneuse antique en Gaule romaine.' *Annales (ESC)* 15 (1960), 1099–1114
Kosinski, D. *Van Gogh's Sheaves of Wheat*. New Haven–London: Yale University Press–Dallas Museum of Art, 2006
Kövecses, Z. *Metaphor: A Practical Introduction*. Oxford: Oxford University Press, 2002
– *Metaphor in Culture: Universality and Variation*. Cambridge: Cambridge University Press, 2005
Kranz, P. *Jahreszeiten-Sarkophage: Entwicklung und Ikonographie des Motivs der Vier Jahreszeiten auf kaiserzeitlichen Sarkophagen und Sarkophagdeckeln*. Berlin: Mann Verlag, 1984 (Die Antiken Sarkophagreliefs, Bd. 5.4)
Krenkel, W. 'Zu den Taglöhnen bei der Ernte.' *Romanitas* 6–7 (1965), 130–53
Kurelek, W. *To My Father's Village: The Last Days and Drawings*. Montreal: Tundra Books, 1988
Laborde, F. 'Les mouvements saisonniers de la population en Tunisie.' *Renseignement coloniale* (1932), 305–16
Lakoff, G., and M. Johnson. *Metaphors We Live By*. 2nd ed. Chicago–London: University of Chicago Press, 2003
Lakoff, G., and M. Turner. *More Than Cool Reason: A Field Guide to Poetic Metaphor*. Chicago–London: University of Chicago Press, 1989
Lambert, G. *Le Luxembourg romain: documents choisis*. Andenne: Magermans, 1990
Lana, I. *L'idea del lavoro a Roma*. Turin: G. Giappichelli, 1984
Lancel, S. 'Suburbures et Nicibes: une inscription de Tigisis.' *Libyca (arch-épigr.)* 3 (1955), 289–98
Landes, D. *The Unbound Prometheus: Technological Change and Industrial Development in Western Europe from 1750 to the Present*. Cambridge: Cambridge University Press, 1969; 2nd ed. 2003
Lane Fox, R. *Travelling Heroes: In the Epic Age of Homer*. New York: Knopf, 2009
Langdon, J. *Horses, Oxen and Technological Innovation: The Use of Draught Animals in English Farming from 1066 to 1500*. Cambridge: Cambridge University Press, 1986
Lassère, J.-M. 'Miracles et vie économique en Afrique au Ve s. A propos d'un troupeau de cochons (*De miraculis Sancti Stephani protomartyris libri duo*, 1, 14).' *AfrRom* 8 (1991), 305–12
– 'Recherches chronologiques sur les épitaphes païennes de l'Africa.' *AntAfr* 7 (1973), 7–151
Lattimore, R. *The Iliad of Homer*. Trans. Richmond Lattimore. Chicago: University of Chicago Press, 1951

Lebel, P. 'Moisson et fenaison en Gaul.' *Revue archéologique de l'Est et du Centre-Est* 11 (1960), 72–5

Leclercq, H. 'Moissonneur.' *DACL* 11.1. Paris, 1934, 1715–18

Lefebvre des Noëttes, R. *L'attelage. Le cheval de selle à travers les âges: contribution à l'histoire de l'esclavage.* 2 vols. Paris: A. Picard, 1931

Lefèvre, F. 'L'agriculture chez les Rèmes à l'époque romaine.' *Mémoires de la Société d'Agriculture, Commerce, Sciences et Arts de la Marne* (1978), 49–57

Le Gall, J. 'Les *falces* et la faux.' *Annales de l'Est* 22 (1959), 55–72

Leglay, M. 'La Gaule romanisée.' Chap. 2 in G. Bertrand, ed., *La formation des campagnes françaises des origines aux XIVe siècle*. Paris: Seuil, 1975, 192–319. Vol. 1 of Duby, ed., *Histoire de la France rurale*

– (*SAM* 1) *Saturne africain: Monuments, 1: Afrique proconsulaire*. Paris: Arts et métiers graphiques, 1961

– (*SAM* 2) *Saturne africain: Monuments, 2: Numidie-Maurétanies*. Paris: Arts et métiers graphiques, 1966

– *Saturne africain: Histoire*. Paris: E. de Boccard, 1966

Legros, R. 'Ordre romain et techniques celtes au service de la production agricole chez les Rèmes.' *Latomus* 30 (1971), 696–702

Lejeune, L. *Le Musée Archéologique luxembourgeois Arlon: à la découverte des plus belles collections*. Arlon: Institut Archéologique du Luxembourg, 2009

Lepelley, C. *Les cités de l'Afrique romaine au Bas-Empire*. 2 vols. Paris: Etudes Augustiniennes, 1979 and 1981

– 'Décline ou stabilité de l'agriculture africain au Bas-Empire? A propose d'une loi de l'empereur Honorius.' *AntAfr* 1 (1967), 135–44 = *Aspects de l'Afrique romaine: les cités, la vie rurale, le christianisme*. Bari: Edipuglia, 2001, 217–32

– 'Quelques parvenus de la culture de l'Afrique romaine tardive.' In L. Holtz and J.-C. Fredouille, eds., *De Tertullien aux Mozarabes, 1: Antiquité tardive et christianisme ancien (IIIe–VIe siècles)*. Paris: Institut d'études Augustiniennes, 1992, 583–94

Lerche, G. 'Observations on Harvesting with Sickles in Iran.' *Tools and Tillage* 1.1 (1968), 33–49

Le Roy Ladurie, E. *The Peasants of Languedoc*. Trans. J. Day. Urbana: University of Illinois Press, 1974; Engl. trans. of selections from *Les paysans de Languedoc*. 2nd ed. Paris: Mouton, 1966

Lescohier, D.D. *Conditions Affecting the Demand for Harvest Labor in the Wheat Belt*. Washington, DC: U.S. Department of Agriculture, 1924 (USDA Department Bulletin, no. 1230)

– 'The Farm Labor Problem.' *Journal of Farm Economics* 3 (January 1921), 10–15

– 'Hands and Tools of the Wheat Harvest.' *Survey* 50 (August 1923), 376–82; 409–12

– *Harvest Labor Problems in the Wheat Belt*. Washington, DC: United States Department of Agriculture, 1922 (USDA Department Bulletin, no. 1020)

- 'Harvesters and Hoboes.' *Survey* 50 (1923), 482–7; 503–4
- *Sources of Supply and Conditions of Employment of Harvest Labor in the Wheat Belt.* Washington, DC: U.S. Department of Agriculture, 1924 (USDA Department Bulletin, no. 1211)

Lesko, L.H. 'The Field of Hetep in Egyptian Coffin Texts.' *JARCE* 9 (1971–2), 89–101

Letaille, J. 'Découverte à Maktar de l'inscription dite du Moissonneur.' *BCTH* (1885), 529

Leveau, P. 'L'*Agricola* de Biha Bilta: à propos d'une inscription récemment découverte dans le region de Mateur.' *RT* 26 (1978), 7–13

Levi, D. 'The Allegories of the Months in Classical Art.' *Art Bulletin* 23 (1941), 251–91

Levine, L.I. *The Ancient Synagogue: The First Thousand Years.* 2nd ed. New Haven–London: Yale University Press, 2005

Lightfoot, J.L. *The Sibylline Oracles: With Introduction, Translation, and Commentary on the First and Second Books.* Oxford: Oxford University Press, 2007

Liungman, W. *Traditionswanderungen, Euphrat-Rhein: Studien zur Geschichte der Volksbräuche.* 2 vols. Helsinki: Suomalainen Tiedeakatemia, 1937–8

Lloyd, G.E.R. *The Ambitions of Curiosity: Understanding the World in Ancient Greece and China.* Cambridge: Cambridge University Press, 2002

Lombardo, S. *Homer: Iliad.* Trans. Stanley Lombardo, intro. Sheila Murnaghan. Indianapolis–Cambridge: Hackett Publishing Company, 1997

Longnon, J., and R. Cazelles intro., M. Meiss pref. *The Très Riches Heures of Jean, Duke of Berry: Musée Condé, Chantiilly.* New York: George Braziller, 1969; reprint 1989

Lowe, E.A. (*CLA*) *Codices Latini Antiquiores: A Palaeographical Guide to Latin Manuscripts prior to the Ninth Century: Supplement.* Oxford: Clarendon Press, 1971

Lukits, R. 'Die Schnitterinschrift von Maktar (CIL VIII 11.824).' In E.M. Ruprechtsberger and R. Lukits, *Antikes Mactaris und die Schnitterinschrfit, CIL VIII 11.824.* Linz: Nordico-Museum der Stadt Linz, 2008, 76–113

Lumsden, J. *Through Canada in Harvest Time: A Study of Life and Labour in the Golden West.* London: T. Fisher Unwin, 1903

Lyne, R.O.A.M. *Words and the Poet: Characteristic Techniques of Style in Vergil's Aeneid.* Oxford: Clarendon Press, 1989

MacCormack, S. 'The Virtue of Work: An Augustinian Transformation.' *AnTard* 9 (2001), 219–37

MacKenzie, A.A. *The Harvest Train: When Maritimers Worked in the Canadian West, 1890–1928.* Wreck Cove, NS: Breton Books, 2002

MacMullen, R. *Roman Social Relations.* New Haven: Yale University Press, 1974

Macqueron, J. *Le travail des hommes libres dans l'antiquité romaine.* Aix: Centre régional de documentation pédagogique: Service d'éditions, 1958; reprint 1964

Mahoney, J. 'Path Dependence in Historical Sociology.' *Theory and Society* 29 (2000), 207–48

Malcolmson, A.W. *Life and Labour in England, 1700–1780.* London: Hutchinson, 1981

Malrain, F., V. Matterne, and P. Méniel. *Les paysans gaulois.* Paris: Errance, 2002

Mane, P. *Calendriers et techniques agricoles: France-Italie, XIIe–XIIIe siècles.* Paris: Le Sycomore, 1983

– 'Comparaison des thèmes iconographiques des calendriers monumentaux et enluminés en France, aux XIIe et XIIIe siècles.' *Cahiers de civilisation médiévale* 29 (1986), 257–64

– *L'outil et le geste: iconographie de l'agriculture dans l'Occident médiévale, IXe–XV siècles.* 3 vols. Lille: Atelier national de reproduction des thèses, 2002

– *La vie dans les campagnes au moyen âge à travers les calendriers.* Paris: Editions de La Martinière, 2004

Manning, W.H. 'The Plough in Roman Britain.' *JRS* 54 (1964), 125–36

Marbach, A. *Les instruments aratoires des Gaules et de Germanie Superieure: catalogue des pièces métalliques.* Oxford: BAR International Series no. 1236, 2004

– *Recherches sur les instruments aratoires et le travail du sol en Gaule Belgique.* Oxford: BAR International Series no. 1235, 2004

Marcone, A. 'Tra archeologia e storia economica: il mausoleo dei Secundini a Igel.' *Athenaeum* 88 (2000), 485–512

Martin, R. *Recherches sur les agronomes latins et leurs conceptions économiques et sociales.* Paris: Les Belles Lettres, 1971

Mastino, A. 'La ricerca epigrafia in Tunisia (1973–1983). Il caso di Mactaris.' *AfrRom* 1 (1984), 73–128

Matterne, V. *Agriculture et alimentation végétale durant l'âge du fer et l'époque gallo-romaine en France septentrionale.* Paris: Université de Paris I, 2000

Matthews, L.G. 'Harvesting by the Gauls: The Forerunner of the Combine Harvester.' *Agricultural History Review* 18 (1970), 52–3

Mattingly, D.J. 'Maximum Figures and Maximizing Strategies of Oil Production? Further Thoughts on the Processing Capacity of Roman Olive Presses.' In Marie-Claire Amouretti and Jean-Pierre Brun, eds., *La Production du vin et de l'huile en Méditeranée.* BCH Suppl. 26, Paris, 1993, 483–98

Mayerson, P. *The Ancient Agricultural Regime of Nessana and the Central Negeb.* London: British School of Archaeology in Jerusalem, 1961

Mazzarino, A. *Introduzione al De agri cultura di Catone.* Rome: Atlante, 1952

M'Charek, A. *Aspects de l'évolution démographique et sociale à Mactaris aux IIe et IIIe siècles ap. J.-C.* Tunis: Université de Tunis, 1982 (Publications de l'Université de Tunis, Faculté des lettres et sciences humaines, no. 13)

– 'Documentation épigraphique et croissance urbaine: l'exemple de Mactaris aux trois premiers siècles de l'ère chrétienne.' *AfrRom* 2 (1985), 213–24

– 'Maghrâwa, lieu de provenance des stèles punico-numides dites de la Ghorfa.' *MEFRA* 101 (1988), 731–60

– 'Un itinéraire inédit dans la région de Maktar: tronçon de la voie augustéenne Carthage – *Ammaedara.*' *BCTH* 22B (1992), 153–67

McCormick, C. *Century of the Reaper: An Account of Cyrus Hall McCormick, the Inventor of the Reaper.* Boston–New York: Houghton Mifflin Co., 1931

Meeks, D., and D. Garcia, eds. *Techniques et économie antiques et médiévales: le temps de l'innovation.* Paris: Editions Errance, 1997 (Colloque international de CNRS, Aix-en-Provence, 21–3 mai, 1996: Travaux du Centre Camille Jullian, no. 21)

Mehl, A. 'Wirtschaft, Gesellschaft, Totenglauben: die "Igeler Säule" bei Trier und ihre Grabherren. Mit einem Anhang. Das Grab des Trimalchio.' *Laverna* 7 (1997), 59–92

Meiss, M. *French Painting in the Time of Jean de Berry: The Limbourgs and their Contemporaries.* 2 vols. New York: George Braziller, 1974

Merridale, C. *Night of Stone: Death and Memory in Twentieth-Century Russia.* London: Granta Books, 2000; New York: Viking, 2001; Harmondsworth: Penguin, 2002

Mertens, J. 'Eine antike Mähmaschine.' *Zeitschrift für Agrargeschichte und Agrarsoziologie* 7 (1959), 1–3

– 'La moissonneuse de Buzenol (Eine römische Mähmaschine).' *Ur-Schweiz/La Suisse Primitive* 22 (1958), 49–53

– 'Nouveaux monuments funéraires de Buzenol.' *Académie Royale de Belgique: Bulletin de la classe des lettres et des sciences morales et politiques* (1959), 35–47

– 'Le refuge antique de Montauban-sous-Buzenol.' *Archaeologia Belgica* 16 (1954), 3–32

– 'Römische Skulpturen von Buzenol, Provinz Luxemburg.' *Germania* 36 (1958), 386–92

– 'Sculptures romaines de Buzenol.' *Le Pays Gaumais* 19 (1958), 17–53

– 'Le *vallus*: moissonneuse mécanique des Trévires.' *Ogam: Tradition celtique* 10 (1958), 217–20

Merton, R.K. 'Singletons and Multiples in Scientific Discovery.' *Proceedings of the American Philosophical Society* 105 (1961), 470–86

Mesnage, P.J. *L'Afrique chrétienne: évêchés et ruines antiques d'après les manuscrits du Mgr. Toulotte et les découvertes archéologiques les plus récents.* Paris: E. Leroux, 1912

Meurers-Balke, J., and C. Leonnecken. 'Zu Schutzgeräten bei der Getreideernte mit der Sichel.' *Tools and Tillage* 5.1 (1984), 27–42

Mitchell, S. 'The Cult of Theos Hypsistos between Pagans, Jews, and Christians.' In P. Athanassiadi and M. Frede, eds., *Pagan Monotheism in Late Antiquity.* Oxford University Press, 1999, 81–148

Moatti, C. 'Le contrôle de la mobilité des personnes dans l'empire romain.' *MEFRA* 112 (2000), 925–58

Moatti, C., W. Kaiser, and C. Pébarthe, eds. *Le monde de l'itinérance en Méditerranée de l'Antiquité à l'époque moderne: procédures de contrôle et d'identification.* Bordeaux: Pessac; Paris: de Boccard, 2009

Mócsy, A. 'Zu den *prata legionis*.' In *Studien zu den Militärgrenzen Roms* = Bonner Jahr-bucher, Beiheft no. 19. Graz-Cologne: Böhlau, 1967, 211–14

Modéran, Y. 'La renaissance des cités dans l'Afrique du VIe siècle d'après une inscription récemment publiée.' In C. Lepelley, ed., *La fin de la cité antique et le début de la cité médiévale*. Bari: Edipuglia, 1996, 85–114

Möller, C. 'Die *mercenarii* in der römischen Arbeitswelt.' *ZRG* 110 (1993), 296–329

Montevecchi, O. *I contratti di lavoro e di servizio nell'Egitto greco-romano e bizantino*. Milan: Vita e pensiero, 1950

Moore, K. 'The Grim Reaper, Working Stiff: The Man, the Myth, the Everyday.' MA Thesis, Bowling Green State University, 2006

Morgan, D.H. *Harvesters and Harvesting, 1840–1900: A Study of the Rural Proletariat*. London: Croom Helm, 1981

– 'The Place of Harvesters in the Ninteenth-Century Village Life.' In R. Samuel, ed., *Village Life and Labour*. London, 1975, 29–72

Morgenstern, F. 'Die Auswertung des *opus agriculturae* des Palladius zu eigenen Fragen der spätantiken Wirtschaftsgeschichte.' *Klio* 71 (1989), 179–92

Mou, M'hamed. 'Amazigh Harvest Izlan (Songs) of the Amagha Region.' In *Amzigh Voice* (June 1996) = http://www.ece.umd.edu/~sellami/JUNE 96/amagha.html

Müller, H.H. 'Zur Rekonstruktion des gallo-römischen Erntemaschine.' *Zeitschrift für Agrargeschichte und Agrarsoziologie* 19 (1985), 191–6

Nelson, M. *The Barbarian's Beverage: A History of Beer in Ancient Europe*. London–New York: Routledge, 2005

Nilsson, M.P. 'The Sickle of Kronos.' *BSA* 46 (1951), 122–4 = *Opuscula Selecta*. Vol. 3. Lund: Gleerup, 1960, 215–19

Nollé, J. 'Boars, Bears, and Bugs: Farming in Asia Minor and the Protection of Men, Ani-mals, and Crops.' Chap. 2 in S. Mitchell and C. Katsari, eds., *Patterns of the Economy of Roman Asia Minor*. Swansea: Classical Press of Wales, 2005, 53–82

Novotny, F. *Die Monatsbilder Pieter Bruegel der Altere*. Vienna: F. Deutike, 1948

Olck, F. 'Ernte.' *RE* 6.1 (1907), 472–82

Orenstein, N., ed. *Pieter Bruegel the Elder: Drawings and Prints*. Exhibition Catalogue. New York: Metropolitan Museum of Art, 2001

Osborne, R. 'The Economics and Politics of Slavery at Athens.' Chap. 2 in A. Powell, ed., *The Greek World*. London: Routledge, 1995, 27–43

Overton, M. *Agricultural Revolution in England: The Transformation of the Agricultural Economy 1500–1850*. Cambridge: Cambridge University Press, 1996

Pagels, E. *Revelations: Visions, Prophecy and Politics in the Book of Revelation*. New York: Viking Penguin, 2012

Pannoux, S. 'La représentation du travail: récit et image sur les monuments funéraires des Médiomatriques.' *DHA* 11 (1985), 293–328

Parke, H.W. *Sibyls and Sibylline Prophecy in Classical Antiquity.* Ed. B.C. McGing. London–New York: Routledge, 1988

Parrish, D. *Season Mosaics of Roman North Africa.* Rome: Giorgio Bretschneider, 1984

– 'Two Mosaics from Roman Tunisia: An African Variation of the Season Theme.' *AJA* 83 (1979), 279–85

Percival, J. *The Roman Villa: An Historical Introduction.* London: Batsford, 1976

Peyras, J. 'Le *Fundus Aufidianus*: étude d'un grand domaine romain de la région de Mateur (Tunisie du Nord).' *AntAfr* 9 (1975), 181–222

Pflaum, H.G. 'La romanisation du territoire ancien de la Carthage punique à la lumière des découvertes épigraphiques récentes.' *AntAfr* 4 (1970), 74–116 = *Afrique romaine: Scripta Varia I.* Paris: Harmattan, 1978, 300–44

Pickvance, D. *Van Gogh in Saint-Rémy and Auvers.* New York: Metropolitan Museum of Art, H.N. Abrams distributor, 1986

Pikhaus, D. 'Les carmina latina epigraphica païens et chrétiens: renouvellement thématique et contexte socio-culturel.' *Miscellanea Historiae Ecclesiasticae* 6 (1983), 325–7

– 'Literary Activity in the Provinces: The Carmina Epigraphica from Roman Africa (1st–7th Century).' *Euphrosyne* 15 (1987), 171–94

– 'Littérature latine et bourgeoisie municipale: l'épigramme funéraire du moissonneur (CLE 1238 = CIL VIII 11824).' In *Studia Varia Bruxellensia*, vol. 1. Leuven, 1987, 81–94

– 'Les origines sociales de la poésie épigraphique latine: l'exemple de provinces nord-africaines.' *AC* 50 (1981), 637–54

– 'La poésie épigraphique latine. Quelques points de vue nouveaux.' In F. Decreus and C. Deroux, eds., *Hommages à Josef Veremans.* Brussels: Collection Latomus, 1986, 228–37

– *Répertoire des inscriptions latines versifiées de l'Afrique romaine, I: Tripolitaine, Byzacène, Afrique proconsulaire.* Brussels: Epigraphica Bruxellensia, 1994

Pinker, S. *How the Mind Works.* New York: Norton, 1997

– *The Language Instinct.* New York: William Morrow; London: Allen Lane, 1994

– *The Stuff of Thought: Language as a Window into Human Nature.* Harmondsworth: Penguin, 2008

Pleket, H. 'Wirtschaft.' In F. Vittinghoff, ed., *Europäische Wirtschafts- und Sozialgeschichte in der römischen Kaiserzeit.* Stuttgart: Klett-Cotta, 1990, 25–160

Pohanka, R., *Die eisernen Agrargeräte der römischen Kaiserzeit in Österreich: Studien zur römischen Agrartechnologie in Rätien, Noricum und Pannonien.* Oxford: BAR International Series, no. 298, 1986

Poelaert, M., F. Puissant, and P. Vander Linden. 'Le témoignage de Pline l'Ancien.' In Raepsaet and Lambeau, eds., *La moissonneuse*, 5–7

Pomeroy, S. *Xenophon Oeconomicus: A Social and Historical Commentary.* Oxford: Clarendon Press, 1994

Poovey, M. *Genres of the Credit Economy: Mediating Value in Eighteenth and Nineteenth-Century Britain*. Chicago: University of Chicago Press, 2008

Poque, S. *Le langue symbolique dans la prédication d'Augustin d'Hippone: Images héroïques*. 2 vols. Paris: Etudes Augustiniennes, 1984

Postan, M., ed. *(CEH) The Cambridge Economic History of Europe, 1: The Agrarian Life of the Middle Ages*. 2nd ed. Cambridge: Cambridge University Press, 1966/1971

Prat, G.-F. *Histoire d'Arlon*. 2 vols. Arlon: P.-A. Bruck, 1873–4; reprint Brussels: Editions Culture et Civilisation, 1973

Prévot, F. *Recherches archéologiques franco-tunisiennes à Mactar, V: Les inscriptions chrétiennes*. Rome: Ecole française de Rome, 1984

Précheur-Canonge, T. *La vie rurale en Afrique romaine d'après les mosaïques*. Tunis: Publications de l'Université de Tunis, Faculté des lettres, Ier sér., archéologie-épigraphie, no. 6, 1962

Quick, G., and W. Buchele. *The Grain Harvesters*. St Joseph, MI: American Society of Agricultural Engineers, 1978

Raepsaet, G. *Attelages et techniques de transport dans le monde gréco-romain*. Brussels: Livre Timperman, 2002

– 'The Development of Farming Implements between the Seine and the Rhine from the Second to the Twelfth Centuries.' Chap. 3 in Astill and Langdon, eds., *Medieval Farming and Technology*, 41–68

– 'Les prémices de la mécanisation agricole entre Seine et Rhin de l'antiquité au 13e siècle.' *Annales (HSS)* 50 (1995), 911–42

– 'Propos d'épilogue: le vallus en devenir.' In Raepsaet and Lambeau, eds., *La moissonneuse*, 107–13

Raepsaet, G., and C. Rommelaere, eds. *Brancards et transport attelé entre Seine et Rhin de l'antiquité au Moyen Age: aspects archéologiques, économiques et technique*. Treignes: Dire, 1995 (Actes du colloque de Bruxelles et Treignes, 1er et 2 octobre 1993)

Raepsaet, G., and F. Lambeau, eds. *La moissonneuse gallo-romaine*. Brussels: Université Libre de Bruxelles, 2000 (Journée d'études, Université Libre de Bruxelles, 24 avril 1999)

Rasmussen, H. 'Grain Harvesting and Threshing in Calabria.' *Tools and Tillage* 1 (1969), 93–104

Rathbone, D. *Economic Rationalism and Rural Society in Third-Century A.D. Egypt: The Heroninos Archive and the Appianus Estate*. Cambridge: Cambridge University Press, 1991

– 'Prices and Price Formation in Roman Egypt.' In J. Andreau, P. Briant, and P. Descat, eds., *Economie antique. Prix et formation des prix dans les économies antiques*. Saint-Bertrand-de-Comminges: Musée archéologique départemental, 1997, 183–244

Raven, S. *Rome in Africa*. 3rd ed. London–New York: Routledge, 1993

Reay, B. *The Last Rising of the Agricultural Labourers: Rural Life and Protest in Nineteenth-Century England*. Oxford–New York: Oxford University Press, 1990
– *Rural Englands: Labouring Lives in the Nineteenth Century*. New York: Palgrave Macmillan, 2004
Rebuffat, R. 'Comme les moissons à la chaleur du soleil.' *AfrRom* 6 (Sassari, 1989), 113–33
Reddé, M. 'Les scènes de métier dans la sculpture funéraire Gallo-romaine.' *Gallia* 36 (1978), 45–63
Reekmans, T. *A Sixth-Century Account of Hay (P. Iand. Inv. 653)*. Brussels: Fondation Egyptologique Reine Elisabeth, 1962
Rees, S.E. *Agricultural Implements in Prehistoric and Roman Britain*. 2 vols. Oxford: BAR British Series, no. 69i–ii, 1979
– 'The Harvest: Sickles, Hooks and Scythes, Pitchforks and Rakes.' Chap. 4 in *Ancient Agricultural Implements*. Aylesbury: Shire Archaeology Publications, 1981, 22–30
– 'The Roman Scythe Blade.' In G. Lambrick and M. Robinson, eds., *Iron Age and Roman Riverside Settlements at Farmoor, Oxfordshire*. Oxford: Oxfordshire Archaeological Unit and Council for British Archaeology, 1979), 61–4 (Oxfordshire Archaeological Unit Report, no. 2; CBA Research Report, no. 32)
Reigneiz, P. 'Histoire et techniques: l'outil agricole dans la periode du Haut Moyen-Age (Ve–Xe siècle).' In Barceló and Sigaut, eds., *Making of Feudal Agriculture*, 33–120
– *L'outile agricole en France au Moyen Age*. Paris: Editions Errance, 2002
Renard, M. 'Scènes de comptes à Buzenol.' *Le pays Gaumais* 20 (1959), 1–45
– *Technique et agriculture en pays trévire et rémois*. Brussels–Berchem: Collection Latomus, no. 38, 1959
– (1959a), 'Technique et agriculture en pays trévire et rémois.' *Latomus* 18 (1959), 77–109
– (1959b), 'Technique et agriculture en pays trévire et rémois.' *Latomus* 18 (1959), 307–33
– '*Vallus* de Trèves.' *Latomus* 26 (1967), 486–7
Richlin, A. *The Garden of Priapus: Sexuality and Aggression in Roman Humor*. Rev. ed. New York: Oxford University Press, 1992
Ricoeur, P. *The Rule of Metaphor: Multidisciplinary Studies of the Creation of Meaning in Language*. Trans. P. Czerny, assist. K. McLaughlin and J. Costello. Toronto–Buffalo: University of Toronto Press, 1977
Rikoon, J.S. *Threshing in the Midwest, 1820–1940: A Study of Traditional Culture and Technological Change*. Bloomington–Indianapolis: Indiana University Press, 1988
Rives, J.B. *Religion and Authority in Roman Carthage from Augustus to Constantine*. Oxford: Clarendon Press, 1995
Rivière, Ch., and H. Lecq. *Traité pratique d'agriculture pour le Nord de l'Afrique*. 2 vols. Paris: Société d'éditions géographiques, maritimes et coloniales, 1928–9

Roberts, M. 'Sickles and Scythes: Women's Work and Men's Work at Harvest Time.' *History Workshop* 7 (1979), 3–28

– 'Sickles and Scythes Revisited: Harvest Work, Wages, and Symbolic Meanings.' Chap. 3 in P. Lane, N. Raven, and K.D.M. Snell, eds., *Women, Work, and Wages in England, 1600–1850*. Rochester, NY: Boydell Press, 2004, 68–101

Rommelaere, C., and G. Raepsaet. 'Les techniques de traction animale. De l'Antiquité au Moyen Age.' In Barceló and Sigaut, eds., *Making of Feudal Agriculture*, 121–30

Romanelli, P. 'La vita agricola tripolitana attraverso le rappresentazioni figurate.' *Africa Italiana* 3 (1930), 53–75

Rositani, A. *Harvest Texts in the British Museum = Rivista degli Studi Orientali*. Pisa–Rome: Fabrizio Serra editore, 2011 (nuova serie 82, supplemento no. 1, vol. 82)

Ross, D. 'The *Culex* and *Moretum* as Post-Augustan Literary Parodies.' *HSCPh* 79 (1975), 235–63

Rostovtzeff, M.I. 'Conductor.' *DE* 2 (1900), 578–97

– 'Frumentum.' *RE* 7.1 (1910), 126–87

– *(SEHRE) Social and Economic History of the Roman Empire*. Oxford: Clarendon Press, 1926; rev. ed. P.M. Fraser, Oxford: Clarendon Press, 1957

Roth, J. *The Logistics of the Roman Army at War (264 B.C.–A.D. 235)*. London–Boston: Brill, 1999

Rüpke, J. *Kalendar und Offentlichkeit: Die Geschichte der Repräsentation und religiösen Qualifikation von Zeit in Rom*. Berlin–New York: de Gruyter, 1995

Saez Fernandez, P. *Agricultura romana de la Bética*. Ecija: Monografias del Departamento de Historia Antigua de la Universidad de Sevilla, 1987

Sahin, M. 'Neue Beobachtungen zum Felsrelief von Ivriz/Konya. Nicht in den Krieg, sondern zur Ernte: der Gott mit der Sichel.' *Anatolian Studies* 49 (1999), 165–76

Salvemini, B. 'Migrants saisonniers et pouvoirs territoriaux: les pouilles à l'époque moderne.' In Moatti, Kaiser, and Pébarthe, eds., *Monde de l'itinérance*, 161–80.

Salzman, M.R. *On Roman Time: The Codex-Calendar of 354 and the Rhythms of Urban Life in Late Antiquity*. Berkeley–Los Angeles: University of Calfornia Press, 1990

Schefold, K., and F. Jung. *Die Urkönige: Perseus, Bellerophon, Herakles und Theseus in der klassischen und hellenistischen Kunst*. Munich: Hirmer, 1988

Scheid, J. 'Les réjouissances des calendes de janvier d'après le *sermon* Dolbeau 26. Nouvelles lumières sur une fête mal connue.' In G. Madec, ed., *Augustin Prédicateur (395–411)*. Paris: Institut d'Etudes Augustiniennes, 1998, 353–65

Scheid, J., and J. Svenbro. *The Craft of Zeus: Myths of Weaving and Fabric*. Trans. C. Volk. Cambridge, MA: Harvard University Press, 1996; Engl. trans. of *Métier de Zeus: mythe du tissage et du tissue dans le monde gréco-romain*. Paris: Editions La Découverte, 1994

Scheidel, W. 'Grain Cultivation in the Villa Economy of Roman Italy.' In J. Carlsen et al., eds., *Landuse in the Roman Empire*. ARID Supplement 22; Rome, 1994, 159–66

– 'In Search of Roman Economic Growth.' *JRA* 22 (2009), 46–70

– 'The Most Silent Women of Greece and Rome: Rural Labour and Women's Life in the Ancient World.' *G&R* 42 (1995), 202–17

– 'Real Wages in Early Economies: Evidence for Living Standards from 1800 BCE to 1300 CE.' *JESHO* 53 (2010), 425–62

Schiavone, A. *The End of the Past: Ancient Rome and the Modern West.* Trans. M.J. Schneider. Cambridge, MA: Harvard University Press, 2000; Engl. trans. of *La storia spezzata: Roma antica e Occidente moderno.* Rome: Laterza, 1996

Schmidt, J. 'Additamenta ad Corp. vol. VIII.' *Eph. epigr.* 5 (1884), 276, no. 279

– 'Essai d'interpretation d'une inscription trouvée à Maktar, Mactaris.' *BCTH* (1891), 575

Schmid, W. 'Ein Vergilanklang in einer neupublizierten Inschrift aus Mactaris.' *Philologus* 106 (1962), 277–80

Schneider, H. *Einführung in die antike Technikgeschichte.* Darmstadt: Wissenschaftliche Buchgesellschaft, 1992

– 'Technology.' Chap. 8 in W. Scheidel, I. Morris, and R. Saller, eds., *The Cambridge Economic History of the Greco-Roman World.* Cambridge: Cambridge University Press, 2007, 144–71

Schnebel, M. *Die Landwirtschaft im hellenistischen Aegypten, 1: Der Betrieb der Landwirtschaft.* Munich: Beck, 1925 (Münchener Beiträge zur Papyrusforschung und antike Rechtsgeschichte, no. 7)

Schörner, G. 'Neue Bilder für alte Rituale: Die Saturn-Stelen als Kultmedien im römischen Nordafrika.' In O. Hekster, S. Schmidt-Höfner, and C. Witschel, eds., *Ritual Dynamics and Religious Change in the Roman Empire.* Leiden: Brill, 2009, 285–306; Engl. trans. 'New Images for Old Rituals: Stelae of Saturn and Personal Cult in Roman North Africa,' *TRAC = Proceedings of the Sixteeenth Annual Theoretical Roman Archaeology Conference, Cambridge, 2006.* Oxford: Oxbow, 2007, 92–102

Schwartz, J. *Les archives de Sarapion et de ses fils: une exploitation agricole aux environs d'Hermoupolis Magna (de 90 à 133 p. C.).* Cairo: Imprimerie de l'Institut française d'archéologie orientale, 1961

Seaford, R. *Money and the Early Greek Mind: Homer, Philosophy, Tragedy.* Cambridge: Cambridge University Press, 2004

Servier, J. *Tradition et civilisation Berbères: les portes de l'année.* Monaco: Editions du Rocher, 1985

Seyrig, H. 'Invidiae Medici.' *Berytus* 1 (1934), 10–11

– 'Notes archéologiques.' *Berytus* 2 (1935), 42–50

Shaw, B.D. 'Cult and Belief in Punic and Roman Africa.' In W. Adler, ed., *The Cambridge History of Religions in the Ancient World,* vol. 2. Cambridge: Cambridge University Press, 2013

– 'Latin Funerary Epigraphy and Family Life in the Later Roman Empire.' *Historia* 33 (1984), 457–97

- 'Pastoralists, Peasants and Politics in Roman North Africa.' PhD Dissertation, Cambridge University, 1978
- *Rulers, Nomads, and Christians in Roman North Africa.* Aldershot: Variorum, 1995
- 'Rural Markets in North Africa and the Political Economy of the Roman Empire.' *AntAfr* 17 (1981), 37–83 = chap. 1 in *Rulers, Nomads, and Christians*
- 'Sabinus the Muleteer.' *CQ* 57 (2007), 132–8
- *Sacred Violence: African Christians and Sectarian Hatred in the Age of Augustine.* Cambridge: Cambridge University Press, 2011
- 'Seasonal Mortality in Imperial Rome and the Mediterranean: Three Problem Cases.' Chap. 4 in G.R. Storey, ed., *Urbanism in the Preindustrial World: Cross-Cultural Approaches.* Tuscaloosa: University of Alabama Press, 2006, 86–109
- 'Soldiers and Society: The Army in Numidia.' *Opus: Rivista internazionale per la storia economica e sociale dell'antichità* 2.1 (1983), 133–59 = chap. 9 in *Rulers, Nomads and Christians*
- 'A Wolf by the Ears.' Introduction to M.I. Finley, *Ancient Slavery and Modern Ideology.* Rev. ed. Princeton: Markus Weiner, 1998, 3–74
- Sigaut, F. 'L'évolution des techniques.' In Barceló and Sigaut, eds., *Making of Feudal Agriculture*, 1–31
- 'Identification des techniques de récolte des graines alimentaires.' *Journal d'Agriculture Traditional et de Botanique Appliquée* 25 (1978), 145–61
- 'Les spécificités de l'épeautre et l'évolution des techniques.' In J.-P. Devroey and J.-J. van Mol, eds., *L'épeautre (Triticum spelta): Histoire et ethnologie.* Treignes: Editions DIRE, 1989, 29–49
- 'Les techniques de récolte des grains: identification, localisation, problèmes d'interprétation.' *Rites et rythmes agraires: séminaire de recherches* (1991), 31–43
- Silver, L. *Peasant Scenes and Landscapes: The Rise of Pictorial Genres in the Antwerp Art Market.* Philadelphia: University of Pennsylvania Press, 2006
- Singer, C., et al., eds. *A History of Technology, 2: The Mediterranean Civilizations and the Middle Ages, c. 700 B.C. to c. 1500 A.D.* Oxford: Clarendon Press, 1954
- Slicher van Bath, B.H. *The Agrarian History of Western Europe, A.D. 500–1850.* Trans. O. Ordish. London: Edward Arnold, 1963
- Smith, J.M.H. *Europe after Rome: A New Cultural History, 500–1000.* Oxford: Oxford University Press, 2005
- Snell, K.D. *Annals of the Labouring Poor: Social Change and Agrarian England, 1660–1900.* Cambridge: Cambridge University Press, 1987
- Söderstrom, G.A. *Epigraphica Latina Africana de titulis sepulcralibus prosa oratione compositis provinciarum Byzacenae et Proconsularis quaestiones selectae.* Uppsala: Appelberg, 1924
- Sontag, S. *Illness as Metaphor.* New York: Farrar, Straus and Giroux, 1978
- Spiro, M. *Critical Corpus of the Mosaic Pavements on the Greek Mainland, Fourth/Sixth*

Centuries, with Architectural Surveys. 2 vols. New York–London: Garland Publishing, 1978

Spurr, M.S. *Arable Cultivation in Roman Italy, c. 200 B.C.–c. A.D. 100.* London: Society for the Promotion of Roman Studies, 1986

Stabler, E. *A Brief Narrative of the Invention of Reaping Machines; and an Examination of the Claims for Priority of Invention by a Maryland Farmer and Machinist.* Chicago: W.B. Conkey, 1897; original: Baltimore: Mills and Cox, 1854

Steensberg, A. *Ancient Harvesting Implements: A Study in Archaeology and Human Geography.* Copenhagen: Nordisk Forlag, 1943

Stephens, S.A. 'Linus Song.' *Hermathena* 172 (2002), 13–27

Stern, H. *Le calendrier de 354: étude sur son texte et sur ses illustrations.* Paris: Imprimerie nationale, 1953

– 'Un calendrier romain illustré de Thysdrus (Tunisie).' *Quaderni dell'Accademia Nazionale dei Lincei*, 365, no. 105 (1968), 176–200

– 'Les calendriers romains illustrés.' *ANRW* 2.12.2 (1981), 431–75

– 'Le cycle des mois de la Porte de Mars à Reims.' In M. Renard, ed., *Hommages à Albert Grenier*, 3. Brussels: Collection Latomus, no. 58, 1962, 1441–6

– 'L'image du mois d'octobre sur une mosaïque d'el-Djem.' *JS* (1965), 117–31 = *CT* 45–6 (1964), 21–33

Steward, J.F. *The Reaper: A History of the Efforts of Those Who Justly May Be Said to Have Made Bread Cheap.* New York: Greenberg, 1931

Stoll, S. *Larding the Lean Earth: Soil and Society in Nineteenth-Century America.* New York: Hill and Wang, 2002

Stone, D. 'Culture and Investment in the Rural Landscape: The North African *bonus agricola*.' *AntAfr* 29 (1998), 103–13

Stone, D. *Decision-Making in Medieval Agriculture.* Oxford: Oxford University Press, 2005

Straw, C. 'Augustine as Pastoral Theologian: The Exegesis of the Parables of the Field and the Threshing Floor.' *Augustinian Studies* 14 (1983), 129–51

Sullivan, K.K. *Weaving the Word: The Metaphorics of Weaving and Female Textual Production.* Selinsgrove, PA: Susquehanna University Press, 2001

Sullivan, M.A. *Bruegel's Peasants. Art and Audience in the Northern Renaissance.* Cambridge: Cambridge University Press, 1994

Sweeney, D., ed. *Agriculture in the Middle Ages: Technology, Practice, and Representation.* Philadelphia: University of Pennsylvania Press, 1995

Swift, R.B. *Who Invented the Reaper? An Answer to the Protest Statement Said to Have Been Filed at the Treasury Department.* Chicago: Private Printer, 1897

Syme, R. 'Pliny the Procurator.' *HSCPh* 73 (1969), 201–36 = chap. 55 in E. Badian, ed., *Roman Papers*, vol. 2. Oxford, 1979, 742–73

Tilley, C.Y. *Metaphor and Material Culture.* Oxford: Blackwell, 1999

Thirsk, J., ed. *The Agrarian History of England and Wales, Vol. 4: 1500–1640.* Cambridge: Cambridge University Press, 1967

– 'Making a Fresh Start: Sixteenth-Century Agriculture and the Classical Inspiration.' Chap. 1 in M. Leslie and T. Raylor, eds., *Culture and Cultivation in Early Modern England: Writing and the Land*. Leicester: Leicester University Press, 1992, 15–34

Thompson, J.H. 'Bringing In the Sheaves: The Harvest Excursionists, 1890–1929.' *Canadian Historical Journal* 59 (1978), 467–89

Tissot, C. *Géographie comparée de la province romaine d'Afrique*. 2 vols. Paris: Imprimerie nationale, 1884–91

– 'Les missions archéologiques en Afrique.' *Archives des Missions scientifiques*, 3e sér., 11 (1885), 253–6

– 'Quatrième rapport sur les missions archéologiques en Afrique.' *CRAI* (1884 [1885]), 64–8

Trousset, P. 'Les centuriations romaines.' In *Tunisie: Carrefour*, 70–81

Tunisia. London: Naval Intelligence Division, Geographical Handbook Series, no. 523, 1945

La Tunisie: Carrefour du monde antique. Dijon: Editions Faton, 1994

Turner, M. *Death Is the Mother of Beauty: Mind, Metaphor, Criticism*. Chicago: University of Chicago Press, 1987; reprint e-version Christchurch, NZ: Cybereditions, 2000

– *The Literary Mind: The Origins of Thought and Language*. New York: Oxford University Press, 1996

Ulansey, D. *The Origins of the Mithraic Mysteries: Cosmology and Salvation in the Ancient World*. New York–Oxford: Oxford University Press, 1989

Valensi, L. *Fellahs tunisiens: l'économie rurale et la vie des campagne aux 18e et 19e siècles*. Paris–La Haye: Mouton, 1977

Valenze, D. *The Social Life of Money in the English Past*. Cambridge: Cambridge University Press, 2006

Van Dam, R., *Saints and Their Miracles in Late Antique Gaul*. Princeton: Princeton University Press, 1993

Van Gogh, V. *Vincent Van Gogh: The Letters: The Complete Illustrated and Annotated Edition*. 6 vols. Ed. L. Jansen, H. Luijten, and N. Bakker. London: Thames and Hudson, 2009

Van Ooteghem, J. 'La moissonneuse gauloise.' *Les études classiques* 27 (1959), 129–32

Vannier, O. 'Les circoncellions et leurs rapports avec l'église donatiste d'après le texte d'Optat.' *RAfr* 67 (1926), 13–28

Varda, A. *Les glaneurs et la glaneuse*. Cinéma Tamaris, 2000; Engl. release title 'The Gleaners and I'; reprised in 2002 with the addition: 'The Gleaners and I: Two Years Later'

Vardi, L. 'Construing the Harvest: Gleaners, Farmers, and Officials in Early Modern France.' *AHR* 98 (1993), 1424–47

– 'Imagining the Harvest in Early Modern Europe.' *AHR* 101 (1996), 1357–97

Varilioglu, G. 'Une inscription de Mercure aux Portes de Cilicie.' *EA* 11 (1988), 59–64

Verlinden, C. *Les statuettes anthropomorphes crétoises en bronze et en plomb, du IIIe mil-*

lénaire au VIIe siècle av. J.-C. Louvain-la Neuve: Institut supérieur d'archéologie et d'histoire de l'art, 1984

Vermaseren, M.J. *Mithriaca, I: The Mithraeum at S. Maria Capua Vetere.* Leiden: Brill, 1971

Vermeule, E. *Aspects of Death in Early Greek Art and Poetry.* Berkeley–Los Angeles: University of California Press, 1979

Versnel, H.S. *Transition and Reversal in Myth and Ritual.* 2nd ed. Leiden–New York: Brill, 1994

Veyne, P. 'Les cadeaux des colons à leur propriétaire: la neuvième bucolique et le mausolée d'Igel.' *RA* (1981), 245–52

Vido, P. 'Biomechanics and Hand Mowing.' http://www.scytheconnection.com/adp/techn2.html

Vignet-Zunz, J. 'La moisson à faucille chez les Jbala (Bni Gorfet) du Rif Occidental (Maroc) et dans l'Ouarsenis (Tell Algérien).' In Amouretti and Comet, eds., *Transmission des connaissances,* 219–34

Volp, U. *Tod und Ritual in des christlicher Gemeinden der Antike.* Leiden: Brill, 2008

Warmington, B.H. *The North African Provinces from Diocletian to the Vandal Conquest.* Cambridge: Cambridge University Press, 1954; reprint Westport, CT: Greenwood Press, 1971

Weber-Kellerman, I. *Erntbrauch in der ländlichen Arbeitswelt des 19. Jahrhunderts auf Grund der Mannhardtbefragung in Deutschland von 1865.* Marburg: N.G. Elwert, 1965

Webster, J.C. *The Labors of the Months in Antique and Medieval Art to the End of the Twelfth Century.* Princeton: Princeton University Press, 1938

Weightman, G. *The Industrial Revolutionaries: The Making of the Modern World, 1776–1914.* New York: Grove Press, 2007

Weiss, Z. *The Sepphoris Synagogue: Deciphering an Ancient Message through Its Archaeological and Socio-Historical Contexts.* Jerusalem: Israel Exploration Society, Hebrew University of Jerusalem, 2005

Weiss, Z., and E. Netzer. *Promise and Redemption: A Synagogue Mosaic from Sepphoris.* 2nd ed. Jerusalem: Israel Museum, 1998

West, M.L. *Ancient Greek Music.* Oxford: Oxford University Press, 1992

– *Hesiod, Theogony.* Edited with prolegomena and commentary. Oxford: Clarendon Press, 1966

– *The Orphic Poems.* Oxford–New York: Oxford University Press, 1983

White, K.D. *Agricultural Implements of the Roman World.* Cambridge: Cambridge University Press, 1967

– 'The Economics of the Gallo-Roman Harvesting Machines.' In J. Bibauw, ed., *Mélanges à Marcel Renard,* vol. 2. Brussels: Collection Latomus, no. 102, 1967, 804–9

– *Farm Equipment of the Roman World.* Cambridge: Cambridge University Press, 1975

– 'Gallo-Roman Harvesting Machines.' *Latomus* 26 (1967), 634–47

– *Greek and Roman Technology*. London: Thames and Hudson, 1981; Ithaca: Cornell University Press, 1984

– 'Roman Agricultural Writers.' *ANRW* 1.4 (1973), 539–97

– *Roman Farming*. London: Thames and Hudson, 1970

– 'Wheat Farming in Roman Times.' *Antiquity* 37 (1963), 207–10

Wickham, C. *Framing the Early Middle Ages: Europe and the Mediterranean, 400–800.* Oxford: Oxford University Press, 2005

Wightman, E.M. *Gallia Belgica*. Berkeley–Los Angeles: University of California Press, 1985

– *Roman Trier and the Treviri*. New York: Praeger, 1971

Williams, William Carlos. *Pictures from Brueghel and Other Poems: Collected Poems, 1950–1962*. New York: New Directions, 1962

Wilson, A. 'Machines, Power and the Ancient Economy.' *JRS* 92 (2002), 1–32

Wyman, M. *Hoboes, Bindlestiffs, Fruit Tramps, and the Harvesting of the West*. New York: Hill and Wang, 2010

Younger, J.G. *Music in the Aegean Bronze Age*. Jonsered: Paul Aströms Förlag, 1998.

Žižek, S. *Violence: Six Sideways Reflections*. New York: Picador, 2008

Index

The author's mother assisting in reaping and stooking operations on the farm of her
brother, Andrew Brown, at Everdale, Alberta, in the summer of 1939, the year before his
enlistment in the Royal Canadian Air Force.

Milton Keynes UK
Ingram Content Group UK Ltd.
UKHW020519291024
450383UK00010B/236